Sociology
of
Health Care
in
Canada

Sociology
of
Health Care
in
Canada

B. Singh Bolaria
Harley D. Dickinson
University of Saskatchewan

Harcourt Brace Jovanovich
Toronto Orlando San Diego London Sydney

Copyright © 1988 by Harcourt Brace Jovanovich Canada Inc.,
55 Horner Avenue, Toronto, Ontario M8Z 4X6

Edited by MAGDA KRYT
Cover design by MICHAEL GRAY
Composed and laserprinted by ON-LINE EDITORIAL
    AND COMPOSITION SERVICES
Printed and bound by THE ALGER PRESS LTD.

Canadian Cataloguing in Publication Data

Main entry under title:

Sociology of health care in Canada

Includes bibliographies.
ISBN 0-7747-3078-1

1. Medical care - Canada.   I. Bolaria, B. Singh,
1936-   . II. Dickinson, Harley D., 1951-   .

RA395.C3S6 1988   362.1'0971   C87-095228-5

Printed and bound in Canada
5 4 3 2   92

PREFACE

The Canadian health-care system presents the observer with a paradox. On the one hand it is generally acknowledged that the Canadian health-care system is one of the best in the world. At the same time, however, it is recognized that the system is in a state of crisis: costs are rising, demands for services are increasing, waiting lists are lengthening, doctors and other health-care workers are striking, and there is a general concern that the quality of health care may be jeopardized.

This book has two interrelated purposes. The first is to provide the student with an understanding of some of the major factors and forces which have shaped, and which continue to shape, the Canadian health-care system. The second is to show that health and illness are not entirely individual phenomena. Rather, the cause, distribution, and consequences of injury and illness are at least partly the product of social, economic, and political factors.

The focus of the book is the sociology of health care and medicine, rather than the sociology for medicine. Historically, medical sociology has developed as an adjunct to medicine. That is, sociological concepts and research were used to assist doctors and, in some cases, other health-care professionals to understand how social factors influence help-seeking and illness behaviour. Although this type of research greatly extended our understanding of the role that various socio-demographic factors played in sickness and health behaviour, it did not provide much insight into the social, economic, and political determinants of disease, and it left completely unexamined the social, economic, and political determinants of health-care policy. Thus, the nature and organization of health-care delivery remained taken for granted.

The magnitude of struggle and the intensity of conflict surrounding the birth of medicare in this country laid to rest the naïve notion that provision of medical and other health-care services could be taken for granted or left entirely to the medical profession. The infamous Saskatchewan doctors' strike was the medical professions' response to the institution of a universal, comprehensive, state-administered medical care insurance plan in July 1962. For patients medicare meant that all necessary physician services were available regardless of an individual's ability to pay. For doctors it meant treatment decisions could be made on purely medical grounds. Physicians no longer had to worry about whether an individual could or would pay for medical treatment, whether a person had private medical insurance, or whether a particular therapeutic procedure was covered. This immediately raises a number of interesting questions. For example, why would a profession dedicated by oath to serving the sick and healing the afflicted refuse to participate in a plan that made their services available to all regardless of ability to pay? Why would doctors withdraw their services over the implementation of a medical care insurance plan that would greatly increase their incomes? Obviously opposition of the organized profession was not based on a desire to deny services to the sick. Rather, the majority of doctors opposed medicare because they saw it, and, to some degree, continue to see it as a threat to their professional power and autonomy. The organized medical profession correctly realized that once the funding for health-care services in general and medical services in particular came out of government revenues, these services would have to compete with other government programmes for money. Funds available for any purpose, including health care, depend in part on the political balance of power and the values and priorities of the government of the day.

Thus it became apparent in the medicare crisis that professional self-interest, as well as altruism, motivated doctors and other health-care professionals. These and subsequent events have made it abundantly clear that the nature and organization of health-care delivery cannot adequately be understood or explained exclusively in terms of the medical need of the sick, or as a manifestation of humanitarian benevolence on the part of a selfless medical profession. It is important to reassert that these comments do not deny that those in the health-care professions are motivated by humanitarian concern and benevolence, but are rather intended to point out that doctors and other health-care professionals are not solely motivated by these concerns. Any attempt to understand or explain the development of health care which does not recognize these other factors will be incomplete and therefore inadequate.

Sociology in general, and this book in particular, also contribute to an understanding of the social determinants of disease and illness. In this sense this book makes a contribution not only to the sociology of health care, but also to the sociology of illness and health. Traditionally, as indicated above, sociology has identified a number of factors influential in illness and health behaviour of patients. This traditional body of literature has not had much to say concerning the social etiology or distribution of illness. Until recently, and with few exceptions, sociologists have remained silent concerning the ways in which social, political, and economic structures are implicated in disease causation and distribution. Recognition of the fact that illness and disease are not simply individual problems caused by accidents or 'germs' is important if we are to achieve the goal of effective prevention. The achievement of effective preventative strategies requires our understanding of the impact which social, economic, and political relations in society have upon a person's health status. This entails more than simply stating that individuals should choose healthy lifestyles. Although it is undoubtedly true that the choice of healthy living patterns will have positive consequences for a person's wellbeing, many of the factors that contribute to disease, injury, and death are rooted in social structures over which an individual, as an individual, has little or no control. In some cases it is fair to say that individuals may be completely unaware of the various structural factors which directly or indirectly influence their health status. One of the goals of this book is to draw attention to some of these less visible social structural factors.

All but two of the chapters have been written especially for this book and the two chapters that are reprinted have been revised and edited. The topics have been chosen by the editors to reflect major issues in the field of medical sociology. Introductory and concluding chapters are written by the editors. The remaining 32 chapters of the book are organized into 10 sections, each of which has an introduction written by the editors. Added features in these chapters are suggested readings that direct students to relevant and related literature, and study questions that will assist them in identifying major themes and issues. The concluding chapter provides a summary of the main analytical themes that have been developed in the book and also points toward areas in need of further research.

Every book is the product of the work of a large number of people and we would like to thank some of them. First we want to thank all the contributors for their co-operation in making this book a reality. We are grateful to Associate Dean Marvin Brown, College of Arts and Science, University of Saskatchewan for academic advice, encouragement, and financial support. We are also grateful to Rolly Muir, Director of Research Services, College of Graduate Studies and Research, University of Saskatchewan for a grant from the President's Publication Fund for the typing of the manuscript. Susan Knight and Sherry Stuber typed sections of the manuscript and we would like to thank them for their good work. We are also grateful to Susan Knight, Shannon Skinner, and Eric Kempthorne for their careful assistance in research and the preparation of bibliographic sources.

Of course, we want to thank HBJ Press, and especially Heather McWhinney, who saw the book through from its inception to completion. We are most impressed with her professional and efficient manner and with her enthusiasm, support, and constant prodding to meet deadlines. We also wish to thank the editorial staff at HBJ Press, especially Darlene Zeleney, Julie Canton, Jean MacDonald, and copy editors and reviewers, whose careful work greatly improved the final product. Finally we would like to thank our families for their patience, understanding, and support.

CONTENTS

Part IV: Women, Family, and Health

1

SOCIOLOGY, MEDICINE, HEALTH, AND ILLNESS: An Overview

B. Singh Bolaria
University of Saskatchewan

INTRODUCTION

Medical sociology covers a wide range of substantive areas and encompasses a diversity of issues pertaining to health and illness, medical institutions, the structure and organization of the health-care sector, and the political, economic, and social determinants of the nature and composition of the health-care delivery systems. Medical sociologists and others interested in this area approach and examine these essential topics and issues from various theoretical perspectives and paradigms and use varying levels of analyses and methodologies. Despite this diversity, certain paradigms and orientations are still dominant in the field of medical sociology. The purpose of this chapter is, by way of introduction, to outline these paradigms and discuss their policy implications. Specifically, the following topics are examined: Evolution and the dominant paradigm of scientific medicine, the definition and etiology of health and illness, and the focus and levels of analyses. In conclusion, the policy implications of dominant paradigms and levels of analyses are considered in the context of current fiscal constraints and the health-care "crisis."

EVOLUTION AND THE DOMINANT PARADIGM OF SCIENTIFIC MEDICINE

The knowledge of modern scientific medicine is founded on the work of Koch, Pasteur, and other bacteriologists. The germ theory of disease, which gained prominence in the late nineteenth century, had a profound impact on the practice of medicine. As Waitzkin (1979:684) states: "The isolation of specific bacteria as the etiologic agents in several infectious diseases created a profound change in medicine's diagnostic and therapeutic assumptions. A unifactorial model of disease emerged. Medical scientists searched for organisms causing infections and single lesions in non-infectious disorders." Renaud (1977:139) emphasizes the same point:

> Contemporary medical knowledge is rooted in the paradigm of the "specific etiology" of disease, that is, diseases are assumed to have a specific cause to be analyzed in the body's cellular and biochemical systems. This paradigm developed out of the germ theory of disease of Pasteur and Koch.

While the germ theory helped to develop the prevention of infectious diseases and improved medical practice, this paradigm

> gave support to the idea of specific therapies, from which rose the essentially curative orientation of current medical technologies toward specific illness rather than the sick person as a whole, and the belief that people can be made healthy by means of technological fixes; i.e., the engineering approach. (Renaud, 1977:139)

This paradigm basically adopted a "mechanistic model" of the human body. This approach has a long history. Philosophers like Descartes (1596–1650) established the philosophical base for a machine model of the human body; that is, that the human body is assumed to work in the same way as a machine. As McKeown (1965:38) states:

> The approach to biology and medicine established during the seventeenth century was an engineering one, based on a physical model. Nature was perceived in mechanistic terms, which led in biology to the idea that a living organism could be regarded as a machine which might be taken apart and reassembled if its structure and function were fully understood. In medicine, the same concept led further to the belief that an understanding of disease processes and of the body's response to them would make it possible to intervene therapeutically, mainly by physical (surgery), chemical, or electrical methods.

Disease, then, is an alteration, a pathological change in the body machinery that must be "fixed" (Navarro, 1986:166). Many diseases are viewed as mere technical defects; treatments are oriented toward restoring the "normal" functioning of the human machine. This approach basically ignores social causes of much ill health. The mechanistic-individualistic paradigm narrows and limits the medical task. As Doyal and Pennell (1979:30) state:

> The adoption of a mechanistic paradigm of this kind did limit the nature and boundaries of what is conceived as the medical task. Thus, scientific medicine ultimately became curative, individualistic and interventionist, objectifying patients and denying their status as social beings.

This mechanistic conception brought about a shift from the consideration of illness as a breakdown of the total system to the notion that ill health could be caused by malfunctioning of one particular part of the body machinery — in other words, localized pathology (Doyal and Pennell, 1979). This idea led to the medical fragmentation of the delivery of health care. Again, it is based on the premise that the human body is like a machine, and can, like any mechanical system, be broken down into different parts for repair (Rossdale, 1965). Many instruments were developed (thermometer, stethoscope) to examine the interior of the body machinery. This shift toward localized pathology had a profound impact on the division of labour (specialization) in medicine.

The specialization in medical knowledge and practice tends to focus on specific parts of the body machine, such as the nervous system, the cardio-vascular system, the gastro-intestinal system, and so forth (Navarro, 1986:167).

The work of bacteriologists and other scientists undeniably had a positive impact on the control of infectious diseases and led to improvements in medical practice. However, recent studies tend to cast doubt on the historical importance of these discoveries (Powles, 1973; Carlson, 1975). It is argued that the major decline in mortality and morbidity was due to better nutrition and sanitation and other environmental improvements, and that the decline in mortality and morbidity patterns, rather than following significant diagnostic and therapeutic discoveries, in fact preceded them (Waitzkin, 1979). Whatever the sequence of events, laboratory medicine with its emphasis on an individualistic, scientific, machine model of the human body achieved ascendancy. It should be noted that the dominant scientific paradigm is not mere linear evolution of scientific discoveries. As Navarro (1986:167) and others have argued, the form and nature of medicine is determined by class and power relations in the society and not by scientific imperatives. The ascendancy of scientific laboratory-based medicine and the dominant position of allopathic medicine in

North America in the beginning of this century is attributed by some writers to the publication of the Flexner Report (Brown, 1979; Berliner, 1977; Kunitz, 1974; Waitzkin, 1979; Kelman, 1977).

Abraham Flexner visited medical schools both in the United States and Canada in 1904–1905. The Flexner Report (1910) was critical of the medical schools that did not have the facilities to teach laboratory-based scientific medicine. It called for the reorganization or, failing that, closure of such institutions. Ninety-two medical schools were closed (mainly in the United States) or reorganized between 1904 and 1915 (Waitzkin, 1979). Some of these institutions taught alternative forms of healing, such as homeopathy, midwifery, and herbalism. This report was highly critical of these alternative practices and helped to relegate them to subordinate status vis-à-vis the allopathic practice of medicine (Kelman, 1977; Berliner, 1975; Kunitz, 1974). The norm for medical education and practice became the laboratory-based scientific medicine. The Flexner report was hailed "as the document that helped change modern medicine from quackery to responsible practice" (Waitzkin, 1979:685).

Before the report's recommendations were implemented, the allopathic physicians had faced stiff competition, which affected their incomes, from practitioners trained in a variety of alternative healing traditions. The costs of delivering premedical education, as well as the necessity for expensive laboratory facilities, led to high tuition fees in medical schools, making medical education all but inaccessible to working-class students. As Waitzkin (1979:686) notes:

> The American Medical Association strongly supported and subsequently helped enforce the Flexner Report's recommendations. The closure of many medical schools not based in laboratory science led to fundamental changes in the class composition of the profession, changes that went hand in hand with reduced competition and higher individual incomes for doctors.

The Carnegie Foundation also helped support Flexner's tour and subsequent publication of the report. In addition, the General Education Board of the Rockefeller Foundation provided financial support to medical schools which implemented the report's recommendations (Nielsen, 1972). The philanthropic support of the Foundations was, according to Waitzkin (1979:686–87), based upon a number of considerations:

> The humanitarian image of this philanthropic work helped justify the exploitation of workers and the environment by which the parent industries accumulated high profits. . . . Secondly, the development of laboratory based medical science diverted attention away from the illness-generating condition of capitalist production and class structure. . . . A third reason for support of scientific medicine by the capitalist class was the need for a work force healthy enough to participate in the production process.

The Flexner Report, supported by the medical profession and by philanthropic foundations, helped to consolidate the dominance of the allopathic practitioners and to establish laboratory-based scientific medicine as the norm for medical education and practice. This mechanistic-individualistic conception is currently pervasive in medical practice and research. As Rodberg and Stevenson (1977:113) point out: "Modern medicine operates according to an individualistic, scientistic, machine model. Humans receive medical treatment outside of, and abstracted from, their normal social and environmental context."

HEALTH AND ILLNESS

The mechanistic view of the human organism has dictated a similar vision of health and illness. For instance, Dorland's Medical Dictionary defines health as "a normal condition of body and mind, i.e., with all the parts functioning normally"; and disease is defined as "a definite morbid process having a characteristic strain of symptoms — it may affect the whole body or any of its parts, and its etiology, pathology, and prognosis may be known or unknown" (Inglefinger, 1982).

This mechanistic view of health and illness is of particular significance with regard to the etiology of health and illness as well as the treatment. As Doyal and Pennell (1979:34) note: "Ill health is now defined primarily in terms of the malfunctioning of a mechanical system, and treatment consists of surgical, chemical or even electrical intervention to restore the machine to normal working order." Medical experts' advanced training permits them to recognize a "malfunction" and prescribe appropriate treatment to correct it and thus make the body "functional." In functional terms, health means "the state of optimum capacity of an individual for the effective performance of the roles and tasks for which he has been socialized" (Parsons, 1972:117). In Parsons' definition, this "capacity to perform" appears to be the sole criterion of health. The experience of ill health in itself does not constitute illnesses.

Others have argued that health in capitalist society is tied to production and capital accumulation process. As Kelman (1977:12) comments:

At any point in time functional "health" is that organismic condition of the population most consistent with, or least disruptive of, the process of capital accumulation. At the individual level, this means the capacity to effectively do productive (contributing to accumulation) work.

Health viewed in this way has important implications in terms of the level of health-care services. Employers want to keep workers in good working order. As Rodberg and Stevenson (1977:112) indicate: "From the point of view of capital, the health-care system does not have to satisfy workers and it is not important that they feel well, as long as they are able to work hard." The definition of health and illness in relation to the accumulation process is an important aspect of the capitalist value system, which regards workers primarily as producers — "they are machines, one dimensional contributors to the accumulation process" (Rodberg and Stevenson, 1977:112). This view is well illustrated in the following passage in an occupational medicine text:

Chickens, race-horses, and circus monkeys are fed, housed, trained, and kept up to the highest physical pitch in order to secure a full return from them as producers in their respective functions. The same principle applies to human beings; increased production cannot be expected from workers unless some attention is paid to their physical environment and needs.
The object of this book is to show those who manage plants and are, therefore, responsible for the management of medical departments, how the workers' health may be maintained and improved as means of increasing production. (Hacket, 1925:11 quoted in Kelman, 1977:17)

Viewed in this context the investments to maintain healthy and productive workers are considered the same way as investments in other factors of production, and have to be balanced against returns. If workers are hard to replace or reproduction costs are high, employers are greatly concerned about the health of the workers and are interested in prolonging their productive life span. Conversely, if workers are easily replaceable, employers are less concerned about their health. Workers are kept healthy so long as the cost of health care is less than the cost of replacing them.

If workers are "owned" by the employers, such as slave labour, the employers are deeply interested in protecting their property. For instance, slaves in the United States had more systematic access to health care and enjoyed somewhat better health status than the freed slaves and poor whites (Postell, 1961; Stampp, 1956). However, health expenditures were tempered with return on this investment. Slaves were kept healthy so long as the cost of health care was less than the cost of replacing them. This is illustrated in the following passage:

Physicians provided prepaid contracts to slaveholders to cover the cost of caring for the slaves, and an entire holding of slaves would often be moved to a more healthy location in times of epidemic, even at the cost of a whole year's production. Irish labourers were sometimes hired in order to save the slaves from working in malaria-infested areas. However, medical care was withheld from slaves when the anticipated cost (times the probability of failure) did not seem justified in the eyes of the slaveholder. (Kelman, 1977:16–17)

In addition to this instrumental view of health and fitness of the workers, "under capitalism, health is also defined in an individualistic way. It is always individuals who become sick, rather than social, economic or environmental factors which cause them to be so" (Doyal and Pennell, 1979:35). As Stark (1977:V) has commented:

> Disease is understood as a failure in and of the individual, an isolatable "thing" that attacks the physical machine more or less arbitrarily from "outside" preventing it from fulfilling its essential "responsibilities." Both bourgeois epidemiology and "medical ecology" ... consider "society" only as a relatively passive medium through which "germs" pass en route to the individual.

This individualistic and functional definition of health provides the basis for the essentially curative focus of medicine itself, which has important social and economic significance (Doyal and Pennell, 1979). For instance, the expansion of technologically curative medicine provides the base for a profitable health-care industry.

This type of analysis would suggest the termination of health resources to the elderly and infirm who no longer work and contribute little to the accumulation process because investment in their health will produce few, if any, returns (Kelman, 1977; Rodberg and Stevenson, 1977; Dreitzel, 1971). To be sure, such policies, strictly speaking, have not been politically and culturally feasible. Even in the United States, where there is no universal health-care programme as in Canada, the elderly, chronically unemployed, and poor receive certain health services, however limited, under the medicare and medicaid programmes. A strictly functional definition of health and sickness purely in terms of the worker's ability to perform cannot always be operationalized because of political and cultural considerations. It is of no less significance to note that nursing homes and other health-care institutions which provide services to the aged

population also provide opportunities for capital investments and profits, particularly those nursing homes that are privately owned and operated but subsidized by public funds.

REDUCTIONISM IN MEDICINE

The mechanistic-individualistic conception of disease, which attributes disease to "malfunctioning" of the human body, absolves the economic and political environment from responsibility for disease. Waitzkin (1979:686) points out the reductionist tendencies of this understanding:

> Scientific medicine, fostered by the Flexner Report and the great philanthropies, tended toward reductionism. It shifted the focus of research and action from societal problems — a topic that implied potential threats to the organization of capitalist production and class structure — to pathophysiological disturbance at the level of the individual patient — much less threatening subject matter.

A similar reductionist approach has emerged which emphasizes individual lifestyle. In Canada in 1974, the publication of Lalonde's paper "A New Perspective on the Health of Canadians," gave prominent attention to health risks associated with individual lifestyles and consumption patterns. Lifestyle was also one of the foci of a recent health policy, "Achieving Health For All: A Framework For Health Promotion" (Epp, 1986). While the clinical model attributes disease to the "malfunctioning" of the human body, the new reductionism introduces the idea that the causes of disease lie in individual lifestyles and behaviours. In the former case the normal functioning of the body can be restored through "technological fixes," while in the latter the solution lies primarily in changing individual behaviours and patterns of consumption. It is argued that since the major risk factors causing much of mortality are under the personal discretion of the individuals, there would be considerable reduction in mortality if individuals would focus their attention on changing those aspects of their lifestyles which are injurious to their health. This focus on individual etiology and individual solutions is being promoted also in other countries (Doyal and Pennell, 1979; Waitzkin, 1983). Both approaches obscure the social nature of disease and fail to recognize the important relationships between social and work environments and health and sickness.

Recent studies from the historical materialistic epidemiological perspective have focussed on illness generating conditions.

SOCIAL ORIGINS OF ILLNESS

Social medicine is primarily concerned with the conditions in the society that produce illness and mortality. While "traditional epidemiology has searched for causes of morbidity and mortality that are amenable to medical intervention ... historical materialistic epidemiology [has] found causes of disease and death that derive from social conditions" (Waitzkin, 1983:64). Social epidemiology and the environmental approach to health are in conflict with the biological and individual orientation of the predominant paradigm. Several social conditions that generate illness are the focus of this approach. These include social class, economic cycles, socially produced stress, production process, and work and profit (Waitzkin, 1983; Navarro, 1986). For instance, cancer and other chronic diseases are substantially related to environmental factors and the workplace. There is also evidence that links incidence of illness to economic cycles and levels of employment. Disruptions of stable community relations have consistently led to an increase in hypertension rates. Rather than focussing on the individual life cycle and its relation to stress, "historical materialist epidemiology shifts the level of analysis to stressful forms of social organization connected to capitalist production and industrialization" (Waitzkin, 1983:63). Studies in the area of occupational health and safety provide persua-

sive evidence that links work environment and the labour process to illness and disease and points to basic contradictions between profit and safety. Differential mortality rates and life expectancy of men and women and among racial groups is related to their varying work experience and social environment.

TYPES OF ANALYSIS

A plethora of sociological and behavioural studies is devoted to analyzing the "medical behaviour" of individuals. These studies have produced a large body of theoretical and empirical literature. Much of this literature concerns the study of differential attitudes toward health and illness, differential health practices, variability of reactions to symptoms and illnesses, and variability in the use of health services.

Another kind of analysis focuses on the behaviour of the provider of services and health-care institutions. The health sector, however, is integrally related to the larger society. It is therefore argued that to study the health-care system without attention to its linkages to broad political, economic, and social forces is misleading. These studies try to transcend the individual level of analysis to find how these linkages determine the nature, composition, and function of the health-care sector and the very definition of health and illness.

A significant portion of past research in medical sociology has been about the "medical behaviour" of consumers of health-care services and the social process which influence the decisions of individuals to use medical services (Albrecht et al., 1979; Cockerham, 1978; Coe, 1970; Krause, 1977; Tuckett, 1976). A number of authors have identified socio-psychological, socio-demographic, and socio-economic variables to account for variability in health behaviour and illness behaviour. According to Kasl and Cobb (1966:246): "health behaviour is any activity undertaken by a person believing himself to be healthy for the purpose of preventing disease or detecting it in an asymptomatic stage" and "illness behaviour is an activity undertaken by a person who feels ill, to define the state of his health and to discover a suitable remedy." Kasl and Cobb state that the likelihood of one's engaging in any particular behaviour is a function of the perceived amount of threat (perceived susceptibility and perceived seriousness) and the attractiveness of the behaviour (perceived probability of amelioration). Social class status, education, occupation, and income levels are important variables in influencing these perceptions.

King (1962) also emphasizes the importance, in any health related action, of the way one "sees or perceives the situation of disease and all of the social ramifications that accompany it." Mechanic's (1962, 1963) concept of illness behaviour has a similar basis, and is concerned with "the ways in which given symptoms may be differentially perceived, evaluated and acted (or not acted) upon by different kinds of persons."

Rosenstock (1966) as well suggests that preventive health behaviour is determined by one's perception of the seriousness of and susceptibility to the problem, perceived benefits of taking action, barriers to taking action, and cues to action. Rosenstock's (1966:98) health behaviour model is based on individual motivation and beliefs and includes two classes of variables: the individual's readiness (psychological) to act and the belief that a particular course of action will, on the whole, be beneficial in reducing the threat of illness. Rosenstock (1966:119) states that an individual's decision to participate in preventive health behaviour will not be made unless the individual is psychologically ready to take action concerning a particular health condition, believes that the action is feasible and appropriate, and encounters a stimulus that triggers the response.

Zola (1964), approaching the problem from a somewhat different perspective, presents a sequential model consisting of "five triggers" in an individual's decision to seek medical care. These are:

1. interpersonal crisis (whereby attention is called to the symptom);

2. social interference (the symptom threatens the individual's social activity);

3. the presence of sanctioning (some other person telling him or her to seek help);

4. perceived threat of the symptom (cognitive response); and

5. the nature and quality of the symptom (involves comparison of symptoms to previous ones, or to those of his or her friends and relatives in order to decide whether to seek help).

Zola also reports that these triggers are viewed differently in importance by various social strata and ethnic groups. Among the Italians the predominant triggers were "interpersonal crisis" and "social interference"; "sanctioning" was the predominant Irish trigger, and "nature and quality of the symptom" was the most significant trigger for Anglo-Saxons.

Suchman (1965b) presents stages of illness and medical care, discerning five stages "demarcating critical transition and decision making points in medical care and behaviour." These stages are symptom experience, sick-role, medical-care contact, dependent-patient role, and rehabilitation. Mechanic (1968) has identified a list of socio-psychological and socio-economic factors which affect individual coping response to illness.

Andersen's (1968:14) "behaviour model of families' use of health services" is composed of predisposition, ability, and need. The model suggests that a sequence of conditions contribute to the volume of health services used. Use of health services is dependent on: ". . . the predisposition of the family to use health services, . . . their ability to secure services, and . . . their need for such services."

Other writers have emphasized the role of cultural, ethnic, and social class differences in health and illness behaviour. These writers primarily view health and illness behaviour as a socially learned response. Thus Koos (1967:160) observed that "the health attitudes and behaviour of a family are related to its. position in the social class hierarchy of the community, and are significantly affected by the prescriptions and proscriptions regarding health shared by those who are members of the same social class." Koos underlines the variation of health related activities from one social stratum to another based on differential perception of health and illness. For instance, upper-class persons were more likely than lower-class persons to view themselves as ill when they had particular symptoms and were more likely to seek medical advice. In brief, Koos (1967) emphasized two factors: (1) social class differences in opinions, attitudes, and behaviour and (2) perceptions of illness and health which are dictated by culture and environment. These factors also influence what the individual "will or will not, can or cannot, expect or accept from those who make his health their professional concern" (Koos, 1967:156–157).

Saunders (1954) notes the differences between Spanish-speaking Americans and Anglos in their attitudes and response to illness and in their use of health facilities. The Anglos preferred modern medicine for many illnesses while Spanish-speaking people were more likely to use home remedies or folk medicine and family care. Similar observations have been made concerning other groups in various cultural contexts (Clark, 1959; Paul, 1955; Leighton and Leighton, 1945; Mead, 1953; Joseph, 1964; Adair et al., 1957; Stone, 1962; Rubel, 1960; Hartly, Straus, and Mead, 1961).

The role of cultural and ethnic differences in illness behaviour is described by Zborowski (1952) in his study of Jewish, Italian, Irish, and "old Americans." Both the Jewish and the Italian patients respond emotionally to pain and tend to exaggerate the pain experience, the Irish tend to deny pain, and "old Americans" tend to be stoical and "objective." Zborowski views these behavioural differences in light of the familial response to children's health and illness among the Jewish and Italian families.

Ethnic differences in illness behaviour have been described in a variety of other studies (Croog, 1961; Mechanic, 1963; Suchman, 1964, 1965b). These studies show a considerable variation in illness behaviour according to ethnicity.

The response to illness may also take the form of self-help or self-medication and consulation with relatives, friends, and neighbours (Phillips, 1965). Some writers also relate the delay in seeking medical help to particular medical orientations and to socio-economic factors (Polgar, 1959; King, 1962; Suchman, 1965a; Goldsen, 1957, 1963; Kutner et al., 1958; MacGregor, 1961).

However, the socio-psychological models with their emphasis on characteristics of individuals, their value systems, perceptions, health beliefs, and orientations are of limited use because they tend to overlook the importance of class inequalities (except indirectly as they affect perceptions and values), availability of and accessibility to medical services, organization and delivery of health-care services, and other structural factors. These inequalities continue to exist even in Canada, where the principle of universality was a major impetus to the introduction of medical care in the sixties (See for example, Wilkins and Adams, 1983; Shah and Farkas, 1985). While a number of studies in this book attest to these inequalities, it is worth quoting at length from a statement by Jake Epp, Minister of Health and Welfare, in a recent policy paper entitled "Achieving Health For All: A Framework For Health Promotion." Epp (1986:398) states:

> The first challenge we face is to find ways of reducing inequities in the health of low- versus high-income groups in Canada.
> There is disturbing evidence which shows that despite Canada's superior system, people's health remains directly related to their economic status. For example, it has been reported that men in the upper income group live six years longer than men with a low income. The difference is a few years less for women. With respect to disabilities, the evidence is even more startling. Men in upper income groups can expect 14 more disability-free years than men with a low income; in the case of women, the difference is eight years.

Among low-income groups, people are more likely to die as a result of accidental falls, chronic respiratory disease, pneumonia, tuberculosis and cirrhosis of the liver. Also, certain conditions are more prevalent among Canadians in low-income groups; they include mental health disorders, high blood pressure and disorders of the joints and limbs.

Within the low-income bracket, certain groups have a higher chance of experiencing poor health than others. Older people, the unemployed, welfare recipients, single women supporting children and minorities such as natives and immigrants all fall into this category. More than one million children in Canada are poor. Poverty affects over half of single-parent families, the overwhelming majority of them headed by women. These are the groups for whom "longer life but worsening health" is a stark reality.

Rather than studying the behaviour of the consumers, others have analyzed the behaviour of the providers of health services and the interaction among different interest groups within the health sector. Focus is primarily on what "goes on" within the health sector without reference to the linkages between the health sector and the broader society. Studies in this area have focussed on such topics as organization and distribution of health-care services, medical education, health-care institutions (e.g., hospitals and nursing homes), professional domination and medical division of labour, and racial inequality in the health sector (See for example, Freidson, 1970a, 1970b; Fee, 1983).

Other analysts question the clinical effectiveness and technical claims of modern scientific medicine. Illich's work, *Medical Nemesis*, has received considerable attention in mass media and in professional circles. Illich (1976) provides considerable evidence of the ineffectiveness of modern medicine in reducing morbidity and mortality and in improving the health of the population. He portrays medicine as a coercive institution and has taken the view that current medical practices are generally doing more harm than good. Illich's analysis centres around three categories (clinical, social, and structural) of iatrogenesis (disease caused or induced by a physician or medical treatment).

He feels that iatrogenesis is clinical when "pain, sickness, and death result from the provision of medical care"; social when "health policies reinforce an industrial organization which generates dependency and ill health"; and structural when "medically sponsored behavior and delusions restrict the vital autonomy of people by undermining their competency in growing up, caring for each other and aging" (Illich, 1976:165).

According to Illich, clinical iatrogenesis includes "all clinical entities for which remedies, physicians or hospitals are the pathogens or 'sickening' agents." Medical domination has led to loss of autonomy and creation of dependency for patients. The responsibility for health is expropriated from individuals by the medical profession.

Illich attributes these iatrogenic effects to the industrialization, bureaucratization and monopoly power of the medical profession, and the over-medicalization of life which perpetuates the addictive dependency of the populace on medicine and medical institutions. The solution, therefore, lies in de-bureaucratization, de-industrialization, and de-monopolization. He proposes de-medicalization, and the return of more autonomy and responsibility to individuals for their health and self-care (For critique, see Starr, 1981; Navarro, 1977:38–58; Waitzkin, 1976). He confines the solutions to the health-care system itself without reference to the structural tendencies and political, social, economic, and class forces in the broader society which perpetuate this system. As Waitzkin (1983:5) notes: "Without attention to these connections, the health system falsely takes on the appearance of an autonomous, free-floating entity, whose defects purportedly can be corrected by limited reforms in the medical sphere."

In recent years, a considerable volume of literature has in fact emerged which does focus on the linkages between the political, economic, and social systems and the health-care sector. (See for example, Navarro, 1986; Waitzkin, 1983; Doyal and Pennell, 1979). This approach is predicated on the fact that the contradictions in medicine reflect the contradictions in society;

that is, the health sector is so integral to the broader society that the attempt to study the one without attention to the other will be misleading. As Waitzkin (1983:5) comments: "Difficulties in health and medical care emerged from social contradictions and rarely can be separated from those contradictions." For instance, one of the contradictions in this society is between profit and safety. If it interferes with profits, an improvement in occupational health and safety is not very likely to be implemented. Gender and other inequalities in the health sector are reflections of these inequalities in the society. While in the discussion of escalating health-care costs the focus is generally on consumers and the health-sector labour force, little attention is given to the corporate invasion of the medical sector, usually referred to as the "medical–industrial complex." A high-technology mentality has encouraged costly and expensive medicine. To fully understand the escalating costs in medicine, one must consider the nexus of societal contradictions. As Waitzkin (1983:37) states:

> While physicians' earnings are important, it is an error to overrate them. Professional fees have their impact within a nexus of social contradictions that encourage practices, inappropriate technology, uncritical acceptance of innovations, corporate exploitation of illness, and the public subsidization of private medicine.

Others have noted the role of the capitalist state, class contradictions, ideology of medicine, medicalization, and illness related to the capitalist production process (For example, see Berliner, 1977; Fee, 1983; Salmon, 1977; Swartz, 1977; Walters, 1982; Kelman, 1971, 1975, 1977; Navarro, 1986, 1977, 1976; Turkshew, 1977; McKinley, 1984; Waitzkin, 1983; Waitzkin and Waitzkin, 1974; Minkler, 1983; Crawford, 1980).

It is increasingly being recognized that the socio-psychological models of consumer behaviour and studies with exclusive focus on the health sector and its contradictions do not provide an adequate and comprehensive analysis of the current health crisis which is characterized by escalating costs and diminishing returns. By focussing on individuals and the health sector, these analyses tend to portray individuals and the health sector as though they existed in a vacuum. They tend to decontextualize the individuals and the health sector. The health-care policies which flow from these analyses would further increase the disparities in health status and health-care utilization in the populace. For instance, those who depend upon public sponsored health services would be adversely affected by any rationing of services or promotion of self-care. As Waitzkin comments:

> ... the medicalization of social problems has many damaging effects, but the demedicalization of medical problems promises even worse repercussions. Self-care is fine, but it does not substitute for health services when needed. Nor can self-care offset the necessity of struggle against illness generating conditions in the workplace, environment, and organization of society.

It is argued that because of the close linkages between medicine and the social, economic, political, and class forces in the broader society, attempts to reform and transform medicine must be tied to wider strategies of change in the societal structure. The contradictions in medicine reflect contradictions of larger society and they cannot be resolved by focussing on the health sector alone or on individual clinicians. As Waitzkin (1983:8) notes:

> It is the structure of the system, rather than decision making by individual entrepreneurs and clinicians, that is the appropriate level of analysis. This distinction makes all the difference for policy and social action.

SUMMARY AND CONCLUSIONS

It was noted that the mechanistic view of human organism is still the prevalent and dominant paradigm in scientific medicine. This is of significance with regard to the etiology of health and illness as well as the treatment. Ill health in this context means the breakdown and malfunctioning of the machine (human body) and the treatment consists of surgical or chemical interventions to restore normal functioning. In functional terms, the sole criterion of health is the capacity of the individual to perform as he or she has been socialized to perform. The experience of ill health in itself does not constitute illness.

Others have argued that health in capitalist society is tied to production and the capital accumulation process. Health viewed in this way has important implications in terms of the levels of health services. Employers want to keep workers in good working order and "it is not important that they feel well as long as they are able to work hard." Viewed in this context, the investments to maintain healthy and productive workers are considered the same way as investments in other factors of production, and have to be balanced against returns.

While the clinical model attributes disease to "malfunctioning" of the human body, the new reductionism introduces the idea that disease lies in individual lifestyle and behaviour. In the former case, the normal functioning of the body can be restored through "technological fixes," while in the latter, the solution lies primarily in changing individual behaviour and patterns of consumption. Both approaches obscure the social nature of disease, which is the subject matter of historical materialistic epidemiology, which identifies social conditions in society that produce illness, disease, and mortality.

This chapter also discussed the various socio-psychological, socio-demographic, and socio-economic factors that influence the medical behaviour of consumers. Other studies have focussed upon the health sector and its contradictions, and recently a body of literature has emerged that focusses on the linkages between the political, economic, social, and class forces in the broader society and in the health-care system.

The collection of essays in this book examines the essential topics in medical sociology from a variety of theoretical perspectives and at varying levels of analysis. Their common intention is to provide an understanding of medicine, health, illness, and the health-care system.

REFERENCES

Adair, John, et al. "Patterns of Health and Disease Among the Navajos." *Annals of the American Academy of Political Science* 311 (May 1957): 80–94.

Albrecht, Gary L., and Paul C. Higgins, eds. *Health, Illness, and Medicine.* Chicago: Rand McNally, 1979.

Anderson, Ronald. *A Behavioral Model of Families' Use of Health Services.* Center for Health Administration Studies Chicago: University of Chicago Press, 1968.

Berliner, Howard S. "Emerging Ideologies in Medicine." *Review of Radical Political Economics* 9, no. 1 (1977): 116–24.

———. "A Larger Perspective on the Flexner Report." *International Journal of Health Services* 5 (1975): 573–92.

Brown, E.R. *Rockefeller Medicine Men: Medicine and Capitalism in The Progressive Era.* Berkeley, California: University of California Press, 1979.

Carlson, Rick. *The End of Medicine.* New York: Wiley Interscience, 1975.

Clark, M. *Health in the Mexican-American Culture.* Berkeley: University of California Press, 1959.

Cockerham, William C. *Medical Sociology.* Englewood Cliffs, New Jersey: Prentice-Hall, 1978.

Coe, Rodney M. *Sociology of Medicine.* New York: McGraw-Hill, 1970.

Croog, S.H. "Ethnic Origins, Educational Level, and Responses to a Health Questionnaire." *Human Organization* 20 (1961): 65–69.

Crawford, R. "Healthism and the Medicalization of Everyday Life." *International Journal of Health Services* 10, no. 3 (1980): 365–88.

Doyal, Lesley, with Imogen Pennell. *The Political Economy of Health*. London: Pluto Press, 1979.

Dreitzel, H.P., ed. *The Social Organization of Health*. New York: Macmillan Company, 1971.

Epp, Jake. "Achieving Health For All: A Framework For Health Promotion." *Canadian Journal of Public Health* 77, no. 6 (November–December 1986): 393–407.

Eyer, Joe. "Capitalism, Health, and Illness." In *Issues in the Political Economy of Health Care*, edited by John B. McKinlay, 23–59. New York: Tavistock Publications, 1984.

Fee, Elizabeth, ed. *Women and Health: The Politics of Sex in Medicine*. Farmingdale, New York: Baywood Publishing Co., 1983.

Flexner, A. *Medical Education in the United States and Canada*. New York: Carnegie Foundation, 1910.

Freidson, E. *Professional Dominance*. New York: Atherton Press, 1970a.

———. *Profession of Medicine*. New York: Dodd Mead and Company, 1970b.

Goldsen, R. "Patient Delay in Seeking Cancer Diagnosis: Behavioral Aspects." *Journal of Chronic Diseases* 16 (1963): 427–36.

———. "Some Factors Related to Patient Delay in Seeking Diagnosis for Cancer Symptoms." *Cancer* 10 (1957): 1–7.

Hackett, J.D. *Health Maintenance in Industry*. Chicago: Shaw, 1925.

Hartly, E., R. Straus, and M. Mead. "Determinants of Health Beliefs and Behavior." *American Journal of Public Health* 51 (October 1961): 1541–54.

Illich, Ivan. *Medical Nemesis: The Expropriation of Health*. New York: Pantheon, 1976.

Inglefinger, F.J., ed. *Dorland Medical Dictionary*. New York: Holt, Rinehart and Winston, 1982.

Joseph, Alice. "Physicians and Patients, Some Aspects of Interpersonal Relationships between Physicians and Patients with Special Regard to the Relationship between White Physicians and Indian Patients." *Applied Anthropology* 1 (July–August–September 1964): 1–6.

Kasl, Stanislav V., and Sidney Cobb. "Health Behavior, Illness Behavior, and Sick-Role Behavior." *Archives of Environmental Health* 12 (February 1966): 246–66; and 12 (April 1966): 531–41.

Kelman, Sander. "Toward the Political Economy of Medical Care." *Inquiry* 8, no. 3 (1971): 30–38.

———. "The Social Nature of the Definition of Health." In *Health and Medical Care in the U.S.: A Critical Analysis*, edited by Vicente Navarro, 3–20. Farmingdale, New York: Baywood Publishing Co., 1977.

———. "The Social Nature of the Definition Problem in Health." *International Journal of Health Services* 5, no. 4 (1975): 625–42.

King, Stanley H. *Perceptions of Illness and Medical Practice*. New York: Russell Sage Foundation, 1962.

Koos, Earl L. *The Health of Regionville*. New York: Hafner Publishing Company, 1967.

Krause, Elliott A. *Power and Illness: The Political Sociology of Health and Medical Care*. New York: Elsevier, 1977.

Kunitz, S.J. "Professionalism and Social Control in the Progressive Era: The Case of Flexner Report." *Social Problems* 22 (1974): 16–27.

Kutner, B., et al. "Delay in the Diagnosis and Treatment of Cancer: A Critical Analysis of the Literature." *Journal of Chronic Diseases* 7 (1958): 95–120.

Lalonde, Marc. *A New Perspective on the Health of Canadians*. Ottawa: Information Canada, 1974.

Leighton, A., and D. Leighton. *The Navaho Door*. Cambridge: Harvard University Press, 1945.

MacGregor, G. "Social Determinants of Health Practices." *American Journal of Public Health* 51 (November 1961): 1709–14.

McKeown, T. *Medicine in Modern Society*. London: Allen and Unwin, 1965.

McKinlay, John B., ed. *Issues In The Political Economy of Health Care*. London: Tavistock Publications, 1984.

Mead, Margaret. *Cultural Patterns and Technical Change*. UNESCO, World Federation for Mental Health, 1953.

Mechanic, David. "The Concept of Illness Behavior." *Journal of Chronic Diseases* 15 (February 1962): 189–94.

———. *Medical Sociology*. New York: The Free Press, 1968.

———. "Religion, Religiosity, and Illness Behavior: The Special Case of The Jews." *Human Organization* 22 (1963): 202–8.

Minkler, Meredith. "Blaming the Aged Victim: The Politics of Scapegoating in Times of Fiscal Conservatism." *International Journal of Health Services* 13, no. 1 (1983): 155–68.

Navarro, Vicente. *Crisis, Health, and Medicine*. New York: Tavistock Publications, 1986.

———, ed. *Health and Medical Care in the U.S.: A Critical Analysis*. Farmingdale, New York: Baywood Publishing Co., 1977.

———. "The Industrialization of Fetishism or the Fetishism of Industrialization." In *Health and Medical Care in the U.S.: A Critical Analysis*, edited by Vicente Navarro, 38–58. Farmingdale, New York: Baywood Publishing Co., 1977.

———. *Medicine Under Capitalism*. New York: Prodist, 1976.

Nielsen, W.A. *The Big Foundations*. New York: Columbia University Press, 1972.

Parsons, Talcott. "Definitions of Health and Illness in the Light of the American Values and Social Structure." In *Patients, Physicians, and Illness*, edited by E. Gartly Jaco, 2nd ed., 107–27. New York: Free Press, 1972.

Paul, B., ed. *Health, Culture and Community*. New York: Russell Sage Foundation, 1955.

Phillips, D.L. "Self-Reliance and the Inclination to Adopt the Sick Role." *Social Forces* 43 (May 1965): 555–63.

Polgar, S. "Health and Human Behavior." *Current Anthropology* 3 (April 1959): 159–205.

Postell, W.D. *The Health of Slaves on Southern Plantations*. Baton Rouge, Louisiana: The Louisiana State University Press, 1961.

Powles, John. "On the Limitation of Modern Medicine." In *Science, Medicine and Man*, London: Pergamon, Vol. 1, no. 1 (1973): 1–30

Renaud, Marc. "On the Structural Constraints to State Intervention in Health." In *Health and Medical Care in the U.S.: A Critical Analysis*, edited by Vicente Navarro, 135–46. Farmingdale, New York: Baywood Publishing Co., 1977.

Rodberg, Leonard, and Gelvin Stevenson. "The Health Care Industry in Advanced Capitalism." *Review of Radical Political Economics* 9, no. 1 (1977): 104–15.

Rosenstock, Irwin M. "Why People Use Health Services." *Milbank Memorial Fund Quarterly* 44, (July 1966): 94–127.

Rossdale, M. "Health in a Sick Society." *New Left Review* 34 (November–December 1965): 82–90.

Rubel, A.J. "Concept of Disease in Mexican-American Culture." *American Anthropologist* 62 (October 1960): 795–814.

Salmon, J. Warren. "Monopoly Capital and the Reorganization of the Health Sector." *Review of Radical Political Economics* 9, no. 1 (1977): 125–33.

Saunders, L. *Cultural Differences and Medical Care*. New York: Russell Sage Foundation, 1954.

Shah, C.P., and C. P. Farkas. "The Health of Indians in Canadian Cities: A Challenge to the Health Care System." *Canadian Medical Association Journal* 133 (1985): 859–63.

Stampp, K.M. *The Peculiar Institution*. New York: Knopf, 1956.

Stark, Evan. "Introduction to the Special Issue on Health." *Review of Radical Political Economics* 9, no. 1 (Spring 1977).

Starr, P. "The Politics of Therapeutic Nihilism." In *The Sociology of Health and Illness: Critical Perspectives*, edited by P. Conrad and R. Kern, 434–48. New York: St. Martin's Press, 1981.

Stone, Eric. *Medicine Among the American Indians*. New York: Hafner Publishing Company, 1962.

Suchman, E. A. "Health Orientations and Medical Care." *American Journal of Public Health* 56 (November 1965a): 97–105.

———. "Sociomedical Variations Among Ethnic Groups." *American Journal of Sociology* 70 (1964): 319–31.

———. "Stages of Illness and Medical Care." *Journal of Health and Human Behavior* 6 (Fall 1965b): 114–28.

Swartz, D. "The Politics of Reform: Conflict and Accommodation in Canadian Health Policy." In *The Canadian State: Political Economy and Political Power*, edited by L. Panitch. Toronto: University of Toronto Press, 1977.

Tuckett, David, ed. *An Introduction to Medical Sociology*. Tavistock Publications, 1976.

Turshen, Meredith. "The Political Ecology of Disease." *The Review of Radical Political Economics* 9, no. 1 (1977): 45–60.

Waitzkin, Howard. "Recent Studies in Medical Sociology: The New Reductionism." *Contemporary Sociology* 5 (1976): 401–5.

———. *The Second Sickness*. New York: Free Press, 1983.

———. "The Marxist Paradigm in Medicine." *International Journal of Health Services* 9, no. 4 (1979): 683–98.

Waitzkin, Howard, and B. Waterman. *The Exploitation of Illness in Capitalist Society*. Indianapolis: Bobbs-Merrill, 1974.

Walters, V. "State, Capital and Labour: The Introduction of Federal-Provincial Insurance for Physician Care in Canada." *Canadian Review of Sociology and Anthropology* 19 (1982): 157–72.

Wilkins, R. and O. Adams. *Healthfulness of Life*. Montreal: Institute For Research on Public Policy, 1983.

Zborowski, M. "Cultural Components in Responses to Pain." *Journal of Social Issues* 8 (1952): 16–30.

Zola, I. "Illness Behavior of the Working Class: Implications and Recommendations." In *Blue Collar World: Studies of the American Worker*, edited by A. Shostak and W. Gomberg, 350–61. Englewood Cliffs, New Jersey: Prentice-Hall, 1964.

PART I

HEALTH STATUS, HEALTH POLICY, AND DELIVERY OF HEALTH CARE

INTRODUCTION

There are currently a number of questions being raised about the national health insurance programme and the health-care system in Canada. Because of the current economic crisis in Canada, the problems of overall health-care costs and the financing of health-care services tend to dominate the discussion. Issues relevant to financing include: federal-provincial cost-sharing arrangements, extra-billing, income and wages of health personnel, user fees, and other institutional costs. Also under debate is the inequality of health status between various socio-economic groups. It is argued that some of the cost-reduction proposals currently being advanced are, if implemented, likely to adversely affect the sick and the poor, and further increase the disparity of health status between high and low socio-economic groups. These concerns are addressed by readings in this section, which provide an overview of the health status of the Canadian population, the development of the health-insurance programme, utilization of health-care resources, and the structure and cost of health care.

In Chapter 2, Hay provides an overview of the health status of the Canadian population and the relationship between selected socio-demographic variables and certain health status indicators. There is a general improvement in the health status of the population, with an increase in life expectancies and decrease in mortality rates for males and females. However, females continue to be characterized by greater life expectancies than males, partly due to lower female mortality rates from most of the major causes of deaths in all age groupings. The evidence presented in Chapter 2 indicates that substantial disparities in life expectancies and mortality rates persist across income and occupational groups, for the unemployed, and for Native Canadians.

Northcott, in Chapter 3, briefly reviews the development of Canada's health insurance programme and the five principles upon which it rests: universality, accessibility, comprehensiveness, portability, and public administration. He goes on to examine issues associated with the financing of the health-care system, with particular emphasis on extra-billing and user fees. Northcott points out that user fees will affect primarily the poor, the sick, and the elderly, who will be deterred from seeking needed care. Furthermore, total costs are not reduced by deterrent fees, because under a fee-for-services system, the providers of health care tend to compensate for lost income by generating extra demand.

Dickinson and Hay, in Chapter 4, broaden the discussion of initiatives and strategies for containment of health costs. They present an overview of the sources and levels of funding for selected health-care and medical services — both doctor-provided and hospital services. They discuss the initiatives taken by various levels of government to lower, or at least contain, health costs and to make delivery of health care more efficient. To achieve these objectives, three general strategies have been adopted: 1) attempts to reduce the episodes of illness requiring medical and/or hospital care, 2) attempts to reduce the number of contacts between the patient and providers of health care during an episode of illness, and 3) attempts to reduce the cost per contact. After an examination of the major consequences of different cost-reduction strategies for the nature and organization of the health-care system, Dickinson and Hay conclude that current cost-containment strategies threaten the principles upon which medicare was founded.

Given that there are already substantial disparities in health status between different socio-economic groups, any cost-containment strategies which impose additional financial burdens on the low socio-economic groups (e.g., user fees, extra-billing) and restrict the accessibility or availability of various health services will adversely affect those who in fact need them most.

Health-care costs, "return" on health dollars, equality of health status, the organization and structure of health-care delivery, and the general principles on which the health-insurance programme was founded are likely to continue to be dominant issues in medical sociology.

2

MORTALITY AND HEALTH STATUS TRENDS IN CANADA

David A. Hay
University of Saskatchewan

Death, its causes, and its deferral have been persistent concerns for humans throughout history. The history of the human race has been one of struggle for survival, with the mortality of humankind reflecting our success or failure in that struggle.

Although it is difficult to pinpoint the origin of the routine collection and analysis of information on the causes and frequencies of deaths, the first systematic analysis of death records may be that of John Graunt, who in 1662 examined burial records for urban and rural locations in England (Peron and Strohmenger, 1985:90). The establishment of national vital statistics accounts and regular population censuses in several European countries in the nineteenth century appears to coincide with the onset of the modern decline in mortality (Peron and Strohmenger, 1985:80).

Such record-keeping, along with the analysis of fertility, mortality, and other vital rates and trends, has continued on a regular basis in the majority of the developed or developing countries in the world today. Indicators such as life expectancy, infant mortality, and other related rates are routinely used as measures of social and economic progress.

This chapter will examine some aspects of the mortality and life expectancy of the Canadian population. A number of relevant indicators of health status, such as life expectancy at birth and related mortality rates, will be utilized.

LIFE EXPECTANCY AT BIRTH

Life expectancy at birth is a widely used indicator of the overall health status of a population. It summarizes the present mortality experiences of a particular birth cohort. As Wilkins (1980:6) indicates, life expectancy at birth is one of the best measures of the health status of a population and is particularly useful for historical, regional, international, and other comparisons.

Table 1 indicates that life expectancy at birth in Canada has improved steadily for both females and males over the period from 1931 to 1981. The improvements in life expectancy have been attributed to substantial reductions both in infant mortality and in deaths due to infectious and parasitic diseases.

The largest gains in life expectancy for both sexes were made between 1931 and 1951;

Table 1. Average Life Expectancy at Birth, Canada, 1931–1981, by Sex

Year	Female	Gain	Male	Gain	Female-Male Difference in Life Expectancy
1931	62.1		60.0		2.1
1941	66.3	4.2	63.0	2.3	3.3
1951	70.8	4.5	66.3	3.3	4.5
1956	72.9	2.1	67.6	1.3	5.3
1961	74.2	1.3	68.3	0.7	5.9
1966	75.2	1.0	68.7	0.4	6.5
1971	76.4	1.2	69.3	0.6	7.1
1976	77.5	1.1	70.2	0.9	7.3
1981	79.0	1.5	71.9	1.7	7.1

Sources: Statistics Canada, 1978(b), Vital Statistics, Vol. 3, Deaths 1976
Statistics Canada, 1983, Vital Statistics, Vol. 3, Mortality 1981

from 1951 the gains in life expectancy occurred at a slower rate. This slowdown has been a cause for concern among health professionals. Peron and Strohmenger (1985:120) indicate that the slowdown may be indicative of an imminent or inevitable stabilization of average longevity, and that future gains may be more difficult to achieve.

However, the modest upturn in life expectancies since 1966, as well as the relatively larger gains experienced in the United States about the same time (Peron and Strohmenger, 1985:120) may indicate that the "plateau" has not been reached. According to Peron and Strohmenger, the gains in the United States were due to the campaign to discourage sedentary lifestyles and reduce exposure to risk factors such as cigarette smoking and the consumption of animal fats, alcohol, and drugs. Future Canadian gains are likely to be derived from these sources and from decreases in mortality from motor vehicle accidents and, especially among the more advanced age groups, from cardiovascular diseases and cancers (Dumas, 1984:83–84).

During the period from 1931 to 1976, the gains in life expectancy at birth for females exceeded those for males. As a result, the differences in life expectancy increased from 2.1 years in 1931 to 7.3 years in 1976. This is due to the well-known lower mortality rates for females from birth.

From 1976 to 1981, however, for the first time in the Canadian experience, the 1.79 years gain in life expectancy for males exceeded the 1.5 years gain for females. This modest relative advantage in gains for males over females is possibly due to a slower decrease, or to a potential increase, in female mortality rates in comparison to male mortality rates from certain causes in certain age groups. For example the convergence of female and male lifestyles in the use of tobacco and alcohol (Abelson et al., 1983:11) is expected to result in an increase in the female death rate attributable to these risk factors.

Although the overall utilization of cigarettes by both sexes is decreasing due in large part to anti-smoking campaigns, the rate for females is not decreasing as rapidly as that for males. The percentage of females between the ages of 20–29 who smoke daily increased up to 1985. (Health and Welfare Canada, 1986:61). This is the only population group which has experienced an increase in cigarette consumption in recent years.

Table 2. Standardized Death Rates* per 1000 Population, Canada, 1931–1981 by Sex, All Causes

Year	Females		Males	
	Standardized Rate	% Change	Standardized Rate	% Change
1931	11.7		12.7	
1941	10.2	−12.8	12.0	−5.5
1951	8.0	−21.5	10.0	−16.7
1956	7.0	−12.5	9.4	−6.0
1961	6.3	−10.0	9.0	−4.2
1966	5.7	−9.5	8.8	−2.2
1971	5.2	−8.8	8.4	−4.5
1976	4.8	−7.7	8.1	−3.6
1981	5.0	+4.2	7.4	−8.6

* Standardized on 1956 Canadian Population

Sources: Statistics Canada, 1976, General Mortality 1950–1972
   Statistics Canada, 1978(b) Vital Statistics, Vol. 3, Deaths 1976
   Statistics Canada, 1983 Vital Statistics, Vol. 3, Mortality, Summary List of Causes, 1981

As indicated in Table 2, the standardized death rate for females increased by 4.2 percent between 1976 and 1981, whereas the comparable rate for males decreased by 8.6 percent. The changes in death rates are generally consistent with the gains in life expectancy. The largest declines occurred up to 1951, with subsequent standardized death rates decreasing at a slower rate, particularly for males up to 1976.

TRENDS IN MORTALITY BY CAUSE, SEX, AND AGE GROUP

In addition to the substantial declines in infant mortality rates, the overall trends in mortality rates have been achieved by the virtual disappearance of parasitic diseases, diseases of the digestive system, tuberculosis, and other infectious diseases. These have been supplanted by other causes of death, such as accidents, poisoning, violence, chronic degenerative diseases of the circulatory system, and cancers. Concentra-

tion of chronic degenerative diseases of the circulatory system and cancers in the older age groups, combined with the decline in mortality in the younger, especially the infant, age groups, has resulted in a shift in the proportion of all deaths occurring at particular ages, as indicated in Table 3.

The percentage of all deaths occurring declined in the infant (under 1 year of age) group from 11.7 percent in 1951 to 2.1 percent in 1981. The relative number of deaths also decreased moderately for the 1-to-4 and 5-to-14 age groups. The relative percentages of all deaths remained relatively constant for the 15-to-24, 25-to-44, and 45-to-64 age groups. The percentages of all deaths which occurred in the age group 65 years and over increased from 53.6 percent in 1951 to 67 percent in 1981. The latter percentage and the overall mortality rates may be expected to rise in the future as the proportion of elderly Canadians continues to grow.

The general examination of improvements in life expectancy and death rates tends to imply a steady overall progress in health status. How-

Table 3. Percentage of All Deaths by Age Group, Canada, 1951–1981, Both Sexes

Age/Year	1951	1956	1961	1966	1971	1976	1981
Under 1 year	11.7	10.9	9.2	6.0	4.0	2.8	2.1
1 to 4 years	2.0	1.8	1.4	1.2	0.8	0.6	0.4
5 to 14 years	1.5	1.4	1.3	1.4	1.3	0.9	0.7
15 to 24 years	2.2	1.8	1.8	2.3	2.8	2.8	2.7
25 to 44 years	7.0	6.3	5.8	5.8	5.8	5.4	5.5
45 to 64 years	22.0	21.1	21.4	22.5	23.0	23.0	21.6
65 years and over	53.6	56.8	59.1	60.9	62.3	64.1	67.0
Total Deaths ('000s)	125.8	132.0	141.0	149.9	157.3	167.0	171.0

Sources: Statistics Canada, 1976: General Mortality 1950 to 1972
    Statistics Canada, 1978a: Causes of Death 1976
    Statistics Canada, 1982: Causes of Death 1981

ever, as Wilkins (1980:10–12) indicates, this tends to obscure important differentials in the relative causes of death by age groupings and sex. A comparison of the female and male mortality experiences for selected age groups will now be considered.

Infant Mortality

The death rate for the group under 1 year of age shows consistent improvement over the period from 1931 to 1981. As indicated in Figure 1, the infant mortality rate for both females and males declined by approximately 89 percent. However, the male rate decreased at a slightly faster rate than the female. As a result, the discrepancy between the sexes also declined over the fifty-year period from a differential of 19.7 per 1000 live births in 1931 to 2.4 per 1000 live births in 1981.

The steepest declines occurred in the period from 1931 to 1951, with subsequent declines up to 1981 occurring at a slower rate, which is also observable in the life expectancies at birth. The substantial declines in infant mortality up to 1951 were primarily "due to lower mortality from diarrhoea and enteritis, influenza, bronchitis, pneumonia, and the virtual elimination of whooping cough as a leading cause of death,"

most of which had been achieved by 1951 (Dominion Bureau of Statistics, 1967:9). Improvements since that date have been somewhat slower, due to the relative increase in causes such as immaturity, congenital problems, asphyxia, and accidents (Dominion Bureau of Statistics, 1967:9).

Figure 1: Infant Mortality Rates per 1000 Live Births by Sex, Canada, 1931–1981

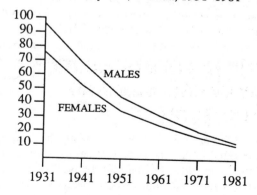

Sources: Statistics Canada, 1978(b) Vital Statistics, Vol. 3, Deaths 1976
    Statistics Canada, 1983, Vital Statistics, Vol. 3, Mortality, 1981

The infant mortality rate has shown the greatest improvement in comparison to the rates for other age groups over the period from 1931 to 1981. However, the infant mortality rate is still greater than comparable rates for all other Canadian age groups up to the 65-year-and-over group. The Canadian infant mortality rate is also higher than that for countries such as Iceland, Sweden, and Japan (Wilkins, 1980:13–14).

15-to-24 Year Age Group

The percentage of all Canadian deaths attributable to the 15-to-24 age group has been relatively constant from 1951 to 1981, as shown in Table 3. This age group does, however, deserve special attention because of the relative prevalence of deaths from preventable causes, and the tragic loss of productive years of life for Canada in an age group which is about to begin, or has embarked upon, productive careers.

The total mortality rate for this age group decreased by more than 80 percent for females and by more than 50 percent for males between 1931 and 1961 (Dominion Bureau of Statistics, 1967:9–10). According to this source, the most important factor in these changes was the elimination of tuberculosis as a leading cause of death, along with reductions in deaths due to influenza, bronchitis, and pneumonia.

Since achieving its lowest value in 1961, the male mortality rate increased to 1971 (Wilkins, 1980:4) and then decreased by approximately 4.9 percent to 1981, as indicated in Table 4. The female mortality rate showed little or no improvement from 1961 to 1971 (Wilkins, 1980:14) but as indicated in Table 4, the overall female mortality rate declined by approximately 20 percent between 1971 and 1981.

Motor vehicle accidents were the leading cause of death for both females and males in 1971 and 1981, accounting for over 39 percent of all deaths for both sexes. This age group also accounted for the largest percentage of all traffic accident deaths in both years under consideration. In 1971 approximately 28 percent of all female and approximately 36 percent of all male deaths attributed to vehicular accidents occurred between the ages of 15 and 24. In 1981 the comparable figures were 30 percent for females and approximately 40 percent for males.

A substantial portion of the motor vehicle accidents and resultant fatalities in this and other age groups is attributable to the increased consumption of alcohol by Canadians of both sexes. For example, McSheffrey (1981:78) found that alcohol was involved in approximately 38 percent of fatal traffic accidents and in 47 percent of motor vehicle accidents involving injuries in Saskatchewan between 1970 and 1977. Likewise, for Canada in 1977, 38 percent of traffic accident fatalities were attributable to hazardous drinking (Statistics Canada, 1980:43).

McSheffrey (1981:73) also indicated that the number of impaired driving offences in Saskatchewan had increased by over 370 percent during the period from 1970 to 1977. A roadside survey conducted by the Department of Transport in 1974 found that the largest proportion of impaired drivers was in the 20-to-24 age group, followed by the 25-to-29 and 30-to-34 age groups (Statistics Canada, 1980:43).

Both the female and male death rates due to motor vehicle accidents decreased over the ten-year period. These reductions have been attributed to the compulsory use of seatbelts in most provinces, reductions in distances travelled by motorists as a result of higher fuel prices, lower speed limits, and more severe penalties for traffic violations such as speeding and impaired driving (Dumas, 1984:88).

Accidental deaths (other than in motor vehicles and by suicide) were the second leading cause of death for both females and males in the 15-to-24 age group during the period from 1971 to 1981.

The third leading cause of death for males in 1971 and 1981 and for females in 1981 was suicide. In 1971, the 15-to-24 age group accounted for approximately 12 percent of all female suicides and about 19 percent of all male suicides. In 1981, the percentage of all suicidal deaths occurring in this age group had increased to 13 percent for females and approximately 25 percent for males.

Table 4. Mortality Rates* and Percentage of Selected Causes of Death by Sex, 15-to-24-Year Age Group, 1971 and 1981

| | 1971 | | | | 1981 | | | |
| | Female | | Male | | Female | | Male | |
Cause of Death	Mortality Rate	% of Deaths	Mortality Rate	% of Deaths	Mortality Rate	% of Deaths	Mortality Rate	% of Deaths
Motor vehicle accidents	22.6	39.5	72.7	46.0	18.0	39.1	66.3	44.1
Other accidental deaths	9.2	16.1	39.9	25.3	8.2	17.8	35.3	23.5
Suicide	4.3	7.6	17.6	11.1	4.9	10.6	27.9	18.1
All cancers	5.9	10.2	9.6	6.1	4.6	9.9	6.4	4.4
All cardiovascular diseases	3.1	5.4	3.6	2.3	2.0	4.2	3.1	2.0
Respiratory system diseases	2.6	4.5	2.2	1.4	1.2	2.5	2.0	1.3
All other causes	9.6	15.9	12.4	6.6	7.1	15.9	9.2	6.6
TOTAL	57.3		158.0		46.0		150.2	

* Rates per 100 000 population

Sources: Statistics Canada, 1972: Causes of Death 1971
       Statistics Canada, 1982: Causes of Death 1981

The long-term trend in suicidal death for females was relatively stable from 1930 to 1960, with a slight increase occurring up to 1970 (Statistics Canada, 1977:77). The female suicide rate increased by approximately 14 percent between 1971 and 1981, as indicated in Table 4. In 1971, suicides accounted for 7.6 percent of all female deaths in this age group, with the percentage increasing to 10.6 in 1981.

The male suicide rate, which was four to five times greater than the female rate in 1971 and 1981, has been more erratic than the female rate since the 1930s. The overall male suicide rate declined by approximately 40 percent from 1930 to 1945, but has since then increased at a relatively constant rate (Statistics Canada, 1977:77). As shown in Table 4, the male suicide rate increased by approximately 59 percent from 1971 to 1981 while accounting for 11.1 and 18.1 percent of all male deaths, respectively.

The death rates for the other causes included in Table 4 remained relatively constant over the ten-year period, with the death rate due to all cancers declining by 22 percent for

females and 33 percent for males from 1971 to 1981. Cancer, with a mortality rate of 5.6, was the third leading cause of death for females in 1971.

25-to-44 Year Age Group

This age group, which accounted for between 7.0 to 5.5 percent of all deaths between 1951 and 1981, appears to be a transition ground between the 15-to-24-year group and the older age groupings. While retaining some of the mortality patterns of the previous group in relation to the relative importance of deaths due to accidents, poisoning, and violence, as indicated in Table 5, the death rates due to causes such as cancer for both sexes and ischaemic heart diseases for males have increased substantially. These latter causes are generally more prevalent in the older population.

Deaths due to motor vehicle and other accidents are important in this age group. However, the emergence in the relative importance of cancer for both sexes, and of ischaemic heart

Table 5. Mortality Rates* and Percentage of Selected Causes of Death by Sex, 25-to-44-Year Age Group, 1971 and 1981

| | 1971 | | | | 1981 | | | |
| | Female | | Male | | Female | | Male | |
Cause of Death	Mortality Rate	% of Deaths	Mortality Rate	% of Deaths	Mortality Rate	% of Deaths	Mortality Rate	% of Deaths
Motor vehicle accidents	11.8	10.0	38.1	17.5	9.2	10.6	32.6	18.7
Other accidental deaths	12.4	10.5	46.4	21.3	10.3	11.9	34.3	19.7
Suicide	9.5	8.0	24.2	11.1	8.5	9.8	26.2	15.0
All cancers	37.8	31.9	29.1	13.3	28.3	32.7	23.6	13.3
Ischaemic heart disease	5.2	4.4	32.4	14.8	4.4	5.0	21.7	12.5
Cerebrovascular heart disease	6.8	5.8	5.6	2.6	4.7	5.4	4.2	2.4
Other cardiovascular diseases	6.5	5.5	7.7	3.5	3.2	3.7	5.8	3.3
Respiratory system diseases	4.7	4.0	5.9	2.7	3.0	3.4	3.0	1.7
All other causes	23.5	19.9	28.7	13.2	15.1	17.5	23.0	13.4
TOTAL	118.2		218.1		86.7		174.4	

* Rates per 100 000 population

Sources: Statistics Canada, 1972: Causes of Death 1971
          Statistics Canada, 1982: Causes of Death 1981

diseases for males, indicate that lifestyle factors such as smoking, alcohol consumption, and sedentary habits are increasingly significant risk factors.

In 1971 and 1981, the premature death rate due to cancer for females is approximately three times greater than the rates for the two next most important causes. Over the period from 1971 to 1981, the cancer rate for females declined by approximately 25 percent, while that for males decreased by approximately 19 percent.

Accidental deaths, other than those due to motor vehicles and suicides, were the most important cause of death for males and the second most important cause for females for 1971 and 1981. Over the decade, the mortality rate due to these causes decreased by over 26 percent and 16 percent for males and females respectively.

Motor vehicle accidents were the second most important cause of death for males and the third most important cause for females in both years. As with the 15-to-24 age group, mortality rates from vehicular accidents decreased over the ten-year period, and for similar reasons. Over 20 percent of all deaths due to motor vehicle accidents in 1971 and 1981 occurred in this age group.

Suicide was the next most important cause of death for both sexes in 1971 and 1981. While the mortality rate due to this cause decreased by approximately 10 percent for females over the ten-year period, the rate for males increased by approximately 8 percent and was approximately 2.5 to three times greater than the female rate in the two years under study. Of all deaths due to suicide in Canada in 1971 and 1981, over 35 percent occurred in this age group, exceeding the percentages occurring in the 15-to-25 age group.

During the period from 1931 to 1981, the overall mortality rate due to all causes in the

25-to-44 age group decreased by approximately 80 percent for females and by 57 percent for males. As with the infant and the 15-to-24 mortality rates, the greatest changes occurred up to 1951. These declines were attributed to the reduction in infectious diseases and maternal deaths, which were particularly high in the early part of the fifty-year period (Dominion Bureau of Statistics, 1967:10). Since 1951, reductions in the overall mortality rate for this age group have been more difficult to achieve, due to the increased relative importance of cancer, cardiovascular diseases, and accidental causes of death.

65-Years-and-Over Age Group

The proportion of all deaths in Canada which occurred in the segment of the population 65 years and older has increased over the period 1951 to 1981, as shown in Table 3. This does not, however, mean that the mortality rates for this age group have increased; rather, it is due to the aging of the Canadian population. In 1971, 8.1 percent of the Canadian population was over 65 years of age; this increased to 9.7 in 1981.

The numerical and relative size of this older age group has increased due to a decline in fertility rates and the decrease in mortality rates at the younger ages. The combination of these two is referred to as "aging from the bottom up." The elderly population has also increased from the top down as a result of a decline in the overall mortality rates in the 65-years-and-over age group. As indicated in Table 6, the overall mortality decreased by approximately 14 percent for females and by slightly over 12 percent for males from 1971 to 1981.

This was a continuation of the downward trend in the total mortality rates for both sexes which commenced in 1941. Prior to that date, the mortality rates for both sexes had been increasing (Dominion Bureau of Statistics, 1967:10).

As a result of the higher mortality rates for males in all age groups commencing at birth, the number of elderly females is greater than the number of males. In 1981, there were approxi-

mately 134 females over 65 years of age for every 100 males. In 1971, the ratio of females to males was approximately 1.2:1.0. The imbalance in the number of females and males becomes more pronounced with increasing age.

Deaths due to cardiovascular diseases and all types of cancer are the most important causes of death for this elderly age group. Ischaemic heart diseases were the most prevalent cause of death for both sexes in 1971 and 1981, accounting for approximately 37 percent of all deaths in 1971 and about 33 percent of all deaths in 1981. The male mortality rate due to ischaemic heart diseases, which was approximately 1.5 times greater than the female rate in both 1971 and 1981, declined by approximately 22 percent. The female mortality rate due to this cause decreased by about 24 percent over the ten-year period.

Deaths due to all types of cancer were the second most important cause for both sexes in 1971 and 1981. The cancer mortality rate for males increased by 5 percent, with the female rate increasing by approximately 3 percent from 1971 to 1981. The female mortality rate due to cancers was approximately 57 percent lower than the male rate in both 1971 and 1981.

Cerebrovascular heart diseases were the next most important cause of death for females in 1971 and 1981 and for males in 1971. In 1981, male deaths from this cause ranked fifth behind other diseases of the cardiovascular and respiratory systems. The mortality rates of cerebrovascular diseases showed considerable improvement for both sexes over the period from 1971 to 1981. The male mortality rate declined by approximately 32 percent, with the female rate improving by about 29 percent. The mortality rates for other cardiovascular diseases also showed an improvement for both sexes over the decade.

Accidents, poisonings, and violence accounted for less than 3 percent of all deaths for females and males in both 1971 and 1981. (Within the younger age groups, these causes comprised a more substantial proportion of all deaths.) The mortality rates for motor vehicle

Table 6. Mortality Rates* and Percentage of Selected Causes of Death by Sex, 65-Years-and-Over Age Group, 1971 and 1981

| | 1971 | | | | 1981 | | | |
| | Female | | Male | | Female | | Male | |
Cause of Death	Mortality Rate	% of Deaths	Mortality Rate	% of Deaths	Mortality Rate	% of Deaths	Mortality Rate	% of Deaths
Ischaemic heart disease	1696.2	36.3	2554.0	37.7	1290.7	32.0	1982.8	33.3
All cancers	786.4	16.8	1348.4	19.9	810.4	20.1	1416.1	23.8
Cerebrovascular heart disease	755.9	16.2	795.3	11.7	535.3	13.3	542.2	9.1
Other cardiovascular diseases	541.5	11.6	647.8	9.6	527.9	13.1	617.2	10.4
Respiratory system diseases	267.4	5.7	601.7	8.9	239.3	5.9	564.7	9.5
Other accidental deaths	99.2	2.1	118.0	1.7	80.6	2.0	102.1	1.7
Motor vehicle accidents	22.1	0.5	46.2	0.7	15.6	0.4	32.2	0.5
Suicide	7.3	0.2	24.7	0.4	9.0	0.2	30.3	0.5
All other causes	495.9	10.6	642.7	9.4	524.1	13.0	664.2	11.2
TOTAL	4671.9		6778.8		4033.1		5951.8	

* Rates per 100 000 population

Sources: Statistics Canada, 1972: Causes of Death 1971
　　　　　Statistics Canada, 1982: Causes of Death 1981

and other accidental causes decreased for both sexes. Suicide, which accounted for a small proportion of all deaths in this elderly age group, did, however, increase by approximately 23 percent for females and males from 1971 to 1981.

All Age Groups

In order to summarize the mortality patterns for 1971 and 1981, Table 7 presents the mortality rates and percent of deaths due to selected causes. As indicated in the table, over 79 percent of all deaths for both sexes in 1971 and 1981 are due to cardiovascular diseases, cancers, and accidents, poisonings, and violence.

Cardiovascular diseases were the primary cause of death for both sexes in 1971 and 1981, with deaths due to all types of cancer being the second most important causal grouping in both years.

Ischaemic heart diseases were the most important cause of death within the cardiovascu-

lar group in accounting for approximately 55 percent of all female and approximately 67 percent of all male cardiovascular deaths in 1971 and 1981. Acute myocardial infarctions (heart attacks) were the most frequent of all ischaemic diseases for males and females in both 1971 and 1981.

During the ten-year period under consideration, the mortality rate for ischaemic heart diseases declined by 7.4 percent for females, while the male mortality rate decreased by 14.4 percent. The mortality rates for cerebrovascular diseases also declined, at rates of 14.3 percent and 22.7 percent, respectively, for females and males. The greater reduction in male mortality rates from ischaemic and cerebrovascular heart diseases over the decade has resulted in a convergence of the female and male rates. According to Dumas (1984:86), these improvements during the 1970s were unexpected and have been attributed to medical advances, healthier

Table 7. Crude Mortality Rates* and Percentage of Selected Causes of Death by Sex, All Ages, 1971 and 1981

| | 1971 | | | | 1981 | | | |
| | Female | | Male | | Female | | Male | |
Cause of Death	Mortality Rate	% of Deaths	Mortality Rate	% of Deaths	Mortality Rate	% of Deaths	Mortality Rate	% of Deaths
Ischaemic heart disease	174.4	28.7	279.6	32.9	161.4	26.8	239.3	29.8
All cancers	128.2	21.1	162.4	19.1	148.1	24.6	187.5	23.3
Cerebrovascular heart disease	78.4	12.9	70.6	8.3	67.2	11.1	54.6	6.8
Other cardiovascular diseases	57.8	9.5	60.1	7.1	65.5	10.9	65.9	8.2
Respiratory system diseases	34.0	5.6	61.3	7.2	32.4	5.4	58.0	7.2
Other accidental deaths	20.8	3.4	45.6	5.4	18.2	3.0	37.9	4.7
Motor vehicle accidents	14.7	2.4	37.3	4.4	11.1	1.8	32.6	4.1
Suicide	6.4	1.1	17.3	2.0	6.8	1.1	21.3	2.6
All other causes	92.8	15.3	116.4	13.6	91.9	15.3	107.1	13.3
TOTAL	607.5		850.6		602.6		804.2	

* Rates per 100 000 population

Sources: Statistics Canada, 1972: Causes of Death 1971
       Statistics Canada, 1982: Causes of Death 1981

diets, and reductions in smoking.

While the mortality rates for the above cardiovascular diseases have declined during the period from 1971 to 1981, the same cannot be said for other cardiovascular diseases and for cancers. The mortality rates for other cardiovascular diseases increased by slightly over 13 percent for females and by approximately 10 percent for males.

Cancer, which was the second most important cause of death for both males and females in 1971 and 1981, increased by over 15 percent for both sexes during the decade. The majority of deaths due to cancer occur in the older age groups (over 50 years) according to Dumas (1984:87), with the relative importance of different types of cancer varying by age and sex.

In the early 1980s, lung cancer accounted for approximately one third of all male cancer deaths. Cancers of the digestive system were the second most important, accounting for slightly more than 11 percent of the male deaths due to cancer (Health and Welfare Canada, 1984:2).

Breast cancer was the most important type for females in the early 1980s, according to Health and Welfare Canada (1983:2), causing over 19 percent of the female deaths due to cancer, with cancers of the digestive system and lung cancer being the next most important causes. These latter accounted for 13.5 and 12.9 percent of all female cancer deaths, respectively.

The higher male mortality rates due to lung cancer and heart diseases are generally attributed to higher levels of cigarette smoking and alcohol consumption by men, and factors related to this. In the period from 1966 to 1983 the proportion of males aged 15 and over who smoke on a regular basis declined to approximately the same level as for females, for whom the incidence of smoking has stabilized or increased in certain age groups (Statistics Canada, 1980:43).

As a result of an expected relative decline

in the rates of breast cancer, and the increased level of smoking by women, it was predicted that lung cancer would become the leading source of cancer deaths for Canadian females by 1987 (Health and Welfare Canada, 1985:33). This source further predicts that as the male lung cancer rate gradually declines, due to reduced levels of smoking, in conjunction with an increase in the female rate, the female and male rates will converge by the year 2000.

The mortality rates due to other accidental causes and motor vehicle accidents declined for both males and females during the period from 1971 to 1981, while the suicide rates increased for both sexes.

Although the mortality rates for these causes rank considerably below those for cardiovascular diseases and cancer in a relative and numeric sense, it is necessary to consider the ages at which these deaths occur, as emphasized by Wilkins (1980:15). The younger ages at which the majority of these deaths occur results in a greater loss of productive years of life for Canada than do more numerous deaths in the older groups.

The overall mortality rate due to all causes also showed an improvement for both sexes during the period from 1971 to 1981. The overall male rate declined by approximately 5 percent, the female rate by slightly less than 1 percent. This is the first decade since 1931 in which the improvements for males exceeded those for females, and is reflected in the greater gains in life expectancies made by males from 1976 to 1981.

The above comparisons must, however, be interpreted with some degree of caution. First, the mortality rates in Table 7 are crude rates and, therefore, have not been adjusted for differences in the male and female age structure or for changes in the age distributions over the period under consideration.

Second and possibly more important, the period from 1971 to 1981 is short and the above changes as well as those examined previously may be short-term random fluctuations, not necessarily representing a significant long-term

improvement. They do, however, give an indication of recent trends in the mortality of the Canadian population.

The improvements in the mortality rates for cardiovascular diseases and motor vehicle and other accidental deaths do, however, provide an optimistic picture for the future if they can be continued. Other improvements may be more difficult to achieve — particularly in the areas of suicide (especially for the younger male age groups) and cancers, which up to the present time appear to be more difficult to control.

REGIONAL COMPARISONS

The comparison of mortality rates and life expectancies in relation to geographical regions is of general concern to health-care practitioners, policy-makers, and other relevant groups. Their concerns focus on differentials in medical programmes and services, degrees of urbanization and industrialization, unemployment rates, and other social and economic disparities between the regions.

The life expectancies at birth presented in Table 8 indicate that the regional differences evident in 1931 have been substantially reduced in 1981 for both males and females. In 1931, the difference between the lowest and highest regions was approximately seven to eight years, compared to a difference of less than two years for the sexes in 1981. The largest gains in life expectancies for both sexes over the fifty-year period were made in the Atlantic and especially in the Quebec regions, both of which in 1931 were below the national average.

In Quebec, where the life expectancy at birth in 1931 was approximately four to five years below the Canadian average for males and females respectively, the gains in life expectancy were approximately 21 years for females and 15 years for males up to 1981. The life expectancies in the Maritime provinces were comparable to the Canadian average in 1931, but had fallen approximately two years below the national figure by 1941. From 1931 to 1981, the Atlantic region experienced improvements

Table 8. Average Life Expectancy at Birth by Region and Sex, 1931–1981

Year	Canada Female	Canada Male	Atlantic Provinces* Female	Atlantic Provinces* Male	Quebec Female	Quebec Male	Ontario Female	Ontario Male	Prairies† Female	Prairies† Male	British Columbia Female	British Columbia Male
1931	62.1	60.0	61.9	60.2	57.8	56.2	63.9	61.3	65.5	63.5	65.3	62.2
1941	66.3	63.0	64.6	61.7	63.1	60.2	68.4	64.6	68.2	65.4	69.0	63.7
1951	70.8	66.3	70.5	66.6	68.6	64.4	71.9	66.9	72.3	68.4	72.4	66.7
1956	72.9	67.6	72.9	67.9	71.0	66.1	73.6	67.8	74.2	69.3	79.3	68.1
1961	74.2	68.4	73.9	68.6	72.8	67.3	74.4	68.3	75.7	69.8	75.4	68.9
1966	75.2	68.8	74.9	68.5	73.9	67.9	75.5	68.7	76.3	70.1	75.8	69.2
1971	76.4	69.3	76.1	69.0	75.2	68.3	76.7	69.6	77.3	70.5	76.7	69.9
1976	77.5	70.2	77.7	69.8	76.5	69.1	77.7	70.5	78.1	71.0	78.4	70.9
1981	79.0	71.8	78.8	71.3	78.7	71.1	79.0	72.3	79.1	72.1	79.5	72.6
GAIN 1931–1981	16.9	11.8	16.9	11.1	20.9	14.9	15.1	11.0	13.6	8.6	14.2	10.4

* Weighted average of Newfoundland, Prince Edward Island, Nova Scotia and New Brunswick.
  Newfoundland not included prior to 1949.
† Weighted average of Manitoba, Saskatchewan and Alberta

Sources: Statistics Canada, 1974c, Vital Statisics, Vol. 3, Deaths 1971
         Statistics Canada, 1978b, Vital Statisics, Vol. 3, Deaths 1976
         Statistics Canada, 1983, Vital Statisics, Vol. 3, Mortality: Summary List of Causes, 1981

in life expectancies of approximately 17 years for females and 11 years for males.

The other regions, which were above the Canadian average in 1931, experienced smaller gains in life expectancy up to 1981. The smallest gains were evident in the Prairie region, which had the highest life expectancy in 1931. In 1981, as in 1931, the two western regions and Ontario had a relative advantage in life expectancies at birth over the Atlantic and Quebec regions.

The overall levelling of life expectancies across the geographical regions represents, according to Wilkins (1980:18), "a more even distribution of social and economic environmental factors contributing to health status, and thus point[s] to a more even spatial distribution of the overall objective quality of life."

One of the most important contributions to this trend has been the extension of universal medicare programmes to all regions.

The gradual disappearance of life expectancy differentials across the Canadian geographical regions tends to indicate that regional disparities may be of lesser importance in explaining health status inequities, in comparison to other factors, such as age and sex, examined previously. According to Wilkins and Adams (1983a:1078), disparities in family incomes, and employment and occupational status are more relevant at the present time. These and other socio-economic factors which may underlie the present regional differences will be examined below. Comparisons of health status indicators for the Native Indian and the rest of the Canadian population will also be examined.

INCOME AND OCCUPATIONAL AND EMPLOYMENT STATUS

The extension of comprehensive health and medical care to potentially all Canadians since the late 1960s does not necessarily mean that health status disparities due to education, income, or occupational and employment status have been eliminated (Wilkins and Adams, 1983a:1078). This is difficult to determine, all the more since breakdowns of mortality and life expectancy data for the above socially significant variables are generally not available in Canada (Wilkins, 1980:20).

Information available from other countries such as Great Britain and the United States will, therefore, be utilized to supplement the limited number of Canadian studies.

One Canadian study which examined the relationship between income levels and life expectancy was conducted by Wilkins and Adams (1983a) for the late 1970s. The results of the study are presented in Table 9.

Table 9. Life Expectancy at Birth by Sex and Income Level (Quintile), Canada, Late 1970s

	Life Expectancy	
	Female	Male
First quintile	76.6	67.1
Second quintile	77.6	70.1
Third quintile	78.5	70.9
Fourth quintile	79.0	72.0
Fifth quintile	79.4	73.4
TOTAL	78.3	70.8

Source: Adapted from Wilkins and Adams (1983b:1078)
Table 3

The results of another Canadian study conducted by Wigle and Mao (1980) in the 21 Census Metropolitan Areas (CMA's) are reported by Wilkins and Adams (1983b:14–16). The disparities in life expectancies at birth found by Wigle and Mao for 1971 are of a similar magnitude to those found by Wilkins and Adams for the late 1970s. Although the research methodologies in the two studies differed to some extent and the time period of concern is short, these results suggest that the life expectancy differentials across income groups did not diminish appreciably during the 1970s.

In the United States, comparisons of mortality rates and life expectancies across income, educational, and racial groupings by Kitagawa and Hauser (1973) and by Kitagawa (1977) indicated that the differentials in these rates had decreased between 1930 and 1940, but that the disparities had increased during the period from 1940 to 1960. According to Kitagawa (1977:387) the reversal in these socio-economic differentials was not unexpected, because of the transition from infectious to chronic degenerative diseases as the major causes of death. As these latter causes became more important, "access to medical care, preventive medical action, health knowledge and prompt medical treatment" became more critical in combatting mortality. The lower socio-economic groupings are at a relative disadvantage in their access to and utilization of these factors (Kitagawa, 1977:381).

In Great Britain, similar disparities in age-adjusted mortality rates were observed for British males across occupational groupings for the period from 1970 to 1972. These comparisons, as quoted by Wilkins (1980:21), indicated that males in the professional and related occupations had age-adjusted mortality rates approximately 1.8 times lower than comparable rates for males in the unskilled occupational groups. According to the sources being quoted by Wilkins, this disparity in the mortality ratios between the highest and lowest occupational classes was as high as or higher than the ratio observed in Britain 50 years previously.

A further socio-economic factor that has not been extensively studied in relation to life expectancies or mortality rates is employment status, or, more particularly, unemployment. In recent years, however, a number of studies which examine the relationship between unemployment and health status have been conducted in Canada and the United States.

Two Canadian studies by D'Arcy and Siddique (1985) and D'Arcy (1986) utilized data drawn from the Canada Health Survey and indicated substantial health differences between unemployed and employed individuals. In particular the unemployed experienced significantly greater psychological problems such as anxiety and distress, and more short- and long-term disabilities, and they reported more health problems than did employed individuals. The unemployed respondents also showed a higher incidence of hospitalization and utilization of health services.

In addition to the self-reported health problems, physician-diagnosed measures indicated that unemployed persons, as compared to employed individuals, were also prone to more serious physical ailments such as heart trouble, heart and chest pains, bone-joint problems, and hypertension. Although varying in magnitude, these features generally persisted across other socio-economic and demographic conditions.

Wilkins (1980:21) cites two other studies which indicated a similar inverse relationship between unemployment and the overall health status of the population. One of the studies, which examined mortality rates in the United States from the 1920s to the 1970s, indicated that as the levels of unemployment increased, the death rates also increased to levels above those that would otherwise be expected.

Results similar to the above were obtained in a Canadian study cited by Wilkins (1980:21) for the period from 1931 to 1974. In general, the results indicated that age-specific death rates increased as unemployment rates rose in most age groups 15 years and over. General mortality was also found to be directly related to the unemployment rate across all geographical regions in Canada since the Second World War.

In addition to the more obvious economic costs of unemployment, the above results indicate that unemployment also incurs socio-psychological and health-related costs. According to Wilkins (1980:21) the loss in self-esteem and socio-economic status and the changes in social roles which accompany unemployment may be important factors underlying the increase in mortality rates and health problems in times of increasing or high unemployment.

It must be recognized, however, that the vulnerability to unemployment is not equal across all social or economic groups. The adverse health effects of unemployment tend to fall most heavily on those occupational, educational, and income groups already bearing greater health risks. The differential unemployment rates across the geographical regions in Canada may also partly account for disparities in life expectancies between the Atlantic and Quebec and the Ontario and western regions in Canada.

Although comprehensive health and medical care has been in theory extended to all Canadians since the late 1960s, the above results indicate that socio-economic disparities in health status have not been eliminated.

NATIVE CANADIAN HEALTH STATUS

Canadians of Native origin have shared to some extent in the improved health standards experienced by all Canadians. However, substantial disparities between the two populations were still evident in the 1970s and early 1980s.

The life expectancy of registered Indian females increased from 63.5 years in 1960 to about 69 years in 1981 (Siggner, 1986:64). This was ten years below the life expectancy for all Canadian females in 1981 given in Table 1. The 1981 figure for the Indian females was also below the level achieved by the national population in 1951.

A similar ten-year disparity between the registered Indian and overall Canadian population was evident for males in 1981. In 1981, the registered Indian male life expectancy was 62 years (Siggner, 1986:64) in comparison to 72 years for the Canadian male population from Table 1. The life expectancy of the registered Indian males in 1981 was also lower than that achieved by the national male population in 1941.

The above results suggest that the registered Indian population of both sexes is 30 to 40 years behind in attempting to achieve parity with the average Canadian in terms of life expectancy at birth.

Between 1960 and 1981, the infant mortality rate for registered Indians declined from 79.0 per 1000 live births to 15.0 in 1981 (Siggner, 1986:64). During the same period, the infant mortality rate for the total Canadian population declined at a slower rate, from 39.0 in 1960 to approximately 10 in 1981, as indicated in Figure 2. However, the registered Indian infant mortality rate, which was over twice as great as that for non-Indians in 1960, was still approximately 1.5 times greater in 1981.

A study of infant mortality on Canadian Indian reserves by Morrison et al. (1986) compared neonatal and postnatal rates for the reserve and non-reserve populations from 1976 to 1983. Their results indicated that the neonatal rate (death within 28 days of birth) for the reserve population was approximately 1.4 times greater than that for the general Canadian population.

Figure 2: Infant Mortality Rates* for Registered Indians and Canadian Populations, 1960, 1975, and 1981

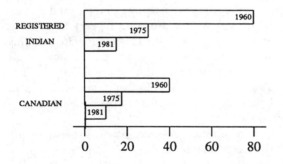

* Rate per 1000 live births.

Sources: 1960 and 1975 adapted from Statistics Canada, 1977. Perspective Canada II, Chart 10.13
1981 Registered Indian, Siggner, 1986:64
1981 Canada, Statistics Canada, 1983. Vital Statistics, Vol. 3, Mortality, 1981

Postneonatal (infant deaths occurring between 28 days and one year of age) mortality rates for the reserve Indians were, however, approximately 3.8 times those of the non-reserve population. According to Morrison et al. (1986:272), postneonatal deaths are more attributable to social, economic, and environmental

factors than are neonatal mortalities.

In examining specific causes of infant deaths for the reserve and non-reserve populations, Morrison et al. (1986:272) observed that reserve infants experienced a higher than expected number of deaths from accidental causes, especially fires. Significantly higher death rates on the Indian reserves were also noted for infectious and respiratory diseases and pneumonia.

The high level of Indian infant deaths due to these latter causes was attributed to low Indian socio-economic status, parental attitudes to medical care, and to parental smoking. Morrison et al. (1986:272) maintain that the high rate of infant deaths on reserves tends to have social and economic rather than biological origins, and is probably due to the isolation and poverty which characterize Indian reserves in Canada.

Mortality rates for other age groups for the registered Indian population also declined over the period from 1960 to 1981. The age-standardized death rate per 1000 population in 1981 was 9.5 for registered Indians in comparison to a rate of 6.1 for the overall Canadian population (Siggner, 1986:66).

Similar discrepancies in the standardized death rates between the registered Indian and non-Indian populations were also observed by Brady (1984:15) in Saskatchewan from 1966 to 1978. As indicated in Table 10, the registered Indian population has experienced more erratic changes in these rates in comparison with the more uniform and consistent declines observed for the non-Indian population.

During the time period under consideration, the non-Indian standardized rates declined by over 10 percent, whereas the 1978 rate for the registered Indians was approximately 16 percent greater than the rate in 1966.

Admittedly, these results for the registered Indian and non-Indian populations of Saskatchewan may not be representative of the respective populations for Canada. They do, however, correspond to some extent with other studies comparing the mortality experiences of the registered Indian and non-Indian populations. More importantly, they indicate that the health status of the Native Indians has not achieved parity with that of the non-Native population in the late 1970s and early 1980s.

Table 10. Standardized Mortality Rates* for the Registered Indian and Non-Indian Populations of Saskatchewan, 1966–1978

Year	Registered Indians	Non-Indians	Indian/Non-Indian Ratio
1966	9.9	6.6	1.5
1968	10.3	6.5	1.6
1970	10.7	6.4	1.7
1972	10.3	6.3	1.6
1974	10.0	6.4	1.6
1976	8.7	6.2	1.4
1978	11.5	5.9	1.9

* Rate per 1000 population standardized on 1956 Saskatchewan population.

Source: Adapted from Brady (1984:152) Table 10.2

The mortality experience of the registered Indian population differs significantly from that of the total Canadian population presented previously. The results in Table 11 indicate that accidents, poisonings, and violence were the most important causes of death for the registered Indian population in 1976 and 1983. For the total Canadian population, these causes ranked a distant third, behind cancers and cardiovascular diseases. Approximately 75 percent of all deaths involving accidents, poisoning, and violence in the registered Indian population have been attributed to alcohol abuse (Health and Welfare Canada: 1986:8).

The crude death rates due to accidental causes for the registered Indian population declined by approximately 30 percent from 1976 to 1983. According to Siggner (1986:66), this improvement may be attributed to programmes to counteract alcohol and drug abuse imple-

mented on Indian reserves during this time period.

Diseases of the circulatory system and cancers were the second and third leading causes of death for registered Indians in 1978 and 1983. The crude death rates were 30 to 40 percent lower than the rates for the Canadian population in both years. Deaths due to these causes generally occur in more advanced age groups. The relatively low average age of death for the registered Indian population, arising from higher mortality rates in the younger age groups due to accidents, suicides, and infant causes, tend to suggest that cancers and diseases of the circulatory system have not had the same opportunity to appear as in the non-Indian population.

Other distinctive differences in the mortality patterns of the registered Indian and non-Indian populations are evident in the incidence of infectious and parasitic diseases. Among registered Indians, the death rate due to these causes declined by approximately 62 percent from 1976 to 1983, but was still 1.8 times greater than the Canadian rate in 1983. Tuberculosis, which has been virtually eliminated as an important cause of death in Canada, continues to be a problem in the Native Canadian population.

The registered Indian population, due to respiratory diseases such as pneumonia, influenza, and bronchitis, also had slightly greater death rates than was evident for the Canadian population in 1976 and 1983.

The continuing disparities in health status indicators between the registered Indian and non-Indian populations, and the relative prevalence of preventable deaths in the Indian population suggest that a variety of factors may be preventing this population from receiving the same quality of health care as the non-Native population. Some of the factors which were noted previously are the extreme poverty, high unemployment rates, low levels of education, and inadequate housing (Brady, 1981:29–40).

Shah and Farkas (1985:861) believe that in addition to these factors, cultural and communicative differences between the Native and non-Native populations are important considerations.

Table 11. Crude Death Rates* for Selected Causes for Registered Indian and Canadian Populations, 1976 and 1983

	1976			1983		
Cause of Death	Registered Indian	Canada	Indian/ Canadian Ratio	Registered Indian	Canada	Indian/ Canadian Ratio
Accidents, poisonings, violence	247.7	66.8	3.7	174.3	57.5	3.0
Circulatory systems diseases	153.2	355.2	0.4	141.5	326.4	0.4
All cancers	54.0	151.5	0.4	56.0	172.0	0.3
Respiratory system diseases	75.1	51.3	1.5	52.0	49.7	1.1
Digestive system diseases	34.5	27.2	1.3	28.1	28.2	1.0
Infectious and parasitic diseases	18.2	4.4	4.1	6.9	3.8	1.8

* Rate per 100 000 population

Source: Adapted from Siggner (1986:67) Table 5.

These factors, in combination with a general lack of knowledge about the availability and utilization of existing health-care programmes, serve as further impediments to the realization of equality in the health status of the Native Canadian populations.

SUMMARY

Canada has experienced substantial gains in life expectancies and reductions in infant mortality rates during the period from 1931 to 1981. These trends are generally taken as indicative of economic and social development or progress at the societal level. However impressive these gains may be, studies also indicate that important disparities in the health status of Canadians continue to exist at the intra-societal level.

Canada and Great Britain have both implemented comprehensive medical care programmes during the past 25 to 30 years and have experienced impressive gains in general health status indices such as infant mortality rates and life expectancies. The continued existence of health status disparities across income, occupational, educational, and other status groupings tends to suggest that the mere provision of uni-

versal medical or health care is not sufficient to overcome the social and economic inequalities and other barriers to good health status faced by these groups. In addressing this problem, Angus and Manga (1986:84) indicate that there is no doubt that lower-income groups have lower health status than those at higher income levels, despite the relative equality of access to health-care services. As a result these authors emphasize that

> equalization of access to health care services does not result in equality of health status. This paradox may become more significant over time, since lifestyle modification in the seventies has been more effective among the higher educated and income groups in the population, where, for instance smoking cessation and increased physical activity have been most noticeable.

Future improvements in mortality rates and life expectancies are likely to be more difficult to achieve, considering the increasing average age of the Canadian population and the relative concentration of the major causes of death in the older age groups. It is also necessary to recognize that mortality levels and life expectancies are a complex product of biological, social, economic, cultural, and environmental factors.

Some of these factors are more readily controlled than are others in the attempt to enhance the health status of the Canadian population.

Biological factors such as sex, race, and ethnicity are factors which cannot be controlled by the individual. Age may also be considered as a biological factor but it is to a large extent determined by the mortality experiences of the population.

Lifestyle factors such as cigarette smoking, alcohol consumption, dietary and exercise habits, and motor vehicle accidents to a large extent are under the control of the individual and are, therefore, preventable. For example, smokers are more likely than non-smokers to suffer heart attacks, strokes, respiratory problems, and cancers of the lungs and digestive system. Cigarette smoking is considered to be the single most important preventable cause of death. Cigarettes, according to Abelson et al. (1983:17), are a legal product which kill when used as intended.

Environmental factors such as occupational hazards, unemployment, poverty, housing conditions, educational opportunities, and so forth are external to the individual, and the individual, therefore, has little or no control over them.

A further important factor is the availability and utilization of health-care services and programmes. As indicated above, the provision of medical and health-care services does not ensure that they will be utilized to an optimal level by the intended recipients. The potential utilization and, hence, benefits to the Canadian population, are to a large extent determined by certain biological factors such as sex, race, and ethnicity and more importantly by economic, social, and cultural factors.

Future improvements in the health status of the Canadian population will depend on potential reductions in occupational hazards and in contributory factors in the lifestyle category. The elimination of social, economic, and cultural inequalities which limit the ability of the poor, the unemployed, Native Canadians, and other lower-status groups to achieve the optimal benefits from our present medical and health-care system will be a most important challenge for the future.

STUDY QUESTIONS

1. Outline and discuss some of the factors that may be related to the differentials in life expectancies at birth for females and males.

2. Indicate some of the factors responsible for the relatively high suicide rate for the 15-to-24 age group. Also indicate why the male suicide rate is higher than that for females.

3. Outline and discuss several programmes that could be implemented to reduce the suicide rate.

4. This chapter indicates that cigarette smoking is one of the most important preventable causes of death in Canada at the present time. Outline several reasons why people smoke and indicate what could be done to reduce the level of smoking.

5. This chapter states that substantial inequalities in health status indicators continue to exist in Canada across income, employment status and occupational groupings, and for the Native populations. Outline and discuss several policies and programmes that could be implemented to reduce these inequalities.

6. The differentials in life expectancies at birth for the geographical regions in Canada have been reduced over the period from 1931 to 1981. However, Ontario and the western regions (Prairies and British Columbia) continue to experience higher life expectancies in comparison to Quebec and the Atlantic Provinces. Outline and discuss some of the factors that could be responsible for the historical and present disparities in life expectancies between East and West.

RECOMMENDED READING

Angus, Douglas E., and Pran Manga. "National Health Strategies: Time for a New 'New Perspective'." *Canadian Journal of Public Health* 77 (March/April 1986): 81–85.

Morrison, H.I., R.M. Semeciw, Y. Mao, and D.T. Wigle. "Infant Mortality on Canadian Indian Reserves 1976–1983." *Canadian Journal of Public Health* 77 (July/August 1986): 269–73.

Peron, Yves, and Claude Strohmenger. Demographic and Health Indicators. Statistics Canada Catalogue 82–543E. Ottawa: Ministry of Supply and Services, 1985.

Shah, C.P., and C.S. Farkas. "The Health of Indians in Canadian Cities: A Challenge to the Health Care System." *Canadian Medical Association Journal* 133 (November 1, 1985): 859–63.

Siggner, Andrew J. "The Socio-Demographic Conditions of Registered Indians." In *Arduous Journey: Canadian Indians and Decolonization*, edited by J. Rick Ponting. McClelland and Stewart, 1986.

Wilkins, Russell, and Owen B. Adams. "Health Expectancy in Canada. Late 1970s: Demographic, Regional, and Social Dimensions." *American Journal of Public Health* 73, no. 98 (September 1983a):1073–80.

REFERENCES

Abelson, Janet, Peter Paddon, and Claude Strohmenger. *Perspectives on Health*. Statistics Canada, Catalogue 82–540E. Ottawa: Ministry of Supply and Services, 1983.

Angus, Douglas E., and Pran Manga. "National Health Strategies: Time for a New 'New Perspective'." *Canadian Journal of Public Health* 77 (March/April 1986): 81–85.

Brady, Paul D. "The Health Status of the Registered Indian Population of Saskatchewan 1959–1978." M.A. diss., Saskatoon: Department of Sociology, University of Saskatchewan, 1981.

———. "Contradictions and Consequences: The Social and Health Status of Canada's Registered Indian Population" In *Contradictions in Canadian Society*, edited by John A. Fry. Toronto: John Wiley & Sons, 1984.

D'Arcy, Carl. "Unemployment and Health: Data and Implications." *Canadian Journal of Public Health* 77 supplement 1 (May/June 1986): 124–31.

D'Arcy, Carl, and C.M. Siddique. "Unemployment and Health: An Analysis of 'Canada Health Survey' Data." *International Journal of Health Services* 15, no. 4 (1985): 609–35.

Dominion Bureau of Statistics. *Life Expectancy Trends 1930–1932 to 1960–1962*. Ottawa: Minister of Trade and Commerce, 1967.

Dumas, Jean. *Report on the Demographic Situation in Canada, 1983*. Ottawa: Ministry of Supply and Services, 1984.

Health and Welfare Canada. *Chronic Diseases in Canada*. Vol. 4, no. 3 (December 1983).

———. Vol. 5, no. 1 (June 1984).

———. Vol. 6, no. 1 (June 1985).

———. Vol. 7, no. 1 (June 1986).

Kalbach, Warren E., and Wayne W. McVey. *The Demographic Bases of Canadian Society*. 2nd ed. Toronto: McGraw-Hill Ryerson, 1979.

Kitagawa, Evelyn M. "On Mortality." *Demography* 14 (November 1977): 381–89.

Kitagawa, Evelyn M., and D.M. Hauser. *Differential Mortality in the United States: A Study in Socioeconomic Epidemiology*. Cambridge: Harvard University Press, 1973.

McSheffrey, Grace. "The Effectiveness of Health Education in Reducing Health Care Costs." M.A. diss., Saskatoon: Department of Sociology, University of Saskatchewan, 1981.

Morrison, H.I., R.M. Semeciw, Y. Mao, and D.T. Wigle. "Infant Mortality on Canadian Indian Reserves 1976–1983." *Canadian Journal of Public Health* 77 (July/August 1986): 269–73.

Peron, Yves, and Claude Strohmenger. *Demographic and Health Indicators*. Statistics Canada Catalogue 82–543E. Ottawa: Ministry of Supply and Services, 1985.

Shah, C.P., and C.S. Farkas. "The Health of Indians in Canadian Cities: A Challenge to the Health-Care System." *Canadian Medical Association Journal* 133 (November 1, 1985): 859–63.

Siggner, Andrew J. "The Socio-Demographic Conditions of Registered Indians." In *Arduous Journey: Canadian Indians and Decolonization*, edited by J. Rick Ponting. Toronto: McClelland and Stewart, 1986.

Statistics Canada. *Causes of Death 1971*. Catalogue 84–203. Ottawa: Ministry of Supply and Services, 1972.

———. *Causes of Death 1976*. Catalogue 84–203. Ottawa: Ministry of Supply and Services, 1978a.

———. *Causes of Death 1981*. Catalogue 84–203. Ottawa: Ministry of Supply and Services, 1982.

———. *General Mortality 1950 to 1972*. Catalogue 84–531. Ottawa: Ministry of Supply and Services, 1976.

———. *Life Tables, Canada and Provinces 1970–72*. Catalogue 84–532. Ottawa: Ministry of Supply and Services, 1974a.

———. *Life Tables, Canada and Provinces 1975–77*. Catalogue 84–532. Ottawa: Ministry of Supply and Services, 1979.

———. *Life Tables, Canada and Provinces, 1980–82*. Catalogue 84–532. Ottawa: Ministry of Supply and Services, 1984.

———. *Perspective Canada*. Catalogue 11–507. Ottawa: Information Canada, 1974b.

———. *Perspective Canada II*. Catalogue 11–508E. Ottawa: Minister of Supply and Services. 1977.

———. *Perspective Canada III*. Catalogue 11–811E. Ottawa: Minister of Supply and Services, 1980.

———. *Vital Statistics Vol. 3. Deaths 1971*. Catalogue 84–206. Ottawa: Ministry of Supply and Services, 1974c.

———. *Vital Statistics Vol. 3. Deaths 1976*. Catalogue 84–206. Ottawa: Ministry of Supply and Services, 1978b.

———. *Vital Statistics Vol. 3. Mortality: Summary List of Causes 1981*. Catalogue 84–206. Ottawa: Ministry of Supply and Services, 1983.

Wilkins, Russell. *Health Status in Canada, 1926–1976*. Montreal: Institute for Research on Public Policy. Occasional Paper no. 13 (1980).

Wilkins, Russell, and Owen B. Adams. "Health Expectancy in Canada. Late 1970s: Demographic, Regional, and Social Dimensions." *American Journal of Public Health* 73, no. 98 (September 1983a): 1073–80.

———. *Healthfulness of Life*. Montreal: Institute for Research on Public Policy, 1983b.

3

HEALTH-CARE RESOURCES AND EXTRA-BILLING: Financing, Allocation, and Utilization

Herbert C. Northcott
University of Alberta

This chapter begins with a brief review of the development of hospital and medical care insurance in Canada and of the principles guiding Canada's health insurance programme. A discussion follows on the various means of financing health care and on selected funding issues. Next, certain debates regarding the allocation and utilization of health care are examined. Finally, the extra-billing question is explored, with a focus on the experiences of Ontario and of Alberta.

THE DEVELOPMENT OF HEALTH-CARE INSURANCE IN CANADA

Residents of Canada currently enjoy a universal health-care insurance plan which covers a wide range of hospital and medical care expenses (for a discussion of the development of Canada's

health policy, see Weller and Manga, 1983a; Taylor, 1978). Before medicare, health care was financed primarily on a so-called user-pay basis. That is, when a person required hospitalization or the services of a physician, that person was billed accordingly. While most users paid their bills, some did not, often because they lacked sufficient financial resources (Taylor, 1978). The poor, the elderly, and the chronically ill were often unable to meet their health-care expenses, and indeed, treating major illness could threaten to reduce even the reasonably well-off to poverty and a dependence on charity. Not only did the consumers of health care, that is, the sick, face financial difficulties, but so also did the providers of health care. Hospitals, physicians, and so on had to absorb losses from unpaid accounts and often offered their services on a basis of charity, knowing that the user could not meet expenses. Accordingly, by the end of the first third of this century, there was a wide-spread sentiment, shared by both users and providers of health care, favouring the concept of public health insurance (National Council of Welfare, 1982:5–7; Taylor et al., 1984:2–3).

Following World War II, a wide variety of private and public insurance programmes for hospital and medical care came into being. However, many Canadians remained uninsured, and many of the insured had only limited and inadequate coverage (National Council of Welfare, 1982:7; Taylor et al., 1984:3–5). In 1946 (1947),[1] Saskatchewan became the first province to institute a public hospital insurance plan (Taylor, 1978). In 1957, the federal government passed the Hospital Insurance and Diagnostic Services Act, which provided for the federal-provincial cost-sharing of provincial hospital programmes. This Act was implemented in 1958, and by 1961 all provinces were enrolled (Taylor, 1978).

Medical care insurance developed separately from and later than hospital insurance. Again, Saskatchewan led the way, establishing in 1961 (1962) the first provincial medical care insurance programme in Canada — and precipitating the 1962 Saskatchewan doctors' strike (Badgley and Wolfe, 1967; Soderstrom, 1978:159; Taylor, 1978). In 1961, the federal government established the Royal Commission on Health Services under the chairmanship of Mr. Justice Emmett M. Hall. The Royal Commission's report was released in 1964 and laid the groundwork for the federal government's 1966 (1968) Medical Care Act, which provided for the federal-provincial cost-sharing of provincial medical care programmes. By 1971, all ten provinces and the Northwest Territories had joined the plan; the Yukon followed finally in 1972 (Taylor, 1978).

Canada's medicare programme was established on several principles: some sources identify four (Taylor, 1978:364–5; Soderstrom, 1978:132–3), while other sources list five (Hall, 1980:39–46; National Council of Welfare, 1982:15; Taylor et al., 1984:5). The four principles common to all sources are: (1) universality

— coverage of all Canadians; (2) comprehensiveness — a broad range of insured services; (3) portability — coverage could be carried from one province to another; and (4) public administration — the programme was to be publicly administered on a non-profit basis without the involvement of the private sector. A fifth principle — accessibility — is often also listed, although actually, accessibility, that is, reasonable access to services, is already included in the concept of universality. It would not make sense to provide universal coverage, that is, to make all Canadians eligible for benefits, and then to allow barriers such as excessive cost or distance to disenfranchise certain segments of the population. In short, universal coverage implies universal access to services. These five principles were reaffirmed in Mr. Justice Emmett Hall's federally commissioned review (1980) of the state of health services in Canada.

COSTS: THE FINANCING OF HEALTH CARE

The intent of the hospital and medical care insurance programmes was to provide comprehensive health-care coverage to all Canadians by removing financial barriers to care and by reducing the financial risks of illness. In other words, the individualistic user-pay concept — payment for services when and only when obtained — was judged to be incompatible with the concept of "insurance" and the collective sharing of risks and costs.

While health care in Canada is a provincial jurisdiction, the two federal health-insurance acts oblige the federal government to share the costs of provincial hospital and medical services and to dictate certain guidelines, including the five principles listed above. Canada's health-care insurance system has been financed by a variety of mechanisms which have varied from province to province and from time to time (Soderstrom, 1978:131–42). Funding for this public insurance plan is derived at the federal level from general tax revenues (and, increasingly, from deficit financing, i.e., borrowing).

Provincial funding is based upon some combination of general tax revenues, premiums, and user fees. User fees have been charged by hospitals and/or by physicians. Premiums, especially user fees, have generated fierce debate and are discussed in more detail later in this chapter.

Hospitals generally provide services according to the budgets provided them by government. From time to time, various provinces have allowed hospitals to charge user fees. Physicians, on the other hand, generally bill the provincial health-care agency on a fee-for-service basis, according to a fee schedule negotiated by the provincial government and the provincial medical association representing the province's physicians. Again, variations on this theme have existed. The National Council of Welfare (1982:25–26) found in the early 1980s that: (1) certain provinces, e.g., Alberta, allowed doctors to bill both the patient *and* the provincial health-care agency — a practice known as "extra-billing"; (2) certain other provinces, e.g., Ontario and Manitoba, allowed doctors to "opt out" of medicare and to bill patients directly, with the patient seeking (often only partial) reimbursement from the provincial health-care agency — that is, reimbursement was according to the negotiated fee schedule and doctors often billed "extra"; and (3) Quebec allowed doctors to opt out and directly bill patients but allowed for no reimbursement at all. In the early 1980s, the federal government waged a campaign against extra-billing, finally implementing legislation discouraging the practice in the form of the 1984 Canada Health Act (Brown, 1986:111). By 1986, extra-billing by physicians had virtually come to an end.[2] The Ontario and Alberta experiences with extra-billing are discussed in more detail shortly.

While the founders of Canada's medicare system did not want cost to be a barrier to services, the cost of health insurance has nonetheless been a continuing concern. Before medicare, fears were expressed that without financial deterrents, people would overuse the system and costs would therefore rise exorbitantly. In retrospect, these fears of frivolous and

excessive overuse have proven to be unfounded (Enterline et al., 1973; Barer et al., 1979:30–35). Costs did rise, nevertheless, following the initial introduction of medicare, though not from demonstrably frivolous utilization. Rather, the costs of services, and, therefore, the incomes of the providers of health care rose initially, although the growth of these costs has subsequently been relatively constrained (Evans, 1984:100; Soderstrom, 1978:248; Naylor, 1982:14; Barer et al., 1979:4).

Various models have been used to suggest mechanisms by which the costs of health care might be contained. In the classical laissez-faire free-enterprise model, consumers are said to "demand" services, and providers to compete with one another to "supply" the services demanded. In this model, it is argued that when demand is high, relative to supply, costs will tend to rise, and vice versa — when supply exceeds demand, costs will decline. In order to restrain costs, then, this model suggests that increasing the supply of physicians, hospital beds, and so on will reduce the unit cost of services. Of course, ideally, this model also implies increased competition among providers of services, i.e., the demonopolization of medicine, and also implies reprivatization, i.e., the termination of the state's role in the provision of health care (for a discussion of the "push for reprivatization," see Weller and Manga, 1983b). Evans (1984:23–24) calls this model "the naïve economic model" because it is, as he says, "not particularly realistic." The problem is basically that demand for health care is not the same as demand for automobiles or television sets. While advertising and "keeping up with the Joneses" influence my perceptions of need, in the end, *I* decide if I need a new car or not, and whether I can afford it. Health care is different. When I am sick, I go to the doctor and it is the *doctor* who decides what care I need. When faced with a choice between life or death, sickness or health, cost, while not irrelevant, tends to play only a peripheral role.

These criticisms of the naïve economic model suggest that, alternatively, cost can be viewed as a function of the public's real need for health care, which, in turn, is accurately assessed and adequately serviced by the various providers of medical care. Evans (1984:21–23) calls this "the naïve medico-technical model" and notes that it too is "not particularly realistic." This model fails for the same reason that the economic model fails; that is, the definition of "need" is not solely a function of the patient's real or even perceived state of health. The providers of health-care services tend to have the ability to generate as much "need" as they can service (Evans, 1984:88, 97, 99). To this point, Evans (1984:85, 87) discusses Roemer's Law — "A built (hospital) bed is a filled bed" — and its parallel extension to physician services. In short, a more realistic model of the relationship among health care supply, demand, and cost takes into account that the providers of health care themselves play a critical role in the determination of both demand and cost. I will refer to this model as the "professional control model."

A fourth model might be labelled the "socialized medicine model." Under this model, the state controls the health-care system, determining the level of services and therefore utilization and cost. While Canada's current health-care system is occasionally described as socialized medicine, Weller and Manga (1983b:495) argue that it is, in fact, a "mixed system, where demand [is] socialized via publicly funded health insurance schemes, but where the supply side [consists] of an essentially private delivery system." Such a mixed system contains tensions which motivate various proponents to argue for movement either back towards a private enterprise system or further in the direction of the social medicine model.

Various solutions to the problem of costs are proposed. Those who adopt the rhetoric of the naïve economic model identify consumer demand as the problem and argue for user fees to raise revenues and to reduce "unnecessary" demand. Critics of this proposal argue that user fees deter precisely those who most need services — the poor, sick, and elderly. Alternatively, those who adopt the rhetoric of the

professional control model identify the power and monopoly of the medical profession as the problem, and argue for increased intervention against the suppliers of services. For example, some argue that hospital beds be closed, that geographic quotas be instituted to control the number and distribution of physicians, and that government payments in the form of hospital budgets and physician fee schedules, or even better, salaries, be carefully rationed. Such intervention by the state, of course, follows the socialized medicine model. However, critics of this model argue that such restrictions will result in an insufficient level of services, such that legitimate medical needs will go untended. It is claimed that quality of care will suffer, people will die in the streets awaiting services, and so on. This last criticism reflects the basic assumption of the naïve medico-technical model, which assumes that medical practitioners identify and service only real medical needs, and which has been criticized for assuming that the suppliers of services respond only to real needs and play no other role in the generation of demand for services. And so, round and round the debate goes with various proponents crying: "Control demand and thereby control costs!" or "Control supply and thereby control costs!" or "Control costs and thereby control both supply and demand!" Two things are certain: (1) supply, demand, and cost are intimately intertwined, and (2) the problem goes far beyond economics and lands squarely in the realm of politics and conflicting ideologies (Weller and Manga, 1983b:514). In other words, the problem may be economic; the solution, however, is political.

As a final note, as governments attempt to limit health-care costs, allegations of underfunding become widespread. Physicians claim that their real incomes are being diminished by inflation, or that they are losing ground relative to other professions. Accordingly, physicians argue that the fee schedule must be altered substantially and/or that they must be allowed the right to directly charge patients in addition to the fee paid them by government. Hospitals also often argue that they are inadequately funded and consequently have to cut valuable services and/or increase waiting times, with compromised patient health the result. Again, solutions are sought either through increased government financing and/or through the implementation of user fees. User fees, however, tend to be viewed as a violation of the basic principles of Canada's health-care programme (equitable access, portability — see Hall, 1980:32) and, consequently, have generated heated discussion. I will return to the issue of user fees shortly.

SUPPLY:
THE ALLOCATION OF
HEALTH-CARE RESOURCES

While the medical profession at one time endorsed the concept of national health insurance (National Council of Welfare, 1982:1; Taylor et al., 1984:2–3), and while Mr. Justice Emmett Hall in his 1980 review of medicare "found no one," not even the medical profession, arguing for the termination of medicare (Hall, 1980:2), the medical lobby has, just the same, frequently voiced its opposition to the idea of, or to various aspects of, government-sponsored insurance programmes (see for example, Badgley and Wolfe, 1967; Blishen, 1969; Taylor et al., 1984; Stevenson and Williams, 1985). Underlying this resistance is the issue of professional autonomy and the model of the physician as a private entrepreneur.

Ultimately, the state controls medicine. It is the state that creates legislation that defines and regulates the medical profession. Further, the state funds the university medical schools, the hospitals, and the health-care insurance system. However, the state delegates its authority to the medical profession itself. In this fashion, the medical profession gains control over admissions to professional schools and over membership in the profession through licensing and through disciplinary mechanisms. This delegation of authority from the state to the profession allows for professional "autonomy"; further, most physicians engage in "private practice" and

bill the health-insurance commission on a "fee-for-service" basis. All of these practices support the notion of the physician as a private entrepreneur in a free-enterprise marketplace. Of course, this model ignores the fact that the medical profession enjoys a state-endorsed monopoly with severely curtailed competition and price-fixing in the form of negotiated fee schedules. Nevertheless, the free-enterprise rhetoric is regularly employed in order to protect the notion and image of professional autonomy.

In certain other respects, the physician fits the model of the "civil servant." For example, some doctors are paid salaries by hospitals or health units, and virtually all physicians, whether paid by salary or on a negotiated fee-for-service basis, are reimbursed ultimately by government funds. Further, major physical facilities used by health-care providers, such as hospitals and their support staff, are provided and funded by the state. Note that the doctor or nurse, who is employed by a hospital, is paid a salary, and can be terminated from employment by the hospital, more clearly fits the model of the civil servant than that of the private entrepreneur. While many physicians are not employed by the hospital per se, nevertheless, fee-for-service physicians working in the hospital must have "hospital privileges" which can be revoked.

Of course, the medical profession finds the civil servant model distasteful and threatening. The typical medical professional has little interest in becoming a salaried employee of the state who is told when and where to practise or how much to charge for services rendered. Nevertheless, there are those who believe that "rational" allocation of health-care resources requires severe restrictions on the autonomous professional's freedom to practise where, when, and how (s)he chooses (see, for example, Weller and Manga, 1983b:515). There are those who have little faith that the forces of the free marketplace or of the medical profession will solve the problems of underservicing in rural areas or of overservicing in urban areas. Such persons argue that the adequate allocation of health-care resources depends on the intervention of the state, an intervention which threatens, increasingly, to transform the physician from a private entrepreneur into a civil servant. Not that this scenario is all bad! After all, the civil servant enjoys relatively high levels of job security, remuneration, and benefits such as a pension plan, paid holidays, predictable hours, and paid overtime — perks that the private practitioner often complains (s)he lacks.

DEMAND: THE UTILIZATION OF HEALTH CARE

Just as both the private entrepreneur and civil servant models can be applied, to certain degrees, to the physician, so also can the private consumer and civil service client models be applied, to certain degrees, to the patient. The patient is a free-market consumer in that (s)he usually decides when services are required and generally has a relatively free choice of practitioner or service agency. The consumer model views demand for services as a personal choice, but recognizes that personal choices may be frivolous or unwise. Consumers may make personal decisions that result in the overuse or underuse of the health-care system. On the other side of the coin, consumers may be persuaded by health-care providers to make excessive use, or, by means of deterrents such as user fees, to lower utilization.

On the other hand, there is a sense in which the patient becomes the client of a state-funded civil-service bureaucracy. Being a "client" implies entitlement to services offered or funded by the state. In short, the client has a "right" to health care, and health-care providers have an obligation of sorts to provide services to the client. In that the client model sees services as a right, it ideally allows no barriers to services. Some argue that such undeterred "clients" will tend to abuse/overutilize the health-care system, or, on the other side of the coin, that the health-care system might seek out clients and provide

them with "appropriate" care whether they want it or not.

It is, however, hardly clear what constitutes overuse or underuse. Similarly, it is difficult to define "need" in black-and-white terms. When a person falls and breaks a leg, it is clear to both the victim and the health-care provider that there is a legitimate need. But does a person need, for instance, a regular checkup? The answer will vary from person to person and from practitioner to practitioner. In other words, the definition of need is often subjective in nature. This means that the definitions of overutilization and underutilization are also often subjective in nature, and that what one considers legitimate use, another might consider overuse or even underuse.

Despite the difficulties of defining legitimate need, appropriate use, overuse, underuse, and abuse, it is often argued that user fees will deter people from seeking unnecessary health care. There is evidence that if user fees are high enough, utilization will go down (Badgley and Smith, 1979:7), although there tends to be a "rebound effect" as physicians shift their patients to more expensive care categories (Badgley and Smith, 1979:7, 32) or otherwise generate more demand (Barer et al., 1979:34; Manga, 1981:672, 675; National Council of Welfare, 1982:33). There is evidence that medical needs differ by social class, tending to be greatest among the poor (National Council of Welfare, 1982:9–11, 16–20; Canadian Sickness Survey, 1960:150; Barer et al., 1982:19–20, 62–66; Soderstrom, 1978:184). There is also evidence that the deterrent effect of user fees varies by social class, again being greatest among the poor (Badgley and Smith, 1979:7; Naylor, 1982; National Council of Welfare, 1982; Hall, 1980; Evans, 1984:91, 334; Barer et al., 1979:33–34). In short, those who need services most are most deterred from seeking them. Before medicare, while the poor were more likely to be sick, they were less likely to see a doctor. After medicare, the level of service obtained by the poor rose (Enterline et al., 1973; Greenhill and Haythorne, 1972; Beck, 1973; McDonald, 1974; Boulet and

Henderson, 1979; Soderstrom, 1978:179–82; Manga, 1981). These studies suggest that the wealthier classes are not as likely to be affected by deterrent fees, while user fees do deter (often necessary) utilization among the poor, resulting in underutilization.

Barer et al. (1979:116) examined the use of a variety of charges directed to patients in order to control health care costs, and concluded that "the scope for deployment of direct charges as a strategy for cost containment . . . is extremely limited." These authors went on to note that "most proposals for 'patient participation in health care financing' reduce to misguided or cynical efforts to tax the ill and/or to drive up the total cost of health care while shifting some of the burden out of government budgets."

In short, user fees (synonyms include extra-billing, balance billing, authorized patient charges, patient participation fees, deductibles, deterrent fees, utilization fees, co-payment, co-insurance, and so on — see Barer et al., 1979:4; Badgley and Smith, 1979:32; Hall, 1980:4) are ineffective in discouraging unnecessary use, and indeed, tend to deter necessary utilization by the poor, sick, and elderly. Such deterrence violates the principle of equal access to health care. In rebuttal, some argue that the poor, sick, and elderly should be exempt from direct charges. The counter-rebuttal states that this proposal would create a two-tiered health-care system, with a public social welfare tier for the poor and a private free-enterprise user-pay tier for the wealthy, who could purchase (more and better) services (Hall, 1980:27; National Council of Welfare, 1982:37).

THE ISSUE OF EXTRA-BILLING

In spite of the establishment of a universal health-care insurance programme, Canada's physicians have preserved the right to directly bill their patients, although certain provinces require that the physician "opt out" of medicare to do so. Further, physicians have preserved the right to charge whatever fee the market will bear, although the majority of physicians in Canada have remained in medicare and charged according to negotiated fee schedules (see Brown, 1986:123–25).

With the high inflation of the 1970s and the recession of the early 1980s, and with the 1977 Established Programs Financing Act, which extricated the federal government from the inflationary cost spiral and shifted more of the responsibility for health-care decisions to the provinces (Brown, 1980:525–26; 1986:112), allegations that the health-care system was underfunded became widespread. Inasmuch as the 1977 Act placed fewer conditions on the transfer of funds for health care from the federal to the provincial governments, Brown argues that one consequence of this change was an increase in extra-billing by doctors, especially in the provinces of Ontario and Alberta (1980:522–30; 1986:112; for a contrary opinion, see Weller and Manga, 1983a:237 and 1983b:507). As extra-billing became more widespread, it began to attract more and more attention. It was argued increasingly that extra-billing deterred precisely those who needed medical services — the poor, sick, and elderly — from seeking care and thereby violated one of the basic principles of Canada's health-care programme, that is, the principle of accessibility. Several studies examining this allegation will be reviewed here.

For the 1980 review of medicare, Mr. Justice Emmett Hall commissioned Professors Stoddart and Woodward to conduct a study of extra-billing in Ontario (Hall, 1980:24–25). A sample was drawn from the residents of four Ontario counties. These counties were chosen because they had high percentages of opted-out general practitioners and because they varied along the rural-urban dimension. Interviews were conducted by telephone and several thousand households were contacted. The findings, as reported by Hall (1980:24–25), include the following: (1) about one third of households in the areas surveyed had been extra-billed; (2) physicians practising among high-income populations were more likely to opt out and extra-bill; (3) both poor and non-poor alike indicated reluctance to negotiate fees with physicians; (4) of those persons who had been extra-billed, the poor were more likely to indicate that they had "reduced utilization and/or delayed in seeking medical care because of cost" (p.25); (5) further, the poor were twice as likely as the non-poor to say that doctors' fees presented a financial problem for them; (6) satisfaction with the quality of medical care was lower for those who had been extra-billed, especially for the poor; and finally (7) more than one quarter of the poor expressed difficulty in finding a doctor whose services they could afford. Hall (1980:25) concluded that extra-billing violates the principle of accessibility in that it deters people, in particular the poor, from obtaining medical care.

About the time that the Stoddart and Woodward survey was done in Ontario, a related study was conducted in Alberta. Remember that extra-billing had become especially visible in the provinces of Ontario and Alberta (Brown, 1980:522), although Ontario physicians had to opt out to extra-bill while Alberta physicians could extra-bill without having to opt out.

The Alberta study (Northcott, 1982) was conducted early in 1980 as part of the annual Edmonton Area Survey and involved face-to-face interviews with a representative sample of 428 adult residents of the city of Edmonton. This study found that: (1) the great majority of respondents had seen a doctor at least once in the past year and, of these, 46 percent had been extra-billed at least once; (2) two thirds of all respondents were opposed to extra-billing, with one third registering "strong" disagreement with the practice (only 19 percent were supportive of extra-billing; another 14 percent were neutral on the subject); (3) there was some evidence that those persons opposed to extra-billing tended to either avoid seeking medical care or sought out non-billing doctors; and finally, (4) the poor were most opposed to extra-billing.

In addition to the extra-billing issue, this study explored the public's perceptions of and attitudes towards physicians' incomes. The public exhibited a fairly accurate perception of the level of net income reported by physicians generally and was supportive of income increases approaching the then high levels of inflation. In other words, there was no evidence of public hostility directed towards physicians on account of their high incomes or income increases.

In summary, the findings of the 1980 Edmonton study indicated strong opposition to the practice of extra-billing as a means of raising physician incomes; nevertheless, perhaps paradoxically, the public was supportive of the high levels of income enjoyed by physicians. These findings lend public opinion support to Hall's (1980:27) two recommendations that extra-billing be banned and that physicians be "adequately compensated."

A second study (Northcott and Snider, 1983) was conducted in Alberta in 1982, again as part of the annual Edmonton Area Survey. This 1982 survey involved face-to-face interviews with 507 adult residents of the city of Edmonton. The study found that: (1) the great majority of respondents had visited a doctor at least once in the past year, and of these, 37 percent had been extra-billed at least once; (2) there was evidence that the elderly were less likely to be extra-billed than the non-elderly; (3) those persons who reported that their health was poor made more visits to the doctor; (4) the elderly, in comparison to the non-elderly, made more visits to the doctor; (5) the poor, however, who were more likely to report health problems and who were expected therefore to make more visits to the doctor, did not; (6) while two thirds of all respondents disagreed with the practice of extra-billing (44 percent strongly disagreed, only 18 percent were supportive, 17 percent were neutral on the subject), the elderly and the poor were even more likely to be opposed to extra-billing; (7) one third of respondents felt that their own health care suffered as a result of extra-billing and 40 percent of these cited financial deterrence as the reason; (8) those who had actually been extra-billed, especially the poor, sick, and elderly, were more likely to perceive a deterioration in medical care than were those who had not experienced extra-billing; (9) conversely, the experience of being extra-billed had little impact on perceived quality of care for the non-poor, non-sick, and non-elderly; and finally, (10) the greater majority of respondents felt that the health care of Albertans generally had suffered as a result of extra-billing, primarily due to the financial barrier to seeking care. In short, this study in Alberta in 1982 found strong opposition to the practice of extra-billing. Respondents, especially the poor, sick, and elderly, considered extra-billing to be a threat both to accessibility to and to the quality of health care.

As the evidence increased in support of the allegation that extra-billing or user fees deterred needy persons from seeking necessary medical care, thereby violating the basic health-care insurance principle of equal accessibility, the federal government increasingly pressured the offending provinces to ban extra-billing and user fees. This pressure culminated in the April 1, 1984 Canada Health Act which, starting on July 1, 1984, imposed a dollar-for-dollar penalty. That is, the federal government would withhold from its transfers to the provinces the equivalent of the amounts raised by extra-billing and other user fees (Brown, 1986:111). The federal government promised to refund these withheld payments provided the provinces ban extra-billing and user fees before April 1, 1987. Given that the funds withheld by the federal government amounted to millions of dollars a month, this placed the provinces under considerable pressure. Nova Scotia acted first, outlawing extra-billing in June of 1984. Manitoba and Saskatchewan followed suit in August of 1985. By January of 1986, only Ontario, Alberta, and New Brunswick were continuing to allow extra-billing.

Following months of heated debate between the government of Ontario and Ontario physicians, represented by the Ontario Medical Association, the Ontario Health Care Accessibility Act was passed on June 20, 1986, legislating an end to extra-billing. Ontario's physicians responded with a walkout that began on June 12, 1986 and lasted 25 days, ending officially on July 7, 1986 — the longest doctors' strike in Canadian history.[3] Nevertheless, not all doctors participated and physician support for the strike declined as time passed, with many returning to work before the walkout's official conclusion. By the end of 1986, relations between the Ontario Medical Association and the Ontario government had more or less returned to normal.

By the fall of 1986, only New Brunswick and Alberta continued to allow extra-billing, with the practice being in fact relatively inconsequential in New Brunswick. Extra-billing in Alberta, however, amounted to millions of dollars yearly, and while the Alberta government had opposed the federal government's attempts to end extra-billing, under the pressure of federal withholding of funds, the Alberta government began to campaign for an end to extra-billing. Alberta physicians argued strongly in favour of their right to extra-bill; nevertheless, the Alberta government and the Alberta Medical Association eventually, and in fact relatively peacefully, worked out an agreement ending extra-billing. This agreement was endorsed by a vote of the AMA membership and came into effect on October 1, 1986.

And so the extra-billing issue, which many thought a threat to the entire medicare programme, was settled. It remains to be seen whether the "medicare crisis" is resolved or averted or whether other serious issues such as alleged underfunding, pressures to control or limit demand, and the opposing pulls of reprivatization versus civil-service medicine will threaten or destroy the viability of Canada's health-care insurance programme.

CONCLUSION

Canada's health-care insurance programme was founded on the five principles of universality, accessibility, comprehensiveness, portability, and public administration. Health care is expensive (although Canada's medicare system is apparently less expensive than America's free-enterprise system) and financial issues have led to numerous struggles between various levels of government, in particular the federal and provincial governments, and to many struggles between provincial governments and the providers of services, in particular, hospitals, doctors, and nurses. Allegations of underfunding have become widespread, and in part, have led to the imposition or escalation of user fees. Among the most controversial of user fees were those charged by physicians in the form of extra-billing. Many felt that user fees in general, and extra-billing in particular, violated the basic principles of accessibility and portability and threatened to destroy medicare. While few want to dismantle medicare entirely, there are many who advocate a return to a more free-enterprise system of medicine, with less intervention from the state, more professional autonomy, and more emphasis on the user-pay concept (although with a public insurance "safety net" provided by the government for the poor, sick, and elderly). Proponents of this model (often referred to as the "two-tiered model") advocate "reprivatization" and argue that the problem of costs should be resolved in a free marketplace (free, that is, from government intervention, although not free in the sense of free competition) where providers of services charge according to demand for services. There are many others, however, who oppose these demand-side adjustments, and instead, emphasize supply-side reforms. First of all, proponents of supply-side change argue that the providers of services must not impose user fees, which violate the principle of equitable access. Further, in their attempts to shore up medicare, arguments are made against any movement towards reprivatization or emphasis on free-market mechanisms. Instead, it is argued that there must be greater constraints on the providers of health care. Many of the supply-side suggestions (for example, salary rather than fee-for-service, or quotas on the number of practitioners who can practise in a given area) imply the transformation of health care into a civil service, a direction which is opposed by the medical profession.

And so the debates continue. Canada's health-care programme is currently neither free-enterprise medicine nor socialized medicine. Rather, it is something in between. The practice of extra-billing, which threatened to undermine medicare and move the health-care system back toward the free-enterprise marketplace, has been banned. For now, the principles on which medicare were founded remain firmly in place.

Acknowledgements: I am grateful to Earle Snider for suggestions regarding the outline/conceptualization of this chapter, to Jan Storch for her comments, to Caterina Pizanias for research assistance, and to Judy Mitchell for transforming my handwriting into readable copy.

NOTES

1. The reader will note apparent discrepancies in the dates reported for various insurance programmes. Some sources report the date that the legislation was passed; other sources report the date that the legislation came into effect. I will report both dates with the date of implementation in brackets.

2. At time of writing, late in 1986, New Brunswick was the only province which still allowed extra-billing, although the practice was rare, involved a relatively small amount of money in total, and tended to be limited to a few procedures, such as cosmetic and dental surgery and vasectomies.

3. The 1962 doctors' strike in Saskatchewan lasted 23 days. A 1970 strike in Quebec lasted ten days and involved specialists only.

STUDY QUESTIONS

1. What were the circumstances and events that led to the implementation of Canada's national health-insurance programme? Be sure to distinguish between hospital insurance and medical care insurance. Why do you suppose these two related programmes developed separately?

2. Discuss the five principles on which Canada's health-care insurance programme is based. Assess the relevance of these principles for a national health insurance programme.

3. Discuss the relationship between social class, health status, utilization of health services, and user fees. Discuss the tension between extra-billing and the principles of accessibility and portability.

4. Compare and contrast the free-enterprise economic model, the medico-technical model, the professional control model, and the socialized medicine model. How does each of these models view the demand for services, the supply of services, and the issue of cost?

5. Discuss the problems in defining terms such as need, overuse, underuse, abuse, necessary and unnecessary or frivolous demand, underservicing, overservicing, and so on. In practice, what roles are played by the public, the media, and the providers of services in defining these terms?

6. Compare and contrast the perspectives of government, the providers of health care, and the general public with respect to allegations of underfunding.

RECOMMENDED READING

Barer, Morris L., R.G. Evans, and G.L. Stoddart. *Controlling Health Care Costs by Direct Charges to Patients: Snare or Delusion?* Toronto: Ontario Economic Council, 1979.

Blishen, Bernard R. *Doctors and Doctrines: The Ideology of Medical Care in Canada.* Toronto: University of Toronto Press, 1969.

Evans, Robert G. *Strained Mercy: The Economics of Canadian Health Care.* Toronto: Butterworths, 1984.

Hall, Emmett M. *Canada's National-Provincial Health Program for the 1980s: A Commitment for Renewal.* Ottawa: Health and Welfare Canada, 1980.

National Council of Welfare. *Medicare: The Public Good and the Private Practice.* Ottawa: National Council of Welfare, 1982.

Taylor, Malcolm G. *Health Insurance and Canadian Public Policy: The Seven Decisions that Created the Canadian Health Insurance System.* Montreal: McGill-Queen's University Press, 1978.

Taylor, Malcolm G., H.M. Stevenson, and A.P. Williams. *Medical Perspectives on Canadian Medicare: Attitudes of Canadian Physicians to Policies and Problems of the Medical Care Insurance Program.* Toronto: York University, 1984.

REFERENCES

Badgley, R.F., and R.D. Smith. *User Charges for Health Services.* Toronto: Ontario Council of Health, 1979.

Badgley, R.F., and S. Wolfe. *Doctors' Strike: Medical Care and Conflict in Saskatchewan.* Toronto: Macmillan, 1967.

Barer, M.L., R.G. Evans, and G.L. Stoddart. *Controlling Health Care Costs by Direct Charges to Patients: Snare or Delusion?* Toronto: Ontario Economic Council, 1979.

Barer, M.L., P. Manga, E.R. Shillington, and G.C. Siegel. *Income Class and Hospital Use in Ontario.* Toronto: Ontario Economic Council, 1982.

Beck, R.G. "Economic Class and Access to Physician Services Under Public Medical Care Insurance." *International Journal of Health Services* 3 (1973): 341–55.

Blishen, B.R. *Doctors and Doctrines: The Ideology of Medical Care in Canada.* Toronto: University of Toronto Press, 1969.

Boulet, J., and D.W. Henderson. *Distributional and Redistributional Aspects of Government Health Insurance Programs in Canada.* Ottawa: Economic Council of Canada, 1979.

Brown, M.C. "Health Care Financing and the Canada Health Act." *Journal of Canadian Studies* 21 (1986): 111–32.

———. "The Implications of Established Program Finance For National Health Insurance." *Canadian Public Policy* 6 (1980): 521–32.

Canadian Sickness Survey. *Illness and Health Care in Canada.* Ottawa: Queen's Printer, 1960.

Enterline, P.E., V. Salter, A.D. McDonald et al. "The Distribution of Medical Services Before and After 'Free' Medical Care — the Quebec Experience." *New England Journal of Medicine* 289 (1973): 1174–78.

Evans, R.G. *Strained Mercy: The Economics of Canadian Health Care.* Toronto: Butterworths, 1984.

Greenhill, S., and D. Haythorne. *Alberta Health Care Study: Health Care Utilization Patterns of Albertans, 1968 and 1970.* Edmonton: University of Alberta, 1972.

Hall, E.M. *Canada's National-Provincial Health Program for the 1980s: A Commitment for Renewal.* Ottawa: Health and Welfare Canada, 1980.

Manga, P. "Income and Access to Medical Care in Canada." In *Health and Canadian Society,* edited by D. Coburn et al. Toronto: Fitzhenry and Whiteside, 1981.

———. "Arbitration and the Medical Profession: a Comment on the Hall Report." *Canadian Public Policy* 6 (1980): 670–77.

McDonald, A. "Effects of Quebec Medicare on Physician Consultation for Selected Symptoms." *New England Journal of Medicine* 291 (1974): 649–52.

National Council of Welfare. *Medicare: The Public Good and the Private Practice.* Ottawa, 1982.

Naylor, C.D. "In Defence of Medicare." *Canadian Forum* 61 (April 1982): 12–16.

Northcott, H.C. "Extra-Billing and Physician Remuneration: A Paradox." *Canadian Public Policy* 8 (1982): 200–06.

Northcott, H.C., and E.L. Snider. *Deterring Physician Utilization: Medical Care User Fees in Canada.* Edmonton Area Series Report Number 26. Edmonton: Population Research Laboratory, Department of Sociology, University of Alberta, 1983.

Soderstrom, L. *The Canadian Health System.* London: Croom Helm, 1978.

Stevenson, H.M., and A.P. Williams. "Physicians and Medicare: Professional Ideology and Canadian Health Care Policy." *Canadian Public Policy* 11 (1985): 504–21.

Taylor, M.G. *Health Insurance and Canadian Public Policy: The Seven Decisions that Created the Canadian Health Insurance Sys-*

tem. Montreal: McGill-Queen's University Press, 1978.

Taylor, M.G., H.M. Stevenson, and A.P. Williams. *Medical Perspectives on Canadian Medicare: Attitudes of Canadian Physicians to Policies and Problems of the Medical Care Insurance Program.* Toronto: York University, 1984.

Weller, G.R., and P. Manga. "The Development of Health Policy in Canada." In *The Politics of Canadian Public Policy,* edited by M. Atkinson and M. Chandler. Toronto: University of Toronto Press, 1983a.

———. "The Push for Reprivatization of Health Care Services in Canada, Britain, and the United States." *Journal of Health Politics, Policy and Law* 8 (1983): 495–518.

4

THE STRUCTURE AND COST OF HEALTH CARE IN CANADA

Harley D. Dickinson and David A. Hay
University of Saskatchewan

INTRODUCTION

Since the Second World War, Canada has developed a state-financed system of health insurance. Under this system, known as medicare, every citizen of Canada is eligible to receive "free" necessary medical and hospital services. In addition, certain groups, such as the elderly and the young, are eligible for various other health-related services, including dental care, eye care, and prescription drugs. Constitutionally, health care is a provincial responsibility; therefore, the specifics of health insurance are slightly different for each province. In the past, the federal government has attempted to ensure a degree of uniformity between provinces through a number of cost-sharing arrangements (Soderstrom, 1978). These arrangements make the receipt of federal funds contingent upon the provinces' meeting certain minimum standards of comprehensive coverage, universality, portability of benefits, and public administration on a non-profit basis. An additional consequence of

federal health policy has been the entrenchment of doctors' services and hospital care at the centre of the Canadian health-care system. This has contributed to a growing fiscal crisis in the delivery of health care (Evans, 1984).

In this chapter, we examine the cost of health care in Canada, especially the cost of medical, that is, doctor-provided and hospital, services. We also look at a number of cost-control strategies and some of the consequences of these for the nature and organization of health-care delivery. The chapter, accordingly, has three main sections. In the first we outline the cost of the health-care system over time. In the second we look at the cost of physician services and various cost-control strategies directed at doctors. The third section contains information on the types, numbers, size, and cost of hospital care, as well as a brief discussion of the chief cost-containment initiatives undertaken in this sector. On the basis of this discussion, we suggest that the form and content of health care are influenced by social, economic, and political forces at least as much as they are by scientific knowledge and medical considerations.

Note: Tables are listed at the end of the chapter.

THE COST OF HEALTH CARE

Table 1 (see p. 62) shows that by 1982 total expenditures for health care in Canada were over $30 billion. This was a 16.8 percent increase over 1981 expenditures and amounted to 8.44 percent of the Gross National Product (GNP).[1] In comparison, total health-care costs in the United States were approximately 10.5 percent of the GNP in 1982. Although the rate of increase in health expenditures has been slower in the United States than in Canada, between 1970 and 1982, total per capita expenditures in the United States were about 1.2 times higher than in Canada. This is significant because of the fact that health-insurance coverage is much less comprehensive in the United States than it is in Canada. In fact, it is estimated that 30 million Americans under the age of 65 have no health insurance of any kind (Pear, 1987). This suggests that the argument that state-administered health insurance is less efficient than privately administered schemes is incorrect, because more is spent on health care in the United States than in Canada, even though coverage in Canada is more comprehensive. In addition, the Canadian system is more effective in delivering necessary health-care services because to a great extent it has removed financial barriers to seeking help. For those people in the United States who have no insurance, or only limited insurance coverage, large doctor or hospital bills can mean financial ruin. As a result, these people may be deterred from seeking necessary medical services simply because they cannot afford to pay.

As stated, medicare has essentially removed this obstacle for Canadians. In fact, it has resulted in a reduction in the proportion of family income spent on health care, as shown in Table 2 (see p. 63). Table 2 also shows, however, that as family income rises, the absolute amount spent on health care increases as well. The amount spent decreases, on the other hand, when expressed as a proportion of family income. This suggests that although medicare has effectively removed financial barriers to the receipt of necessary medical and hospital services, a degree of income-related inequality remains (Grant, this volume). In addition it has been argued that inequalities related to gender (Trypuc, this volume), race (Frideres, this volume), and age (Ujimoto, this volume) also characterize the Canadian health-care system.

The recent trend toward reprivatization (Weller and Manga, 1983) likely will exacerbate these inequalities by creating a two-tiered system of health care, one for the rich and one for the poor. Privatization is generally promoted by the political right as a cost-cutting measure that will result in savings in health-care delivery because of greater efficiency. The claim that the private sector is inherently more efficient than the public sector, however, may be based more on ideology than fact. As we have already seen, in the United States, where there is no universal, comprehensive, state-administered health insurance, expenditures for health care are higher than in Canada. And as shown in Figure 1, private-sector health expenditures in the United States are more than double those in Canada. It is also instructive to note that between 1970 and 1982, prepayment administration costs in the United States have generally been about 2 1/2 times greater than in Canada. This seems to belie the claim that the private sector is necessarily more efficient than the public sector.

The trend toward reprivatization has been accompanied by a reduction in the proportion of total state expenditures devoted to social welfare and health programmes (albeit within the context of overall increases in government expenditures); at the same time, tax breaks, rebates, and other direct subsidies to business have increased. To illustrate: expenditures on health care, considered as a proportion of total gross general expenditures for all levels of government, decreased from about 12.6 percent in 1976 to 12.1 percent in 1982. During that same time period, expenditures on hospital care as a proportion of total gross general expenditures also dropped, to 7.3 percent from 8.2 percent (Statistics Canada, *Consolidated Government Finance*,

1976, 1982). As can be seen from Table 3 (see p. 63), provincial and local levels of government are picking up a larger share of the health-care bill, and given their limited tax base, this generates tremendous pressure to reduce health-care expenditures. Because of this, provincial governments may find reprivatization increasingly attractive. Although few politicians openly espouse dismantling medicare, this may be one of the consequences of some of the cost-control strategies currently being employed.

Figure 1: Private-Sector Shares of Total Health Expenditures, Canada and United States, 1960–1982*

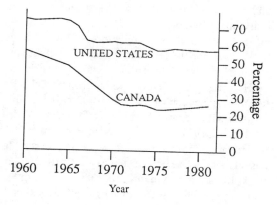

* 1981 for Canada is provisional

Source: National Health Expenditures in Canada, 1970–1982. Health and Welfare Canada, n.d., p.27.

Since the early 1970s it has been agreed that health-care costs can be controlled in three ways: (1) by reducing the episodes of illness requiring medical or hospital care, (2) by reducing the number of contacts between the patient and medical personnel during any episode of illness, and (3) by reducing the cost per contact (Task Force, Vol. 3, 1970).

There are, of course, many different ways in which these three strategies can be implemented, and it is not possible to discuss them all here. Instead, we will examine what we feel are the most significant trends in both the medical (doctor) and hospital-services sectors. We will also discuss some of the possible consequences of different cost-reduction tactics for the nature and organization of health-care delivery in Canada.

DOCTORS AND MEDICARE

Doctors are the principal providers of health care in Canada. Not only are they usually the first point of contact for those seeking care, they are also the "gatekeepers" to hospitals, most health-care institutions, and many professional services. It has been estimated, for example, that physicians directly control approximately 80 percent of total health-care costs, even though their incomes account for only 15 percent of those costs (Chappell et al., 1986:100). Thus, doctors' decisions concerning who will be admitted to hospital, how long they stay, and the type and number of tests and treatments provided to a considerable extent dictate the cost of health-care delivery. In addition, because physicians have a legislative monopoly on drug prescription, they largely control the patterns and costs of drug use. Thus, it is evident that the containment of health-care costs will require changes to the nature and organization of physicians' practices.

As can be seen in Table 4 (see p. 64), which shows total health-care expenditures in Canada by category between 1970 and 1982, doctors' services alone cost over $4.4 billion in 1982. Table 5 (see p. 65) shows income levels for selected occupations in Canada between 1968 and 1980. Doctors have consistently had the highest incomes, although in 1980 dentists' incomes surpassed those of doctors by a small amount. Interestingly, if we break doctors' and dentists' incomes down by sex, we find that the average income for male physicians and surgeons in 1980 was $59 834, compared to $36 115 for female physicians and surgeons. (Dentists' average incomes for that year were $58 121 and $40 510 for males and females respectively.)

The reasons for these gender-based income differences are unclear. Undoubtedly, however, they are related to patterns of specialization: females are channelled into, or choose, the less lucrative specialties or geographical areas of practice. They may also be related to non-work factors such as patterns of child care and responsibility for other domestic duties. More research into these factors is needed. Given these high income levels, however, and the growth in the number of doctors, it is not surprising that considerable attention has been devoted to controlling costs both by reducing the number of contacts people have with doctors, and by reducing the cost per contact.

Reducing the Number of Contacts and Services

There are two sources of demand for doctors' services: the consumer/patient and, after the initial contact has been made, the service-provider/doctor.

Consumer-Generated Demand

There are a number of ways to limit consumer-generated demand for medical and other health-care services. The most obvious is to improve the health status of the population so that people do not need as much care. Although the determinants of health status are many and complex, it is generally agreed that they include the following four components and the interactions between them: human biology, environment, lifestyles, and health-care organization (Lalonde, 1974). We will examine efforts in the first three categories in this section. Initiatives in the area of health-care organization will be discussed in the next section, under the heading Provider-Generated Demand.

Although it is obvious that genetic and biochemical processes of the body are implicated in a wide range of disorders, including many chronic diseases such as diabetes, arthritis, and atherosclerosis, as well as congenital malformations and mental retardation, in the short run, these must be considered fixed. Having said this, however, it should be noted that much money and research are devoted to discovering the secrets of human biology and genetics to

enable the control and modification of these processes.

The environment, which is defined as those things "which are external to the human body and over which the individual has little or no control" (Lalonde, 1974:18), also influences health and illness. Aspects of the environment include: levels and types of air, water, and food pollution and contamination; product safety; the nature and organization of work; levels and duration of unemployment; incomes, housing conditions, etc. These, and other so-called environmental factors, are rooted in particular social, economic, and political relationships. Thus, health and illness must be understood as being partly the product of social, economic, and political processes, as well as the result of individual pathologies. This point is made clearly in several of the chapters in this volume: by Weston and Jeffery with regard to AIDS, and by Currie in her discussion of anorexia nervosa, by Harding with reference to environmental pollution and cancer rates, and by Dickinson and Stobbe with regard to the link between work-related injury and illness, and control over the nature and organization of work processes. It has also been demonstrated recently that high rates of unemployment are related to higher rates of psychological distress, greater short-term and long-term disability, increased susceptibility to a wide range of health problems, and more hospitalization and utilization of health care (D'Arcy and Siddique, 1985; Hay, this volume). It is in recognition of these relationships that full employment, workplace democracy, and environmental protection have been proposed as part of an attempt to improve people's health and reduce the cost of health-care delivery. Evidence seems to suggest, however, that the balance of political and economic forces in society do not support — and in many cases actively oppose — such actions. It is at least partly because of the political nature of environmental approaches to improved health that many reformers have emphasized, to the virtual exclusion of environmental reforms, the importance of individual lifestyles in the determination of health and illness.

Lifestyles, considered as the third determinant of health, are conceptualized as the "aggregation of decisions by individuals which affect their health and over which they more or less have control" (Lalonde, 1974:32). It is argued that

> personal decisions and habits that are bad from a health point of view, create self-imposed risks. When those risks result in illness or death, the victim's lifestyle can be said to have contributed to, or caused, his own illness or death.

Although it is obvious that certain elements of an individual's lifestyle, such as poor diet, smoking, excessive alcohol consumption, and sedentary lifestyle, will contribute to illness, injury, and death, an overemphasis on these factors at the expense of the social, political, and economic environment within which these behaviours and decisions take place, exaggerates their significance in causing injury and illness and may degenerate into ideological obfuscation and victim-blaming (Bolaria, this volume).

Provider-Generated Demand

The improvement of health and individual behaviour modification are not the only ways to reduce consumer-generated demand for health-care services. It is recognized that the organization and operation of the health-care system are influential in determining levels of demand and patterns of utilization. Thus, much effort is directed toward organizational and operational changes intended to reduce cost by reducing utilization. A common strategy in this regard has been the imposition of financial barriers to utilization of services, in the form of user fees, deterrent charges, and extra-billing. Advocates of these tactics argue that making consumers pay discourages frivolous and unnecessary use of "free" health-care services. What has been observed, however, is that very few people demand unnecessary services and that the only real consequence of user fees is to dissuade the poor from seeking necessary services. This, of course, violates the principles of universality and accessibility upon which medicare rests. In

order to protect these principles, the 1984 Canada Health Act among other things imposed financial penalties on those provinces that allowed doctors to extra-bill or hospitals to charge user fees. As a result, these practices have disappeared.

There are, however, other ways to limit consumer-generated demand for necessary health-care services which have not been banned, and in some cases are actively pursued in the name of efficiency and economy. These practices include waiting lists for various hospital and medical services, capping health-care budgets, not insuring certain services, and limiting the number of services of a particular type that will be covered. Other, largely unintended, forms of rationing result from regional maldistribution of medical personnel and facilities. It is generally known, for example, that both doctors and hospitals are concentrated in urban areas. As a result, people who live in non-urban areas do not have ready access to these medical services and facilities. This, like extra-billing, violates the principles of universality and accessibility. A number of attempts have been made to counter this inequity. As of May 31, 1985, the government of British Columbia refused to issue new doctors billing numbers, which allow them to be remunerated from the provincial medical insurance system, unless they agreed to practise in underserviced areas of the province. Although there was some opposition from that segment of the profession directly affected, it appeared not to be an issue over which the majority of doctors were willing to fight, at least not at that time. One suspects that unless doctors show some willingness to address the problem of maldistribution themselves, more provincial governments will follow the lead of British Columbia and unilaterally impose a solution.

Doctors, however, are notoriously jealous of their professional autonomy. They argue that the nature of their work requires complete freedom to determine what they do and how they do it. They also claim that the doctor-patient relationship is a relationship of trust that should not be subject to intervention or surveillance by any third party, whether that third party is a private insurance company or a state agency. This position is based upon the claim that doctors, and only doctors, have the special knowledge and technical expertise to determine what medical procedures are required and appropriate in any given situation. They argue further that the potential abuse and conflict of interest that are inherent in such a situation are not an issue because, as a profession, they are motivated by altruism and a commitment to community service rather than by baser pecuniary considerations (Frankel, this volume). Drawing upon this professional ideology, doctors have vigorously resisted any encroachments upon their professional autonomy and incomes (Stevenson and Williams, this volume). The best-known examples of this are the infamous Saskatchewan doctors' strike, occasioned by the introduction of the country's first state-sponsored prepaid medical care insurance plan in 1962 (Badgley and Wolfe, 1967; Tollefson, 1963), and the 1986 strike of Ontario doctors against the banning of extra-billing (Northcott, this volume).

Politicians, ever concerned about the political consequences of confronting doctors, have decided that the least controversial way to reduce the cost of doctors' services is simply to limit the number of doctors. This strategy, which is supported by many practising physicians, indicates a significant change of opinion, because historically (until the 1970s) it had been maintained that the major problem facing the health-care system was a shortage of physicians; effort was thus concentrated on increasing the number of doctors (see Table 6, p. 65). This has been achieved by training doctors in Canada and by importing them from abroad (Bolaria, this volume). As experience has demonstrated, however, simply increasing the number of doctors is no guarantee that the health status of the population will improve, or even that medical services will be equally available to everyone. There are two reasons for this: (1) doctors may not locate their practices in the geographic areas where they are required, and/or (2) they may not be trained in appropriate areas of specialization.

For example, although there were 49 916 practising doctors in Canada in 1984, the ratio of population to active physicians (excluding interns and residents) varied from a high of 830:1 in New Brunswick to a low of 527:1 in British Columbia. The national average was 596:1 (*Health Manpower Directorate*, 1985). To the extent that there is any shortage of doctors, it is with primary-contact physicians, not specialists. Despite this, only about 44 percent of practising doctors were primary-contact physicians in 1984, down from about 54 percent in 1968 and 67 percent in 1955. As we have stated, this not only contributes to escalating costs because of differential fee schedules, it also exacerbates the problem of physician maldistribution: specialists' practices are concentrated in the larger urban areas, leaving non-urban residents underserviced.

The continuing growth in the number of specialists is indicative of the contradiction between the self-interest of the medical profession and the interest of society in available, accessible, appropriate, and affordable health-care services. Recognition of this has resulted in a number of recommendations for the reorganization of health-care delivery. In 1972, for example, a report prepared for the Conference of Health Ministers recommended the creation of a system of Community Health Centres. These were to employ multi-disciplinary teams composed of physicians, social workers, nurses, and other health-care professionals on a salaried basis in the provision of "initial and continuing health care of high quality" (Hastings, 1972:1). The Community Health Centres were to provide an alternative to the solo medical practitioner and hospital-based health-care services. Doctors vigorously resisted their implementation, however, and in the few cases where this type of facility already existed, such as the Community Clinics in Saskatchewan, doctors would only work if they had complete autonomy and control. Young (1975) provides an interesting account of the mass resignation of the doctors at the Regina Community Clinic when an active lay board of directors and a change in budgeting procedures threatened the doctors' autonomy and control. Thus, as a result of physician opposition, the Community Health Centres, heralded as the remedy to rising health-care costs and an overemphasis on curing sickness rather than promoting health, have not materialized on a significant scale. There are about 120 Community Health Centres in the entire country and about 100 of those are in Quebec (Naylor, 1986:245). Although a substantial minority of practising physicians in Canada are salaried employees of various types of organizations, about two thirds are self-employed on a fee-for-service basis (Naylor, 1986:245–6).

The Community Health Centre, or any other institution that employs doctors and other health-care professionals on a salaried basis, is one means of controlling health-care costs. This is because employed professionals are more easily monitored than are fee-for-service practitioners. Monitoring of doctors' work patterns enables evaluation and comparison of patterns of diagnosis and treatment, and can eliminate unnecessary or inappropriate services. A case in point is the prescription of medication. As the Task Force on the Cost of Health Services in Canada (1970:72) noted, "drugs are a major component of the therapeutic armamentarium of most doctors, and doctors' habits are the major determinants of the use and abuse of drugs." Doctors' prescription habits are conditioned by a number of factors, including perceived medical indications, training, and the advertising and marketing activities of the pharmaceutical industry. The major drug companies, however, are in business to maximize profits and, therefore, may encourage doctors to overprescribe and, whenever possible, to prescribe expensive brand names over inexpensive generic equivalents (Lexchin, this volume). Experience with various drug plans has shown that the external monitoring of doctors' drug prescription patterns can substantially lower the medication component of overall health-care costs. Similarly, external monitoring of physicians' and surgeons' patterns of practice have resulted in changes in levels of surgery and diagnostic test-ing (Myers and Schroeder, 1981; Dyck, 1977). The reduction of unnecessary medical intervention not only reduces costs of health-care delivery, it also reduces the incidence and rate of iatrogenic, that is, doctor-produced, disease and injury (Illich, 1976), and may thereby contribute to an improvement in the health status of Canadians.

The recent growth in the effectiveness of medical technology has produced a different set of ethical and financial concerns, namely, should life always be extended if the technology exists, or are there conditions under which people should be allowed to die and, if so, who should decide? At present many of these decisions, by default, are made by the medical profession. It is likely that many doctors do not wish to bear this awesome responsibility. At the same time, however, doctors do not want to lose control over the nature and organization of their work and, therefore, these issues remain highly contentious. These and a number of other issues are discussed in this volume by Roy.

As we have seen, doctors are generally loath to permit changes which threaten their power, pay, or prestige, even if proposed changes would bring about greater equity in the availability and accessibility of required health services (Hamowy, 1984). The development and deployment of various alternative health-care professions is believed by many to be the best solution to inequity in availability of and accessibility to health-care services. Historically, doctors have attempted to limit competition from other independent health professions by having their practices declared illegal (and the practitioners labelled "quacks"), or by making them directly subordinate to physician authority. Many non-medical health-care professions have resisted this medical domination, with varying degrees of success. Some of their efforts are described in this volume: Burtch, for example, discusses the case of midwives who have thus far been unsuccessful in their fight for legitimacy in Canada; Biggs looks at the case of chiropractors, who have achieved greater success; Dickinson and Andre discuss the case of clinical psychologists and social workers in the field of community psychiatry; and Croucher provides an interesting examination of how dentists, using arguments similar to those employed by doctors, resisted the development of a dental plan for schoolchildren which would have required the extensive use of independent dental nurses.

The reasons for this differential success are varied and complex. Given the present political and economic climate, however, the promise made by most non-medical health-care professions that they can provide effective services at less expense than doctors is extremely attractive to legislators. In the future, therefore, we may see increased utilization of various non-medical health professions in the delivery of health-care services. The 1984 Canada Health Act (CHA), in fact, provides for this possibility.

The CHA enables the provinces to include under their various medical insurance plans services provided by non-physicians. Interestingly, it allows the providers of these services to be reimbursed on a fee-for-service basis. A fee-for-service system of reimbursement makes it difficult to control costs, because after the initial contact is made, utilization patterns are largely provider-determined. Thus, although part of the rationale for including non-physician services under medicare is cost reduction, the allowance of access to a fee-for-service system to non-physicians will likely contribute to rising costs. In addition it will produce a unity of interests among a wide array of potentially competing health-care professions in the perpetuation of the inflationary fee-for-service system; this, in turn, will render any cost-containment strategies less effective.

THE STRUCTURE OF HOSPITAL SERVICES AND THE CONTAINMENT OF COSTS

The federal government became actively involved in hospital construction in 1948 under the terms of reference of the National Health Program. Table 7 (see p. 66) shows the number, size by number of beds, and the total number of beds in Canadian public general hospitals. As can be seen, since 1965 the trend is toward more larger and fewer smaller hospitals. And although the total number of beds available has increased from 101 775 to 125 592, they tend to be concentrated in hospitals of 200 beds or more which, in turn, tend to be concentrated in larger urban centres.

Following the Second World War, and especially since the passage of the Hospital Insurance and Diagnostic Services Act in 1958, the general and acute care hospital has been the primary locus of medical treatment. Consequently expenditures on general and allied special hospitals have consistently accounted for the largest proportion of total health expenditures (see Table 4, p. 64). There is a wide variation, however, in the amount spent for hospital care, as well as in the cost per patient day, as can be seen in Table 8 (see p. 67). As in other sectors of the health-care system, cost increases in hospitals are linked to patterns both of service utilization and of service provision.

Patterns of Hospital Utilization

Table 9 (see p. 68) shows separation rates and average days per separation by sex and province for 1980–81. Wide variation can be observed by both sex and region. Table 10 (see p. 69) shows separation rates and average days per separation by age and sex for 1980–81. Separation rates vary markedly by age and sex, with the separation rates for females being much higher in the middle age groups and the rates for males being higher in the younger and older groupings. The higher rate of separations for females in the 15-to-44 age group is most likely linked to the fact that pregnancy and childbirth are largely considered medical matters requiring medical intervention and hospitalization (Pollock, this volume). It also suggests the possibility of substantial savings to the health-care system by a shift to the use of midwives for normal, low-risk births.

Table 11 (see p. 70) shows the separation rates, percentage of all separations, and average days per separation by sex for the eight leading causes of hospitalization in 1980–81. Again one sees substantial variation in separation rates and average length of stay by sex. Thus, not only are men and women hospitalized for different reasons, but also the length of time they stay in hospital varies, even if they are admitted for the same causes. These and many other sources of variaton are important for policy-makers and planners interested in controlling hospital costs and developing alternatives to inpatient hospital treatment. Characteristics of health-care consumers and related utilization patterns, however, are only one component of costs in the health-care system. In fact, Vayda et al. (1979) suggest that the primary source of cost increases in the hospital sector in Canada is *not* increased utilization, but rather increasing unit costs of hospital care. Unit costs are related to many factors, including admission and discharge practices, the type and number of tests and treatments, the cost of drugs, the nature and organization of the hospital labour force, and, of course, wage levels of hospital employees.

Table 12 (see p. 71) shows operating expenditures by type of expense for reporting public hospitals in Canada between 1963 and 1983–84. It is clear that the largest proportion of hospital expenditure is composed of salaries and wages. This category, as a proportion of total hospital expenditures, has decreased from 76 percent to 74 percent between 1978–79 and 1983–84. In fact, except for medical and surgical supplies, there has been a slight downward trend in all categories of expenditures expressed as a proportion of total expenditures, even though in absolute terms more money is being spent overall.

Cost-Containment Strategies in the Hospital Sector

Cost-containment strategies in the hospital sector are generally of two types: (1) attempts to reduce the number of hospitalizations, and (2) attempts to reduce the cost per hospitalization.

The number of hospitalizations can be reduced either by improving the health of the population or by restricting admissions. Under the existing system, admission to and discharge from hospital are medical prerogatives directly linked to the professional power, pay, and prestige of doctors and, therefore, are difficult to control or change. Rather than challenging doctors for control of these processes, politicians and lay administrators have opted to limit admissions in other ways, including leaving available beds empty and actually reducing the number of beds available. Between 1974 and 1985, for example, roughly 20 percent of available hospital beds in Canada were empty (Canadian Hospital Directory, 1986). Hastings (1972:11) has stated, however, that "the chief means of controlling costs within the hospital sector is to be found in a reduction in the present acute bed/population ratio and a consequent reduction of in-patient services and facilities." This is achieved through direct limits placed on hospital budgets by provincial governments. It is recognized that simply reducing the number of hospital beds available, or leaving available beds empty, may result in people being denied access to necessary services and care. Consequently, the policy of restricting admission to hospital beds has been accompanied by the development of a range of Special Care Homes. These include facilities such as homes for the aged, the physically handicapped, the mentally handicapped, alcoholics, drug addicts, unmarried mothers, and emotionally disturbed children, as well as various community-based services such as Home Care. Although these facilities and services were developed as part of an attempt to reduce hospital costs, they have become the fastest-growing component of Canadian health-care expenditures (see Table 4, p. 64). This might be partly explained by the fact that the previously noted trend towards privatization of health care is well advanced in this sector, and by the changing demographic composition of the Canadian population. Tarman (this volume), for example, examines the privatization of non-hospital institutional care for the elderly and suggests that the provision of profit-based institutional care for the elderly has a tendency to degenerate into simple warehousing of the aged. Experience also shows that where the need for profit supersedes the needs of people, the result is degradation and dehumanization.

Other attempts to reduce expenditures for hospital services have focussed on reducing the cost per hospitalization. It is generally accepted that increases in the size of hospital work forces, combined with wage increases achieved through unionization, were responsible for rising costs in the hospital sector (Hall, 1982). As Wotherspoon (this volume) points out, however, even after substantial wage gains throughout the 1960s and 1970s, nurses' average income, and incomes of other hospital workers, are *below* the Canadian average income. Despite this, nurses' and other hospital workers' incomes do account for the major proportion of hospital costs. Consequently, attempts at work rationalization have been largely directed at these workers.

Wage-related costs can be reduced in either absolute or relative terms. Absolute wage reductions can be achieved by cutting the size of the work force or cutting wages, or some combination of the two. Relative wage reductions can be achieved through intensification of the work process, that is, by getting more work out of a worker in a given time period. This can be achieved through either organizational or technological means. Currently both types of cost-containment strategies are evident in Canadian hospitals.

Reducing the number of workers or decreasing their wages, of course, are effective means of reducing costs in any workplace. This, however, is a difficult strategy to implement because workers, especially unionized workers, will struggle against both layoffs and wage rollbacks. Politicians and hospital administrators, therefore, seldom pursue this policy in a very aggressive manner. Rather, staff reductions are generally achieved through attrition; that is, by not replacing people who retire or leave for other reasons. Wage reductions are achieved through job reclassification and by replacing full-time workers with part-time workers.

Table 13 (see p. 71) shows that there has been an increase in the employment of part-time workers in hospitals, which mirrors an increase in the number of part-time workers in general. The growth in the employment of part-time workers occurs for two reasons. First, part-time workers are less expensive than full-time workers (even if they are paid at the same rate, which is unlikely) because employers are not required to make compulsory contributions for various non-wage benefits for these workers. Second, part-time employees are attractive to employers because they tend not to be union supporters and are therefore usually unwilling to support union struggles. This contributes to a lack of unity among hospital workers, which in turn limits their ability to achieve wage increases, job security, or other improvements in the terms and conditions of employment.

A fragmented and non-unified work force facilitates management attempts to reduce relative wage costs through intensifying the work process. The intensification of work, i.e., the process of getting more work from workers in a given time period, can, as we have suggested, be achieved through both organizational and technological means. Campbell (this volume), for example, shows how various management-initiated organizational changes, intended to increase the "efficiency" of nurses' work, have increased the stress experienced by nurses to the point where not only is their own health undermined, but the level and quality of care provided to patients is also jeopardized. Dickinson and Brady (1984) discuss how "labour-saving" technology used in intensive-care units may have the same results. In addition, there is some indication that "labour-saving" technology may also contribute to the deskilling of some aspects of nursing work, with the consequence that nurses can be replaced by less well trained, less skilled, and less expensive technicians.

The joint threat to nurses' working conditions and the quality of patient care produced by management efforts to reduce hospital costs leads Warburton and Carroll (this volume) to suggest that nurses are strategically located to bridge the gap that traditionally separates producers from consumers and, therefore, to lead the struggle for a fair and just health-care system. Whether such an alliance can be forged, and if forged, can be effective, remains to be seen. What is clear is that the struggle for effective and equitable health care is far from over.

CONCLUSIONS

In this chapter we have examined health-care costs in Canada, with a special focus on the cost of doctor-provided and hospital services. We have also seen how decisions taken at the political and administrative level have consequences for — in fact, largely determine — the nature and organization of health-care delivery systems. We have also suggested that since at least 1970, the primary motivating force in the health-care system has been cost-containment and, although few would argue that the provision of the best possible health-care services at the lowest possible price is not desirable, there is little agreement on how that can best be achieved. Having stated this, however, it seems evident that the dominant trend is towards increasing privatization and decentralization of control. The Meech Lake Constitutional Accord essentially restricts the role of the federal government to providing money for whatever the provinces decide to do, and essentially destroys the ability of the federal government to insist on national standards in social and health-care programmes. If such an arrangement had been in place in the mid-1960s, the federal government would have been unable to establish medicare, due to the degree of provincial opposition that existed at that time.

When this political emasculation of the federal government is combined with the dominance of the cult of efficiency and the push towards privatization at the provincial level, one cannot help but be concerned that medicare and the principles upon which it stands are being eroded.

Acknowledgements: This paper was partly funded by the University of Saskatchewan President's Social Sciences and Humanities Research Council Fund, the support of which is gratefully acknowledged. We are also grateful to Janice Remai and Shannon Skinner for their assistance in collection and tabulation of data and to Terry Wotherspoon and Glenn Andre for their valuable suggestions and comments on earlier drafts of this chapter. We are completely responsible, however, for any errors or omissions in the paper.

NOTES

1. Gross National Product (GNP), by totalling all costs arising in production, measures the market value of all goods and services produced in the current period by Canadian (i.e., resident in Canada) factors of production. It is equal to wages and salaries, profits, interest, net rent, net income of farm and nonfarm unincorporated business, indirect taxes (less subsidies), capital consumption allowances, and miscellaneous valuation adjustments (National Health Expenditures, n.d.: 106).

STUDY QUESTIONS

1. Health and illness are at least as much the products of social, economic, and political forces as they are the result of individual pathologies. Discuss.

2. Health-care costs cannot be controlled without first limiting the power and autonomy of the medical profession. Discuss.

3. Privatization of health-care delivery is preferable to state-administered medicare. Discuss.

4. Outline and discuss the two main cost-containment strategies currently being applied to the hospital sector. What are some of the possible negative consequences for caregivers and patients?

5. What are the major forms of cost control in the health-care sector, and what are the limitations of each strategy?

Table 1. Total Health Expenditures, Health Expenditures as a Percentage of GNP, and Percentage Increase over Previous Year, Canada and United States, 1970–1982 (Billions of Dollars)

Year	Total Expenditures*		Percentage of GNP		Percentage Increase over Previous Year	
	Canada	U.S.	Canada	U.S.	Canada	U.S.
1970	6.26	74.7	7.30	7.52	—	—
71	7.12	83.3	7.54	7.73	13.8	11.5
72	7.80	93.5	7.40	7.88	9.4	12.2
73	8.72	103.2	7.06	7.78	11.9	10.4
74	10.25	116.4	6.95	8.12	17.5	12.8
75	12.38	132.7	7.49	8.57	20.8	14.0
76	14.16	149.7	7.38	8.71	14.4	12.8
77	15.53	169.2	7.39	8.82	9.7	13.0
78	17.09	189.3	7.36	8.75	10.1	11.9
79	19.07	215.0	7.21	8.89	11.5	13.6
80	22.18	249.0	7.48	9.46	16.3	15.8
81†	25.77	286.6	7.60	9.70	16.2	15.1
82†	30.09	322.4	8.44	10.49	16.8	12.5

* Includes for Canada: personal health care; institutions (general and allied special hospitals, mental hospitals, tuberculosis hospitals, federal hospitals, homes for special care); professional services (physicians, dentists, chiropractors, optometrists, podiatrists, osteopaths, nursing, physiotherapists); drugs and appliances (prescribed drugs, non-prescribed drugs, eyeglasses, hearing aids, health appliances and other prostheses); other health costs (prepayment administration, public health, capital expenditures, health research, miscellaneous health costs).

Includes for the United States: all institutions (hospitals, homes for special care); all professional services (physicians, dentists, other professionals); all drugs and appliances (drugs and medical sundries, eyeglasses and appliances); all other health costs (prepayment administration, public health, capital expenditures, health research, miscellaneous health costs).

† Provisional

Source: National Health Expenditures in Canada 1970–1982, Ottawa: Health and Welfare Canada, n.d.

Table 2. Family Expenditures on Health Care by Income Level (Quintile), Canada, 1972–1978

Average Dollar Expenditure	1972 Dollars	%	1974 Dollars	%	1976 Dollars	%	1978 Dollars	%
First quintile	105.8	2.8	135.2	2.7	137.3	2.3	151.4	2.1
Second quintile	219.7	3.0	240.3	2.4	291.8	2.4	318.0	2.3
Third quintile	268.2	2.6	296.3	2.2	336.9	2.0	391.2	2.0
Fourth quintile	350.1	2.7	352.3	2.1	425.3	2.0	471.9	1.9
Fifth quintile	455.0	2.3	474.8	1.8	561.2	1.7	625.7	1.7

Source: Abelson, J. et al. *Perspectives on Health*, Statistics Canada, Catalogue 82–540E, Table 94.

Table 3. Federal and Provincial/Local Government Share of Health-Care Costs, Canada, Selected Years, 1962–1982

	Gross General Expenditures, All Levels of Gov't ('000s)	Federal Expenditure ('000s)	%	Provincial/Local Expenditure ('000s)	%
1962	1 153 250	425 376	36.9	727 874	63.1
1967	2 275 823	617 829	27.1	1 657 994	72.9
1972	7 492 790	1 603 418	21.4	5 889 790	78.6
1977	14 577 704	3 305 048	22.7	11 272 704	77.3
1982	27 581 940	4 740 707	17.2	22 840 940	82.8

Figures for 1962–1967 were calculated from tables in *Consolidated Government Finance*. Figures for 1972–1982 were calculated by subtracting the gross federal expenditure cited in *Federal Government Finance* from the gross general expenditures of all levels of government cited in *Consolidated Government Finance*.

Sources: *Federal Government Finance*, Statistics Canada, Cat. 68–211 Annual;
     Consolidated Government Finance, Statistics Canada, Cat. 68–202 Annual.

Table 4. Total Health Expenditures, Canada, by Category, 1970–1982 (Millions of Dollars)

Category	1970	1971	1972	1973	1974	1975	1976	1977	1978	1979	1980	1981*	1982*
Total health expenditures	6 255.9	7 122.3	7 790.2	8 720.3	10 247.5	12 381.4	14 158.7	15 532.6	17 094.1	19 067.2	22 178.6	23 769.3	30 087.7
Personal health care	5 452.7	6 209.1	6 851.0	7 671.2	8 994.1	10 931.2	12 507.5	13 703.7	15 073.8	16 825.3	19 364.0	22 551.9	26 427.1
Institutions	3 263.1	3 668.8	4 066.5	4 603.5	5 584.6	6 940.3	8 008.7	8 671.6	9 488.6	10 532.9	12 195.1	14 255.1	16 587.7
General & allied special hospitals	2 291.2	2 585.5	2 858.8	3 235.2	3 952.9	4 970.4	5 778.4	6 355.1	6 929.3	7 696.9	8 920.4	10 364.8	12 045.4
Mental hospitals	407.7	443.2	475.6	529.7	605.8	696.8	650.6	413.3	414.0	394.9	418.5	194.9	230.1
Tuberculosis hospitals	23.7	21.2	12.7	9.7	6.4	7.1	0	0	0	0	0	0	0
Federal hospitals	92.2	102.8	109.5	115.7	124.0	130.5	142.5	160.0	140.2	147.6	145.9	164.7	194.5
Homes for special care	448.3	516.0	609.9	713.2	895.5	1 135.6	1 437.2	1 743.3	2 005.1	2 293.4	2 710.4	3 530.7	4 117.7
Professional services	1 410.1	1 675.4	1 859.6	2 038.6	2 291.2	2 691.8	3 006.3	3 357.8	3 740.9	4 236.3	4 902.7	5 613.0	6 564.1
Physicians	1 040.7	1 250.4	1 386.2	1 483.4	1 659.7	1 914.1	2 103.2	2 309.0	2 544.0	2 843.5	3 284.7	3 741.0	4 414.3
Dentists	265.0	311.5	350.6	419.1	483.9	596.6	699.8	827.6	954.1	1 106.0	1 288.0	1 482.9	1 682.6
Chiropractors	34.2	39.3	43.5	49.5	56.8	66.5	77.4	87.8	96.6	115.4	128.8	151.5	181.1
Optometrists	45.7	49.1	53.2	57.8	64.2	71.9	80.5	87.3	88.4	102.7	119.9	142.6	170.2
Podiatrists	7.9	4.2	4.7	6.3	8.4	13.2	14.4	14.9	15.2	17.3	18.9	20.1	22.1
Osteopaths	1.9	2.1	2.1	2.3	2.1	1.3	1.4	1.5	1.5	1.5	1.4	1.6	1.8
Nursing	18.7	18.8	19.2	20.1	16.1	28.1	29.5	29.7	33.2	36.5	44.5	55.3	70.9
Physiotherapists	—	—	—	—	—	—	—	—	7.9	13.3	16.5	18.1	21.2
Drugs and appliances	779.4	865.0	924.9	1 029.1	1 118.3	1 299.1	1 492.6	1 674.3	1 844.2	2 056.1	2 266.1	2 683.8	3 275.3
Prescribed drugs	368.7	402.5	421.1	466.9	498.0	578.7	667.1	746.0	822.2	918.2	1 011.2	1 205.3	1 473.4
Non-prescribed drugs	329.4	361.6	379.9	424.8	459.5	536.8	617.7	689.4	759.6	845.4	928.6	1 109.9	1 357.7
Eyeglasses	58.6	74.1	92.6	102.9	120.0	137.2	158.0	181.8	197.4	214.8	241.7	272.1	333.4
Hearing aids	9.7	10.0	10.7	11.3	13.3	14.9	13.6	15.7	20.2	28.1	30.3	35.7	42.1
Health appliances & other prostheses	13.0	16.7	20.5	23.3	27.5	31.5	36.2	41.3	44.9	49.5	54.3	61.1	68.6
Other health costs	803.7	913.2	939.2	1 049.1	1 253.3	1 450.1	1 651.1	1 828.9	2 020.3	2 241.9	2 814.6	3 217.4	3 660.6
Prepayment administration	99.2	123.4	134.1	146.4	175.3	211.6	216.3	256.5	251.5	273.8	311.0	403.3	441.4
Public health	197.2	214.7	231.2	249.0	284.9	369.4	484.6	544.5	594.7	697.1	762.6	872.1	952.8
Capital expenditures	364.8	420.2	400.0	456.7	567.8	604.5	646.2	668.3	765.9	822.7	1 219.8	1 332.4	1 585.4
Health research	70.3	78.3	89.7	100.5	112.6	125.7	139.2	168.3	191.8	206.2	243.4	290.2	327.1
Miscellaneous health costs	71.8	76.7	84.2	96.5	112.7	138.9	164.8	191.4	216.3	242.1	277.8	319.4	353.9

— Data not available

* Provisional

Source: *National Health Expenditures in Canada, 1970–1982.* Ottawa: Health and Welfare Canada, n.d., p. 32.

Table 5. Average Employment Incomes of Selected Professionals, Canada, Selected Years, 1968–1980

	Physicians	Dentists	Nurses	Lawyers & Notaries	Accountants
1968	28 283	19 336	5 532	22 057	15 964
1970	33 905	21 926	6 488	25 213	18 137
1972	39 396	27 006	7 583	28 521	18 845
1974	41 721	33 174	8 888	38 811	28 215
1976	46 757	41 569	12 874	41 734	33 746
1978	52 499	46 173	15 307	41 865	36 351
1980	56 537	56 877	n.a.	39 035	n.a.

Source: Abelson, J., et al. *Perspectives on Health*. Statistics Canada, Catalogue 82–540–E, Table 95; Abella, R. S. *Equality in Employment: A Royal Commission Report*. Ottawa: Minister of Supply and Services, 1984, p. 74.

Table 6. Number of Medical Schools, Number of Medical Degrees Awarded, Canada, by Sex, Selected Years

Years	Medical Schools Canada*	M.D.s Awarded by Canadian Universities, by Sex			
		Total	Men	Women	% Women
1940–1944	10	3080	2929	151	4.9
1945–1949	11	2791	2570	221	7.9
1950–1954	12	4116	3870	246	6.0
1955–1959	12	4366	4094	272	6.2
1960–1964	13	4168	3805	363	8.7
1965–1969	16	4866	4318	548	11.3
1970–1974	16	6373	5331	1042	16.4
1975–1979	16	8464	6179	2285	27.0
1980–1984	16	8840	5747	3093	35.0

* The years medical schools were established are: U. of A., 1913; U. of C., 1966; U. of B.C., 1950; U. of M., 1883; Memorial, 1967; Dalhousie, 1868; McMaster, 1965; U. of O., 1945; Queen's, 1854; U. of T., 1843; U. of W.O., 1882; Laval, 1852; McGill, 1829; U. of Montreal, 1843; U. of Sherbrooke, 1961; U. of S., 1926.

Source: *Canadian Medical Education Statistics*, Vol. 6. Association of Canadian Medical Colleges, 1984, Table 33.

Table 7. Number and Size by Number of Beds and Total Bed Capacity of Public General Hospitals,* Canada, Selected Years, 1965–1980

	1965	1970	1975	1980
1–24 beds				
Number	238	227	209	215
Total beds	3 584	3 530	3 202	3 302
25–49 beds				
Number	194	200	197	186
Total beds	6 599	6 844	6 877	6 496
50–99 beds				
Number	142	141	137	137
Total beds	9 821	9 874	9 478	9 583
100–199 beds				
Number	128	132	127	121
Total beds	17 681	18 092	17 070	16 446
200+ beds				
Number	150	172	192	203
Total beds	64 090	73 339	84 326	89 765
TOTAL				
Number	852	872	862	862
Total beds	101 775	111 679	120 953	125 592

* Applies to hospitals generally recognized by the province as "public hospitals," not generally operated for profit; provides for *primary* diagnosis and short-term treatments for a wide range of diseases or injuries and is not restricted by sex or age.

Source: *List of Canadian Hospitals and Special Care Facilities*, Statistics Canada.

Table 8. Total Expenditure for General and Allied Special Hospitals and Cost per Patient Day for General Hospitals, Canada,* by Province, 1972–82

YEAR	Canada Total† Expenditure Millions of Dollars	Canada Cost per Patient Day	Saskatchewan Total Expenditure Millions of Dollars	Saskatchewan Cost per Patient Day	British Columbia Total Expenditure Millions of Dollars	British Columbia Cost per Patient Day	Alberta Total Expenditure Millions of Dollars	Alberta Cost per Patient Day
1972	2 858.8	73.17	109.1	51.69	237.9	59.89	217.6	60.56
73	3 235.2	81.32	117.6	57.55	278.0	66.83	251.0	67.74
74	3 953.0	96.39	143.4	70.37	376.5	82.67	288.6	79.77
75	4 970.4	117.22	171.0	87.16	493.8	99.77	391.8	110.22
76	5 778.4	139.68	207.4	104.71	560.4	110.11	440.6	126.07
77	6 355.1	‡	230.5	‡	626.9	‡	486.2	‡
78	6 929.3	152.01	245.4	113.63	693.8	121.45	543.8	140.75
79	7 696.9	166.19	272.4	129.26	783.9	134.72	637.1	160.96
80	8 920.4	181.87	320.2	139.31	964.3	147.27	779.6	183.06
81	10 364.8	208.42	369.6	167.75	1 155.4	184.45	944.1	224.05
82	12 045.4	244.69	427.3	196.59	1 315.4	216.86	1 158.0	275.79

YEAR	Manitoba Total Expenditure Millions of Dollars	Manitoba Cost per Patient Day	Ontario Total Expenditure Millions of Dollars	Ontario Cost per Patient Day	Quebec Total Expenditure Millions of Dollars	Quebec Cost per Patient Day	New Brunswick Total Expenditure Millions of Dollars	New Brunswick Cost per Patient Day
1972	127.4	68.35	1 094.4	75.97	840.3	92.12	75.1	62.07
73	139.2	76.73	1 205.6	85.40	977.9	98.14	86.1	67.24
74	161.5	93.13	1 449.1	101.60	1 212.7	112.68	100.3	79.95
75	210.2	116.59	1 797.3	124.41	1 504.2	129.83	125.7	99.29
76	239.3	132.26	2 017.2	142.67	1 841.7	179.87	148.8	111.48
77	260.7	‡	2 203.8	‡	2 014.0	‡	166.6	‡
78	271.3	149.81	2 361.5	155.15	2 225.5	182.96	177.5	129.27
79	295.6	157.97	2 551.7	167.87	2 499.6	197.25	192.1	142.34
80	340.2	173.72	2 848.1	182.81	2 921.0	217.28	215.5	155.65
81	419.3	206.26	3 340.7	204.34	3 258.6	235.86	256.6	178.62
82	490.8	251.17	3 943.3	237.68	3 652.9	269.47	311.6	211.07

(continued)

Table 8. *continued*

	Nova Scotia		Prince Edward Island		Newfoundland	
YEAR	Total Expenditure Millions of Dollars	Cost per Patient Day	Total Expenditure Millions of Dollars	Cost per Patient Day	Total Expenditure Millions of Dollars	Cost per Patient Day
1972	91.6	65.72	11.0	48.09	52.2	66.63
73	101.5	74.84	12.1	55.19	63.2	78.22
74	123.3	89.74	14.2	65.21	80.0	94.04
75	154.5	112.44	16.9	77.31	101.1	123.03
76	181.1	133.61	19.6	87.54	118.2	137.45
77	202.7	‡	21.9	‡	135.7	‡
78	231.9	142.58	24.2	102.04	147.6	164.68
79	261.7	163.73	27.0	119.03	166.5	200.44
80	295.2	177.16	31.0	133.99	194.6	201.06
81	355.8	198.36	34.4	151.22	217.3	230.23
82	427.5	250.72	40.5	167.82	261.6	302.15

* Excluding Yukon and NWT
† Average cost of operating expenditures including building depreciation and interest.
‡ In 1977 reporting period changed from calendar year ending 31 December, to fiscal year ending 31 March.

Sources: *National Health Expenditures in Canada*, 1970–1982. Ottawa: Health and Welfare Canada, n.d.
         Saskatchewan Hospital Services Plan Annual Report, 1972–1982.

Table 9. Separation Rates* and Average Days per Separation, Canada, by Sex and Province, 1980–81

	Separation Rate		Average Days per Separation	
	Female	Male	Female	Male
Newfoundland	19 546	13 082	8.2	9.3
Prince Edward Island	22 889	18 822	7.1	7.4
Nova Scotia	18 995	15 108	9.3	10.2
New Brunswick	18 890	14 319	10.3	11.5
Quebec	13 636	9 410	14.2	16.0
Ontario	17 239	12 935	11.2	11.6
Manitoba	17 587	13 198	11.2	12.5
Saskatchewan	23 677	17 764	9.8	10.5
Alberta	20 405	13 914	10.1	12.0
British Columbia	17 490	13 665	13.0	11.8
Canada	17 047	12 539	11.7	12.4

* Rates per 100 000 population

Source: *Hospital Morbidity.* Statistics Canada, Catalogue 82–206.

Table 10. Separation Rates* and Average Days per Separation, Canada, by Age Group and Sex, 1980–81

	Separation Rates		Average Days per Separation	
	Female	Male	Female	Male
Under 1 year	28 279	36 321	8.0	7.4
1 to 4 years	10 425	14 339	4.9	4.6
5 to 14 years	5 417	6 352	4.9	5.1
15 to 19 years	12 107	6 403	7.1	5.3
20 to 24 years	22 621	7 163	5.4	7.7
25 to 34 years	23 088	6 986	5.8	8.1
35 to 44 years	13 966	8 832	8.1	9.2
45 to 64 years	15 768	17 051	12.4	12.5
65 to 74 years	24 483	32 626	19.9	17.5
75 years and over	39 643	51 878	37.7	28.1
TOTAL	17 047	12 539	11.7	12.4

* Rates per 100 000 population

Source: *Hospital Morbidity*. Statistics Canada, Catalogue 82–206, Table 1.

Table 11. Separation Rates,* Percentage of all Separations, and Average Days per Separation by Sex for Eight Leading† Causes of Hospitalization, Canada, 1980–81

	Separations				Average Days per Separation	
	Female		Male		Female	Male
	Rate	% of Total	Rate	% of Total		
System Diseases:						
Digestive	1 692	9.9	1 844	14.7	8.9	7.8
Genitourinary	1 669	9.8	807	6.4	6.4	8.7
Circulatory	1 436	8.4	1 818	14.5	29.6	20.3
Respiratory	1 369	8.0	1 720	13.7	7.7	8.1
Injuries and poisonings	1 063	6.2	1 590	12.7	12.9	9.1
All neoplasms	999	5.8	818	6.5	15.2	17.6
Mental disorders	706	4.1	621	4.9	26.5	22.7
Nervous & sense organs	675	3.9	633	5.0	19.1	17.4
All other diseases	7 438	43.9	2 688	21.6	—	—
TOTAL	17 047		12 539		11.7	12.4

* Rates per 100 000 population
† Ranked by separation rates and percent of total separations for females.

Source: *Hospital Morbidity*. Statistics Canada, Catalogue 82–206, Table 1.

Table 12. Operating Expenses as Percentage* of Total Expenditure by Type of Expense for Public Hospitals, Canada, Selected Years, 1963–1983/4

	No. of Hospitals	Total Expenditure ('000s)	Gross Salary and Wages†	Medical and Surgical Supplies	Drugs	Supplies and Other Expenses	Other Non-Departmental Expenses‡
1963	978§	879 390	65.9	3.1	3.9	19.8	7.3
1968	1 042§	1 719 064	67.4	3.1	3.3	21.6	4.6
1973	1 004§	3 074 209	70.7	3.2	2.6	17.8	—
1978/9	1 043¶	6 965 205	76.1	3.1	2.3	18.5	—
1983/4	1 008¶	13 455 633	73.7	3.6	2.5	19.1	—

* Numbers may not add up to 100 due to rounding.
† Gross Salary and Wages includes salary for medical and other staff and employee benefits.
‡ Nondepartmental Expenses include interest on loans, depreciation, rentals and other miscellaneous expenses.
§ Operating hospitals
¶ Reporting hospitals
— not reported

Source: *Hospital Annual Statistics*, Statistics Canada, Catalogue 83–232, 1978/9 and 1983/4; Hospital Statistics Preliminary Annual Report, Statistics Canada, Catalogue 83–217, 1963 and 1968.

Table 13. Total Number of Full-Time and Part-Time Hospital Workers and Nurses, Canada, 1976/7–1983/4

Year	Total No. of Hospital Employees*			Nurses	
	Total No.	Full-time	Part-time	Full-time	Part-time
1976/7	364 770	292 411	72 359	124 348	40 719
1977/8	375 025	293 471	81 554	123 478	45 809
1978/9	381 368	294 340	87 028	124 604	49 720
1979/80	381 439	293 027	88 412	124 315	50 330
1980/1	396 514	299 832	96 682	124 960	54 636
1981/2	412 883	305 814	107 069	127 291	61 068
1982/3	417 190	304 405	112 785	125 539	64 305
1983/4	426 750	306 692	120 058	127 015	68 591

* Includes hospitals in the public, proprietary and federal sector.

Source: *Hospital Statistics, Annual*. Statistics Canada, Catalogue 83–232, 1976/7–1983/4.

RECOMMENDED READING

Evans, R.G. *Strained Mercy: The Economics of Canadian Health Care*. Toronto: Butterworths, 1984.

Hamowy, R. *Canadian Medicine: A Study in Restricted Entry*. Vancouver: Fraser Institute, 1984.

Naylor, C.D. *Private Practice, Public Payment: Canadian Medicine and the Politics of Health*

Insurance, 1911–66. Kingston and Montreal: McGill-Queen's University Press, 1986.

Soderstrom, L. *The Canadian Health System*. London: Croom Helm, 1978.

Task Force Reports on the Cost of Health Services in Canada. Vols. 1–3. Ottawa: Information Canada, 1971.

REFERENCES

Abella, R.S. *Equality in Employment: A Royal Commission Report*. Ottawa: Minister of Supply and Services, 1984, p. 74.

Abelson, J., P. Paddon, and C. Strohmenger. *Perspectives on Health*. Statistics Canada, Catalogue 82–540E. Ottawa: Ministry of Supply and Services, 1983.

Badgley, R.F., and S. Wolfe. *Doctors' Strike: Medical Care and Conflict in Saskatchewan*. Toronto: Macmillan, 1967.

Canada. *Health Manpower Directorate*. Ottawa: Minister of National Health and Welfare, 1985.

———. *National Health Expenditures in Canada, 1970–1982*. Ottawa: Health and Welfare Canada, n.d.

Canadian Hospital Directory. Canadian Hospital Association, 1986.

Canadian Medical Education Statistics, Vol. 6. Association of Canadian Medical Colleges, 1984.

Chappell, N.L., L.A. Strain, and A.A. Blandford. *Aging and Health Care: A Social Perspective*. Toronto: Holt, Rinehart and Winston, 1986.

D'Arcy, C., and C.M. Siddique. "Unemployment and Health: An Analysis of Canada Health Survey Data." *International Journal of Health Services* 15 (1985): 609–35.

Dickinson, H.D., and P.D. Brady. "The Labour Process and the Transformation of Health Care Delivery." In *Contradictions in Cana-

dian Society*, edited by J.A. Fry. Toronto: Butterworths, 1984.

Dyck, F.J. "Effects of Surveillance on the Number of Hysterectomies in Saskatchewan." *New England Journal of Medicine* 296 (1977): 1326–28.

Evans, R.G. *Strained Mercy: The Economics of Canadian Health Care*. Toronto: Butterworths, 1984.

Hall, E.M. "The Future of Health Services in Canada." In *Issues in Canadian Social Policy: A Reader*. Vol. 1. Ottawa: Canadian Council on Social Development, 1982.

Hamowy, R. *Canadian Medicine: A Study in Restricted Entry*. Vancouver: Fraser Institute, 1984.

Hastings, J.E.F. "The Community Health Centre in Canada." *Report of the Community Health Centre Project to the Conference of Health Ministers*, 1972.

Illich, I. *Limits to Medicine: Medical Nemesis, The Expropriation of Health*. Toronto: McClelland and Stewart, 1976.

Lalonde, M. *A New Perspective on the Health of Canadians: A Working Document*. Ottawa: Queen's Printer, 1974.

Myers, L.P., and S.A. Schroeder. "Physician Use of Services for the Hospitalized Patient." *Milbank Memorial Fund Quarterly* 59 (1981): 481–507.

Naylor, C.D. *Private Practice, Public Payment:*

Canadian Medicine and the Politics of Health Insurance, 1911–1966. Kingston and Montreal: McGill-Queen's University Press, 1986.

Pear, R. "Reagan, Apostle of Less, Assures Expanded Health Care for Elderly." *New York Times* 15 February 1987: 19.

Saskatchewan Hospital Services Plan. *Annual Report*. Regina: Government of Saskatchewan, 1975–1985/86.

Soderstrom, L. *The Canadian Health System*. London: Croom Helm, 1978.

Statistics Canada. *Consolidated Government Finance*. Ottawa: Minister of Supply and Services Canada, 1962, 1967, 1976, 1982.

———. *Federal Government Finance*. Ottawa: Minister of Industry, Trade, and Commerce, 1972, 1977, 1982.

———. *Hospital Annual Statistics*. Ottawa: Minister of Supply and Services, 1976/77–1983/4.

———. *Hospital Morbidity*. Ottawa: Minister of Supply and Services, 1981.

———. *Hospital Statistics Preliminary Annual Report*. Ottawa: Minister of Trade and Commerce, 1963, 1968.

———. *List of Canadian Hospitals and Special Care Facilities*. Ottawa: Minister of Supply and Services, 1965, 1970, 1975, 1980.

Task Force Reports on the Cost of Health Services in Canada. Vols. 1–3. Ottawa: Information Canada, 1970.

Tollefson, E.A. *Bitter Medicine: The Saskatchewan Medicare Feud*. Saskatoon: Modern Press, 1963.

Vayda, E., R.G. Evans, and W.R. Mindell. "Universal Health Insurance in Canada: History, Problems, Trends." *Journal of Community Health* 4 (1979): 217–31.

Weller, G., and P. Manga. "The Push for Reprivatization of Health Care Services in Canada, Britain, and the United States." *Journal of Health Politics and Law* 8 (1983): 495–518.

Young, T.K. "Lay-Professional Conflict in a Canadian Community Health Centre: A Case Report." *Medical Care* 13 (1975): 897–904.

PART II

DOCTORS, PATIENTS, AND HEALTH-CARE DELIVERY

INTRODUCTION

Physicians, dentists, nurses, therapists, pharmacists, nurses' aides, and other health professionals constitute an important component of the professional/technical and scientific labour force in the health sector. It is quite costly to produce this labour force. One way to economize on educational and training costs is to import immigrant and migrant workers.

The evidence presented in Chapter 5 indicates that there has been a large influx of health-care professionals to Canada. The importation of these workers, already produced and paid for elsewhere — ready-made workers, so to speak — means a considerable saving for Canada. In the case of physicians and dentists, for example, hundreds of millions of dollars are saved on educational costs alone. Immigrant physicians and other health professionals on their initial entry fill particular labour needs within the health-care sector. Evidence suggests that foreign medical graduates are represented at the lowest levels of the medical hierarchy, ending up in less desirable jobs and in less desirable locations, primarily those in which non-immigrant medical graduates prefer not to practice. Foreign medical graduates help to ease the situation in the labour market and reduce maldistribution of physicians.

The labour force in the health sector is stratified along occupational, gender, and racial lines. While immigrant professionals end up in low-status and less lucrative specialties and in less desirable locations, unskilled foreign workers in general, and women and minority workers in particular, are more likely to end up in low-paying and arduous jobs. Consequently, foreign workers, whether professional or unskilled, help to reduce the cost of provision of health services.

Physicians occupy a dominant position among the providers of health care. They are usually the first point of contact for the patient and they are also the "gatekeepers" to hospitals, most health-care institutions, and many other professional services. Because of this position, it is important to know the attitudes of the practising physicians toward various health-care policy issues. In Chapter 6, Stevenson and Williams present such data from a survey of 2087 physicians. Their analysis indicates the influence of ideology on these attitudes by documenting the marked consensus on questions of professional autonomy versus government control of the health-care system, and the opposition to medicare in principle, as opposed to a relatively favourable assessment of the administration and effectiveness of medicare in practice. Their analysis shows, further, that variation in the intensity of professional criticism of medicare is grounded, as the theoretical understanding of ideology suggests, not in objective differences of occupational experience, but in subjective perceptions of occupational stress, threats to professional status, and differences in values concerning the definition of health problems and policy priorities.

While the attitudes of practising physicians towards overall health policy issues are important, also significant is the interaction between doctors and patients. The individual physicians come face to face with individual patients in the process of medical practice. The dynamics of the patient-physician relationship are the subject of Chapter 7. Gail Frankel presents a brief review of the history of interaction between patients and medical practitioners, and discusses structural-functionalist, conflict, and interaction models postulated by various theorists. Each of these perspectives provides some understanding of the dynamics of the doctor-patient relationship. It is then pointed out that the interaction between doctors and patients must be studied in the social framework within which it occurs; it cannot be seen as separate from that context. The author demonstrates this by her review of the modification of the traditional interaction between patients and health-care practitioners, brought about by third-party insurance and other legislative initiatives and by the consumer movement, which emphasizes individual patients' rights.

5

THE MEDICAL BRAIN DRAIN TO CANADA

B. Singh Bolaria
University of Saskatchewan

INTRODUCTION

Migrant and immigrant workers now constitute a significant part of the labour force in many advanced countries. The nature and composition of this labour force vary, however, depending upon the labour needs and other structural requirements of the economies of the labour-importing countries. Immigration laws determine admission criteria, and thus the quantity and the composition, as well as the legal/political status, of foreign labour. While a large majority of these workers would be classified as unskilled or semi-skilled, in recent years there has been a marked increase in the international circulation of professional and skilled workers. Canada is one of the major recipients of this labour.

The immigration data show that there has been a large influx of entrepreneurs and managerial, professional, and skilled workers during the period 1960–83. For the period 1961–67, the proportion of immigrant workers in this category varied between 21.8 percent to 28.3 percent of the total immigrant workers (Bolaria, 1987). The figures for the period 1968–72 show that an even higher proportion, almost one third of all the immigrant workers, were in the professional/technical, managerial category. The data for the next decade show that the proportion of immigrant workers in this category remains high — between nearly one quarter to one third of all immigrant workers (Bolaria, 1987). A significant number of workers with professional skills are also entering Canada under the Non-Immigrant Employment Authorization Program (Bolaria, 1984, 1987).

Medical brain drain is an important aspect of the entry of professionally skilled workers to Canada since the 1960s. Data are presented here on immigrant physicians, dentists, graduate nurses, therapists, pharmacists and other health professionals, and technically skilled health workers. These data are discussed in the context of international movement of labour resources across national boundaries, with particular emphasis on immigration laws and regulations, which govern the flow and composition as well as the legal/political status of immigrant workers, and on a unified educational system, patterned after the developed countries, which fosters transferability of skills and produces an easily substitutable work force.

INTERNATIONAL LABOUR MIGRATION

The international circulation of workers has usually been studied in demographic terms rather than in terms of labour resources. The primary focus of demographic studies is to compile a list of characteristics, such as age and sex, of the migrants. Other studies tend to adopt the perspective of the individual migrant, trying to account for migration in individualistic terms. The individual migrant's motivation and choices are the primary focus of these studies. For instance, in analyzing why people migrate, the tendency is to compile a list of "push" and "pull" factors and present them as a theory of migration. As for the destination of migrants, attention is focussed on the consequences for migrants after arrival — adaptation, acculturation, assimilation, and integration. Many of these studies provide governments and social scientists with valuable and useful information about the nature and composition of migrants; this information can also be used for determination of immigration levels and other policy decisions.

Demographic studies are sometimes criticized for their limited focus and scope. With their primary focus on migrations as movement of people, demographic studies neglect the economic role that migrants play in the receiving country. Movements of people are essentially migrations of labour, that is, of individuals who move to sell their labour capacity in the receiving countries (Portes, 1978). Therefore, the issue is not adaptation or assimilation of new immigrants, but their role as labour and how structural constraints of the labour market (for example, the tendency to shunt immigrants into job ghettos, and the persistence of racial, ethnic, and gender differentiation) make permanent integration impossible (Burawoy, 1976). Demographic studies of migration also do not explain the structural determinants involved in patterned migration movements (Portes, 1978). Contrary to the assertions of demographers, aggregate immigrant flow of people is not a random collection of "individual choices" to migrate (Cockcroft, 1982).

Patterned migration and migratory flow arise from conditions of unequal development between countries, and will continue so long as these conditions persist. As Sassen-Koob (1978:514–515) notes, "the nature of migratory flow depends on the nature of those conditions, not on those of the migrants themselves, these being a consequence of those conditions." Thus, "migrants can be viewed as stepping or falling into a migratory flow, rather than initiating or constituting such a flow through their individual decisions and action" (Sassen-Koob, 1978:515).

Recent studies of international circulation of labour have adopted the so-called world-system perspective. The capitalist world system is characterized by gross disparities and unequal accumulations of capital (Elling, 1981; Jonas and Dixon, 1979). The political and economic forces which produce wealth in core capitalist countries simultaneously sustain and produce underdevelopment, unemployment, and poverty in peripheral countries. The transfer of labour is one aspect of the unequal and exploitative relations between labour-importing and labour-exporting countries. Underdevelopment and blocked development create high unemployment and a surplus of labour, forcing many workers to migrate. As Bonacich and Cheng (1984:2) state, "migration is a product not of discrete and unconnected factors in the sending and receiving countries, but of historical connections between the countries. It is not fortuitous; it is systematic."

Capitalism is increasingly international in character (Navarro, 1986; Elling, 1981; Barnet and Muller, 1974; Turner, 1973). Internationalization of capital is accompanied by internationalization of labour. Therefore, the core countries have access to a labour pool not only within their own boundaries, but also internationally. International economic disparities encourage the flow of labour from the periphery to the core. The professional and skilled labour force is part of the general migration of labour across national boundaries.

In addition to the above considerations, it is important to take into account the role which the state plays in regulating the flow of labour, as well as to recognize the "cultural hegemony" of the Western educational system, which facilitates the transfer of professional and skilled labour across national boundaries.

Migratory flows are regulated by the state through immigration policy and laws. These laws determine the quantity and composition, as well as the admissibility and the legal/political status, of foreign labour (Zolberg, 1979; Dixon et al., 1982). Canadian immigration regulations have been changed from time to time to accommodate Canada's varying labour needs (Bolaria, 1984; Bolaria and Li, 1985). For instance, during the 1960s and 1970s, many Western countries required a professionally skilled and highly specialized labour force for rapid industrial development and to meet needs in some professions such as medicine and education. To accommodate the recruitment of professional and scientific labour, immigration regulations were changed. For instance, the McCarren-Walter Act of 1952 in the United States, which restricted the admission of Asian immigrants, was changed in 1965 to make it easier for professionals from Asia to enter the United States. Likewise, in Canada, the Immigration Act of 1967 stressed educational and technical qualifications for immigration.

Immigration laws also determine the legal/political status of foreign labour. For instance, in addition to regular immigrant settler labour, Canada also relies upon migrant workers to meet labour needs in the agricultural sector (Bolaria, 1984; Bolaria and Li, 1985). The Employment Authorization Regulations, introduced in 1973, allow admission of non-residents for temporary employment in Canada. Thousands of workers annually are being admitted to Canada under this programme. Through the use of entry regulations, the Canadian state has been successful in converting what otherwise would be permanent settlers into migrant contract labour (Bolaria and Li, 1985; Bolaria, 1987). A large number of professional and skilled workers are admitted to Canada under this programme (Bolaria, 1984, 1987).

Another important factor which facilitates the flow of professional labour across national boundaries is the international "cultural hegemony" of the Western educational system, an important element of which is the control of and setting of standards for educational institutions. As Third World countries are major recruitment sources in the international brain drain, the pattern of education in those countries is of crucial significance in understanding the circulation of this labour force. The educational system in many Third World countries is patterned after that of the developed countries. The paradigms of medical curriculum, training, and priorities in medical education which predominate in the advanced countries are uncritically adopted in the developing countries (Navarro, 1986; Ozlak and Caputo, 1973). This standardized educational system fosters transferability of skills and produces an easily interchangeable labour force (Kaiwar, 1982; Aidoo, 1982; Ishi, 1982; Doyal and Pennell, 1979; Dale, 1982; Rashid, 1983).

In summary, it is by considering labour as a resource that the circulation of labour across national boundaries can most fruitfully be analyzed and discussed. Professional and skilled workers are part of the general migration of labour, which involves the transfer of valuable human resources from one country to another. This transfer obviously represents a very large economic cost for the countries of emigration. The entry of labour is regulated by the state through various immigration laws and regulations. A unified educational system facilitates the transfer of the professional and skilled labour force across national boundaries.

THE MEDICAL BRAIN DRAIN TO CANADA

The medical brain drain is part of the general migration of a professional and skilled labour force which flows from the peripheral to the core countries. All advanced countries now rely upon foreign workers. For example, in the United

Table 1. Immigrant Physicians, Dentists, Graduate Nurses, Therapists, Pharmacists, and Other Health Professionals, 1962–1984

Year	Physicians & Surgeons	Dentists	Graduate Nurses	Therapists	Pharmacists	Other Health Professionals
1962	530	61	1621	177	39	75
1963	687	42	1879	177	56	178
1964	668	55	1967	198	63	449
1965	792	60	2829	219	87	134
1966	995	78	3723	266	106	25
1967	1213	99	4262	317	142	22
1968	1277	99	3375	198	132	405
1969	1347	92	3248	162	95	423
1970	1113	72	2274	155	81	434
1971	987	55	989	165	71	313
1972	988	87	892	159	73	306
1973	1170	72	1418	274	138	38
1974	1081	83	1702	331	65	1241
1975	806	83	1839	334	75	966
1976	401	102	1130	275	101	725
1977	312	97	607	267	46	630
1978	264	69	405	177	43	457
1979	300	72	467	187	74	512
1980	380	69	653	249	117	574
1981	389	68	977	283	115	527
1982	463	70	999	286	90	551
1983	355	43	358	120	39	318
1984	337	49	300	115	40	250

Figures in each category are by intended occupation

Source: Immigration Statistics: 1962–65, Department of Citizenship and Immigration; 1966–77, Department of Manpower and Immigration; 1978–84, Department of Employment and Immigration.

States, Britain, Germany, and Switzerland, foreign-born health professionals and other health workers constitute a significant portion of the health-sector work force (Navarro, 1986:23).

Immigrants are an important source of physicians in Canada. Data in Table 1 show that a large number of foreign medical graduates have entered Canada since the early 1960s. Figures are particularly noteworthy for the period 1966–70, because during this time period, the number of foreign medical graduates entering Canada exceeded the number of Canadians graduating from medical schools (Association of Canadian Medical Colleges, 1984). The figures for M.D. degrees awarded in Canada during 1966–70 are 882 (1966); 918 (1967); 1016

(1968); 1018 (1969); 1074 (1970). The total volume of immigrant physicians and surgeons remained high during 1971–75. However, since 1976 there has been a sharp decline in the number of foreign medical graduates entering Canada. This decline may be due partly to the pressure of the Canadian Medical Association on the federal government to curb the number of immigrant physicians, ostensibly at an annual saving of $250 000 for each physician kept out (Swartz, 1977). In spite of this decline, foreign physicians continue to be an important source of medical man/womanpower in this country.

Another dimension of the medical brain drain is the influx of foreign graduate nurses. The immigration of graduate nurses corresponds to the general patterns of immigration of physicians and other professionals. Again, during the 1960s and early 1970s, a large number of foreign graduate nurses entered Canada. The volume of immigrants is particularly noteworthy for the years 1965–1970. After some decline in 1971–72, immigration increased during the period 1973–76. While the number of immigrant graduate nurses has declined since 1977, foreign graduate nurses continue to be an important source of nursing personnel in this country.

Data in Table 1 also show that during the period 1962–84 a significant number of foreign dentists arrived in Canada, along with a large number of therapists and pharmacists. Though figures are not reported here, it should be noted that foreign-born and foreign-trained optometrists, osteopaths, chiropractors, and veterinarians also have immigrated to this country.

As Table 1 reveals, a significant number of immigrant workers are classified under the Other Health Professionals category. The number of health professionals admitted under this general category is relatively high during the late 1970s and early 1980s.

Data reported in Table 2 for the period 1962–73 indicate that immigrants contributed significantly to man/womanpower in capacities such as medical and dental technicians and nurses' aides. Since 1974, the categories reported in Table 2 have been combined into the single category of "Nursing, Therapy, and Related Assisting Occupations." These figures are reported in Table 3.

Table 2. Immigrant Medical and Dental Technicians and Nurses' Aides, 1962–1973

Year	Medical & Dental Technicians	Nurses' Aides
1962	227	292
1963	242	213
1964	193	29
1965	309	325
1966	389	603
1967	431	1079
1968	1169	893
1969	969	924
1970	905	840
1971	749	502
1972	674	467
1973	811	1085

Immigrant Figures for each category by intended occupation

Source: Immigrant Statistics: 1962–65, Department of Citizenship and Immigration; 1966–73, Department of Manpower and Immigration.

It is evident from these data that immigrant physicians, dentists, graduate nurses, other health professionals, and skilled workers constitute an important percentage of the work force in the health sector.

It is important to point out that these data represent "intended occupation" of immigrants. Some of them may not actually enter their intended occupations; immigrating physicians, for example, may not obtain their licence to practise in the year of entry, and they may be required to undergo additional training before being granted a licence to practise. Some immigrants may be underemployed or obliged to take jobs which are not consistent with their qualifications, background, and training. The point is that, whatever the specific nature of their employment, the services of this professional/technical and highly trained labour force are often lost to the countries of emigration.

Table 3. Immigrant Nursing, Therapy, and Related Assisting Occupations, 1974–1984

Year	Nursing, Therapy, and Related Assisting Occupations
1974	1745
1975	1392
1976	967
1977	544
1978	432
1979	570
1980	556
1981	455
1982	451
1983	329
1984	288

Figures by intended occupation

Source: Immigrant Statistics: 1974–77, Department of Manpower and Immigration; 1978–84, Department of Employment and Immigration.

Whereas in the case of immigrant workers there may not be exact correspondence between intended occupation and the actual employment, the non-immigrant work authorizations are more clearly tied to the particular jobs. As noted before, Employment Authorization Regulations were introduced in 1973 to allow admission of non-immigrants for temporary employment in Canada. Since then, thousands of workers have been admitted under this programme (Bolaria, 1984; Bolaria and Li, 1985). While many workers under this programme are specifically recruited for work in low-paying and hazardous jobs, such as seasonal farm labour or domestic and textile work, almost half of them are recruited for professional/technical and highly skilled jobs (Bolaria, 1984).

To illustrate the significance of Non-Immigrant Employment Authorization Program, selected data for the period 1980–84 are reported in Table 4. It is apparent that a large number of work authorizations are granted each year in the areas of medicine and health, teaching, natural sciences, engineering and mathematics, and social sciences and related disciplines. Of particular significance for our purposes are the data pertaining to medicine and health. It is important to note that in addition to health professionals and other health workers who are admitted as immigrants (permanent settler labour), a large number are imported under the Non-Immigrant Employment Authorization Program (temporary migrant labour).

In summary, whatever the legal/political status of foreign workers, foreign physicians, dentists, and other health professionals and technically skilled workers are an important dimension of total health man/womanpower in this country.

DISCUSSION

In view of the theoretical framework outlined earlier, it is important to place our discussion in the context of general labour migration across national boundaries, since, after all, circulation of professional, scientific, and technically skilled individuals is part of overall migration patterns. There are several political and economic advantages of imported labour to the recipient countries.

For instance, with imported labour, the costs of reproduction of labour, (educational and other costs) are externalized to another country and economy. Second, unskilled foreign workers end up in low-paying, dangerous, and "dirty" jobs. In some instances they are used by employers as scabs and as a buffer against unions and organized labour. Third, because of their tenuous legal/political status, foreign workers are often submissive and docile, and are subjected to racial, gender, and social subordination which is socially unacceptable in the case of indigenous labour. These factors and conditions contribute to a reduction in the cost of labour (Burawoy,

Table 4. Non-Immigrant Employment Authorization in Medicine and Health, Teaching, Natural Sciences, Engineering and Mathematics, and Social Sciences and Related, 1980–84

Occupational Groups	Year				
	1980	1981	1982	1983	1984
Medicine and health	2 992	4 414	2 876	2 582	2 854
Teaching	14 797	22 682	14 674	15 215	15 827
Natural science, engineering and mathematics	7 722	16 191	8 119	8 560	9 106
Social sciences and related	1 622	3 025	1 598	1 741	1 600

Figures for 1980 and 1981 are based upon the sum total of work authorizations issued to "long-term" and "short-term" visitors.

Source: Immigration Statistics 1980–84, Employment and Immigration Canada.

1976; Sassen-Koob, 1978; Berger and Mohr, 1975; Portes, 1978; Carney, 1976; Dixon et al., 1982; Cockcroft, 1982). If the use of immigrant labour is profitable politically and economically, the use of migrant labour is even more so (Bolaria, 1984; Bolaria and Li, 1985).

It is in the context of the above general remarks that the circulation of professional technical and scientific work force can most effectively be discussed. It should be emphasized, however, that there are significant differences between the status and work conditions of professional and skilled workers and of unskilled labour. For instance, highly paid professional workers cannot be considered as being subjected to the same degree of exploitation and racial subordination as unskilled low-cost labour. Nevertheless, as the following discussion indicates, the existence of a foreign-born and foreign-educated sector in the professional-scientific work force is advantageous to the countries of immigration. Because of the scope of this volume, our discussion is confined to the medical brain drain. Besides, the medical profession provides one of the clearest illustrations of international circulation of professional workers as well as of cultural hegemony in education, which produces and facilitates easily transferable skills across national boundaries.

The data presented here show that there has been a large influx of health man/womanpower in Canada. Immigration of these workers involves the transfer of valuable human resources to Canada, and this transfer represents a very large economic loss for the countries of emigration. It must be noted that in the context of the international circulation of workers, the migration generally flows from peripheral to core countries, with stop-overs in semi-peripheral countries. All advanced countries benefit from this migration of physicians from the poor to the advanced countries. As Moore (1977:41) states: "There is something of a chain exploitation in that America recruits British doctors whilst Britain recruits doctors from the Indian sub-continent. Thus each nation received 'cheap' doctors and the poorest countries experienced a net loss." The number of immigrant physicians in the United States is comparable to the total output of American medical schools (Irigoyen and Zambrana, 1979). Most of these physicians come from the Third World. In 1972 about 70 percent of the foreign medical graduates came from Asia (Dublin, 1974). Data also show that while more than 10 000 physicians from Asia and Africa were practising in Britain, only about 1500 doctors from Britain were practising in developing countries (Bader, 1977).

British loss through emigration is compensated by immigration from developing Commonwealth countries (Watanabe, 1969; Fortney, 1970). Similarly, Canadian loss through emigration is compensated by immigration from England and other sources. As Fortney (1970:227) states, "the effect of emigration is far greater in the developing countries than it is on the industrialized nations where out-migration of professionals is largely compensated for by in-migration from developing countries."

It is quite costly to produce professional labour. This cost is borne by the country of emigration, which has invested considerable sums of money in training its professionals. The transfer of these valuable human resources represents a very large economic loss for countries of emigration and is considered as "capital export," similar to the export of other factors of production. The countries of immigration thus transfer the cost of reproduction of labour to countries of emigration. There are savings of hundreds of millions of dollars in educational costs alone (Weiss, 1974). Since the flow of workers is primarily from poor to rich countries, this is in fact a form of exploitation of the poor countries (Ahmed, 1983; Rashid, 1983). According to a United Nations study, it would "cost the developing nations $11.4 billion to replace the skilled persons these countries have lost to Canada between 1963 and 1972" (cited in Law Union of Ontario, 1981:43). It was noted in Parliament in 1964: "There were 6000 doctors entering Canada since 1945 . . . The cost of training these doctors would be approximately $84 million in Canada. This is a gift" (Parai, 1965). As has been noted before, this exploitation is facilitated by the political, economic, cultural, and technological hegemony of core countries over the peripheral countries, and further widens the gap between rich and poor countries.

Immigrant physicians on their initial entry fill particular needs for labour within the health sector. Evidence suggests that foreign medical graduates are represented at the lowest levels of the medical hierarchy (Irigoyen and Zambrana, 1979). Data from England indicate that many overseas doctors, (as well as, incidentally, women physicians) end up in low-grade posts and unpopular specialties (Elston, 1977). Immigrant physicians end up in less desirable medical jobs and in less desirable locations, primarily the tasks and locations where native medical graduates prefer not to practise (Mick, 1975; Ishi, 1982). In Canada, a disproportionate number of immigrant physicians end up working in isolated and underserviced areas in the North and in rural areas, or in cities in outpatient clinics where they provide service to predominantly poor patients (Roos et al., 1976).

Foreign medical graduates are asked to fulfill various additional requirements such as residency and internships, and to pass additional examinations before being licensed to practise. The Report of the Special Task Force Committee on Visible Minorities in Canada (1984) notes that the evaluation of foreign degrees and credentials is such that minority immigrants do not receive due recognition of their training and face undue delay in becoming licensed. Their education is devalued. Also, through licensing and other evaluation procedures, many foreign medical graduates end up at the low end of professional hierarchies, facing problems of underemployment, economic exploitation, and social subordination. The subordinate status of immigrant physicians is artificially prolonged through various state licensing requirements. The Committee recommended that the practice of evaluation of non-Canadian degrees and credentials and the licensing of professions be investigated (*Report of the Special Task Force Committee on Visible Minorities in Canada*, 1984:40–41).

Finally, it is important to examine the universal educational system which produces easily transferable skills and an easily interchangeable work force. As has been noted before, the educational system in most Third World countries is patterned after the Western model. As India's education system is fairly typical of that in many other developing countries, it will be used here as an example.

The post-colonial period saw the expansion of higher education systems in many Third

World countries (Ishi, 1982). Higher education became a priority in many underdeveloped countries, including India, as part of the general overall policy of development (Ilchman, 1974; Tobias, 1968). As the United States became a dominant force in the world politically and economically, its influence over educational and research institutions became apparent (Sreenivasan, 1978). For instance, both state and private funds in India were used to finance the activities of the Indian Institute of Technology and the All-India Institute of Medical Sciences (Sreenivasan, 1978; Ishi, 1982). Grants from the Rockefeller Foundation were given to the Indian Association for the Advancement of Medical Education and to medical colleges and institutes for the purchase of research equipment (Sodeman, 1971).

These investments produced a glut of university graduates, which the Indian labour market has to this day failed to absorb (Puttaswamaih, 1977). Low wages, a high rate of unemployment, and low effective demand for costly professional services force many to emigrate. Indeed it has become a state policy in many Third World countries to encourage large-scale export of workers in order to earn much-needed foreign exchange to service foreign debts. For instance, Pakistan has set up a Bureau of Emigration to facilitate employment abroad (Ahmed, 1983). The employment structure for the professions, inherited from the British colonial model, also limits young professionals' opportunities for advancement: "elite feudalism" maintains the status quo of the established professionals (Khadria, 1978). These conditions contribute further to emigration. The significance of the outflow of Indian doctors, scientists, and engineers was well documented in a 1973 study (Kabra, 1976). Many of the doctors produced in Pakistan are working overseas (Ahmed, 1983).

By importing ready-made workers, the host countries economize on the reproduction of high-cost labour. It is cheaper and quicker, for example, to import foreign medical graduates than to produce the graduates domestically

(Reddy, 1974).

It is pointed out by Doyal and Pennell (1979) and Navarro (1986) that maintaining a system of medical education and health care based upon the Western model benefits primarily the core countries. Many of the teachers in peripheral medical schools are trained in core countries, and there is a strong desire on the part of the medical school to establish an "international reputation" which will meet with the approval of Western countries. The adoption of medical curricula from core countries further facilitates the recruitment of health personnel from peripheral countries (Aidoo, 1982). The training, based upon Western curriculum and its emphasis on curative medicine, produces physicians whose services are in "effective demand" by a small portion of upper-income and urban elites. Such training and priorities in education are divorced from the health needs of the majority of the population, who live in rural areas. Western medical education and professional socialization produces physicians who have a "trained incapacity for rural practice" (Johnson, 1973). Also, a very high proportion of students who are admitted to medical schools are likely to be from urban areas and upper-income groups. Because of their social, cultural, and economic background, they have little in common with the rural masses (Doyal and Pennell, 1979). Consequently, medical education for physicians is more appropriate to medical practice in industrialized, developed core countries than in the rural peripheral nations. Many students aspire to become doctors in order to work abroad.

The concentration of resources in core countries assures a relatively comfortable standard of living for physicians and other elites, making it attractive for medical personnel to migrate. While recipient countries benefit from this situation, the outflow of expensive labour exacerbates health problems of the poor countries (Elling, 1981; Aidoo, 1982).

Our focus in this chapter has been primarily on physicians, dentists and other health professionals and skilled workers. It should be pointed out that there are other foreign workers who are employed in the lower echelons of the health sector in many core countries. These workers are predominantly from Third World countries or are women and non-white minorities. They are employed as service workers, kitchen helpers, sanitation workers, janitors, and other health auxiliaries (Navarro, 1986:23; Doyal and Pennell, 1979:262–265). A labour force composed mostly of immigrants, women, and minorities can be hired cheaply. This helps to reduce the cost of provision of health services by reducing the cost for a large segment of the health sector's workers (Brown, 1983; Navarro, 1986).

As the labour force in the health sector is stratified in terms of occupation, gender, and race, immigrant professionals end up in low-status and less lucrative specialties and in less desirable work locations. Unskilled foreign workers in general, particularly women and minority workers, are more likely to end up in low-paying, menial, and arduous jobs. Thus, foreign workers, whether professional or unskilled, help to reduce the cost of provision of health service.

SUMMARY AND CONCLUSIONS

The data presented here show that immigrant physicians, dentists, graduate nurses, therapists, pharmacists, nurses' aides, and other health professionals are important sources of professional/technical and scientific labour in the health sector. While in recent years there has been some decline in the number of health professionals admitted as immigrants (permanent settler labour), a large number of professionals in the area of medicine and health are being admitted under the Non-Immigrant Employment Authorization Program (temporary migrant labour).

The quantity and composition of immigrant workers as well as their legal/political status is regulated by the state through various immigra-

tion laws and regulations. A unified educational system, patterned after the Western model, facilitates the transfer of professional/technical and scientific workers across national boundaries.

Migration of workers involves the transfer of valuable human resources from one country to another, and this transfer represents a very great economic loss for the countries of emigration. The importation of professional/technical and scientific workers, already produced and paid for elsewhere — ready-made workers, so to speak — means a considerable saving for Canada. In the case of physicians and dentists, for example, hundreds of millions of dollars are saved on educational costs alone. Canadian loss of health professionals through emigration is compensated by immigration from other countries.

Immigrant physicians and other health professionals on their initial entry fill particular labour needs within the health sector. Evidence suggests that foreign medical graduates are at the lowest levels of the medical hierarchy and end up in less desirable jobs and in less desirable locations, primarily the tasks and locations where native medical graduates prefer not to practise.

Immigration of health personnel may help to ease the situation in the labour market and reduce the maldistribution of physicians. However, the outflow of physicians, nurses, and other health-care workers from poor countries exacerbates extant international inequalities in the distribution of medical personnel and resources.

This chapter has been confined to discussion of the brain drain in the medical field. While the medical profession provides one of the clearest illustrations of international circulation of professional labour, as well as of cultural hegemony in education which produces and facilitates easily transferable skills across national boundaries, the general analysis and arguments given here apply to other sectors of the professional, scientific, and technically skilled labour force as well.

STUDY QUESTIONS

1. Outline the demographic and world-system perspectives on the study of international circulation of workers across national boundaries.

2. Discuss the disadvantages to the peripheral countries of the outflow of professional and skilled workers.

3. The quantity and composition of the labour force are regulated by the state to accommodate labour needs and other structural requirements of the Canadian economy. Discuss the statement in the context of the Canadian Immigration policy.

4. Discuss the advantages which accrue to the recipient countries due to the influx of professional and skilled foreign workers with particular emphasis on the medical brain drain.

5. Discuss the role of immigrant workers in the health sector and in the delivery of health services.

6. How does the "cultural hegemony" of the West facilitate the flow of professional and skilled workers from peripheral to core countries?

RECOMMENDED READING

Bolaria, B. Singh. "The Brain Drain to Canada: The Externalization of the Cost of Education." In *The Political Economy of Canadian Schooling*, edited by Terry Wotherspoon, 301–22. Toronto: Methuen, 1987.

Brown, Carol A. "Women Workers in the Health Service Industry." In *Women and Health: The Politics of Sex in Medicine*, edited by Elizabeth Fee, 105–16. Farmingdale, New York: Baywood Publishing Co., 1983.

Gish, O. "Medical Brain Drain Revisited." *International Journal of Health Services* 6, no. 6 (1976): 231–37.

Horn, James J. "The Medical Brain Drain and Health Priorities in Latin America." *International Journal of Health Services* 7, no. 3 (1977): 425–42.

Navarro, Vicente. *Crisis, Health and Medicare: A Social Critique*. New York: Tavistock Publications, 1986.

Weaver, Jerry L., and Sharon D. Garrett. "Sexism and Racism in the American Health Care Industry: A Comparative Analysis." In *Women and Health: The Politics of Sex in Medicine*, edited by Elizabeth Fee, 79–104. Farmingdale, New York: Baywood Publishing Co., 1983.

REFERENCES

Ahmed, Feroz. "The New Dependence." In *Pakistan: The Roots of Dictatorship*, edited by Hassan Gardezi and Jamil Rashid, 192–227. London: Zed Press, 1983.

Aidoo, Thomas Akwasi. "Rural Health Under Colonialism and Neocolonialism: A Survey of the Ghanian Experience." *International Journal of Health Services* 12, no. 4, (1982): 637–57.

Association of Canadian Medical Colleges (A.C.M.C.) *Canadian Medical Education Statistics — 1984*. Vol. 6 (1984).

Bader, Michael B. "The International Transfer of Medical Technology — An Analysis and A Proposal For Effective Monitoring." *International Journal of Health Services* 7, no. 3 (1977): 443–58.

Barnet, R.J., and R.E. Muller. *Global Reach: The Power of the Multinational Corporations.* New York: Simon and Schuster, 1974.

Berger, John, and Jean Mohr. *A Seventh Man: Migrant Workers in Europe.* New York: Viking Press, 1975.

Bolaria, B. Singh. "Migrants, Immigrants, and the Canadian Labour Force." In *Contradictions in Canadian Society*, edited by John A. Fry, 130–39. Toronto: John Wiley and Sons, 1984.

———. "The Brain Drain to Canada: The Externalization of the Cost of Education." In *The Political Economy of Canadian Schooling*, edited by Terry Wotherspoon, 301–22. Toronto: Methuen, 1987.

Bolaria, B. Singh, and Peter S. Li. *Racial Oppression in Canada.* Toronto: Garamond Press, 1985.

Bonacich, Edna, and Lucie Cheng. "Introduction: A Theoretical Orientation to International Labour Migration." In *Labour Immigration Under Capitalism: Asian Workers in the United States before WW I*, edited by Edna Bonacich and Lucie Cheng, 1–56. Berkeley: University of California Press, 1984.

Brown, Carol A. "Women Workers in the Health Service Industry." In *Women and Health: The Politics of Sex in Medicine*, edited by Elizabeth Fee, 105–16. Farmingdale, New York: Baywood Publishing Co., 1983.

Brown, E. Richard. "Exporting Medical Education: Professionalism, Modernization and Imperialism." *Social Science and Medicine* 13a (1979): 585–95.

Burawoy, Michael. "The Functions and Reproduction of Migrant Labour: Comparative Material from Southern Africa and the United States." *American Journal of Sociology* 81 (1976): 1050–87.

Carchedi, Guglielmo. "Authority and Foreign Labour: Some Notes on a Late Capitalist Form of Capital Accumulation and State Intervention." *Studies in Political Economy* No. 2 (Autumn 1979): 37–74.

Carney, John. "Capital Accumulation and Uneven Development in Europe: Notes on Migrant Labour." *Antipode* 8 (1976): 30–38.

Castells, Manuel. "Immigrant Workers and Class Struggles in Advanced Capitalism: the Western European Experience." *Politics and Society* 5 (1975): 33–66.

Castles, Stephen, and G. Kosack. *Immigrant Workers and Class Structure in Western Europe.* Oxford: Oxford University Press, 1973.

Cockcroft, James D. "Mexican Migration, Crises, and the Internationalization of Labour Struggle." In *The New Nomads: From Immigrant Labour to Transnational Working Class*, edited by Marlene Dixon and S. Jonas, 48–61. San Francisco: Synthesis Publications, 1982.

Dale, Roger. "Learning to Be . . . What? Shaping Education in 'Developing Societies.'" In *Sociology of Developing Societies*, edited by Hamza Alavi and T. Shanin, 408–21. London: Macmillan, 1982.

Dixon, Marlene, S. Jonas, and E. McCoughan. "Reindustrialization and the Transnational Labour Force in the United States Today." In *The New Nomads: From Immigrant Labor to Transnational Working Class*, edited by Marlene Dixon and S. Jonas, 101–15. San Francisco: Synthesis Publications, 1982.

Donaldson, Peter J. "Foreign Intervention in Medical Education: A Case Study of the Rockefeller Foundation's Involvement in a Thai Medical School." In *Imperialism, Health and Medicine*, edited by Vicente Navarro, 107–26. Farmingdale, New York: Baywood Publishing Co., 1981.

Doyal, L., and I. Pennell. *The Political Economy of Health.* London: Pluto Press, 1979.

Dublin, J.D. "Foreign Physicians: Their Impact on U.S. Health Care." *Science* 2 (1974): 407–14.

Elling, Ray H. "The Capitalist World System and International Health." *International Journal of Health Services* 2, no. 1 (1981): 21–51.

Elston, Mary Ann. "Women in The Medical Profession: Whose Problem?" In *Health and The Division of Labour*, edited by Margaret Stacey et al., 115–38. London: Croom Helm, 1977.

Fortney, Judith A. "International Migration of Professionals." *Population Studies* 24 (1970): 217–32.

Gorz, Andre. "Immigrant Labour." *New Left Review* 61 (1970): 28–31.

Ilchman, Warren F. " 'People in Plenty': Educated Unemployment in India." In *The Higher Learning in India*, edited by Amrik Singh and Philip G. Altbach, 119–36. Delhi: Vikas Publishing House, 1974.

Irigoyen, Matilde, and Ruth E. Zambrana. "Foreign Medical Graduates (FMGs): Determining Their Role in the U.S. Health Care System." *Social Science and Medicine* 13a (1979): 775–83.

Ishi, T.K. "The Political Economy of International Migration: Indian Physicians to The United States." *South Asian Bulletin* 2, no. 1 (1982): 39–58.

Johnson, T. "Imperialism and the Professions." In *Professionalization and Social Change*, edited by P. Halmos. Sociological Review Monograph No. 20, University of Keele, 1973.

Jonas, S., and M. Dixon. "Proletarianization and Class Alliances in the Americas." *Synthesis* 3, no. 1 (1979): 1–13.

Kabra, Kamal Nayan. *Political Economy of Brain Drain: Reverse Transfer of Technology.* New Delhi: Arnold Heinemann, 1976.

Kaiwar, Vasant. "Some Reflections on Capitalism, Race and Class." *South Asian Bulletin* 2, no. 1 (1982): 1–5.

Khadria, Binod Kumar. "Brain Drain — The Missing Perspectives: A Comment." *Journal of Higher Education* 4, no. 1 (1978): 101–5.

Law Union Of Ontario. *The Immigrant's Handbook.* Montreal: Black Rose Books, 1981.

Mick, Stephen S. "The Foreign Medical Graduates." *Scientific American* 232, no. 2 (1975): 14–21.

Moore, Robert. "Migration and Class Structure of Western Europe." In *Industrial Society: Class, Cleavage and Control*, edited by Richard Scase, 136–49. London: George Allen and Unwin, 1977.

Navarro, Vicente. *Crisis, Health and Medicine: A Social Critique.* New York: Tavistock Publications, 1986.

Ozlak, O., and D. Caputo. "The Migration of Medical Personnel From Latin America to the United States: Toward An Alternative Interpretation." In *Pan-American Conference on Health Manpower Planning, Background Documents.* Vol. 3, Chap. 4. Pan-American Health Organization, Washington D.C., 1973.

Parai, L. *Immigration and Emigration of Professional and Skilled Manpower During the Post-War Period.* Ottawa: Queen's Printer, 1965.

Portes, Alejandro. "Migration and Underdevelopment." *Politics and Society* 8, no. 1 (1978): 1–48.

Puttaswamaih, K. *Unemployment in India: Policy for Manpower.* New Delhi: Oxford and IBH Publishing Co., 1977.

Rashid, Jamil. "The Political Economy of Manpower Export." In *Pakistan: The Roots of Dictatorship*, edited by Hassan Gardezi and Jamil Rashid, 213–27. London: Zed Press, 1983.

Reddy, A.K.N. "The Brain Drain." In *The Higher Learning in India*, edited by Amrik Singh and Philip S. Altbach, 373–94. Delhi: Vikas Publishing House, 1974.

Report of the Special Task Force Committee on Visible Minorities. Equality Now! Canada: House of Commons, 1984.

Roos, N., et al. "The Impact of Physician Surplus on the Distribution of Physicians Across Canada." *Canadian Public Policy* 11, no. 2 (1976).

Sassen-Koob, Saskia. "The International Circulation of Resources and Development: The

Case of Migrant Labour." *Development and Change* 9 (1978): 509–45.

Sodeman, William A. "United States Programs to Strengthen Medical Education in Developing Countries." In *Migration of Medical Manpower*, edited by John Z. Bower and Lord Rosenheim, 163–72. New York: Josiah Macy Jr. Foundation, 1971.

Sreenivasan, Sheillu. "Foreign-Aided ITT Education." *Journal of Higher Education* (India) 4, no. 2 (1978): 187–200.

Swartz, Donald. "The Politics of Reform: Conflict and Accommodation in Canadian Health Policy." In *The Canadian State*, edited by Leo Panitch, 311–43. Toronto: University of Toronto Press, 1977.

Tobias, George. *India's Manpower Strategy —*
Revisited, 1947–1967. Bombay: N.M. Tripathi, 1968.

Turner, L. *Multinational Companies and the Third World*. New York: Hill and Wang, 1973.

Watanabe, S. "The Brain Drain From Developing to Developed Countries." *International Labour Review* 99, no. 4 (1969): 401–33.

Weiss, R.J. "The Effect of Importing Physicians — Return to a Pre-Flexnerian Standard." *New England Journal of Medicine* 290 (1974): 1453–58.

Zolberg, Aristide R. "International Migration Policies in a Changing World System." In *Human Migration: Patterns and Policies*, edited by William H. McNeill and Ruth Adams, 241–86. Bloomington: Indiana University Press, 1979.

6

PHYSICIANS AND MEDICARE: Professional Ideology and Canadian Health-Care Policy

H. Michael Stevenson and A. Paul Williams
York University

INTRODUCTION

Conflict between governments and the medical profession over the introduction and administration of medicare in Canada is well documented. When the Depression first brought government health-insurance programmes onto the political agenda, the Canadian Medical Association insisted (1934) that such programmes should be administered so as to guarantee the dominance and autonomy of the profession within the health-care delivery system (Taylor, 1978:24). Draft federal legislation for a national health-insurance programme presented in 1943 more or less accommodated this professional insistence, and the Canadian Medical Association Council was willing on this basis to endorse government health insurance. However, the proposed legislation foundered as a result of federal-provincial

disagreements over the financial arrangements required, and in 1949 the CMA backtracked from its earlier position. It now declared that government involvement in health insurance should be restricted to paying into voluntary private insurance plans part or all of the premiums of those unable to pay (Taylor, 1978:26–27, 198). Professional criticism was relatively subdued in response to the 1957 Hospital Insurance Act, but escalated rapidly when the success of hospital insurance and the proliferating profession-controlled medical care prepayment plans stimulated government initiatives to provide more comprehensive and universal medical care insurance (Shillington, 1972).

Saskatchewan's pioneering efforts in this field were met in 1962 by the withdrawal of all but emergency services by physicians in that province (Badgley and Wolfe, 1967). The introduction of a federal-provincial medical insurance programme, achieved under the 1966 Medical Care Insurance Act, was opposed by professional association spokespersons appearing before the Royal Commission and parliamentary committees involved (Taylor, 1978: Ch. 6). Professional opposition was, however, checked by the essential continuity, under the new legislation, of the dominance and autonomy of the profession, and by the windfall professional income gains realized in the early years under the new system of guaranteed payments (Coburn, Torrance, and Kaufert, 1983).

While this general pattern of conflict between governments and the medical profession over health policy is familiar to most observers, the content and intensity of professional positions on issues of health policy are not well documented. The public statements of professional association spokespersons may not be a good guide to the attitudes of all practising physicians, and there are few publicly available opinion surveys of physicians. Such information is important, however, if any accurate diagnosis of the scope and degree of conflict over health-care policy is to be made, and if any effective measures for the resolution of such conflict are to be initiated. This, at any rate, was the impetus behind the survey of 2100 physicians which we conducted with Professor Malcolm Taylor in 1983, the general results of which are described in the report entitled Medical Perspectives on Canadian Medicare (Taylor, Stevenson, and Williams, 1984).

The purpose of this chapter is to analyze more closely the structure of professional attitudes to questions of health policy posed in that survey. More specifically, we seek to establish the extent to which professional attitudes are grounded in ideology, and by extension, the degree to which the present political conflict over medicare can be resolved by rational accommodation on concrete issues rather than by purely political strategies, which mobilize public support for or against a resolution by legislative fiat.

PROFESSIONAL IDEOLOGY AND HEALTH-POLICY ATTITUDES: THEORETICAL CONSIDERATIONS

In the general sense, ideology involves the distorted or biased and rationalized rather than objectively reasoned evaluation of issues. More specifically, the source of ideological distortion — the nature of the rationalization involved — is that it serves to justify and defend relations of domination (Larrain, 1979). In this sense, ideology has a specifically political character, although ideological expression tends to mask its true character behind non-political discourse. From this widely accepted understanding of the nature of ideology, it follows that ideological perspectives on issues assume an increased significance when relations of dominance are threatened, and that the intensity with which ideological perspectives are held varies individually with the extent to which individuals perceive that their dominance in some system of social relations is threatened.

As regards the attitudes of physicians towards medicare, these preliminary remarks suggest attention to sources of actual or potential threat to professional dominance in the health-care system, and to factors accentuating the extent to which individual physicians perceive such threats.

The effect of the public health-insurance programmes of the late 1950s and 1960s on professional dominance has not generally been noted. The transfer of the financial administration of the hospital and medical services delivery system from private to public agencies has not, that is, changed the fundamental autonomy of the profession in relation to the content and division of labour in medical work, or to the control over patients. Fee-for-service remains the basic method of payment; medical doctors, as "gatekeepers" to the system, are the prime decision-makers in the allocation of health resources (tests, x-rays, drugs, hospital admissions, and treatment), and the colleges of physicians and surgeons (although some have been opened up to public representatives) maintain the independence of a self-governing profession.

The main effect of the transfer of financing has been an increase in the resources allocated to the treatment system, accompanied by a substantial proportional decrease in resources allocated to overhead administrative costs.

The loss of financial control, nevertheless, represents a threat to professional dominance, especially as the general fiscal crisis since 1974 has forced governments to consider means of controlling burgeoning costs of medical services by controlling the supply side of the health-care system. This threat to professional dominance is reflected most obviously in the gap between the pricing of medical services by the profession and by government. Although the profession retains more or less complete control over the structure of the fee schedule — i.e. the types of services and their relative prices — governmental control over inflation adjustments to those prices limits professional control over incomes.

Other limitations on professional autonomy, prompted by the need to contain health-care costs, include government regulation of hospital residences and hospital beds, the regional allocation of medical technology, and labour regulation to favour underserviced areas. Potential threats include government acknowledgement of the eligibility of para-professionals (non-physicians) to handle services currently monopolized by physicians, and the imposition of income and workload ceilings beyond which physicians would receive zero or marginally decreasing payments.

In addition to these actual and potential threats attributable to government involvement in health insurance, there are broader cultural threats to the profession. The dominance of the medical profession is grounded historically in the biomechanical paradigm of health. This paradigm presumes that symptoms of ill health have their origin in lesion, which in turn is caused by a pathogenic agent (White, 1981). The historical hegemony of this model is illustrated by the massive commitment of social resources

to the treatment of disease, the ever-increasing reliance upon technological medicine, and the elevated social status enjoyed by medical professionals who master the diagnostic and curative technology. Alternative models of health organization stress behavioural and socio-environmental causes of illness, and preventive rather than curative approaches to health problems. Such models de-emphasize the value of technological "cures" and imply a reduced status for the physician. Although the supremacy of the biomedical disease model has not yet been seriously undermined by such alternative perspectives, there has been growing skepticism in recent years about the benefits attributable to the increasing medicalization of contemporary life (Illich, 1976; McKeown, 1976).

Ideological resistance to medicare is also likely to be reinforced by socio-psychological pressures on physicians that encourage their scapegoating of medicare as the source of frustrations specific to medical practice. Blishen (1969) has examined the pressures and role strains experienced by physicians as a result of the technically and emotionally demanding nature of medical practice and the inevitable divergence between actual professional experience and role expectations.

This role strain is complicated by perceptions among physicians of the declining social status of the profession and declining public esteem for medical practitioners. Although all professions have experienced a decline in public esteem as the population has become more educated, and although physicians collectively remain the highest-earning population subgroup, doctors may tend to see in the recent conflict over physicians' incomes and in the general threats to medical dominance a cause of declining public respect for their profession.

Finally, there are strains related to the normal work environment and routine (or lack thereof) in medical practice. Working conditions in the office of the practitioner entail stress for those doctors not competent as business managers. Hours of work, the inability to schedule leisure time, and the associated pressures of personal and family responsibility also contribute significant amounts of stress. Work in the complex environment of the modern hospital involves strain due to the need to conform to institutional routine and control. More generally, physicians must cope with the prospect of increasing government and peer review of their practices, with increasing economic and professional competition from paramedical personnel and nurse practitioners, and with the general level of tension that characterizes contemporary medical politics.

The occupation stress and role strain experienced by physicians as a result of such factors encourages a high degree of reliance on an ideology based upon the principle of professional autonomy. This principle emphasizes the freedom of the practitioner and professional organizations from external control, particularly control by the state.

AN EMPIRICAL MODEL OF PROFESSIONAL IDEOLOGY

The preceding discussion outlines reasons to expect ideological resistance to medicare on the part of physicians. It should be clear, however, that the factors stimulating ideological defensiveness within the profession in general are not experienced universally or with equal intensity among physicians. In order, therefore, to examine empirically the nature and extent of their ideological response to medicare, we have constructed a model in which professional attitudes towards health-policy issues are conceptualized and measured in a number of dimensions, and in which variation in these attitudes is conceived as being determined independently by "subjective" socio-psychological factors associated with ideological thinking, and by "objective" structural factors in occupational life, associated with different "interests" in health-policy questions.

The "objective" professional differences we examine are: the province in which physicians practise, their specialization, the proportion of their income derived from fee-for-service, their country of birth, age, experience in

medicare, and involvement in national and provincial medical associations.

The "subjective" factors in the analysis measure physicians' concerns about their personal and professional status by questions which ask whether physicians are "losing ground" economically and suffering from declining public esteem. They measure occupational stress and role strain by questions which ask about the extent of stress experienced in medical practice and about difficulties encountered with patients and health-insurance administrations. And finally, they measure commitments to different models of health by questions which ask about the relative funding priorities assigned to acute care hospitals, the acquisition of advanced medical technology, community health centres, public health, and so on.

Finally, the policy attitudes we examine deal with: (1) medicare in principle — i.e., the degree to which the programme meets the needs of equitable access, planning and administrative efficiency, and so on; (2) medicare in practice — i.e., the effects of the programme on the quality of health-care services and physician satisfaction in medical practice; (3) the financing of health services through the imposition of premiums, user fees, and health insurance deductibles; (4) extra-billing; (5) regulation of the geographic allocation of medical man/woman-power; (6) workload guidelines; and (7) professional association organization and tactics vis-à-vis income negotiations with governments.

DATA ANALYSIS

The data reveal a generalized commitment within the medical profession to a mode of health care which emphasizes institutional, curative services under the direction of physicians over community-based organizations employing allied health professionals. There is also a tendency to discount the importance of factors under the control of physicians or directly related to their treatments as causes of the increasing utilization of medical services. An apparent exception to this pattern of support for the dominant biomedical model of health is doctors' approval of increased efforts to reduce threats to public health posed by environmental pollution and poor sanitation. However, such efforts do not imply any restructuring of the health-care system and do not, therefore, constitute a direct threat to the status of the physician or to the autonomy of the medical profession. In this connection the data reveal widespread feelings of status insecurity and occupational stress among physicians. These conditions seem, however, to be tied more to dealing with patients, to perceptions of the attitudes of the general public, and to comparisons of income with other professional groups, than to strained relations with health bureaucracies. Apart from the minority of physicians for whom such problems are serious, the sense of threatened professional status and role expectations for most physicians is not attributable to routine interventions by government in their professional lives.

To investigate the extent to which these beliefs influence physicians' attitudes on issues of health-care policy, we use least squares regression, analysis of variance, and statistics associated with these methods. Province, specialization, method of payment for services, year of entry into practice, country of birth, and medical association membership are represented by dummy variables in a multiple classification analysis, the results of which are summarized in Table 1. The top half of the table contains raw (unadjusted) mean scores of the dependent variables for each category of the explanatory variables measuring "objective" occupational characteristics. These mean scores provide a simple description of the topography of professional opinion on key health-care policy issues.

The data reveal moderate levels of approval of medicare in practice but a general tendency to disapprove of medicare in principle. The mean score of 3.2 on the first multiple-item variable indicates a relatively high level of satisfaction among physicians with professional practice under conditions of medicare and favourable evaluations of provincial health insurance programmes. The mean score of 2.9 on the second multiple-item variable shows, however, the tendency for physicians to argue against medicare in principle on the grounds that government intervention results in the reduction of individual responsibility for health, that it threatens the physician's control of medical decisions, and that a return to private, commercial health insurance is preferable.

There is widespread approval among physicians of the principle that consumers of medical care should assume responsibility for the costs of those services (through hospital user fees, premiums, and insurance deductibles). There is also a consensus justifying the practice of extra-billing as a means of maintaining professional incomes and autonomy. In each instance, mean scale scores exceed 3.5, a substantial measure of approval for these policies.

The next pair of dependent variables concerns proposals for the regulation of the conditions of medical practice. The first involves government economic incentives or penalties meant to stream physicians into underserviced geographic areas; the second, increased peer review of physicians' workloads and hospital practices. There is marginally greater support for the latter policy — average scale scores are 2.4 and 3.0 respectively — probably reflecting a preference for regulation by one's associates, but in both cases support for such regulation is clearly limited.

The final policy variable measures approval for proposals to reconstitute medical associations as labour unions under provincial law and for the withdrawal of professional services in the event of deadlock with governments on income issues. Support for union and strike activity is not strong among physicians in the survey: the average score on the five-point scale is 2.6.

Taken together, these results suggest that professional criticism of medicare is grounded more in a principled opposition to government involvement in health insurance than in negative evaluations of the conditions of professional practice or the standards of medical services under medicare; that there is strong support for an increase in the proportion of private (as

Table 1. Regression of Policy Attitudes on Background Characteristics and "Subjective" Perceptions*

Independent Variables in Regression	Dependent Variable†						
	Satisfaction Under Medicare	Approval of Medicare	Approve User Pay	Approve Extra-Billing	Approve Manpower Regulation	Approve Peer Review	Approve Unions, Strikes
Province (alone)							
Nova Scotia	3.69‡	3.08‡	3.67	3.68	2.48‡	3.39‡	2.25‡
Quebec	3.17	3.17‡	3.47‡	3.27‡	2.62‡	3.18‡	3.00‡
Ontario	3.17¶	2.79¶	3.64¶	3.61¶	2.24¶	2.92¶	3.60¶
Alberta	3.29	2.74	3.99‡	3.72	2.33	2.94	2.35
British Columbia	3.21	2.86	3.87‡	3.49§	2.53‡	3.17‡	2.44§
Specialization (alone)							
General practitioner	3.23	2.90§	3.59‡	3.51	2.43	2.97‡	2.73‡
Specialist	3.25¶	2.98¶	3.73¶	3.51¶	2.44¶	3.20¶	2.55¶
Method of payment (alone)							
<20% fee-for-service	3.35§	3.23‡	3.40‡	3.09‡	2.77‡	3.34‡	2.52‡
20–80% fee-for-service	3.41‡	3.11‡	3.65	3.34‡	2.46§	3.30‡	2.37‡
>80% fee-for-service	3.17¶	2.84¶	3.71¶	3.64¶	2.34¶	2.98¶	2.73¶
Year began practice (alone)							
Pre-1970	3.31¶	2.97¶	3.64¶	3.45¶	2.51¶	3.08¶	2.53¶
1970 or later	3.14‡	2.89	3.68	3.60‡	2.30‡	3.09	2.80‡
Country of birth (alone)							
Canada	3.22¶	2.93¶	3.67¶	3.51¶	2.39¶	3.08¶	2.65¶
Britain	3.30	2.86§	3.70	3.58	2.47	3.09	2.46‡
Other country	3.26	3.02	3.59	3.49	2.52‡	3.08	2.71
Association membership (alone)							
Association non-member	3.35§	3.21‡	3.39‡	3.09‡	2.59‡	3.21§	2.53
Association member	3.21¶	2.95¶	3.65¶	3.53¶	2.42¶	3.07¶	2.64¶
Association executive	3.25	2.73‡	3.82‡	3.71‡	2.36	3.05	2.69
Fund alternative health structures	.073‡	.192‡	−.151‡	−.143‡	−.039	.107‡	−.002
Fund established health structures	−.080§	−.063§	.049	.094‡	−.120‡	−.054	.101‡
Approve public health measures	.065§	.075‡	−.064§	−.080‡	.123‡	.235‡	−.056
MD-initiated use important	.053§	−.006	.022	−.142‡	.183‡	.134‡	−.103‡
MDs losing economic ground	−.159‡	−.194‡	.115‡	.273‡	−.120‡	−.080‡	.300‡
Public esteem declining	−.183‡	−.174‡	.050	−.009	.059	.044	−.089§
High levels of professional stress	−.117‡	.022	.019	.047	−.011	−.051	.091‡
Difficulties with patients	−.069‡	−.107‡	.058‡	.094‡	−.048§	−.050§	.119‡
Complaints against bureaucracy	−.280‡	−.214‡	.096‡	.167‡	−.103‡	−.044	.111‡

* Dependent variable means are presented for each categorical variable; standardized regression coefficients for "subjective" perceptions.

† Dependent variables are continuous multiple-item scales ranging from 1 to 5, where high scores indicate strong satisfaction or approval.

‡ Significant at .01.

§ Significant at .05.

¶ Omitted category in regression.

opposed to public) financing of the health-care system; that physicians resist any government control on the conditions of medical practice and that they also tend to resist professional self-regulation; that there is widespread insistence upon the freedom to determine income by extra-billing, but that physicians, for professional reasons or otherwise, do not, in the main, support overt labour union-style actions to produce more favourable income settlements.

Provincial variation in these results shows that doctors in Nova Scotia are, on average, more satisfied in professional practice under medicare than physicians in all other provinces, and that they are also more approving of medicare in principle than physicians in any province other than Quebec. Doctors in Nova Scotia are also more likely than their colleagues to approve of government regulations to stream physicians into underserviced areas, and of peer review of their practices. They are also less supportive of the proposal to reconstitute medical associations as labour unions and to sanction the withdrawal of professional services. Physicians in Quebec are more supportive than their colleagues in other provinces of medicare in principle, but they are least satisfied with their provincial plan in practice. Quebec doctors also generally approve of the proposals for labour allocation and peer review, but unlike physicians in Nova Scotia, they strongly support unionization and strike activities. Finally, physicians in Alberta more strongly support the policies of user pay and extra-billing than physicians in other provinces and they are relatively less likely to approve of union and strike activities.

However intelligible these provincial differences may be, they are not for the most part substantial. The much-remarked regionalism of Canada, the obvious differences in the political character and economic power of different provincial governments, and the differences in health-care administration appear to have very little impact on the policy attitudes of physicians across the country. Similarly, looking at the other hypothesized influence of background experience in different political systems, there

are no substantial differences in the policy attitudes of physicians born in different countries. British-born doctors are, however, noticeably less likely to approve of medicare in principle and less likely to support militant professional activity in income negotiations with government.

There are also no sizeable differences in the policy attitudes of specialists as compared to general practitioners, although a consistent pattern is evident in our results. General practitioners are less approving of provincial health-insurance programmes and of proposals for government and peer regulation, and they are more supportive of union and strike activities to settle income disputes. The responses of younger medical doctors (i.e., those who entered practice after 1970) are similar to those of general practitioners, which may be indicative of the relatively disadvantaged status of both groups within the medical profession. General practitioners and younger doctors earn, on average, less than specialists and older doctors with more established practices; they are less likely to hold high status within the medical profession, and more likely to encounter difficult patients since they constitute, especially in primary practice, the main point of entry into the health-care delivery system.

Method of payment, measured by proportion of fee-for-service remuneration, and involvement in medical associations, measured by medical association membership or executive membership, have comparatively strong effects on policy attitudes. Physicians who derive more than 80 percent of their professional incomes from fee-for-service are much less satisfied in practice under conditions of medicare, less approving of the aims and impact of the programme, less accepting of government and peer regulation of the conditions of medical practice, and more strongly in favour of union and strike activities. Similar views are expressed by physicians who have served as executive officers of national or provincial medical associations or on committees of these associations within the last decade. This suggests, first, the greater sensitivity of fee-dependent physicians to policies which are perceived to threaten their economic discretion and hence their ability to maximize incomes; and, second, a greater concern on the part of the medical association leaders with the collective interests and autonomy of the profession.

The bottom half of Table 1 contains standardized regression coefficients measuring the impact of physicians' perceptions of health and health status on their policy attitudes. All of the "subjective" variables were entered into the multiple regressions as a group to produce these coefficients. They show that approval of the increased funding of alternative health organizations, approval of increased public health measures, and the belief that doctor-initiated treatments are an important cause of the increasing utilization of medical services are each indicative of greater satisfaction in practice under medicare, lower levels of approval for user pay and extra-billing, greater support for government and peer regulation of medical practice, and greater opposition to job action. Conversely, support for the increased funding of established health institutions such as acute hospitals predisposes physicians to resist government and peer regulation and to support policies like extra-billing which protect the corporate autonomy of the medical profession.

The group of five variables measuring beliefs about the economic and social status of the medical profession and problems with patients and the health-care bureaucracy exert an even more marked impact on policy choice. For example, physicians who believe that they are "losing ground" economically, even though the average net income of physicians in Canada remains substantially higher than that of any other professional group, are much less satisfied in practice under medicare and much more strongly favour policies perceived to strengthen the autonomy of the medical profession. In particular, large positive regression coefficients confirm that extra-billing and union and strike activities are viewed by doctors as primary means of protecting professional incomes

against a perceived decline in comparison with other professional groups. In the same way, physicians who feel that public esteem for the profession has diminished are also less likely to express approval of medicare in principle or in practice. Finally, physicians who report greater numbers of problems with patients and with health-care bureaucracies are also less likely to give positive evaluations of medicare, more likely to resist government and peer regulation of medical practice, and more likely to approve of user pay, extra-billing, and the withdrawal of professional services.

Table 2 presents the analysis of variance for the regressions reported above. The "unadjusted" effects measure the statistical impacts of the "objective" demographic or "subjective" perceptual factors on policy attitudes when entered into the regressions alone; the "adjusted" effects measure the marginal increase in the explanatory power of the regressions upon entering a second factor. By decomposing the variance in this way we can establish the degree to which the circumstances of professional practice are associated with physicians' subjective perceptions of professional status, occupational stress, and health-care priorities, and the extent of their joint influence on policy attitudes.

These results demonstrate the relative independence of the influence of the two factors. The measured impact of the demographic variables, although relatively small and reduced slightly by controlling the perceptual variables, remains significant, indicating that in large part the effects are direct and are not substantially mediated by physicians' beliefs about health organization, professional status, or frustrations in practice. The results also emphasize the strong impact of the subjective factors on policy attitudes. In each case, the variance estimate for the subjective factors exceeds the corresponding estimate for the demographic variables. With respect to satisfaction with medicare in practice, approval of medicare in principle, and approval of extra-billing, the impact of the subjective factors is the order of three to eight times as large.

Table 2. Analysis of Variance for Regression of Policy Attitudes*

Dependent Variable	Unadjusted Effect†		Adjusted Effect‡		Total Variance Explained
	Background Characteristics	"Subjective" Perceptions	Background Characteristics	"Subjective" Perceptions	
Satisfaction in practice under medicare	.049	.197	.018	.166	.215
Approval of medical principles	.089	.228	.055	.194	.283
Approve user-pay	.077	.083	.066	.072	.149
Approve extra-billing	.118	.235	.077	.194	.312
Approve manpower regulation	.071	.089	.058	.076	.147
Approve peer review	.066	.094	.051	.079	.145
Approve unions, strikes	.101	.125	.060	.084	.185

* Table entries are proportions of explained variance. All coefficients are statistically significant at .01.

† Unadjusted effects are calculated without controlling the influence of any other variables.

‡ Adjusted effects measure the marginal increase in the explained variance upon entry of an additional group of dependent variables into the regression after the other group has already been entered.

CONCLUSIONS

These findings increase our understanding of the characteristics and function of medical belief systems. Despite the essential continuity of the organization of the health-care delivery system before and after the introduction of medicare, the ideological resistance within the profession toward government intervention in this area remains an important constraint upon change and reform of health programmes. The extent of this resistance is demonstrated by physicians' opposition to medicare in principle, their qualified approval of Canadian medicare programmes in practice, their strong support for user pay and extra-billing, and their resistance to regulation of the conditions of medical practice.

It is not in itself original to argue that such attitudes are primarily a defensive ideological reaction to the currently limited, but potentially greater, encroachment by the state upon the autonomy of the medical profession. What is, we hope, more interesting, is the systematic documentation of the extent of the consensus against state intervention in the health-care system: how little this consensus is affected by the growing heterogeneity of occupational specialization and recruitment to the profession; how medical politicians lead, but not by much, their constituents in adherence to these positions; and how little the variation in provincial health programmes diversifies the attitudes of physicians toward health-care policy issues.

We have also shown that the intensity of commitment to the medical consensus on health policy is strongly influenced by subjective perceptions of the professional status, occupational stress, and different models of health organization. The analysis demonstrates that the impact of these subjective perceptions on professional policy attitudes is largely independent of, and stronger than, objective differences in physicians' occupational experience. This isolation and apparent pre-eminence of the subjective-ideological realm minimizes the potential effect on medical politics of the growing heterogeneity of the profession. It also reduces the range of initiatives that governments can hope to adopt to reform the health-care system without significant opposition from the medical profession.

The constraint set by professional ideology on possible government reforms is suggested, for example, by doctors' reports of difficulties with health-care bureaucracies. Our data indicate that only a minority of physicians have serious complaints against the administration of their provincial health-care programmes, but that the frequency of such complaints is very strongly associated with the intensity of opposition to medicare. In other words, these few complaints assume, through the lens of medical ideology, a significance which is much greater than the importance attached by most physicians to bureaucratic problems per se. Such complaints may reasonably stimulate policy-makers to streamline administrative procedures, but it is not clear from our analysis that such reforms would reduce professional opposition to government control of the health-insurance system. In the same way, there is little guarantee that increases by governments in insured fee schedules would do anything to dispel the widely held perception of physicians that they are "losing ground" economically if, as our analysis suggests, this perception reflects concern not just about absolute income levels, but about government restrictions on the right of physicians to determine them.

We should not overstate the restrictive effect of professional ideology on public policy decisions. There is some evidence in our survey that physicians do tend to accommodate themselves, at least in some degree, to government policies which they initially oppose. For instance, in British Columbia and Quebec,

where extra-billing was prohibited at the time of the survey, there is less professional support for this practice than in Nova Scotia, Ontario, and Alberta, where extra-billing was still allowed. Professional opposition to the Canada Health Act may therefore be expected to diminish as physicians in affected provinces adapt themselves to the new legislation or otherwise compensate for its negative economic effects through manipulation of professional workloads. Similarly, physicians who are primarily salaried and who are, therefore, already subject to a form of income control, are less critical of medicare and are less concerned with the defence of professional autonomy than their fee-dependent colleagues. The growing number of physicians in salaried and institutional practice, and the growing heterogeneity of the profession in this and other respects, may therefore serve to moderate professional opposition to medicare.

However, it should be clear that these findings and speculations only qualify, and do not substantially alter, the strength of the fundamental professional consensus against government involvement in the health-care field. Given this strong opposition in principle, it seems unlikely that governments can produce any substantial proposals for reform of medicare which will not be resisted by the medical profession. The insistence of the profession upon its autonomy and its continued dominance of health care leave little room for policy-makers to manoeuvre if public opinion and the fiscal crisis of the state continue to pressure for ways to rationalize the Canadian health-care system. As in the case of the Canada Health Act, such pressures are likely to lead governments to legislative action in spite of strong professional opposition, relying upon the support of public opinion and the long-term adaptive capacity of physicians.

Acknowledgements: This is the much-revised version of a paper which first appeared in *Canadian Public Policy* XI, 3:504–21, 1985. The survey of physicians reported in this paper was conducted at the Institute for Social Research, York University, under a grant from the National Health Research Development Program, Health and Welfare Canada. The principal investigators were Malcolm G. Taylor and H. Michael Stevenson. We wish to acknowledge the substantial contribution of Professor Taylor to an earlier discussion paper on which the present analysis is based; we are indebted to him for his assistance and comments on this paper.

STUDY QUESTIONS

1. What are some of the principal sources of stress in contemporary medical practice?

2. To what extent has government health insurance had an impact on the clinical and economic authority of physicians?

3. On what grounds do physicians criticize government involvement in the health-care field?

4. Discuss the argument that physicians' criticism of medicare is an ideological rather than rational response to government policy?

5. What do the findings in this paper suggest about the role of the medical associations in the debate over the future of Canadian medicare?

6. In what ways does the strength of physicians' ideological opposition to medicare affect the capacity of governments to rationalize health-services delivery?

RECOMMENDED READING

Badgley, Robin F., and Samuel Wolfe. *Doctors' Strike*. Toronto: Macmillan, 1967.

Blishen, Bernard R. *Doctors and Doctrines*. Toronto: University of Toronto Press, 1969.

Coburn, David, George M. Torrance, and Joseph M. Kaufert. "Medical Dominance in Canada in Historical Perspective: The Rise and Fall of Medicine?" *International Journal of Health* 13 (1983): 407–32.

Evans, Robert R. *Strained Mercy*. Toronto: Butterworths, 1984.

Navarro, Vicente. *Medicine Under Capitalism*. London: Croom Helm, 1976.

Taylor, Malcolm G. *Health Insurance and Canadian Public Policy: The Seven Decisions That Created the Canadian Health Insurance System*. Montreal: McGill-Queen's Press, 1978.

REFERENCES

Badgley, Robin F., and S. Wolfe. *Doctors' Strike: Medical Care and Conflict in Saskatchewan*. Toronto: Macmillan, 1967.

Blishen, Bernard R. *Doctors and Doctrines*. Toronto: University of Toronto Press, 1969.

Coburn, David, George M. Torrance, and Joseph M. Kaufert. "Medical Dominance in Canada in Historical Perspective: The Rise and Fall of

Medicine?" *International Journal of Health Services* 13 (1983): 407–32.

Evans, Robert R. *Strained Mercy*. Toronto: Butterworths, 1984.

Hall, E.M. *Canada's National Provincial Health Program for the 1980s: A Commitment for Renewal*. Ottawa: Dept. of National Health and Welfare, 1980.

Illich, Ivan. *Limits to Medicine: Medical Nemesis. The Expropriation of Health*. Toronto: McClelland and Stewart, 1976.

Larrain, Jorge. *The Concept of Ideology*. London: Hutchinson, 1979.

McKeown, T. *The Role of Medicine: Dream, Mirage or Nemesis*. London: Nuffield Provincial Hospital Trust, 1976.

Navarro, Vicente. *Medicine Under Capitalism*. London: Croom Helm, 1976.

Shillington, Howard. *The Road to Medicare in Canada*. Toronto: Del Graphics, 1972.

Taylor, Malcolm G. *Health Insurance and Canadian Public Policy: Seven Decisions That Created the Canadian Health Insurance System*. Montreal: McGill-Queen's University Press, 1978.

Taylor, Malcolm G., H. Michael Stevenson, and A. Paul Williams. *Medical Perspectives on Canadian Medicare*. Toronto: Institute for Behavioural Research, York University, 1984.

White, Norman F., ed. *The Health Conundrum: Explorations in Health Studies*. Toronto: Ontario Educational Communications Authority, 1981.

7

PATIENT-PHYSICIAN RELATIONSHIPS: Changing Modes of Interaction

B. Gail Frankel
University of Western Ontario

INTRODUCTION

The most fundamental interaction in the health-care system is that between patient and physician. In earlier times, physicians did not possess the technical skills and knowledge to offer their patients the cures that are available to us today, nor did they occupy the relatively high position in the social hierarchy enjoyed by their contemporary counterparts (Shorter, 1985; Starr, 1982). Major progress toward improving the health of the general population tended to be the result of public health measures (nutrition, sanitation, pasteurization, regulation of working conditions, housing, etc.) rather than of medical practice per se (McKeown, 1976). However, scientific advances in the area of vaccination for the prevention of the spread of some diseases, and drugs for the treatment of others, made it possible for doctors to actually begin to cure disease. Because of this phenomenon, it was the physician, not the public health advocate or the general scientist, who eventually came to be viewed as the ultimate authority in the health-care system. The physician became a figure of power, not only relative to the patient, but also among other health-care professionals.

The purpose of this chapter is to review some of the major theoretical approaches to the dynamics of the patient-physician relationship. It will show how power came to be invested in the role of the physician, and how the traditional power relationship with the patient seems to be changing, albeit slowly. The review begins with the work of Talcott Parsons, and proceeds through other major theoretical perspectives on the patient-practitioner relationship. We then address changing roles of both physicians and patients in modern medical practice, and consider the impact of financial arrangements (the involvement of third-party insurers particularly) on the patient-physician relationship. Finally, we offer some speculations about the future of the interaction between patients and practitioners in the health-care system.

TALCOTT PARSONS AND THE SICK ROLE

Writing from the functionalist perspective, Parsons (1951) outlines a series of expectations that govern the relationship between physician and patient and prescribe behaviour for both parties in that relationship. Caring for the sick is "not an incidental activity of other roles — but has become functionally specialized as a full-time 'job' " (Parsons, 1951:434). Physicians are seen as the professionals who possess the high levels of technical competence necessary to perform this primary function in society. Because they (the physicians) are the only people who are recognized as possessing this essential technical competence, they are accorded higher status than the patients in the social structure, resulting in an asymmetric relationship between these functionaries in the health-care system.

According to Parsons (1951), the high level of technical competence required of the physician necessitates "specificity of function." He argues that the time and effort required to become expert in the field of health preclude comparable expertise in other fields. Thus one ought not to expect the physician to be more knowledgeable about issues outside of medicine than "any other comparably intelligent and well-educated citizen" (Parsons, 1951:435). Even within medicine, there are subspecialties that require the physician to become expert in one specific area, often precluding functioning in other subspecialties.

Physicians are expected to behave in a universalistic fashion, treating all patients who present themselves for care in the same manner regardless of age, sex, social class, or other characteristics. The personal likes and dislikes of a physician vis-à-vis a specific patient should not interfere with the delivery of service to that patient. As an objective scientist, the physician must function from an affectively neutral stance. Parsons sees the physician as an individual who treats objective problems in objective terms, who maintains social distance from patients, and who does not become emotionally involved with patients.

Finally, the physician's role is seen as having a strong "collectivity-orientation." In Parsons' words, the physician is obligated "to put the 'welfare of the patient' above his personal interests, and [to regard] 'commercialism' as the most serious and insidious evil . . . ." (Parsons, 1951:435). Thus, the profit motive ought not to be part of the medical professional's thinking.

From the point of view of the patient, Parsons believes that "being sick" constitutes a social role, not merely a state or condition. He identifies a set of four "institutionalized expectations," composed of two rights and two obligations, that govern this "sick role." First, the individual who is sick is seen to be exempt from the usual responsibilities and demands of social roles, relative to the nature and severity of the illness involved. This exemption requires legitimation, which often comes from the physician, but which may also come from others, especially when the sick individual attempts to deny the sickness.

Second, Parsons argues that the individual who is sick cannot be expected to get well simply by deciding to do so, or by willing the illness to go away. Sick individuals are thus exempted from direct responsibility for their cures; it is up to others to take care of them. Thus, not only the attitude, but the "condition" of the sick individual must be altered (Parsons, 1951). It is this "right" of non-responsibility for the cure of the illness that leads to consideration of the obligations inherent in the sick role.

The third "institutionalized expectation" is based on the assumption that the state of being ill is undesirable and carries with it the obligation to want to get well. Only when this obligation is accepted are the first two elements, the rights of the sick person, legitimated. Finally, there is the obligation to seek "technically competent" help and to co-operate with the helper in the process of getting well (Parsons, 1951:437). For Parsons, the physician is the most appropriate source of help necessary for the patient to get well. Once the patient has called on the physician for help, the patient "has assumed the obligation to cooperate with that physician in what may be regarded as a common task" (Parsons, 1951:438).

In summary, then, the Parsonian model of patient-physician interaction is based on two basic beliefs. The first is that the patient is in an undesirable role — the so-called sick role — that requires him or her to co-operate with others in order to leave that role. The undesirable nature of the sick role places the patient in a powerless position, relative to the physician. The second basic belief is that, although the physician's behaviour is dictated by certain expectations, the physician is always in a more powerful position than the patient, and this power is legitimated by the sick role model.

The Parsonian formulation has been criticized on a number of grounds. These criticisms have been summarized by Gallagher (1976), among others. It should be kept in mind that the value of a theoretical formulation lies, at least in part, in the extent to which it conforms to reality, and to which it can be generalized. Gallagher notes three of the major limitations of the sick role theory, all of which indicate that gaps exist between theory and reality, and that the sick role cannot be widely generalized.

First, the theory fails to account for the circumstance of individuals with chronic physical illness, or some types of mental illness. Individuals with chronic arthritis, for example, may never "get well," despite their acceptance of its undesirability and their diligent co-operation with physicians' advice. Individuals who have developed lung cancer may, in many instances, actually be held responsible for their illness; after all, to hold that a heavy smoker is not responsible for his or her lung cancer flies in the face of scientific evidence. Mental illnesses are still not always amenable to treatment that leads to cure. Thus, at best, the sick role paradigm is limited to cases of acute physical illness.

Parsons' formulation also fails to account for preventive health care, or to use Gallagher's term (1976:209), health maintenance. Much of health "care" today involves practices designed to maintain health and to preclude adverse

health phenomena. Such practices have become normative, yet appear to have no place in the Parsonian model, which really only deals with individuals who are "sick." This failure to account for a major health practice limits the usefulness of the sick role model.

The third major criticism outlined by Gallagher (1976:209) is that the model "presents a relatively undifferentiated picture of the social structure of health care." The role of the physician is seen as invariable, and no consideration is given to the potential effect of variations in the organization of medical practice. Freidson (1961) also notes that the definition of the sick role is seen entirely from the physician's perspective. As noted earlier, the physician's role is seen as limited to the treatment of illness, and not in the broader context of total health behaviour. As well, little attention is paid to variations in patient roles and expectations. Cultural values are not considered at all, and we must be cognizant of the fact that health and illness are not universally interpreted as they are in modern Western societies (see also Freidson, 1970b).

Yet Parsons' approach to the relationship between patients and their physicians remains the cornerstone of work in this area. It provides valuable insight and has also generated considerable effort to further our knowledge about the interaction between functionaries in the health-care system.

A PSYCHOANALYTIC/ INTERACTIONIST PERSPECTIVE

Szasz and Hollender (1956) consider the relationship between patients and physicians to be an abstraction rather than a "function" or a "thing." They believe that this abstraction is "appropriate for the description and handling of certain observational facts . . . [and] presupposes concepts of both structure and function" (Szasz and Hollender, 1956:585). The relationship involves the encounter of two persons or roles in which there is joint participation. Such an interaction is conditioned by the attitudes, beliefs, and needs of both participants, and varies according to the particular circumstances.

Szasz and Hollender describe three basic models of patient-physician interaction that, they believe, are analogous to certain relationships among individuals in general. The first is the model of "activity-passivity," in which the physician actively does something to the patient, who is essentially passive. It is an interaction that takes place "irrespective of the patient's contribution and regardless of the outcome" (Szasz and Hollender, 1956). Such an approach to treatment is seen as entirely appropriate for certain medical situations, such as emergency care for the severely injured or comatose patient. The authors liken this model to the interaction between parents and helpless infants.

The second model, called "guidance–cooperation," is what characterizes much of general medical practice. In such a model, the patient recognizes that he or she has symptoms of illness that require intervention, and that the physician is the most appropriate agent of this intervention. By seeking help, the patient to some extent places the physician in a position of power, because the physician has knowledge and skills that the patient does not possess. The physician offers advice or guidance and the patient is expected to follow that advice, and neither to question nor to disagree with it. Szasz and Hollender (1956) believe that such interaction corresponds to that between parents and adolescent children.

The third model, called "mutual participation," is based on the philosophical belief in equality among human beings. Szasz and Hollender (1956) argue that the participants in such interactions have approximately equal power, that they need one another in some way, and that the interaction is satisfying to both of them. It is a model that seems apt for the care of individuals with chronic illnesses, since the patients' experiences provide valuable input into the kinds of treatment that work. These patients often know more about how their illnesses respond to various interventions than do their

physicians (equal "power"), although they still need the physicians' assistance to obtain appropriate therapy. The relationship is mutually satisfying to the extent that both parties seek the best possible outcome for the patient. It is a relationship that most resembles adult-adult interactions in the general sense.

It seems that in all three models, however, the power or authority rests in the hands of the physician. While this observation is especially clear in the first two models, some clarifying comment is warranted regarding the third. Clearly, when both parties take an active role in the relationship, the distribution of authority is more equal. Yet, in contemporary medical care, the physician still retains the power to prescribe medication, to make referrals to many ancillary services, and to control admissions to hospital. Thus, even in the model of mutual participation, to the extent that the patient requires services other than those provided by the physician, the power in the relationship rests in the hands of the physician.

THEORETICAL VIEWS OF PROFESSIONAL DOMINANCE: CONFLICT PERSPECTIVES

There is no single definitive "conflict" perspective on the patient-physician relationship. In fact, some of the work that appears to be conflict-oriented may be more appropriately treated in the interactionist perspective (especially the work of Freidson). Nonetheless, because of a common emphasis on professional dominance, power, and authority among theoretical points of view, we have chosen to examine a number of them under the general rubric of conflict perspectives.

Eliot Freidson (1961, 1970a, 1970b), has written extensively on the issue of medical dominance. He argues that the physician and patient are always potentially in conflict, not because they differ in their understanding of the goal of their interaction (i.e., solving the patient's problem), but because the means at their disposal to solve the problem are very different, and because their perceptions and definitions of the problem may vary considerably. On the basis of experience, the physician may see the problem as rather more routine than will the patient (Freidson, 1970b). What for the patient is a new and disturbing circumstance of pain and suffering is likely to be a situation that the physician has encountered and dealt with successfully in the past.

Freidson (1970b) also argues that it is not merely technical competence and knowledge that legitimate the physician's power and authority over the patient. The gap in knowledge between the patient and physician also contributes to the differential distribution of power in the relationship. Moreover, he suggests that medicine possesses the authority to determine when illness exists; in fact, he states, "medicine may be said to be engaged in the creation of illness as a social state which a human being may assume" (Freidson, 1970a; 205). Thus, while Parsons (1951) argues that medicine has the power to legitimate illness in patients, Freidson goes further to suggest that medicine has a monopoly on defining what illness really is, thus creating "illness as an official social role" (Freidson, 1970a: 206).

Increasingly in North America, human behaviour is becoming the context of definitions of health and illness, in part because of the social value placed on individual health. Medicine appears to intervene in more and more disruptions in human behaviour and more and more of these disruptions thus become labelled health problems or illnesses (Freidson, 1970a). Physicians are assuming control over a greater range of human behaviour that may previously have been in the domain of the church or the law. As the social value of health rises, so inevitably does a profession to claim jurisdiction over the maintenance of that value. The medical profession, then, may be viewed as creating its own ideas of illness, and the social values attached to those ideas. The patient comes to see that not only does the physician define what illness is, he or she also controls the "cure," and thus is the

agent of the return to health, which society argues is paramount (Freidson, 1970a).

Twaddle and Gill (1978) discuss the concept of alienation within the interaction between patients and physicians. They note that Freidson (1970a) suggests that physicians' autonomy was achieved through a variety of circumstances, before a reasonable case for medical effectiveness could be made. They argue that technical competence ought not to justify autonomy and that the sources of physician autonomy may be found in patient alienation.

According to Twaddle and Gill (1978), autonomy is a function of the power and control that one social group exerts over another. Increases in autonomy in one group are associated with increases in alienation in the other. Thus they see that growing autonomy of physicians in the control and distribution of medical services has resulted in growing alienation among patients in the patient/physician encounter. This alienation has four dimensions: clinical, organizational, economic, and lifestyle.

Clinical alienation is described as being at least partially irreducible because it stems from the fact that medicine possesses a body of knowledge not immediately available to, and rarely shared by, patients. There is an assumption of inequality between patients and physicians with respect to medical knowledge. "Physicians know more and are better trained in important skills which are (a) not shared by other occupations or the lay public and (b) are thought to be effective in prolonging life and minimizing incapacity" (Twaddle and Gill, 1978:45). In such a situation, the alienation of the patient is clear.

Organizational alienation for the patient is a direct result of the changing nature of medical practice. Modern medicine tends to be based in clinics and hospitals, settings that are largely controlled by the providers of medical care. In the past, much of the delivery of heath care was centred in the home, in surroundings familiar to the patient. Contrast that circumstance with the situation today, where patients are subjected to a variety of complex tests and examinations, organized often for the convenience of the practitioner rather than that of the patient. These tests are not easily understood by the patient, and many times, the results are not communicated to the patient in understandable terms; quite frequently, they are not communicated at all. "In short, the patient is more organizationally alienated than was the case in earlier times" (Twaddle and Gill, 1978:47).

In the United States (and to a lesser extent in Canada), the medical profession sets the terms of the financial arrangements between patients and the health-care system. Costs of all aspects of health-care delivery are escalating and are rendering health services unavailable to many. This is especially true where the fee-for-service system of payment prevails. Most importantly, no matter what the payment system, the public has little control over the economics of health care, and patients become increasingly alienated in an economic sense.

The final dimension of alienation discussed by Twaddle and Gill (1978) is termed lifestyle alienation. Essentially, what the authors refer to here is the widening gap in social class between physicians and most of their patients. Physicians' incomes have grown substantially over recent decades, especially relative to the incomes of others in the general population. Accordingly, there seems little likelihood that patients and physicians will understand or appreciate each others' lifestyles. It is also probable that they will have difficulty in communicating with one another, since they are unlikely to have a common language.

As Twaddle and Gill (1978:47) state,

> the patient must not only bridge the gap in knowledge, deal with organizations and settings that are strange and threatening, and accept the financial terms dictated by the medical profession, he must also bridge a widening gulf of social class as well.

It is little wonder then that the relationship between patients and physicians is not harmonious; rather, it is an interaction that is characterized by an increasing dissatisfaction growing out of the alienation of the patient.

A final theoretical formulation in terms of conflict is provided by Howard Waitzkin (1984), who focusses on the issue of medicalization and the use of social control as means of maintaining the dominant ideology of society. Medicalization refers to the tendency among physicians to convert the personal suffering of patients into medical problems, largely ignoring the social roots of such suffering. Those who criticize medicalization argue that medicine, by depoliticizing health, has become an agent of social control in many societies. As Waitzkin (1984:340) states, "medicalization of social problems involves the expansion of health professionals' activities to include control over wide areas of social and personal life." It is primarily in the patient-physician relationship that this activity occurs.

The principal mechanism with which medicine reinforces the dominant ideology in Western society is by its definition of health as the ability to work (Waitzkin, 1984). There are others, including government, who promote this definition of health, emphasizing the importance of economic forces and the ideology that is "crucial in sustaining and reproducing the social relations of production, and especially the patterns of domination" (Waitzkin, 1984:340). On a macro level, public health policies, government agencies, and the media emphasize the importance of a healthy work force in capitalist society, and a definition emerges of the healthy person as one who maintains maximum capacity to work and produce.

Waitzkin (1984) argues that interactions between doctors and patients may reinforce this definition of health as the ability to work. Frequently, when people become sick, they stop working, and it is the doctor who certifies that the patient is too ill to work, and later that the patient is fit to return to work. The physician, rather than attempting to investigate the social causes (and "cures") of the problem, may cast the patient's complaints or problems in terms of whether or not they interfere with work. Over time, patients too begin to see their problems in relation to their capacity to perform productive work, and thus the medicalization of social problems is complete. This, coupled with the kind of alienation described by Twaddle and Gill (1978), clearly shows that the interaction between patients and physicians is one characterized by considerable distance (intellectual, motivational, lifestyle) with consequent dissatisfaction and distrust on the part of the patient.

CHANGING PHYSICIAN ROLES AND THE RISE OF CONSUMERISM

The practice of medicine has changed radically in the latter part of the twentieth century (Freidson, 1986; Waitzkin, 1984). Modern medical practice is increasingly fragmented, with the growth of numerous specialties and subspecialties. In many cases, scientific knowledge and technology have rendered these subspecialties incomprehensible to one another. There is a widening gap between patients and practitioners in this "high-tech" environment. At the same time, however, there is evidence, especially in the United States, that health-care consumers are not satisfied with the situation. Part of this evidence is the radical increase in malpractice suits over the past decade, especially against physicians who are involved in the delivery of highly specialized care (Twaddle, 1981).

Other evidence is the rapid growth of anti-authority trends in the public at large. Haug and Lavin (1983) argue that public willingness to question the authority of medicine may in part be due to increased levels of education in the general public. As well, there has been a proliferation of health magazines, health information on television and in the print media, and general public-awareness programmes with respect to health issues. Consumers of health care are beginning to act like consumers of other products; they question the assertions of authority figures, request second opinions, and require that they be given information about the risks and benefits of their choices (Haug and Lavin, 1983).

The rise of consumerism in health care has resulted in other changes in the health-care system. Not only are patients questioning their doctors, they are involved to a much greater extent in self-care activities, and are turning more often to paraprofessionals for more of their basic health-care needs. The traditional relationship between patients and doctors is changing because of the challenge to physician authority. This challenge is likely to continue and may have the effect of increasing physician accountability.

When patients question medical authority, several outcomes are possible, some positive and some negative. Clearly it will be incumbent upon physicians to inform their patients more completely with respect to the diagnosis they give and the treatment they recommend. The increase in the seeking of second opinions may lead to "doctor-shopping," to inefficiencies in the health-care system, to increased costs, and possibly to confusion for the patient, who is bombarded with conflicting information. On the other hand, it could result in greater sensitivity of physicians to patients' needs, to reductions in unnecessary surgery and tests, and to more knowledgeable, better-informed, and more satisfied patients.

THE EFFECT OF THIRD PARTIES ON THE PATIENT-PHYSICIAN RELATIONSHIP: HEALTH INSURANCE IN CANADA

Many physicians believe that their relationships with their patients are sacrosanct, that there is no place in that relationship for a third party. Yet, as Blishen (1969) notes, some third-party intervention has occurred throughout history, typified by the legal prescription of rewards and penalties described in the ancient code of Hammurabi some 4300 years ago. What seems to be at issue for physicians today is not the media reports of malpractice suits or the legal requirement that physicians violate patient confidentiality in certain well-defined circumstances (Blishen, 1969), but the entry of third parties into the financial arrangements between doctors and their patients. Nowhere is this more apparent than in the history of government health insurance in Canada.

Since the focus of this discussion is on the patient-physician relationship, we cannot here discuss health insurance in great detail. However, since the funding of health care has a considerable impact on that relationship, we will examine briefly the historical background of the Canada Health Act of 1984, the ensuing legislation in Ontario (Bill 94: The Health Care Accessibility Act of 1986) and the effect of physicians' responses to the government's interference in patient-physician interaction.

The funding of health care in Canada is a matter of provincial jurisdiction. Initial federal funding involved a cost-sharing arrangement with the provincial governments for the planning and construction of hospitals (Vayda and Deber, 1984). By 1961, all provinces had adopted universal hospital insurance, which made them eligible to receive from the federal government half of the costs of all hospital-based health services under the terms of the Hospital Insurance and Diagnostic Services Act. The federal government moved into insurance for physician services with the Medical Care Act of 1968 (Vayda and Deber, 1984). Because of the jurisdictional boundary, participation in the plans was voluntary. However, in order to qualify for federal-provincial cost sharing, the provincial programmes had to meet four criteria:

1. Universal coverage on uniform terms and conditions that does not impede, or preclude, either directly or indirectly, whether by changes made to insured persons or otherwise, reasonable access to insured services by insured persons

2. Portability of benefits from province to province

3. Insurance for all medically necessary services

4. A publicly administered non-profit programme (Vayda and Deber, 1984:193).

The formula for determining the extent of federal contributions is complex and need not be discussed here. It amounts to an approximate 50–50 split between the two levels of government.

Over time, some erosion of the criteria occurred, particularly the first. A small but significant proportion of physicians began to charge fees above the rate set by government plans ("extra-billing"), especially in Ontario, New Brunswick, and Alberta. Many of these physicians were specialists, and in some areas, entire specialties were charging extra fees for their services. In addition, hospitals in some provinces charged "user fees" to hospital patients. These actions prompted new federal action in the form of the 1984 Canada Health Act, which provided fiscal penalties for provinces that continued to allow extra-billing and user fees. For each dollar collected above the rates set by provincial plans, the federal government was to withhold one dollar in transfer payments. Legislation to ban extra-billing in Ontario followed with the Health Care Accessibility Act of 1986.

The first provincial health insurance plan in Canada was introduced in Saskatchewan in 1962. The Saskatchewan College of Physicians and Surgeons opposed the plan, arguing that such government involvement would destroy the mutual trust of the doctor-patient relationship, and erode physicians' professional autonomy (Blishen, 1969). To make their point, the physicians withdrew their services, calling Canada's first doctors' strike. The strike lasted 23 days, and at the end, the legislation remained in place, although physicians did retain the right to bill their patients directly.

History repeated itself in Ontario following the introduction of Bill 94 to the provincial legislature. The physicians began by attempting to solicit the support of their patients in fighting the proposed legislation. This action was seen as coercive, an abuse of power, inappropriate, and unethical (*Globe and Mail*, May 2, 1986). Further, the Ontario Medical Association threatened strike action if the bill became law (*London Free Press*, May 30, 1986). As the final reading progressed in Parliament, the physicians withdrew their services on June 12, 1986. The bill passed on June 20, 1986.

It was never clear how extensive the strike was; its short duration (about two weeks) may be a reflection of fairly limited support. Many physicians did not close their offices or withdraw hospital services. Perhaps this lack of consensus among physicians contributed to the failure of the strike. However, an important factor in ending the strike was the attitude of the public towards it. Before the beginning of the strike, when the physicians were arguing against the bill, a poll indicated that about half the population surveyed believed that the physicians were fighting for important principles and the other half felt that the primary focus of objections to the bill was financial. After the strike began, however, public support dropped drastically, with only 29 percent of the population surveyed supporting the strike action (*London Free Press*, June 27, 1986). A larger proportion of the general public came to see the doctors' opposition to the bill as motivated by greed.

The impact that this collective action on the part of physicians has had on their relationships with patients has not yet been investigated. Nevertheless, one can speculate that the view of doctors held by Parsons as collectivity-oriented and universalistic must be challenged. Patients who found their physicians unavailable during the strike may have had their faith in the medical profession severely shaken. Those who had to wait for treatment in understaffed emergency rooms may begin to question more seriously the authority of physicians and the meaning of professionalism among them.

SUMMARY AND CONCLUSIONS

We have reviewed some of the major theories on the relationship between patients and physicians. We have seen that each of these perspectives provides some assistance in understanding the dynamics of that relationship. Finally, we have attempted to show how social movements such as consumerism and political events such as government interventions have had an impact on the relationship. What we can conclude from our review is that the interaction between doctors and patients must be studied in the social context within which it occurs, that it cannot be seen as separate from that context. The simplest, and yet the most complex overall conclusion, is that this basic relationship in the health-care system is in a state of flux, and will likely continue to change in response to socio-political events in the future.

STUDY QUESTIONS

1. Using as a basis the criticisms of the sick role paradigm that have been discussed, critically evaluate Parsons' description of the expectations of physicians in the context of modern medical practice.

2. Do you see any ways that patient alienation, as described by Twaddle and Gill, can be reduced in today's health-care system?

3. What do you see as the positive and negative effects of the consumer movement in health care? Consider this question from the perspective of the patient, the physician, and the health-care system as a whole.

4. How can we apply Max Weber's concepts of traditional, charismatic, and legal-rational authority to explain physician dominance in the patient-practitioner relationships?

5. Why do you think doctors are so strongly opposed to government health insurance plans?

6. How do you see the future of the relationship between doctors and patients?

RECOMMENDED READING

Badgley, R.F., and S. Wolfe. *Doctors' Strike.* Toronto: Macmillan, 1967.

Illich, I. *Limits to Medicine: Medical Nemesis, The Expropriation of Health.* Toronto: McClelland and Stewart, 1976.

McKinlay, J.B. "Toward the Proletarianization of Physicians." In *Professionals as Workers: Mental Labor in Advanced Capitalism,* edited by C. Derber. Boston: G.K. Hall, 1982.

Navarro, V. *Medicine Under Capitalism.* New York: Prodist, 1976.

Soderstrom, L. *The Canadian Health System.* London: Croom Helm, 1978.

Waitzkin, H. *The Second Sickness: Contradictions of Capitalist Health Care.* New York: Free Press, 1983.

———. "Information-giving in Medical Care." *Journal of Health and Social Behavior* 26 (June 1985): 81–101.

REFERENCES

Badgley, R.F., and S. Wolfe. *Doctors' Strike.* Toronto: Macmillan, 1967.

"Bid to Enlist Patients in Fight on Extra-Billing Causes Stir." *Globe and Mail,* 2 May, 1986.

Blishen, B.R. *Doctors and Doctrines: The Ideology of Medical Care in Canada.* Toronto: University of Toronto Press, 1969.

"Doctors Warn of Indefinite Second Strike." *London Free Press,* 30 May 1987.

Freidson, E. *Patients' Views of Medical Practice.* Philadelphia: Russell Sage Foundation, 1961.

———. *Profession of Medicine.* New York: Harper & Row, 1970a.

———. *Professional Dominance.* New York: Atherton Press, 1970b.

———. "The Medical Profession in Transition." In *Applications of Social Science to Clinical Medicine and Health Policy,* edited by L. Aiken and D. Mechanic. New Brunswick, N.J.: Rutgers University Press, 1986.

Gallagher, E.B. "Lines of Reconstruction and Extension in the Parsonian Sociology of Illness." *Social Science and Medicine* 10 (1976): 207–18.

Haug, M., and B. Lavin. *Consumerism in Medicine: Challenging Physician Authority.* Beverly Hills: Sage Publications, 1983.

Illich, I. *Limits to Medicine: Medical Nemesis, The Expropriation of Health.* Toronto: McClelland and Stewart, 1976.

McKeown, T. *The Role of Medicine: Dream, Mirage or Nemesis?* London: Nuffield Provincial Hospitals Trust, 1976.

McKinlay, J.B. "Toward the Proletarianization of Physicians." In *Professionals as Workers: Mental Labor in Advanced Capitalism,* edited by C. Derber. Boston: G.K. Hall, 1982.

Navarro, V. *Medicine Under Capitalism.* New York: Prodist, 1976.

Parsons, T. *The Social System.* New York: Free Press, 1951.

"Public Opposes Strike But Extra-Billing Gains." *London Free Press,* 27 June 1987.

Shorter, E. *Bedside Manners: The Troubled History of Doctors and Patients.* New York: Simon and Schuster, 1985.

Soderstrom, L. *The Canadian Health System.* London: Croom Helm, 1978.

Starr, P. *The Social Transformation of American Medicine.* New York: Basic Books, 1982.

Szasz, T.S., and M.H. Hollender. "The Basic Models of the Doctor-Patient Relationship." *Archives in Internal Medicine* 97 (1956): 585–92.

Twaddle, A.C. "Sickness and the Sickness Career: Some Implications." In *The Relevance of Social Science for Medicine*, edited by L. Eisenberg and A. Kleinman. Dordrecht, Holland: Reidel, 1981.

Twaddle, A.C., and D.G. Gill. "The Concept of Alienation." *Sociological Symposium* 23 (Summer 1978): 41–60.

Vayda, E., and R.B. Deber. "The Canadian Health Care System: An Overview." *Social Science and Medicine* 18 (1984): 191–97.

Waitzkin, H. *The Second Sickness: Contradictions of Capitalist Health Care.* New York: Free Press, 1983.

———. "The Micropolitics of Medicine: A Contextual Analysis." *International Journal of Health Services* 4 (1984): 339–78.

———. "Information-giving in Medical Care." *Journal of Health and Social Behavior* 26 (June 1985): 81–101.

PART III

INEQUALITY AND HEALTH CARE

INTRODUCTION

In the period following the Second World War, several countries developed national health insurance programmes which were manifestly concerned with equalizing access to health services and assuring that minimum levels of medical care were available to all citizens on the basis of demonstrated medical need, rather than the ability to pay. In formulating such a policy, it was believed that the removal of financial barriers to medical care would equalize access to medical services, and that ultimately, this would go a long way to equalizing health status among the population.

Grant, in Chapter 8, asks the question: "Has medicare narrowed the gap in access to services and in health status among the Canadian population?" The conclusion is that it has not, and that "the inverse care law" is operating in this country; that is, those with the greatest medical need often have the least access to care, even under medicare. Selected evidence is presented to show that the distribution of health and illness in Canada has not been significantly altered by medicare. Many of those groups with a history of heightened susceptibility to disease, disability, and death before medicare remain in a highly vulnerable position today. Medical services in Canada are poorly distributed throughout the country, with large pockets of the nation being undoctored or underdoctored. And even where access has been more or less equalized, equalizing health remains an elusive goal. Grant concludes with a discussion of some of the reasons why programmes designed to equalize outcomes by equalizing access do not necessarily succeed.

While disparities in health status continue to persist among different socio-economic groups, these disparities are even more pronounced between the Native and non-Native populations. The health status of the Native population is the subject of Chapter 9 by Frideres.

High infant mortality rates, premature adult deaths, low life expectancy, and excessive acute respiratory and chronic disease provide a grim picture of the health status of the Native population. Frideres attributes this low health status to a number of factors which include: colonial and racist practices, destruction of the indigenous health system and imposition of Western high-technology curative medicine, emphasis on individual etiology of disease, low socio-economic status, and the divergent cultural ethos of Native people.

Diseases of poverty, overcrowding, poor housing, and unsanitary living conditions continue to take a heavy toll among Native people. Yet because government health programmes tend to focus on individual etiology of disease, failing to acknowledge social, economic, and political causes, the health policies and practices have not significantly improved the health status (to achieve parity at least with the rest of the population) of the Native people.

Both Grant and Frideres emphasize that to achieve equality of health status it is necessary to address questions of social, economic, and political inequality in society and to move beyond individual etiology of disease to the recognition of environmental and social origins of illness.

8

THE INVERSE CARE LAW IN CANADA: Differential Access under Universal Free Health Insurance

Karen R. Grant
University of Manitoba

INTRODUCTION

In 1958, in response to the observation that a segment of the Canadian population faced economic barriers to health care, national legislation was passed to cover the cost of hospital care for all Canadians, regardless of age, sex, race, creed, geographic location of residence, or socio-economic status. Subsequently, in 1968, following the success of hospital insurance, comprehensive health insurance was introduced, so that by 1971 no Canadian would be denied access to necessary medical services for reasons having to do with the ability to pay for medical care. This programme of compulsory universal health care, initiated on the basis of a policy for distributive justice, sought to provide citizens with the highest possible standards of care by breaking down economic barriers to health-care services.

Almost 30 years after the introduction of the hospital insurance plan, and more than a decade after all medical services became covered by national insurance, Canadian society boasts a reasonably healthy population, and ranks eighth among 21 Western developed nations in terms of life expectancy and rates of mortality, and in particular premature death (Bennett and Krasny, 1981:40). Equity in the *availability* of health services (but as yet, not necessarily *accessibility* to such services) has more or less been achieved by the Canadian policy, while maintaining high standards of quality. As a result, Canada has been viewed as a model for other nations which are trying to rectify inequalities in health and access to health services.

However, there are some epidemiological data indicating that even in Canada, under "universal free health care," equality of health has yet to be realized. The removal of economic barriers was a substantial step toward resolving problems of maldistribution and unequal utilization and access to services (Beck, 1973, 1974; Crichton, 1980; Enterline et al., 1973a, 1973b, 1975; Hatcher, 1981; LeClair, 1975; Manga, 1981; McDonald et al., 1974; Siemiatycki et al., 1980). Yet problems of access to and utilization of health and medical services remain. Indeed, recent disputes in Ontario and Alberta concerning extra-billing once again raise the spectre of inequalities in health.

This sounds particularly familiar to those who have studied the British National Health Service (NHS), and sounds all too much like "the inverse care law," a thesis presented by Julian Tudor Hart in 1971. According to Tudor Hart, although the NHS had eliminated inequalities, "the availability of good medical care tends to vary inversely with the need for it in the population served" (1971:412). He qualified his statement, however, by noting that the problems of the United Kingdom would have been considerably worse under a private, fee-for-service, market-based system such as that found in the United States (1971).

Following a brief description of the Canadian health-care system, the basic components of the inverse care law will be examined in conjunction with available evidence on achieving equity under Canada's universal free health-insurance programme. Finally, some of the reasons for the "failure of the equity objective in health" (Manga and Weller, 1980) will be considered.

UNIVERSAL FREE HEALTH CARE IN CANADA

There is a long history of government intervention in the maintenance of Canadian institutions. In part, this reflects a strong belief in public responsibility, as opposed to the more pragmatic ethos of private responsibility common to the United States (Blishen, 1969; Hatcher, 1981). Canada, like Britain, subscribes to a collectivistic social philosophy in which common goals are viewed as primary, with individual interests secondary. Thus, government is regarded as an agent of the people, legislating in the interests of the common good (Presthus, 1974).

In the wake of the Depression and the general social reconstruction which followed the Second World War, Canadian policy-makers saw the need to introduce broad social reforms. The most notable examples were social welfare programmes, old age pensions, and government health insurance (Crichton, 1980; Hatcher, 1981; Lee, 1974; Torrance, 1981). These programmes reflected the belief that government had a responsibility to promote equality and equity.

Health care in Canada is, with only minor exceptions, a provincial responsibility, as stipulated in both the British North America Act of 1867 and the recently patriated Canadian Constitution. As such, there is no "national" health-delivery system, per se; rather, each province has developed programmes designed to serve the needs of its particular populations (Hatcher, 1981; Lalonde, 1974; LeClair, 1975; Lee, 1974).

The insurance programme originally involved two major components. The Hospital Insurance and Diagnostic Services Act of 1958 provided all Canadians with comprehensive coverage for inpatient or outpatient care in any of Canada's hospitals and clinics, as well as limited hospitalization insurance when travelling. The Medical Care Act of 1966 provided all Canadians with comprehensive and universal health insurance, covering all medically required services provided by licensed physicians (LeClair, 1975).

In 1983, the Hospital and Medical Insurance Acts were replaced by a more comprehensive Canada Health Act (CHA). Remaining true to the original principles of the health-insurance programme, the CHA ensures that all Canadians may receive medical services without prejudice.

Prior to the passage of the CHA, the costs of medical services were shared by the federal and provincial governments on a 50–50 cost-sharing basis. The CHA changed that formula, and now, the federal government provides block funds to the provinces, based on the size of their populations. Provinces, then, supplement federal funds with revenues generated through taxation. In order to receive federal funding, however, provincial programmes must meet the following criteria:

1. *Comprehensiveness*: All medically required services rendered in hospitals or in private offices by physicians are covered, without dollar limit or other restrictions, and are available solely on the basis of demonstrated medical need. Co-payments, though admissible and imposed in some provinces, thus must not set up financial barriers to care.

2. *Universality*: Health and hospital insurance must be available to all residents who are eligible on uniform terms and conditions. At present, nearly 100 percent of the Canadian population is covered by the mandatory health-insurance programme.

3. *Portability*: Benefits must be portable in the sense that persons travelling or in the process of moving interprovincially are eligible for hospital and medical care insurance coverage.

4. *Administration by a public authority*: Each plan must be operated on a non-profit basis and be administered by an agency or commission directly accountable to the provincial governments.

5. *Accessibility*: Services must be made available so as not to impede or preclude reasonable access to insured services (Crichton, 1976; Lalonde, 1974; LeClair, 1975).

Most physicians in Canada are paid on a fee-for-service basis, though a small proportion work in salaried positions. Annual negotiations are held between the provincial governments and professional associations to determine fee schedules. While physicians in some provinces reserve the right to opt out of the government plans, only a minority have chosen to do so. Physicians enjoy a high degree of autonomy, which they have fiercely protected over the years (Blishen, 1969). There are almost no restrictions on physicians' location of practice or on their choice of specialties. Just as the patient has the freedom to choose his or her physician, so too, physicians have few restraints imposed upon them by government (Andreopoulos, 1975; Lalonde, 1974). This relatively lax attitude of the government towards physicians' behaviour has meant that in Canada there is, in essence, "private medicine with the public paying the health care bills" (Manga and Weller, 1980:255).

This universal insurance programme is considered by many to be a model plan (Marmor, 1975), though it is not without its problems.

In terms of quality of care, the Canadian system of health delivery certainly ranks with that of other Western nations.[1] It boasts high-quality and humane medical care available to all citizens, and some of the most progressive medical researchers and facilities, along with the favourable health statistics already mentioned. This would suggest that medicare has successfully blended therapeutic effectiveness with social responsibility.

However, there is a certain price paid for this quality. One of the most serious dilemmas facing the Canadian governments, both federal and provincial, is the ever-larger percentage of the GNP that is consumed by health services, and which inflation has exacerbated in recent years. In 1973, second only to Sweden, which allocated 7.38 percent of its GNP to health care, Canada outspent 11 other developed nations — devoting 7.02 percent of its GNP to medical care (Newhouse, 1977). By 1982 (the most recent year for which cost estimates are available), national health expenditures in Canada consumed 8.4 percent of the GNP (Evans, 1984).

Efforts are now underway to curb the costs of medical care. Some provinces charge patients user fees at the time of service and/or monthly premiums (Ontario, Quebec, Alberta, and British Columbia), which are intended to increase patient awareness and deter overutilization.[2] Whether or not such deterrent charges can effectively curb inappropriate utilization without, at the same time, undermining the basic objective of Canada's medicare programme (i.e., equity) remains uncertain. We will return to this topic after outlining Tudor Hart's inverse care law.

THE INVERSE CARE LAW

In 1971, Julian Tudor Hart proposed the inverse care law to describe how the British NHS had failed to achieve its goal of reducing inequalities in health care. Contrary to the work of Rein (1969a, 1969b), which contended that inequities had been abolished, Tudor Hart noted that many of the indicators of mortality and morbidity showed a clear class gradient. Corroborative evidence was sought in the work of Titmuss, who noted that although discriminatory barriers had been effectively removed by the universalistic policy of the NHS, equality of outcomes remained to be achieved:

> We have learnt from fifteen years' experience of the health service that the higher-income groups know how to make better use of the service .... Universalism in social welfare, though a needed prerequisite toward reducing and removing formal barriers of social and economic discrimination, does not by itself solve the problem of how to reach the more-difficult-to-reach with better medical care.... (1968:196–97)

In order to assess whether the inverse care law applies within the context of Canadian society, we will first need to discuss briefly its major components. These are: the distribution of health needs, the availability and utilization of health services, and finally, the quality of medical care.

The Distribution of Health Needs

What are health needs? Are health needs the same as the demand for health care? What factors influence needs and demands for health and health care? And how are such needs and demands distributed within Canadian society? These and related questions involve complexities that may not be readily apparent. Consider the following remarks of Matthews (an economist) on the subject:

> The "need" for medical care must be distinguished from the "demand" for care and from the use of services or "utilization." A need for medical care exists when an individual has an

illness or disability for which there is an effective and acceptable treatment or cure. It can be defined either in terms of the type of illness or disability causing the need, or of the treatment or facilities for treatment required to meet it. A demand for care exists when an individual considers that he has a need and wishes to receive care. Utilization occurs when an individual actually receives care. Need is not necessarily expressed as demand, and demand is not necessarily followed by utilization, while on the other hand, there can be demand and utilization without real underlying need for the particular service used. (Cited in Williams, 1978:32)

Very basically, the demand for health care is derived from the demand for health itself (Becker, 1965; Phelps, 1975). Assuming that individuals can make informed decisions about the nature and quality of services available, as well as their needs, economic theory tells us that the demand for health care amounts to a form of utility maximization in which one makes "rational" choices among commodities and services[3] (McGuire, no date; Cullis and West, 1979). Whether such a calculated model applies to health remains an empirical question, and one that is beyond the scope of the present discussion.

It is hardly news that health needs (however defined) and health itself are *not* randomly distributed throughout society. A number of analysts have documented a greater susceptibility among the poor, certain minority groups, and the elderly to particular forms of morbidity and mortality, as well as the existence of patterns of differential treatment as a function of, among other things, age, race, social class, and area of residence (Antonovsky and Bernstein, 1977; Berkanovic and Reeder, 1974; Bergstrand, 1979; Cole, 1979; Dohrenwend, 1966; Fiedler, 1981; Hollingshead and Redlich, 1958; Hollingsworth, 1981; Kadushin, 1964; Kitagawa and Hauser, 1973; Kleinman et al., 1981; McKinlay, 1974; Morris, 1979; Pratt, 1971; Stroman, 1976; Syme and Berkman, 1981; Weeks, 1977; U.S. DHEW, 1979). In their review of the literature, Syme and Berkman have found that low socio-economic status[4] is associated with higher rates of infectious and parasitic diseases, lower life expectancy, and higher mortality from all causes — a finding first noted in the twelfth century (1981:35–36).

Minority groups (e.g., Native Indians and Inuit, blacks, and Hispanics) have consistently higher rates of overall and infant mortality, lower life expectancy at birth and beyond, and higher morbidity rates, in terms of disability days and chronic morbid conditions, than is the case for the rest of the population (Syme and Berkman, 1981; U.S. DHEW, 1979; Weeks, 1977). According to Health and Welfare Canada, the health status of Native peoples as compared with the remainder of the population is markedly inferior. The rates of death due to infectious and respiratory diseases and to accidents are alarmingly high among Native peoples, and the infant mortality rate is more than twice that of all Canadians. Though rates of death due to cancer and heart disease are lower among Native Canadians than in the rest of the population, a glance at statistics of the median age at death yields the grim explanation for this pattern: Native men's and women's median age at death in 1976 was approximately 46 years, as compared to 68.6 years for Canadian males and 75.9 years for Canadian females in that same year. Native people die so early that there is no opportunity for chronic disease to become a cause of death.

When poverty and minority group status are combined with old age and residence in either an urban ghetto or a rural area, individual socio-demographic characteristics may be said to coalesce into "multiple jeopardy." Despite improvement in living standards, and advances in medical care, substantial differences in health status persist. In all likelihood, the problems of the poor, the minorities, the aged, and ghetto and rural residents are the result of a combination of reduced access and/or failure to benefit from medical care. In addition, living in a toxic, hazardous, and non-hygienic environment that is socially, medically, and psychologically pathogenic no doubt only exacerbates vulnerability to specific diseases and morbid conditions (Syme and Berkman, 1981:37–40).

Access to and Utilization of Health Care

The second part of Tudor Hart's inverse care law concerns the differential availability of health services, in terms of both quantity and quality of medical care, as a function of non-medical criteria. Here, we refer to the issue of *equality of access* to medical care. A perusal of the "equity" literature reveals that it is still difficult to operationalize concepts such as "equity," "access," and "availability" of health services (Aday and Andersen, 1981; Andersen et al., 1975; Davis et al., 1981; Gutmann, 1981; Vladeck, 1981; Wyszewianski and Donabedian, 1981).

According to Aday and Andersen, access may be defined as "those dimensions which describe the potential and actual entry of a given population group to the health-care delivery system" (1981:5–6). This framework holds that in order for equity of access to exist, services must be made available according to people's medical needs for such services. One of the ways in which equality of access is evaluated is by the characteristics of the health-delivery system, specifically:

1. *Structural indicators*, which include the volume and distribution of hospital and clinic facilities and the health labour force;

2. *Process indicators*, which refer to the measure of ease in obtaining care; i.e., whether individuals have a regular source of care, the length of time one must wait to obtain care (waiting and travel time), and the nature of individuals' health insurance coverage;

3. *Utilization/objective indicators* and *satisfaction/subjective indicators* (Aday and Andersen, 1981; Andersen et al., 1981).

In discussing the applicability of the inverse care law in the context of Canadian health care, some of these dimensions of access will be elaborated with particular attention to access under universal free health care (medicare).

Regarding the utilization of health services, there are two myths which we need to dispel. The first is that utilization is a reflection of the nature and distribution of pathology. According to this notion, individuals uniformly respond to symptoms and morbidity. More than a few studies in medical sociology have questioned this assumption (McKinlay, 1974; Davidson, 1970; Zola, 1966). The second myth equates utilization with access to health services. Utilization is only evidence that access has occurred, and reveals nothing of the circumstances which motivate help-seeking behaviour (Fiedler, 1981). In other words, "demand may be only a proportion of the need that exists, it may only be the iceberg's surface above the water" (Stroman, 1976:46). Furthermore, one cannot assume that utilization necessarily produces similar outcomes within the population. Townsend's comments regarding British health and human services seem particularly cogent in this regard:

> Like other major institutional systems of society the health system is organized in a hierarchy of values and status. *No-one today would argue that the heavy utilization of secondary-modern schools by the working classes constitutes evidence of equality of educational provision.* (1974:1186. Emphasis added)

The Dimension of Quality

Despite repeated claims to the contrary throughout this century by the medical profession, the substantial reductions in mortality and improvements in life expectancy observed may be attributed primarily to public health measures, i.e., improvements in nutrition, living and housing standards, and the control of water- and air-transmitted infections, rather than to personal medical services (Fuchs, 1974; McKeown, 1965; 1979; McKinlay and McKinlay, 1977). McKeown, in fact, has argued that social measures have done as much in reducing morbidity and mortality as has any advance in medical policy (1965; 1979). Similar conclusions have been reached by Haggerty (1972), and Powles (1980). In reality, there are diminishing returns even in the face of growing efforts within the medical

field to combat disease, disability, and death.

The point is, however, that if there are medical measures which can be shown to be effective in treating and/or preventing morbidity and mortality, these services should be made available in an equitable manner to all groups who exhibit similar need (Wyszewianski and Donabedian, 1981; Aday and Andersen, 1981). Measures of the equitable distribution of quality care include consideration of factors such as the technical appropriateness of treatment, i.e., whether interventions maximize benefits and minimize risks to the patient, and interpersonal components of the therapeutic relationship (Aday and Andersen, 1981; Wyszewianski and Donabedian, 1981; McKinlay, 1979).

It is important to acknowledge that there is very definitely a relationship between quantity and quality of care. It makes little sense to talk of the quality of care if minimum basic levels of service have not been met. That is, "quantity is a necessary, though not sufficient, prerequisite of quality" (Donabedian, 1976:322). There are reports in Canada, the United States, and abroad suggesting that disparities in the quantity of care available to the poor and non-poor have diminished somewhat, though serious gaps persist (Aday and Andersen, 1981; Andersen et al., 1981; Davis et al., 1981; Siemiatycki et al., 1980; Townsend, 1974, 1981). Assuming that medical care is currently more widely distributed, focus should then turn to whether the care available is necessary, technically appropriate, and delivered to all in the same manner. We will return to several of these points when examining the applicability of the inverse care law to the Canadian scene, and in discussing the issue of equity in general.

THE INVERSE CARE LAW: DOES IT APPLY IN CANADA?

Despite being an egalitarian social policy, universal free health insurance is still not a guarantee of equality of health outcomes. Crichton has noted that the availability of health services to all Canadians on equal terms:

Table 1. Prevalence of Selected Health Problems by Economic Family Income, Canada, 1978–1979

Type of Health Problem	TOTAL ('000s)	Economic Family Income (Quintiles)					
		1st (%)	2nd (%)	3rd (%)	4th (%)	5th (%)	Not Known (%)
At least one problem	12 510	20.0	17.8	17.9	19.2	20.2	4.9
No problems	10 513	17.4	20.0	19.9	18.4	17.2	7.1
Mental disorders	1 000	34.2	18.0	11.8	18.4	13.5	4.1
Hypertension	1 551	25.7	18.4	15.0	17.3	18.0	5.5
Heart disease	847	31.1	20.7	14.4	14.6	16.4	2.9
Dental problems	1 697	25.8	17.6	18.5	17.2	17.2	3.7
Gastric and duodenal ulcers	482	24.7	14.8	15.0	22.1	18.6	4.8
Acute respiratory	781	22.0	18.5	20.6	14.9	18.1	5.9
Bronchitis/emphysema	562	27.8	23.0	11.8	18.2	15.2	4.1
Anaemia	417	30.1	16.7	14.2	16.9	16.9	5.2
TOTAL PROBLEMS	25 526	23.6	18.0	16.7	18.2	19.4	4.2

Source: *Canada Health Survey*, 1981:117.

obviously . . . is a value easier to legislate than to accomplish, given the still prevailing, though less inequitable maldistribution of physicians. But at least there is no longer a direct financial barrier to access to essential services. (1980:248)

Indeed, the failure to produce uniform health outcomes cannot be attributed solely to Canada's health-delivery system. Despite any and all welfare-state interventions to promote equality, health is dependent on much more than the reduction or elimination of barriers to access. It is much more difficult, as policy-makers have discovered, to rid the system of social, psychological, informational, and institutional barriers to care (Andersen et al., 1981; Badgley et al., 1967; Berkanovic and Reeder, 1974; Davidson, 1970; Fiedler, 1981; Lalonde, 1974; Manga, 1981; McKinlay, 1974; Morris, 1979; Pratt, 1971; Suchman, 1964; Wildavsky, 1977; Zola, 1966). Essentially, the Canadian programme has had the primary effect of equal-izing access to health care through the removal of direct payments at the time of service — nothing more and nothing less. An interesting question arises here as to the effect of the removal of financial barriers on health outcomes.[5]

Health Status

As noted previously, health status varies within the population and may reflect the availability of health services, although medical care alone cannot necessarily reduce all pain and suffering, or cure all ills. Tables 1–3 present data from the Canada Health Survey (1981) on the prevalence of selected health problems by economic family income and major activity. Looking first at health problems by income (Table 1), a class gradient is present for several of the forms of morbidity listed, for example, mental disorders, cardiovascular disorders, and dental problems. Table 2 indicates that there is a persistent pattern of higher morbidity among those engaged in

Table 2. Prevalence of Selected Health Problems by Major Activity, Canada, 1978–1979

Type of Health Problem	TOTAL ('000s)	Major Activity					
		Work-ing (%)	House-keeping (%)	School (%)	Inactive Health (%)	Inactive Other (%)	Child/ Baby (%)
At least one problem	12 510	40.2	24.1	17.6	3.9	8.9	5.3
No problems	10 513	38.9	11.1	32.7	—	4.0	13.4
Mental disorders	1 000	26.4	39.1	8.1	11.8	13.8	—
Hypertension	1 551	32.6	41.2	0.7	7.6	17.9	—
Heart disease	847	25.5	29.4	1.7	18.4	24.3	0.9
Dental problems	1 697	42.5	23.7	17.6	4.7	7.5	4.1
Gastric and duodenal ulcers	482	54.8	21.8	3.4	8.3	11.7	—
Acute respiratory	781	29.4	14.7	32.1	0.9	3.4	19.5
Bronchitis/emphysema	562	33.7	23.1	11.1	11.0	16.3	4.6
Anaemia	417	25.3	51.9	6.8	5.8	5.8	—
TOTAL PROBLEMS	25 526	36.3	29.5	12.4	7.2	11.3	3.3

Source: *Canada Health Survey*, 1981:116.

Table 3. Annual Disability Days by Sex and Education Level, Canada, 1978–79

Education Level	Total Days					
	Number Incurred			Days Per Person		
	Total	Male	Female	Total	Male	Female
Secondary or less	284 136	110 027	174 109	17.81	14.26	21.14
Some post-secondary	16 266	5 085	11 181	11.23	6.59	16.52
Degree or diploma	35 109	13 525	21 585	11.56	8.45	15.03
Education unknown	2 873	2 129	—	14.15	20.40	—
Baby/child	23 827	11 790	12 037	9.99	9.61	10.39
TOTAL	362 211	142 556	219 655	15.73	12.49	18.93

Source: *Canada Health Survey*, 1981:121.

housekeeping compared with other activities, though this finding should be regarded cautiously since more women than men were interviewed for the survey. Table 3, showing disability days by education, indicates a class gradient in that those with lower education show a higher degree of disability.

These data, while far from ideal or comprehensive, are useful in showing that health status is associated with socio-economic status in a systematic way. It appears that socio-economic status is inversely related to morbidity, despite Canada's programme of universal free medical care. Without further longitudinal and cross-sectional data, it is difficult to specify the relationship in greater detail.

The Distribution of Physician Services and Medical Facilities

One of the great anomalies of the Canadian health-delivery system is that although improving overall access to the best possible medical services is desired, physicians are free to practise whatever and wherever they choose. As a result, physicians are maldistributed among the ten provinces and two territories and there are gross disparities between rural and urban Canada, despite the fact that in the time since medicare was introduced, there has been an overall increase in the number of physicians. (In 1961, the physician/population ratio was 1:858. In 1971, when medicare became universal throughout Canada, the ratio was 1:670. As of 1981, this ratio has continued to narrow to 1:563 [Coburn et al., 1983; Weller and Manga, 1983a].) Table 4 reports comparative data for the provinces and territories in physician/population ratios. In keeping with the findings of Wolfe and Badgley (1974), this table illustrates the unequal distribution of physicians throughout Canada. Physicians in Canada, as elsewhere, are attracted to metropolitan areas, and to teaching and research facilities; these, of course, are seldom found in sparsely populated areas.

Consider, for example, the situation in Manitoba as of December 1985, described by Horne (1986). In Winnipeg, the physician/population ratio was 1:422, while in the Eastman health region (an area in south-central Manitoba, due east of Lake Winnipeg), the physician/population ratio was 1:1596, and in the Norman health region (the area beyond the 53rd parallel), the ratio was 1:1183. On the surface, these differences would suggest a significant maldistribution of physicians. Yet, Horne assures us that access to services throughout Manitoba has not been severely compromised, and the province's Standing Committee on Medical Manpower (1986) considers current physician/population ratios to be acceptable (implying no severe shortage of physicians). Nonetheless, media and anecdotal reports continue to point to chronic problems in the recruitment and retention of physicians in rural communities, particularly in remote areas in Manitoba and elsewhere in the country.

A similar problem is evident in the distribution of medical facilities. In essence, the problem stems from trying to satisfy the principle of equality of access and equity, simultaneously trying to co-ordinate the most efficient health-care system possible. Crichton has described this perplexing problem:

> So far as equity is concerned, how can "fair shares" of services be provided to a scattered population? It is not feasible to have tertiary referral hospitals in every small town or specialized educational institutions except in centres of dense populations. Canada's history and geography have had much to do with the unequal supply of services. . . . (1980:246)

Indeed, one of the greatest challenges for the Canadian system concerns efforts to overcome the problems of the maldistribution of services and facilities, so that needs can be met equitably without imposing undue tax burdens on the consumer, or draining dwindling national revenues on health expenditures.

Utilization of Health Services

Given the paucity of utilization (particularly longitudinal) data, and also the fact that no national data exist describing the influence of universal free health care on utilization, it is

Table 4. Physician/Population Ratios,* Selected Years

	1951	1961	1971	1980
British Columbia	1:847	1:758	1:614	1:511
Alberta	1:1118	1:982	1:690	1:627
Saskatchewan	1:1278	1:973	1:813	1:677
Manitoba	1:926	1:823	1:645	1:547
Ontario	1:857	1:776	1:621	1:516
Quebec	1:990	1:853	1:639	1:520
New Brunswick	1:1445	1:1314	1:1048	1:903
Nova Scotia	1:1094	1:1044	1:733	1:539
Prince Edward Island	1:1342	1:1149	1:1145	1:816
Newfoundland	1:2424	1:1991	1:1101	1:674
Territories (Yukon & N.W.T.)	1:1394	1:1542	1:1182	1:946
CANADA	1:977	1:857	1:659	1:544
Ratio of largest to smallest	2.86	2.63	1.93	1.85

* For all active civilian physicians, including interns and residents.

Source: Health and Welfare Canada, Health Manpower Inventory.

instructive to examine the research by Beck (1973; 1974) on the Saskatchewan experience, as a case study of utilization patterns. Beck has shown that while positive effects on access were not felt immediately with the introduction of medicare, over time, the programme resulted in a narrowing of the gap between the poor and non-poor in terms of utilization of all services, general practitioners' services, and minor surgery. The impact was less dramatic, though still substantial, in the use of specialist services, complete and regional examinations, laboratory testing, home and emergency visits, and major surgery (figures not shown; see Beck 1973: 346–53). Beck notes that "disparity in access to services by income class will not disappear immediately upon the introduction of medical care insurance" (1973:347). Mediating factors such as cultural background and belief in the efficacy of medical treatment in comparison with other modalities (Davidson, 1970; Suchman, 1964; Zola, 1966), for example, play as

much a part in determining utilization behaviour as does the issue of direct payment versus government-financed service. Even recently published data from the Canada Health Survey suggests that factors other than cost (e.g., time, or belief that one's condition is not serious enough to merit medical attention) are more important determinants of utilization than cost per se. The point is, as stated by Beck, that "the removal of income barriers to services allows an erosion of behavioural patterns or habits, which were previously reinforced by income" (1973:347).

In an effort to prevent overutilization of the health system and as a cost-containment measure, the Saskatchewan government introduced utilization fees in 1968. This allowed physicians to charge patients $1.50 per office visit, and $2.00 for emergency, home, and hospital outpatient visits. Initially, these user fees resulted in a reduction of hospital days of 2.5 percent for two years. After that time, days of care and office visits returned to their previous levels, and admission rates increased some 10 percent (Hatcher, 1981:80). The available evidence suggests that the introduction of co-payments results in only short-term reductions in utilization rates. Insofar as this was the goal of the programme, one might say it was a success. However, Beck maintains that a financial barrier was created to the poor, as evidenced by a proportionally greater drop in their utilization rates, as compared with the population at large. There was an 18 percent reduction in the use of physicians' services by the poor, as compared to a 6–7 percent reduction for the entire population (Beck, 1974).

In 1971, the user fees were discontinued, having failed to beneficially alter utilization patterns. In essence, the co-payments reconstructed the very barriers that universal free health insurance had been designed to destroy. There are at least two lessons to be learned from the Saskatchewan experiment. First, presumably co-payments were introduced to make consumers more cost-conscious and to curb "unnecessary" utilization. Such efforts, it is argued, are doomed to failure if the source of demand is not the point at which intervention takes place. As Enthoven, among others, has noted,

> physicians receive only about 20 percent of the health care dollar, but they control or influence most of the rest . . . physicians are the primary decision makers in the health care system. But the present structure of the system assigns very little responsibility to them for the economic consequences of their health care decisions. . . if the decision makers in a system are not concerned with cost effectiveness, the system will not be cost effective. (1978:652)

This is not to suggest that consumers play no role in the decisions made by physicians, but there is little more than anecdotal evidence implicating patient demand (in lay, not economic, terms) in the spiralling cost of health care. Incentives should be applied where they have had the greatest impact — on physicians.

Second, if the purpose of universal free health care was and is to remove financial barriers, co-payments, however small, can only be

expected to adversely affect those with the least resources. It is difficult to differentiate overuse or abuse from true medical need. Until such time as this distinction can be made, penalizing those who can least afford the added costs is at best unfair, at worst a travesty. It is noteworthy that with the passage of the CHA, this type of co-payment is no longer permitted. The June 1986 doctors' strike in Ontario hinged on the question of whether the Ontario government's Health Care Accessibility Act (which made extra-billing illegal) compromised physician autonomy. From the standpoint of patients, however, the end to extra-billing was a victory. A similar bill has also been passed recently in Alberta. Such legislative efforts serve to forestall any further erosion of the principle of equity that was and is the cornerstone of Canada's universal free health-insurance programme.

CONCLUSIONS

Despite the strides made in Canada in reducing differentials in the availability of care, equality of access and health outcomes have not yet been realized, nor has equity been achieved among status groups throughout the country, whether distinguished by income, race, sex, or geography. The "failure of the equity objective" in Canada, according to Manga and Weller (1980; Weller and Manga, 1983a, 1983b), is due to three factors. First, programmes such as medicare were not really intended to produce equity, per se, but rather to provide some basic minimum standard of care to citizens. Second, these programmes are too narrow in focus. They equate more doctors' services and hospitals with health (Fuchs, 1978; Wildavsky, 1977), without examining the place of preventive services in health promotion and protection, and they minimize the role of non-economic barriers to health and utilization of health care. Moreover, the health-care system is treated as a fully independent institution in society, which it is not, and access to health services is seen as the single most important objective. Yet if individuals are socially deprived (i.e., have different opportunities) then health care is only one of many possible areas in which equity may be at issue. And, third, there continues to be some reluctance among providers of health care (particularly physicians) and government to embrace equity as the objective in health (Wahn, 1984; Guttmann, 1981). It can be argued that physicians are more interested in protecting professional incomes and privileges than they are in furthering equity. As for government, it is no secret that since the mid-1970s, reforms to Canada's insurance programme have been prompted more by the desire to curb costs than by a concern to redistribute health, wealth, justice, or anything else.

Where does this leave us? We have a system that enjoys popular support, but which falls short of producing equal access to health care or health. Maldistribution of services and the health labour force continues, technologically dependent curative medicine dominates the system, and obtaining minimal levels of primary care still eludes some segments of the population. An old Chinese proverb states that "it is better to light a single candle than to curse the darkness." Likewise, although the inverse care law may be operating in Canada, one could envision a far worse scenario without medicare.

Acknowledgements: This is the revised version of a paper published previously in *Sociological Focus* (Volume 17, Number 2, 1984, pp. 137–55). The author wishes to thank the Social Sciences and Humanities Research Council of Canada and the National Health Research and Development Program for their support when this manuscript was first prepared.

NOTES

1. Alternatively, there is a distinct possibility that unnecessary services are as common in Canada as they are in the United States. Excessively high rates of surgery, often linked to iatrogenic disease (Larned, 1977, 1978; Illich, 1977), have led Vayda to conclude that the organization and payment of health services cannot be discounted as a possible explanation of higher surgical rates in Canada (1973:1224). Perhaps there is some truth to "Bunker's Law": "If surgeons are in good supply, and if they are paid on a fee per operation basis by patient insurance, there will not be any tonsils, appendices, or Fallopian tubes left in the population" (cited in Cullis and West, 1979:15).

2. Co-payments must not impose a financial burden on prospective patients such that they deter those in need from obtaining necessary care. When we look specifically at the issue of access in the Saskatchewan health plan, the influence of co-payments on utilization will be examined more carefully.

3. The question of the appropriateness of economic models to study medical care, while of importance and interest, does not fall within the scope of this paper. Suffice to say, however, that there is some disagreement among analysts as to the validity of economic assumptions with respect to the medical market (e.g., Cullis and West, 1979; Feldstein, 1979). Outka, in disputing the assumption of informed choice, has put it this way: "When lumps appear on someone's neck it usually makes little sense to talk of choosing whether to buy a doctor's service rather than a color television set" (cited in Aday and Andersen, 1981:7).

4. The inverse relationship between socio-economic status and higher morbidity, higher mortality, and lower life expectancy holds independent of whether SES is measured using singular variables (income or education or occupation), or composite indexes of social position.

5. Owing to the problems in obtaining comprehensive national data on the health of Canadians, the data presented in the following section are largely drawn from secondary sources and independent research reports, and on a limited basis, from published data derived from the Canada Health Survey (1981). This survey of approximately 12 000 Canadian households was conducted from July 1978 to March 1979, and was designed in response to recommendations of the Lalonde report *A New Perspective on the Health of Canadians* (1974). Empirical studies examined include the following: Hatcher's in-depth study of universal free health insurance (1981), Beck's study of access and the effects of co-payments in Saskatchewan (1973, 1974), Wolfe and Badgley's study of payment schemes (1974), and Horne's study on physician shortages in Manitoba (1986).

STUDY QUESTIONS

1. What barriers exist to achieving universal access to health services in Canada? How does this compare with societies which embrace a "free enterprise" system in regard to health-care provision (e.g., the United States)?

2. Studies show that even after cost barriers have been removed, the health of the poor continues to lag behind that of the middle and upper classes. Why?

3. What kinds of policy initiatives would you suggest to overcome the problems associated with the inverse care law? What are the political, economic, and social impediments to rational policy-making in health and health care?

4. Julian Tudor Hart proposed the inverse care law in 1971. How have circumstances changed in Canada and in Britain since 1971? Does the inverse care law apply in some provinces more clearly than in others? Why? Does it apply to other social policies (e.g., education, social welfare, etc.)?

RECOMMENDED READING

Anderson, O.W. *Health Care: Can There Be Equity?* New York: Wiley, 1972.

Department of Health and Social Security. *Inequalities in Health: Report of a Research Working Group (Black Report).* London: Her Majesty's Stationery Office, 1980.

Manga, P., and G.R. Weller. "The Failure of the Equity Objective in Health: A Comparative Analysis of Canada, Britain, and the United States." *Comparative Social Research* 3 (1980): 229–67.

Syme, S.L., and L.F. Berkman. "Social Class, Susceptibility and Sickness." *American Journal of Epidemiology* 104 (1976): 1–8.

Titmuss, R.M. *Commitment to Welfare.* London: Allen and Unwin, 1968.

REFERENCES

Aday, L., and R.M. Andersen. "Equity of Access to Medical Care: A Conceptual and Empirical Overview." *Medical Care* 12 (1981/supplement): 4–27.

Andersen, R.M., J. Kravits, and O.W. Anderson. *Equity in Health Services.* Cambridge, Massachusetts: Ballinger, 1975.

Andersen, R.M., S. Lewis, A.L. Giachello, L. Aday, and G. Chiu. "Access to Medical Care Among the Hispanic Population of the Southwestern United States." *Journal of Health and Social Behavior* 22 (1981): 78–89.

Andreopoulos, S., ed. *National Health Insurance: Can We Learn from Canada?* New York: Wiley, 1975.

Antonovsky, A., and J. Bernstein. "Social Class and Infant Mortality." *Social Science and Medicine* 11 (1977): 453–70.

Badgley, R.F., R.W. Hetherington, V.L. Matthews, and M. Schulte. "The Impact of Medicare in Wheatville, Saskatchewan, 1960–1965." *Canadian Journal of Public Health* 58 (1967): 101–08.

Badgley, R.F., and S. Wolfe. *Doctors' Strike.* Toronto: Macmillan, 1967.

Beck, R.G. "Economic Class and Access to Physician Services Under Public Medical Care Insurance." *International Journal of Health Services* 3 (1973): 341–55.

———. "The Effects of Co-Payments on the Poor." *Journal of Human Resources* 9 (1974): 129–42.

Becker, G.S. "A Theory of the Allocation of Time." *Economic Journal* 75 (1965): 493–517.

Bennett, J.E., and J. Krasny. "Health Care in Canada." In *Health and Canadian Society*, edited by D. Coburn, C. D'Arcy, P. New, and G. Torrance, 40–66. Toronto: Fitzhenry and Whiteside, 1981.

Bergstrand, C.R. "Victim-Blaming and the 'Looping' Effect of Social Policy: The Case of Physician Maldistribution and Underserved Rural Communities." *Social Problems* 27 (1979): 62–68.

Berkanovic, E., and L.G. Reeder. "Can Money Buy the Appropriate Use of Services? Some Notes on the Meaning of Utilization Data." *Journal of Health and Social Behavior* 15 (1974): 93–99.

Blishen, B.R. *Doctors and Doctrines.* Toronto: University of Toronto Press, 1969.

Coburn, D., G.M. Torrance, and J.M. Kaufert. "Medical Dominance in Canada in Historical Perspective: The Rise and Fall of Medicine?" *International Journal of Health Services* 13 (1983): 407–32.

Cochrane, A.L. *Effectiveness and Efficiency.* London: Nuffield Provincial Hospitals Trust, 1972.

Cole, P. "Morbidity in the United States." In *Patients, Physicians and Illness*, 3rd ed., edited by E.G. Jaco, 30–52. New York: Free Press, 1979.

Crichton, A. "The Shift from Entrepreneurial to Political Power in the Canadian Health System." *Social Science and Medicine* 10 (1976): 59–66.

———. "Equality: A Concept in Canadian Health Care: From Intention to Reality of Provision." *Social Science and Medicine* 14c (1980): 243–57.

Cullis, J.G., and P.A. West. *The Economics of Health: An Introduction.* New York: University Press, 1979.

Davidson, K.R. "Conceptions of Illness and Health in a Nova Scotia Community." *Canadian Journal of Public Health* 61 (1970): 232–42.

Davis, K., M. Gold, and D. Makuc. "Access to Health Care for the Poor: Does the Gap Remain?" *Annual Review of Public Health* 2 (1981): 159–82.

Dohrenwend, B.P. "Social Status and Psychological Disorder: An Issue of Substance and an Issue of Method." *American Sociological Review* 31 (1966): 14–34.

Donabedian, A. "Effects of Medicare and Medicaid on Access to and Quality of Health Care." *Public Health Reports* 91 (1976): 322.

Enterline, P.E., J.C. McDonald, A.D. McDonald, L. Davignon, and V. Salter. "Effects of 'Free' Medical Care on Medical Practice — The Quebec Experience." *New England Journal of Medicine* 288 (1973a): 1152–55.

Enterline, P.E., V. Salter, A.D. McDonald, and J.C. McDonald. "The Distribution of Medical Services Before and After 'Free' Medical Care — The Quebec Experience." *New England Journal of Medicine* 289 (1973b): 1174–78.

Enterline, P.E., J.C. McDonald, A.D. McDonald, and V. Henderson. "Physicians' Working Hours and Patients Seen Before and After National Health Insurance: 'Free' Medical Care and Medical Practice." *Medical Care* 13 (1975): 95–103.

Enthoven, A. "Consumer Choice Health Plan." *New England Journal of Medicine* 298 (1978): 650–58.

Evans, R.G. *Strained Mercy: The Economics of Canadian Health Care*. Toronto: Butterworths, 1984.

Feldstein, R.J. *Health Care Economics*. New York: Wiley, 1979.

Fiedler, J.L. "A Review of the Literature on Access and Utilization of Medical Care with Special Emphasis on Rural Primary Care." *Social Science and Medicine* 15C (1981): 129–42.

Fuchs, V.R. "The Growing Demand for Medical Care." *New England Journal of Medicine* 279 (1968): 190–95.

———. *Who Shall Live? Health Economics and Social Choice*. New York: Basic Books, 1974.

———. "The Supply of Surgeons and the Demand for Operations." *Journal of Human Resources* 13 (1978): 35–56.

Government of Canada. *The Health of Cana-*

dians: Report of the Canada Health Survey. Ottawa: Minister of Supply and Services, 1981.

Gutman, A. "For and Against: Equal Access to Health Care." *Milbank Memorial Fund Quarterly/Health and Society* 59 (1981): 542–60.

Haggerty, R.J. "The Boundaries of Health Care." *Pharos* 35 (1972): 106–11.

Hatcher, G.H. *Universal Free Health Care in Canada, 1947–1977*. Washington, D.C.: U.S. Department of Health and Human Services, NIH pub. no. 81–2052, 1981.

Hollingshead, A.B., and F.C. Redlich. *Social Class and Mental Illness: A Community Study*. New York: Wiley, 1958.

Hollingsworth, J.R. "Inequalities in Levels of Health in England and Wales, 1891–1971." *Journal of Health and Social Behavior* 22 (1981): 268–83.

Horne, J.M. "Searching for Shortage: A Population-Based Analysis of Medical Care Utilization in 'Underdoctored' and 'Undoctored' Communities in Rural Manitoba." Paper presented at the 3rd Canadian Conference on Health Economics, Winnipeg, 1986.

Illich, I., I.K. Zola, J. McKnight, J. Caplan, and H. Shaiken. *Disabling Professions*. London: Marion Boyars, 1977.

Kadushin, C. "Social Class and the Experience of Ill Health." *Sociological Inquiry* 34 (1964): 67–80.

Kitagawa, E.M., and P.M. Hauser. *Differential Mortality in the United States*. Cambridge: Harvard University Press, 1973.

Kleinman, J.C., M. Gold, and D. Makuc. "Use of Ambulatory Medical Care by the Poor: Another Look at Equity." *Medical Care* 19 (1981): 1011–29.

Lalonde, M. *A New Perspective on the Health of Canadians: A Working Document*. Ottawa: Minister of Supply and Services, 1974.

Larned, D. "The Epidemic of Unnecessary Hysterectomy." In *Seizing Our Bodies*, edited by C. Dreifus, 195–208. New York: Vintage,

1978a.

⸻. "Caesarean Births: Why They are Up 100 Percent." *MS Magazine*, October, 1978b.

LeClair, M. "The Canadian Health Care System." In *National Health Insurance: Can We Learn from Canada?* edited by S. Andreopoulos, 11–96. New York: Wiley, 1975.

Lee, S.S. "Health Insurance in Canada — An Overview and Commentary." *New England Journal of Medicine* 290 (1974): 713–16.

Manga, P. "Income and Access to Medical Care in Canada." In *Health and Canadian Society*, edited by D. Coburn, C. D'Arcy, P. New, and G. Torrance, 325–42. Toronto: Fitzhenry and Whiteside, 1981.

Manga, P., and G.R. Weller. "The Failure of the Equity Objective in Health: A Comparative Analysis of Canada, Britain, and the United States." *Comparative Social Research* 3 (1980): 229–67.

Manitoba Health Services Commission. *Standing Committee on Medical Manpower, Annual Report, 1985.* Winnipeg, 1986.

Marmor, T.R. "Can We Learn from Canada?" In *National Health Insurance: Can We Learn from Canada?* edited by S. Andreopoulos, 231–50. New York: Wiley, 1975.

McDonald, A.D., J.C. McDonald, V. Salter, and P. Enterline. "Effects of Quebec Medicare on Physician Consultation for Selected Symptoms." *New England Journal of Medicine* 291 (1974): 649–52.

McGuire, T.G. "Patients' Trust and the Quality of Physicians." Unpublished paper. Boston University: n.d.

McKeown, T. *Medicine in Modern Society.* London: Allen and Unwin, 1965.

⸻. *The Role of Medicine.* Oxford: Basil Blackwell, 1979.

McKinlay, J.B. "The Help-Seeking Behavior of the Poor." In *Poverty and Health*, edited by J. Kosa and I.K. Zola, 224–73. Cambridge: Harvard University Press, 1974.

⸻. "Epidemiological and Political Determinants of Social Policies Regarding the Pub-

lic Health." *Social Science and Medicine* 13a (1979): 541–48.

McKinlay, J.B., and S.M. McKinlay. "The Questionable Contribution of Medical Measures to the Decline of Mortality in the United States in the Twentieth Century." *Milbank Memorial Fund Quarterly/Health and Society* 55 (1979): 405–28.

Morris, J.N. "Social Inequalities Undiminished." *The Lancet* 1 (1979): 87–90.

Mott, F.D. "Prepaid Medical Care Under Government Auspices in Saskatchewan." *Canadian Journal of Public Health* 41 (1950): 403–10.

Newhouse, J.P. "Medical Care Expenditures: A Cross-National Survey." *Journal of Human Resources* 12 (1977): 115–25.

Phelps, C.E. "Effects of Insurance on Demand for Medical Care." In *Equity in Health Services*, edited by R.M. Andersen, J. Kravits, and O.W. Anderson, 105–30. Cambridge, Massachusetts: Ballinger, 1975.

Powles, J. "On the Limits of Modern Medicine." In *Readings in Medical Sociology*, edited by D. Mechanic, 18–44. New York: Free Press, 1980.

Pratt, L. "The Relationship of Socioeconomic Status to Health." *American Journal of Public Health* 61 (1971): 281–91.

Presthus, R. "Interest Group Lobbying: Canada and the U.S." *Annals of the American Academy of Political and Social Science* 44 (1974): 44–57.

Rein, M. "Social Class and the Health Service." *New Society* 14 (1969a): 807–10.

⸻. "Social Class and the Utilization of Medical Care Services." *Hospitals* 43 (1969b): 43–54.

Roemer, M. "Prepaid Medical Care and Changing Needs in Saskatchewan." *American Journal of Public Health* 46 (1956): 1082–88.

Siemiatycki, J., L. Richardson, and I.B. Pless. "Equality in Medical Care Under National Health Insurance in Montreal." *New England Journal of Medicine* 303 (1980): 10–15.

Stroman, D.F. *The Medical Establishment and Social Responsibility*. London: Kennikat Press, 1976.

Suchman, E.A. "Sociomedical Variations Among Ethnic Groups." *American Journal of Sociology* 70 (1964): 319–31.

Syme, S.L., and L.F. Berkman. "Social Class, Susceptibility and Sickness." In *Sociology of Health and Illness*, edited by P. Conrad and R. Kern, 35–44. New York: St. Martin's Press, 1981.

Titmuss, R.M. *Commitment to Welfare*. London: Allen and Unwin, 1968.

Torrance, G.M. "Socio-Historical Overview: The Development of the Canadian Health System." In *Health and Canadian Society*, edited by D. Coburn, C. D'Arcy, P. New, and G. Torrance, 9–28. Toronto: Fitzhenry and Whiteside, 1981.

Townsend, P. "Inequality and the Health Service." *The Lancet* 2 (1974): 1179–89.

———. "Toward Equality in Health Through Social Policy." *International Journal of Health Services* 11 (1981): 63–75.

Tudor Hart, J. "The Inverse Care Law." *The Lancet* 1 (1971): 405–12.

U.S. Government. *Health, United States, 1979*. Washington, D.C.: U.S. Department of Health, Education and Welfare pub. no. (PHS) 80–1232, 1979.

Vayda, E. "A Comparison of Surgical Rates In Canada and In England and Wales." *New England Journal of Medicine* 289 (1973): 1224–29.

Vladeck, B.C. "Equity, Access and the Costs of Health Services." *Medical Care* 12 (1981/supplement): 69–80.

Wahn, M. "Losing Medicare: Why Worry?" *Canadian Dimension* 18 (1984): 5–6.

Weeks, A.H. "Income and Disease — The Pathology of Poverty." In *Medicine in a Changing Society*, 2nd ed., edited by L. Corey, M.F. Epstein, and S.E. Saltman, 53–65. St. Louis: C.V. Mosby, 1977.

Weller, G.R., and P. Manga. "The Development of Health Policy in Canada." In *The Comparative Study of Canadian Public Policy*, edited by M. Atkinson and M. Chandler, 223–46. Toronto: University of Toronto Press, 1983a.

———. "The Push for Reprivatization of Health Care Services in Canada, Britain and the United States." *Journal of Health Politics, Policy and Law* 8 (1983b): 495–518.

Wildavsky, A. "Doing Better and Feeling Worse: The Political Pathology of Health Policy." *Daedalus* 106 (1977): 105–23.

Williams, A. "'Need' — An Economic Exegesis." In *Economic Aspects of Health Services*, edited by A. J. Culyer and K.G. Wright, 32–45. London: Martin Robertson, 1978.

Wolfe, S., and R.F. Badgley. "How Much is Enough? The Payment of Doctors — Implications for Health Policy in Canada." *International Journal of Health Services* 4 (1974): 245–64.

Wyszewianski, L., and A. Donabedian. "Equity in the Distribution of Care." *Medical Care* 12 (1981/supplement): 28–56.

Zola, I.K. "Culture and Symptoms — An Analysis of Patients' Presenting Complaints." *American Sociological Review* 31 (1966): 615–30.

9

RACISM AND HEALTH: The Case of the Native People

J.S. Frideres
University of Calgary

INTRODUCTION

The present chapter will demonstrate how colonialism and racism destroyed most Native institutions, in particular their traditional health-care system and health practices. We will also show that the health-care policies of the government contain a fundamental bias that reinforces the belief that sickness is located in the individual's body. This, in turn, reinforces the tendency for Canadians to view health care and health risks in terms of the individual, rather than in the context of society or of the actions taken by vested interest groups such as the Canadian Medical Association or large multinational corporations (Turshen, 1977). As Bolaria (1979) points out, this individual-centred conceptualization has led to a curative orientation, where technical medical solutions are offered to solve the individual's problems, and the social, economic, and political causes of ill health are ignored. He goes on to point out that this position obscures the extent to which health and illness depend upon socially determined ways of life.

According to the 1981 census, nearly one-half million people were identified as being at least partially of Native origin. Table 1 identifies the different classifications of Native people.

Table 1. Different Categories of Native People by Origin, 1981

	Single Origin	Multiple Origin	Total
Inuit	23 200	2 190	25 390
Status Indian	266 425	26 275	292 700
Non-Status Indian	47 235	27 875	75 110
Métis	76 515	21 745	98 260
TOTAL	413 380	78 080	491 460

Source: 1981 Census of Canada, (Catalogue 99–937)

Demographically speaking, there are many respects in which Native people are quite different from the remainder of the population. First of all, nearly half of the Native population is found in rural or rural non-agricultural areas. Having more children but not living as long as other Canadians, Native people show a high dependency ratio. (This is the number of people who are either too young or too old to work relative to the number of people of working age — usually defined as ages 15–65.) Nearly 40 percent of Native people (22 percent of non-Native) are under 15 years of age and only 3 percent are over 65 (9 percent for non-Native people). Almost 70 percent of the Native population is under 30, compared to less than 50 percent of non-Native people. For the Native population, the average age is about 23, while for the non-Native population, it is 33 (Frideres, 1983).

Native people as a group can be considered to occupy the lower-status positions in Canadian society. For those over 15 years of age and not attending school full-time, nearly half have less than a Grade 9 education, with only 6 percent ever having received a high school diploma. Comparable figures for the non-Native population are 22 and 14 percent, respectively (Canada, 1985). Labour force participation is affected by the lack of education. Native people show high rates of unemployment (averaging 60 percent) everywhere in Canada, with rates as high as 90 percent in some areas of northern Saskatchewan and in the Atlantic provinces. They are also disproportionately represented in the job market. Only about half of those working were employed for more than 40 weeks per year, and they were twice as likely as other Canadians to have worked less than 13 weeks. The educational and occupational status of Native people are reflected in their annual income. On the average, Native incomes are less than two thirds of non-Native incomes. In addition, nearly one fourth of all Native people had no income. However, for those reporting an income, nearly 20 percent of this income was not earned; i.e., it was a result of government transfers — family allowance, old age pension, or welfare. At the other end of the income scale, we find about 15 percent of Native people making over $20 000 per year and 4 percent making over $30 000 (Abella, 1984). Comparable figures for non-Natives are 35 and 23 percent, respectively. The high unemployment and lower incomes are also evident in the quality of housing among Native people: one house in every six is considered

crowded (more than one person per room) compared to one in 43 among the non-Native population. In addition, one quarter of Native homes require major repairs, over one half lack central heating, and nearly one third lack an indoor bathroom (Canada, 1985).

In summary, our statistics show that Native people have a low participation rate in the labour force, low educational attainments, low job status, and low incomes. They are further restricted by geographic concentration in rural and isolated areas. Native people are, for the most part, concentrated at the bottom of the class hierarchy of Canadian society. This position is primarily a result of government policies that have created and maintained a relationship of perpetual dependency (Dunning, 1959; Carstens, 1971). Paine (1977) has referred to this relationship as one of "welfare colonialism." As Tanner (1983) points out, the colonial structure emerged over an extended period, first with the French, then the British, and more recently with a rapidly expanding industrial state. The central goal of the federal government in dealing with Native people has always been to maintain close control over them in almost all aspects of their lives.

NATIVE HEALTH CARE

The involvement of government in health care is a relatively recent phenomenon. As Meilicke and Storch (1980) point out, prior to Confederation there was limited government involvement with health-care issues. The government's position was that health and social needs of Canadians were family concerns and were to be dealt with by families and voluntary or religious organizations. As Heagerty (1934, 1943) pointed out, there is no reference to any measures taken by the provincial or federal government to prevent the spread of smallpox, typhus, and other diseases that frequently decimated the Indian population. Only when various epidemics threatened the local non-Native population would the provinces and/or cities become involved in health care (Hasting and Mosley, 1964).

Traditional Indian Health Care

For many Indians, the traditional understanding of illness was embedded in the system of religious beliefs. Illness was the result of some kind of action taken by an individual, for example, breaking of taboos and allowing an evil spirit to enter the body. Native people traditionally identified three kinds of illness. First, there were visible injuries that were a result of physical causes, such as bone fractures and lacerations. Secondly, there were diseases caused by some invisible external event, confirmed indirectly by the behaviour of the sick person, e.g., smallpox, influenza, or cancer. Finally, there was a residual category, which included mental illness.

The traditional Native health-care practitioner generally applied routine medicines at the outset of his or her curative regimen. The assumption was that there was some biological basis for the illness and that the medicines administered would have a curative power. There were many different medicines developed to treat a variety of illnesses. However, if the illness did not pass, shamanistic methods — prayers and chants — would be employed (Sealey and McDonald, no date). Because Native people viewed illness as a result of some foreign object or spirit having entered the body, the task of the medicine man or woman or shaman was to remove the foreign object or spirit.

As the colonialization of Native people inexorably continued, it eroded the Native health-care system. This demise began slowly, and under seemingly benign conditions, during the Treaty Period (1850–1920) when some health-care benefits were included in the terms of the treaties with the colonizers. Traditional health-care activities were increasingly discouraged and discontinued as various government agencies defined them as inappropriate or sometimes illegal. The period after World War II found Indians still living in isolated rural communities with local subsistence economies, e.g., hunting, fishing, and trapping, supplemented by seasonal labour in the dominant technological society. During this time, the government Indian Affairs department was the sole provider of educational and medical activities on the reserves. The major problem confronting Native people was the precipitous intrusion of white society on their way of life; high rates of neurosis and alcoholism resulted as they attempted to deal with the rapid changes imposed upon them. As Eyer and Sterling (1977) point out, the economic and cultural forces imposed on Native people by the government and its agencies created a great deal of stress by disrupting communal ties and by trying to mould competitive, striving individuals.

Current Health Care Responsibility

The responsibility for providing direct health services to Indians was transferred to Health and Welfare Canada in 1945 and has remained there since. In 1962, Indian Health Services was merged with six other federal health programmes to form the Medical Services Branch, a branch of National Health and Welfare. Full medical services to Indians are provided, although these vary from province to province according to the standards set by each provincial legislation. In 1964, Treaty Indians were regarded as insured persons under provincial medicare. Four years later a health plan for Indians was produced, recommending the user-pay concept and the total transfer of the programme to the provinces. In addition it restated that the government had no formal obligation to provide Indians with free medical services. Later, in 1971, the federal government stopped paying for Indian patients in provincial mental hospitals. In 1974, The Department of Indian Affairs and Northern Development (DIAND) once again issued a statement which spelled out its policy toward Indians: even though the federal government currently covers health-care costs for Indians, there are no federal statutes, including the Indian Act, which compel it to do so.

During the 1960s, several factors changed the Native view of Canadian society. Increased transportation and communication (i.e., roads and television) reduced the isolation of Indian communities. Second, Native society experienced a baby boom. Third, counterculture values were introduced into the reserves. As a result, with the arrival of the 1970s, Native people began to demand more and different health, social, and occupational services: opportunities and changes which would allow them to better adapt to the new political economy. Although the 1970s saw a shift of power from DIAND to band councils, DIAND still retains a great deal of control over Native people in all aspects of their lives. (Ponting and Gibbins, 1980). In 1981, a proposal to transfer responsibility for health-care services to Indian communities was approved by the federal Cabinet on a two-year experimental basis — since renewed. Over 30 communities are now involved in this community-based health-demonstration programme. In addition, Medical Services Branch has developed a professional health Career Development Program through which Native people can enter professions in the health sciences and learn to administer community health programmes. Special training programmes to provide Native para-professional health workers and programmes in the area of alcohol and drug abuse treatment and rehabilitation are also funded by DIAND. These activities are carried out within the $150 million annual budget of Medical Services Branch.

A federal-Native conference on Indian health care was held in 1984 in an attempt to further develop the funding and delivery of health services to Indians. Although a number of recommendations were agreed upon, they have yet to be enacted, because of their lack of endorsement by the Assembly of First Nations. Constitutional issues and questions of self-government have now emerged which need to be dealt with before specific health-care programmes can be enacted.

Programmes of Medical Services

Medical services for Native people are provided through three government structures. The first is the provincial health-care programme. All services provided to Native people by the provinces are fully reimbursed by the federal government. The other two major agencies which deal with Native health-care services are the Medical Services Branch and DIAND. The Medical Services Branch has nearly 200 doctors (11 of them Native), over 1000 nurses (150 Native), and over 500 community health workers on their payroll. Today about 20 percent of the full-time employees of the Medical Services Branch are Native, although fewer than 200 qualified Native health professionals are in the top seven health professions. On a per capita basis, Medical Services Branch spends about $350 per year, about the same as spent on non-Native people by the federal and provincial governments (Grescoe, 1981). Indian and Northern Health services (the subdivision of Medical Services Branch) provides health-care services for Indians through a variety of means including physicians, health educators, dental therapists, and community health representatives. These services consist of medical care to Indians on reserves, in special hospitals (located both on and off reserves), and to Native people in the Northern Territories. (See Figure 1 for the structure of National Health and Welfare Canada, Medical Services Branch.)

Services are also provided through contributions and contract arrangements with Native organizations, bands, and universities. They carry out this programme under four main activities: (1) health care and treatment services, (2) public health services, (3) involvement of Indians in the health-care system, and (4) the provision of physical facilities. (DIAND, 1984).

Today the major programme for health care under DIAND for Native people is the Indian and Northern Health Services. Its budget of over $300 million has four major subcomponents: Community Health Services, Environmental Health and Surveillance, the National Native Alcohol and Drug Abuse Program, and Hospital Services. Two additional components are the Universal Health Benefit and the Capital Construction. The former covers dental services, drugs, eyeglasses, and the payment of health-care premiums. The cost for this subprogramme

Figure 1: Health and Welfare Canada: Structure for Medical Services to Indians

Level of
Responsibility

NATIONAL   Cabinet   Treasury Board

                                  Minister

          Deputy Minister   Deputy Minister
             Welfare   Health

                          Assistant Deputy Minister

                  Director General   Director General
                  Policy and Evaluation   Operations

      Director, Indian/   Director   Director
        Inuit Policy   Planning   Evaluation

PROVINCIAL   Regional Director

REGIONAL   zone   zone   zone

                  (Nurse, Doctor, Environmental Health Officer)

LOCAL   Band Council

                                  Indian Patients

Source: Castellano, 1982, p. 117.

has escalated from less than $36 million in 1979–80 to more than $130 million in 1985–86. The latter programme covers the cost of building, upgrading, and expansion of health centres, e.g., hospitals and nursing stations (Canada, 1985). Through this latter programme, the federal government has also established special hospital facilities for Native people, e.g., Cardston, Alberta, and Sioux Lookout, Ontario. Some of these, such as the Charles Camsell Hospital for treatment of tuberculosis, have since been turned over to the province, and are now operated as regular provincial health facilities.

In addition, DIAND operates three related programmes which provide funds and services to Native people to assist them in maintaining health, safety, dignity, and family unity. These three subprogrammes are Social Assistance, Welfare Services, and Capital Facilities and Community Services. The Social Assistance programme makes up $260 million (16 percent of the total DIAND budget). Welfare Services make up an additional 5 percent, or $81 million, and Capital Facilities and Community Services make up an additional $450 million. An individual faced with a deficit between needs and resources is eligible for assistance under the above programmes. Today, nearly 60 percent of the reserve population is receiving some form of social assistance. Finally, in addition to the above programmes, DIAND has created several joint health-care programmes with other federal and provincial departments. One of the best known is the National Native Alcohol Abuse Program (with Medical Services Branch) established in 1976. This programme provides Native communities with both financial and technical resources. At present, nearly 300 community projects are funded by this programme.

HEALTH CONDITIONS OF NATIVE PEOPLE

Many of the statistics about disease and illness among Native people have been published and are well known. (See Graham-Cumming, 1966 and "Mortality and Health-Status Trends in Canada" by David Hay in this volume.) Diseases of poverty, overcrowding, and poor housing have led to chronic and acute respiratory diseases, which take a heavy toll among Native people. The standardized death rate for the Native population is more than double the general Canadian population — 15.9 vs. 6.6 deaths per 1000 population, (Nuttall, 1982; Brady, 1983) with an average age of death more than twenty years below that of the average non-Native Canadian.

Rates of infant and perinatal mortality for Native people are also much higher than those for the overall population. For the average Canadian, the four most important causes of death before age 70 are (in order of importance): (1) diseases of the circulatory system, (2) neoplasms, (cancer) (3) accidents, poisoning, and violence, and (4) diseases of the respiratory system. Native people share the same four leading causes but not in the same order. Accidents, poisoning, and violence are the major causes of death and account for nearly 40 percent of Native deaths compared to 12 percent for non-Natives. Infectious diseases, gastroenteritis, and colitis are also frequent causes

of death for Native people, while among non-Indians, diseases associated with degenerative causes, e.g., heart disease and cancer, are most important. A comparison of life tables (length of life) between the Native and non-Native populations over the past 20 years shows that there has been little improvement for Native people, and even a deterioration in the past decade (Nuttall, 1982). Today, the life expectancy of a Native person is 30 years less than that of a non-Native.

Brady (1983) shows that in Native society, compared to the rest of the population, suicide and self-inflicted injuries are three times higher (six times higher for the 15–24 age group), homicide rates are twice as high, congenital anomalies are 1.5 times higher, tuberculosis is over nine times higher, and pneumonia over three times higher. Native people have five times the rate of child welfare, four times the death rate, three times the violent death, juvenile delinquency, and suicide rate, and twice the rate of hospital admissions of the average Canadian population. Native people are also exposed to severe environmental hazards: industrial and resource development have polluted water and disrupted fish and game stock for many reserve communities, seriously affecting quality of life. For example, residents of the White Dog and Grassy Narrows reserves in Ontario were found to have 40 to 150 times more mercury in their blood than the average Canadian (Bolaria, 1979). Various environmental disturbances have upset other Native communities such as Cluff Lake (uranium pollution), Serpent River (acid discharge), and St. Regis (fluoride pollution). Obviously, the Native lifestyles vary considerably from those of non-Natives.

In summary, statistics show that the quality of life experienced by Native people is far inferior to that of non-Natives. How have they found themselves in this position? These conditions have come about as a result of the cultural imperialism of the Canadian government and the racist philosophy that promoted the dominant society's insistence on the inferiority of Native people.

PERSPECTIVES ON NATIVE HEALTH AND ILLNESS

Traditional health care, as practised by Native societies, was not only a way of dealing with private troubles and uncertainties, it was an integral part of social relationships and cultural patterns of belief. It involved both a practitioner and a patient, and the actions taken by the medical practitioner reinforced the existing social order (Birenbaum, 1981). Native people used their traditional health-care system as a form of social control. Like others, it aimed to produce a healthy person who could work and produce goods for domestic consumption and economic surplus.

Over the years, traditional Native health-care practices have been ridiculed by the practitioners of the dominant society. Non-natives, unfamiliar with the substances and methods used in Native medicine, saw its practices as primitive, irrational, and ignorant. From their ethnocentric and racist perspective, the use of shamans was evidence of paganism and heathenism; they persistently argued that shamans were evil and that Christian prayers were more efficacious in curing illness (Sealey and McDonald, no date). These moral entrepreneurs, who carried out their destruction of Native health-care practices with relentless zeal, were aided by the government's willingness to accept the medical profession's definition of what was appropriate and acceptable in health-care methods. To secure the primacy of this definition, laws were introduced which would ensure that traditional Native ways would be phased out, and new ways legitimized. As a result, the Western medical model became the dominant accepted model. As a result, over the years many traditional medicinal practices and products have been forced underground, and in certain communities, much of the knowledge has disappeared altogether. The dominant society's medical system may be utilized by Native people, but their traditional health care provides them with a sense of security not obtainable through modern practices. Thus, they tend to retain and utilize some of the traditional approaches — under specific conditions, along with the more modern health-care practices. On many of the reserves, traditional health care remains viable, if not universally used. To the extent that Native people are isolated and institutionally complete, use of such traditional techniques is reinforced.

The basic elements upon which Canadian medical thinking, and hence the health-care system, rest are the acceptance of germ theory and the ability of people to diagnose and take steps to cure an illness. Both these presuppose that health is the concern of the individual. Most members of the population accept the first condition with little reservation; the second also does not seem to be problematic for many people. However, there are certain sectors of the population, i.e., Native people, who do not accept the first assumption and find the second difficult to implement. Obviously, those who reject or are unable to accept or implement both these assumptions are at a distinct disadvantage in maintaining good health, and consequently in quality of life. The most serious consequence is a mortality rate considerably greater than among those people who accept germ theory and practise preventive medicine and who are in any case already in a position of low risk with regard to life-threatening illnesses.

The health of an individual is influenced by four factors: lifestyle, environment, organizational structures of health care, and biological (genetic) makeup (LaFramboise, 1980). Lifestyle is comprised of decisions made by an individual which have an impact on overall health, for example, use of alcohol and tobacco, occupation, and physical fitness. There is a tendency to define this component in terms of only "voluntary" decisions. However, it must be pointed out that many of these seemingly voluntary decisions are actually involuntary or at least severely circumscribed. For example, smoking is a means to reduce hunger pangs, unskilled labourers are forced to take jobs with a high risk of accidents, and the nutritional value of one's diet may be determined by financial resources. The environmental element is the individual's physical and social environment, which includes factors such as air quality, potable water, place of residence, and housing. Health-care organization refers to the quality, arrangement, nature, and relationships of people and resources within society to health-care services. This component, usually referred to as the "health-care delivery system," includes such factors as medical practices, the existence and availability of hospitals and extended care facilities, and the availability and use of antibiotics and other drugs. The final component — human biological makeup — refers to the individual's physical and genetic makeup. There is a tendency to view this component as a constant, and to consider all people biologically the same.

Health problems experienced by the individual are, theoretically, the result of a "crack" in any one of the above four components. However, we will quickly come to see that each of these components can contribute differentially to illness for different groups of people. As noted above, there is a tendency to assume that all Canadians have access to the same health-care system and have the same biological makeup, so that these two components are constant. To a certain extent, environment is also viewed as a constant. As a result, there is a tendency for researchers to focus on the individual's lifestyle as determining the quality of health, since it is considered the only variable in the formula (Wirick, 1966).

In other words, politicians, health-care practitioners, and the employment system view the Canadian population as homogeneous, or soon to become so. There is a continued insistence that one health-care model (the individual technical curative model) is correct and no others are to be recognized. Policy decisions and programmes established by the government reflect this fundamental bias. However, it is clear that many social classes and cultural groups aside from middle-class whites have fundamental problems in adapting to the health-care model propounded by the medical profession. Native people are in double jeopardy — they tend to be shunted into a lower social class, and

they are culturally separate from the dominant society. We will examine below how socioeconomic and cultural factors influence Native people's access to health-care services and affect their health.

ETIOLOGY IN SOCIETY

The definition of disease and illness or health has a social as well as pathological component. The physical condition of an individual must be defined as one of illness before the individual can perceive that he or she is ill (Berliner, 1977). If the group, neighbourhood, or community defines the condition as an illness, then certain steps are necessary to correct the condition. On the other hand, if it is not so defined by the individual's reference group, it would be inappropriate for the individual to assume a sick role and so the individual would not seek treatment (Kane, Kasteler, and Gray, 1976). If we accept this proposition, then the definition of illness for a community will determine the norm of health or state of health considered normal for its members. A Native individual living in a Native community thus interprets his or her own health status as do others in the community. What constitutes illness or sickness will be determined by the definition of the group and the group's reaction to people who exhibit certain symptoms or behaviour. As Kane et al. (1976) argue, the Native definition of reality means living with other Native people who take on and share the same perspective, values, and beliefs. These beliefs and values are passed from one generation to the next.

There is also a middle-class mentality prevalent among professional health-care practitioners. Any patient not sharing these values is at a distinct disadvantage. First, the practitioners do not understand the attitudes and lifestyle of lower-class patients. Health-care professionals, socialized in a middle-class milieu with the modern medical ethic, are ill-prepared to deal with patients whose behaviour does not conform to middle-class values. They assume that Native patients share their perspective on illness and health care, and that they have the same resources (or access to the same resources) as the middle-class patient or the medical professional. In reality, however, Native people are usually poor and materially can manage only the barest of necessities; heat, food, and clothing. Thus their desires are for material improvements, and health is not a high priority; they are not concerned about health in a specific sense. The day-to-day experience of medical practitioners clearly reinforces the notion that Native patients do not follow their orders and heal themselves. As a result, Native people are stereotyped as irresponsible, dirty, and incapable of carrying out orders or taking responsibility for themselves. Negative attitudes are expressed more or less openly, making encounters with health-care providers unpleasant for Native people. Every time they return to the health-care facility, they must suffer through this experience. The alternative strategy, usually chosen, is to avoid the unpleasant situation by not coming back.

Culture creates rules of behaviour for its members, dictating what is expected, encouraged, or allowed. Among various subcultures, there may be different rules. The extent to which a group is institutionally complete, or isolated from other cultural influences, will determine the extent to which the norms will differ from those of the dominant society and the extent to which they are enforced. Cross-cultural influences or memberships will reduce the influence and redefine the situation. Native people, since they retain residence in rural areas, remain an isolated group with a high frequency of contact within the group. All of this has created tight social networks which reinforce their collective definition of reality. Thus, Native people's attitude and behaviour toward illness and their strategy for dealing with it are a response to how their culture (and the community) defines it and to the types of social support or pressure they receive (Knowlton, 1971).

Because of their poverty and cultural ethos, Native people have a very tolerant attitude toward what middle-class culture defines as ill-

ness. However, when it becomes clear that there is little they can do to prevent an illness or to heal it, they learn to define certain conditions as not illness or not requiring the seeking-out of health-care services. In other words, poor people learn to live with certain "illnesses" as long as they are not physically incapacitated. Since all people in the community take this perspective and share these attitudes, all members of the community learn to view certain debilitating physical conditions as normal.

Native people, with both lower-class status and a culture different from the dominant society, do not respond well to professional health-care workers. Native people prefer to deal with others from a more holistic perspective — taking note of all the aspects of the person with whom they are interacting. In the health-care system of the dominant society, there is an elaborate division of labour: nurses are only interested in one aspect of the patient, the X-ray technician in another, the orthopedic surgeon still another. Native people find this a foreign experience, both confusing and frustrating (Suchman, 1963). They also perceive the rational, objective, and unemotional manner of health-care professionals, inculcated at medical school, as the mark not of a good professional but rather of a cold, heartless person, unsympathetic to the patient (Knowlton, 1971).

In addition, Native patients tend to resent and resist professional health-care workers' extracting private and personal information from them, which in addition, sometimes seems irrelevant to them. They do not want health-care workers to have access to private information about them without any reciprocity and without being able to control how this information is used — both in the present context and in the future (Baca, 1969). Native women also find that they prefer to deal with women physicians rather than men, so that, unless they are experiencing an acute illness, they tend not to visit male doctors. One other factor which affects the overall health of Native people is the perception of health-care facilities. Because a pattern of health service provided to them has been well established over the years, Native people have learned to gauge their state of health very differently from non-Natives. Until very recently, medical services were provided to Native people by the federal government on a nine-to-five, five-days-a-week basis. There were no home visits and no referrals, nor were any preventive services carried out. If a Native person got sick at night or on a weekend, he or she would have to define the illness as not serious and wait until morning or Monday. However, if it were in fact life-threatening, he or she would be forced to seek attention from medical personnel at the nearest hospital. For this reason, hospitals, not day clinics or doctors' offices, have become defined as the most appropriate place to seek health care (Ryan, 1987).

Native people do not utilize health-care services partially as a result of their perception of "health" and "illness." They operate from a different mentality than non-Natives. For example, many Indian people do not believe in immunization of their children. They view the injection of a foreign substance into the body as harmful or potentially harmful. The major utilization of health-care services for Native people generally occurs when a person experiences acute pain or finds him or herself in a life-threatening situation. Native people, because of their particular economic and cultural attitudes, adopt a sick role under different conditions than do middle-class, non-Native people. This is particularly true when the sick role is defined as a manifestation of weakness, or when it means that the individual would have to be removed from the community and isolated in health-care facilities far from friends and kin (Dutton, 1986).

CONCLUSION

Successful adaptation of Native people to the dominant society requires the denial or at least repression of traditional models of health care in favour of those of the dominant society. In this process, there is a fundamental inequity and dehumanization (Weidman, 1980). The dominant group has taken the position that its patterns of behaviour and institutions are not only the best, but morally superior. Behaviours that do not match the dominant group norms are viewed as undesirable. As a result, while Native people publicly utilize the dominant society's medical services, it is not uncommon for individuals to seek help simultaneously from the traditional health-care system. While Native people use the dominant health-care systems, they continue to regard their own understanding of the natural world as antecedent and superior knowledge (Press, 1978). Unfortunately, modern orthodox practitioners ignore the existence of a traditional health-care culture in Native communities. They are not trained to be aware of it, nor do they have any ability to evaluate it; they deny its existence, or if they acknowledge it, discount its significance to the medical world or to those people using it (Lam, 1980).

Because middle-class white Canadians have accepted germ theory as a legitimate causal explanation for illness, the Canadian lifestyle is organized in such a way as to minimize the adverse impact of germs; e.g., sanitation, refrigeration. However, those who do not accept this perspective, or are unable to implement the preventive strategies based on such assumptions, cannot avoid certain diseases or illnesses. Native people, because of cultural differences and poverty, find themselves unable to implement the preventive strategies.

The dominant society, and in particular our health-care practitioners, dismiss medicine men or women or shamanism among Native people as meaningless, though there are many prescribed medicines in the modern world that are used which are pharmacologically inert (Sealy and McDonald, no date). Despite this, the dominant medical profession still relies upon these medicines and, what is perhaps more startling, the patients using them get well. This suggests that medicine is not just a function of its pharmacological ingredients but also of suggestion and social support.

We also find health services tend to be concentrated in urban areas, yet most Native people live in rural areas. When health professionals enter the rural areas, the "drop-in" mentality is seldom conducive to delivery of adequate service. Medical specialists have little understanding of Native culture, and language also poses a barrier to communication. When Native people have to travel to distant urban centres to obtain health services, disruptions are even more acute.

Most service and delivery systems are centralized and insensitive to input from local communities, operating on the assumption that Native patients are passive recipients with little or no say in what services are offered, by whom, or where. The bureaucracy of the Medical Services Branch (see Figure 1) shows that policies emanate from Ottawa and are then implemented by regional administrators and on-site health-care workers. There is little in which the bureaucracy can be responsive to local concerns or issues. In addition, professional autonomy in medical issues at the local level inhibits involvement of Native clients. Those services that are offered undermine Native culture by explicitly or implicitly providing incentives for Native people to abandon their heritage and be assimilated into the larger, non-Native society. The dominant society perpetuates this situation despite the obvious fact that one of the most effective ways of improving a people's health lies in individual maintenance. This is more important than having more doctors per capita or improving environmental conditions. An individual's quality of life is highest when he or she functions at a high level, is free from morbidity or impairment, and when his or her vitality and emotional health are high (Lerner, 1973). Rather than denigrating traditional medicine, the dominant society should spend more time learning about Native health care and how to utilize and integrate it with modern health-care practices.

Intergovernmental and interdepartmental divisions of responsibility generate debate and delay when dealing with issues that are health-related but not traditionally defined as such, e.g., mercury pollution, where DIAND and Health and Welfare are jointly responsible (Castellano, 1982). The effectiveness of the entire health-care system is related as much to the environmental conditions of Native communities as to the treatment and facilities provided. Too often, the need for care is engendered by problems associated with overcrowded living conditions leading to contagion and/or infection, by generally poor nutrition associated with chronic unemployment, by family and community violence, and by the re-emergence of medical problems after effective treatment, when the patient returns to the conditions from which the problems arose. Nevertheless, the Medical Services Branch treats the symptoms and little is done to address the basic causes of poor health conditions in areas of housing, economic development, employment opportunities, and sanitation — all of which lie within the mandate of DIAND (Canada, 1985).

STUDY QUESTIONS

1. What are some of the reasons why Native people do not use modern health practices?

2. How has the federal government tried to provide Indians with health-care services?

3. What are the health conditions of Indians compared to non-Indians?

4. How does the dominant health-care system fail Native people?

5. How is modern health care similar to traditional health-care practices used by Native people?

6. Why is it valuable for a health-care professional to have an understanding of traditional Native approaches to health care?

RECOMMENDED READING

Boldt, M., J. Long, and L. LittleBear, eds. *The Quest for Justice*. Toronto: University of Toronto Press, 1985.

Driben, Paul, *We Are Métis*. New York: AMS Press, 1985.

Frideres, J. *Native People in Canada*. Scarborough: Prentice-Hall, 1983.

Li, P., and B. Bolaria, eds. *Racial Minorities in Multicultural Canada*. Toronto: Garamond Press, 1983.

Morse, B., ed. *Aboriginal Peoples and the Law*. Ottawa: Carleton University Press, 1985.

Ponting, J.R., ed. *Arduous Journey: Canadian Indians and Decolonization*. Toronto: McClelland and Stewart, 1986.

REFERENCES

Abella, Rosalie. *Report of The Commission on Equality in Employment*. Ottawa: Government of Canada, October 1984.

Baca, J. "Some Health Beliefs of the Spanish-Speaking." *American Journal of Nursing* 69 (1969): 2172–76.

Berliner, H. "Emerging Ideologies in Medicine." *Review of Radical Political Economics* 9, no. 1 (1977): 189–218.

Birenbaum, A. *Health Care and Society*. Allanheld, New Jersey: Osmund Publishing, 1981.

Bolaria, B. Singh. "Self-Care and Lifestyles: Ideological and Policy Implications." In *Economy, Class and Social Reality*, edited by J.A. Fry. Toronto: Butterworths, 1979.

Brady, P. "The Underdevelopment of the Health Status of Treaty Indians." In *Racial Minorities*, edited by P. Li and B. Bolaria. Toronto: Garamond Press, 1983.

Carstens, P. "Coercion and Change." In *Canadian Society, Pluralism, Change and Conflict*, edited by R. Ossenberg. Scarborough: Prentice-Hall, 1971.

Castellano, M. "Indian Participation in Health Policy Development: Implications for Adult Education." *Canadian Journal Of Native Studies* 2, no. 1 (1982): 113–28.

Department of Indian and Northern Development. *Annual Report 1983–84*. Ottawa: Ministry of Supply and Services, 1984.

Dunning, R. "Ethnic Relations and the Marginal Man in Canada." *Human Organization* 18, no. 3 (1959): 117–22.

Dutton, P. "Financial Organizational and Professional Factors Affecting Health Care Utilization." *Social Science and Medicine* 23, no. 7 (1986): 721–35.

Eyer, J., and P. Sterling. "Stress-Related Mortality and Social Organization." *Review of Radical Political Economics* 9, no. 1 (1977).

Frideres, J. *Native People in Canada*. Scarborough: Prentice-Hall, 1983.

Graham-Cumming, G. "The Influence of Canadian Indians on Canadian Vital Statistics." Ottawa: Medical Services Department of National Health and Welfare, 1966.

Grescoe, P. "A Nation's Disgrace." In *Health and Canadian Society*, edited by D. Coburn, C. D'Arcy, P. New, and G. Torrance. Toronto: Fitzhenry and Whiteside, 1981.

Government of Canada. *Indians and Native Programs, A Study Team Report to the Task Force on Program Review*. Ottawa: Supply and Services, 1985.

Hasting, J., and W. Mosley. "Introduction: The Evolution of Organized Community Health Services in Canada." Royal Commission on Health Services. Ottawa: Supply and Services, 1964.

Heagerty, J. "The Development of Public Health in Canada." *Canadian Journal of Public*

Health 25 (1934): 53–59.

———. *Report of the Advisory Committee on Health Insurance*. Ottawa: March, 1943.

Kane, R., J. Kasteler, and R. Gray. *The Health Gap: Medical Services and the Poor*. New York: Springer Publishing Company, 1976.

Knowlton, C. "Cultural Factors in the Non-Delivery of Medical Services to Southwestern Mexican Americans." In *Health-Related Problems in Arid Lands*, edited by M. Riedesel. Tempe, Arizona: Arizona State University Press, 1971.

LaFramboise, H. "Health Policy: Breaking the Problem Down into More Manageable Segments." In *Perspectives on Canadian Health and Social Services Policy: History and Emerging Trends*, edited by C. Meilicke and J. Storch. Ann Arbor, Michigan: Health Administrative Press, 1980.

Lam, A. "Traditional Chinese Medicine and Western Medical Practice: Personal Observations." In *Doctors, Patients and Society*, edited by M. Staum and D. Larsen, 147–51. Waterloo, Ontario: Wilfrid Laurier University Press, 1980.

Lerner, M. "Conceptualization of Health and Social Well-Being." In *Health Status Indexes*, edited by R.L. Berg. Chicago: Hospital Research and Educational Trust, 1973.

Meilicke, C., and J. Storch. *Perspectives on Canadian Health and Social Services Policy: History and Emerging Trends*. Ann Arbor, Michigan: Health Administration Press, 1980.

Nuttall, Richard. "The Development of Indian Boards of Health in Alberta." *Canadian Journal of Public Health* 73 (1982): 300–03.

Paine, R., ed. *The White Arctic: Anthropological Essays on Tutelage and Ethnicity*. St. John's: Memorial University of Newfoundland, Institute of Social and Economic Research, 1977.

Ponting, J.R., and R. Gibbins. *Out of Irrelevance: A Socio-Political Introduction to Indian Affairs*. Scarborough: Butterworths, 1980.

Press, I. "Urban Folk Medicine: A Functional Overview." *American Anthropologist* 80 (1978): 71–84.

Ryan, J. personal correspondence with author. Department of Anthropology, Calgary, University of Calgary, 1987.

Sealey, B., and N. McDonald. *The Health Care Professional in a Native Community*. Ottawa: Department of National Health and Welfare, no date.

Suchman, E. *Social Patterns of Health and Medical Care*. New York: New York City Department of Health, 1963.

Tanner, A., ed. *The Politics of Indianness*. St. John's: Memorial University of Newfoundland, Institute of Social and Economic Research, 1983.

Turshen, M. "The Political Ecology of Disease." *Review of Radical Political Economies* 10, no. 1 (1977): 250–67.

Weidman, H. "Dominance and Domination in Health Care: A Transcultural Perspective." In *Doctors, Patients, and Society*, edited by M. Staum and D. Larsen, 133–45. Waterloo, Ontario: Wilfrid Laurier University Press, 1980.

Wirick, G. "A Multiple Equation Model of Demand for Health Care." *Health Services Research* (Winter 1966): 301–46.

PART IV

WOMEN, FAMILY, AND HEALTH

INTRODUCTION

Four readings in this section discuss a wide range of issues with respect to women as patients and consumers of health-care services. One common theme runs through these chapters; that is, gender inequality and women's subordinate position in the society dictate the inequality of treatment which women receive in the health sector. There are several manifestations of this, including: medical definition of women's health problems, male definition of women's sexuality and fertility, and the medicalization of social problems. It should be noted that practices within the health sector not only observe but also reinforce gender inequality in the society. Four chapters in this section address women's health issues in a variety of contexts.

Chapter 10 by Trypuc begins with the basic premise that women's position in society has consequences for their health as well as for their experiences as consumers of health care.

The author examines three areas. First, an analysis of sex differences in Canadian mortality and morbidity patterns indicates that in general, women have greatly benefitted from health improvements and disease control. There is a decline in women's mortality and an increase in life expectancy; as a matter of fact, women tend to live longer than men. Women also seem to use the health-care system more than men. The major cause of morbidity differs between the sexes, with men suffering from more chronic conditions and women suffering from more acute conditions.

Second, the author critically examines the various explanations that have been proposed to explain the sex mortality differentials. These include: the "genetic superiority of women" hypothesis, male socialization (wherein males ostensibly are socialized to be more aggressive than females), and the "male lifestyle" hypothesis (which suggests males engage more frequently in life-endangering behaviour).

Third, the author further examines various explanations which shed light on women's morbidity patterns. These include: the negative effects of the social role of women, the hypothesis that women are actually "sicker," the hypothesis that women are *made to believe* they are sicker (due to medicalization of procedures), the notion that women have a greater knowledge and interest in health (and thereby take better care of themselves), and the hypothesis that the concept of the health ethic is masculine (making it, therefore, easier for a woman to be sick).

The chapter concludes by noting that women increasingly are challenging the health-care system and the society that supports this system. As long as women remain a devalued group in society, their health will continue to suffer.

Recent feminist investigations of women's health reveal the ways in which health practices reflect and perpetuate gender inequality. This is clearly illustrated in Chapter 11, *Feminism and Reproduction*, by Scarlet Pollock.

This chapter focusses specifically on male domination of women's sexuality and fertility. This domination is reinforced by other aspects of gender inequality which are expressed in hierarchical relations of privileges and authority. Pollock notes that the control over women's reproductive capacity is critical to the perpetuation of male domination and, conversely, women regaining control over their own sexuality and fertility is a vital factor in achieving women's liberation. This dynamic, according to Pollock, characterizes recent feminist debate on issues of reproduction and reproductive health.

Pollock, based upon her analysis of "medical treatment" of women's reproduction, demonstrates the ways in which health-care structure and practices perpetuate women's subordination.

Feminist principles, on the other hand, promote women's participation and control in health care. They assert the necessity of the widespread availability and accessibility of women-centred services and the accumulation of knowledge based upon women's experiences.

The social analysis of health care from a feminist perspective contrasts sharply with the medical model which dominates the organization of health care in Canada, and challenges the legitimacy of this model. It is noted that the hierarchical structuring of information and services which protects and gives status to the "expert" is revealed to be inversely related to the promotion of health. Existing social inequalities are perpetuated by the discriminatory availability of services. The structuring of health-care relationships in terms of medical heroes and passive patients involves often unnecessary and unsafe intervention in reproductive processes.

The feminist critique of the medical model represents a reassessment of sexual inequality and its perpetuation through health-care organization. It is grounded in the contradiction between the ideology of health-care services and the reality of women's experiences. The alternative being created by feminist groups is the organization of health care on principles of equality. The feminist health-care model offers an understanding of the possibilities of achieving health through social equality.

Chapter 12, by Ahluwalia and MacLean, examines the evolution of domestic violence from a legitimate and private form of violence against women to its current status as a medical illness. Three distinct periods within this evolution are traced, from legitimacy, to the recognition of wife abuse as a social problem which was criminalized, to its medicalization as an individual pathology.

The paper argues that due to the cultural belief that domestic disputes were private affairs, legal intervention served only to underestimate the frequency, blame the victim, and privatize the problem, thus reinforcing the domination of women. Due to the rise of feminist scholarship and the interest in the breakdown of the nuclear family, domestic violence has been "rediscovered" and become an important political issue. The "explosion of activity" surrounding this issue has sensitized the medical intervention.

The essay goes on to argue that due to the lack of diagnostic categories, the medical institution, in facing a crisis for cure, developed the Battered Wife Syndrome. Equipped with the panoply of a biomechanical model of medicine,

traditional sex-role stereotypes of women, and various other diagnostic tools, such as a medical conceptual framework within which privatization, individualization, and redefinition of the problem were facilitated, the medical institution effectively transformed spouse abuse into self-abuse.

The authors conclude that present therapeutics in the area of domestic violence have not only contributed to the problem, but have treated the consequences of the illness as the cause of the illness, and in so doing have mystified the nature of interspousal violence, while reinforcing the relations of domination.

Once a rare disease of mysterious causation, anorexia nervosa is currently reported as widespread. Usually manifested in adolescent girls from professional families, anorexia has a very poor prognosis. Less than half of all cases are completely "cured," and a significant number of treated cases develop a stable, but chronic, condition. In Chapter 13, Currie examines the failure of modern medicine to eradicate this disease. She argues that this failure stems from the tendency of medical approaches to treat the symptoms of this disorder rather than the cause. In order to illustrate this, Currie overviews traditional approaches to anorexia, which include medical models, psychoanalytic explanations, and family systems theory. Common to all of these explanations is a focus upon the individual or the individual's family. In contrast to micro-level analyses, recent approaches have begun to examine the socio-cultural roots of the problem. Within this emergent critical school, feminist authors examine cultural stereotypes of women and our society's obsession with thinness, especially in women. However, although these works have significantly broadened our understanding of anorexia as a "socio-" rather than "psycho-" somatic disorder, Currie notes that they leave unanswered the question of why some women rather than all women exposed to these cultural pressures develop eating disorders. In particular, data indicate that girls from professional, achievement-oriented families are selectively at risk. Building upon socio-cultural approaches, Currie continues by examining a sociological explanation for anorexia which moves beyond cultural images to examine the material position of women in contemporary capitalist society. Within this exploration Currie explains why only radical social, rather than individual, change can eradicate anorexia.

10
WOMEN'S HEALTH

Joann M. Trypuc
Director, Ontario Hospital Association

INTRODUCTION

If illness were viewed only from a medical or biological point of view, questions of power, resources, beliefs, and attitudes would be unimportant. However, the fact that sociology views illness as socially defined, with the medical system incorporating social relationships, makes it necessary to examine health care within a broader social context.

Women's position in society has consequences for their health as well as for their experiences as consumers of health care. Essentially, women wield less economic and political power than men. Women are also more likely to be socially and psychologically dependent and economically disadvantaged. In our society, certain institutions and practices, reinforced by socialization processes, favour men over women in the achievement of power and authority. This sexual inequality has led to concerns by feminists regarding women's health and the care women receive.

One Canadian critic has observed that women get inferior health care mainly because of their upbringing and conditioning. Girls are taught not to question, to be unaggressive, and to defer to men and to authority figures. Most doctors are both. Furthermore, women are faced with conflicting societal expectations, feeling guilty about participating in the paid labour force while trying to fulfill the traditional role expectations of mother and homemaker. Often

stressed and overworked, women have difficulty controlling their lives. Demanding more control within the medical system, which is supposed to provide care, is a struggle (Carver, 1984: 38–45).

There are a large number of important issues surrounding women as patients and consumers of health care. This chapter will begin by presenting Canadian mortality (death) and morbidity (illness) statistics, and will then explore in more detail the issues surrounding the mortality and morbidity experiences of Canadian women.

SEX DIFFERENCES IN MORTALITY AND MORBIDITY

Women have greatly benefitted from health improvements and disease control. Before the turn of the century, females faced higher risks of dying than males. Although this was a time of high overall death rates due to infectious disease (e.g., tuberculosis, influenza), for women repeated pregnancies, lengthy breast-feeding, and prolonged childbearing made them even more susceptible to illness and death (Omran, 1977:30). Better sanitation and medical technology gradually lowered infectious disease rates for both sexes. As well, women's health benefitted from the declining birth rate, and the increase in degenerative diseases (e.g., cancer, heart disease) seemed to affect men at higher rates than women. A noticeable increase in the sex mortality differential appeared. For

Table 1. Major Causes of Death in Canada, 1982

	Women		Men	
	No.	%	No.	%
Diseases of the heart	25 527	33.4	33 856	34.5
Malignant neoplasms (cancer)	18 515	24.2	23 449	23.9
Cerebrovascular diseases (strokes)	8 186	10.7	6 334	6.5
Respiratory diseases	4 664	6.1	7 574	7.7
Accidents (including poisonings and violence)	4 120	5.4	10 045	10.2
Sub-total	61 012	79.9	81 258	82.9
Other causes	15 347	20.1	16 796	17.1
TOTAL	76 359	100.0	98 054	100.0

Source: *Vital Statistics*, Statistics Canada Catalogue 84-206.

example, in 1931, Canadian women's life expectancy was 62.1 years, compared to 60.0 for men. By 1981, the differential increased to seven years, with women expected to live to 79 years of age and men to 71.9 years of age (Life Tables, Statistics Canada Catalogue 84-515; Vital Statistics, Statistics Canada Catalogue 84-206).

Today, the major causes of death for Canadian women are similar to those for men. As Table 1 shows, the two major causes of death are chronic diseases of the circulatory system (e.g., heart disease, strokes) and malignant neoplasms (i.e., cancer). Accidents, which include poisonings and violence, and which are avoidable deaths, are the fifth major killer of Canadian women, and the third major killer of Canadian men.

Unlike mortality, the major causes of morbidity differ between males and females. Table 2 compares the 20 leading causes of hospitalization of women and of men. Hospitalization due to pregnancy, childbirth, and diseases of the reproductive organs account for a large proportion of women's hospitalization rates. In contrast, heart disease, a chronic condition and the major cause of hospitalization for men, is only the seventh major cause for women.

Men are hospitalized for more chronic conditions than females, whereas females suffer

from more acute causes of hospitalized illness. In other words, the diseases of females are less likely to lead to death (Nathanson, 1977; Verbrugge, 1976b).

One of the most notable morbidity differences between the sexes is the fact that females more commonly admit to symptoms of both mental and physical illness than do males (Clancy and Gove, 1974:210; Nathanson, 1975:57; Verbrugge, 1976a:400; Nathanson, 1977:15; D'Arcy and Schmitz, 1979:19). In the 1978–1979 Canada Health Survey, 54.3 percent of females reported at least one health problem, compared to 45.7 percent of men. In addition, women reported more major activity days lost because of illness than did men. Women reported losing 83 188 000 major activity days compared to 30 977 000 reported by men, a ratio of 2.7 to 1 (Health and Welfare Canada and Statistics Canada, Catalogue 82-538E).

Women also use doctors and hospitals more frequently than do men (Rosenstock, 1966:96; Andersen and Anderson, 1967:40-41; Nathanson, 1975:57; Nathanson, 1977:15; Mechanic, 1978:196; Verbrugge, 1979:61). In Canada in 1980–1981, for every day spent in the hospital by a male, females spent 1.3 days. This differential use of hospitals has been shown to persist even with the exclusion of hospitalization for pregnancy (Rosenstock, 1966:96; Andersen and Anderson, 1967:36–37; Nathanson, 1975:58).

WHY DO SEX DIFFERENCES IN DEATH EXIST?

Various explanations have been proposed to shed light on the sex mortality differential.

Genetic Superiority of Women

Genetics have often been used to explain the fact that males have higher mortality rates than females in many different species (Waldron, 1976:3). Although more males are conceived than females (Bentzen, 1963:93; Taylor et al., 1972:216; Williamson, 1978:4; Ortmeyer, 1979:123), the death rate of male fetuses is higher (Fuchs, 1974:47–48; Ortmeyer, 1979: 124–125; Waldron, 1976:3). For example, research has shown that more male than female fetuses are spontaneously aborted (Rasmuson, 1971:43). Similarly, the number of male still-births is higher than that for females (Yerushalmy, 1963:151; Rasmuson, 1971:43), and in the first year of life, the male death rate is higher than the female death rate.

All of the above findings seem to point to a female genetic advantage. It has been suggested that the chromosomal arrangement may be a major factor in this advantage: if a gene on the males' X chromosome is defective, there may be no countering gene on the Y chromosome, whereas a female may have a corresponding gene on the second X chromosome acting as protection (Ortmeyer, 1979:124). This explanation may have some validity. One study showed that out of 187 neonatal abnormalities identified in a study of 15 000 patients, 71.8 percent occurred predominantly among males, 25.1 percent among females, and only 3.1 percent had an equal sex distribution (Singer et al., 1968:109).

Although more than 50 pathological conditions do occur exclusively in males, most of these pathologies are not common, and those that are common are seldom lethal; in fact, deaths due to these causes are less than 2 percent of excess male deaths up to the end of the repro-

ductive years (Waldron and Johnston, 1976:22–23).

Although higher male fetal death rates seem to point to a female genetic advantage, care must be taken not to overemphasize genetics as a major contributor to the longer life expectancy for women. Retherford has noted that the increases in the human sex mortality differential over the past 50 years could not have been due to biological differences, for genetic structures do not change that quickly (1975:12).

Male Socialization

It has been suggested that males are socialized to be more aggressive than females. "Boys and men (more than girls and women), have been encouraged to consume alcohol, drive cars, use guns, be adventurous, act unafraid, be brave, and if need be, take risks" (Ortmeyer, 1979:129). As mentioned above, this type of socialization may have a major effect on death rates as measured by accident and suicide fatalities. As Table 1 indicates, 10.2 percent of all Canadian male deaths in 1982 were a result of accidents, in contrast to 5.4 percent of female deaths.

Gender differences in death rates due to motor vehicle accidents in particular may be explained by the fact that men both drive more and drive less safely than women (Waldron and Johnston, 1976:19). Furthermore, men consume more alcohol than women. For example, in Canada in 1978–79, 75.2 percent of Canadian men were current drinkers compared to 55.7 percent of women. Of these men, 57.9 percent consumed seven or more drinks per week, as compared to 35.2 percent of women who consumed this much (Health and Welfare Canada and Statistics Canada, Catalogue 82–538E). Needless to say, this drinking has deadly consequences. Half of all fatal motor vehicle accidents involve drunken drivers; other accidents, as well as suicides, are also associated with alcohol use (Waldron and Johnston, 1976:20). One can hypothesize that males are victims of a socialization which stresses being aggressive and engaging in risky behaviour. Unfortunately, the deaths which do

Table 2. Twenty Leading Causes of Hospitalization by Number of Separations for Women and Men, Canada, 1982–1983

Women	%	No.
Complications in labour and delivery	6.3%	130 613
Normal delivery	5.5%	115 458
Indication for care in pregnancy, labour, and delivery	4.8%	100 064
Other complications relating to pregnancy	4.2%	87 918
Other diseases of female genital organs	3.2%	66 693
Cholelithiasis	2.0%	41 459
Other forms of heart disease	1.9%	39 115
All other forms of ischaemic heart disease	1.8%	38 055
Contact with health services related to reproduction and development	1.8%	37 670
Chronic diseases of tonsils and adenoids	1.6%	33 913
Disorders of menstruation	1.5%	32 063
Non-infective enteritis and colitis	1.5%	30 828
Pneumonia	1.4%	28 834
Asthma	1.3%	27 418
All other diseases of urinary system	1.2%	26 067
Neurotic and personality disorders	1.2%	25 925
Other arthropathies and related disorders	1.2%	25 673
Other diseases of intestine and peritoneum	1.2%	24 982
Diabetes mellitus	1.1%	23 818
Other late effects of cerebrovascular disease	1.1%	23 277
Sub-total	46.0%	959 843
Other causes	54.0%	1 126 016
TOTAL	100.0%	2 085 859

occur as a result of these actions are violent, and for the most part preventable.

The "Male Lifestyle"

Closely related to socialization is a traditional male lifestyle that more women are beginning to emulate. Table 1 shows that the two major causes of death today in Canada are diseases of the circulatory system (e.g., heart disease, strokes), and neoplasms (i.e., cancers). As mentioned previously, males tend to suffer from these "killer" diseases at higher rates than females. Excessive tobacco use by males, haz-

ardous occupational conditions, and stress have increased death rates due to these lifestyle-related diseases. Increasingly, women's health is being affected by these conditions as well.

"Smoking trends have played an important role in the evolution of the sex mortality differential during this century" (Retherford, 1972:205). This trend has exacerbated the incidence of coronary heart disease, lung cancer, and emphysema (Waldron, 1976:10). Since middle-class women were discouraged from smoking, at least until the twentieth century, women were less vulnerable than men to

Table 2. *continued*

Men	%	No.
All other forms of ischaemic heart disease	4.0%	60 721
Inguinal hernia	3.2%	47 815
Other forms of heart disease	2.9%	44 030
Pneumonia	2.3%	35 190
Acute myocardial infarction	2.2%	33 573
Fractures of the skull and intracranial injury	2.0%	30 756
Hyperplasia of prostate	2.0%	30 700
Asthma	2.0%	29 776
Chronic diseases of tonsils and adenoids	1.9%	29 244
Other arthropathies and related disorders	1.9%	28 912
Acute upper respiratory infections	1.8%	26 503
Non-infective enteritis and colitis	1.7%	26 275
All other diseases of respiratory system	1.7%	26 009
All other diseases of urinary system	1.7%	25 045
Other and late effects of cerebrovascular diseases	1.6%	24 657
Other diseases of intestine and peritoneum	1.4%	20 693
Diabetes mellitus	1.3%	19 033
Intervertebral disc disorders	1.2%	18 439
Other injuries, early complications of trauma	1.2%	18 398
Appendicitis	1.2%	18 242
Sub-total	39.2%	594 011
Other causes	60.8%	920 118
TOTAL	100.0%	1 514 129

Source: *Hospital Morbidity 1981–1982 and 1982–1983*, Statistics Canada, Catalogue 82-206

smoking-related illnesses. This is rapidly changing, however. The average consumption of cigarettes by Canadian males 15 years of age and older in 1931 was 1113 cigarettes, compared to 78 for females of the same age. By 1975, however, these figures had risen to 4311 cigarettes for males and, much more dramatically, to 2592 cigarettes for females (Abelson et al., 1983:30). Between 1970 and 1983, in Canada, male smoking declined 15 percent, while female smoking declined only 4 percent. Furthermore, in 1985, 25 percent of teenage girls smoked daily, compared to 21 percent of teenage boys. The results of this trend towards smoking can be seen in

female disease trends: in the past ten years, Canadian women's lung cancer mortality increased by 45 percent; within the next five, it is estimated to exceed breast cancer as the leading cancer in women (Edwards, 1986:9).

Why are women smoking more? A number of reasons have been suggested: smoking may be viewed as a symbol of emancipation (as stated in one brand's slogan: "You've come a long way, baby"); smoking may also be a way to cope with the increasing stresses which women face in trying to fulfill home and paid work responsibilities.

Along with cigarette smoking, industrial

pollutants have contributed to higher lung cancer rates (Waldron, 1976:10), and to increases in cancer and heart and lung disease in general (Ortmeyer, 1979:130). With greater numbers of women moving into non-traditional occupations, industrial pollutants may begin to have a greater impact on women's death rates. In addition, it has been suggested that the stress associated with women's greater upward mobility in the paid labour force will increase female lifestyle death rates. The findings of a recent study, however, do not support this hypothesis. Although further research is needed, the authors point to the notion that the effects of occupational stress which women undergo may be minimized as long as mobility is seen as a positive development (Sorensen et al., 1985:390). It must be pointed out, however, that women may also experience stress as a result of frustrated ambition due to limited upward mobility.

Suicides have also been regarded as the deadly consequence of a stressful lifestyle. In Canada today, more men than women die by their own hand. For example, in 1982 for every 100 000 Canadian men between 15 and 24 years of age, approximately 27 committed suicide, compared to five Canadian women. For those 25 years of age and over, the rates increased to 29 male suicides and nine female suicides (Statistics Canada, Catalogue 89–503E).

It has been postulated that one cause of the higher suicide rate among men is the stress of competition for jobs (Waldron and Johnston, 1976:20). Women presumably experience less stress in adopting the homemaker role. This assumption may not hold true, however, since females attempt suicide four times more often than males; on the other hand, males are three times more likely to complete the act (Garai, 1970:138; Gove, 1972:205; Furnass, 1977:15; Ortmeyer, 1979:129). A higher male "completed" suicide rate may be a result of methods used (men tend to use immediately fatal methods, such as guns, whereas women tend to use more "reversible" methods, such as poisons and drugs). Furthermore, women may use the suicide attempt as a cry for help rather than as an act to fulfill the need to kill themselves, whereas men, finding it more difficult to "cry for help," carry the suicidal act through to its conclusion (Waldron and Johnston, 1976:20–22).

WHY DO SEX DIFFERENCES IN MORBIDITY EXIST?

Numerous attempts have been made to explain women's illness patterns. There seems to be a contradiction in the fact that women live longer and are, therefore, presumably healthier, yet report more illness and use more medical services than men. Consequently the popular view exists that the high rates of morbidity among women are artifactual (Gove and Hughes, 1979:129), with women using health services and spending health dollars needlessly. Several reasons have been proposed to explain women's illness behaviour. A number of these are explored below.

The Social Role of Women

It is part of a woman's role as a parent to take children to the doctor; women become accustomed to being there, are more familiar with the doctor, and possibly become more dependent on him or her (D'Arcy, 1977:216; Simkin, 1978:11). Thus, the finding that women are more likely than men to seek medical help even for minor illnesses may be due to this acquired dependency on the doctor, as well as to the opportunity that their role as the primary caregiving parent creates.

Related to this analysis is the fairly widely held assumption that the social role of women entails fewer time constraints than that of men. This presumably allows women to seek medical attention and to restrict activity more readily than males (Mechanic, 1965:256; Verbrugge, 1976b:292; Verbrugge, 1979:66). Although it may be easier for women who do not work fixed hours to schedule medical appointments, the premise that women have fewer obligations and therefore more free time to be sick is unfounded. In fact, on the average, women work longer hours than men. Married women working for pay also fulfill their domestic responsibilities; as Luxton (1980:11) has noted, women take "on a double day of work, labouring as both wage workers and domestic workers."

As domestic workers, women take on the major role of being health-care workers in the home. In her study of 240 British women, Roberts (1985) points out that women are not only consumers but are also producers of health care. As producers, women take the major responsibility for keeping other people healthy, yet there seems to be little recognition that fulfilling this duty might actually make women sick. The study notes that overworked, stressed women were encouraged to quit work and stay at home to "rest," even though other findings suggest that women's unpaid work is more stressful than their paid labour. Therefore, the prescription for these women to stay home actually had the potential to make them sick.

Women Are Sicker

In view of the social role of women discussed above, women may actually be sicker, displaying more symptoms of illness as a result of pressures associated with their role demands. Gove and Hughes (1979:127,134) found that the apparent higher rates of morbidity among women were based almost exclusively on higher rates of mild transitory disorders, such as colds, headaches, and dysmenorrhea. These illnesses, it is postulated, are physical disorders which are a reaction to psychological distress. Assuming the female's role entails an obligation to care for others which may interfere with her ability to care for herself, and because she has more role obligations which require ongoing activity (i.e., with children, spouse, and others), Gove and Hughes (1979:132,144) hypothesize that a woman's self-care will be interrupted, leading to a negative effect on her health. After control of the data for marital status, living arrangements, psychiatric symptoms, and nurturant role obligations, health differences between women and men disappeared. The authors conclude that sex differences in physical health are due to sex differences in nurturant role demands and mental

health. Furthermore, these differences reflect real rather than artifactual differences in physical health (Gove and Hughes, 1979:126, 141–143).

Women may also experience more sickness due to their reproductive functions. Verbrugge (1985:164) notes that reproduction gives women unique morbidity risks not experienced by men. Furthermore, women's reproductive systems are more complex than men's, which increases the risk of female-specific disorders.

It has been suggested that women's morbidity rates are higher because the symptoms of some of women's illnesses are more easily detectable (Mechanic, 1978:187). For example, Omran (1977:32) notes that certain female cancers (e.g., of the cervix, uterus, and breast) produce more noticeable symptoms than certain male cancers (e.g., of the colon, lung, and prostate), where the organ is concealed and not routinely examined and produces symptoms only in the advanced stages of malignancy. Women, noticing these overt symptoms, are able to respond much more quickly than if the symptoms were not easily detectable.

Women Are Made to Believe They Are Sicker

The nature of Canadian health-care delivery may actually make women believe that they are sicker than is actually the case. We live in a society where high rates of hospital use have been said to reflect partly social custom rather than necessary medical procedure (Allentuck, 1978:8). For example, unnecessary drug prescription, procedures, and surgery do occur. Unfortunately, these actions carry the implicit message that the recipient is sick and in need of treatment.

Canadian women take more prescription and non-prescription drugs than do men. The Canada Health Survey found that 55 percent of Canadian females use drugs of all types, compared to 41 percent of males. The rate of tranquillizer use by females is more than double the rate of use by males (Abelson et al., 1983:40–42). Another study found that physicians were more likely to offer tranquillizers to women than to men presenting the same complaints (Cooperstock, 1979:33). And in a third study, when Ontario general practitioners were questioned about the higher mood-modifying prescription rate for women, doctors' replies ranged from biological vulnerability, to differential life stress, to self-indulgence, to male reluctance to seek help (Cooperstock, 1971:239–40).

Drug advertising, especially in medical journals, presents a negative view of women. Some of the themes of these ads include the notions that women cannot cope, that women are "dumb," that women can be a real nuisance to others, and that a woman's biology is her destiny (Rochon Ford, 1986:14–17). Besides this, the overall message comes through that many of life's ills can be remedied with a drug (Chesher, 1977:35). Thus, rather than trying to change the stressful circumstances of one's life, a person will use drugs to enable toleration of this life.

Taking drugs can actually make one feel physically, emotionally, and psychologically sicker. Many drugs are toxic with "physical side effects, interaction effects with other substances, as well as effects on the emotion and behaviour of individuals" (Owen, 1977:45). Furthermore, although many drugs are on the market, "in only a few cases can it be said that we know how the drug is working . . . in some cases it is still uncertain if the drug therapy is any more effective than placebo" (Chesher, 1977:34).

In addition to drug use, women can be made to feel sicker through unnecessary operations and the overmedicalization of particular functions. For example, uncomplicated delivery of a baby is not a sickness so much as a normal part of life. It can be argued that low-risk, normal pregnancies do not require extensive medical backup. In fact, one consequence of such backup is that it can further medicalize childbirth. For example, the Caesarian rate as a percentage of live births has been gradually rising in Canada. In 1970, 6 percent of live births were by Caesarian. By 1980, this figure had risen to 14.9 percent.

Another example of a female experience which is unnecessarily medicalized is abortion.

The rate of therapeutic abortions, which can only be performed legally in accredited Canadian hospitals, has risen from 8.5 per 100 live births in 1971 to 17.8 per 100 live births in 1982 (Statistics Canada, Catalogue 89-503E). It can be argued that an expensive, technological hospital setting is not necessary for performing abortions safely within the first 16 weeks of pregnancy.

A close examination of Table 2 shows that childbirth and sex-specific ailments are important factors in female hospitalization rates. It seems reproduction and related functions consistently introduce a bias into women's use of health services. It can be argued that women consume disproportionately more health resources and facilities largely as a result of needs associated with their reproductive systems. In fact, they have been socialized to depend on the system for these particular functions, with the view that these functions constitute illness.

Women Have a Greater Knowledge of and Interest in Health

Women may be more aware of disease and health issues because they have a greater knowledge of and interest in health (Mechanic, 1978:187). Since women tend to be responsible for their families' health, they, as domestic health-care workers, may have a better understanding of medical problems than do men. In one study, female patients were more likely to ask questions after a physician's explanation than were male patients; those questions were also more likely to elicit informative answers (Wallen et al., 1979:139). Another study found that twice as many men as women ignore newspaper and magazine health columns, as well as health programmes on radio and television. Furthermore, women proved to be better informed about the symptoms of cancer, polio, and diabetes, leading the authors to conclude that the broad area of health and illness is more of a feminine concern (Feldman, 1966:112–13; also Lewis and Lewis, 1977:866).

The Concept of the Health Ethic is Masculine

In contrast to the notion that health and illness are feminine concerns is the notion that healthiness is part of masculinity. It has been suggested that perhaps defining oneself as ill is more appropriate to the social role of the woman than to that of the man (Phillips, 1964:687; Phillips and Segal, 1969:59, 69; Wilson, 1970:77; Verbrugge, 1976a:398; Gove and Hughes, 1979:126; Verbrugge, 1979:63,66). Because of socialization patterns, women are allowed to complain more readily and to appear less stoic (Cooperstock, 1971:241; Mechanic, 1978:197), whereas males "suffer in silence." Thus, supposedly, women more readily admit symptoms and distress (Mechanic, 1976:30). They report more illness because it is culturally more acceptable for them to be ill; the norm of health is masculine (Nathanson, 1977:25), with men feeling more inhibited about reporting certain symptoms (Mechanic, 1976:33).

In studies which have examined reporting of symptoms, methodological problems confound the issue somewhat. Women may be more responsive in interviews, more likely to perceive symptoms, and more likely to report them (Verbrugge, 1976b:295). Similarly, proxy reporting tends to underestimate the illness of the absent person (Verbrugge, 1976a:398; Nathanson, 1977:20). Women are more likely to respond to illness surveys, and thus they may underestimate the illness experience of both their spouses and their children (Mechanic, 1976:33; Verbrugge, 1979:65). It seems sex-based differences in illness either disappear or become smaller when objective measures of illness are used, when symptoms are more "tangible and visible," or when a large degree "of incapacity or impairment is evident" (Mechanic, 1978:188). It has further been suggested that if women are regarded as more willing to express distress, then the definition of distress should include characteristically male behavioural dimensions of distress as well, such as expressions of anger, violence, and drinking (Mechanic, 1976:33).

This would serve to provide a more accurate measure of impairment, as defined by the existence of distress.

An argument could be made that the concept of the health ethic as masculine originates from the structure of our system rather than from the socialization process itself. There are greater economic costs associated with males being sick as compared to females not in the labour force or in very low-level positions. Thus, the emphasis on remaining healthy is directed toward the more economically productive group. By viewing health as congruent with the male social role and using this argument to explain differences in health-care use, blame is misplaced. Rather than blaming the system, we end up blaming the socialization of the individual. The appropriateness of illness to the social role of women, structurally speaking, points to the essentially devalued position of women in society.

CONCLUSION

Challenging the health-care system and the society that supports it is a difficult task. But for women as a group, the challenge is important, since their health and well-being depend on the outcome.

Women are increasingly analyzing both the physical and mental health-care systems from a feminist perspective. For example, many drugs, once taken without question, are being viewed as a way to individualize and make women's structural role strains "manageable." One study quotes a woman as saying,

> In the early years when I was so obviously unhappy with what was happening in my life the solution to the doctors was so obviously a drug solution. And I had to push everybody I knew, including the doctors, except my psychiatrist who supported me all the way, that the solution for me was going to be really to quite radically change my life and not to make me comfortable with the life I was in. (Cooperstock and Lennard, 1981:155)

This woman highlights some familiar themes: the medical model with the medical cure for any problem; the professionals whose "expert advice" should be followed unquestioningly; and the struggle of the patient to participate in determining his or her own treatment. Beyond these themes, however, is the added dimension of the patient as female. Since women have less value and less power as a group in our society, they run a greater risk of being taken less seriously.

It has been difficult for women to have their mortality and morbidity experiences legitimized. The fact that Canadian women outlive men, yet use more health services, has been used to suggest that perhaps women are feigning illness. They are not really sick. They are pretending. This view can adversely affect the quality of health-care a woman receives. One instance of such a consequence was a study of 498 female rheumatoid arthritis patients. All of them presented symptoms to their physicians, yet 87 percent went 12 years or longer without a diagnosis, with most of them being told they were neurotic (Simkin, 1978:12).

It cannot be denied that health-care advances have greatly benefitted women. However, there is a need for improvement, especially in the areas of consumer/patients' rights and regaining control over one's body. Inherent in the women's health movement, which emerged in the early 1970s, is this emphasis on knowledge and self-determination (McDonnell, 1985:18–21). Self-help groups, the natural childbirth movement, the fight to legalize midwifery, and viewing health beyond the constraints of the medical model are some of the issues that have either been initiated by or incorporated into the women's health movement.

Fighting for better health care and having their illness experiences legitimized are part of the larger issue which women face. This issue is women's struggle for equality. As long as women are not allowed equal participation in public life and in the financially empowered sector of the economy, they will continue to be devalued as a group, and their health will continue to suffer.

STUDY QUESTIONS

1. Based on the information from this chapter, what are your predictions for the mortality and morbidity profiles of men and women in the year 2010? Support your answer.

2. Using medical journals (e.g., Canadian Medical Association Journal), examine how women are depicted in drug advertisements. What themes do you note? Compared to ten years ago, have these depictions changed?

3. This chapter examines women as consumers of health care. Investigate the position women hold as health-care workers in the hospitals and in the professions.

4. Give evidence to support the argument that women's health care will not improve until women's position in society improves.

RECOMMENDED READING

Barrington, Eleanor. *Midwifery is Catching.* Toronto: NC Press, 1985.

Boston Women's Health Book Collective. *The New Our Bodies, Ourselves.* New York: Simon and Schuster, 1984.

Carver, Cynthia, M.D. *Patient Beware: Dealing with Doctors and Other Medical Dilemmas.* Scarborough: Prentice-Hall, 1984.

Dreifus, Claudia, ed. *Seizing Our Bodies: The Politics of Women's Health.* New York: Random House, 1978.

Ehrenreich, Barbara, and Deirdre English. *For*

Her Own Good: 150 Years of the Experts' Advice to Women. Garden City: Anchor Press/Doubleday, 1979.

Healthsharing: A Canadian Women's Health Quarterly. Published quarterly by Women Healthsharing Inc., 101 Niagara St., No. 200A, Toronto, Ontario. M5V 1C3.

McDonnell, Kathleen, and Mariana Valverde, eds. *The Healthsharing Book: Resources for*

Canadian Women. Toronto: Women's Press, 1985.

Penfold, P. Susan, and Gillian A. Walker. *Women and the Psychiatric Paradox.* Montreal: Eden Press, 1983.

Ruzek, Sheryl Burt. *The Women's Health Movement: Feminist Alternatives to Medical Control.* New York: Praeger, 1979.

REFERENCES

Abelson, Janet, Peter Paddon, and Claude Strohmenger. *Perspectives on Health.* Statistics Canada, Catalogue 82-540E. Ottawa: Minister of Supply and Services, 1983.

Allentuck, Andrew. *Who Speaks for the Patient?* Don Mills: Burns and MacEachern, 1978.

Andersen, Ronald, and Odin W. Anderson. *A Decade of Health Services.* Chicago: University of Chicago Press, 1967.

Bentzen, Frances. "Sex Ratios in Learning and Behaviour Disorders." *American Journal of Orthopsychiatry* 33 (January 1963): 92–98.

Bermosk, Loretta S., and Sarah E. Porter. *Women's Health and Human Wholeness.* New York: Appleton-Century-Crofts, 1979.

Carver, Cynthia. *Patient Beware: Dealing With Doctors and Other Medical Dilemmas.* Scarborough: Prentice-Hall, 1984.

Chesher, Greg. "The Psychotropic Drugs; Part I: Pharmacological Aspects." In *The Magic Bullet,* edited by Mark Diesendorf, 33–43. Canberra: Society for Social Responsibility in Science, 1977.

Clancy, Kevin, and Walter Gove. "Sex Differences in Mental Illness: An Analysis of Response Bias in Self-Reports." *American Journal of Sociology* 80, no. 1 (1974): 205–16.

Cooperstock, R. "Sex Differences in the Use of Mood-Modifying Drugs: An Explanatory Model." *Journal of Health and Social Behavior* 12 (September 1971): 238–44.

———. "A Review of Women's Psychotropic

Drug Use." *Canadian Journal of Psychiatry* 24 (February 1979): 29–34.

Cooperstock, Ruth, and Henry L. Lennard. "Role Strains and Tranquilizer Use." In *Health and Canadian Society: Sociological Perspectives,* edited by David Coburn et al., 142–57. Toronto: Fitzhenry and Whiteside, 1981.

D'Arcy, Carl. "Patterns of Delivery of Psychiatric Care in Saskatchewan 1971–1972: Part III: Patient Socio-Demographic and Medical Characteristics." *Canadian Psychiatric Association Journal* 22 (August 1977): 215–22.

D'Arcy, Carl, and Janet A. Schmitz. "Sex Differences in the Utilization of Health Services for Psychiatric Problems in Saskatchewan." *Canadian Journal of Psychiatry* 24 (February 1979): 19–27.

Edwards, Peggy. "Cigarettes: A Feminist Issue." *Healthsharing* 7:3 (Summer 1986): 8–12.

Feldman, Jacob J. *The Dissemination of Health Information.* Chicago: Aldine Publishing Co., 1966.

Fuchs, Victor R. *Who Shall Live?* New York: Basic Books, Inc., 1974.

Furnass, Bryan. "Changing Patterns of Health and Disease." In *The Magic Bullet,* edited by Mark Diesendorf, 5–32. Canberra: Society for Social Responsibility in Science, 1977.

Garai, J.E. "Sex Differences in Mental Health." *Genetic Psychology Monographs* 81 (Jan/June 1970): 123–42.

Gove, Walter R. "Sex, Marital Status and Suicide." *Journal of Health and Social Behavior* 13 (June 1972): 204–13.

Gove, Walter R., and Michael Hughes. "Possible Causes of the Apparent Sex Differences in Physical Health." *American Sociological Review* 44 (February 1979): 126–46.

Health and Welfare Canada and Statistics Canada. *The Health of Canadians: Report of the Canada Health Survey*, Catalogue 82-538E, 1981.

Lewis, Charles E., and M.A. Lewis. "The Potential Impact of Sexual Equality on Health." *New England Journal of Medicine* 297 (October 1977): 863–69.

Luxton, Meg. *More Than A Labour of Love*. Toronto: Women's Press, 1980.

McDonnell, Kathleen. "The Women's Health Movement." In *The Healthsharing Book: Resources for Canadian Women*, edited by Kathleen McDonnell and Mariana Valverde, 18–21. Toronto: Women's Press, 1985.

Mechanic, David. "Perception of Parental Responses to Illness: A Research Note." *Journal of Health and Human Behavior* 6 (Winter 1965): 253–57.

———. "Sex, Illness, Illness Behaviour and the Use of Health Services." *Journal of Human Stress* 2 (December 1976): 29–40.

———. *Medical Sociology*. New York: Free Press, 1978.

Nathanson, Constance A. "Illness and the Feminine Role: A Theoretical Review." *Social Science and Medicine* 9 (February 1975): 57–62.

———. "Sex, Illness and Medical Care — A Review of Data, Theory and Method." *Social Science and Medicine* 11 (January 1977): 13–25.

Omran, Abdel R. "Epidemiologic Transition in the U.S.: The Health Factor in Population Change." *Population Bulletin* 32, no. 2. Population Reference Bureau, Inc., Washington, D.C., 1977.

Ortmeyer, Linda E. "Female's Natural Advantage, Or the Unhealthy Environment of Males? The Status of Sex Mortality Differen-

tials." *Women and Health* 4 (Summer 1979): 121–33.

Owen, Alan. "The Psychotropic Drugs; Part II: Psychosocial Aspects." In *The Magic Bullet*, edited by Mark Diesendorf, 44–48. Canberra: Society for Social Responsibility in Science, 1977.

Phillips, Derek L. "Rejection of the Mentally Ill: The Influence of Behaviour and Sex." *American Sociological Review* 29 (October 1964): 679–87.

Phillips, Derek L., and Bernard E. Segal. "Sexual Status and Psychiatric Symptoms." *American Sociological Review* 34 (February 1969): 58–72.

Rasmuson, Marianne. "Men, the Weaker Sex?" *Impact of Science on Society* 21 (January/March 1971): 43–54.

Retherford, Robert D. "Tobacco Smoking and the Sex Mortality Differential." *Demography* 9 (May 1972): 203–16.

———. *The Changing Sex Differential in Mortality*. Westport: Greenwood Press, 1975.

Roberts, Helen., *The Patient Patients: Women and Their Doctors*. London: Pandora Press, 1985.

Rochon Ford, Anne. "In Poor Health." *Healthsharing* 7, no. 2 (Winter 1986): 13–17.

Rosenstock, Irwin M. *Why People Use Health Services*. Reprinted from the *Milbank Memorial Fund Quarterly* 44, no. 3, part 2 (July 1966).

Simkin, Ruth J. *The Inadequacy of Health Care of Women*. Unpublished paper (June 1978):1–16.

Singer, Judith E., Milton Westphal, and Kenneth R. Niswander. "Sex Differences in the Incidence of Neonatal Abnormalities and Abnormal Performance in Early Childhood." *Child Development* 39 (June 1968): 103–12.

Sorensen, Gloria, et al. "Sex Differences in the Relationship Between Work and Health: The Minnesota Heart Survey." *Journal of Health and Social Behavior* 26 (December 1985): 379–94.

Statistics Canada. *Life Tables for Canada and Regions, 1941 and 1931*, Catalogue 84-515, 1947.

———. *Women in Canada: A Statistical Report*, Catalogue 89-503E, 1985.

———. *Hospital Morbidity*, Catalogue 82-206, 1986.

———. *Vital Statistics*, Catalogue 84-206, 1986.

Taylor, David C., and Christopher Ounsted. "The Nature of Gender Differences Explored Through Ontogenetic Analyses of Sex Ratios in Disease." In *Gender Differences: Their Ontogeny and Significance*, edited by Christopher Ounsted and David C. Taylor, 215–40. London: Churchill Livingstone, 1972.

Verbrugge, Lois M. "Females and Illness: Recent Trends in Sex Differences in the United States." *Journal of Health and Social Behavior* 17 (December 1976a): 387–403.

———. "Sex Differentials in Morbidity and Mortality in the United States." *Social Biology* 23 (Winter 1976b): 275–96.

———. "Female Illness Rates and Illness Behaviour: Testing Hypotheses About Sex Differences in Health." *Women and Health* 4 (Spring 1979): 61–79.

———. "Gender and Health: An Update on Hypotheses and Evidence." *Journal of Health and Social Behavior* 26 (September 1985): 156–82.

Waldron, Ingrid. "Why Do Women Live Longer Than Men? Part I." *Journal of Human Stress* 2 (March 1976): 2–13.

Waldron, Ingrid, and Susan Johnston. "Why Do Women Live Longer Than Men? Part II." *Journal of Human Stress* 2 (June 1976): 19–30.

Wallen, Jacqueline, Howard Waitzkin, and John D. Stoeckle. "Physician Stereotypes About Female Health and Illness: A Study of Patient's Sex and the Informative Process During Medical Interviews." *Women and Health* 4 (Summer 1979): 135–46.

Williamson, Nancy E. "Boys or Girls? Parents' Preferences and Sex Control." *Population Bulletin* 33, no. 1 (1978).

Wilson, Robert N. *The Sociology of Health: An Introduction*. New York: Random House, 1970.

Yerushalmy, Jacob. "Factors in Human Longevity." *American Journal of Public Health* 53, no. 2 (1963): 148–62.

11

FEMINISM AND REPRODUCTION

Scarlet Pollock
Dalhousie University

The significance of a feminist approach to reproduction lies in its understanding that social
inequality characterizes the relationship between
women and men in most societies today. Feminism asserts that the personal is political; that is,
individuals' experiences in the world (however
private and personal they may feel) belong to a
set of social relations highly structured by political conflicts. These provide the context of
norms, expectations, economic relations, legal
sanctions, and possible alternatives within which
individuals act and understand their relationships with other people. Sexual or gender
inequality is only one form of inequality in society, but it is a fundamental one, upon which our
economic, political, legal, religious, and familial
institutions are based.

SEXUAL INEQUALITY

To speak of social inequality between the sexes
expresses a hierarchical relation of privilege and
authority which discriminates in favour of men.
Individuals are treated as members of the group
of men or women, irrespective of their intentions
or expressed wishes. As members of each group,
people have privileges granted or withheld, and
are subjected to organized sets of rules and sanctions which influence their opportunities and

experiences.

Sexual inequality takes many forms. These
include:

1. men's privileged access to economic and
   political resources;

2. a rigid sexual division of labour which
   excludes women from certain jobs and tasks
   reserved for men, and compels women
   towards serving others;

3. the devaluation of women and the things that
   women do in favour of an inflated valuation
   of maleness and masculinity;

4. an ideology of women's subordination to
   men where women are depicted as being, and
   are instructed to be or to act, subservient to
   men;

5. prioritizing men and boys — giving central
   importance to male wants, needs, problems,
   and experiences, while trivializing the consequences for the lives of women and girls;

6. men's rights of access to and control over
   women's bodies for sexual and reproductive
   purposes;

7. the use of violence against women as a male
   prerogative.

It is the combination of these factors which make women's lives a great deal more difficult than men's. Marilyn Frye (1983) explains this relationship in terms of the bars which make up a cage. A single bar would not appear to be an insurmountable obstacle, but the structure which connects many bars to form a cage significantly limits the mobility of those confined within it. It is necessary to be aware of the structure as a whole to appreciate the relationship between the groups who exist on either side of this set of barriers. The concept of oppression expresses the position of those people whose lives are confined by such a structure; it is the experience of having one's alternatives continually shaped and reduced by systematic discrimination. Those outside these barriers may also suffer from some of the rules of the system, but they benefit from the restricted movement allowed to those within the cage. Thus it would not make sense to speak of men, who have most to gain from the cage around women's lives, as being oppressed by it, however they may suffer by restricted roles or the "responsibilities" of privilege.

This chapter will focus specifically upon male domination of women's sexuality and fertility, remembering that the full effect would be far less significant if it were not supported by the other aspects of sexual inequality described above. Control over women's reproductive capacity and the care of children is critical to the perpetuation of male domination. Conversely, feminists assert that women's regaining control over their own sexuality and fertility is a vital factor in achieving liberation. This dynamic characterizes recent feminist debate on issues of reproduction and reproductive health.

REPRODUCTION AND HEALTH

The question of health, reproductive health in particular, is interesting in assessing social inequality. This is because it may appear to be a primarily biological phenomenon, with secondary social consequences. Health and illness are often perceived to be physiological experiences which promote or restrict our ability to work and relate to others in our society. Yet biological and social phenomena are more closely intertwined than this view would suggest. Social relationships inform our perception of biology and give it social value. Biological reactions are defined, interpreted, and treated in the context of our social and political structures.

Questions of inequality raise vital issues with regard to the social constructions of health and illness, and what is deemed knowledge in these matters. In reproductive health care it is important to ask, for example: Who defines whether pregnancy is a healthy state or a sickness? What is a "normal" birth? Which contraceptive symptoms are legitimated as interfering with a woman's health, and which are considered "side effects" to be tolerated? Is a woman giving birth or seeking an abortion or consulting for contraception or undergoing a sterilization procedure, considered to be of sound mind and body? If she is regarded as healthy, which procedures are likely to be made available to her? If she is defined as ill, what decision-making power is she granted? When is a healthy woman treated as if she is ill and in need of medical intervention? What types of treatment will be made available to her, and what alternatives does she have?

These kinds of questions surround all health care. They are particularly significant when the "patient" is said to be both healthy and ill at the same time. With reproductive health care, they are pivotal. To what extent are forms of medical intervention necessary, and who should decide if and when particular procedures will be carried out?

Reproductive health and health care are embedded in social dimensions far more than is often recognized. The reproductive physiology of men and women is biologically different, but what we make of this difference is social. Our experience of reproduction is inseparable from our social constructions of sexuality, reproduction, and health. Whatever social inequalities exist in our society will be reflected and affirmed in these areas.

Fundamental to reproductive health is the social issue of who controls reproduction: Who reproduces? How? Where? When? And under what circumstances? From a feminist point of view, it is essential to identify and analyze the values and practices which promote sexual inequality and disallow women's control over their sexuality and reproduction. Health care is assessed in terms of its consequences for women, its ideology of sexual relations, and its potential for change. From sexual activities to family structures, from health care to child-care facilities, the question of who controls reproduction is very serious.

FEMINIST PRINCIPLES OF HEALTH CARE

Beginning from the awareness of sexual inequality as a social formation, and the physiological differences between women and men, feminist arguments tend to rest upon the following principles:

1. Women should have control over their bodies, particularly over their sexuality and reproduction.

2. Women should be the ultimate decision-makers regarding their reproductive capacities because it is primarily their lives which will be affected by pregnancy, birth, and childrearing.

3. The knowledge which is accumulated in reference to health care for women must be centred in women's experience, on terms which take women seriously and which redefine women in contrast to the traditional sexist valuation of women.

4. Information should be made as widely available as possible to give women the necessary background to make decisions about their bodies, the available alternatives, and their possible consequences.

5. Health-care facilities for women should be woman-centred; they must address the experience and needs of women as defined by women.

6. These principles should apply equally to *all* women. This means taking into consideration how different groups of women may be discriminated against on the basis of age, race, marital status, economic class, religion, nationality, or disability.

This is an overview of a feminist perspective on health care. It brings together understanding in the area of sexuality, reproduction, health-care services and policies, health knowledge, and the differences which exist amongst women living in various situations. Let us look in more detail at each of these principles, and to their relevance to sexuality and reproduction in the lives of women in Canada.

1. Women should have control over their bodies. Sexuality and reproduction are central areas in which women's bodies may be used — and abused — by others. Because it is primarily their bodies which will be affected by pregnancy and birth, women must have control over sexual activity, fertility decision-making, and health-care organization.

(a) Sexuality Far from being simply a biological "doing what comes naturally," sex is a highly structured ritual governed by social rules and sanctions. In relations of sexuality we encounter double standards of sexual morality. Sexual activities are geared primarily towards what stimulates men. Sexual behaviour is centred upon what men find attractive about women, which itself is constructed around the sexual appeal of feminine dependence upon men.

It is possible for individuals to challenge these rules. But institutional support for male dominance in heterosexuality and family life makes it difficult for women who do not conform. While social norms maintain that sex is or should be fun for all, they also assume that women should enjoy what men enjoy about sex. The onus to challenge male-dominant concepts of "normal" sexual activities thus rests upon the woman. This places her in a defensive position, where she risks being perceived by her male partner as "rejecting" and/or "abnormal." Either possibility protects male-dominant definitions of what sex is and what sexual activities should take place, while focussing upon the woman as the problem. The evidence of women's experience is redirected from the conclusion that there is something wrong with what sex is defined to be, and turns into the question: what is wrong with the women who do not find these heterosexual activities satisfying?

Despite the difficulties encountered, many women do confront stereotypical attitudes and insist that their sexual relationships be conducted on a more equal footing. Clearly, where individuals are willing, some change is possible. The question of whether individual sexual relationships can become equal, however, must take into account the institutional supports which accrue privileges to men and deny them to women. This includes the overwhelming protection of male-dominant forms of sexuality, from the promotion of pornographic imagery to economic discrimination against women. As long as it remains men's prerogative to "enjoy" or "give up" their privileges, relationships remain based upon inequality. Equality in sexuality can only exist when mutual consideration, as equal privilege, is incorporated into the organization of our social, economic, and legal institutions — not when it is dependent upon granting or withholding by one of the parties involved.

(b) Reproduction Men and women do not have an equivalent participation in the reproductive process. While this difference should not be taken to imply that relations of dominance/subordination are in any way obvious or natural, it is a physiological factor which must be taken into account in our social analysis.

For example, a woman may wish to share responsibility for contraception with her partner as an obvious basis for equality between two people involved in a heterosexual relationship. Yet the consequences will be very different for each. Should a pregnancy occur, it is the woman alone whose body is affected, who will be confronted with the need to seek out health-care services, whether she carries the pregnancy to term or seeks an abortion. She alone cannot walk away from the situation, and it is her life which will be most affected by child-care responsibilities. Social and biological differences are addressed, and at the same time affirmed, by the higher reliability of female-oriented contraceptives. The reluctance of men to use contraceptives which interfere with their sexual enjoyment leaves women in the position of seeking out those contraceptives which offer high reliability and control, despite the health risks involved.

The ways in which a woman's body is treated by others plays a significant part in her self-esteem and her perception of herself as a healthy and independent being. It is critical that a woman be able to control how her body is used by others, especially in sexual and reproductive matters. The ability of others to invade a woman's body is a violation of her independence as a person and as a woman. It is a coercive affirmation of her subordinate position in society and it is extremely detrimental to both physical and mental health.

Sterilization without consent is one of many examples of such abuse of women's bodies. It is a practice most commonly used against women and girls considered to be unfit to have children or whose menstrual periods are thought to be a burden upon others. These judgements are made by the medical and legal establishments and they are imposed upon those women and girls selected. Alison Sawyer (1981) offers evidence to suggest that Inuit and Native women in Canada and in the United States have frequently been sterilized without proper consent. Kathleen Ruff (1986) examines recent Canadian cases where females who have been labelled mentally retarded have been subjected to sterilization without their consent. She argues that this abuse is carried out without reliable (i.e., impartial) evidence that it is in these individuals' best interests, and without legal protection for them. Sawyer indicates that the justifications used for sterilization of mentally handicapped women include sparing them "from the 'traumas' of mothering ... [and] ... avoiding the strain the potential children of such 'unfit' mothers would put on community social services" (1981:93).

Gisela Bock (1984) analyzes a similar approach to those considered unfit to reproduce, in Nazi Germany. The eugenic philosophy of selective breeding to "improve" the human race occurs in conditions of social inequality. In this context, as Ruth Hubbard (1985) points out, eugenic intent fuels racist thinking and social practices. The definition of "unfit" may be extended by those who have the power to impose sterilization to include anyone considered socially undesirable. This may include those groups seen to be or to cause social problems or to deviate from socially acceptable norms of behaviour, and more generally, groups perceived as inferior. In recent years, evidence is emerging in many countries of sterilization abuse on the basis of economic conditions and racial prejudice (Mass, 1976; Davis, 1981; Rodriguez-Trias, 1982; Savage, 1982; Clarke, 1984; Zurbrigg, 1984; Corea, 1985).

2. Women should be the ultimate decision-makers regarding their own reproductive capacities.

The birth of a child affects all of the people who must live with him or her, especially those who take on the responsibilities of parenting. It also affects others in the society who may be involved in the provision and financing of day care, health care, education, etc. But mostly it affects the mother.

Unlike other people, the mother is inseparable from the pregnancy and, if she carries the pregnancy to full term, the birth. Unless she gives up the baby at birth it becomes her responsibility to tend to its needs. She may share some of these tasks with one or more other parenting figures, such as the father, a friend, a sister, or her parents. Yet, as the child's mother, she is legally and socially the primary person expected to care for the child's everyday needs and to pro-

tect the child from harm.

Obviously, having a child dramatically changes a woman's life. It may be a positive, negative, or ambivalent experience, depending upon her feelings about having children and the social conditions in which she lives. The extent of the change will also depend upon the resources and facilities available to her, such as sharing of or assistance with child care, work prospects, support systems, living situation, and personal relationships. Her marital status is likely to influence how others see and treat her, regardless of how she sees herself and her child.

The consequences of having children in terms of work patterns vary with the flexibility and security of the job which a woman has when she becomes pregnant. Men's privileged access to economic resources, including better pay, better working conditions, and more possibilities of promotion, make it difficult for most women to raise children without a male's income. Dorothy Smith argues that this leads to women's subordination: "Where men are wage earners and women cannot earn enough outside the home to provide for their children independently of a man and his wage, dependency permeates every aspect of the interpersonal process in the home" (1985:6).

Pat Armstrong (1984) examines the consequences of the growing economic crisis on women's work in the household and the labour force. Her analysis indicates that increasing unemployment and risk of unemployment for both women and men increases women's workload. It increases the financial necessity for women to continue in paid employment while caring for young children, as women cannot afford to lose their jobs. Unemployment rates are higher for women than men, pushing many women out of the labour market. Making the money stretch further at home compounds daily chores. Armstrong points out that it is women who bear this burden of domestic work and the rising tension in the home, who are the likely victims of increasing violence at home, and whose control over their bodies is threatened by state policies of reproductive rights and day-care facilities. The position of women, she concludes, is deteriorating.

In this context, it is clear that women need to have as much control as possible over the circumstances in which they will have children. This involves control in two senses. First, control over reproduction as a potential biological event — birth control, abortion, assistance with infertility. These may be achieved through herbal medicines, massage, vacuum aspiration, hormones, implanted devices, artificial insemination, among other techniques. Second, control over decision-making — regarding whether and with whom to have sex, what sexual activities take place, which method of birth control to use, and access to abortion, sterilization, and infertility treatment facilities. In all these situations, someone takes a decision; in all these situations it should be the women — not the men, religious bodies, the medical profession, or the state — who take the final decision over their reproductive actions. There is always room for debate on these issues — their morality and ethical implications, advantages and disadvantages, and the possible alternatives — but ultimately it is the woman who has to decide what she will do. The decision should not be forced upon her by others.

The debate on the abortion question has revealed conflicting world views on the position of women. Susan McDaniel (1985) argues that abortion is quintessentially a women's issue because the proponents of each side of the issue are arguing primarily about the reproductive role of women in a male-dominated society. The anti-abortion argument, she states, is informed by the perspective that women's central purpose is "as vessels for carrying out other people's wishes, those of their family, husbands and society," i.e., to bear children, while the pro-choice side maintains that women have the right to choose or refuse pregnancy and motherhood, to decide if, when, and in what situations they will bear children. As Janice Tait (1985) points out, the decision to abort must remain with the woman whose life stands to be most affected, especially since society and the state leave the

tasks and responsibilities of child care almost entirely to women.

Medical doctors are the gatekeepers to contraception, abortion, sterilization, and birthing facilities, as well as to the new reproductive technologies. Their control over access to prescription drugs and health-care facilities enables them to prescribe who will give birth and under what circumstances; of course individuals may go on to seek health care outside the financed services available, if they can afford it, and outside the law, as in the case of illegal abortion. Doctors are free to impose upon their women patients male-dominant opinions on morality, ethical procedures, and the proper place and the best interests of women. At the same time, their professional interests include preserving their own status as experts, their authority, autonomy, and their financial rewards. None of these interests favour the achievement of woman-centred and woman-controlled health care.

Women's control over their reproduction has been vigorously opposed by the medical profession. The history of the provision of birth control and birthing services shows much medical contention over three issues: first, women's potential sexual activity, the breakdown of the family unit, and women's subordination to their husbands; second, the quality of population control, the racist and eugenic concern with the degeneration of the population and the threat of white "race suicide"; and third, the potential for midwifery and related woman-centred health care by woman healers (Oakley, 1976; Ehrenreich and English, 1978; Scully, 1980; McDonnell, 1984; McLaren and McLaren, 1986).

Reproductive health care, for the most part, involves patients who are healthy. Whether negotiations centre upon contraception, abortion, or birthing practices, medical authority cannot be justified in defining and treating women as ill. The medical profession's active opposition to the demedicalization of contraception, abortion, and birthing practices has been maintained on grounds of the risks to women's health. Yet efforts to expand these services have been resisted on grounds that it is a social and perhaps moral issue, rather than a medical priority. The monopolization of service provision has enabled the medical profession to selectively control women's access to available health services. In this way, doctors have been able to wield both social and moral influence over the lives of the healthy, as well as the sick.

These issues continue to be raised with regard to recent "advances" in reproductive technology. The scientific possibility of in vitro fertilization (removal of a woman's ova, fertilization with sperm in a Petri dish, and implantation into her or another woman's womb), embryo transfer (from one woman's womb to another), and the future possibility of ectogenesis (fetus developed in an artificial uterus) is rife with the potential for abuse. Mary O'Brien (1985) warns us that the development of reproductive technology cannot be separated from the questions of power and control. As long as technology remains a male preserve and the law is used to legitimate these procedures, we cannot expect them to support women's control over their lives. Indeed, the historical development of reproductive technology may best be understood as a strategy to consolidate male control of reproduction.

The physiological differences between men and women, especially in the context of sexual inequality, must be recognized as highly relevant to reproductive health care. In this context, it is essential for women to be in a position to make the vital decisions about whether to become pregnant and carry the pregnancy to term, where and how to give birth, whether to breast-feed the infant, and so on. Health-care services must be sensitive to the potential for conflict on these issues between heterosexual partners and between women and medical personnel. Every effort should be made to support the woman in the decisions she makes, for it is she who will live with them, and she who will bear the consequences of any actions which are or are not taken.

3. The knowledge which is accumulated in reference to reproductive health care for

women should be centred in women's experience.   Feminist health care begins by taking women and women's experiences seriously, and assumes that women's control over their fertility and reproductive health care is essential to health. Self-help health groups and health-care services are directed towards (a) understanding health issues in context of the social conditions of women's lives, (b) awareness of the available and potential alternatives for action, and (c) taking decisions which will strengthen women's position and increase women's control over their lives.

In Canada, the women's health movement has been redefining women's health needs and exploring the potential for feminist health care since the early 1970s. The Vancouver Women's Health Collective, Centres de Santé des Femmes across Quebec, The Women's Health Education Network in Nova Scotia, and many others across the country have been involved in the exciting exploration of a new woman-centred knowledge. This knowledge is based upon women's experiences, an understanding of sexual inequality and the socio-economic and environmental context of health, a vision of woman-controlled alternatives to health care, and a commitment to radical social change. As Kathleen McDonnell declares in *The Healthsharing Book*: "We aim at nothing less than a health system transformed from an instrument of human oppression into a vehicle for human liberation" (1985:21).

In contrast, medical knowledge rests upon definitions of women, reproduction, and women's reproductive needs that are found to be gravely misogynistic. The language and concepts of medicine rely upon a stereotype of women as ruled by their reproductive hormones, as inferior and uninteresting, and as dependent upon men. Analyses of medical education (Weiss, 1978; Scully, 1980), medical perceptions of women (Elston, 1981; Graham and Oakley, 1981; Arditta et al., 1984; Corea, 1985), and the advice offered to women (Ehrenreich and English, 1978) reveal that these stereotypes are reinforced with tedious regularity. Medicine as a profession has historically and in modern times been central in defining women as intellectually incapable, lacking in physical stamina, periodically polluting, sexually dangerous, and emotionally unstable. This portrayal is based solely on the condition of being female and not male, irrespective of any individual's state of health.

Women's health care suffers greatly as a result of this prejudice, which leads to the misreading of symptoms, overprescription of tranquillizers and other drugs, and to inappropriate medical intervention (Cooperstock and Hill, 1982; Pollock, 1984; Ford, 1986). In the case of contraceptive side effects, for example, medical studies often assume that women are unreliable in assessing and reporting changes in their health. It is believed that women are likely to "over-report," that is, to complain of symptoms simply because they have the opportunity rather than because they have good cause. Women are not taken seriously and their symptoms are easily dismissed as "subjective"; indeed, women are made to appear and to feel at fault for complaining. The standard low-risk-few-side-effects view of oral, injectable, and intra-uterine contraceptives remains unchallenged, despite women's reports of negative experiences with them. This can, and frequently does, result in the failure to assess symptoms which have the potential to develop into complicated health problems. It forces women to live with unnecessary discomfort and pain. Worse yet, the prospects for improvement with this approach are minimal: the invalidation of women's experiences precludes the possibility of developing knowledge about side effects and the evaluation of them as health risks (Bunkle, 1984; Pollock, 1984).

The use of patriarchal stereotypes and sexist values in health care belies the rhetoric of medical objectivity. In spite of the language and claims of expertise, medical "knowledge" reflects male-dominant perspectives of women. In the course of medical examinations, advice, and treatment, doctors' attitudes towards women are clearly expressed and imposed. While doctors may interpret women's symptoms as evidence of either female weakness or unladylike behaviour, women experience this approach as a

lack of understanding and of competence in dealing with the problems at hand. The invalidation which women experience in their relations with physicians gives rise to conflicts which interfere with their health needs. It also encourages women to look beyond traditional medicine for alternatives in health care.

The individualism of the medical model of care discourages a wider understanding of the social issues involved in health care. As Sheila Zurbrigg (1984) points out, good intentions are not sufficient; what is necessary is a reconsideration of health care from an awareness of the conditions in which people live and an understanding of the social inequalities which give rise to specific health needs. Until these inequalities are addressed, health "knowledge" remains faulty and incomplete, while health-care services developed upon such knowledge will necessarily be inappropriate.

4. Information should be made as widely available as possible. One of the major achievements of feminist health groups has been to break through the medical monopoly of knowledge, or what has been taken to be knowledge. Its method is simply for women to begin to communicate with each other. Increasingly this route has been used to affirm women's experience, to gather and to share information, and to lessen women's dependence upon men and male-dominated medical perspectives. In challenging medical knowledge, women's health groups have shared new understandings and the means of achieving these understandings in workshops, newsletters, information-sharing kits, books, and films. This activity has involved co-ordinating resources across Canada, and combining efforts with women in many other countries (see, for example, *The Healthsharing Book*, 1985).

The medical model imposes a hierarchy upon health care, setting up the doctor as expert, and the recipient of health services as lacking in knowledge and, thereby, dependent. This has the effect of isolating patients from each other. What is needed among women is the understanding which comes from sharing experiences, respecting their own awareness and expertise about their bodies, and recognizing the social conditions which influence health and illness.

Medical claims of professional expertise are legitimated and perpetuated by cultivating the ignorance of health-care recipients. The patient's ignorance may be actual, as a result of the withholding or mystification of knowledge, or it may be a misperception founded on denial of the patient's wisdom and assertion of the superior wisdom of the physician. Health guides to women have been notorious in their attempts to undermine the expertise women acquire from friends, mothers, women who have much experience — claiming that women should ignore "old wives' tales" in favour of the advice of their doctors. Yet it is well known that medical knowledge has been misinformed by sexist values, patriarchal stereotypes, fads and fashions, glorification of technology, and ignorance of social and environmental conditions responsible for health and illness (Corea, 1985; Romalis, 1985).

The withholding from women of information about their bodies and of the means to care for themselves and others has a long history. One of the most violent assertions ever of men's rights over women's bodies and health care was the burning of wisewomen healers, or witches, as they were labelled, during the late fifteenth and the sixteenth centuries, and the development of a male-only medical profession in its wake. The history of the medical profession reveals not so much the establishment of men's dominance in healing as a process of transferring control from women to men — from laywoman to male professional. The medical profession continued to exclude women from its ranks for 400 years (Oakley, 1976).

By the late nineteenth century this exclusion was being rationalized by medical "science," which emphasized women's frailty as dictated by their ovaries (Ehrenreich and English, 1978). It was considered indecent for women to have knowledge of anatomy and physiology since, as Lorna Duffin succinctly

puts it: "Femaleness involved purity. Purity involved innocence and innocence meant ignorance" (1978:46). The exclusion of women from knowledge and status as healers made women dependent upon men for information and health care. It purported an ideology of femininity which may have appealed to men but which has done much to disarm women and girls from protecting themselves and each other.

Mary Petty (1986) explains the importance of sharing information amongst women as a means "to reclaim our life events from the medical sphere." Central to a feminist model of health care is women's access to all information, and women's participation in their own care as far as possible. With the self-help model, women share information which is gathered from many sources; self-help is based upon mutual support and respect for women's knowledge of their own bodies. In feminist clinics, women learn to examine themselves, do basic tests and measurements, and to share any recordings. Taking part in feminist health care has the result of increasing women's confidence and their willingness to ask questions and share information. Through feminist analysis and the development of health-care alternatives, Petty concludes, women's health groups work to combat the medicalization of women's lives.

5. Health-care facilities for women need to be woman-centred. This principle is an affirmation of women in contrast to male-dominant definitions of the needs of women. It poses the question: who benefits from current health-care practices? For example, are hospital obstetrical procedures designed to support women giving birth, or do they centre upon the comfort and convenience of physicians and hospital workers? Do health-care policies give priority to women's health, or to the socio-economic status of the medical profession and hospital administrators?

The fight for midwifery illustrates the conflict which women face in many areas of women's health care. In recent years, growing numbers of women giving birth and of women practicing midwifery have been battling for the legalization of midwifery and the preservation of home births. They have been opposed in large part by the medical establishment fearing competition and loss of authority and control over women's birthing process. Yet, the rationale for midwifery is strong, and some argue that legalization is inevitable. It is supported by demand — the popularity of midwifery amongst women, by the high cost of obstetrical institutions, technology, and obstetricians, and by the fewer risks involved with midwifery care than in modern obstetrics (Barrington, 1985; Romalis, 1985).

Midwifery, as opposed to modern technological obstetrics, is a woman-centred approach to health care. Its existence offers women a greater choice of where, with whom, and under what conditions to give birth. Emphasis is placed upon providing women with information and personalized care at a reasonable cost. The difference between modern obstetrics and midwifery is in this woman-centred, woman-controlled approach. As Eleanor Barrington (1985) states in the preface of her book *Midwifery is Catching*: "According to midwifery philosophy, credit for 'delivering' a baby belongs to the mother. Her midwife is there to aid and abet, and then to gently 'catch' the arriving infant." Diane Scully's study of obstetricians/gynecologists reveals the opposite to be true of modern obstetrics where the obstetrician is perceived as expert, authority, and deliverer of the baby; the mother is portrayed as the more or less co-operative, passive, and grateful patient (Scully, 1980).

Shelly Romalis (1985) argues that contemporary obstetrics has been shaped by the needs and ideologies of pathologically oriented practitioners. Despite medical claims that intervention improves the survival of babies, fetal mortality rates do not bear this out. Routine hospital practices, including "invasive diagnostic procedures, induction and acceleration of labour, reliance on drugs for pain reduction, routine electronic fetal monitoring, dramatically increased Caesarean-section rates, and separation of mother and baby

after the birth . . . [have] been shown to be problematic, if not dangerous" (1985:185). Women are encouraged to rely upon their doctors and on anaesthetic drugs to cope with labour; besides, doctors are untrained in non-medicated births. Women come to expect that their labour will develop complications and that medical interference will be necessary. Although, as Romalis points out, safety of the baby is an amorphous notion, involving "more guesswork and judgment than science," it remains the ultimate weapon which doctors wield to achieve the resignation of women in labour to medical intervention.

Associated with the expansion of large-scale hospital units is the lower priority placed upon primary prevention and the massive funding of high-risk management. Having set up this form of care, the tendency is to treat all women going into these hospital units "as if they were high risk — the 'just-in-case' approach" (Romalis, 1985). Dianne Patychuk (1985) questions the necessity of routine obstetrical ultrasound examinations, demonstrated to cause cellular changes comparable to exposure from 250 chest X-rays. Like other forms of medical intervention in childbirth, she argues, the new prenatal technologies separate the mother from her child. Increasingly we are seeing a wedge being driven between women and their future children.

Who benefits from the growth of these technologies? Patychuk argues that the primary benefactors are not childbearing women, but rather those whose profits and status are derived from the increasing employment of technology. This allows for the invasive heroics on the part of obstetricians, who may bypass the woman's experience in favour of independent "objective" observation, control, and delivery of the baby. The risks to health remain with the women, as do the consequences when things go wrong.

6. The preceding five principles should apply equally to *all* women. In taking control from women and monitoring health-care facilities and treatment, it has been possible to differentially treat groups of women according to factors such as race or economic class. Women are treated as reproductive objects; those who are going to be carrying the children of white middle-class men are encouraged or coerced to bear children, while others, seen as unfit because of their disability, poverty, marital status, or race, are discouraged or prevented from having children. Women's reproductive capabilities are used as a means of control over women in general, as well as control over specific racial and economic class groups.

Janice Tait (1985) asks why it is that in the development of reproductive technology, the pain, suffering, and violence inflicted on women's bodies has been ignored. The assumptions behind this scientific "progress" include the untested view that this reproductive technology is "safe enough," that the means justifies the end, and that the end involves the eugenic view of handicapped people (and others considered inferior) as a blight on society. Further, the assumption that men and women are equal in the area of reproduction "elevates the importance of men and downgrades the central role of women." The new technologies have been used to increase the monitoring of women, their bodies, and their babies. Women are treated as reproductive machines, and their babies as products of men's operation of and control over these machines.

The reproductive rights issue affects women, according to their relation to the particular group of men who constitute the ruling class, on an international scale. For some women it has involved a struggle over the right to contraception, abortion, and sterilization services. For others, it is the fight against coercive measures of population control and for the right to have children. For all women the issue is control over their bodies and their lives.

Coercive measures of population control include enforced sterilization, the use of Depo-Provera, and other measures which reduce women's control over their fertility and their bodies. Depo-Provera is a three-month injectable contraceptive produced and marketed by Upjohn, a multinational American drug company. Its use as a contraceptive method in the United States has been banned on grounds that it involves an unacceptably high risk of cancer. However, the testing and widespread dissemination of this drug continues among Third World women, poor women, and women of colour, which clearly indicates the racist use of methods of reproductive control. Indeed, the "advantages" of Depo-Provera are heralded to be its low cost in terms of service provision, and the fact that women have little control over its use (Rakusen, 1981). Its reported side effects include infertility, heavy bleeding, diabetes, uterine disease, pituitary damage, deformities to offspring, severe depression, lowered immunity, and cancer, among others. These are not considered sufficiently serious to population programmes in 80 countries administering it to over 10 million women. It can be and is administered without women's knowledge of what is being injected into them (Bunkle, 1984). In Canada, Depo-Provera has been used to preclude menstrual bleeding among handicapped women, often without their consent (DAWN, 1986; Lalonde and Wittstock, 1986). Upjohn is currently lobbying for the acceptance of Depo-Provera for contraceptive use in Canada, amidst much opposition from feminist health groups.

Sexism and racism are inseparable. This relationship is explored in *Reproductive Wrongs: Male Power and the New Reproductive Technologies*. The authors point out that the patterns of abuse evidenced by oral contraceptive experiments, Depo-Provera, selective abortion, and sterilization programmes offer a clear perspective on the likely future use of the new reproductive technologies. For example: "Racism in the male supremacist cultures which have produced new reproductive technologies means that some women (white, Gentile, middle-class, and able-bodied) may be judged genetically superior and selected as egg donors, while black women and women of colour (i.e., non-valuable women) can be sterilized and used as breeders or incubators for white (and preferably male) embryos" (1985:13). The tools developed by

Western medicine and science to support male dominance over women's bodies may be used to "advance" control over women and over certain racial and economic class groups.

THE FEMINIST CHALLENGE

Feminism offers a profound challenge to the organization of health care, both in Canada and internationally. In its analysis of the consequences of contemporary health policy and services for women, feminism points to the need for fundamental restructuring of health care. The demand is more than a reminder that health-care services should be patient-centred. It contains two fundamental assertions: first, women should have control over reproductive health-care facilities and services; and second, health care should become a means of achieving social equality, rather than legitimating and promoting inequality.

This has far-reaching effects and strikes at the heart of the hierarchical organization of health care. Feminism challenges the practices, the knowledge, and the use of medicine within our social order. This involves questioning all of the following aspects of health services often taken for granted:

1. The right of individuals or social institutions to impose their moral views upon women, including whether, how, and with whom women will have or avoid having children;

2. The medical model of disease emphasizing individual pathology and cures and trivializing the social conditions in which people live and take decisions about their reproductive health;

3. The definition and treatment of women's "normal" reproductive cycles as disease conditions requiring invasive medical procedures, especially during childbearing and menopause;

4. The perception of women as ruled by their reproductive capacity and/or as reproductive vessels for the fulfillment of other people's

wishes or morality;

5. The exploitation of women and their bodies for financial, experimental, or status reasons;

6. The goals of selective breeding (eugenics) which classify people as inferior according to race, economic class, physical or mental ability, religion, nationality, marital status, and sex.

7. The use of health care as a form of social control, legitimated by the state and justified under the rubric of "helping";

8. The competence of doctors and other health-care professionals to promote and protect women's health, particularly reproductive health.

Feminists are making the claim that the structure of medicine and health care has evolved historically according to political and economic interests outside of women's health. Sexually, racially, and economically, inequality continues to permeate developments in the organization of health care. In part, this is a reflection of widespread social attitudes. But more than this, the institutions of health care, and the profession of medicine in particular, have actively pursued and jealously guarded the powers of decision-making, quality of information, and distribution of health-care facilities. This is very serious for those who require but do not receive health care designed to meet their needs as autonomous and equal participants in society.

Approaching questions of health and health care in Canada from a feminist understanding offers a new direction for analysis and research. First, we learn that one of the central questions which must be posed is how our definitions of health, health practices, and health-care institutions may reflect and perhaps promote sexual inequality. Second, we come to reassess health and the quality of health care from the point of view of the recipients. In reproductive health, this means largely from the point of view of women. Finally, it becomes evident that improvements in health-care services need to take on the strategy of affirmative action, or positive discrimination, to reach a point of equal balance. Insofar as the health policies and institutional hierarchies do not seem capable of achieving equality and recipient-centred/controlled health care, they must be transformed into new structures which do meet these requirements.

STUDY QUESTIONS

1. This chapter presents a feminist approach which differs from the traditional medical model for reproductive health care. What do you think are the most important differences?

2. How do you think experiences can best be shared? What types of information are most useful and what format would you use to share experiences?

3. What is recognized as knowledge, and how is knowledge about reproductive health developed? Why is it necessary to bring together different experiences to gain an overall understanding of health and health care?

4. What is meant by "control," based on the feminist assertion that women should have control over reproduction? Why is this pivotal to women's position in society?

RECOMMENDED READING

Arditta, Rita, Renata Duelli Klein, and Shelley Minden, eds. *Test-Tube Women: What Future for Motherhood?* London: Pandora Press, 1984.

McDaniel, Susan A. "Implementation of Abortion Policy in Canada as a Women's Issue." *Atlantis* 10, no. 2 (1985): 74–91.

McDonnell, Kathleen. *Not an Easy Choice: A Feminist Re-examines Abortion*. Toronto: Women's Press, 1984.

McDonnell, Kathleen, and Mariana Valverde, eds. *The Healthsharing Book: Resources for Canadian Women*. Toronto: Women's Press, 1985.

O'Brien, Mary. "State Power and Reproductive Freedom." *Canadian Woman Studies* 6, no. 2 (1985): 62–66.

Romalis, Shelly. "Struggle Between Providers and Recipients: The Case of Birth Practices." In *Women, Health and Healing: Toward a New Perspective*, edited by E. Lewin and V. Olesen. New York: Tavistock, 1985.

Williams, Linda. "But What Will They Mean for Women? Feminist Concerns About the New Reproductive Technologies." *CRIAW Feminist Perspectives*, no. 6. Ottawa: Canadian Research Institute for the Advancement of Women, 1986.

REFERENCES

Achilles, Rona. "New Age Procreation." *Healthsharing* 6, no. 4 (1985): 10–14.

Arditta, Rita, Renata Duelli Klein, and Shelley Minden, eds. *Test-Tube Women: What Future for Motherhood?* London: Pandora Press, 1984.

Armstrong, Pat. *Labour Pains: Women's Work in Crisis*. Toronto: Women's Press, 1984.

Barrington, Eleanor. *Midwifery is Catching*. Toronto: NC Press, 1985.

Bart, Pauline. "Seizing the Means of Reproduction: An Illegal Feminist Abortion Collective

— How and Why It Worked." In *Women, Health and Reproduction*, edited by H. Roberts. London: Routledge and Kegan Paul, 1981.

Bock, Gisela. "Racism and Sexism in Nazi Germany: Motherhood, Compulsory Sterilization and the State." In *When Biology Became Destiny: Women in Weimar and Nazi Germany*, edited by R. Bridenthal, A. Grossmann, and M. Kaplan. New York: Monthly Review Press, 1984.

Boston Women's Health Book Collective. *The New Our Bodies, Ourselves*. New York: Touchstone, 1984.

Bunkle, Phillida. "Calling the Shots? The International Politics of Depo-Provera." In *Test-Tube Women: What Future for Motherhood?* edited by R. Arditta, R. Duelli Klein, and S. Minden. London: Pandora Press, 1984.

Clarke, Adele. "Subtle Forms of Sterilization Abuse: A Reproductive Rights Analysis." In *Test-Tube Women: What Future for Motherhood?* edited by R. Arditta, R. Duelli Klein, and S. Minden. London: Pandora Press, 1984.

Clarke, Juanne N. "Sexism, Feminism and Medicalism: A Decade Review of Literature on Gender and Illness." *Sociology of Health and Illness* 5, no. 1 (1983): 62–82.

Cohen, Leah, and Constance Backhouse. "Women and Health: The Growing Controversy." *Canadian Women's Studies* 1, no. 4 (1979): 4–10.

Cole, Susan G. "The Real Abortion Issue." *This Magazine* 17, no. 2 (1983): 4–8.

Collins, Larry D. "The Politics of Abortion: Trends in Canadian Fertility Policy." *Atlantis* 7, no. 2 (1982): 2–20.

Cooperstock, Ruth, and Jessica Hill. *The Effects of Tranquillization: Benzodiazepine Use in Canada*. Ottawa: Health and Welfare Canada, 1982.

Corea, Gena. *The Hidden Malpractice: How American Medicine Mistreats Women*. New York: Harper and Row, rev. ed., 1985.

———. *The Mother Machine: Reproductive Technologies from Artificial Insemination to Artificial Wombs*. Toronto: Fitzhenry and Whiteside, 1985.

DisAbled Women's Network. *Over Our Dead Bodies*. Toronto: D.A.W.N. 1986.

Davis, Angela. *Women, Race and Class*. New York: Random House, 1981.

Doyal, Lesley, with Imogen Pennell. *The Political Economy of Health*. London: Pluto Press, 1979.

Duffin, Lorna. "The Conspicuous Consumptive: Woman as an Invalid." In *The Nineteenth-Century Woman*, edited by S. Delamont and L. Duffin. London: Croom Helm, 1978.

Dworkin, Andrea. *Right-Wing Women: The Politics of Domesticated Females*. London: Women's Press, 1983.

Ehrenreich, Barbara, and Deirdre English. *For Her Own Good: 150 Years of the Experts' Advice to Women*. New York: Doubleday/Anchor, 1978.

Elston, Mary Ann. "Medicine As 'Old Husbands' Tales': The Impact of Feminism." In *Men's Studies Modified*, edited by D. Spender. Oxford: Pergamon, 1981.

Ford, Anne Rochon. "In Poor Health." *Healthsharing* 8, no. 1 (1986): 13–17.

Frye, Marilyn. *The Politics of Reality: Essays in Feminist Theory*. Trumansburg, N.Y.: Crossing Press, 1983.

Graham, Hilary, and Ann Oakley. "Competing Ideologies of Reproduction: Medical and Maternal Perspectives on Pregnancy." In *Women, Health and Reproduction*, edited by H. Roberts. London: Routledge and Kegan Paul, 1981.

Hubbard, Ruth. "Prenatal Diagnosis and Eugenic Ideology." *Women's Studies International Forum* 8, no. 6 (1985): 567–76.

Lalonde, Michelle, and Melinda Wittstock. "Depo-Provera To Be Dumped on Canada?" *Dalhousie Gazette* (November 20, 1986): 12.

Lorber, Judith. "Women and Medical Sociology: Invisible Professionals and Ubiquitous Patients." In *Another Voice: Feminist Per-*

spectives on Social Life and Social Science, edited by M. Millman and R.M. Kanter. Garden City, N.Y.: Anchor, 1975.

Mass, Bonnie. *Population Target: The Political Economy of Population Control in Latin America.* Toronto: Women's Press, 1976.

McCrea, Francis B. "The Politics of Menopause: The 'Discovery' of a Deficiency Disease." In *The Sociology of Health and Illness: Critical Perspectives,* 2nd ed., edited by P. Conrad and R. Kern. New York: St. Martin's, 1986.

McDaniel, Susan A. "Implementation of Abortion Policy in Canada as a Women's Issue." *Atlantis* 10, no. 2 (1985): 74–91.

McDonnell, Kathleen. *Not an Easy Choice: A Feminist Re-examines Abortion.* Toronto: Women's Press, 1984.

McDonnell, Kathleen, and Mariana Valverde, eds. *The Healthsharing Book: Resources for Canadian Women.* Toronto: Women's Press, 1985.

McLaren, Angus, and Arlene Tiger McLaren. *The Bedroom and the State: The Changing Practices and Politics of Contraception and Abortion in Canada 1880–1980.* Toronto: McClelland and Stewart, 1986.

Oakley, Ann. "Wisewoman and Medicine Man: Changes in the Management of Childbirth." In *The Rights and Wrongs of Women,* edited by J. Mitchell and A. Oakley. Harmondsworth: Penguin, 1976.

———. *The Captured Womb.* Oxford: Basil Blackwell, 1984.

O'Brien, Mary. *The Politics of Reproduction.* London: Routledge and Kegan Paul, 1981.

———. "State Power and Reproductive Freedom." *Canadian Woman Studies* 6, no. 2 (1985): 62–66.

Patychuk, Dianne. "Ultrasound: The First Wave." *Healthsharing* 6, no. 4 (1985): 25–28.

Petty, Mary. "Women Resisting Medicalization." *Dalhousie Gazette* (November 20, 1986): 11.

Pollock, Scarlet. "Refusing to Take Women Seriously: Side Effects and the Politics of Contraception." In *Test-Tube Women: What Future for Motherhood?* edited by R. Arditta, R. Duelli Klein, and S. Minden. London: Pandora Press, 1984.

Rakusen, Jill. "Depo-Provera: The Extent of the Problem. A Case Study in the Politics of Birth Control." In *Women, Health and Reproduction,* edited by H. Roberts. London: Routledge and Kegan Paul, 1981.

Reproductive Wrongs: Male Power and the New Reproductive Technologies. Pamphlet available from Sisterwrite, 190 Upper St., London, England, 1984.

Rodriguez-Trias, Helen. "Sterilization Abuse." In *Biological Woman — The Convenient Myth,* edited by R. Hubbard, M.S. Henefin, and B. Fried. Cambridge: Schenkman, 1982.

Romalis, Shelly. "Struggle Between Providers and Recipients: The Case of Birth Practices." In *Women, Health and Healing: Toward a New Perspective,* edited by E. Lewin and V. Olesen. New York: Tavistock, 1985.

Ruff, Kathleen. "Sterilization Without Consent." *Just Cause,* Canadian Legal Advocacy Information and Research Association of the Disabled (CLAIR), 3, no. 4 (1986): 22–25.

Ruzek, Sheryl Burt. *The Women's Health Movement: Feminist Alternatives to Medical Control.* New York: Praeger, 1979.

Savage, Wendy. "Taking Liberties with Women: Abortion, Sterilization, and Contraception." *International Journal of Health Services* 12, no. 2 (1982): 293–307.

Sawyer, Alison. "Women's Bodies, Men's Decisions." *Canadian Women's Studies* 3, no. 2 (1981): 92–93.

Scully, Diane. *Men Who Control Women's Health: The Miseducation of Obstetrician-Gynecologists.* Boston: Houghton Mifflin, 1980.

Smith, Dorothy E. "Women, Class and Family." In *Women, Class, Family and the State.* Toronto: Garamond Press, 1985.

Tait, Janice. "Ethical Issues in Reproductive Technology: A Feminist Perspective." *Canadian Woman Studies* 6, no. 2 (1985): 40–45.

Weiss, Kay. "What Medical Students Learn about Women." In *Seizing Our Bodies: The Politics of Women's Health*, edited by C. Dreifus. New York: Vintage, 1978.

Williams, Linda. "But What Will They Mean for Women? Feminist Concerns About the New Reproductive Technologies." *CRIAW Feminist Perspectives*, no. 6. Ottawa: Canadian Research Institute for the Advancement of Women, 1986.

Zurbrigg, Sheila. *Rakku's Story: Structures of Ill-Health and the Source of Change*. Madras: George Joseph, 1984. (Available from 6270 Lawrence St., Halifax, N.S.)

12

THE MEDICALIZATION OF DOMESTIC VIOLENCE

Seema Ahluwalia and Brian D. MacLean
University of Saskatchewan

INTRODUCTION

In recent years, the subject of family violence has been receiving increasing attention from citizens, politicians, the media, the criminal justice system, and the medical community (Klaus and Rand, 1974). Despite this wave of interest, however, family violence is by no means a recent phenomenon, and it remains a serious social problem about which little is understood or known with any certainty (Schlesinger, 1974). The frequency and scope of domestic violence have been difficult to measure historically (Ahluwalia and MacLean, 1986), although there are three main sources of information from which estimates might be made.

Because wife-battering is a criminal offence, one source of information on these occurrences is the records which come to be made by the agencies of justice. These data tend to grossly underestimate domestic violence, however, and probably tell us more about the police response to domestic violence than about domestic violence itself (Jones et al., 1986). Hospital records and transition house statistics are a valuable second source of information,

although again due to underreporting by victims, these data, as well, lead to underestimates (MacLeod, 1980). A final source of information is located in data produced by victimization surveys (Klaus and Rand, 1974), and while these provide more accurate estimates, they too underreport a large proportion of domestic violence, despite methodological innovations designed to improve upon rates of disclosure (MacLean et al., 1986).

As long as the frequency and scope of domestic violence remain unclear, causal theories will not be firmly grounded in empirical evidence, and the success of different intervention programmes will be at best dubious. This chapter argues that while most domestic violence remains hidden, that proportion of it which does surface does so only through official institutional channels. As a result, the official problem of domestic violence is given a colouration which suggests more about the institutional response than it does about domestic violence.

In examining the history of intervention in domestic violence, we show that while wife-battering has a long history, only recently has it been viewed as a problem requiring state intervention. Agencies charged with the responsibility of managing domestic violence have tended to incorporate their own conventional wisdom into strategies of intervention, and can be faulted for not basing their policies on solid sociological research.

We briefly examine three distinct phases in which domestic violence has elicited differential social responses. The first is characterized by non-intervention. Intervention by the criminal justice apparatus marks the second phase; the dissatisfaction with which paves the way for medical intervention in the third phase.[1] The medicalization of a social phenomenon has been predated by the two periods of problem identification followed by criminalization and legal intervention. We argue that like judicial intervention, medical intervention has been characterized by the imposition of institutional practices and assumptions which serve to exacerbate rather than resolve domestic violence. In both instances, the victim, seen as precipitating the violence used against her, must in the end take the responsibility for her own safety.

An analysis of the subordinate position of women in class and patriarchal societies and their struggles against these authorities is a worthwhile but onerous task which cannot be undertaken in its entirety here. Yet we believe that changes pertaining to the legality of their subordination are central to understanding the process by which legitimate violence against women becomes transformed into a social problem. In the following section we review this historical process.

THE PROBLEM IDENTIFIED

In her analysis of state intervention practices, Patricia Morgan notes that

> certain behaviours or conditions may exist in a society for decades and never blossom into problematic issues ... the shifts in public awareness of particular issues, and the transformation of the problems' images import and consequences can be charted within a general process of state intervention. (1985:60–61)

Violence against women in the family has a long history, and rather than being viewed as a social problem, such violence was seen in most cases as legitimate (Bauer and Ritt, 1983; Dobash et al., 1986; Dobash and Dobash, 1979; Martin, 1978; Pleck, 1979; Schechter, 1982; Schwendinger and Schwendinger, 1983). In England and Europe, husbands traditionally possessed the legal right to chastise their wives; in North America, the adoption of English common law neither confirmed nor denied this right until 1824, when wife-beating was made legal in the state of Mississippi (Dobash and Dobash, 1979).

Since men were held legally responsible for the behaviour of their wives, public attitudes held that restraint and punishment were expected in order to preserve their subservience to men. Such belief was reinforced by the church, and

> male dominance was perceived as the natural order and when women attempted to speak out against their husbands or other men in the community, including church leaders, they risked being defined as public nuisances, shrews, nags and viragos. (Dobash et al., 1986:19)

The "common scold" was legitimately punished in a variety of ways both by local magistrates and church leaders, and the ducking stool was often used to restrain such evil (Dobash et al., 1986). Dobash et al. describe another form of punishment which was commonly employed in the seventeenth century:

> A more brutal and painful method of punishing the "common scold" ... was through the application of the scold's or gossip's bridle. The branks was an iron cage placed over the head, and most examples incorporated a spike or pointed wheel that was inserted into the offender's mouth in order to "pin the tongue and silence the noisiest brawler" ... The common form of administering this punishment was to fasten the branks to a woman and parade her through the village, sometimes chaining her to a pillar. (1986:19)

The idea that the family was private and the domain of male authority was deeply entrenched in public, religious, and legal attitudes, and although such punishments as described above were carried out in public, they were linked to household domination. Dobash and Dobash (1979) have suggested that throughout the seventeenth, eighteenth, and nineteenth centuries, as long as a husband did not exceed certain tacitly recognized limits, there was no community objection to his using force on his wife.

It was not until the late nineteenth century that wife-beating began to be recognized as a social problem, although even then only for the most extreme cases. In the United States, judges would only imprison the most violent of men, and it was not until 1871 that wife-beating was declared illegal — though only in the two states of Alabama and Massachusetts (Schechter, 1982). In England, the absolute power of husbands to chastise their wives was abolished in 1829 (Schechter, 1982); however, this had no real effect on the frequency of wife-beating, since women were not protected legally from violence in the marriage, and there was no legal escape from such marriages (Dobash and Dobash, 1979). Finally, in 1895, with the passage of the Married Woman's Property Act in England, conviction for assault became legitimate grounds for divorce (Schechter, 1982), although as Dobash and Dobash suggest, "it was, of course, very difficult to get a conviction for assault and the standard of proof was often so high as to make a conviction almost impossible" (1979:63). Schechter argues that such legal reforms came about as a consequence of "agitation from women who were demanding rights to divorce, separation, control of their property, and custody of their children" (1982:218). In Canada, the National Council of Women recommended a set of similar reform measures for adoption in the Dominion and Provincial Parliaments of 1912 (Strong-Boag, 1976).

Legal reforms in the area of family law and family violence helped to reduce the moral and legal control that men held over their wives (Schechter, 1982), but did little to reduce the frequency of family violence. For example, Linda MacLeod (1980) estimates that presently at least one woman in ten is a victim of domestic violence. Jones et al. (1986) suggest that one family in four is characterized by at least one incident of serious domestic violence in any given year, and Dobash and Dobash (1979) found that in a study of 3020 cases of assault, 25 percent were cases in which wives had been assaulted by husbands.

From the early twentieth century, when wife-battering became criminalized, until the mid-1970s, when it was "rediscovered" (Dobash and Dobash, 1979), the responsibility for state intervention rested largely with the police and other agencies of criminal justice. Since the recording of domestic disputes by police seriously underrepresented the frequency of wife-battery and because intervention by law enforcement agencies remained largely informal, the bulk of family violence remained a hidden and private problem (Ahluwalia and MacLean, 1986). Combined with the ideology of the sanctity of the private domain, criminal justice responses resulted in the individualization of this social problem, while the ubiquity of family violence escaped public attention.

The recognition of wife abuse as a problem, then, was slow in developing; however, after the legal reforms of the early twentieth century, which criminalized wife-battery, the problem became a latent one. The extent to which the practices of criminal justice contributed to the submergence of this problem is discussed in the next section.

LEGAL RESPONSES TO DOMESTIC VIOLENCE

There are two critical moments in the process by which domestic violence is officially constructed by justice agencies. First, someone must report an incident to the police, and second, the police must respond to an incident that comes to their attention.[2] Studies of domestic violence have helped to identify numerous reasons why women do not report an incident to the police. Both the Islington Crime Survey (1986) and the Canadian Urban Victimization Survey (1985) found that two common reasons for not reporting incidents of wife-battery to the police were fear of reprisal from the offender, and the the perception that the police could not do anything about it anyway (Jones et al., 1986; CUVS, 1985). Other reasons given are that the victims do not want to "get the offender into trouble" (CUVS, 1985) and that the victim felt it was a personal matter (Klaus and Rand, 1974; Langan and Innes, 1986). Sometimes, victims will not report the incident to the police because they fear that they or their children may suffer embarrassment, financial loss, or some other serious repercussion (Thompson and Gilby, 1980).

When victims of domestic violence do report to the police, the most common reason given is that they hope police intervention will prevent further incidents of violence, or simply that police intervention will stop the current dispute (Langan and Innes, 1986). The police, on the other hand, have a dismal record of success when called upon for such intervention (Martin, 1978). According to Martin (1978), the police tend to arrest only those cases they think they might win in court. She states that in Oakland only one in 100 cases ever makes it to court, while in Detroit during one year only 300 out of 4900 complaints were tried in court. Results of study after study of police response to domestic violence have indicated that either down-criming[3] occurs (McCabe and Sutcliffe, 1978), or the police exercise a policy of non-arrest (Bell, 1985).[4]

Thompson and Gilby (1980) have suggested that there are at least six justifications for the police policy of non-arrest:

1. Often the victim does not desire an arrest or charges to be laid, but she has involved the police in the hope that they may intimidate the offender, have him removed from the home temporarily, or, where required, be taken to the hospital for treatment.

2. If the offender is arrested, he may retaliate with further violence.

3. Arrest and conviction might result in eco-

nomic setbacks for the victim. Expenses such as legal fees, fines, or loss of wages due to incarceration can adversely affect the victim.

4. Often, the victim will change her mind before conviction, resulting in what is considered by the police to be a waste of resources. Thompson (1978) reports that at least 50 percent of all cases appearing in family court for wife-battery are withdrawn by the plaintiff.

5. The police are really only able to lay charges if they themselves witness the assault, or if they are successful in gathering sufficient evidence that will likely lead to a conviction.

6. According to Parnas (1970), the usual approach used by the courts in obtaining facts and imposing fines is not appropriate for the problem.

Even if the police do make an arrest, securing a conviction is not always possible, since, as one Family Court judge suggests, judges face a number of dilemmas, such as dealing with a serious criminal matter as a family problem, or attempting to induce deterrence when the matters are dealt with in secrecy (Thompson and Gilby, 1980).

Bell suggests that police departments "assign a low priority to domestic disputes, fail to reward officers for effective intervention, and imply that domestic dispute intervention is not a legitimate police function" (1985:302). Thus, arrest is only exercised when serious violent injury has occurred (Martin, 1978), and as Loving (1980) argues, the police remain resistant to the idea of wife-battering as a legitimate police concern.

The history of justice agency intervention into cases of domestic violence is one of selective law enforcement guided by a set of prescribed institutional responses. These, in turn, have tended to blame the victim for her plight, leaving her to her own resources in the resolution of the domestic crisis. The result has been a misrepresentation to the public of the frequency, scope, quality, and location of domestic violence, which has only become visible as studies of domestic violence have begun to be compiled.

Dobash and Dobash (1979) observe that in the mid-1970s there was an "explosion of activity" around the issue of battered women, generated by women's aid groups that were not only expanding in number, but also gaining supportive, albeit sensationalist, coverage in the media. This explosion of activity led in Britain to the appointment of a Select Committee on Violence in Marriage in 1974 by the House of Commons (Dobash and Dobash, 1979). In Canada, a similar process was underway which led to the formation of a number of committees aimed at investigating the extent of family violence, and the Canadian Advisory Council on the Status of Women commissioned its own investigation into wife-battering (MacLeod, 1980).

It seems that the "rediscovery" of wife-battering as a social problem coincided with a growing awareness of the inferior status of women generally, and women's groups which were becoming increasingly politicized commanded investigations which illustrated the failure of the judicial system to deal with the problem. What was once legitimate was now being recognized as a serious social problem requiring a form of intervention other than criminal justice. What had been effectively privatized since the beginning of the twentieth century as a personal problem was beginning to rear its head in public with no apparent institutional resolution. In the next section we will examine the way in which this social problem became individualized as a medical pathology.

THE MEDICALIZATION OF DOMESTIC VIOLENCE

The term "medicalization" has been used by critics of the health-care system to refer to a process which is characterized by "a tendency to 'naturalize' social causes of illness by constraining them within static and reified categories" (Stark, 1984:61). Such a tendency leaves the physician with a limited repertoire of pathologi-

cal categories within which the patient can be diagnosed, and obscures the historically specific and contradictory social relations which give substance to the illness. As a result, the conception that all illness is an individual pathology is maintained, and it is the individual rather than these social relations which is considered the appropriate object of medical practice.

The idea that the medical institution serves to mystify fundamental social contradictions (Stark, 1984) is well illustrated by the problem of wife abuse. Despite the fact that family violence is rooted in contradictory social relations (Dobash and Dobash, 1979; Stark, 1984; Stark et al., 1979; Szechtman, 1985), it is the individual victim that has been traditionally assigned a category of illness, one in need of treatment by the medical institution. When battered women become the object of medical scrutiny, the social context within which the assault takes place is ignored.

Such a strategy of medical practice fits the biomechanical model of health care which has dominated the field of medicine (Stevenson and Williams, 1985). According to Stark et al., the aim of medical science is "to aggregate immediate symptoms and relevant physiological data . . . into pre-existing 'scientific' categories. These, in turn, suggest a particular therapeutic response in accord with recognized precepts of medical practice" (1979:469). Thus, the conventional wisdom of health practice dictates that victims of domestic violence, once identified, must be cured. The particular problem which the battered woman presents to the clinician, however, is an array of widely disparate symptoms which cannot be immediately attributed to some "natural cause." The inability of the clinician to categorize these symptoms "into available diagnostic categories, coupled with the patient's persistence for the practitioner to offer a solution, create a 'crisis of the cure'" (Stark et al., 1979:470). Whether or not the clinician recognizes the case as one of battery determines the way in which this crisis is resolved.

A woman who is seeking medical treatment for the first time for injury or other somatic ailments resulting from domestic assault is very unlikely to disclose the assault to her physician, and will likely be misdiagnosed.

> The one-way hierarchical nature of the medical examination which excludes dialogue makes it very unlikely that women will raise the problem and that general practitioners are not likely to do so either. (Dobash et al., 1984:159)

In such instances, the woman's inability or reluctance to disclose the battering, in combination with the vagueness of her symptoms, leads the doctor to assign labels to her chart for which treatment strategies are implicit. Labels such as "somatization disorder" (Swanson, 1986), "patient with multiple vague medical complaints," or "multiple symptomatology with psychosomatic overlay" (Stark et al., 1979:469) have been documented. For example, one physician reports:

> Battered women visit their physicians often, usually with somatic or conversion symptoms, or psycho-physiological reactions. Their most frequent complaints are headache, insomnia, a choking sensation, hyperventilation, abdominal pain, chest pain, pelvic pain, and back pain. They may also show signs of anxiety, neurosis, depression, suicidal behaviour, drug abuse and non-compliance with medications. (Swanson, 1985:824)

Flitcraft (1977) has argued that in these situations, the practitioner, unable to structure symptoms to fit available diagnostic categories, may label the patient's problem as hysteria, hypochondriasis, or neurosis. Stark et al. (1979) suggest that such labelling has little therapeutic value in that it does nothing to prevent future suffering, while masking the real problem of abuse. For such diagnoses, pharmacotherapy and/or psychiatric referral are the main treatment strategies. Both the diagnosis and treatment are entered on the patient's medical chart, which itself becomes an important diagnostic tool for future visits.

Should she continue to visit the physician and should the battering continue to be unrecognized by the doctor, the patient may develop other medical problems which are cited in her medical record. Stark et al. (1979) found that

these include drug and alcohol abuse, attempted suicide, and depression, while Swanson (1986) records various manifestations of hysterical conversion reaction. Since visits for these subsequent ailments are recorded chronologically in the patient's medical record, the practitioner now has the opportunity to organize the information logistically. What previously might have been perceived as a series of unrelated events now takes on the appearance of a causal chain, well before the abuse has been established. For example, drug or alcohol abuse may be seen as the cause of the patient's anxiety, depression, or even injuries when clearly these are not the causes but the effects of domestic violence. Similarly, the "real" medical problem is considered to be the substance abuse, and when the battering is identified it is seen as one outcome of the substance abuse.

The tendency to interpret correlational evidence as causal pervades the medical literature on domestic violence. In one study of 60 battered women, Hilberman and Munson found that

> nine women had classic depressive illness, one was manic-depressive, two schizophrenic, four alcoholic, and four severely character-disordered ... most had been treated ... with sedative-hypnotics, tranquilizers, and/or antidepressants. (1977/78:464)

In addition, Rounsaville and Weissman (1977/78) found 37 percent with depressive neurosis, 6 percent with psychotic depression, 10 percent with depression with alcohol abuse, and 6 percent drug abusers.

In order to illustrate the way in which the cause–effect relationship is inverted by standard medical practice, Stark et al. (1979) compared reported secondary symptoms of abuse between battered and non-battered women both before the first record of assault (Table 1) and after (Table 2).

Table 1 illustrates that prior to the onset of abuse there are no significant differences (except for alcohol abuse) between non-battered and battered women for other symptoms which are commonly associated with battery. In Table 2, however, there is a significant difference on all

Table 1. Problem Incidence and Referrals of Non-Battered Women and of Battered Women Prior to First Recorded Assault (per 100 Women)

Problem/Referral	Non-Battered Women	Battered Women Before Assault
Suicide attempt	3	6
Drug abuse	1	2
Alcohol abuse	1	7*
Psychiatric emergency service	7	9
Community mental health centre	3.6	4
State mental hospital	1	2
Psychosocial labels	2	4

* χ^2 significant at <.001

Source: Stark et al., 1979:468

Table 2. Overall Problem Incidence and Referrals of Non-Battered and Battered Women (per 100 Women)

Problem/Referral	Non-Battered Women	Battered Women
Suicide attempt	3	26*
Drug abuse	1	7*
Alcohol abuse	1	16*
Psychiatric emergency service	7	37*
Community mental health centre	3.6	26*
State mental hospital	1	15*
Psychosocial labels	2	22*

* χ^2 significant at <.001

Source: Stark et al., 1979:468

secondary symptoms between battered and non-battered women indicating that it is only after the physical abuse that these labels of psychiatric disorder are found in the medical record. The importance of these data is twofold. First, they illustrate that psychiatric symptoms of abuse are the effects and not the precipitators of abuse, contrary to the predominant medical wisdom on the subject. Second, they show that medical intervention is inadequate and in most instances probably exacerbates the problem of battery for the woman. Thus the pattern of abuse is heavily influenced by medical intervention, as Stark et al. have observed.

Since the pattern is invisible to medicine and emerges primarily only after the first apparent incident of abuse, and since repeated medical interventions are ineffective at best and at worst may contribute to the victim's diminishing options, the medical encounter must be carefully considered in an analysis of the evolving pattern of abuse. (1979:469)

THE BATTERED WIFE SYNDROME

The redefinition by the medical community of wife abuse into self-abuse equips the physician with a clinical classification that provides a therapeutic strategy for an otherwise diagnostic anomaly. Known as the *Battered Wife Syndrome*, this classification provides a resolution to the crisis of the cure. Stark et al. explain:

> Medicine now recognizes battering as part of a "syndrome" to which it gives a distinct materialist and social form ... by using "syndrome," battering appears as a phenomenon whose individual components are interdependent and wherein the logic of interdependence can be specified. (1979:476–77)

Viewed as a disease, the Battered Wife Syndrome can be found listed in the International Classification of Diseases: Clinical Modification, Ninth Revision (1978, Vol. 1, p. 867). In essence, this syndrome is a complex of symptoms, many of which are the result of earlier medical intervention. For example, many women diagnosed within this category are considered to be also suffering from substance abuse. Stark et al. (1979) report that battered women are more likely to receive prescriptions (24 percent) than non-battered women (9 percent), Swanson (1986) reports that 75 percent of his battered patients are using neurotropic drugs such as Valium and various antidepressants, Gayford (1975) found that 71 percent of a sample of battered women were using antidepressant drugs or tranquillizers, and a Saskatoon transition house reports that in 1986 at least 30 percent of their residents used these drugs. Since these drugs are prescribed by doctors, (and, as the above discussion illustrates, probably prior to the diagnosis of Battered Wife Syndrome), the dependency is a *product* of medical intervention, not a cause. What starts as

treatment is later interpreted as a symptom. In this way, the medical community has constructed a condition which is considered an individual pathology, and which requires individualized treatment. The social problem of wife abuse has become the individual problem of self-abuse.

There is a variety of reasons why the individualization of this social problem is possible within the medical institution and why the "blaming the victim" ideology becomes medicalized. One reason, the idea that abused women are of a Hobbesian mentality, requiring the strictest of controls for their own protection, is a common theme in the medical literature on spouse abuse. For example, in his study of 100 battered women, Dr. J. J. Gayford claimed that these women were often in need of "protection against their own stimulus-seeking activities ... they have the ability to seek violent men or by their behaviour to provoke attack from the opposite sex" (1975:197). This portrayal of battered women as deviant personalities who even enjoy their victimization is further illustrated by Snell, Rosenwald, and Robey:

> A husband's behaviour may serve to fill a wife's need even though she protests it ... such wives [are] ... aggressive, efficient, masculine, and sexually frigid ... masochism ... is typical ... The periods of violent behaviour by the husband served to release him momentarily from his ineffectiveness as a man, while at the same time giving his wife apparent masochistic gratification and helping probably to deal with the guilt arising from intense hostility expressed in her controlling, castrating behaviour. (1964:111)

In direct contrast to the victim-precipitation theory implicit in the Battered Wife Syndrome and made explicit in the above citations, Dobash and Dobash conclude that "all women ... see the injustices done to them and deny that they deserved to be hit or punished simply because their behaviour was not totally submissive" (1979:136–37).

It is the battered woman, not the abuser, who comes to the attention of the clinician, and while many physicians only diagnose a case as

Battered Wife Syndrome after many visits, many are reluctant to diagnose the abuse at all. Thus, patients are either blamed for their plight, or a medical record of misdiagnosis continues to be constructed:

> Physicians usually respond to interpersonal violence with disinterest, blame, or disbelief. They tend to stereotype the patient, blaming her for inviting the violence ... physicians may feel that domestic violence is a private concern. (Swanson, 1985:825)

Various erroneous beliefs about domestic violence, combined with negative stereotypes of women and the female role, then, have contributed to the process by which domestic violence is defined as an individual pathology.

THE CYCLE OF VIOLENCE

Another factor which has facilitated the transformation of wife abuse into self-abuse is the variety of conceptions of cause found in the medical literature. Tables 1 and 2 illustrate that the process of medical intervention led to an erroneous conception of causation. Gelles and Straus (1977) have listed fifteen theories of domestic violence, none of which adequately explains all instances of battery. However, because there is recognition that accurate causal explanations are multifaceted and involve non-medical factors, a fully medical theory of spouse abuse has yet to emerge, and the existing theories do not lend themselves to therapeutic intervention. Indeed, some researchers have concluded that causal theory is not really necessary for successful intervention because the characteristic pattern of abuse provides certain times at which intervention may be most effective (Walker, 1978).

Lenore Walker (1978) has developed what she calls the Cycle Theory of Battering Incidents. Briefly, the cycle unfolds in three distinct phases. In phase one, the "tension-building phase," the victim suffers from psychological stress as she anticipates the impending violence. In the second phase, the "explosion of acute battering incidents," the tension accumulated in the

first phase erupts into specific acts of violence. In the third phase, the "calm loving respite," the abuser is sorry and loving, while the victim wants to believe that this kind and loving behaviour will last (Walker, 1977/78).

Referred to most commonly in the literature as the "cycle theory of violence," this conception can hardly be termed a theory, in that it does little to explain the causes of interspousal violence. At best a description of the process of battery, the cycle theory of violence was developed as a predictive tool (Walker, 1977/78), and seems to fit the medical conception of disease. Many chronic illnesses, for instance, multiple sclerosis, are described in medical terms as proceeding through a cycle with three distinct phases. In phase one, the "Prodome Phase," premonitory symptoms of the disease develop. In phase two, the "Acute Phase," the illness erupts. In phase three, the "Remission Phase," the acute illness has passed and remains latent, until symptoms begin to re-emerge. Given that domestic violence is usually unrecognized until it has become chronic, it is not difficult to see why the cycle of violence theory has been so readily adopted by medical practitioners. (Ganley and Harris, 1978; Hilberman and Munson, 1977/78; Rounsaville and Weissman, 1977/78; Swanson, 1985). Figure 1 illustrates this cycle.

Figure 1: The Cycle of Violence

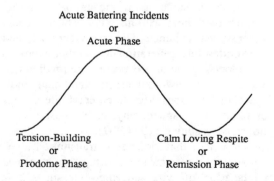

Acute Battering Incidents
or
Acute Phase

Tension-Building
or
Prodome Phase

Calm Loving Respite
or
Remission Phase

The cycle of violence theory may fit the medical paradigm, but it fails to consider the role that medical intervention itself plays in shaping the patterns of domestic violence as demonstrated by Stark et al. (1979) above. Furthermore, in their study of abuse victims Dobash and Dobash (1979) conclude that there is no evidence to support this theory:

> Only a small percentage (8%) of the husbands almost always expressed remorse immediately following the violent event; 22% usually expressed regret after a few days ... expressions of regret or contrition, apologies or helpful behavior were not typical of the men. Instead, they rarely or never expressed remorse or contrition regarding their violent actions. (1979:117)

While the cycle of violence theory is not a theory per se but a description, it does not even accurately describe the process of wife abuse. Rather, it serves to separate interpersonal violence from the social fabric in which it is embedded, thereby reducing a social process to an individual pathology. In so doing, it not only ignores the contribution of medical intervention in the shaping of the patterns of abuse, it also ignores the role that other institutions, such as the police or social services, might play in constructing this apparent cycle through selective and systematic non-intervention.

Another explanation which portrays violence as a cyclical phenomenon is the intergenerational transmission of violence. Downey and Howell (1976) have suggested that children who have been raised in a familial environment characterized by violence are more likely to resort to violence as a means of resolving conflict than those who have not. This approach suggests that violence is learned vicariously and transmitted intergenerationally, so that exposure to violence in childhood becomes a predictor of adult violence. Swanson asserts that "many individuals who witness violent parental interactions as children engage in physically abusive relationships as adults" (1984:709).

The idea that violence is transmitted intergenerationally contributes little to a causal explanation of wife-battering, but since it is often considered as one aspect of the Battered Wife Syndrome, it contributes to the conception that the abused precipitate their own victimization. Such an idea is implicit in the analysis of

marital violence by Hilberman and Munson.

> Life-long violence was the pattern for many of these women ... physical and/or sexual abuse of these women as children were described ... Although there is less access to information about husbands, they too had early exposure to emotional deprivation ... and violence, both as witnesses and as abused children. (1977/78:461)

Adopting the theory of intergenerational transmission of violence, in combination with the cycle theory of violence, suggests that violence is not only a learned response but that, from the perspective of the victim, it is an inevitable aspect of life from which there can be no escape without expert assistance. The concept of "learned helplessness," advanced by Walker (1979), which arises from theories of violence offers, besides, certain therapeutic strategies:

> experiences in childhood and those from living in a battering relationship have an impact on the woman's current state ... they appear to interfere with the battered woman's ability to successfully stop the batterer's violence towards her after he initiates it ... perceptions of helplessness can be learned ... from experiences of uncontrollability or non-contingency between response and outcome. (Walker, 1979:82–93)

The concept of learned helplessness has been readily adopted by the medical community because it suggests individual psychotherapy as the most effective treatment. As such, it contributes to the resolution of the "crisis of the cure," but it does so at the cost of redefining wife abuse as a psychopathology located in the victim. As one doctor suggests, removal to a safe environment and psychotherapy to reverse learned helplessness and low self-esteem are the "cornerstones of treatment" (Swanson, 1986).

In summary, victims of domestic violence present a particular problem for medical intervention, in that diagnostic categories into which the disparate symptoms might be interpreted are non-existent. As a result, the proper course of action remains ambiguous and leads to the "crisis of the cure." In attempting to resolve this crisis, the medical establishment has constructed the category of Battered Wife Syndrome, which, in combination with the theory of intergenerational violence, the cycle theory of violence, and learned helplessness, provide a medical conceptual framework within which treatment alternatives were developed. This process has resulted in the reorganization on the medical record of the effects of wife-battery as its causes, and wife abuse has effectively been transformed into self-abuse — an individual pathological state.

SUMMARY AND CONCLUSIONS

Violence against women in the family is a historical fact. During most of history, domestic violence was seen as a legitimate aspect of private life, and while there is no evidence to suggest that the frequency of this phenomenon has changed radically over time, its status as a social problem has altered significantly. This paper has presented the argument that the medical construction of domestic violence as an illness is a relatively recent historical development, but it is not the first institutional response to this social problem.

From the late nineteenth century, when wife abuse was "discovered" as a social problem and effectively criminalized, there was a certain reluctance on the part of justice agencies to intervene in domestic violence. In part due to patriarchal assumptions about the privacy of the home and the cultural belief that "a man's home is his castle," and in part because the victims of domestic violence were seen as precipitating their own plight, police forces exercised a policy of non-intervention. This institutional practice reinforced the domination of women in the home, and much of domestic violence remained a personal problem removed from social scrutiny. When cases did come to the attention of justice agencies, their response was one which blamed the victim, effectively privatizing the problem as an individual shortcoming.

During the 1970s, as social science, informed by feminist debate, turned its attention to the breakdown of the nuclear family, domestic violence was "rediscovered" and once more

elevated to the status of a social problem, only this time requiring a more effective form of state intervention than was offered by the agencies of justice. As government-appointed committees investigated the problem politically, the medical community was increasingly sensitized to the issue as one requiring medical attention.

Our paper suggests that the medical response to domestic violence was very similar to the earlier judicial response. Unable to resolve the problem of battered women and characteristic of traditional practices, medicine associated wife abuse with individual pathology. Stark has coined the term "institutional projection" to refer to this process of translating the failure of medicine into the personal failure of the patient.

> Helping professionals project their failures to comprehend or cope with abuse onto patients and then, when institutional failure and discipline combine with physical brutality to subdue patient initiative, read their failure back as the patient's own through diagnostic categories and treatment modalities that allegedly characterize "the victim." (1981:2)

The creation of the Battered Woman Syndrome can be viewed as a device employed by the clinician to resolve the "crisis of the cure." An amalgamation of conventional wisdom, stereotypical images of women, and naturalized patterns such as the cycle theory of violence and the intergenerational transmission of violence, the Battered Wife Syndrome effectively negates the historical struggle of women, and reduces interspousal violence to an individual pathology which can be treated and managed by the practitioner.

In the contemporary context of medical care, the clinician's practice is organized around treating individuals, not effecting social or political change. In this manner, social problems are individualized so that they will conform to the current paradigms of health care, yet these paradigms are not adjusted to adequately address the problems (Stimson, 1977). Like the judicial intervention which preceded it, the medicalization of domestic violence has not only failed to meet the social, psychological, and medical needs of the patient, but it has also incorrectly redefined them for her. In this way, the relations of domination that characterize her existence have been reinforced and legitimated. As Patricia Morgan notes:

State intervention ... acts to promote individualistic definitions of problems, their causes and "cures." In this light it can be argued that the state manages not just the problem itself, but also the image of the problem; that is, an image of social problems which supports the state's legitimacy and guards against definitions which may threaten social order. (1985:61)

NOTES

1. Clearly, the historical process does not move from one phase to the next consecutively. Rather, these phases are to be seen as parts of a process and, as such, overlap considerably. Nevertheless, there is sufficient distinction between these parts to treat them as phases for purposes of this discussion.

2. For a detailed discussion of the process by which events come to be recorded in police statistics see Sparks (1979). For a discussion of the priorities which police attach to incoming calls for help, and the proportion of class which are social-service related see Jones et al. (1986). For purposes of this discussion, the process has been somewhat simplified. There are a number of incidents in which it is some-

one other than the victim who may contact the police. Also, it is very unlikely that the police will happen upon an incident of domestic dispute without it first being reported to them.

3. Jones et al. (1986:78) have defined this as a practice whereby an action is recorded as a less serious offence than is actually the case.

4. It is only very recently that some studies of police intervention have reported upon the ways in which altering policing practice may provide for deterrence of future domestic assault by the offender. See D. Bell, 1985, Burris and Jaffe, 1986, and Langan and Innes, 1986.

STUDY QUESTIONS

1. In what ways do battered women present a problem for medicine?

2. Traditionally, victims of domestic violence have received assistance from justice agencies, social services, and the medical establishment. Which, if any, of these agencies offers the best form of intervention, and why?

3. Discuss some possibilities as to the causes of spouse abuse. In what ways do the perceived causes lead to a specific form of intervention?

4. Can you think of any ways, besides those discussed in this chapter, by which the process of medicalization constructs wife abuse?

5. This chapter has illustrated that while violence against women in the family has a long history, it is only relatively recently that it has been criminalized, and only recently that it has gained recognition as a social problem, which has been medicalized. What political and economic processes have accompanied these changes?

6. What are the factors which contribute to the bulk of domestic violence being hidden from view? In what way does hidden domestic violence differ from that which has been recorded?

7. The medical institution has failed to deal effectively with spouse abuse as a social problem and projects this failure in its strategies of intervention. Discuss.

8. What is meant by the "crisis of the cure"? Describe the process by which this crisis has been resolved in medical practice.

RECOMMENDED READING

Dobash, R. Emerson, and R. Dobash. *Violence Against Wives: A Case Against the Patriarchy.* New York: Free Press, 1979.

Johnson, N., ed. *Marital Violence.* Sociological Review Monograph no. 31. London: Routledge and Kegan Paul, 1985.

Martin, D. *Battered Wives.* San Francisco: Glide, 1976.

Pahl, J. *Private Violence and Public Policy.* London: Routledge and Kegan Paul, 1984.

Penfold, S., and G. Walker. *Women and the Psychiatric Paradox.* Montreal: Eden Press, 1983.

Walker, L. *Battered Women.* New York: Harper and Row, 1979.

REFERENCES

Ahluwalia, S., and B.D. MacLean. "Racial Biases in Policing: The Case of the Female Victim." In *The Administration of Justice*, edited by D.H. Currie and B.D. MacLean, 64–89. Saskatoon: Social Research Unit, 1986.

Bauer, C., and L. Ritt. " 'A Husband is a Beating Animal' Frances Power Cobbe Confronts the Wife Abuse Problem in Victorian England." *International Journal of Women's Studies* 6, no. 2 (1983): 99–118.

Bell, D. "A Multiyear Study of Ohio Urban, Suburban, and Rural Police Dispositions of Domestic Disputes." *Victimology: An International Journal* 10, nos. 1–4 (1985): 301–10.

Burris, C., and P. Jaffe. "Wife Abuse as a Crime." In *Crime in Canadian Society*. 3rd ed., edited by R. Silverman and J. Teevan, 115–19. Toronto: Butterworths, 1986.

Canada, Ministry of The Solicitor General. *Canadian Urban Victimization Survey: Female Victims of Crime.* Bulletin 4, Ottawa: Programs Branch/Research and Statistics Group, 1985.

Dobash, R. Emerson, and R. Dobash. *Violence Against Wives: A Case Against the Patriarchy.* New York: Free Press, 1979.

Dobash, R., R. Emerson Dobash, and S. Gutteridge. *The Imprisonment of Women.* Oxford: Basil Blackwell, 1986.

Dobash, R. Emerson, R. Dobash, and K. Cavanagh. "The Contact Between Battered Women and Social and Medical Agencies." In *Private Violence and Public Policy*, edited by J. Pahl, 142–65. London: Routledge and Kegan Paul, 1984.

Downey, J., and J. Howell. *Wife Battering: A Review and Preliminary Enquiry into Local Incidence, Needs, and Resources.* Vancouver: United Way of Greater Vancouver, Social Policy and Research, 1976.

Flitcraft, A. *Battered Women: An Emergency Room Epidemiology With a Description of a Clinical Syndrome and Critique of Present Therapeutics*, Doctoral thesis, Yale University School of Medicine, New Haven, 1977.

Ganley, A., and L. Harris. *Domestic Violence: Issues in Designing and Implementing Programs for Male Batterers.* Paper presented at the Annual Meeting of the American Psychological Association, August, 1978.

Gayford, J.J. "Wife Battering: A Preliminary Survey of 100 Cases." *British Medical Journal* 1 (January, 1975): 194–97.

Gelles, R., and M. Straus. "Determinants of Violence in the Family: Toward a Theoretical Integration." In *Contemporary Theories About the Family*, edited by W. Burr et al. New York: Free Press, 1977.

Hilberman, E., and K. Munson. "Sixty Battered Women." *Victimology: An International Journal* 2, nos. 3–4 (1977/78): 460–70.

Jones, T., B.D. MacLean, and J. Young. *The Islington Crime Survey: Crime Victimization and Policing in Inner-City London.* London: Gower, 1986.

Klaus, P., and M. Rand. *Family Violence.* Bureau of Justice Statistics Special Report, U.S. Department of Justice, 1974.

Langan, P., and C. Innes. *Preventing Domestic Violence Against Women.* Bureau of Justice Statistics Special Report, U.S. Department of Justice, 1986.

Loving, N. *Responding to Spouse Abuse and Wife Beating.* Washington D.C.: Police Executive Research Forum, 1980.

MacLean, B.D., T. Jones, and J. Young. *The Preliminary Results of the Islington Crime Survey.* London: The London Borough of Islington Police Sub-Committee, 1986.

MacLeod, L. *Wife-Battering in Canada: The Vicious Circle.* Report of The Canadian Advisory Council on The Status of Women. Ottawa: Ministry of Supply and Services, 1980.

Martin, D. "Battered Women: Society's Problem." In *The Victimization of Women*, edited by J. Chapman and M. Gates, 111–42. Beverly Hills: Sage, 1978.

McCabe, S., and F. Sutcliffe. *Defining Crime.* Oxford: Basil Blackwell, 1978.

Morgan, P. "Constructing Images of Deviance: A Look at State Intervention into the Problem of Wife Battery." In *Marital Violence*, edited by N. Johnson, 60–76. Sociological Review Monograph 31. London: Routledge and Kegan Paul, 1985.

Parnas, R. "Judicial Response to Intra-Family Violence." *Minnesota Law Review* 54 (1970): 585–645.

Pleck, E. "Wife Beating in Nineteenth-Century America." *Victimology: An International Journal* 4, no. 1 (1979): 60–74.

Rounsaville, B., and M. Weissman. "Battered Women: A Medical Problem Requiring Detection." *International Journal of Psychiatry in Medicine* 8, no. 2, 1977/78): 191–202.

Schechter, S. *Women and Male Violence.* Boston: South End Press, 1982.

Schlesinger, S. *Family Violence.* Bureau of Justice Statistics Special Report, U.S. Department of Justice, 1974.

Schwendinger, J., and H. Schwendinger. *Rape and Inequality.* Beverly Hills: Sage, 1983.

Snell, J., R. Rosenwald, and A. Robey. "The Wifebeater's Wife." *Archives of General Psychiatry* 11 (1964): 107–12.

Sparks, R. *Research on Victims of Crime: Accomplishments, Issues, and New Directions.* Crime and Delinquency Issues: A Monograph Series. Maryland: U.S. Department of Health and Human Services, 1982.

Stark, E. *The Battering Syndrome: Social Knowledge, Social Therapy and The Abuse of Women.* Doctoral dissertation, Department of Sociology, SUNY, Binghamton, 1984.

———. "Battered Women as Victims of the Helping Services." Paper presented at the Seventh Annual Conference of the National Organization for Victim Assistance, Toronto, 1981.

Stark, E., A. Flitcraft, and W. Frazier. "Medicine and Patriarchal Violence: The Social Construction of a Private Event." *International Journal of Health Services* 9, no. 3 (1979): 461–93.

Stevenson, H., and A. Williams. "Physicians and Medicare: Professional Ideology and Canadian Health Care Policy." *Canadian Public Policy* 11, no. 3 (1985): 504–21.

Stimson, G. "Social Care and The Role of the General Practitioner." *Social Science and Medicine*, 11, (1977): 485–90.

Strong-Boag, V. *The Parliament of Women: The National Council of Women of Canada 1893–1929*, The National Museum of Man, Mercury Series, History Division, Paper 18. Ottawa: National Museum of Canada, 1976.

Swanson, R. "Signs and Symptoms of Abuse." Paper presented at Saskatchewan Health Department Conference entitled *The Spouse Abuse Victim as a Hospital Patient*. Saskatoon, 1986.

———. "Recognizing Battered Wife Syndrome." *Canadian Family Physician* 31, no. 1 (1985): 823–25.

———. "Battered Wife Syndrome." *Canadian Medical Association Journal* 130 (1984): 709–12.

Szechtman, S. "Wife Abuse: Women's Duties — Men's Rights." *Victimology: An International Journal* 10, nos. 1–4 (1985): 253–66.

Thompson, J., and R. Gilby. "Correlates of Domestic Violence and the Role of Police Agencies." In *Crime in Canadian Society*, 2nd ed., edited by R. Silverman and J. Teevan, 298–306. Toronto: Butterworths, 1980.

Walker, L. *The Battered Woman*. New York: Harper and Row, 1979.

———. "Treatment Alternatives for Battered Women." In *The Victimization of Women*, edited by J. Chapman and M. Gates, 143–74. Beverly Hills: Sage, 1978.

———. "Battered Women and Learned Helplessness." *Victimology: An International Journal* 2, nos. 3–4 (1977/78): 525–34.

13

STARVATION AMIDST ABUNDANCE: Female Adolescents and Anorexia

Dawn Currie

University of Saskatchewan

Surveys indicate that during 1978, 45 percent of American households contained a dieting member. Most of these dieters were women. In fact, 56 percent of American women aged 24 to 54 years of age diet, and 76 percent of these women claim that they do so for "cosmetic" rather than health reasons (Schwartz, Thompson, and Johnson, 1985:95). After polling subscribers, *Glamour* magazine (Feb., 1984) reported that respondents were either "dissatisfied with" or "ashamed of" their stomach, hips, or thighs (Boskind-White, 1985:114).[1] Indeed, many authors claim that the relentless pursuit of thinness is a new "cultural obsession." In unusual cases this obsession can result in life-threatening behaviour when over 25 percent of original body weight is lost, and the psychological effects of malnutrition include depression with suicidal tendencies. The relationship between "normal" dieting and such abnormal preoccupation with weight loss — called anorexia nervosa — is currently a matter of academic dispute. In the more dramatic case of anorexia, research indicates

that this phenomenon of self-induced starvation is increasing, especially among female adolescents.

Epidemiological studies indicate that the diagnosis of anorexia nervosa has increased from 0.55 per 100 000 population in 1970 to 3.26 per 100 000 in 1980. This worldwide trend is reflected in Canadian data. Like American data, Canadian statistics demonstrate dramatic recent increases in the incidence of anorexia, particularly among adolescent girls. Table 1 summarizes Canadian data from 1979 onwards.[2] From this table we can see that almost 800 patients leaving general hospitals[3] in Canada during 1982–83 had been diagnosed as anorexic. Thirty-one cases were treated on the hospital wards in Saskatoon, the major treatment centre for the province of Saskatchewan.[4]

For all eating disorders, outpatient rather than inpatient figures are more important, although unfortunately this type of data is more difficult to collect. Nevertheless, Table 2 provides a "sketch" of treatment patterns for

Table 1. Numbers of Patients Hospitalized as "Anorexia Nervosa" in Canada and Saskatchewan, 1979–1984

Year	Total Cases:	CANADA: Male:		Female:		SASKATCHEWAN: Total:
		No.	%	No.	%	
1983–4	n.a.	n.a.		n.a.		31
1982–3	780	59	7.6	721	92.4	25
1981–2	814	68	8.4	746	91.6	n.a.
1980–1	725	70	9.7	655	90.3	n.a.
1979–80	581	42	7.2	539	92.8	n.a.

Note: These are absolute numbers of separations from general hospitals (excluding psychiatric wards).

Sources: Special Tabulations of Unpublished Data; General Hospital Reports; Statistics Canada Psychiatric Services Branch, Saskatchewan Health, Regina, Saskatchewan

bulimia and anorexia in Saskatoon. This table is based upon cases known to two major specialty practices in Saskatoon, the primary treatment centre in the province. The number of cases under treatment by other psychiatrists throughout the province and the proportion of less serious cases remaining under the care of family physicians is unknown. Even as a conservative estimate, however, Table 2 indicates that official data seriously underestimate the frequency of this disease and remain the proverbial "tip of the iceberg." A self-report survey of Grades 10 and 12 of a Saskatoon high school reveals that a sizeable portion of schoolgirls show "subclinical" signs of eating disturbances.[5] While 35 percent of girls in Grade 10 reported "dissatisfaction" with their current weight, this percentage increased to 56 percent by Grade 12. Correspondingly, 30 percent of Grade 10 and 46 percent of Grade 12 schoolgirls indicated an "intense fear of becoming obese." By Grade 12, 76 percent of subjects reported that they diet, with 12 percent of subjects indicating that they use dieting aids, 17 percent vomiting, and 7 percent purgatives to assist in weight loss. These results are comparable to the findings of Leichner et al. (1984) from a more extensive Manitoba survey, which found that 22 percent of females aged between 12 and 20 years show maladaptive behaviours regarding eating.[6]

The nature of the relationship between anorexia nervosa and bulimia has not yet been clearly established. One specialist reports that, impressionistically, the trend is toward proportionately a greater frequency of bulimia than anorexia, so that anorexics account for about one third of the aggregate figures in Table 2. At the same time, she reports that the age of onset for anorexia may be decreasing, with her youngest recent patient being eight years old.[7]

This chapter will examine anorexia nervosa as a "socio-somatic disease." By labelling it a disease, attention is drawn to the fact that this behaviour is accompanied by a state of physical ill-health and, further, that in terms of intervention this phenomenon has been appropriated by the "medical" rather than the "social" sciences. By labelling this behaviour as "socio-somatic," however, attention is also drawn to the fact that the physiological symptoms are secondary to social ones, despite the tendency of a medical approach to focus upon the former. In order to understand how current medical practice treats the symptoms rather than the cause of anorexia,

Table 2. Persons Treated for Anorexia and Bulimia by Saskatoon Specialists, 1984–1985

Patients in care:	474	(100.0%)
Male:	9	(1.9%)
Female:	465	(98.1%)
Residents of Sask:	441	(79.0%)
New referrals during 1985:	97	(20.0%)
Long-term cases: (over two years)	68	(14.0%)
Number hospitalized:	71	(15.0%)

Notes: Data from unpublished files. It is worth repeating here that Saskatoon specialists attract the majority, but not the total, of cases in the province.

current medical theories about etiology and treatment will be reviewed. From these theories it will be seen that within a medical framework, this "disease" is characterized as a disturbance in the "normal" functioning of individuals or their families, which "predisposes" them to pathology. In terms of understanding the *social* origin of anorexia, a sociological approach will be suggested. Within this approach a model of individual pathology is rejected, arguing instead that anorexia can be seen in relationship to the "normal" functioning of a sexist and consumption-oriented economy. To begin this exploration, the medical "symptomology" and "epidemiology" will be examined.

SYMPTOMOLOGY OF ANOREXIA NERVOSA

In 1873 Laseque provided one of the first medical documentations of the anorexic patient:

Gradually she reduces her food, furnishing pretexts, sometimes in headache, sometimes in temporary distaste, and sometimes in the fear of a recurrence of pain after eating. At the end of some weeks there is no longer a supposed temporary repugnance, but a refusal of food that may be indefinitely prolonged. The disease is now declared, and so surely will it pursue its course that it becomes easy to prognosticate the future. Woe to the physician who, misunderstanding the peril, treats as a fancy without object or duration, an obstinacy which he hopes to vanquish by medicines, friendly advice, or by the still more defective resource, intimidation.

... At this initial period, the only prudent course is to observe, to keep silent, and to remember that when voluntary inanition dates from several weeks it has become a pathological condition, having a long course to run. (in Thoma, 1967:9)

According to more recent accounts, this profile of the willfully languishing patient is little changed, although a more precise understanding of the physiological aspects has been gained.

Thoma (1967:67–76) presents a synopsis of "Henriette," a typical anorexic. At nineteen Henriette was hospitalized with 102 pounds on her 5′ 7″ frame. Her mother reported that she tired easily and had lost her usual vivacity. She ate less and her menses had ceased. Physical examination on admission indicated that Henriette was in a considerably reduced nutritional state. Fat deposits were at a minimum, her collarbones and pelvis jutted out, intercostal spaces were sunken, and her stomach was caved in. Routine tests ruled out hyperthyroidism, metabolic function, or gastric performance as the cause of her weight loss. If her disease had progressed much further, we would add a number of medical effects reported by Dwyer (1985:25) and others. For example, when body protein is reduced by 30 to 50 percent, respiratory muscle function is often impaired so that the patient is predisposed to respiratory infections and pneumonia. Changes in endocrine function can result in electrolyte imbalance so that edema is apparent. Signs of other grave problems include marked hypothermia, hypotension, toxic encephalopathy, dangerously low levels of serum potassium, and electrocardiographic abnormalities. Spack (1985:14–15) reports, in addition to these, anaemia, reversible cerebral and cerebellar atrophy, and nonreversible dental complications.

While not experiencing the extremes described above, Henriette was diagnosed as suffering from anorexia nervosa on the basis of seven symptoms distinguishing this disease from other illnesses which result in emaciation and weight loss. These include: onset of the disorder at puberty; female sex of the patient; psychically determined reduction in nutritional intake; occurrence of spontaneous or self-induced vomiting, usually in secret; amenorrhea; and the presence of physical effects of undernourishment. In severe cases, they can lead to death (Thoma, 1967:21). In terms of the social pattern of the disease, anorexia appears only in advanced industrialized countries, where adolescent women from professional families are selectively "at risk," although recent writers emphasize the "democratization" of this disorder to working-class and black families.

While the physiological status of the anorexic will be managed through medical intervention, for treatment of the primary symptoms of anorexia — obsession with dieting and weight loss — Henriette will be referred for intensive psychiatric therapy. The immediate goal of therapy will be to restore her appetite and weight. The longer-term objective, however, will be to resolve the emotional crisis which underlies her disturbed attitudes towards eating. Judging from many reports, this will be a difficult task, for anorexics characteristically are secretive about their behaviour. As a therapist, Orbach (1985:135) finds that the anorexic avoids discussions of her body size, except to insist that she needs to lose weight, and that she is extremely cagey about her eating habits. Reassuring others that she has just eaten, an anorexic invents whole meals. She finds it almost impossible to acknowledge that she has a problem, and when forced to eat with others, she will hide her food in napkins or under salad leaves. Although she desperately wants to have food, she will not submit to her desire for it. If she does submit, an anorexic may engage in binge eating, followed by a secret purging ritual of self-induced vomiting and laxatives. Overall, therapists consider anorexics to be extremely difficult to treat, which is reflected in follow-up statistics. Less than half (about 40 percent) are cured in a global sense, while approximately 30 percent are significantly improved but continue to lead symptomatic or impaired lives. Fifteen to 25 percent of former anorexics remain significantly underweight (defined as less than 75 percent of average body weight for their height and age). Twenty percent develop an apparently stable but chronic anorexia, while 9 percent die from causes related to their condition — the leading cause of death being suicide (Thompson and Gans, 1985:292–3). Orbach (1985:132) claims that the greatest obstacle to successful treatment is that, to the patient, the anorexia is *not* the problem but rather the solution. The patient continually denies that she has a problem. While others are painfully aware of her wasting away, the anorexic feels powerful and in control, so that to eat is to lose rather than to gain control.

Let us examine in greater detail the "failure" of medical intervention by exploring current psychiatric approaches.

EGO DEFICITS: ANOREXIA AS THE "FAILURE TO DIFFERENTIATE"

Perhaps it is not surprising that the earliest explanations of anorexic behaviour were influenced by the works of Freud, who discussed human development in relationship to biological imperatives. According to Freud, an erotic or "libidinal" energy is associated with various bodily functions and developmental stages. Within a psychoanalytic approach, Bruch (1973:63) argues that all bodily functions, including feeding, are exposed to a variety of appropriate and inappropriate learning experiences, reinforcements, distortions, or even extinctions due to the immaturity of the human neonate and its long period.of dependency. When bodily functions develop normally, they are used to fulfill their proper purposes. However, they may develop abnormally, in which case they are misused in the service of neurotic or psychotic conflicts. A model of early development thus focusses upon the stages necessary for normal progressive maturation and upon factors encouraging or hindering this process. A traditional psychoanalytic view is that a pathological personality structure results from the "fixation" of the instincts at one of the early stages of maturation.

One of the earliest reports of the psychoanalytic treatment of anorexia nervosa appeared in 1929. This case concerned a thirteen-year-old girl whose weight had dropped to 33 kg and who refused to eat. She claimed to have lost the sensation of hunger and she vomited violently after meals. Psychoanalysis revealed an intense fixation on the father (called the Electra complex) and the desire by the patient for a baby from the father: this was seen as the psychic motivation for the vomiting. The intense food refusal, however, was interpreted as relating to the wish for a penis. Thus, the anorexia was viewed as developing out of the desire for a child from the father, representing pathological fixation upon early feminine development (described in Bruch, 1973:216). Other classical psychoanalysts since have similarly viewed the problem as symbolically expressing an internalized sexual conflict. The syndrome is argued to be precipitated by the need for adjustment to adult feminine sexuality, with anorexic patients regressing to an infantile stage of development.

This early view of anorexia as the repudiation of sexuality dominated clinical literature for some time and can still be found in contemporary approaches. Thus when we return to the case of Henriette, we find Thoma's (1967:76) psychiatric diagnosis:

[Her crisis] is due, undoubtedly, to a problem of maturation which has appeared in connection with the physical onset of puberty. It is easy to recognize that the patient is afraid of growing up, chiefly because it means committing herself to womanhood, which she rejects as inferior, constricted, a state of passive dependency. ... In this case, it is not improbable that narcissistic, kinesthetic eroticism, such as latent homosexual leanings, contribute their part. The identification, however, is not exaggeratedly masculine; it would be better to say that a narcissistic, sexless existence is seen as providing a refuge from feminine, genital sexuality.

From this account we can see that although modern psychoanalytic thinking has moved away from a strictly symbolic approach, the avoidance of psychosexual development continues to be an important theme. Crisp (1980) defines anorexia as "a distorted biological solution to an existential problem for an adolescent." Viewed in the adolescent's terms, puberty marks the transition to adult sexual function and roles. This transition is signalled by biological changes. For girls, this means an increase of fat deposits upon specific parts of their body — breasts, hips, and thighs — all hallmarks of biological femininity. Crisp claims that, typically, the anorexic first becomes aware of these changes when the question of sexual freedom emerges. He (1980:65) continues by stating that many anorexics pass briefly and panic-stricken through a phase wherein they find themselves suddenly exposed to demands from others with which they cannot cope. According to Crisp, sexuality becomes a currency that they cannot handle. In support of this argument he cites the personal immaturity of the anorexic, arguing that given the pressures upon her, she is not equipped to be a competent adult. Crisp (1983:17) later specifies these pressures as ones of assuming responsibility for her sexuality and body, together with the development of a dependency upon self rather than family, and an orientation towards peer rather than parental values. To Crisp, the symptoms of anorexia represent a means of avoiding adolescent concerns and responsibilities. For this reason, he characterizes anorexic behaviour as experientially "adaptive" in that it postpones an otherwise imminent crisis.

In more recent approaches, psychoanalytic explanations include the nature of the parent-

child relationship in determining the successful negotiation of the developmental process. Within this literature, what was called "fixation" has been redefined as an inadequate and deficient organization of a body function so that it remains undefined, not able to be used effectively and appropriately. For example, in her studies on eating disorders, Bruch (1973) argues that the experience of hunger contains important elements of learning to differentiate self from other. Disturbances arise when individuals are unable to distinguish hunger from other states of bodily need or emotional arousal. Mothering is central to learning about hunger, because it is the mother who helps the child to establish discriminatory concepts about inner states, such as being "hungry" or "sated." "Good" mothering requires careful attention to a child's biological needs, so that food is given when the baby's cry indicates nutritional need. In contrast, when food is given as a pacifier without regard to the real reason for a child's discomfort or as a reward for "good" behaviour (and conversely withheld as punishment for disapproved actions), the child will grow up confused and unable to differentiate between various needs, feeling unable to control biological urges and emotional impulses (1973:57–58).

Bruch continues by reconstructing the early feeding histories of both obese and anorexic patients in order to argue that as children these patients came to distrust the legitimacy of their own feelings and experiences. Lacking the essential tools to deal with various developmental stages, these children were continuously bewildered and anxious, and incapable of effective self-assertion. Thus any one of the disturbed emotional reactions and defence mechanisms characteristic of a wide variety of psychiatric disorders can develop. In terms of anorexia, the mother superimposes on the child her own concept of the child's needs, so that the ego is weak and stunted. The anorexic remains in a state of arrested development and dependency, with her physical immaturity symptomatic of this failure to individuate from her mother. Because they feel "out of control," anorexics seek self-mastery through very literal control of their bodies.

General criticisms of psychoanalytic theory have been developed by a number of writers. In terms of the discussion at hand, three are important to examine. To begin, Freudian concepts of ego, super-ego, penis envy, and the like are non-empirical: they cannot be measured or tested. For this reason, although psychoanalytic theory can be appraised "rationally," i.e., according to its logic, it cannot be refuted scientifically. While this does not necessarily mean that Freudian theory is not helpful to therapists, it is difficult to read psychoanalytic accounts without suspecting that the diagnostic process is self-validating. For example, when Freudian conflicts are not overtly manifested by the patient, the psychoanalyst's tendency is to report on "latent" (i.e., unconscious to the patient) symptoms of pathology (see Findlay, 1975). At the same time, by taking a completely individualistic approach, psychoanalysts cannot account for the pattern or "epidemiology" of the disease. Historically, anorexia has been confined to young females of the upper and middle classes. In terms of explaining anorexia as a "feminine" disease, writers like Wilson (1983:20) claim that gender differentiation results from

> demands on the woman's maternal ego which confronts the feminine ego with a more complex maturational process than for males. ... The anorexic rage with the mother, which was initially rooted in repression, sadomasochistic oral conflicts, has been externalized and displaced onto food.

I have not been able to find anywhere in the psychoanalytic literature, however, explanations for the occurrence of this psychiatric phenomenon in women from predominantly upper-class families rather than in women generally, nor explanations for recent increases in the disease. Finally, a number of feminists have criticized Freudian theory generally for its sexist assumptions and portrayals of women. Janet Sayers (1982:125) in particular points out that:

> [Freud] sometimes dismissed "emancipated"

women as motivated by unresolved penis envy. He also asserted that, since the incest taboo was not reinforced in girls (as it was in boys) by castration anxiety, girls were therefore "less ready to submit to the great exigencies of life". As a result, he said, "The work of civilization has become increasingly the business of men, it confronts them with ever more difficult tasks and compels them to carry out instinctual sublimations of which women are little capable." He maintained that "We must not allow ourselves to be deflected from such conclusions by the denials of the feminists, who are anxious to force us to regard the two sexes as completely equal in position and worth."

In summary, psychoanalytic theory, when applied to anorexia, has characterized this disorder as an attempt to "avoid femininity." As a consequence, therapy is aimed at the patient's acceptance of socially defined normal "femininity" which, as we shall see, others have identified as the cause of the "illness" in the first place.

PSYCHOSOMATICALLY ORGANIZED FAMILIES: ANOREXIA AS A STRUGGLE TO DIFFERENTIATE

After the 1970s, reflecting the influence of R.D. Laing on psychiatry generally, focus shifted away from an emphasis on mother-daughter relationships to a study of interactions within the family as a whole. While earlier accounts portrayed the families of anorexics as stable, with the adoption of a family dynamics perspective, this veneer of harmony can be peeled back to reveal a multitude of disorders. The most common complaint is that mothers of anorexics are frustrated overachievers whose children are forced to compensate for her disappointments (Bruch, 1973; Taipale et al., 1971). According to Dym (1985) the mother is typically insecure and overprotective, while Taipale et al. (1971) claim that mothers of anorexics are frustrated, set high standards of performance, and cannot tolerate independence in their children. Overall, a portrait of the typical mother of the anorexic

emerges: a woman of achievement frustrated in her own career aspirations, and conscientious in her motherhood to the point of being "over-maternal" (Bruch, 1973:82). Thus the theme which emerges is that mothering interferes with the child's development. Wilson (1983:30) argues that in terms of parenting, children are over-controlled; parents are over-conscientious, emphasizing good behaviour and social conformity in their children; and that these families are successful, professional, and community-minded with a sense of "hyper-morality." In this way, although these families seldom have histories of previous mental illness and are likely to see themselves as "good" families without problems, a picture emerges of a "dysfunctional" family whose pathology is expressed through the "symptomology" of the child. Blitzer (1961) thus describes anorexia as a "family neurosis."

From this perspective, the literature begins to provide detailed profiles of parents of anorexics. However, the most that these data tell us is that anorexics appear to be the product of success-oriented upper middle-class families, an observation which does not take us beyond descriptions provided by demographic profiles. In an attempt to overcome this limitation, by the 1970s a much more structural point of view was developed. Influenced by the work on communication within the families of schizophrenics, Palazzoli studied communication patterns in anorexic families. Through observations of transactional patterns during therapy sessions, she identified five characteristics of families with an anorexic child (1974:205–16). First, she reports that members of these families tend to reject messages sent by others. At the same time, contradictory messages are often communicated to the children, with little resolution of ensuing conflict. Second, Palazzoli reports that parents have difficulty in assuming leadership roles. As a consequence, no one in the family is prepared to assume responsibility when things go wrong. Third, while open alliances between parents and child are prohibited, the child is relegated to the role of secret ally to both father and mother. She refers to this triangle as a "three-way matrimony." Fourth, Palazzoli claims that these families are characterized by a spirit of "self-sacrifice." Finally, she characterizes the marital relationship as a façade of unity which in reality conceals a profound underlying disillusionment. From these observations, Palazzoli suggests that in terms of family dynamics, an extremely rigid pattern exists, from which the anorexic symptom is an ultimate refuge.

Following the works of Palazzoli, Minuchin, Rosman, and Baker (1978) developed an open-systems model to explain childhood disorders, including anorexia nervosa. They argue that three conditions are found in families with children who develop psychotic disorders: a physiological vulnerability on the part of the child, involvement of the child in parental conflict, and a family organization characterized by four interactional patterns which they identify as enmeshment, rigidity, overprotectiveness, and lack of conflict resolution (1978:30–33). Enmeshment is a structural characteristic referring to the intensity of boundaries within the family. Enmeshment and disengagement are viewed as two extremes of a continuum: while in the former boundaries are lacking between individual family members, the latter is characterized by very fixed boundaries, in this case between parents and children. Rigidity is described in terms of the degree of adaptability of family interaction. Rigid family dynamics are pathological in that they fail to change in the face of serious internal or external stresses, which can indeed only be managed through new transactual patterns. Overprotectiveness is described as a high degree of concern of family members for each other's "welfare." In the case of anorexia, the family "hypervigilantly" focusses on the anorexic child, who may be highly protective of one or both parents, and is often involved in conflicts between parents. Finally, lack of conflict resolution is described as a low threshold for overt conflict. By means of triangulation, parent-child coalitions, and detouring, these families avoid and put off conflicts rather than confronting them. Because there are no mechanisms for negotiation, problems in the family remain unresolved. This "structural" point of view thus contains the patterns of communication described by Palazzoli (1974) and the parental descriptions provided by others, providing an explanation for anorexia in terms of family dynamics.

Within the perspective of the family as a system, the anorexic child becomes what Vandereycken and Meerman (1984:48) describe as a "lightning conductor" which is used to maintain family stability and to avoid overt conflicts, especially between parents. Since 1978, the work of Minuchin et al. has guided practitioners in the development of therapeutic interventions. Dym (1985), for example, proposes a "diagnostic model" grounded in general systems theory applied to psychosomatic family dynamics. From his sketch of what he calls prototypical family dynamics (1985:182–83), we can reconstruct the family setting of Henriette's disorder:

> Mother and anorexic daughter are intimately engaged in conversation, perhaps finishing each other's sentences, and acting as if they can read each other's minds. They are enmeshed. They are discussing whether it is reasonable for the daughter to apply for out-of-town colleges. The mother thinks this is a bad idea because her daughter is not very mature. While her daughter secretly agrees, she objects. Mother is being overprotective and, as in the past, will try to enlist her husband's support on this matter. At the moment, father seems preoccupied with his own thoughts and does not join the conversation. Then the conversation becomes heated. The father now enters in one of several ways. He may enter by saying something critical about his daughter. This is likely. But he may enter to criticize the way his wife is handling the situation. In either case, mother and daughter will temporarily suspend their heated discussion to defend the other. They will say that father does not understand. . . . Often the father will leave in frustration at this point. Nothing will have been resolved. . . . This rigid sequence will repeat itself endlessly, rendering the (rigid) family unable to adapt to the developmental crisis represented by the daughter's preparation to leave home.

From this type of "diagnostic model" offered by Dym, Henriette would be referred for "structural family therapy."

Moving beyond the individual, a family systems approach characterizes the anorexic patient as a symptom of psychosomatically organized families. This approach may appear therefore to offer a more sociological view by recognizing the individualized symptoms of anorexia as the consequence of behaviours learned within a social context. By remaining at the micro level of analysis, however, family systems theory does not meet an important criterion of the sociological approach; that is, to explain the social patterns, or "epidemiology," of anorexia nervosa. Family systems theory can only explain the overrepresentation of anorexia in upper-class and professional families, for example, by arguing that such families inhibit autonomy and fail to resolve conflict to a much greater extent than do working-class families. To my knowledge, there is no theoretical or empirical support for this claim. Further, the family systems approach cannot account for recent real increases in anorexia except to imply that the number of "dysfunctional" or psychosomatically organized families is increasing. Although a not implausible assertion, this trend would need to be included within a more completely sociological theory.

As we have seen, psychoanalytical theory has been criticized because of the untestability of its central propositions. From research accounts based on the clinical observations of family behaviour by Palazzoli (1974) and others, a family systems approach may appear as an advance over psychoanalytic theory in terms of its testability as scientific theory. A number of writers, however, have challenged the claims of this approach to empirical testability. Virtually all studies are carried out ex post facto; that is, after diagnosis. There are many reasons why family interaction, as a dynamic process, may change as a consequence of the illness of the anorexic member. Thus many of the so-called dysfunctional characteristics observed in the families of anorexics may be the result of several years of these families trying to cope with the behaviour of one of its members. Vandereycken and Meerman (1984:49) point out

that, up to the present, family theories have been based on clinical observations and impressionistic explorations rather than on methodologically reliable research. It remains to be substantiated that *specific* abnormal patterns of family interaction occur in anorexia nervosa, and that they are *causally* related to the development of the condition. Therefore, they conclude that with family therapy there may be a risk of presenting old psychosomatic personality typologies in new dress, namely, as psychosomatic family typologies.

Finally, we have seen how psychoanalytic theory accused mothers of inducing anorexia in their daughters due to "poor mothering" because they fail to empathize with their baby's needs. In contrast, within family systems theory, mothers "over-empathize." They become too involved with their child, so that anorexic behaviour is rebellion against enmeshment or overprotection and part of a struggle to differentiate self from other. Within this latter perspective, anorexia is not an avoidance of femininity on the part of the daughter, but rather an overinvolvement of the mother in her otherwise appropriate maternal role. In this way, although a "disease of womanhood," within both psychoanalytic and family systems theory, anorexia is a "disease caused by womanhood." In neither case has the very simple but significant observation of anorexia as a gender-specific disorder been used to develop a more sociological approach.

TOWARDS A SOCIOLOGICAL UNDERSTANDING OF ANOREXIA AS A "SOCIO-SOMATIC" DISEASE

Although the study of family systems begins to move beyond a strictly individualistic approach, as we have seen it has not been successful in explaining the social patterns of the disease. For example, what can these theories tell us about the increasing incidence of the disorder? Schwartz, Thompson, and Johnson (1985:101) say little, perhaps nothing at all. Yet it is the epidemiology of anorexia that provides the most compelling argument for the importance of cultural factors: anorexia is a disease which historically has appeared only in advanced consumer economies, where adolescent women from professional families are selectively "at risk." Clearly, a sociological approach capable of explaining the social character rather than the individualistic symptomology of the disease is needed.

In an assessment of cultural forces, most writers emphasize cultural stereotypes of women. In these studies, the 1960s represent a turning point, when models like Jean Shrimpton in Britain and Twiggy (also British) in the United States symbolized a new trend towards a femininity of thinness. Twiggy, in particular, was long legged and pre-adolescent, described by Schwartz, Thompson, and Johnson (1985:97) as an "idealized anorexic." According to Wallechinsky, Wallace, and Wallace (1977), prior to the arrival of these models on the fashion scene our culture's current preoccupation with thinness did not exist. Many other writers have documented a trend towards greater thinness which is apparent over the past two decades. The evidence includes studies of *Playboy* centrefolds, assessments of contestants and winners of Miss America Pageants, and surveys of the public's opinion of the most beautiful women of the world. These types of sources indicate that ideal weight declined over the twenty-year period from 1960 to 1980. Since 1970, Elizabeth Taylor declined in polls as the ideal woman, displaced by Twiggy who ranked number one in 1976 (Schwartz, Thompson, Johnson, 1985:97). This is all the more interesting given that the actual weight of women in the population at large has been in fact *increasing* due to postwar affluence. It is not surprising, therefore, that during this period there has been a steady and parallel increased interest in dieting (Garner et al., 1980). Thus Garner, Garfinkel, and Olmsted (1983:69) note that while thinness has become positively evaluated, obesity has been stigmatized during the same period. They argue that, particularly for women, thinness is a "fetish."

Bennett and Gurin (1982:171) suggest that this new image is symbolic of the women's liberation movement: the liberated woman is athletic, androgynous in her independence, and characterized by a "nonreproductive" sexuality. This image of the liberated woman is furthermore popularized by the fashion industry. In short, anorexia is portrayed as the symptom of our culture's preoccupation with thinness. Dieting is positively sanctioned, and anorexia is one end of the dieting continuum whereby voluntary weight control becomes uncontrollable dieting.

This theme of cultural thinness is especially emphasized in feminist writing about anorexia. Within a feminist perspective, rather than viewing anorexic behaviour as the "rejection" of femininity, authors focus on the anorexic's exaggerated conformity to the female sex role, society's harsh judgement of fat women, and the relationship between women's sense of ineffectiveness and powerlessness and eating disorders. Chernin (1981:2), for example, suggests that "a woman obsessed with the size of her body, wishing to make her breasts and thighs and hips and belly smaller and less apparent, may be expressing the fact that she feels uncomfortable being female in this culture." Thus Orbach (1978) and Lawrence (1979) maintain that controlling weight has become for many women a substitute for dealing with the real issues in their lives over which they lack real control. Overall, the most important gain of a feminist approach has been to identify the way in which anorexia is a gender-differentiated disorder. Feminist perspectives argue for recognition of the devalued position of women in our society as a causal factor.

In terms of the relationship between the social devaluation of women and anorexia, Orbach (1986) examines sociologically the development of psychic structure. She argues (1986:32) that this development is shaped especially by two factors: the social climate of the time and the particular models of parenting that exist. Both of these factors are culturally and historically specific. The social climate of the time is a consumer society which fetishizes the female form. In North America, consumerism is the activity through which individuals participate in their "community." Through advertising, commodities are invested with values of status, power, wealth, and sexuality — all human characteristics. Advertising suggests that acquisition of a commodity endows the purchaser with these "human" values. Within advertising campaigns, the sexuality of women's bodies is one characteristic thus imputed to commodities: by draping an automobile with a sexy model, the advertisement makes the car and therefore, also the owner of the car (traditionally male), sexy, so that he also wins a desirable woman. As a consequence of this type of advertising practice, women are encouraged to view their bodies from the outside, as if they were commodities. In assessing their body in relationship to cultural images, most women will feel discomfort which can be relieved only temporarily by clothing, diet, and cosmetics. In short, the social climate of the time has two effects on women's self-concept: women develop both a distorted assessment of their physical appearance and a sense of separation or disjuncture from their bodies. At the individual level, these effects are determined by the way in which a woman has learned to relate to her body in earlier life. Thus Orbach continues by examining the second factor in the development of psychic structure: contemporary models of parenting.

In terms of parenting, Orbach similarly stresses the fact that modes of parenting are historically specific. In particular, Orbach focusses upon the mother-daughter relationship as affecting the development of a feminine psychology, which is fertile ground for a wide range of eating disorders. Mothers of postwar babies were themselves subject to the postwar idealization of motherhood. Contained within this ideology are two deeply internalized taboos. The first is against women's expression of their own need to be nurtured by others. Girls are taught to defer to others, to anticipate the needs of others, and to seek self-definition through connection with others. These three requirements result in insecurity and an inadequate sense of self. The second taboo is against women's expression of compe-

tence. Girls are encouraged to appear "not to know" — how to change a light bulb or to repair a tire, for instance. Orbach argues that this appearance of incompetence maintains the ideological dictum of men's superiority. As a result of these two taboos, women do not feel good about themselves. Further, as women, mothers also feel ambivalent in their relationships with their daughters. While they are encouraged to push sons towards full adult competence and self-confidence on the one hand, they are required to thwart their daughters' potential on the other. Because her dependency needs, as well as her desires for autonomy are thwarted, the daughter is confused and unsure. This insecurity re-emerges during adolescence as an insecurity about her body. At the same time, many mothers have a difficult time accepting their daughters' developing sexuality. Overall, anorexia is an expression of discomfort with self and a denial of selfhood. Orbach analyzes how food becomes the battleground for this specific psychic conflict, discussing in particular the way in which femininity traditionally is linked to food through women's domestic labour at the same time as cultural standards of femininity dictate self-denial (Orbach, 1986).

In the final analysis, Orbach (1986:102–14) draws an analogy between anorexia and social protest. Anorexia is portrayed as a hunger strike, through which women, both unconsciously and consciously, protest the social conditions of womanhood. Facing a world she feels excluded from and unentitled to enter, the anorexic develops the "needless self." Therefore, the satisfaction derived from dieting concerns denial per se and not thinness. Fat represents the exposure of need, the plenty around her that she feels unentitled to. Secretive eating binges are the other side of her experience — rebellion against denial.

Overall, analyses which focus upon cultural images and values have contributed towards understanding anorexia as a *socio-* rather than *psycho*somatic disorder. Recent writers, especially feminists, have done a great deal to help explain why anorexia is associated with the values propounded by a consumer society which promotes sexist images of women. At the same time, however, although writers like Orbach identify mechanisms whereby these values may become internalized in such a way as to become the basis for psychological disturbance, they raise a number of new questions. First, why do only women from middle-class families, and not all women exposed to these socio-cultural pressures, develop an eating disorder? Further, if cultural portrayals are the central causal factor, how do new stereotypes which are argued to be symbolic of the emancipation of women contribute to continued oppression rather than liberation? The new woman is portrayed as athletic rather than physically incompetent, sexual in a non-procreative way, and androgynous in her independence. According to feminist writers like Orbach and Chernin, it is this new image towards which anorexic (and non-anorexic) women are striving. Feminists struggling against old cultural portrayals of women, however, may ask whether images with these apparently more positive connotations simply result in a new "disease" for women. I believe that the answer to this question lies in understanding the incompleteness of an explanation based entirely on cultural values. The remainder of this chapter will sketch out a more broadly based approach.

Although cultural representations of women now include the competent woman, physically lithe and in control of her destiny, images which emphasize voluptuous sexuality and feminine dependence are not hard to find. Starlets of popular entertainment like Dolly Parton and, more recently, Madonna, can hardly be credited with creating "androgynous" images of women.[8] Perhaps more "competent" than earlier counterparts, these women are seductive in their sexuality and traditional in their physical portrayal of femininity. According to Saskatchewan Consumer and Commercial Affairs (1983:60), "old" stereotypes of women still persist. In studies of television advertising, 77 percent of leading roles in advertisements for food, cleaning products, laundry, or the care of the household and its members were filled by women. Men were shown as incompetent in the kitchen and involved in cleaning only while "the little lady" was away. Women were portrayed primarily as nurturing and serving others. They were also depicted as emotionally, intellectually, and physically dependent and in constant need of advice, as childish, illogical, and frivolous, spending money wildly on luxuries, as jealous, passive and seductive, as incomplete without a man, as obsessed with the approval of a man or her children, worshipped only if young, slender, beautiful, and "shapely", and as decorations or sex objects. What about the liberated "new woman"?

In effect, it seems difficult to conclude that old stereotypes of women have been replaced with new ones. Through careful observation it can be found that there are double messages for women. On the one hand, society has witnessed in the media the debut of women embodying personhood, achieving in the world with competence and a strong sense of self. On the other hand, the old image of women as traditionally dependent and in secondary roles is far from extinct. Thus there are contradictory images of women. What does this tell us about the role and the status of women today?

The autonomy so recently ascribed to the "new woman" reflects actual changes in the material position of women. The increasing participation of women in the labour force is a striking characteristic of postwar employment. By the late 1970s, 60 percent of women at any moment were gainfully employed. Professions like law and medicine were no longer the exclusive domain of men, so that the influx of women into these programmes of study has resulted in a more balanced sex ratio among students in higher education. In Canada, women are increasingly represented in postsecondary institutions (university and non-university). While they made up 38 percent of the enrollment in 1962–63, by 1974–75 this figure rose to 51 percent (Mackie, 1983:189). Accompanying these changes is a steady decline in fertility, so that the typical completed family consists of two children spaced two or three years apart. While traditionally a woman's adult life was consumed in the bearing and rearing of children, today the extent of her care of dependent children represents nine years, or one sixth of the hypothetical adult life span (Daniels and Weingarten, 1983:3). These changes in the roles of women are popularly portrayed as indicators of the "liberation" of women. The new role of women is no longer centred upon reproductive capacity, but emphasizes instead their activities in the labour force and as consumers. This new role is reflected in cultural stereotypes of the "non-maternal" woman, autonomous and fully active in public life.

At the same time that these changes represent a historical improvement in the material position of women, a number of recent assessments suggest that this "liberation" has not been as extensive as may first appear. Although the rates of labour force participation have increased, the types of jobs held by women have not changed very much at all. The Advisory Council on the Status of Women reports that the majority of women working in Canada are in service and clerical jobs, with professional careers being restricted to the traditionally feminine fields of health care and teaching. Within these professions women seldom hold the most prestigious positions, so that very few women are working "at the top." In 1984 only 8 percent of employed women were in managerial or administrative positions. Canadian women remain concentrated in the "female" job ghetto, where chances for promotion are few and wages are low. As a group, women earn about 58 percent of men's earnings. Even after controlling for job training and experience, these earnings do not match those of men, remaining around 80 percent of men's earnings (Phillips and Phillips, 1983:59). Others have shown how this persistence of sexual discrimination is furthermore evident in education, resulting in a "hidden curriculum" which prepares women for traditional aspirations (Sutherland, 1978). Women in post-secondary education continue to enroll mostly in traditional fields such as the arts, education, and nursing. Although the enrollment of women in traditionally male-dominated professions such

as law, medicine, and commerce has increased sharply, the proportion remains small relative to males. Finally, a number of writers have noted that while women are moving into waged employment, the participation of men in domestic labour has changed very little. Women remain primarily responsible for both housework and child care, so that most working women are in reality struggling with two demanding "careers." Thus, women's family responsibilities have been identified as the primary obstacle to the achievement of both *real* equality (measured by achievement in education, income, etc.) and *substantive* equality (measured as quality of life). What does this tell us about the "liberation" of women?

After examining the empirical reality of women's lives rather than simply cultural portrayals, it becomes apparent that the "liberation" of women has been confined to a minority of women rather than women generally. Overall, society prepares women primarily for motherhood and secondarily for autonomy and independence. As Oakley (1979) and Veveers (1980) have argued, the motherhood mandate is alive and well. While it is acceptable for women to achieve vocationally, the prescription for motherhood demands conformity to traditional feminine roles. Like other "opportunities," the opportunity for women to pursue non-traditional roles is confined to those few women with access to resources which enable them to individually negotiate structural barriers (for example, resources which allow a woman to replace her own domestic and child-care labour with purchased labour). Although the media tend to ascribe the success of these women to their personal characteristic of being "liberated," in a consumer economy, most "negotiation" occurs in the marketplace. In this way, new opportunities for women are class-biased in that they are restricted to women who can afford them. For this reason, the conflict resulting from contradictory messages for women about their adult role will be most acute for women from upper- and middle-class families who are the beneficiaries of new choices for women. For most women, their life path is unambiguous because there are few real alternatives. For adolescent girls from success-oriented families who can afford to encourage their daughters academically, the double message may render the transition from prepubescent emotional and economic dependency to the autonomy of adulthood problematic. Weitzman has shown (1979:170–71), for example, that working-class families emphasize conformity to traditional gender roles, while middle-class families value traditional gender roles for daughters, but also encourage independence and assertiveness. For these women, the idealized image of the liberated career woman is accessible. Yet at the same time, its achievement is undermined by processes which continue to reproduce the traditional role expectations for women. Thus Weitzman (1979) also reports that adolescent girls equate intellectual success with a loss of femininity. The source of conflict wrought by these contradictory messages will not be immediately apparent, however, for the reproduction of social inequalities is submerged beneath an appearance of democratic opportunity. Thus conflict is not directed outward, but turned inward. Women individually cannot "control" the contradictory demands placed upon them externally and symbolically through the media. They can, however, struggle continuously to "control" their personal body image. As Orbach (1986) and others have argued, the struggle of the anorexic is not simply to achieve thinness, but to achieve *control*. Sociologically, anorexia can be understood not simply as the *internalization of cultural images of women*, but as the internalization of the *conflict fostered by contradictory images of women*, arising from the contradictory position of contemporary women in capitalist societies.

CONCLUSIONS AND DISCUSSION

What is outlined above is not a theory of anorexia, but a view of anorexia as rooted in social and cultural processes. While viewing anorexia as psychosomatic limits our thinking

about anorexia to a disorder rooted in the psychology of individual women, seeing it as sociosomatic allows us to think about its relationship to the material social world. It is only through the latter perspective that the social and historical patterns can be understood. Anorexia is found only in capitalist societies where women represent 90 to 95 percent of reported cases. While historically a rare disorder, "outbreaks" of anorexia are recorded for two periods during which the roles for women were changing: the 1920s and the 1970s. As now, the twenties were characterized by new autonomy for women, with expanded opportunities in terms of both education and employment. Yet as we have seen, the so-called liberation of women in capitalist society is a contradictory phenomenon. While the rhetoric is one of equality, the utilization of opportunities which impart equality is compromised by women's domestic and child-care roles, so that economically women's earnings remain a fraction of those of their male counterparts, and politically women are underrepresented in positions of authority and decision-making. Some feminists, like myself, believe that women cannot be liberated within a capitalist system, because gender stratification is maintained by processes which perpetuate class hierarchies. While this debate is beyond the scope of this chapter, it does suggest that without radical social change anorexia cannot be eliminated.

While sociologists are not against treating those who suffer from social injustices on an individual basis, they do emphasize that "treatment" must move beyond the individual to the social level if social "diseases" are to be eradicated. It is within this long-term perspective that "feminist" therapies stress consciousness-raising. Returning to the case of Henriette, feminist therapy would enable her to recognize her disorder as a symptom of her oppression as a woman in a capitalist society. From a traditional approach, Thoma claimed that Henriette's problem is chiefly because she rejects a commitment to womanhood which *she sees as inferior, constricted, and a state of passive dependence*. Traditional therapy therefore emphasizes the need for Henriette to change this view of womanhood as a misperception. Within a feminist therapy, however, Henriette would be encouraged to recognize that within contemporary society *women in reality are seen as inferior and are constricted and confined to roles of dependence.* By recognizing the dynamics of her oppression, Henriette would be able to see that her personal conflict stems from her struggle to individually reconcile contradictory messages about the liberation of women. At the same time, it would encourage her to join with the many other women and men who are struggling on many levels to eradicate the cause of her disorder through change at the social rather than the individual level. It is this potential which differentiates a sociological from a strictly medical approach.

Acknowledgements: A number of people have assisted in the preparation of this chapter. In particular I would like to thank Dr. A. Thakur of the Anorexia Nervosa & Bulimia Foundation of Saskatchewan, Dr. P. Matthews of the Department of Psychiatry at the University of Saskatchewan, and Rod Riley of Statistics Canada for invaluable assistance in data collection. Also, I would like to thank Singh Bolaria, Harley Dickinson, and Gerry Pearson for their helpful comments in the write-up of this paper.

NOTES

1. While comparable data for Canadian women do not exist, there are few reasons to expect that Canadian trends are substantively different.

2. 1979 is the first year in which a separate diagnostic category appears in official statistical reports.

3. The numbers of patients separated from psychiatric hospitals are not included in these figures because they are not available for every reported year. Therefore the figures presented here are "conservative" estimates, although the majority of cases are admitted to general hospitals. During 1979–80, 45 separations from psychiatric institutions are reported, a figure which is similar for the years 1981–2 and 1983–4.

4. Saskatoon treats most of the cases of anorexia and bulimia in Saskatchewan for three primary reasons: Saskatoon is the only psychiatric facility with an adolescent unit in Saskatchewan; Saskatoon has specialists who attract patients; and there is an Anorexia and Bulimia Society in Saskatoon.

5. Unpublished survey, personal communication.

6. An unpublished paper "Screening for Anorexia Nervosa and Bulimia in a Canadian School Age Population" by Pierre Leichner, John Arnett, Suja Srikameswaran, and Brent Vulcano, presented to the Department of Psychiatry, University of Manitoba, 1984.

7. Personal communication with author.

8. It is perhaps interesting to ponder Dolly Parton's recent anorexia.

STUDY QUESTIONS

1. What other behaviours besides eating are often thought to be "instinctual"? How does an analysis of anorexia nervosa highlight the shortcomings of studying these behaviours as biological rather than social?

2. Compare and contrast the assumptions and explanations for eating disorders within biomedical, psychoanalytic, socio-psychological, and sociological perspectives.

3. Why might a medical model be inappropriate

for understanding mental illnesses in women generally?

4. What types of social changes do you think are necessary to eliminate a "disease" such as anorexia nervosa?

5. Why are "micro-level" explanations for diseases more common in discussions about health than sociological explanations? What other diseases might be better understood from a sociological rather than a strictly medical approach?

RECOMMENDED READING

TRADITIONAL APPROACHES

Bruch, Hilde. *Eating Disorders: Obesity, Anorexia Nervosa, and the Person Within.* New York: Basic Books, 1973.

Emmett, Steven Wiley. *Theory and Treatment of Anorexia Nervosa and Bulimia: Biomedical, Sociocultural, and Psychological Perspectives.* New York: Brunner/Mazel Publishers, 1985.

Spatz Widom, C. *Sex Roles and Psychopathology.* New York: Plenum Press, 1984.

Wilson, Philip C., ed. *Fear of Being Fat: The Treatment of Anorexia Nervosa and Bulimia.* New York: Jason Aaronson, 1983.

CRITICAL/FEMINIST PERSPECTIVES

Chernin, Kim. *The Obsession: Reflections on the Tyranny of Slenderness.* New York: Harper & Row, 1981.

Lawrence, M. "Anorexia Nervosa — The Control Paradox." *Women's Studies International Quarterly* 2 (1979): 93–101.

Orbach, Susie. *Hunger Strike: An Anorexic's Struggle as a Metaphor for our Age.* New York: W.W. Norton & Company, 1986.

REFERENCES

Bennett, W.B., and J. Gurin. *The Dieter's Dilemma: Eating Less and Weighing More.* New York: Basic Books, 1982.

Blitzer, J.R., N. Rollins, and A. Blackwell. "Children Who Starve Themselves: Anorexia Nervosa." *Psychosomatic Medicine* 23 (1961): 368–83.

Boskind-White, Marlene. "Bulimia: A Sociocultural Perspective." In *Theory and Treatment of Anorexia Nervosa and Bulimia,* edited by S. Emmett, 113–26. New York: Brunner/Mazel Publishers, 1985.

Bruch, Hilde. *Eating Disorders: Obesity, Anorexia Nervosa, and the Person Within.* New York: Basic

Books, 1973.

Chernin, K. *The Obsession: Reflections on the Tyranny of Slenderness.* New York: Harper and Row, 1981.

Crisp, A.H. "Some Aspects of the Psychotherapy of Anorexia Nervosa." In *Anorexia Nervosa: Recent Developments and Research*, edited by Darby, Garfinkel, Garner, and Coscina, 15–28. New York: Alan R. Liss Inc., 1983.

———. *Anorexia Nervosa: Let Me Be.* London: Academic Press, 1980.

Daniels, Pamela, and Kathy Weingarten. *Sooner or Later: The Timing of Parenthood in Adult Lives.* New York: W.W. Norton & Co., 1983.

Darby, P., P. Garfinkel, D. Garner, and D. Coscina, eds. *Anorexia Nervosa: Recent Developments and Research.* New York: Alan R. Liss Inc., 1983.

Dwyer, Johanna. "Nutritional Aspects of Anorexia and Bulimia." In *Theory and Treatment of Anorexia Nervosa and Bulimia*, edited by S. Emmett, 20–50. New York: Brunner/Mazel Publishers, 1985.

Dym, Barry. "Eating Disorders and the Family: A Model." *Theory and Treatment of Anorexia Nervosa and Bulimia*, edited by S. Emmett, 174–93. New York: Brunner/Mazel Publishers, 1985.

Emmett, S. *Theory and Treatment of Anorexia Nervosa and Bulimia: Biomedical, Sociocultural, and Psychological Perspectives.* New York: Brunner/Mazel Publishers, 1985.

Findlay, D. Smith, and S. David, eds. *Women Look at Psychiatry.* Vancouver: Press Gang Publishers, 1975.

Garner, D., P. Garfinkel, and M. Olmsted. "An Overview of Sociocultural Factors in the Development of Anorexia Nervosa." In *Anorexia Nervosa: Recent Developments and Research*, edited by Darby, Garfinkel, Garner, and Coscina, 65–82. New York: Alan R. Liss Inc., 1983.

Garner, D.M., P.E. Garfinkel, D. Schwartz, and M. Thompson. "Cultural Expectations in Women." *Psychological Reports* 47 (1980): 483–91.

Lawrence, M. "Anorexia Nervosa — The Control Paradox." *Women's Studies International Quarterly* 2 (1979):93–101.

Mackie, Marlene. *Exploring Gender Relations.* Toronto: Butterworths, 1983.

Minuchin, Salvador, B. Rosman, and L. Baker. *Psychosomatic Families.* Cambridge: Harvard University Press, 1978.

Oakley, Ann. *From Here to Maternity.* London: Penguin Books, 1979.

Orbach, Susie. *Hunger Strike: An Anorexic's Struggle as a Metaphor For Our Age..* New York: W.W. Norton & Company, 1986.

———. "Visibility/Invisibility: Social Considerations in Anorexia Nervosa – A Feminist Perspective." In *Theory and Treatment of Anorexia Nervosa and Bulimia*, edited by S. Emmett, 127–40. New York: Brunner/Mazel Publishers, 1985.

———. *Fat Is a Feminist Issue.* New York: Paddington Press, 1978.

Palazzoli, M.S. *Self-Starvation.* London: Chaucer, 1974.

Phillips, Paul, and Erin Phillips. *Women and Work: Inequality in the Labour Market.* Toronto: James Lorimer and Co., 1983.

Saskatchewan Consumer and Commercial Affairs. *Advertising.* Education and Communications Branch, 1983.

Sayers, Janet. *Biological Politics: Feminist and Anti-Feminist Perspectives.* London: Tavistock Publications, 1982.

Schwartz, D.M., M.G. Thompson, and C.L. Johnson. "Anorexia Nervosa and Bulimia: The Sociocultural Context." In *Theory and Treatment of Anorexia Nervosa and Bulimia*, edited by S. Emmett, 95–112. New York: Brunner/Mazel Publishers, 1985.

Spack, Norman. "Medical Complications of Anorexia Nervosa and Bulimia." In *Theory and Treatment of Anorexia Nervosa and Bulimia*, edited by S. Emmett, 5–19. New York: Brunner/Mazel Publishers, 1985.

Sutherland, Sharon. "The Ambitious Female: Women's Low Professional Aspirations." *Signs* 3 (1978): 774–94.

Taipale, V., O. Tuomi, and M. Aukee. "Anorexia Nervosa, An Illness of Two Generations." *Acta Paedopsychiat* 38 (1971): 21–25.

Thompson, M.G., and M.T. Gans. "Do Anorexics and Bulimics Get Well?" In *Theory and Treatment of Anorexia Nervosa and Bulimia*, edited by S. Emmett, 291–303. New York: Brunner/Mazel Publishers, 1985.

Thoma, Helmut. *Anorexia Nervosa*. New York: International Universities Press, Inc., 1967.

Vandereycken, W., and R. Meermann. *Anorexia Nervosa: A Clinician's Guide to Treatment*. New York: Walter de Gruyter & Co., 1984.

Veveers, Jan. *Childless by Choice*. Toronto: Butterworths, 1980.

Wallechinsky, D., I. Wallace, and A. Wallace. *Book of Lists*. New York: William Morrow, 1977.

Weitzman, L.J. *Sex Role Socialization*. Palo Alto: Mayfield Publishing Co., 1979.

Wilson, Philip C., ed. *Fear of Being Fat: The Treatment of Anorexia Nervosa and Bulimia..* New York: Jason Aronson, 1983.

Wilson, Philip C., ed. "The Family Psychological Profile and Its Therapeutic Implications." In *Fear of Being Fat*, edited by Philip C. Wilson. New York: Jason Aronson, 1983.

PART V

HEALTH CARE
AND THE ELDERLY

INTRODUCTION

The demographic profile of Canadian society is rapidly changing. It is projected that by the turn of the century the elderly will constitute a significant proportion of the population. Also, the proportion of those commonly referred to as the "old old" or "frail old" is increasing among the elderly group. The increase of the elderly population has important implications for planning and delivery of health-care services.

It should be noted, however, that the elderly population is by no means homogeneous. Socio-economic status, age, and gender influence the need for health care and other services. In addition to socio-economic diversity and gender, ethnic and cultural differences associated with the process of aging must be taken into account when considering health-related issues. Ujimoto, in Chapter 14, examines the relationship between aging, ethnicity, and health.

Ujimoto argues that an understanding of what is meant by ethnicity is important to an understanding of differential adjustment to aging by ethnic minorities, and for an understanding of their attitudes and behaviour towards aging from a health-care perspective. While the concept of ethnicity can be viewed in several different ways, Ujimoto emphasizes that the systematic or integrative approach that draws upon the different conceptions of ethnicity is necessary to comprehend the dynamics of the aging process as it relates to the health status and general well-being of the elderly.

Regardless of ethnic, racial, and cultural differences, all elderly people face some common health problems. There is a normal decline in physical, mental, and functional ability with advancing age. However, as Ujimoto notes, ethnic and cultural differences are important in relation to perceptions of personal health and illness, perceptions of "seriousness" of the problem, responses to illness, health status, utilization of services, and coping responses and medications used to "manage" physical and psychological stress or illness.

Ujimoto argues that it is important for health-care professionals and other "providers" of health care to recognize ethnic or cultural peculiarities in order to avoid any "cultural misunderstandings." This requires a greater sensitivity to the cultural dimensions of how illnesses are viewed in different ethnic groups. In this regard, an excellent start has been made by the Multicultural Health Coalition in Ontario and Doctors' Hospital in Toronto.

While Ujimoto provides a broader discussion of aging, ethnicity, and health, the focus in Chapter 15 by Tarman is on the elderly, specifically in terms of health-care policy and institutional care.

A variety of institutions provide social and health services for the elderly. Despite the importance of such care, in particular for the "old old" group, there is no uniform and coherent Canadian policy or set of regulations to govern the accommodation standards, funding arrangements, and quality of care. Other than certain conditions which have to be met to retain eligibility for federal cost-sharing arrangements, provinces more or less set their own requirements for the operation and funding arrangements of special care facilities for the elderly.

Evidence shows that a large number of special care facilities in Canada are privately owned. There is considerable variation by provinces in type of ownership.

The discussion on the development of health policy regarding nursing homes in Ontario indicates that the provincial policy has not been oriented toward a complete transformation of the nursing home industry. The provincial government for the most part has been content to "regulate" the industry by requiring certain accommodation and health standards. Though these requirements have had beneficial results, they have also led to an increase in the number and size of facilities with private and corporate ownership. This situation has proved to be advantageous for larger units, enabling them to make large profits. The critics charge that the profit motive is incompatible with quality of care; they advocate the complete transformation of all health-care institutions for the aged to public non-profit facilities.

14

AGING, ETHNICITY, AND HEALTH

K. Victor Ujimoto
University of Guelph

INTRODUCTION

It is a well-recognized fact that the demographic profile of Canadian society is rapidly changing. The 1981 census indicates that there were over 2.4 million people in the age category 65 and over. Stone and Fletcher (1980:8) and McDaniel (1986:36) have shown that the proportion of our elderly population has been increasing consistently since 1901. According to Health and Welfare Canada (1983:12), only 5 percent of the total Canadian population was over 65 years of age in 1901, but by 1981, this proportion had increased to 9.7 percent. Stone and Fletcher (1980:10) predict that the population over 65 will continue to grow until 2016, at which time it is expected to decline. This means that, in terms of numbers at least, the elderly are becoming a more significant group today than ever before and will continue to have an important impact on Canadian society in terms of pension benefits, health, and other issues relating to health-care systems.

There is another important aspect of demographic change that is occurring, and that is the multicultural nature of Canadian society. The aging population is no longer homogeneous, and the ethnic cultural differences associated with the processes of aging must be taken into account when considering health-related issues. The heterogeneity of our aging population is illustrated in Figure 1, in which it can be seen that the proportion of those 65 years of age and over is particularly high for certain ethnic groups, such as the Jewish, Polish, and Ukrainian. However, given the present demographic trends, we can expect changes to reflect the current increases in the percentage/age distribution of the foreign-born. Moreover, as shown in Figure 2, recent emigration to Canada has shifted away from the traditionally European countries to predominantly Asian, African, Caribbean, and South American countries. For an aging and culturally diverse society, it is extremely important to begin to understand the cultural variations that exist today, especially as regards provision of health care and the well-being of the ethnic minority. Several general questions will be addressed in this chapter: What do we need to know about ethnic culture to understand the adjustment to aging by ethnic minorities? What do we need to know about atti-

Figure 1. Population 65 Years and Over as a Percentage of the Total Population for Selected Ethnic Groups, Canada, 1981

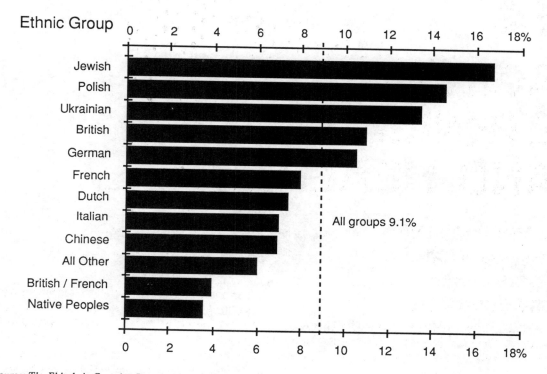

Source: *The Elderly in Canada.* Ottawa: Statistics Canada, 1984, Chart 6, p. 13.

tudes and behaviour towards aging for effective health care and social support? What can be done to bridge the cultural gap in health-care provision?

ETHNICITY AND AGING

Until very recently, the study of ethnic variations in the aging experience has received very little attention in Canadian gerontological literature. Earlier studies that attempted to examine the influence of ethnicity on aging failed to differentiate between the various meanings associated with the term. One of the first attempts to clarify what is usually meant by ethnicity is provided by Rosenthal (1986:19). From an extensive review of the literature, she culled the following three conceptions of ethnicity: ethnicity as culture, especially immigrant culture; eth-

nicity as a determinant of social inequality; and ethnicity as synonymous with "traditional" ways of thinking and behaving. As indicated by Rosenthal, each of the above conceptions of ethnicity will lead to a different model of aging of ethnic families, because of the differential emphasis placed on the concept. Therefore, she argues for an integrative approach in the study of ethnic families, in which connections or linkages between various conceptions of ethnicity can be made. This approach makes considerable sense, especially in the study of some ethnic families in which generational cohorts can be clearly identified, and thus different conceptions of ethnicity can be applied to each generation.

The first conception of ethnicity as culture, particularly immigrant culture, takes on added significance if we reconsider the demographic changes, noted earlier, that are taking place in

Figure 2. Canadian Immigration from World Areas, 1984

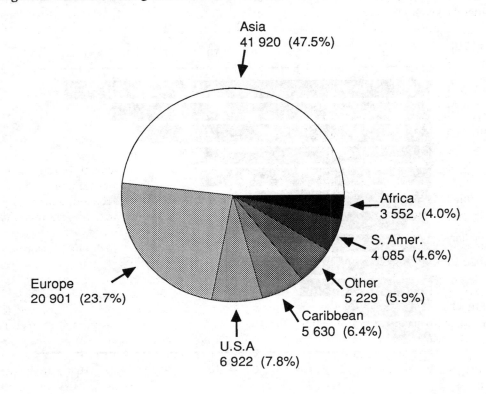

Source: *Immigration Statistics* 1984. Ottawa: Employment and Immigration Canada.

Canadian society. It is fairly safe to assume that there will always be an immigrant or a first generation of the various ethnic groups in Canada. Therefore, the conception of ethnicity as immigrant culture requires a clear understanding of the various elements or components that constitute a given ethnic culture. Most definitions of culture include shared meanings (Gordon, 1964; Fry, 1980; Marshall, 1980; Hagedorn, 1986). As described by Hagedorn (1986:36), meanings are usually shared through the various components of culture such as beliefs, norms, mores, values, and symbols.

An interesting point to be made in the definition of culture, which has been noted by Rosenthal (1986:20), is that while some definitions of culture include both shared meanings and patterns of behaviour, others do not. For our purposes, however, it will be argued that the various components of culture, such as beliefs, norms, mores, values, and symbols that constitute the shared meanings are important only in influencing behavioural outcomes. The extent to which each component of culture influences behaviour will depend on the degree of "institutional completeness," a term developed by Breton (1964:193) to describe the extent to which various social organizations are developed in an ethnic community. For example, depending on the immigrant's age at the time of emigration, beliefs are most likely influenced by the earlier socialization processes. The traditional norms or the rules of behaviour ingrained in the immigrant's mind may or may not be reinforced, depending on the size, density, ethnic composition, and the degree of institutional completeness of his or her ethnic community. Similarly, the enforcement of traditional mores and patterns of social interaction based on a system of mutual obligations is also most likely to be influenced by the degree of institutional completeness.

Another important argument that is advanced by Rosenthal (1986:20) is that further distinction must be made between ethnic culture and immigrant culture. She argues that "if the conception of culture is limited to immigrant culture, then ethnic variability in family life should decrease over successive, new immigrant generations." While we have implied previously that immigrant culture is a "transplanted phenomenon," to use Rosenthal's term, and that its influence on behaviour will depend on the degree of institutional completeness, it must be underscored that ethnic cultural characteristics continue to exist, although in slightly modified forms. Some of these characteristics that impinge on the general positive health status and well-being of the elderly will be discussed later in further detail.

The second conceptualization of ethnicity as a determinant of inequality by Rosenthal (1986:20) draws attention to the ways in which previous research has tended to equate ethnic group with minority group. While the main focus of current debate has been on the lack of distinction between social class and ethnicity (Holzberg, 1982) as key independent variables to account for variations in aging, there are nevertheless several key factors that are relevant to our present discussion on ethnicity and inequality. Since there are several different forms of inequality in Canadian society, we must be extremely careful in selecting the particular one that we wish to address, not so much in terms of ethnicity, but with reference to our dependent variable, for example, the health status and well-being of our elderly.

The most common form of inequality is economic inequality, or the variations in one's income and other material resources. A key to understanding economic inequality with reference to ethnic groups is to understand the long history of their exploitation by the dominant culture, especially of the immigrant or first-generation ethnic group, and in many instances, that of institutional racism (Bolaria and Li, 1983). The effects of institutional racism prevented equal access to many institutions and further increased economic inequality.

Another aspect of continued economic inequality which was deeply rooted in institutional racism was the eventual relegation of some ethnic groups to ethnic minority status. The concomitant effects of economic inequality, deprivation, lack of political power, minority status, and hence, social inequality, all contributed to the lack of the individual's sense of identity. The sense of who we are and how we relate to others depends on the position we occupy in the social structure. Another way of looking at this situation is to see which group or groups occupy a dominant position or a subordinate position in terms of influence and decision-making. The numerical size of the group, where they are located in territory, their role in the economy, their level of education, and the occupational position held all tend to influence not only the identity of the ethnic group members, but also the attitudes of the dominant groups towards the minority group. Attitudes in turn govern social relationships and the degree to which meaningful social interaction can take place. The development of one's ethnic identity and the strengths of this identity in relation to the extent of external or societal constraints is a complex issue that requires further investigation.

The third conception of ethnicity advanced by Rosenthal (1986:20) as synonymous with "traditional" as opposed to the "modern" ways of thinking and behaving is based on several assumptions and misconceptions. As in the first conceptualization of ethnicity as culture, particularly immigrant culture, there is the implicit assumption that the traditional forms of family life and social discourse are retained and that ethnic culture does not change. Thus, there is a very strong tendency for researchers to idealize the ethnic family. Cultural change and generational differences in cultural retention have been subordinated or altogether neglected. This tendency to both generalize and idealize the ethnic family in traditional family typology stems partly from the inclination to equate ethnic group with minority group; this latter labelling implies that the ethnic group is a relative newcomer to Canadian society. This implication has often been based on the lack of appreciation of the history of the ethnic group concerned, which in several instances may go back several generations. By conveniently disregarding the history and social experiences of the ethnic groups in Canadian society, and also by failing to differentiate between various ethnic groups, it has been possible to dichotomize ethnicity in terms of the traditional and modern orientations.

While the limitations of conceptualizing ethnicity in terms of the traditional and modern typology may be fairly obvious, it should be observed that the influence of traditional roles and values is still extremely important to our understanding of the variations in aging, health care, and mental health. Furthermore, it will be equally clear that a simple definition of ethnicity will no longer suffice, and that we must draw upon several different conceptions of ethnicity in order to capture the dynamics of the aging process as it relates to the health status and general well-being of the elderly. However, before we proceed to examine the relationship between the various components of ethnicity and the social aspects of aging as they relate to health, a brief overview of what is meant by health, health care, and mental health will be provided.

AGING AND HEALTH

The well-being of the individual becomes a primary concern especially when one approaches retirement age. Health is a crucial variable in assessing the individual's well-being, regardless of age. What is meant by health? Shanas and Maddox (1985:701) note that health in the aged is usually defined in terms of the presence or absence of disease, or in terms of the ability to function. The determination of health in terms of the presence or absence of disease is generally considered to be an objective assessment, because it is based on medical examinations and laboratory tests to confirm the medical diagnosis. However, Shanas and Maddox also note that a truly objective measure of health is difficult to achieve, and that the administration of the laboratory test to measure health varies from time to time. They provide, as an example, physiological measures such as blood-pressure readings and glucose levels.

Although Canadian data on the objective measures of health for various ethnic groups are not readily available, it may be instructive to use American data to illustrate the differences in the average annual number of deaths by various disease category. These data, which are provided in Tables 1a–1d, are for 1979–1981. While the data presented reflect the health problems of the "visible minorities," namely, blacks, Hispanics, Native Americans, and Asian/Pacific Islanders, they do indicate some of the differences in life expectancy. Life expectancy data for Canadian ethnic minorities have not been reported as yet in recent gerontological publications; however, it has been noted by McDaniel (1986:98) that "life expectancy in Canada for both men and women has increased continuously since 1931."

An alternative way to define health among the elderly, suggested by Shanas and Maddox (1985:701), is based on how well the elderly are able to function in terms of day-to-day activities. They argue that the various things that the elderly can do, or think that they can do, are useful indicators not only of their health, but of the kinds of health services that they may require. This functional approach to the assessment of health is of particular importance especially with respect to ethnic minorities because it assumes that "both the individual and the physicians may have relevant and possibly conflicting information about health status" (Shanas and Maddox, 1985:701). Such conflicting information may easily occur as a result of different perspectives or different cultural perceptions of a given health condition. For example, symptoms

Table 1a. Average Annual Number of Deaths by Disease Category for Ethnic Minorities, United States, 1979–1981

Ethnic Group		CVD*	Cancer	Cirrhosis	Infant Mortality	Diabetes	Unintentional Injuries	Homicide	All Other	Sub-Total‡	Total Deaths
Blacks under Age 45											
Males	Observed	3 236	1 587	961	6 782	201	5 940	6 487	5 900	(31 094)	31 094
	Expected†	1 340	1 204	259	3 465	86	6 000	1 019	3 203	(16 576)	16 576
	Excess	1 896	383	702	3 317	115	−60	5 468	2 697	(14 518)	14 578
Percent of Total Excess§		13	3	5	23	1	0	38	19		100
Females	Observed	2 090	1 790	549	5 540	184	1 905	1 488	3 686	(17 232)	17 232
	Expected†	674	1 366	130	2 679	77	1 991	343	1 838	(9 098)	9 098
	Excess	1 416	424	419	2 861	107	−86	1 145	1 848	(8 134)	8 220
Percent of Total Excess§		17	5	5	35	1	0	14	22		100
Blacks under age 70											
Males	Observed	24 913	16 117	2 706	6 782	1 190	8 429	7 935	16 629	(84 701)	84 701
	Expected†	16 444	10 335	1 344	3 465	544	7 316	1 227	8 914	(49 589)	49 589
	Excess	8 469	5 782	1 362	3 317	646	1 113	6 708	7 715	(35 112)	35 112
Percent of Total Excess§		24	16	4	9	2	3	19	22		100
Females	Observed	17 788	11 946	1 525	5 540	1 786	2 739	1 796	10 817	(53 937)	53 937
	Expected†	8 076	9 677	743	2 679	583	2 605	415	5 614	(30 392)	30 392
	Excess	9 712	2 269	782	2 861	1 203	134	1 381	5 203	(23 545)	23 545
Percent of Total Excess§		41	10	3	12	5	1	6	22		100

* Cardiovascular disease (CVD) combines heart disease and stroke.
† The expected number is calculated from the rate observed in the white population.
‡ Subtotal is the sum of negative and positive excess deaths. Total deaths sums positive excess deaths only.
§ Percentages based on total deaths.

Source: *Report of the Secretary's Task Force on Black & Minority Health.* Washington, D.C.: Department of Health and Human Services, 1985.

Table 1b. Average Annual Number of Deaths by Disease Category for Ethnic Minorities, United States, 1979–1981

Ethnic Group		CVD*	Cancer	Cirrhosis	Infant Mortality	Diabetes	Unintentional Injuries	Homicide	All Other	Sub-Total‡	Total Deaths
Mexican-born Hispanics, Ages 0–64											
Males	Observed	585	334	136	3	32	1 322	848	554	(3 814)	3 814
	Expected†	947	622	106	39	34	769	147	727	(3 391)	3 391
	Excess	−362	−288	30	−36	−2	553	701	−173	(423)	1 284
Percent of Total Excess§		0	0	2	0	0	43	55	0	0	100
Females	Observed	292	367	39	2	40	184	53	309	(1 286)	1 286
	Expected†	331	512	45	28	28	186	33	357	(1 520)	1 520
	Excess	−39	145	−6	−26	12	−2	20	−48	(−234)	32
Percent of Total Excess§		0	0	0	0	38	0	63	0	0	100
Cuban-born Hispanics, Ages 0–64											
Males	Observed	351	243	32	0	12	143	179	204	(1 164)	1 164
	Expected†	540	337	53	1	17	172	31	268	(1 419)	1 419
	Excess	−189	−94	−21	−1	−5	−29	148	−64	(−255)	148
Percent of Total Excess§		0	0	0	0	0	0	100	0	0	100
Females	Observed	114	215	14	0	9	39	25	102	(518)	518
	Expected†	208	307	26	1	16	56	9	158	(781)	781
	Excess	−94	−92	−12	−1	−7	−17	16	−56	(−263)	16
Percent of Total Excess§		0	0	0	0	0	0	100	0	0	100

* Cardiovascular disease (CVD) combines heart disease and stroke.
† The expected number is calculated from the rate observed in the white population.
‡ Subtotal is the sum of negative and positive excess deaths. Total deaths sums positive excess deaths only.
§ Percentages based on total deaths.

Table 1C. Average Annual Number of Deaths by Disease Category for Ethnic Minorities, United States, 1979–1981

Ethnic Group	CVD*	Cancer	Cirrhosis	Infant Mortality	Diabetes	Unintentional Injuries	Homicide	All Other	Sub-Total‡	Total Deaths
Native Americans under Age 45										
Males										
Observed	97	40	95	263	12	715	129	387	(1 738)	1 738
Expected†	81	72	16	214	6	351	60	187	(987)	987
Excess	16	–32	79	49	6	364	69	200	(751)	783
Percent of Total Excess§	2	0	10	6	1	46	9	26		100
Females										
Observed	55	49	77	219	4	252	45	171	(872)	872
Expected†	39	73	7	166	4	109	18	98	(514)	514
Excess	16	–24	70	53	0	143	27	73	(358)	382
Percent of Total Excess§	4	0	18	14	0	37	7	19		100
Native Americans under Age 70										
Males										
Observed	571	225	210	263	57	881	158	732	(3 097)	3 097
Expected†	736	468	66	214	26	412	70	435	(2 427)	2 427
Excess	–165	–243	144	49	31	469	88	297	(670)	1 078
Percent of Total Excess§	0	0	13	5	3	44	8	28		100
Females										
Observed	298	216	156	219	69	302	52	397	(1 709)	1 709
Expected†	319	398	32	166	22	134	21	245	(1 337)	1 337
Excess	–21	–182	124	53	47	168	31	152	(372)	575
Percent of Total Excess§	0	0	22	9	8	29	5	26		100

* Cardiovascular disease (CVD) combines heart disease and stroke.
† The expected number is calculated from the rate observed in the white population.
‡ Subtotal is the sum of negative and positive excess deaths. Total deaths sums positive excess deaths only.
§ Percentages based on total deaths.

Source: *Report of the Secretary's Task Force on Black & Minority Health.* Washington, D.C.: Department of Health and Human Services, 1985.

Table 1d. Average Annual Number of Deaths by Disease Category for Ethnic Minorities, United States, 1979–1981

Ethnic Group	CVD*	Cancer	Cirrhosis	Infant Mortality	Diabetes	Unintentional Injuries	Homicide	All Other	Total Deaths
Asians under Age 45									
Males									
Observed	148	140	15	300	4	378	108	271	1 364
Expected†	240	195	49	405	14	823	152	483	2 361
Excess	–92	–55	–34	–105	–10	–445	–44	–212	–997
Females									
Observed	83	176	3	252	3	152	49	199	924
Expected†	107	221	22	309	13	260	48	271	1 251
Excess	–24	–45	–19	–57	–10	–101	1	–72	–327
Asians under age 70									
Males									
Observed	1 083	873	73	300	51	476	142	642	3 640
Expected†	2 142	1 344	190	405	72	999	181	1 208	6 541
Excess	–1 059	–471	–117	–105	–21	–523	–39	–566	–2 901
Females									
Observed	506	732	31	252	46	216	58	451	2 292
Expected†	914	1 182	96	309	68	335	57	704	3 665
Excess	–408	–450	–65	–57	–22	–119	1	–253	–1 373

* Cardiovascular disease (CVD) combines heart disease and stroke.
† The expected number is calculated from the rate observed in the white population.
NOTE: Percent of total excess was not calculated in this table because excess deaths were virtually all negative.

Source: *Report of the Secretary's Task Force on Black & Minority Health.* Washington, D.C.: Department of Health and Human Services, 1985.

such as a headache may be attributed to a particular disease by an elderly ethnic individual, however, this same symptom may be completely disregarded by the doctor as a sign of old age. Such a problem in the interpretation of the symptom may be doubly troublesome because various ethnic groups have different pain thresholds (Hayashida, 1984).

While both the medical and functional models of health evaluation may provide an overall assessment of the elderly person, caution must be exercised if such health assessments are used to decide whether or not the elderly patient should be placed in a given institution. The time and location of the initial health evaluation may be extremely critical in terms of the assessment outcome. Shanas and Maddox (1985:702) report that "different service settings, for example, institutions or mental health clinics, attract elderly patients with differing assessment profiles." In this regard, it is of interest to examine a few studies that have compared the functional health evaluation of the elderly in different settings.

One such study that compared the self-assessment of health with objective measures of health was conducted by G.G. Fillenbaum (1979:45). In this study, Fillenbaum compared these two measures of health assessment utilizing a sample of older persons who resided in the community and in institutions. The objective measures of health were based on an OARS (Older American Resources and Services) questionnaire which provided an assessment of the various levels of functioning. Some of the items employed by Fillenbaum (1979:46) were as follows:

1. The number of health-related problems reported present in the previous month;

2. The number of different types of medication taken during the previous month;

3. The number of different illnesses and disabilities presently affecting the respondent.

The objective measures were compared against the responses to the following subjective questions:

1. How would rate your health at the present time — excellent (4), good (3), fair (2), or poor (1)?

2. How concerned do you feel about your health troubles — not concerned (4), mildly concerned (3), moderately concerned (2), or very concerned (1)?

3. How much do your health troubles stand in the way of your doing the things you want to do — not at all (3), a little (some) (2), or a great deal (1)?

For the elderly residents of the community, it was found that the self-assessment or subjective evaluations of health reflected the actual state of health as assessed by the objective measures. This probably derives from the fact that those elderly who are able to function independently in the community are also in better health and have a higher degree of self-esteem and life satisfaction than those elderly who are institutionalized. Indeed, this is shown in the Fillenbaum study, which indicates that for the elderly in institutional settings, self-evaluations of health were not consistent with objective measures of health. Fillenbaum (1979:50) concludes that "it is possible that the objective measures used — number of health problems, medicines, illnesses — may not be appropriate where the institutionalized are concerned, or may have a different meaning in institutions."

While the results of the Fillenbaum study may be specific to both time and location, the results from an earlier longitudinal study by Maddox and Douglass (1973:17), which compared the medical and self-assessments of the elderly over a period of 15 years, indicated persistent positive congruency for the two types of health assessment. Of interest is their finding that whenever there was a difference in the physicians' and the patients' assessment of health, the tendency was for the individual to overestimate, rather than underestimate, the state of health. Maddox and Douglass (1973:92) noted the substantial stability over time in both the patients' and physicians' health ratings; however, the patients' health rates showed slightly more stability. Their unexpected finding was "the tendency for self health rating to be a better predictor of future physicians' ratings than the reverse." Maddox and Douglass (1973:92) conclude that although their data did not provide a conclusive pattern to confirm or refute the commonly reported findings regarding the two types of health assessment, the data demonstrated that "self-assessment of health is not random but is persistently and positively related to objective evaluations of health status."

An excellent overview of the literature on recent trends in viewing the health status of the elderly from several different perspectives, as well as from several different levels of function, is provided by Shanas and Maddox (1985:703). They draw our attention to the growing acceptance and merging of the medical and functional models of health assessment, especially by those in geriatrics. To underscore this latter observation, they quote the following from the World Health Organization:

> It is now accepted by the medical profession that morbidity should be measured not only in terms of the extent of the pathological process but also in terms of the impairment of the function in the person affected by a pathological condition . . . Functional diagnosis is one of the most important elements that has been introduced in geriatrics. In this approach a distinction is made between an impairment and a disability caused by a pathological condition.

The utility in employing both models of health assessment becomes evident when we consider the distinction that is made between an impairment and a disability. From the World Health Organization report, Shanas and Maddox (1985:703) note that impairment is "a physiological or psychological abnormality that does not interfere with the normal life activities of the individual." They further note that disability is "a condition that results in partial or total limitation of the normal activities of the individual." It is important to keep these distinctions in mind

when considering the health status of aged ethnic minorities. Some types of impairment may eventually result in disability.

A recent report on Canadian health and disability by Statistics Canada and the Department of Secretary of State of Canada (1986:17) provides data on age distributions among disabled and non-disabled persons. These are shown in Figure 3. While it is clear from Figure 3 that 37.2 percent of those reporting a disability fall in the 65-and-over category, the report notes that only 12.3 percent of the overall Canadian population fall in this age group.

The distribution of disability rates by various age categories for each of the provinces is provided in Table 2. It can also be seen from Table 2 that 12.8 percent of the Canadian adult population reported some level of disability. In terms of actual numbers, this percentage represents 2 448 000 individuals among the Canadian adult population (Statistics Canada and Department of Secretary of State of Canada, 1986:17). It will be further noted from Table 2 that the level of disability is lowest in the 15-to-24 years of age category, at 3.8 percent, and it increases sharply with age, reaching 38.6 percent for those aged 65 and over.

One of the many disadvantages of health disability is that it affects the individual's status in the labour force, which, in turn, directly affects social and economic quality of life. Statistics Canada and the Department of the Secretary of State of Canada (1986:65) report that among those reporting a disability in 1983–1984, 68.4 percent, or 1 675 000 disabled persons were not in the labour force at all. This same report notes that "the percentage rises from 40.8 percent in the 15–34 age group, to 69.5 percent among those 55–64." While participation rates in the labour force differ by age, it is evident that there are also sex differences. It can be seen from Figure 4 that the participation rates are lower for women in both disabled and non-disabled groups. This pattern tends to be borne out in the prevalence of double jeopardy particularly among elderly women. With reference to the health and disability of aged ethnic minori-

Figure 3. Age Distribution Among Those Reporting and Those Not Reporting a Disability

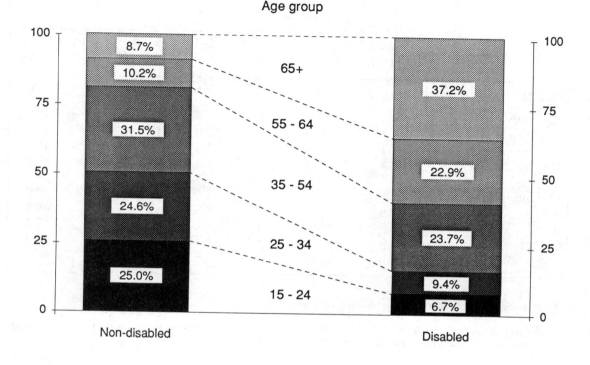

Source: *Report of the Canadian Health and Disability Survey, 1983–1984*. Ottawa: Statistics Canada Health Division and Department of the Secretary of State of Canada, 1986, Figure 2, p. 18.

ties, further research is required to determine the combined effects of age, sex, and ethnicity.

While the physiological or physical aspects of aging are important considerations in terms of the functional capabilities of the elderly, it is also important to examine the effects of aging on one's mental health. In order to study the psychological aspects of aging, it is necessary to have an understanding of exactly what is meant by mental health. D'Arcy (1987:425) defines mental health as

> a state in which a person demonstrates his competence to think, feel and (inter)act in ways that demonstrate his ability to deal effectively with the challenges of life. The mentally healthy person is accepting of himself, able to give as well as receive in relationships and, having realistically evaluated his assets and liabilities, has an

appropriate level of self-confidence, making decisions based on sound judgement and accepting responsibility for his actions.

There are several key components in the above definition that merit our attention, particularly with reference to ethnicity and aging. One such component concerns the individual's ability to think. As noted earlier in our discussion on ethnicity and its synonymity with traditional ways of thinking, it is quite conceivable that misunderstandings can occur if the traditional cultural backgrounds of the ethnic groups are not understood. Social behaviour as outward manifestations of the thinking process may often be interpreted as bizarre, when in one's own cultural group, they may be considered as quite normal.

Table 2. Disability Rates* in the Canadian Population, by Province of Residence

	Age-standardized	Not age-standardized					
	15 years and over	15 years and over	15–24 years	25–34 years	35–54 years	55–64 years	65 years and over
Canada	12.8	12.8	3.8	5.3	9.9	24.7	38.6
Saskatchewan	14.4	15.8	4.1	5.6	10.7	25.6	47.0
Nova Scotia	14.3	14.9	3.9	5.0	12.7	27.6	41.5
New Brunswick	14.1	14.0	3.9	6.0	11.8	27.1	41.4
Newfoundland	13.8	12.4	3.4	6.3	10.1	26.8	43.5
Ontario	13.3	13.6	4.0	6.2	10.7	25.3	38.4
Manitoba	13.0	13.9	4.6	6.0	9.5	21.4	42.0
Alberta	12.8	11.0	3.7	4.9	9.4	25.0	40.3
British Columbia	12.0	12.5	4.3	4.6	7.9	24.9	37.1
Quebec	11.9	11.5	3.2	4.5	9.5	23.4	35.9
Prince Edward Island	10.8	12.0	—	—	—	—	40.0

* Expressed as a percentage of the total population in each age group.

Source: *Report of the Canadian Health and Disability Survey, 1983–1984*. Ottawa: Statistics Canada Health Division and Department of the Secretary of State of Canada, 1986, Table 1.1, p. 18.

Another important component which is noted in D'Arcy's definition of mental health is the ability to deal effectively with various day-to-day situations. As noted elsewhere by Ujimoto (1987:131), there is accumulating evidence that coping plays a central role in reducing stress-related illnesses and in promoting good health. The coping strategies utilized by the elderly who have different socio-demographic characteristics are particularly relevant to the study of aging and health because constant psychosocial adjustments must be made throughout an individual's lifespan. Therefore, an understanding of the cultural context in which these adjustments occur is very important.

The final component of D'Arcy's definition of mental health that will be briefly discussed here concerns the types of social relationships that can realistically occur, given the limited assets and resources of the elderly. The study of social relationships in terms of the cultural con-text in which they occur requires an understanding of the social exchange mechanisms of the particular group. For example, in the case of the elderly *Issei* (immigrant or first-generation Japanese Canadian) and *Nisei* (second-generation or Canadian-born), it has been observed by Kobata (1979:100), Nishio and Sugiman (1983:19), and Ujimoto (1987:116) that traditional Japanese values influence generational relationships. Intergenerational relationships based on a system of mutual and moral obligation as well as on social custom may be applicable only to certain groups, and at the same time, there may be less importance placed on them by subsequent generations. Social relationships based on concepts such as filial piety and familial dependency in old age are other factors that may intervene in social relationships, depending on the ethnic group.

From our brief discussion of the three key components crucial to the definition of mental

Figure 4. Labour Force Participation Rates by Disability Status by Age Group and Sex

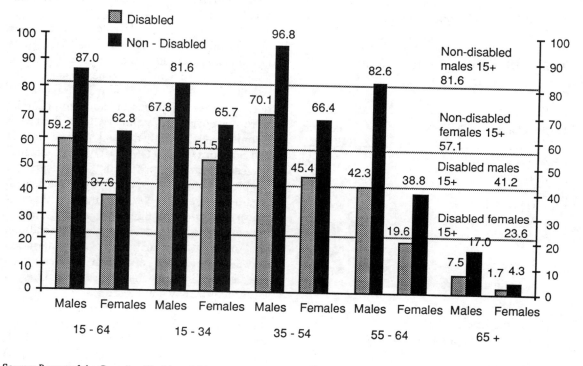

Source: *Report of the Canadian Health and Disability Survey* 1983–1984. Ottawa: Statistics Canada Health Division, 1986, Figure 5, p. 67.

health provided by D'Arcy, it can be hypothesized that the negative effects of daily-life situations will impact more severely on the mental health of recent immigrants to Canadian society than on subsequent generations. The recent arrivals to Canada are the ones who will experience the greatest changes in mental health because of value conflicts and other difficulties of adjustment to their new environment. Support for this observation is provided by Kuo (1986:133) who has documented that "an excessive amount of social stress among immigrants — resulting from social isolation, cultural conflicts, poor social integration and assimilation, role changes and identity crises, low socioeconomic status, and racial discrimination — has led to a high prevalence of ill health and psychological impairment among them." The plethora of factors that affect mental health are

extremely difficult to disentangle. As Chappell, Strain, and Blandford (1986:37) have noted, "changes in mental health as we age are less straightforward. Mental health encompasses numerous aspects, including cognitive, psychological and emotional functioning. It is known to be related to both physiological conditions and social environments." At present, the social environment of aged ethnic minority groups is a relatively unexplored area of study.

Although the data on the health status of ethnic groups are not readily available as yet, substantial progress has been made in recent years in obtaining health-related information at the national level. During 1978 and 1979, Health and Welfare Canada and Statistics Canada (1981:14) conducted a survey to obtain data on the health problems and disability of the Canadian population. The data on the health status of

Canadians were based on a survey of 12 000 households, which provided information on selected health behaviour such as drug use, dis-

Table 3. Distribution of Various Health Conditions

Health Condition	Percent
1. Mental disorders	3.9
2. Diabetes	1.5
3. Thyroid disorders	1.2
4. Anaemia	1.6
5. Headache	4.3
6. Sight disorders	4.7
7. Hearing disorders	4.0
8. Hypertension	6.1
9. Heart disease	3.3
10. Acute respiratory ailments	3.1
11. Influenza	2.7
12. Bronchitis and emphysema	2.2
13. Asthma	2.1
14. Hayfever and other allergies	8.5
15. Dental trouble	6.6
16. Gastric and duodenal ulcers	1.9
17. Functional digestive disorders	2.7
18. Skin allergies and other skin disorders	8.1
19. Arthritis and rheumatism	9.6
20. Back, limb, and joint disorders	9.1
21. Trauma (accidents and injury)	2.4
22. Other	10.4
Total (all conditions)	100.0
N = 12 000 households	

Source: *The Health of Canadians. Report of the Canada Health Survey.* Ottawa: Health and Welfare and Statistics Canada, 1981, Table VI, p. 110.

ability days, accidents, and activity limitations. Table 3 illustrates the distribution of various health conditions.

The data shown in Table 3 refer to the respondents' subjective evaluations of their own health conditions rather than to objective evaluations by physicians. In some instances, the validity and reliability of the responses may be questioned, as symptoms of the health disorder were not clearly differentiated from the health disorder itself. The Health and Welfare Canada and Statistics Canada (1981:109) report includes the cautionary comment that "some degree of double counting is especially suspected with regard to categories 19 (arthritis and rheumatism) and 20 (back, limb, and joint disorders), which were contained in the chronic condition list." A graphic representation of the relationship between prevalence of health problems and selected health behaviour by sex and selected age groups is shown in Figure 5.

In Table 4, a further differentiation of the prevalence of health problems by specific age groups and by sex is provided. Health and Welfare Canada and Statistics Canada (1981:109) information on the proportion of the population that is experiencing a given health problem is also shown. Thus, while it can be seen from Table 4 that 12.5 percent of the health problems are reported by females who are 65 years of age and over, it must also be noted that this group constitutes only 4.9 percent of the total population.

From the data presented in Table 4 on the prevalence of health problems, certain health characteristics for those 65 years of age and older of both sexes can be obtained. The most prevalent health problems appear to be the following: heart disease, 46.5 percent; hypertension, 37.4 percent; diabetes, 35.6 percent; and arthritis and rheumatism, 35.1 percent. As the ethnically diverse Canadian population ages, variations in the perception of health conditions by various ethnic groups will be an important consideration for the provision of appropriate health care, as well as in formulating health-care strategies and social policy.

Figure 5. Prevalence of Health Problems per 100 Persons by Selected Health Behaviours and Sex, for Selected Age Groups, Canada 1978–79

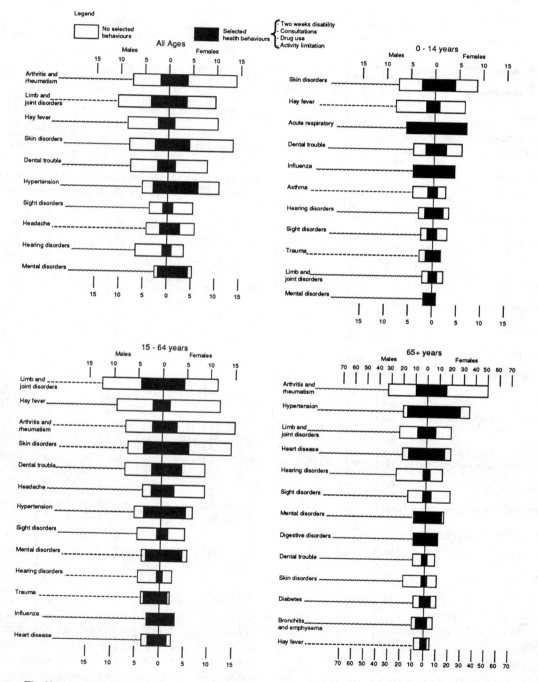

Source: *The Health of Canadians.* Report of the Canada Health Survey. Ottawa: Health and Welfare Canada and Statistics Canada, 1981, Figure VI, p. 112.

Table 4. Prevalence of Health Problems by Age and Sex, Canada 1978–1979

Type of health problem		All ages			Less than 15			15–64			65 and over		
		Both sexes	Male	Female	Both sexes	Male	Female	Both sexes	Male	Female	Both sexes	Male	Female
							in thousands						
Total Population (2)	No.	23 023	11 417	11 606	5 531	2 833	2 699	15 473	7 697	7 775	2 019	887	1 132
	%	100.0	49.6	50.4	24.0	12.3	11.7	67.2	33.4	33.8	8.8	3.9	4.9
At least one problem	No.	12 510	5 714	6 796	1 928	1 005	924	8 853	3 968	4 885	1 729	742	987
	%	100.0	45.7	54.3	15.4	8.0	7.4	70.8	31.7	39.0	13.8	5.9	7.9
No problem	No.	10 513	5 703	4 811	3 603	1 828	1 775	6 620	3 730	2 890	290	145	146
	%	100.0	54.2	45.8	34.3	17.4	16.9	63.0	35.5	27.5	2.8	1.4	1.4
Health problems:													
Total problems	No.	25 526	10 559	14 967	2 634	1 385	1 249	17 692	7 177	10 515	5 200	1 997	3 203
	%	100.0	41.4	58.6	10.3	5.4	4.9	69.3	28.1	41.2	20.4	7.8	12.5
Mental disorders	No.	1 000	363	637	53	39	14	697	249	448	249	75	174
	%	100.0	36.3	63.7	5.4	3.9	1.4	69.7	24.9	44.8	24.9	7.5	17.4
Diabetes	No.	379	149	230	—	—	—	237	102	135	135	45	90
	%	100.0	39.2	60.8	—	—	—	62.5	27.0	35.5	35.6	11.8	23.8
Thyroid disorders	No.	297	41	256	—	—	—	230	24	206	65	15	51
	%	100.0	13.7	86.3	—	—	—	77.4	8.1	69.3	22.0	5.0	17.0
Anaemia	No.	417	52	366	33	—	16	307	24	283	77	11	66
	%	100.0	12.4	87.6	8.0	—	3.9	73.6	5.8	67.9	18.4	2.7	15.8
Headache	No.	1 102	292	809	40	19	21	984	253	732	77	21	57
	%	100.0	26.5	73.5	3.6	1.7	1.9	89.3	22.9	66.4	7.0	1.9	5.1
Sight disorders	No.	1 200	449	750	96	45	51	786	304	482	318	100	217
	%	100.0	37.5	62.5	8.0	3.7	4.3	65.5	25.4	40.1	26.5	8.4	18.1
Hearing disorders	No.	1 028	607	422	127	66	62	549	327	222	352	214	138
	%	100.0	59.0	41.0	12.4	6.4	6.0	53.4	31.8	21.6	34.2	20.8	13.4
Hypertension	No.	1 551	588	963	—	—	—	970	411	559	579	176	403
	%	100.0	37.9	62.1	—	—	—	62.6	26.5	36.1	37.4	11.4	26.0
Heart disease	No.	847	429	418	—	—	7	436	237	199	394	182	212
	%	100.0	50.6	49.4	—	—	.8	51.5	28.0	23.5	46.5	21.5	25.0
Acute respiratory	No.	781	355	426	320	164	156	428	177	251	33	14	19
	%	100.0	45.4	54.6	41.0	21.0	20.0	54.8	22.6	32.1	4.2	1.8	2.4
Influenza	No.	680	296	384	204	100	104	441	189	252	35	7	27
	%	100.0	43.6	56.4	30.0	14.7	15.3	64.8	27.8	37.1	5.1	1.1	4.0
Bronchitis and emphysema	No.	562	279	283	70	42	27	364	158	207	128	79	49
	%	100.0	49.6	50.4	12.4	7.5	4.9	64.8	28.1	36.7	22.8	14.0	8.8
Asthma	No.	547	290	257	141	97	44	327	148	179	79	45	34
	%	100.0	53.1	46.9	25.7	17.7	8.1	59.8	27.1	32.7	14.5	8.3	6.2
Hay fever and other allergies	No.	2 157	987	1 170	390	222	168	1 650	729	921	117	36	81
	%	100.0	45.8	54.2	18.1	10.3	7.8	76.5	33.8	42.7	5.4	1.7	3.7
Dental problems	No.	1 697	739	958	246	104	142	1 267	552	715	184	83	101
	%	100.0	43.6	56.4	14.5	6.2	8.3	74.7	32.5	42.1	10.8	4.9	5.9
Gastric and duodenal ulcers	No.	482	282	199	—	—	—	398	232	166	79	46	33
	%	100.0	58.6	41.4	—	—	—	82.6	48.2	34.5	16.3	9.6	6.8
Digestive disorders	No.	687	286	401	45	26	19	434	178	256	209	83	126
	%	100.0	41.7	58.3	6.5	3.7	2.8	63.1	25.9	37.2	30.4	12.0	18.4
Skin disorders	No.	2 064	756	1 308	426	202	224	1 495	497	998	143	57	86
	%	100.0	36.6	63.4	20.6	9.8	10.9	72.4	24.1	48.4	6.9	2.8	4.2
Arthritis and rheumatism	No.	2 440	844	1 596	13	6	—	1 571	550	1 021	856	288	568
	%	100.0	34.6	65.4	.5	.2	—	64.4	22.5	41.8	35.1	11.8	23.3
Limb and joint disorders	No.	2 334	1 182	1 153	70	39	31	1 833	952	881	432	192	240
	%	100.0	50.6	49.4	3.0	1.7	1.3	78.5	40.8	37.8	18.5	8.2	10.3
Trauma	No.	616	349	268	73	46	27	471	281	190	72	22	51
	%	100.0	56.6	43.4	11.8	7.5	4.3	76.4	45.6	30.8	11.8	3.5	8.2
Other	No.	2 660	945	1 715	254	134	121	1 818	605	1 213	588	207	381
	%	100.0	35.5	64.5	9.6	5.0	4.5	68.4	22.7	45.6	22.1	7.8	14.3

Source: *The Health of Canadians*. Report of the Canada Health Survey. Ottawa: Health and Welfare Canada and Statistics Canada, 1981, Table 57, p. 115.

AGING, ETHNICITY, AND HEALTH

While there are several recent Canadian publications on aging and health, for example, Simmons-Tropea and Osborn (1987:399), D'Arcy (1987:424), Connidis (1987:451), Marshall (1987:473), Chappell (1987:489), Schwenger (1987:505), and Shapiro and Roos (1987:520), the cultural variations in Canadian society and its implications for the future health-care provisions of aging ethnic minorities are not considered. Since this is an important area of study, it is just beginning to receive more attention. As noted by Chappell, Strain, and Blandford (1986:30), "the relevance of subculture (ethnic, minority and racial) for the elderly population and, in particular, for the provision of health care is an under-researched area in gerontology. Even though conceptually and theoretically it has been argued that subcultural cohesiveness is likely to result in more social support for its elderly members, this has not been established empirically."

One recent study that examined the relationship between aging and health as interpreted through culture is the study by Rempel and Havens (1986). In this study, they identified the differential perceptions of health of older persons, based on 12 different ethnic groups in Manitoba. The Rempel and Havens (1986:18) data analysis indicates that ethnicity and education affect health perception. They note that the Asians and northern Europeans have the highest positive rating of their own health and the Middle Eastern and Eastern Europeans the poorest health. Because of the small size of each of the ethnic groups represented in the sample, caution must be exercised in interpreting the data. The study is nevertheless useful, as it suggests several new avenues for future research.

An area of study in health behaviour that is rapidly gaining attention concerns stress and coping behaviour. One study that examines the relevance of ethnicity in relation to stress and coping, particularly with reference to the minority elderly, is the study by Wong and Reker (1985:29). In their comparative study of elderly Chinese and Anglos, Wong and Reker were interested in determining how the Chinese and Anglos differed in their coping behaviour. The three categories of coping strategies that they examined were as follows:

1. *Internal strategies* are one's own instrumental efforts.

2. *External strategies* include various forms of dependence on others to reduce stress.

3. *Palliative strategies* are ways of coping that make one feel better without solving the problem.

Analysis of the Wong and Reker (1985:33) data revealed the presence of several stress-producing health problems noted earlier in Figure 4. In addition to arthritis or rheumatism, eye problems, and other health disorders, other stressful factors that influenced the well-being of the elderly included in-law problems, loss of a spouse, worries about the family, and economic problems. On the basis of their data analysis, Wong and Reker conclude that the "Chinese did not report having more problems, but they perceived their problems, especially the general problem of aging, as more serious than Anglos." The authors note that in addition to the normal biological constraints of aging, there are other compounding factors associated with the minority status of the Chinese aged such as "a language barrier, lack of information, and fear of racial discrimination."

In terms of coping strategies, Wong and Reker (1985:33) found that the Chinese relied more on external and palliative strategies than did Anglos. Although the Chinese relied more on external help, it is noted that the source of the outside help came primarily from family members and relatives. The Chinese also tended to reminisce and seek refuge in the past rather than attempting to solve a given stress situation, except in coping with health-related problems. Wong and Reker suggest that "Chinese elderly not only experience more stress, but possess less adequate coping resources." Since the aged Chinese sample were all first-generation or immigrant Chinese, while the Anglos were either born in Canada or were long-time residents, the results are perhaps not too surprising. However, they do point out the concerns and health-care needs of the first-generation ethnic minority, and therefore, future health-care policies should not be based on the common assumption that the aged are homogeneous.

At present, there is a research project on the well-being of aged Asian-Canadians which includes the coping inventory developed by Wong and Reker (1983, 1984) and noted above. This project (K.V. Ujimoto, H. Nishio, P. Wong, and L. Lam, 1986), entitled "Comparative Aspects of Aging Asian-Canadians: Social Networks and Time Budgets" examines the cultural aspects of ethnicity in relation to the allocation of time to various daily activities. By utilizing time-budget data, those activities most predictive of well-being can be determined. A description of this research is provided elsewhere by Ujimoto (1987:130). Both time-budget and social network data will enable us to identify those individuals who rely upon external resources in order to cope with a stress situation rather than on internal strategies.

More and more research on various aspects of aging and health is being reported in the literature. However, future studies will have to examine the influence of ethnicity on aging and health in greater detail. As reported by Ujimoto (1987:117), difficulties with language and the inability to express innermost feelings by aged immigrants erect formidable barriers that prevent easy access to the available social, economic, and health support services. Whether it is the lack of health services available in one's own language or the cultural and psychological barriers that prevent ethnic minorities from utilizing various services, the net result is underutilization of existing health services and facilities by ethnic minorities. Chan (1983:43) found that although the Chinese elderly women in his study were generally aware of medical and dental services in the Chinese community, they were unaware of other services and resources for the elderly available at other institutions and agencies outside of it.

While the underutilization of health-care services by various ethnic groups has been noted by Wong and Reker (1985:33), Rempel and Havens (1986:9), and Ujimoto (1987:117), this aspect of aging, ethnicity, and health research requires a controlled study to determine why this may be so. Perhaps there are alternative health-care and coping strategies available. We have been alerted to this possibility by a recent study by Hess (1986:314), who investigated the differences in over-the-counter (OTC) drug use by the elderly in two racially and ethnically different groups — the Chinese and the Hispanic. Hess was interested in determining the variety and amount of OTC preparations that were purchased and used by the two groups for "the relief of common symptoms such as pain, constipation, heartburn/indigestion, nervous tension, 'down in the dumps,' and insomnia/difficulty sleeping." A partial list of OTC preparations used by the Chinese and Hispanic elders is provided in Table 5.

Hess (1986:316) reports that "pain preparations used by Chinese were predominantly topical ointments and balms, while the Hispanics tended to take internal medications for pain." As shown in Table 5, for heartburn or indigestion, the Chinese relied more on various kinds of teas than on OTC drugs. This is one important aspect of health care very often overlooked when the patient is admitted to a hospital, and instead of Chinese tea, a more potent form of drug is administered. For the remedy of constipation, it can also be noted from Table 5 that the Hispanics tend to use more OTC drugs than the Chinese. The Chinese tend to rely on natural fruits, vegetables, and folk remedies. Hess concludes that "health care professionals cannot assume that all elderly people are alike in how they approach illness." She argues that "the determination of what preparation to take will depend on a person's perception of the symptoms and their cause." This is usually influenced by the various aspects of ethnicity discussed earlier in

Table 5. Partial List of OTC Preparations Used by Chinese and Hispanic Elders

Symptom	Preparations Used by	
	Chinese Elder	Hispanic Elder
Pain	Absorbine Jr. (topical) Anacin (internal) Ben-Gay (topical) Dr J.H. Volcanic Oil (topical) Essential Balm (topical) Infra-Rub (topical) Tamenton Heating Oil (topical) Tiger Balm (topical)	Alcohol and camphor (topical) Alfalfa tea (internal) Anacin (internal) Aspirin (plain) (internal) Bayer (internal) Bufferin (internal) A.P.C. (internal) Balsamo (topical) Corn husk/barley/Jamaica (topical) Jasmine tea (internal) Lemon juice and brandy (internal) Mejoral (internal) Mentholatum (topical) Ruda/Avocado/Seidajal (topical) Tylenol (internal) Vicks Vaporub (topical)
Constipation	Bok choi (internal) Cascara (internal) Chinese Four-Flavour Teas (internal) Glycerin suppositories (internal) Honey (internal) Maalox (internal) Milk of Magnesia (internal) Po Chai pills (internal) Senna leaves (internal) Wheat and prunes (internal)	Agoral (internal) Ex-Lax (internal) Feen-A-Mint (internal) Gaviscon (internal) Glycerin suppositories (internal) Maalox (internal) Metamucil (internal) Perdiem (internal) Prune juice (internal)
Indigestion (Antacids)	Baking soda (internal) Chrysanthemum crystal tea (internal) Ginseng tea (internal) Maalox (internal) Milk of Magnesia (internal) Mylanta (internal) Po Chai pills (internal) Po Ney tea (internal) Sup Ling Don tea (internal)	Alka-Seltzer (internal) Assorted herbs (internal) Brioschi (internal) Festal (internal) Gaviscon (internal) Maalox (internal) Milk of Magnesia (internal) Mylanta (internal) Pepto-Bismol (internal) Rolaids (internal)
Cold and Cough	Chinese cough syrup (internal)	Vicks Formula 44 (internal)
Skin Problems	Calamine lotion (topical) Desitin (topical) Aveeno Bath (topical) Tashari skin cream (topical)	Tinactin (topical) Hydrogen peroxide (topical)
Eye Strain		Visine
Insomnia/Sleep Difficulties		Warm milk (internal) Sominex (internal)

Source: Patricia Hess, "Chinese and Hispanic Elders and OTC drugs." In *Geriatric Nursing, American Journal of Care for the Aged*, Vol 7, no. 6, November/December, 1986, pp. 314–18.

this chapter.

An important aspect of health practice that Hess (1986:317) draws our attention to is the Chinese folk practices which "revolve around single-dose liquid preparations." In contrast, Western medical practice prescribes multiple dosage of OTC drugs. Hess suggests that this is a confusing concept to the Chinese and that this may explain the Chinese preference for teas and topical preparations for the relief of their health problems.

A theoretical perspective that views the environment and Nature in terms of interacting wholes has created an interest in the holistic approach to medicine and health care. Lock (1978:151) notes that "Western man, having devoted himself for so long to models based on mechanistic and reductionist explanations of the Newtonian tradition can find few examples in his recent history upon which to draw." Therefore, she points to the need "to reach out to other cultures or sub-cultures where illness is not dealt with as though it were reducible to a totally scientific problem." Based upon her extensive research on East Asian medical practices, Lock demonstrates quite forcefully that the concept of holism is culturally determined.

As noted by Ujimoto (1987:117), some ethnic groups, such as the Japanese, Chinese, Koreans, and Filipinos, strongly value the emotional and symbolic support provided the elderly members by their families. Lock (1978:151) notes that in East Asian medical practices "the social and cultural dimensions of the *experience* and *meaning* [emphasis added] of illness are assigned at least equal importance to the naming and removal of a specific disease." In Canadian hospitals, this opportunity to discuss and share the "experience and meaning of illness" with family members is often denied to the ethnic minority patient and his/her family members. Visits by family members to assist with eating, clothing, bathing, etc. are often viewed as interfering with the tasks of the hospital staff. Ujimoto (1987:118) further notes that the situation becomes even more stressful if the aged patient does not understand the medical instructions given by the hospital staff.

SUMMARY AND CONCLUSION

In this chapter, we have examined the relationships among aging, ethnicity, and health. It has been shown that changes in recent immigration to Canada and the rapidly aging population strongly indicate a heterogeneous demographic profile. The implications of demographic change on health care have also been discussed.

In order to understand the adjustment to aging by ethnic minorities and their attitudes and behaviour towards aging from a health-care perspective, we argued that an understanding of what is meant by ethnicity is important. While there are several different conceptions of ethnicity, as noted by Rosenthal (1986:19), as culture, as a determinant of social inequality, and as synonymous with "traditional" ways of thinking and behaving, it was emphasized that the systemic or integrative approach that draws upon the different conceptions of ethnicity was necessary in understanding the dynamics of the aging process as it relates to the health status and general well-being of the elderly.

A discussion on the objective and subjective measures of health has also been provided. Although it was not intended to provide a comprehensive review of the literature on aging and health, selected examples were noted to give some direction for future research considerations. Since Canadian data on the health statistics of ethnic minorities are not readily available, American data were used to illustrate some of the differences in health problems. We were, however, able to obtain recent data on the age distributions among disabled and non-disabled persons in Canada.

The sharing of emotional and symbolic support by the patient with his/her family was an important consideration to be noted particularly in the East Asian ethnic groups such as the Chinese, Korean, and Japanese Canadians. One way in which cultural misunderstandings can be reduced is to enable health-care professionals to recognize the non-verbal aspects of communication in health care. This requires a greater sensitivity to the cultural dimensions, or how illnesses are viewed in different ethnic groups. In this regard, an excellent start has been made in Ontario by the Multicultural Health Coalition, established in 1983 to "promote culturally relevant and appropriate programmes, services and materials." Through a series of seminars, workshops, and publications, health professionals and educators are gradually being made aware of the health beliefs of over one hundred different ethnocultural groups currently residing in the Greater Toronto Metropolitan Area. Another example of the active role provided in the promotion of multicultural health care is that of Doctors' Hospital in Toronto. This hospital serves a community that has some 35 different minority-language groups and the diverse concerns of the community are discussed regularly by the hospital's Director of Community Health Planning.

In this chapter, we have noted only some of the major issues related to cultural misunderstanding that may impact on the well-being and health of the elderly and the provision of health care. Differences in mental health, stress, and coping strategies were discussed with reference to the aged Chinese and Anglos only. Research in this area, particularly about elderly Japanese, Korean, and Chinese Canadians, is currently in progress. It is clear that research on aging, ethnicity, and health can be expanded to include other ethnic groups.

STUDY QUESTIONS

1. What are some of the factors that account for the changing demographic profile of Canadian society?

2. What are some of the ways in which ethnicity can be defined?

3. Why is it important to consider the history of ethnic groups in Canada in order to understand the aging process from a life-span developmental perspective?

4. In what ways do traditional roles and values influence health-care behaviour?

5. What are some of the differences between the medical and functional models of health evaluation?

6. What are the three key components in the definition of mental health?

RECOMMENDED READING

Chappell, N., L.A. Strain, and A.A. Blandford. *Aging and Health Care.* Toronto: Holt, Rinehart and Winston, 1986.

Driedger, L., and N. Chappell. *Aging and Ethni-*

city: Toward an Interface. Toronto: Butterworths, 1987.

Marshall, V.W. *Aging in Canada.* Toronto: Fitzhenry and Whiteside, 1987.

REFERENCES

Bolaria, B.S., and P. Li. *Racial Oppression in Canada.* Toronto: Garamond Press, 1983.

Breton, R. "Institutional Completeness of Ethnic Communities and the Personal Relations of

Immigrants." *American Journal of Sociology* 70 (1964): 193–205.

Chan, Qwok B. "Coping with Aging and Managing Self-Identity: The Social World of the

Elderly Chinese Women." *Canadian Ethnic Studies* 15, no. 3 (1983).

Chappell, N. "Canadian Income and Health-Care Policy: Implications for the Elderly." In *Aging in Canada*, edited by V.W. Marshall. Toronto: Fitzhenry and Whiteside, 1987.

Chappell, N., L.A. Strain, and A.A. Blandford. *Aging and Health Care.* Toronto: Holt, Rinehart and Winston, 1986.

Connidis, I. "Life in Older Age: The View from the Top." In *Aging in Canada*, edited by V.W. Marshall. Toronto: Fitzhenry and Whiteside, 1987.

D'Arcy, C. "Aging and Mental Health." In *Aging in Canada*, edited by V.W. Marshall. Toronto: Fitzhenry and Whiteside, 1987.

Employment and Immigration Canada. *Immigration Statistics.* Ottawa: Ministry of Supply and Services, 1986.

Fillenbaum, G.G. "Social Context and Self-Assessments of Health Among the Elderly." *Journal of Health and Social Behavior* 20, no. 1 (1979): 45–51.

Fry, C.L. *Aging in Culture and Society.* Brooklyn, N.Y.: J.F. Bergin, 1980.

Gordon, M.M. *Assimilation in American Life.* New York: Oxford University Press, 1964.

Hagedorn, R. *Sociology.* Toronto: Holt, Rinehart and Winston, 1986.

Hess, P. "Chinese and Hispanic Elders and OTC Drugs." *Geriatric Nursing, American Journal of Care for the Aging* 7 (November/December 1986): 314–18.

Hayashida, C. "Extending the Medical Center to a Multi-Ethnic Aging Population with Long-Term Care Needs." Paper presented at the thirty-seventh Annual Scientific Meeting, The Gerontological Society of America, San Antonio, Texas, 1984.

Health and Welfare Canada. *Fact Book on Aging in Canada.* 1983.

Health and Welfare Canada and Statistics Canada. *The Health of Canadians: Report of the Canada Health Survey.* Ottawa: Minister of Supply and Services Canada, 1981.

Holzberg, C.S. "Ethnicity and Aging: Anthropological Perspectives on More Than Just the Minority Elderly." *Gerontologist* 22 (1982): 249–57.

Kobata, F. "The Influence of Culture on Family Relations: The Asian American Experience." In *Aging Parents*, edited by P. Ragan. Los Angeles: University of Southern California, 1979.

Kuo, W.H., and Y. Tsai. "Social Networking, Hardiness and Immigrants' Mental Health." *Journal of Health and Social Behavior* 27 (June 1986): 133–49.

Lock, M. "Scars of Experience: The Art of Moxibustion in Japanese Medicine and Society." *Culture, Medicine and Psychiatry* 2 (1978): 151–75.

Maddox, G.L., and E.B. Douglass. "Self-Assessment of Health. A Longitudinal Study of Elderly Subjects." *Journal of Health and Social Behavior* 14 (1973): 87–93.

Marshall, V.W. *Last Chapters: A Sociology of Aging and Dying.* Monterey, California: Brooks/Cole, 1980.

———. "The Health of Very Old People as a Concern of Their Children." In *Aging in Canada*, edited by V.W. Marshall. Toronto: Fitzhenry and Whiteside, 1987.

McDaniel, S.A. *Canada's Aging Population.* Toronto: Butterworths, 1986.

Nishio, H., and P. Sugiman. "Socialization and Cultural Duality Among Aging Japanese Canadians." *Canadian Ethnic Studies* 15, no. 3 (1983): 17–35.

Rempel, J.D., and B. Havens. "Aged Health Experiences as Interpreted Through Culture." Paper presented at the Canadian Sociology and Anthropology Association Annual Meeting, Winnipeg, Manitoba, 1986.

Rosenthal, C. "Family Support in Later Life: Does Ethnicity Make a Difference?" *Gerontologist* 26, no. 1 (1986): 19–24.

Schwenger, C.W. "Formal Health Care for the Elderly in Canada." In *Aging in Canada*, edited by V.W. Marshall. Toronto: Fitzhenry and Whiteside, 1987.

Shanas, E., and G.L. Maddox. "Health, Health Resources, and the Utilization of Care." In *Handbook of Aging and the Social Sciences*, edited by R. Binstock and E. Shanas. New York: Van Nostrand Reinhold, 1985.

Shapiro, E., and N.P. Roos. "Predictors, Patterns and Consequences of Nursing-Home Use in One Canadian Province." In *Aging in Canada*, edited by V.W. Marshall. Toronto: Fitzhenry and Whiteside, 1987.

Simmons-Tropea, D., and R. Osborn. "Diseases, Survival and Death: The Health Status of Canada's Elderly." In *Aging in Canada*, edited by V.W. Marshall. Toronto: Fitzhenry and Whiteside, 1987.

Statistics Canada. *The Elderly in Canada*. Ottawa: Minister of Supply and Services Canada, 1984.

Statistics Canada and Department of the Secretary of State of Canada. *Report of the Canadian Health and Disability Survey 1983–1984*. Ottawa: Minister of Supply and Services Canada, 1986.

Stone, L., and S. Fletcher. *Canada's Older Population*. Montreal: The Institute for Research on Public Policy, 1980.

Ujimoto, K.V. "The Ethnic Dimension of Aging in Canada." In *Aging in Canada*, edited by V.W. Marshall. Toronto: Fitzhenry and Whiteside, 1987.

————. "Organizational Activities, Cultural Factors, and Well-Being of Aged Japanese Canadians." In *Ethnicity and Aging: New Perspectives*, edited by D.E. Gelfand and C. Barresi. New York: Springer Publishing Company, in press (a).

————. "Variations in the Allocation of Time Among Aged Japanese Canadians." In *Daily Life in Later Life: A Comparative Perspective*, edited by Karen Altergott. Beverly Hills: Sage Publication, in press (b).

Ujimoto, K.V., Harry Nishio, Paul Wong, and Lawrence Lam. "Comparative Aspects of Aging Asian-Canadians: Social Networks and Time-Budgets." Research funded by the Social Sciences and Humanities Research Council of Canada, Population Aging, Strategic Grant No. 492–84–0014, in progress.

U.S. Department of Health and Human Services. *Report of the Secretary's Task Force on Black and Minority Health*. Washington, D.C.: U.S. Department of Health and Human Services, 1985.

Wong, P.T.P., and G.T. Reker. "Face Validity of the Coping Inventory." Paper presented at the twelfth Annual Meeting of the Canadian Association on Gerontology, Moncton, N.B., 1983.

————. "Coping Behaviours of Successful Agers." Paper presented at the thirtieth Western Gerontological Society Annual Meeting, Anaheim, California, 1984.

————. "Stress, Coping, and Well-Being in Anglo and Chinese Elderly." *Canadian Journal on Aging* 4 (1985): 29–37.

15

INSTITUTIONAL CARE AND HEALTH POLICY FOR THE ELDERLY

Vera Ingrid Tarman
University of Toronto

INTRODUCTION

An increasing proportion of the Canadian population is composed of the elderly. In 1984, the elderly constituted a little over 10 percent of the population. The projection is that by the turn of the century, this proportion will increase to 13 percent, and by the year 2013, the elderly will constitute almost 24 percent of the population (Messinger and Powell, 1987:570). Of particular significance in the present context is the increase in the number of people aged 80 and over, commonly referred to as the "old old" or "frail old," within the elderly group. For instance, while in 1981 this group made up 19 percent of the population aged 65 and over, it is estimated that by the year 2001, this will increase to 24 percent (Fact Book, 1983:18). The rapid increase of this population has important implications for the planning and delivery of health-care services for the elderly.

There is a decline in the physical, mental, and functional abilities with increased age.

However, it must be emphasized that only a very small minority of the elderly have severe and incapacitating physical and mental conditions. The general notion that old age is synonymous with total dependence on others and that a majority of the elderly are confined to long-term institutional care is not borne out by the data (Chappell et al., 1986).

The elderly population is by no means homogeneous. Socio-economic status, age, and gender variously determine the need for services. For instance, because of higher life expectancy for women and, most likely, for a majority of them, inferior financial status, more women than men are in need of social and health services in old age (Fact Book, 1983). Women stand a greater likelihood than men of living alone. For example, in the 65-to-74 age group, 30 percent of women and 11 percent of men live alone. However, for those 75 years of age and over, 36 percent of women live alone, in contrast to 16 percent of the men. More women than men also end up in institutions and collective dwellings. For those 75 years of age and over, 20 percent of the women, as compared to 13 percent of the men, live in collective dwellings. After the age of 80, there is a sharp increase in the proportion of women living in collective dwellings (Fact Book, 1983:68; Shapiro and Roos, 1987:529). Women, therefore, tend to have a higher rate of institutionalization than men.

As noted before, health continues to decline among elderly persons as they continue to age. There is an increased likelihood of dementia. Overall, approximately 5 to 6 percent of the elderly have dementia; however, these figures increase with advanced age — 20 percent of those 80 years of age and over have dementia. Dementia is progressively debilitating and patients require assistance in their day-to-day existence (Chappell et al., 1986). Functional disability, of course, increases with age, and older people also come to suffer from physical diseases, typically chronic conditions such as heart disease, arthritis, and rheumatism (Chappell et al., 1986).

Most elderly Canadians live in private households in a variety of living arrangements — alone, with a spouse, or with relatives. Family and friends continue to be an important source of social support and care for the elderly. A small proportion of the elderly are under institutional care. The figures for 1981 indicate that a little less than 7 percent of the elderly (percentage 65 years and over) were under institutional care. The "old old" population is more likely to be under institutional care. The data for 1981 indicate that 33 percent of the "old old" (percentage 85+) were under institutional care, which includes nursing homes and institutions for the elderly and the chronically ill (Chappell et al., 1986:83). Overall, it is estimated that 20 to 25 percent of the elderly can expect to spend some time in an institution (long-term care facility) before they die (Chappell et al., 1986). If the current demographic trends hold, the important age and gender differences are likely to be even more significant in terms of need and demand for social and health services for the elderly, not only in the community but also in institutions.

With an increase of the "old old" population, the demand for and reliance on institutional care is likely to increase further, unless, of course, some alternatives to institutional care (such as community-based homemaker services) are developed.

In spite of the importance of institutional care for the elderly, in particular for the "old old" group requiring extended care facilities, there is currently no uniform and coherent policy in Canada to regulate the standard of accommodation, funding arrangements, and quality and standards of care. Institutional care, like most other health services, is a provincial responsibility, and thus is subject to variation across the country.

This chapter provides an overview of the special care facilities in Canada and the provinces. A detailed discussion is presented on the development of health policy regarding nursing homes in Ontario, with particular emphasis on the funding and regulatory arrangements affecting these institutions and the consequences of provincial policy for the nursing home industry.

SPECIAL CARE FACILITIES IN CANADA

There is a variety of institutions providing social and health services for the elderly population. These vary considerably by province. Other than specifying certain conditions which have to be met in order to remain eligible for federal cost-sharing arrangements, provinces make their own decisions regarding the organization and funding of programmes.

Data on special care facilities for the aged are presented in Table 1. It is evident that a large number of special care facilities are privately owned. This includes proprietary, for-profit institutions which are owned by "private individual, partnership or corporation, regardless of financial aid received by owner or residents, and operated for a profit" (Statistics Canada, 1987). Public ownership refers to those institutions which have municipal, provincial, or federal ownership.

There is considerable variation through the provinces in type of ownership. For instance, a large proportion of the number of facilities and the number of beds in the provinces of Quebec, Saskatchewan, and Alberta are under public ownership. On the other hand, in the provinces of Newfoundland, Prince Edward Island, Nova Scotia, Manitoba, and British Columbia, a very large number of special care facilities are privately owned.

Institutions also vary in terms of the type and level of care provided. According to federal guidelines issued in 1973, there are five levels of institutional care. These are: (1) residential, which includes custodial care institutions such as rest homes, hostels, homes for the aged, and the like; (2) extended care, which includes nursing homes and their equivalents; (3) chronic hospitals; (4) rehabilitation; and (5) acute hospital care (Kane and Kane, 1985:58; for a detailed description of Ontario's scheme, see Gross and Schwenger, 1981:28–44).

In spite of these guidelines, there continues to be provincial diversity in funding, health-care provision for the elderly, and even the use of nomenclature for various institutions (Kane and Kane, 1985:59). For instance, the chronic, rehabilitation, and acute hospitals (levels 3 to 5) are automatically funded by all provincial health-insurance programmes. Services provided by levels 1 and 2, however, are fully funded only in the provinces of Manitoba and British Columbia. Nursing-home care, specifically, is funded as a universal benefit in Ontario, Manitoba, British Columbia, Quebec, Saskatchewan, and Alberta, but not in the four Atlantic provinces. Home-care insurance, as well, is developed (or is in the process of developing) in the same provinces which presently fund nursing homes (Kane and Kane, 1985:15).

It is apparent from the above that in spite of some commonality, there continues to be considerable diversity in the organization of institutional and other health facilities for the elderly. Consequently, it is difficult to present a meaningful analysis, given the time and space, of health-care policy for the aged in the Canadian context. Therefore, the remainder of this chapter deals with the special care facilities in Ontario and examines the development of health policy towards nursing homes in that province.

Special Care Facilities in Ontario

Ontario is the most populated province in Canada. A little over 35 percent of the Canadian population lives in Ontario. It also has the largest population of elderly people. Almost 37 percent of Canada's elderly live in Ontario (Kane and Kane, 1985:17). Ontario's "old old" population is also quite high. In 1981, almost 40 percent of the elderly were over 75 years of age.

The data on special care facilities for the elderly in Ontario are presented in Table 2. It is evident that Ontario continues to rely very heavily upon private facilities to provide special care services for the elderly. In fact, there was a substantial increase both in the number of private facilities and beds from 1981 to 1983. This is particularly important in view of the discussion which follows regarding incompatibility between the profit motive and quality of care (Baum, 1977; NDP Task Force, 1984; Social Planning Council of Metropolitan Toronto, 1984).

Various provincial regulations govern the funding and operation of institutions for the elderly in Ontario. Although some services for the elderly are covered by other ministries, long-term care in Ontario is primarily within the jurisdiction of the two provincial ministries, the Ministry of Health and the Ministry of Community and Social Services (ComSoc). Both subsidize residential and extended care services in the community.

Long-term institutional services in Ontario can be placed under the residential, extended care, chronic, and rehabilitation levels of the federal paradigm mentioned earlier. There is some overlapping of services among long-term care institutions. Nursing homes, which fall under the label of extended care (defined as 1.5 hours of nursing and personal care a day in Ontario), are allowed to offer some residential care. Homes for the aged, which are municipal

Table 1. Number of Special Care Facilities* and Beds for the Aged† — Canada and Provinces 1983

PROVINCE	PUBLIC		PRIVATE	
	No.	Beds	No.	Beds
Newfoundland	2	347	76	2 746
Prince Edward Island	6	496	18	481
Nova Scotia	23	1 931	77	3 776
New Brunswick	1	172	179	5 177
Quebec	482	25 608	155	7 092
Ontario	94	18 868	534	42 369
Manitoba	28	936	98	7 342
Saskatchewan	92	5 157	43	3 417
Alberta	160	9 499	58	5 467
British Columbia	5	380	316	18 153
N.W.T. & Yukon	3	69	1	4
CANADA	896	63 490	1 554	96 024

* *Special care facilities* — facilities which provide a measure of care. Data cover residential units only. These facilities are in general maintained for residents who are chronically ill or disabled, in contrast to, for example, a hospital where patients are accommodated on the basis of medical need and are provided with continuing medical care and supporting diagnostic and therapeutic services.

† *Aged* — those who receive a level of care and whose reason for residing is due principally to the aging process.

Source: Statistics Canada, *List of Canadian Hospitals and Special Care Facilities, 1983.*

Table 2. Ontario Special Care Facilities* and Beds for the Aged† — Selected Years

YEAR	PUBLIC		PRIVATE		TOTAL	
	No.	Beds	No.	Beds	No.	Beds
1979	88	17 883	461	32 443	549	50 326
1980	88	17 883	472	33 374	560	51 257
1981	87	17 787	451	33 400	538	51 187
1983	94	18 868	534	42 369	628	61 237

* *Special care facilities* — facilities which provide a measure of care. Data cover residential units only. These facilities are in general maintained for residents who are chronically ill or disabled, in contrast to, for example, a hospital where patients are accommodated on the basis of medical need and are provided with continuing medical care and supporting diagnostic and therapeutic services.

† *Aged* — those who receive a level of care and whose reason for residing is due principally to the aging process.

Source: Statistics Canada, *List of Canadian Hospitals and Special Care Facilities, 1979–1983.*

or charitable non-profit institutions funded and regulated by the Ministry of Community and Social Services, are expected to offer custodial rather than health care (Gross and Schwenger, 1981:36). Individual homes are, however, allowed to offer up to 60 percent of their beds as extended care (Blake, 1972). Total provincial expenditures for homes for the aged in 1980 was approximately $127 million (Liberal Policy Research Office, 1984:4).

The definition of Ontario nursing homes comes from the 1972 Nursing Homes Act, which states that a nursing home is "any premise maintained and operated for persons requiring nursing care, or in which such care is provided to two or more unrelated persons." In order to maintain a license and receive funding, nursing homes must offer at least 75 percent of their beds to patients who require "extended care," that is, 1.5 hours or more of nursing and personal care. In actual fact, nursing homes provide over 94 percent of their beds at this level of health care (Hansard, 1984:4853). In 1983–84, nursing homes received a total of $241.7 million from the Ministry of Health (Social Planning Council, 1984:30).

While the notion of a nursing home as a business is not incorporated into the legislated definition, it must be noted that nursing homes, as opposed to homes for the aged, are and have been, by and large, private, for-profit entities. Currently, 95 percent of homes are private, for-profit entities (Kane and Kane, 1985:76; spokesperson for the Ministry of Health, 1986).

THE DEVELOPMENT OF HEALTH POLICY REGARDING NURSING HOMES IN ONTARIO

The development of health policy concerning nursing homes in Ontario may best be discussed in two parts. The first will examine the time period beginning with the General Welfare Assistance Act of 1949, which represents the provincial government's first involvement with the nursing home industry. The primary concerns raised during this time, which extends until the 1972 Nursing Homes Act, relate to the necessity for provincial licensing, uniformity of standards, and universal funding for nursing homes.

The second part deals with what may be characterized as "quality of care issues." The focus is on the debate between various interest groups — government, the opposition party, nursing home operators, and other interested groups. Provincial policy has been primarily oriented toward reforms. Critics of the proprietary (for-profit) institutions argue that there is a basic contradiction between the profit motive and quality of care which cannot be resolved by reform and more regulation.

I The Call for Provincial Licensing and Insurance

The debate surrounding nursing homes until 1972 was dominated by two issues: the need for provincial license and regulation, and the necessity for nursing home insurance.

Before the amendment to the General Welfare Assistance Act of 1957, which represented the provincial government's first action towards the funding and regulation of homes, nursing homes were for the most part unlicensed, small, private households. The Ontario Health Survey estimated that there were approximately 487 nursing and boarding homes in Ontario, which gave in-bed care suitable for the elderly (Davis, 1950:166).

Upon the implementation of the General Welfare Assistance Act, homes which received payments for their indigents were expected to conform to regulations suggested by a draft provincial bylaw. This Act thus represented the first action of government towards recognizing homes as being more than small businesses. Nursing homes were beginning to be seen as providing care for the old and infirm. This required, therefore, some acknowledged standards of care; however, the proposed standards were not generally accepted as adequate.

The basic problem with the Act was that it

did not address the lack of uniformity of regulations across the province. Homes which did not receive payments did not have to be licensed, or even declare their existence, and of those homes which did receive subsidies, it was up to the individual municipalities to interpret and enforce the suggested provincial regulations.

This variation of standards in nursing homes became an issue shortly after the introduction of the Hospital Insurance and Diagnostic Services Act of 1957 (see LeClair, 1975). Nursing homes were excluded from this federal-provincial cost-shared health-insurance programme because they were too disparate and unregulated. They were also not seen as providing health care (Blake, Dreezer, and Corder, 1986).

Thus, by the late 1950s, two issues emerged which would shape the history of nursing homes until 1972: the issues of inadequate standards, and the desire for more extensive government subsidy. These two issues dominated the debate concerning nursing homes. All the parties — nursing home owners, consumers of nursing home services, government representatives — were in agreement (though for different motives) in their demand for adequate and uniform standards for health-care services for the elderly.

Nursing home proprietors, through a newly formed association, lobbied for the extension of universal hospital insurance to cover nursing homes. They were thus motivated to push for provincial license and uniform regulation of homes in order to receive this funding from the Department of Health, or failing that, to increase their subsidy under the Department of Welfare (Associated Nursing Homes Incorporated, 1964).

The need for provincial licensing and regulations was also becoming obvious to consumers of nursing home care. In the early 1960s, families of patients had begun to write to their Members of Parliament and to the media about the poor conditions that they had found in homes. The Ontario Welfare Council released an interim report in 1965, citing 165 homes out of 425 as giving inadequate care (Hansard, 1965:4444).

There was pressure within the provincial government itself, by officials who worked with nursing homes, to seek uniform regulation. This was because a certain percentage of nursing homes at this time were being used as "auxiliary hospitals," wherever there was a shortage of hospital beds. By 1964, there was also a percentage of homes that were licensed as Homes for Special Care, that is, that housed ex-psychiatric patients. Officials found that when they looked for suitable homes to which they could transfer patients, many were not adequate for their purposes (Blake, Dreezer, and Corder, 1986; Blake, 1972).

Despite the apparent congruity of interests of various parties, the government was somewhat reluctant to take steps to transform private institutions for the elderly. Nursing homes continued to be treated as custodial care institutions rather than as health-care institutions. The government, however, did pass additional regulations and increased funding to the municipalities.

The response in 1965, for example, to the growing concerns over the quality of nursing home care, was simply to tighten up the General Welfare Assistance regulations, and to increase its municipal payments.

The provincial Nursing Home Act of 1966 stipulated that all nursing homes in Ontario be licensed under the Department of Health. But it was still left to the municipalities to interpret, add to, and enforce the provincial regulations (see An Act to Provide for the Licensing and Regulation of Nursing Homes). This Act, therefore, did not establish uniform standards for nursing homes across the province.

Under the Nursing Home Act of 1966, nursing homes were still not considered eligible for provincial hospital insurance, despite their having been taken over by the Department of Health. They were still being funded, on a means-test basis, by the Department of Welfare, now renamed the Department of Family and Social Services. They were still primarily seen as offering custodial rather than health care.

The extension of hospital insurance was seen, however, as necessary for the Nursing Home Act to be effectual. The Act had been modelled after the Homes for Special Care Act, in that nursing homes were now officially expected to act as inexpensive substitutes for hospital beds, of which there was an increasing shortage (Hansard, 1966:1087). However, unlike Homes for Special Care, nursing home beds were not subsidized and consequently could not fulfill the function of a hospital bed, since people were reluctant to transfer patients from the hospital to a facility that they had to pay for.

Despite its failure to provide uniform funding and regulations, this Act did have a significant effect on the nursing home industry in other respects. Many previously unlicensed or smaller homes were forced to close down because they could not afford to adapt to the new regulations. According to one source, as many as 70 homes closed down in the period of a year and a half (Hansard,1968:2342). "In the Canadian nursing home industry," the *Financial Post* forecast, "the days of the 'ma and pa' homes may be numbered" (Bruchovsky, *Financial Post*, 1970:21).

Bruchovsky further states: "Emerging are corporate chains, building large and modern facilities and very intent on expansion." Indeed, by 1970, in the space of less than five years, there were six public investor-owned chains in Canada, with at least two operating in Ontario. There was a growing optimism about the financial feasibility of nursing homes, and of the profit that could be generated from a nursing home business (Bruchovsky, 1970:21).

At this juncture, the provincial government passed additional regulations. The Nursing Home Act of 1972 signalled at last the greater willingness of the provincial government to become involved with nursing home care. These regulations were to be enforced by the Ministry of Health, rather than the municipalities. This Act also provided the extended care hospital insurance for nursing home residents, (and some homes for the aged residents), under the newly amalgamated Ontario Health Insurance Plan (Nursing Home Act, 1972).

The Act thus signalled a turning point for the government in its recognition of the changing function of nursing homes. The role of nursing homes was shifting from profit and "custodial care" to "health-care" institutions for the old and infirm.

An equally important feature of the Act was the control government took over the numbers and allocation of beds to be licensed. There was a systematic effort to distribute beds across the provinces so that rural as well as urban communities would have access to nursing home care. The allocation of beds would be based on demonstrated need. The utilization of the district health councils one year later was an effort to formalize this system of demonstrated need to 3.5 beds per 1000 population (Potter, Hansard, 1973:2170).

There was also a decided effort to control the costs and thus the numbers of beds that government had to subsidize (Hansard, 1972:799; Chatfield, cited by Engel, 1973:17). This was a valid concern as federal aid towards nursing homes would not be forthcoming until the Extended Care Block grant in 1977 (Blake, Dreezer, and Corder, 1986).

Government, by controlling beds in this way, was thus able to provide the popular extended care insurance within its own regional and budgetary constraints. This rationing strategy, however, in some areas inadvertently created a shortage of nursing home beds.

The situation proved to be advantageous for the larger nursing home chains. The smaller "independent" nursing homes could not compete with larger "corporate" institutions, and were forced to close down. It has been estimated that 148 homes closed down after 1971, as a result of the inability of homes, particularly smaller homes, to comply with regulations (Duggan, 1985). According to the Nursing Home Association, the low per diem rates of the extended care subsidy made it difficult for homes to afford the higher standards required by the Act. Nursing homes, in order to be licensed, were required to provide extended care insurance for 75 percent of their beds. Nursing homes could not offset this cost by charging extra fees to their clients, as the 1973 amendment to the Nursing Home Act disallowed any charge which exceeded the fee schedule (Potter, Hansard, 1973:326).

The smaller nursing homes already in existence could not compete with the larger homes. Also, new small enterprises were not viable because of the large capital outlay required to open new premises (Hansard, 1972:1277). These conditions contributed to the increase of larger homes which could afford the capital costs and still make a profit with the extended care subsidy.

It is not surprising to find, therefore, that since 1971 the average size of homes has increased from 44 beds to 89 beds (Scully, 1986:13). By 1983, 41 percent of the nursing home beds in Ontario were owned by the ten largest nursing home companies active in Ontario. (Privatization Project, Feb. 1984). By 1986, there were 157 corporate owned homes (three homes or more owned by one company) out of 332 homes (spokesperson for the Ministry of Health, 1986). The Act thus created a situation which favoured the emergence of larger homes and which enabled them to make, according to the *Financial Post* (Engel, *Financial Post*, 1973), record profits.

Linda McQuaig of the *Globe and Mail* (1984) has analyzed this favourable situation for the large nursing homes as analogous to the taxi-cab business.

Like the taxicab business, nursing homes benefit from a licensing system that limits competition. . . . But the nursing home business has another advantage not enjoyed by the cab industry: a huge and growing demand for its services. In the taxi business, it would be comparable to an ever present and growing line-up of customers ready to jump in as soon as the cab is empty. . . . And payment is guaranteed . . . to continue the taxi analogy, it would be as if all those customers lined up to get into the cab had government charge accounts. . . . under the current system . . . private nursing home operators, in many ways, are enjoying the best that both the private and public sectors have to offer. The firms are assured of government subsidies and provincially set prices but also enjoy benefits of private enterprise profits.

It was also during this time that various interest groups entered into the controversial debate concerning the type of ownership of homes (for-profit versus non-profit) and quality of care. For instance, the private contenders, such as the Nursing Home Association, called for a higher per diem, or for less governmental control of the competitive forces of the private nursing home marketplace (Duggan, 1985; ONHA). The public or non-profit advocates, such as the New Democratic Party (1984) or the Social Planning Council (1984; see also Concerned Friends, 1984), felt that the profit motive was incompatible with quality of care, even in the best of conditions, and called for the creation of non-profit nursing homes (for a review of arguments, see Tarman, 1985).

In summary, the provincial policy, particularly the Nursing Homes Act of 1972, has had some beneficial results. The Act provided uniform operating standards for nursing homes and called for equitable distribution of facilities across the province, so that rural as well as urban residents would have access to nursing homes. Many small nursing homes, because of the costs, could not comply with the standards and had to close down. New small enterprises were not viable because of the large capital outlay required to open new facilities. This situation favoured the emergence of larger homes under corporate ownerships. This created a basic contradiction between the profit motive and provision of quality care for the elderly.

II The Calls for Quality of Care

The second part of this history looks at the issues which emerged as a result of the 1972 Nursing Homes Act. One notes that government remained hesitant to intervene in nursing home matters until the early 1980s, when policy towards homes shifted and became strongly reformist in nature.

Because of the repercussions of the nursing home legislation, the government has, through the years, been somewhat reluctant to enforce regulations and address the suggestions for nursing home reform put forth by many groups. Government has been hesitant to intervene and further jeopardize the profit interests of the nursing home business. This led to a series of confrontations in the late 1970s, between the Ministry of Health, nursing homes, and the public.

The Ministry, for example, was reluctant to prosecute nursing home owners for any violations of standards, particularly if it would result in the closing of homes. The Ministry was not anxious to exacerbate the bed shortage, particularly in rural areas (Hansard, 1978:S–1113). It preferred instead to advise and seek co-operation from nursing home operators. As one spokesperson for the regulatory authority in the Ministry of Health explained: "Let me stress that we are not anxious to close any nursing home because the need for such institutions is great. We would prefer to develop an atmosphere of cooperation which would be of mutual benefit" (cited in Baum, 1977:70).

The Ministry, furthermore, was reluctant to make inspection reports pertaining to nursing homes' compliance with regulations and standards available to the public. The Ministerial response was based on considerations of confidentiality; that is, the records were confidential for medical reasons; instead, only summaries of the reports would be given (Hansard, 1978:4621; Hansard, 1981:584).

The same arguments were made to protect the confidentiality of profits and losses of nursing homes. The provincial government argued that to demand such information was an invasion into private property rights (Hansard, 1983:1189). There was a concern raised by some (Concerned Friends, 1984) that profits generated from nursing home care were not being reinvested into the homes (in terms of upkeep), but were instead going into other business ventures such as life insurance and computer technology.

As a result, beginning as early as 1977, there were calls for an inquiry into nursing homes. The Ministry, however, felt that a highly publicized inquiry was too expensive and quite unnecessary (Timbrell, Hansard, 1977:2454). Instead, it granted slight improvements to the inspections procedure and amended a regulation

in the Nursing Homes Act in 1980 (Hansard, 1978:S–1094; Hansard, 1980:5029).

Calls to make nursing homes non-profit were also continuously opposed. The fundamental and growing concern held by many (NDP, 1984; Concerned Friends, 1984; Social Planning Council, 1984), was that nursing homes, as proprietary institutions, were more interested in making a profit than in providing good quality care. To reduce costs, nursing home operators, for example, followed the practice of contracting out health and maintenance services, to avoid hiring the better-paid unionized workers (Hansard, 1977:629; Hansard, 1983:3039; NDP, 1984:22). To increase their incomes, some institutions were levying additional charges for necessary services, such as laundry or transportation, which are not covered under the extended care or resident co-payment fees (Social Planning Council, 1984:101). Some nursing homes also practised what is referred to as "cream-skimming," that is, accepting only the least problematic and thus least costly patients into their homes (Social Planning Council, 1984:19).

There was an implicit concern in the government, however, that without the profit motive many nursing home operators would lose incentive, close down homes, and thus exacerbate the bed shortage. The general response to the call to make nursing homes non-profit was that the problems in quality of care in nursing homes resulted more from a faulty inspections procedure than from the type of ownership (Hansard, 1978:2409).

The issues which emerged in the late 1970s indicate that government has been reluctant to intervene into the "business matters" of the nursing home industry. The 1972 Nursing Homes Act, which was intended to improve the conditions of nursing homes, was inadvertently the cause for potentially greater problems within nursing homes. Yet government was hesitant to intervene still further, as it seemed that increased state intervention would jeopardize private involvement in nursing home care. It seemed inevitable that even more small homes would close down if forced to conform to regulations;

as well, the larger homes would lose incentive to provide care if their profit-making mechanisms were challenged and/or curtailed.

From the early 1980s, however, there has been a detectable shift in government's priorities regarding nursing home policy. Highly publicized events and the growing strength of public interest groups have elicited a decisive increase in governmental intervention. These interventions have promoted nursing homes as reliable health-service entities.

Some examples of intervention bear mention, as they are in sharp contrast to government's previous reluctance to interfere in the private market. In 1983, the Minister of Health made inspection reports available to the public (Norton, 1983:8). Not incidental to this reform was the nursing home industry's own initiative to accredit nursing homes by the Canadian Council on Hospital Accreditation. The Ministry of Health publicly supported this action (Norton, 1983:15; Hansard, 1984:S–53).

The focus on resident and family input into homes has increased in the last few years. In 1983, the Minister of Health set policy to ensure that residents be informed of their right to form a residents' council (Norton, 1983). In the fall of 1986, the Minister of Health proposed a resident's bill of rights in the Legislature.

The Ministry, as well, saw to the creation of the Nursing Home Resident's Complaint Committee (Hansard, 1984:3625). This committee, an objective body outside the Ministry, deals with complaints regarding the quality of life in nursing homes (Norton, 1984).

Perhaps there will be a shift in policy in the provision of services by the Liberal government, which took office in 1985 after a continuous Progressive Conservative ascendancy in Ontario since 1943. The Minister of Health, Murray Elston, seemed to be receptive to considerations of non-profit homes when he pondered: "It seems a fair question to ask if there is not room in the extended care field for a broader non-profit role" (Elston, 1986).

In the recent past it appears that the government has been more willing to intervene to assure uniform standards through various regulations, as well as to be more receptive to public input and public surveillance of nursing homes. The nursing home industry also has taken the initiative, and is supported by the government, to have nursing homes accredited by the Canadian Council on Hospital Accreditation.

SUMMARY AND CONCLUSIONS

A variety of institutions provide social and health services for the elderly population. In spite of the importance of institutional care for the elderly, in particular the "old old" group, there is a lack of a uniform and coherent Canadian policy and regulation which govern the standards of accommodation, funding arrangements, and quality and standards of care. As in other matters of health care, institutional care is a provincial responsibility. Other than certain conditions which have to be met to maintain their eligibility for federal cost-sharing arrangements, provinces more or less set their own requirements for operation and funding arrangements of special care facilities for the elderly.

Data show that a large number of special care facilities in Canada are privately owned, which includes proprietary, for-profit facilities. There is considerable variation in provinces of type of ownership. For instance, Quebec is one of the provinces with a high proportion of facilities and beds under public ownership. In Ontario, on the other hand, a very large number of the facilities are under private ownership. In fact, there was a substantial increase from 1981 to 1983 in the number of both privately owned facilities and beds in Ontario.

The discussion on the development of health policy regarding nursing homes in Ontario indicates that the provincial policy has not been oriented toward a complete transformation of the nursing home industry. The provincial government for the most part has been content to "regulate" the industry by requiring accommodation and health standards. Though these requirements have had beneficial results, they have also led to an increase in the number and size of facilities under private and corporate ownership. This situation has proved to be advantageous for larger units, enabling them to make large profits. The critics charge that the profit motive is incompatible with quality of care. The data presented above suggest that nursing homes use various strategies to cut costs or levy additional charges to residents for necessary services, or practice what is referred to as "cream-skimming."

This continued reliance on proprietary facilities is particularly significant in view of the current concern about health costs and quality of care. Institutional care is quite expensive, whether provided by public or private facilities.

The proprietary institutions, however, are more likely to be oriented to profit and less concerned about quality of care. The debate about health costs in addition to health-promotion strategies perhaps should also include the current organization and financial arrangements of health-care institutions (in this case special health-care facilities for the elderly) and health-care delivery system. The critics of the proprietary, for-profit institutions advocate their complete transformation to public non-profit facilities. As the "reforms" and other regulations do not alter the basic contradiction between profit and quality of care, nor do they significantly improve the quality of care or reduce the cost of health-care services for the elderly.

STUDY QUESTIONS

1. Briefly discuss the development of policy regarding nursing homes in Ontario and its impact on the provision of health services for the elderly.

2. It is argued that reforms do not resolve the basic contradiction between profits and quality of care. Discuss this in view of the material presented in this chapter.

3. Why, in your opinion, has the provincial government been content to "regulate" the nursing home industry rather than transforming it completely to a non-profit public ownership industry?

4. Discuss briefly the mechanisms used by the owners to reduce costs and how these interfere with the provision of care.

5. How would you explain the continued existence of privately owned special care facilities in the context of universal public funding of health-care services?

RECOMMENDED READING

Chappell, N., L. Strain, and A. Blandford. *Aging and Health Care: A Social Perspective*. Holt, Rinehart and Winston, 1986.

Gross, M., and C. Schwenger. *Health-Care Costs for the Elderly in Ontario: 1976–2026*. Toronto: Ontario Economic Council, Occasional Papers 11, 1981.

Kane, R.L., and R.A. Kane. *A Will and a Way: What Americans Can Learn About Long-Term Care From Canada*. Santa Monica: Rand Corp., 1985.

Social Planning Council of Metropolitan Toronto. *Caring for Profit: The Commercialization of Human Services in Ontario*. Christa Freiler, Project Director. Toronto, October, 1984.

Swartz, D. "The Politics of Reform: Conflict and Accommodation in Canadian Health Policy." Chapter 11 in *The Canadian State: Political Economy and Political Power*, edited by L. Panitch, 311–42. Toronto: University of Toronto Press, 1977.

REFERENCES

Alberta Nursing Home Review Panel. "Report and Recommendations." Ministry of Hospitals and Medical Care, 1982.

An Act to Provide for the Licensing and Regulation of Nursing Homes. Revised Statutes of Ontario, 1966, chap. 99, p. 495.

Associated Nursing Homes Incorporated. "A Report Concerning Nursing Homes and Nursing Home Residents in the Province of Ontario to the Senate of Canada Special Committee on Aging. July, 1964." In *History of Associated Nursing Homes Incorporated* (Ontario): 1959–1964. Toronto, 1964.

Baum, D.J. *Warehouses for Death: The Nursing Home Industry.* Don Mills: Burns and MacEachern, 1977.

Blake, B. Speech to OHA Small Hospital Forum. October 25, 1972.

Blake, B., S. Dreezer, and D. Corder. Interview with spokespersons at Ministry of Health, October, 1986.

Bruchovsky, A. "Nursing Homes Plan to Grow with 'Good Quality Care.'" *Financial Post*, 21 March 1970, 21.

Chappell, N., L. Strain, and A. Blandford. *Aging and Health Care: A Social Perspective.* Holt, Rinehart and Winston, 1986.

Concerned Friends of Ontario Citizens in Care Facilities. "Consumer Concerns and Recommendations Related to Nursing Home Care in Ontario." A Brief to the Honourable Larry Grossman, Minister of Health, September, 1984.

Davis, G. (Chairman). Report of the Ontario Health Survey Committee. Vol. 1, 1950.

Duggan, R. Interview with spokesperson at Ontario Nursing Home Association. September, 1985.

Elston, M. Remarks by the Honourable Murray Elston, Minister of Health, to the Ontario Nursing Home Association. Hamilton, September 9, 1986.

Engel, R. "Nursing Home Concept Catching On." *Financial Post*, 12 May 1973, 17–18.

Estes, C.I., L.E. Gerard, J.S. Zones, and J.H. Swan. *The Political Economy, Health and Aging.* Boston: Little, Brown and Co., 1984.

Fact Book on Aging in Canada. Second Canadian Conference on Aging, Government of Canada, October 24–27, 1983.

Gross, M., and C. Schwenger. *Health Care Costs for the Elderly in Ontario: 1976–2026.* Toronto: Ontario Economic Council, Occasional Papers 11, 1981.

Hansard Official Report of Debates, 1960–1986. Published by the Legislative Assembly of Ontario.

Kane, R.L., and R.A. Kane. *A Will and a Way: What Americans Can Learn about Long-Term Care from Canada.* Santa Monica: Rand Corp., 1985.

LeClair, M. "The Canadian Health Care System." Chapter 1 in *National Health Insurance: Can We Learn from Canada?* edited by S. Andreopoulos. Malabar: Robert E. Krieger, 1975.

Liberal Policy Research Office. *Options for Living: Directions for Change.* Toronto: Queen's Park, June, 1984.

Messinger, H., and B. Powell. "The Implications of Canada's Aging Society on Social Expenditures." Chapter 29 in *Aging in Canada: Social Perspectives*, edited by V.W. Marshall, 569–85. Markham, Ont.: Fitzhenry and Whiteside, 1987.

McQuaig, L. "Nursing Homes Flourish Under Taxpayer's Umbrella." *Globe and Mail*, 17 May 1984, M2.

Ministry of Health. Telephone interview with the spokesperson for the Ministry of Health, in August, 1986.

NDP Caucus Task Force Report. "Aging With Dignity." June, 1984.

Norton, K. Remarks by the Honourable Keith

Norton, Minister of Health, to the Ontario Nursing Home Association. Toronto, September 22, 1983.

————. Remarks by the Honourable Keith Norton, Minister of Health, to the Concerned Friends of Ontario Citizens in Care Facilities, Inc. Toronto, May 7, 1984.

Nursing Homes Act, 1972. Revised Statutes of Ontario, 1972, chapter 11, p. 87.

Ontario Nursing Home Association's Role Study Task Force. Position Paper and Recommendations Regarding the Role of Nursing Homes as Developed by the ONHA, 1983.

Panitch, L. "The Role and Nature of the Canadian State." Chapter 1 in *The Canadian State: Political Economy and Political Power*, edited by L. Panitch, 3–27. Toronto: University of Toronto Press, 1977.

Privatization Project, February, 1984.

Scully, D. "History of Nursing Homes in Ontario." *Ontario Nursing Home Journal* 2, no. 1 (February 1986): 12–15.

Shapiro, E., and N. Roos. "Predictors, Patterns and Consequences of Nursing-Home Use in One Canadian Province." Chapter 26 in *Aging in Canada: Social Perspectives*, edited by V.W. Marshall, 520–37. Markham: Fitzhenry and Whiteside, 1987.

Social Planning Council of Metropolitan Toronto. *Caring for Profit: The Commercialization of Human Services in Ontario*. Christa Freiler, Project Director. Toronto: October, 1984.

Statistics Canada. *List of Canadian Hospitals and Special Care Facilities, 1986*. Statistics Canada, Health Division, Ottawa, 1987.

Swartz, D. "The Politics of Reform: Conflict and Accommodation in Canadian Health Policy." Chapter 11 in *The Canadian State: Political Economy and Political Power*, edited by L. Panitch, 311–42. Toronto: University of Toronto Press, 1977.

Tarman, V.I. "Looking Behind the Rhetoric: Analysis of Ownership Type of Nursing Home and Quality of Care." Paper presented at the 14th Annual Meeting of the Canadian Association of Gerontology, November, 1985.

PART VI

MENTAL ILLNESS, PSYCHIATRY, AND SOCIOLOGY

INTRODUCTION

A number of previous readings in the text indicate that while there has been a general improvement in the health status of the Canadian population, substantial disparities in life expectancies and mortality rates continue to persist across income and occupational groups and for the unemployed and Native Canadians. Evidence presented in Chapter 16 by Stolzman shows that disparities in the rates and types of mental disorders also prevail across social classes, with the rates of mental disorders being highest in the lower classes.

Stolzman discusses different theoretical interpretations of the relationship between class and mental disorder. After a brief outline of the genetic and social selection hypotheses, explanations that emphasize causation are discussed in more detail. The societal reaction model maintains that the purported higher prevalence of mental disorder in the lower classes is primarily an artifact of class bias as to who gets labelled as mentally ill in society. The social stress hypothesis attributes the proclivity of lower-class persons to become mentally disordered to the pressures and deprivations associated with their life circumstances. A modified version of this interpretation argues that lower-class people are more prone to psychological disturbances because they have fewer and less adequate resources for coping with stress than do people in higher social class positions. The examination of all these factors to promote a comprehensive understanding of the connections between social class and mental disorder is stressed.

Stolzman also examines differences in psychiatric treatment by social class. It is contended that a two-tiered mental health care system, in which higher-class patients receive quality psychotherapy, while lower-class patients are regulated to custodial care or less effective organic treatments, persists in North American society. In conclusion, the author proposes some reforms aimed at reducing the unequal allocation of psychotherapy.

One of the reforms proposed by Stolzman suggests that medical students in psychiatry should do substantial course work in the humanities and social sciences. This would expose students to various pyschosocial factors which impinge upon mental health and psychiatric care, and help to alleviate an apparent obliviousness to these factors which is fostered by existing medical education and training. While Stolzman argues for the use of social science research in the training and education of medical students, Hetherington, in Chapter 17, reports the results of a Canadian survey on the utilization of social science research in mental health policy.

The study had two objectives: (1) to examine attitudes of policy-makers, administrators, and social scientists toward the place of social science research in mental health policy formulation, and (2) to examine the utilization of such information by policy-makers and administrators in the mental health field. A two-communities theory underlies the study. The theory states that scientists and policy-makers occupy two different cultures, and the resulting differences in beliefs, values, and attitudes hinder effective use of relevant scientific knowledge in the resolution of policy issues.

Evidence tends to support the existence of two separate cultures, involving differences related to perceptions of the place of science in policy and interpersonal/organizational problems related to perceived quality of social science research. The available evidence suggests that the role which social science research information plays in policy decisions is not a vital one. In terms of information utilization, it is found that consultants and *general* knowledge of social science research and theory are used more frequently by administrators and policy-makers than are the results of specific studies.

What are the motivations for use? Data indicate that motivations are predominantly instrumental rather than legitimating. How do differences between scientists and policy-makers relate to rates and types of use? Perceived problems with quality of scientific evidence are found unrelated to frequency of use, but lead to greater use of "trusted" and "controlled" sources by decision-makers. What are the consequences of accommodation between the two cultures? Accommodation results in reduction of the value differences between the two groups, but increases, rather than reduces, the awareness of problems associated with the utilization of social scientific information in policy making. In conclusion, recommendations based on this research are provided.

From a discussion of the distribution of mental disorders and mental health, and mental health policy, we now turn to the discussion of the institutional transformation of psychiatric practice, characterized by a shift from asylum-based to community-based forms of service delivery.

Dickinson and Andre, in Chapter 18, argue that the demise of the asylum and the development of community psychiatry cannot be understood as a manifestation of the medicalization of deviance, nor can it be understood as the simple substitution of one form of social control with another. Rather, they argue, contemporary psychiatry is characterized by the simultaneous expansion of two distinct but related forms of psychiatric practice. On the one hand, there is a medically dominated, general-hospital–based, private-sector psychiatric services system, and, on the other, a mental-health-clinic–based, public-sector psychiatric services system increasingly dominated by non-medically trained professionals like psychologists and social workers. The basis of this institutional bifurcation is the ambiguity about the cause of mental disorders, which appear to be both biological and social/psychological in origin. This ambiguity vis-à-vis etiology has resulted in jurisdictional battles between competing professions, and between competing specialties within professions, for control over the diagnosis and treatment of those disorders. Drawing upon historical material from the province of Saskatchewan, and analyzing psychiatry as a form of work, this chapter examines how various intra- and interprofessional struggles have influenced the institutional development of psychiatry.

16

THE DISTRIBUTION AND TREATMENT OF MENTAL DISORDERS BY SOCIAL CLASS:
A Review of the Research and Theoretical Interpretations

James D. Stolzman
Dalhousie University

INTRODUCTION

Sociology's distinctiveness as a perspective on human behaviour is founded on the observation that the way in which groups and societies are organized or structured has a profound effect on how its members think, act, and feel. A key aspect of any society's structure is its system of stratification. This term refers to the social arrangements whereby people receive unequal amounts of, and have unequal access to, whatever is considered valuable in that society. Most writers on stratification agree that foremost among the valued resources distributed in society are wealth, social prestige, and power.

Canada, along with most other Western industrial capitalist nations, has what sociologists call a class type of stratification system. In a class system the various occupational positions form a hierarchy based primarily upon inequalities of wealth, property, and income. Compared to other types of stratification systems, class societies are relatively open. This is to say that they permit individuals to move up or down the hierarchy on the basis of their personal qualities and achievements. Consequently, class societies are typically highly competitive. While existing inequalities of power and privilege may interfere with its realization, the ideal of equal opportunity is central to the beliefs that serve to legitimize this type of stratification system.

In class-stratified societies, the inequalities of wealth and power tend to be manifested in a variety of ways. Social research has repeatedly demonstrated that people's standing in the class system partly determines the kinds of lives they lead, the kinds of attitudes they hold, and the kinds of opportunities that are available to them. Indeed, social class has proven to be sociology's most powerful explanatory variable; it correlates with a multitude of behaviour patterns, beliefs, lifestyles, and "life chances." By the latter term I mean the probability of securing resources that will promote and enhance the quality of one's life. These might include the opportunity to get a good education, to hold a rewarding job, to live a long life, to travel extensively, and to be healthy, both physically and mentally.

This last point brings us to the subject matter of this chapter. Other chapters in this volume have no doubt underlined the fact that physical health and illness are unequally distributed across the stratification system. More specifically, "social class gradients of mortality and life expectancy have been observed for centuries, and a vast body of evidence has shown consistently that those in the lower classes have higher mortality, morbidity, and disability rates" (Syme and Berkman, 1981:35). Why this is so is a matter of some controversy that will be considered here only insofar as it bears on one facet of the issue — namely, the relationship between social class and mental disorders.[1] Discussion of this issue will begin by surveying some of the major studies that have helped to establish that such a connection is real. I will then identify and comment upon various interpretations that have

been offered to explain the nature of the relationship between social class and mental disorder. The chapter will conclude with an examination of how social class affects the type and quality of treatment received by the mentally ill.

EMPIRICAL RESEARCH ON CLASS AND MENTAL DISORDER

One of the first systematic studies in the social epidemiology of mental disorder was conducted by Faris and Dunham (1939) in Chicago during the 1930s. They combed the admission records of both public and private mental hospitals to identify approximately 35 000 persons who had received psychiatric care over a twelve-year period. They then plotted the addresses of these individuals on large census maps of the city. What this procedure revealed, among other things, was that the highest rates of schizophrenia were found in inner city districts where persons of low status were concentrated. The more affluent areas of the city, on the other hand, tended to be the districts where the least number of mental patients and ex-patients resided. While Faris and Dunham's conclusion that poverty led to a higher incidence of mental disorder was challenged on a number of methodological and theoretical points, their study did lend credibility to the notion that people's position in the class structure had implications for their mental health.

The most famous study to pursue this implication was carried out by Hollingshead and Redlich (1958) in New Haven, Connecticut in the early 1950s. These authors were concerned that previous research, such as Faris and Dunham's, may have underestimated the extent of mental disorders in the middle and upper classes, because it was based solely on hospital admissions. Hollingshead and Redlich sought to remedy this deficiency by undertaking an ambitious case-finding procedure. A thorough examination of the records of hospitals, clinics, and psychiatrists in private practice enabled them to identify a total "psychiatric population" of almost 2000 New Haven residents. For purposes of comparison, the authors also gathered information on a large random sample of the general population of New Haven. To determine a person's social standing, Hollingshead and Redlich devised a composite index that encompassed occupation, education, and location of residence. Utilizing this index, they divided the community into five social classes. Next they compared the social class distribution of the general (non-patient) population with that of the psychiatric patients. The logic of this research design was that if there were no relationship between social class and the incidence of mental disorders, then each of the five classes should be present in the psychiatric population in roughly the same percentage as it was in the general population. Hollingshead and Redlich's data clearly indicated that this was not the case. Instead, the social class breakdown of the two populations showed that the highest class in New Haven was significantly underrepresented, the three middle or in-between classes were moderately underrepresented, and the lowest class was substantially overrepresented. For example, although the lowest social class, according to Hollingshead and Redlich's index, included just under 18 percent of New Haven's citizens, it contributed nearly 37 percent of the psychiatric patients. What is more, this strong association between social class and being a mental patient still existed after the authors controlled for the effects of sex, age, race, and marital status. Their findings also revealed an interesting pattern with respect to class and the type of mental disorder. What they discovered was that members of the lower classes were more likely to be diagnosed as suffering from relatively severe disorders (psychoses), whereas members of the higher classes were more frequently diagnosed as having milder disorders (neuroses).

As its authors were well aware, a major limitation of Hollingshead and Redlich's study was that their data pertained only to the relationship between social class and the prevalence of *treated* mental disorders. They realized, however, that there are very good grounds for assuming that those who receive psychiatric or other treatment for their problems by no means constitute all of the mentally disordered persons in society. For this reason it is not possible to speak of the "true" or "total" prevalence of mental disorders unless one has taken measures to locate such untreated cases. In the absence of such measures, studies such as Hollingshead and Redlich's do not necessarily indicate that persons of the lower class are more apt to be psychologically disturbed. It might only mean that they are more likely than their higher-class counterparts to visit a psychiatrist or to end up in a mental institution. What is needed to determine the relation between class and the actual prevalence of mental disorders in society is a procedure for assessing mental health in the general population, quite independent of whether those judged to be disordered are receiving treatment of any kind. Despite this shortcoming of their study, Hollingshead and Redlich can be credited with marshalling impressive evidence to suggest that there is an inverse relation between social class and rates of treated mental disorders. They also laid the groundwork for subsequent studies that were designed to approximate the distribution of untreated disorders in the population.

A study conducted by Leo Srole (1962) and a number of his associates in the 1950s attempted to ascertain the true prevalence of mental disorder among a large cross-section of persons who lived in the midtown Manhattan area of New York City. Over 1600 adults in a sample of randomly selected households were interviewed. Information was collected on their personal background, past history of psychological distress and psychotherapy, and responses to an index of psychiatric symptoms that was constructed for the study. The interviewers also rated the respondents' tension level both at the beginning and at the conclusion of the interview. All of these data were then turned over to a team of psychiatrists, which was asked to evaluate the respondents' mental health in terms of four categories, ranging from "well" to "impaired."

Perhaps the most remarkable finding of this study was that less than 20 percent of those interviewed were assessed as well or relatively free from noticeable psychiatric symptoms. This rather amazing fact aside, the research once again showed that class (or what the authors called "socio-economic status") exhibited a substantial and consistent relation to rated psychiatric condition. To illustrate, Srole and his colleagues found that their lowest socio-economic group had almost twice the percentage of respondents considered "psychiatrically impaired" as did the highest socio-economic group. Moreover, the latter had approximately three times the proportion of people diagnosed as "well" compared to the low-status group.[2]

Another major epidemiological survey of mental disorder was the so-called Stirling County survey carried out by Leighton et al. (1963) in a rural and small-town area of Nova Scotia during the late 1950s.[3] One aspect of the study involved examining the records of local hospitals and physicians. Information obtained in this manner permitted the investigators to determine the prevalence of treated cases and to select a sample of previously hospitalized mental patients for interviewing. But, like the researchers of the Midtown Manhattan study, Leighton et al. were interested in the prevalence of untreated disorders. They accordingly developed a questionnaire and inventory of psychiatric symptoms that was administered to a random sample of over 1300 Stirling County residents. The data collected from these interviews were then evaluated by at least two psychiatrists to assess the likelihood of respondents being considered mentally ill if they had been diagnosed by a psychiatrist applying the prevailing standards of the profession. The results of this study again suggested that the incidence of untreated cases in the population at large is extremely high. While it was not the focus of their research, Leighton et al. did include a measure of socio-economic status and, not surprisingly, they found that mental disorder was most common among members of the lowest socio-economic category.

These studies are commonly acknowledged to be the classical research ventures in this area of inquiry. Subsequent research has generally confirmed the patterns reported above. Myers and Bean (1968), for example, did a follow-up study of New Haven ten years after Hollingshead and Redlich's that corroborated the main findings of the original study. In 1974 Dohrenwend and Dohrenwend exhaustively analyzed the findings of all published studies on the true prevalence of psychopathology by social class. While acknowledging the difficulty of comparing results of studies based on what are often very discrepant methodologies, they nevertheless assert that the most consistent finding has been that lower socio-economic status is related to differential rates of mental disorder. The Dohrenwends report that of 33 communities studied by various researchers, 28 yielded the highest rates of psychological disturbance in the lowest class. This general pattern also squares with the results of a variety of social surveys carried out in recent decades that indicate persons in the lower classes are, on average, more unhappy, more worried, and less hopeful about the future than are persons in the middle and upper classes.[4]

To summarize, the proposition that a relationship exists between social class and mental disorder can be regarded as fairly well established. However, the coarse generalization that social class and mental illness are inversely related cannot be accepted without a couple of important reservations or provisos. First of all, it seems clear that this pattern does not apply to all types of disorders. In their aforementioned review of studies in this area, the Dohrenwends found that the relationship held most strongly for personality disorders and schizophrenia. But no relationship was discovered between socio-economic status and the prevalence of affective psychoses (i.e., severe mania and/or depression). They also noted that the situation with respect to the class distribution of less severe disorders, the neuroses, is inconclusive. Slightly more than half of the studies examined showed an inverse relationship between class and the prevalence of neuroses, but a sizeable minority revealed either a positive or no relationship. In other words, some mental disorders and even certain types of disorders appear to be exceptions to the generalization. Secondly, although it is true that most studies have reported the prevalence of serious psychological impairment to be greatest in the lowest socio-economic category, there is at best only a very moderate inverse association among the remaining strata designated in these studies. Again, major differences in both the conceptual frameworks and methodologies employed by the various researchers make the drawing of such conclusions questionable, but it appears that there is insufficient evidence to warrant inferences of the sort that rates of mental disorder are "higher in the middle class than the upper class" or are "lower in the 'upper middle' than the 'lower middle' class." To the extent that the purported inverse relationship between social class and mental disorders implies such notions, the generalization is misleading on a second count.

These cautions and qualifications notwithstanding, I would not quarrel with Grusky and Pollner's (1981:92) observation that "the relation between social class and mental disorder is virtually incontestable." To this point, however, I have only attempted to summarize the body of empirical research that allows one to make this claim. But these research findings still need to be interpreted; the facts do not "speak for themselves" in this regard. So the next task is to look at how these researchers and other social scientists have sought to *explain* the relationship between class and mental disorder.

THEORETICAL INTERPRETATIONS

Several interpretations have been formulated to explain the relationship between social class and mental disorder. As a sociologist, I am inclined to favour interpretations that emphasize the impact of the social environment on people's mental health. Theories along these lines are known as "social causation" explanations. Most of the discussion that follows will be devoted to outlining the rationales of the leading sociological perspectives that fall under this general heading. However, before turning to these social causation explanations, I will briefly mention two other interpretations that seek to explain the class-mental disorder relationship without reference to social or environmental effects.

Genetics

There is, first of all, the genetic explanation which argues that mental disorders are transmitted through heredity. Studies of monozygotic twins and adopted children have established that genetic transmission plays some part in people's susceptibility to schizophrenia and other psychiatric disorders. It is also apparent from these studies that genetic factors alone cannot provide a sufficient explanation of schizophrenia or account for why it is so prevalent in the lower class.

Social scientists have been critical of both the biological determinism and the ideological conservatism implicit in this viewpoint. However, it should be noted that this explanation does not necessarily imply that persons of the lower class are genetically inferior. Rather, one can postulate that if vulnerability to mental disorder is inherited, then there must have been high rates of such disorders among the parents and grandparents of those afflicted. And because disorders such as schizophrenia are usually debilitating, downward social mobility in earlier generations would almost certainly have occurred and thus, eventually resulted in a concentration of genetically susceptible people in the lower class. The rationale of this extrapolation for the genetic hypothesis is in fact very similar to the next interpretation I will consider, the "social selection" hypothesis.

Social Selection

This explanation accepts that there is a definite relationship between social class and mental disorders, but maintains that this is because low class standing is a *consequençe* rather than a cause of poor mental health. One variant of this explanation, dubbed the "downward drift" hypothesis, posits that psychologically disturbed persons typically experience a reduction of their ability to function successfully in their occupations, and therefore gradually drift down the social ladder and into the lower class.

The other version of this school of thought posits that poor mental health works not so much to cause downward mobility as to limit or retard upward mobility. According to this way of thinking, the prevalence of mental disorders in the lower class is largely due to the fact that its mentally healthy members are more likely to achieve upward mobility, thus leaving behind a cohort of persons whose aggregate level of mental health has been diminished by the departure of such individuals.

There are empirical studies that have been made which lend some support to both versions of the social selection hypothesis.[5] That is, it seems true that psychological impairment both restricts some persons from moving up the class hierarchy, and is a contributing factor in the case of some who "skid" downward. Having conceded this point, however, I would hasten to add that social selection, either by itself or in conjunction with the genetic explanation, is not adequate to fully explain the higher incidence of mental disorder in the lower social classes. Furthermore, I concur with Cockerham (1981:187) who states:

> When the question is whether social class position helps to promote mental disorder (social causation) or whether mental disorder causes social class position (social selection), most likely the former . . . is correct. That is, social class position contributes to the onset of mental disorder to a more significant degree than does the mental disorder causing social class position.

It now remains to explore the social causation explanation. This interpretation appears in a number of guises. All of them are in agreement that the preponderance of mental disorder in the lower class is mainly attributable to social factors, but they differ in their assessment of which features of the environment are most salient. In this connection, one can single out the following perspectives: societal reaction, social stress, and differential coping resources. Each of these will be discussed in turn.

Societal Reaction

The first perspective to be considered takes a radically different point of departure when analyzing what is ordinarily called "mental illness." Proponents of the societal reaction model (also known as "labelling theory") fundamentally challenge the medical conception of mental disorder that informs modern psychiatry as well as public attitudes on the subject. The view that most people in our society have come to accept is the one put forth by the medical profession, which essentially contends that mental disorders are illnesses much like cancer, tuberculosis, or influenza. According to the medical model, mental "illness" is either likened or attributed to a disease entity lodged in the individual's mind and/or body, that manifests itself in observable symptoms. Labelling theorists tend to be extremely skeptical about this whole formulation. Echoing the maverick psychiatrist Thomas Szasz (1961) — who went so far as to claim that mental illness is a myth — they view the latter as a label applied to certain people who either violate society's rules or express unacceptable ideas in an unusual idiom. In short, mental disorders are understood as deviant behaviour.

A distinctive aspect of this perspective is that it does not centre its attention on trying to explain what makes the deviant "tick." Its focus is rather on the social context within which such transgressions occur. This alternative vantage point is largely premised on the observation that deviance is a status conferred upon a person by other members of society. Labelling theorists think it telling that many acts of rule-breaking do not result in the rule-breaker being branded as deviant. Such conduct frequently goes unrecognized, or is rationalized away, by members of the community. (For example, middle-class male vandalism may be dismissed as nothing more than "boys will be boys.") On the other hand, if and when labelling takes place, the "deviant" is expected to conform to the prescriptions of the role in which he/she has been cast. Once a person has been labelled as "crazy," for instance, others will expect that person to behave abnormally and may give him/her little chance to act like a "sane" person. As Scheff (1984) has argued, where bizarre behaviour is defined and reacted to as signs of mental illness, a self-fulfilling process is initiated that can culminate with the labelled individual capitulating to social pressures and rewards, and accepting the proffered role of a mentally ill person.

The nature of society's reaction is thus seen as the crucial factor influencing what comes of misbehaviour. If the community response is to ignore or downplay such conduct, labelling theorists would predict that it will be of transitory significance because it is not likely to make a lasting impact on the rule-breaker's self-identity or social status. If, however, displays of such behaviour are acknowledged and responded to by significant others in the community, the individual may be launched on a "career" of ever more extensive and identity-altering deviant acts.

This critical stance causes labelling theorists to take quite a different view on the question of why rates of mental disorder are usually highest in the lower class. To begin with, they allege that such data are not what they pretend to be — that is, objective measures of mental disturbance. In their judgement, these data merely reflect the number of persons who have been classified as mentally ill by the arbitrary standards of the psychiatric profession. On this score, societal reaction theorists are fond of citing research which demonstrates that psychiatric diagnosis is notoriously unreliable. They note that psychiatrists routinely infer the presence of "illness" in their patients from unconventional behaviour and/or beliefs. Their ostensibly objective inference that particular actions or ideas are "symptoms" of an underlying pathology is said to actually entail a subjective judgement that is bound to be coloured by the psychiatrist's own

political and moral standards. To be sure, these ideas may be shared by other members of his/her profession, and beyond; however, labelling theorists will correctly reply that bias can be collective as well as individual.

Defenders of the societal reaction model emphasize that psychiatrists occupy positions of power and privilege in contemporary society. Like other dominant groups, psychiatrists are said to be favourably situated to create and impose their own particular interests, values, and views of the world on other, less privileged members of society. That such efforts are not always successful is said to be attested to by the fact that psychiatry's criteria for evaluating what is "healthy" or "normal" in human beings have come under attack in recent decades as harbouring biases of various types. Blacks and women, for example, have charged that psychiatry's prototype of health belies the fact that its practitioners are overwhelmingly white and male.[6] Following this same logic, it has been argued that the apparent concentration of mental illness in the lower class is at least partly an artifact of a middle-class bias that pervades psychiatric thought and diagnosis. This argument rests upon the truth that a number of attitudes, values, and skills relevant to psychological assessment vary considerably by social class. For example, introspection, emotional control, and intellectual autonomy all tend to be more valued in the middle and upper classes than in the lower class. Given the highly subjective nature of psychiatric diagnosis, these class differences in cognitive abilities and value orientations may have the effect of predisposing psychiatrists to evaluate the mental health of lower-class patients unfavourably. The intrusion of such class prejudice could mean that part of what are seen as psychiatric symptoms in lower-class people are simply their distinctive social class characteristics.

The societal reaction approach by no means regards the sort of class bias just described as confined to the formal procedure of psychiatric diagnosis. Inasmuch as middle-class norms and values tend to to prevail in most spheres of everyday life (e.g., schools, the mass media), lower-class people who act in an odd or obnoxious manner run a greater risk of being labelled "crazy" than do their higher-class counterparts. In other words, if the labelling theorists are right, the middle-class bias of psychiatry only reinforces the prejudices in the society at large, which brings greater numbers of lower-class people to its attention in the first place.

Another relevant feature of this explanation concerns the differential ability of persons by class to resist the labelling process, in the psychiatric setting as well as in society generally. Labelling theorists maintain that even though the severity of their psychological distress may be equivalent, higher-class persons ordinarily enjoy numerous advantages (e.g., access to expert legal counsel) over lower-class persons of having their "symptomatic" behaviour disregarded or minimized by the community, thereby reducing the possibility of their becoming officially designated as psychiatric cases. All of these considerations have led critics of the medical model to assert that the mentally disordered suffer not so much from internal predispositions to "illness" as from external "contingencies" that render them vulnerable to being defined by society as mentally ill.

Social Stress

A second type of social causation explanation is the social stress hypothesis. In contradistinction to the societal reaction hypothesis, this interpretation does not dispute the claim that mental disorder is most prevalent in the lower class. It accepts this as fact and seeks to account for it by suggesting that members of the lower class are subjected to greater stress by virtue of living in deprived social conditions.

The supposition that something about the lower-class environment is stressful appears to be well-founded. However, there is no consensus when it comes to specifying exactly what features of the lower-class life situation produce stress. Overcrowded housing, broken homes, and social isolation are but some of the items mentioned in this connection. The most commonly

cited factor, however, is the economic insecurity of lower-class life. Unemployment and/or the threat of job layoffs are most acutely felt by persons in lower social class positions. Apart from the ample social scientific research attesting to the negative consequences of being without work, it is surely no secret that unemployment tends to erode family relationships and create feelings of despair and worthlessness. Little wonder, then, that fluctuations in the level of unemployment have been shown to be the single most important source of changing admission rates to mental hospitals.[7]

For those in the lower class who manage to find employment, the jobs available frequently have several features believed to be associated with stress. In addition to being low-paid, a majority of lower-class workers hold jobs that are thought to require little skill, are repetitive and monotonous, involve being controlled by others, and are easy to get locked into for life. Moreover, many of these jobs take place in work settings where there are serious problems of comfort, health, and safety.[8] Such working conditions, it is hypothesized, are likely to be hazardous to people's emotional well-being, to say nothing of their physical health.

Other commentators have pointed out that the hazards of belonging to the lower class are not restricted to the material hardships dictated by economic status. A proper assessment of the stresses facing lower-class persons also needs to take into account the whole climate of degradation that envelops low status in a class-stratified society. This is to say that, over and above the disadvantages deriving from lack of money or power, lower-class people must endure repeated affronts to their dignity and selfhood. Where class inequality prevails, people's worth tends to be measured by their financial and occupational success. Honour and esteem are accorded to those who achieve such success; disrepute befalls those who do not. That these judgements are often shared by lower-class persons themselves has been documented by Sennett and Cobb in a study aptly titled *The Hidden Injuries of Class*. Through intensive interviews with a number of blue-collar workers in the Boston area, the authors uncovered a tragic sense of failure and self-devaluation in these people. The depth of these feelings was perhaps most poignantly conveyed by their proclaimed efforts to ensure that their children should not follow in the parents' footsteps. Working-class people, Sennett and Cobb (1972) observe, ask their children to take their parents' lives as a warning rather than as a model.

The stress of such emotional wounds is probably compounded by the tendency, common among lower-class persons, to blame themselves for their subordinate position in society. That is, when asked about the reasons for their low status, they frequently mention their perceived laziness, stupidity, or some other nameless personal deficiency as key determinants.[9] This definition of their predicament means that the anger or sense of injustice that lower-class people commonly feel about their lowly position in society is more likely to be turned inward rather than directed against the social sources of their misery. Sennett and Cobb detected something of this nature in the Boston workers they interviewed. As they put it, "they are both angry and ambivalent about their right to be angry" (Sennett and Cobb, 1972:79). It almost goes without saying that such ambivalence and suppressed rage is frequently the stuff of emotional disturbance.

Coping Resources

It is arguable whether the proclivity of lower-class persons to blame themselves for their disadvantaged situation directly adds to the stresses they already encounter. What seems more certain is that self-blame detracts from their ability to cope effectively with the myriad pressures surrounding life at the bottom of the class hierarchy. This may, in fact, generally be why stress manages to adversely affect the mental health of the lower classes. Langner and Michael (1963), two of Srole's colleagues in the previously discussed Midtown Manhattan study, had found that membership in the lower class did involve being subjected to more measurable

life stress than did membership in the higher classes. However, they further disclosed that at any given level of stress, persons in the lowest socio-economic category were more likely to become mentally disturbed than persons of middle- or upper-class standing. Indeed, Langner and Michael found that the more sources of stress, the greater was the class difference in the proportion of people who manifested psychiatric symptoms. What these findings seemed to be suggesting was that stress affects the mental stability of the underprivileged more severely than it does that of the relatively privileged. This finding has recently been confirmed by Kessler (1979) and other investigators. Realization of this point has, in turn, prompted a shift in thinking among some advocates of the social stress hypothesis. Proponents of this interpretation are now less inclined to subscribe to the notion that the relationship of class to mental disorder is primarily attributable to the sheer amount of stress people endure by virtue of their socio-economic position. The strong suspicion was that there are important class differences in how effectively people deal with stress.

This modified interpretation suggests that irrespective of whether lower-class members are confronted with greater stress as a result of living in deprived social circumstances, they are at a disadvantage in their ability to cope with it. The disadvantage is said to derive from the fewer and poorer coping resources at their disposal. Lower-class people are in a weak position in this respect because the stress-producing circumstances they face are usually less alterable by individual action than are those confronting middle-class persons. It will be recalled that much of the stress in the lower-class environment probably stems from remote, impersonal economic forces over which most members of society, but especially those in the lower class, have precious little control. Similarly, lower-class persons, almost by definition, have little money or power to either escape or mitigate stressful experiences. Recent research by Liem and Liem (1978) has also shown that lower-class people are more prone to find environmental stress psychologically distressing, because their interpersonal relationships and weak ties to the community typically afford less social support to buffer the stress than is enjoyed by the those in the higher classes. All in all, then, the lower class appears to suffer from a poverty of external coping resources, which serves to exacerbate an already stressful situation.

Sociologist Melvin Kohn (1977) has pursued a rather novel tack in analyzing this issue. Kohn persuasively argues that certain features of lower-class life and socialization patterns impair its members' *internal* resources for dealing effectively with stress. Without discounting the liabilities engendered by their lack of external resources, Kohn postulates that the constricted conditions of life experienced by people in the lower class fosters conceptions of social reality which diminish their ability to deal effectively with stress. Kohn's own research demonstrated that there are important social class differences in how children are taught to perceive, assess, and deal with reality. Unlike middle-class parents who encourage their children to act according to their own judgement and moral standards, lower-class parents are less concerned with self-direction and place a much greater emphasis on obedience to external authority. Kohn submits that this fundamental class difference in value orientations — the premium on self-direction at higher-class levels and on conformity at lower-class levels — is not accidental but reflects significant divergences in life circumstances. He is worth quoting at length on this point.

> The essence of higher class position is the expectation that one's decisions and actions can be consequential; the essence of lower class position is the belief that one is at the mercy of forces and people beyond one's control, often, beyond one's understanding. Self-direction — acting on the basis of one's own judgment, attending to internal dynamics as well as to external consequences, being open-minded, being trustful of others, holding personally responsible moral standards — this is possible only if the actual conditions of life allow some freedom of action, some reason to feel in control of fate. Conformity — following the

dictates of authority, focusing on external consequences to the exclusion of internal processes, being intolerant of non-conformity and dissent, being distrustful of others, having moral standards that strongly emphasize obedience to the letter of the law — this is the inevitable result of conditions of life that allow little freedom of action, little reason to feel in control of fate (1977:189).

Kohn does not deny that the conformist value system may in some ways be adaptive for coping with the standard exigencies of lower-class existence. However, rigid adherence to norms or authority can also prove to be disastrous to people when they are confronted with new situations and new problems that require an innovative response. In sum, the conformist value system may be too simplistic to provide people with a sufficient sense of life's complexities, and too inflexible to provide them with the cognitive tools they need to meet the dilemmas and crisis situations that invariably arise in a rapidly changing world. For Kohn, then, insofar as lower-class people subscribe to such an orientation, they may be ill-prepared to adequately cope with the stresses they encounter.

A Note on Theoretical Divergence in Sociology

This completes my survey of the theoretical interpretations that have been advanced to explain why rates of mental disorder are related to social class. Representatives of the contending schools of thought often engage one another in scholarly debate over how adequately the various interpretations are able to account for the presumed facts pertaining to this issue. Such controversy is commonplace in modern social science. Because the competing theoretical perspectives are often tied, wittingly or unwittingly, to different ideological positions and/or social policy implications, the tenor of these debates may give outsiders the impression that the validity of the rival interpretations is mutually exclusive. I think it is accurate to say that the literature on the relationship of class to mental disorder could easily lead one to assume that it is not possible to accept certain interpretations unless one rejects others. I hope that my review of these different theories has discouraged readers from adopting such an assumption. In my opinion, all of the hypotheses discussed contain elements of truth that can contribute to a comprehensive understanding of why mental disorder is more common at the lower end of the social scale. The fact that lower-class persons are more apt to suffer from psychological distress than middle- or upper-class persons may very well be the result of a combination of interacting factors that includes genetic susceptibility, social selection, differential labelling, environmental stress, and inadequate coping resources — and perhaps still others that have thus far eluded our attention. This posture is not meant to deny that some of the foregoing factors will prove to have greater explanatory power than others. By the same token, some of the interpretations I have reviewed will probably prove more influential than others in shaping society's mental health policies. But, given the present state of our knowledge about this complex problem, future theorizing, research, and policy debates will likely stand to benefit from an appreciation of all the perspectives outlined in this chapter. One such policy issue concerns the type of psychiatric treatment people receive when they become mentally disordered. The way in which social class standing affects such treatment will now be explored.

DIFFERENCES IN PSYCHIATRIC TREATMENT BY SOCIAL CLASS

It has long been observed that class differences in the prevalence of mental disorders are compounded by what is tantamount to a two-tiered system of mental health care. That is, the poor are said to be disadvantaged relative to the rich not only because they are more likely to experience some form of debilitating psychological distress, but also because they tend to receive less adequate treatment for their disorders.

This double standard in the distribution of mental health services was most conspicuous in the early decades of this century. Kupers has noted that two quite distinct psychiatries coexisted at that time.

> One was practiced in asylums, the other in consulting rooms. In the asylum inmates were chained to the wall, forced into icy baths, and severely reprimanded for every bizarre act. In the consulting room the analysand was listened to with compassion and taught how to understand anxieties and dreams and how to use that understanding to create a richer life (1981:13).

The clientele of these two psychiatries was clearly differentiated along social class lines. Psychoanalytic therapy "was practised in the consulting room among the affluent, and services for the poor consisted only of asylum practice" (Kupers, 1981:20).

By mid-century, the old-style asylums had given way to the public mental hospitals and veterans' hospitals. In the transition, the line distinguishing the two types of psychiatric treatment became less distinct. However, the persistence of a double standard was attested to by Hollingshead and Redlich's previously discussed study of New Haven. Their research documented that higher-class patients tended to receive individually oriented therapy involving verbal interaction between the patient and the psychiatrist, whereas lower-class patients were far more likely to receive organic therapies (e.g., drugs, electroshock, psychosurgery) or "custodial" care. As Gallagher rightly remarks, the latter category is really a euphemism or "polite term for no treatment at all" (1980:268). An especially telling statistic emerging out of Hollingshead and Redlich's research was that more than 600 persons in their psychiatric population of 1900 plus were judged to have received custodial care only; over 90 percent of these patients were from the two lowest social strata in the study's five-class scheme. Thus, Hollingshead and Redlich concluded with good reason that social class position strongly affects the type of treatment rendered to persons in need of psychiatric help.

This particular finding of the New Haven

study provoked considerable controversy. Some critics seized upon it as ammunition to indict the whole mental health-care system for providing quality therapy to higher-class patients while relegating lower-class patients to custodial care or less effective therapeutic programmes. Defenders of the system argued that the prevailing therapy of choice, psychoanalysis, did not lend itself to treating the sort of severe disorders or psychoses most often found in the lower classes. Others went a step further and claimed that lower-class persons were generally not suitable candidates for social psychological or "talking" therapies aimed at equipping patients with insight into their emotional problems. According to this argument, lower-class people lacked the motivation, verbal skills, and/or self-awareness to benefit from the sort of therapeutic techniques that had proven successful with their more affluent, better educated clients. The critics regarded this defence as itself a sign of the middle-class bias permeating psychiatric thought and practice.

In retrospect, it appears that this issue temporarily subsided because it had arisen at a time when psychiatric treatment and mental health policies were beginning to undergo some rather substantial changes. In the middle 1950s, chlorpromazine and other psychotropic medications were developed. The administration of these drugs enabled many mental patients, including some of the more severely disturbed, to function better without impairing their consciousness. The popularity of these drugs spread rapidly. One of the most significant consequences of their wholesale adoption by psychiatry was that large numbers of patients were helped enough to be discharged from mental hospitals. The diffusion of drug treatments and the declining mental hospital population also gave hope to many psychiatrists and other mental-health professionals who saw in these developments new opportunities to both treat and prevent mental illness. Their belief was that the potential for reducing the severity and duration of mental disorders, if not their cure, was contingent upon returning patients to the community, where family and friends could help create conditions that would permit ex-patients to work and to live more or less normal lives. Institutional mental health care was also increasingly coming under attack as being hopelessly custodial. Such misgivings with the large, overcrowded state/provincial mental hospitals were related — probably not coincidentally — to the recognition that these institutions required enormous and ever increasing outlays of tax revenue for their maintenance alone.[10] By the early 1960s the confluence of all these factors had set the stage for a major shift in social policy: the establishment of community mental health centres. In the decade between 1965 and 1974, a multitude of public clinics and outpatient mental health facilities were set up in communities across North America.[11]

The community mental health movement was partly inspired by a wish that such centres would engender a more democratic dispensation of therapy. The vision was that as the archaic mental hospitals were phased out, sufficient resources would then be available to provide low-income clients with quality mental health care. With the advantage of hindsight, it is today fairly safe to say that the egalitarian ideals of this movement have, by and large, not been translated into reality. To be sure, "deinstitutionalization" has meant the return of many mental patients to the community. Nevertheless, the double standard of mental health care is by no means a thing of the past. By all accounts, the chronically disordered patients who remain warehoused in mental hospitals are still drawn disproportionately from the lowest social strata. Moreover, it is questionable whether life for many of the former mental patients who now reside in the community has been positively affected by this policy. Kupers assesses the situation as follows:

> The treatment they receive at public clinics rarely includes much in-depth psychotherapy, and usually involves the administration of large doses of psychotropic medications plus training in skills of daily living and appropriate behavior. In other words, the goals of treatment are more like the old asylum psychiatry, with its

stress on external constraint and moral training, than they are like the self-discovery and self-expansion of consulting room therapy. The locked doors and straitjackets of the asylum have merely been replaced by the medications prescribed in public clinics. Thus the mental patients have been ghettoized in the community, and many people are wondering whether their plight there is any better than it was in the asylums (1981:22–23).

The trends described by Kupers have been accelerated in recent years by often severe budgetary cutbacks that have been imposed on public clinics and outpatient facilities. Despite such diminished resources, therapists working in such settings are obliged to treat anyone in their geographic or catchment area who cannot afford private therapy. Many of these persons have little or no desire to undergo therapy, but have been pressed into seeking help by parents, schools, the courts, or other authorities. Under these circumstances, staff are only able to see most clients briefly and they manage to cope with the situation by resorting to the prescription of drugs, which many concede serve more as social control mechanisms than as effective psychotherapy.

Psychiatrists and non-medical therapists working in the private sector operate under conditions that are vastly more conducive to the practice of quality psychotherapy. For one thing, therapists in private practice are normally in a position to select their clients from a pool of persons who have voluntarily sought out their services. And, as Szasz (1970) has argued so vociferously, a precondition for avoiding the social control functions of traditional psychiatry is that both parties, client and therapist, freely enter into the therapeutic relationship. In-depth psychotherapy, in which the therapist does not simply dispense advice to clients about how to live their lives, but attempts to help each of them find his or her own path virtually always requires a great deal of time. As long as the client can afford to pay, there is a greater likelihood in private therapy that the time needed to sort out emotional conflicts and to arrive at such self-discovery can be arranged.

On the other hand, this is not to suggest that quality therapy is easily procured. One result of the over-success of the pharmacological revolution referred to earlier has been the rise of a new generation of psychiatrists who have largely given up the psychotherapeutic orientation of their professional predecessors. The once-dominant psychoanalytic view of mental disorders as intrapsychic conflicts rooted in childhood experiences is probably now subscribed to by only a relatively small fraction of North American psychiatrists. In its place, the new psychiatry favours a physiological model of madness and tends to embrace drug treatment as the most promising therapeutic strategy. Of course one can still find psychiatrists who remain committed to psychosocial conceptions of mental disorders and to non-organic therapies. There are also a large number of psychiatrists in private practice who advocate the use of tranquillizers and antidepressant medications as an adjunct to other therapies aimed at self-exploration and self-clarification. This combined approach — which, incidentally, appears to be highly effective — is quite different from the situation in public clinics and hospitals, where the use of drugs is essentially an *alternative* to in-depth therapy.

In sum, to the extent that higher- and lower-class patients are generally treated by psychiatrists working in the private and public sectors respectively, the description of the mental health-care system as "two-tiered" would seem to be justified. Indeed, this charge of a double standard in treatment is even more warranted when one considers the various and sundry non-medical psychotherapies (e.g., Gestalt therapy, psychodrama, primal therapy, etc.) which have gained a following in recent decades. For both economic and cultural reasons these alternative therapies cater almost exclusively to a middle-class clientele.

At this point, it is perhaps worth speculating about what accounts for these class differences in psychiatric treatment. Radicals tend to explain the inequitable distribution of mental health care as a predictable by-product of the dominant socio-economic structure of society. In this view a class-stratified society ensures that important life chances, including the opportunity to receive quality psychotherapy, are bound to be unequally allocated. The double standard is thus understood as an instance of class discrimination against society's underprivileged members. For these critics, the villains in the story are the psychiatrists and other mental health professionals in positions of authority, whose class bias allegedly disposes them to pursue mental health policies that perpetuate inequalities in treatment.

I confess to having some sympathy with elements of the radical critique. More specifically, as long as the economic conditions of life are class-divided, I would contend that it is naïvely unsociological to believe that these divisions will not somehow be reflected in most areas of social life. But having conceded this, I cannot accept the implication of some radicals that the differential psychiatric treatment by social class is a matter of design or deliberate policy. Building on some of the research I have reviewed in this chapter, I would instead offer a more benign interpretation. In this connection I see the double standard as partly attributable to, and reinforced by, a curious affinity that exists between certain aspects of the different world views held by middle-class mental health professionals and their lower-class patients.

On the psychiatrists' side, their characteristic values and view of the world inclines them to truly believe that lower-class people are generally unable or unwilling to take advantage of quality, insight-oriented therapy. And while I would agree that such a presumption is based upon class prejudice, it must be appreciated that if this is how they define the situation, then their practice of treating low-income clients with drugs or some other somatic methods actually makes sense. Strangely enough, the values or world view of their lower-class patients frequently mesh with this definition of the situation. For example, there is plenty of research indicating that lower-class persons tend to view their mental or emotional problems in physical terms. (Attributing psychological distress to one's "nerves" is perhaps the most common expression of this conception.) Richard Lichtman has nicely summarized some significant social class differences in how such matters are typically perceived. In his words,

> the poor are not simply less wealthy than the rich. Their world is qualitatively different. They do not even regard their bodies as the more prosperous do; their bodies are alien, incomprehensible, dangerous, unworthy of care, naturally given to misuse and decay, and a comforting explanation for their social inadequacy. They are far more likely to accept the impairment of their bodily and mental functioning as a "normal" fact of the world, to be borne like other natural hazards of existence, and manipulated for whatever comfort it may offer (1968:47).

This way of thinking may well be generated by ignorance, indoctrination, and/or alienating life circumstances. But again, insofar as such notions are defined as valid, lower-class patients adhering to them are likely to welcome organic treatments as appropriate, and to regard insight-oriented therapies as irrelevant to what they believe ails them.[12]

CONCLUSION

I will conclude by briefly considering the social policy implications of the interpretation just presented. To reiterate, I acknowledge the radicals' polemical point that the double standard in mental health care cannot ultimately be eliminated in the absence of society-wide transformation and "destratification." However, this certainly does not mean that anything short of a full-fledged social revolution will be of no avail in addressing this or related problems. If the argument put forth above is correct, a number of possible reforms might be pursued to ameliorate the situation. To begin with, medical schools could be enjoined to insist that students electing to specialize in psychiatry do substantial coursework in the humanities and social sciences. It is at least arguable that the commonly narrow, exclusively scientific education and training presently received by most psychiatrists fosters obliviousness to the psychosocial factors impinging on mental health and psychiatric care. Secondly, if mental hospitals and public clinics caring for the poor are to do more than medicate and otherwise control their large numbers of clients, massive budgetary increases will obviously be needed. Kupers reports that many mental-health professionals employed in the public sector are initially motivated to provide meaningful psychotherapy to their lower-class patients, but along with the aforementioned inadequacies in their medical training, the obstacles presented daily by swelling caseloads and diminishing financial resources eventually produce staff "burnout" or demoralization. Finally, I would recommend that governments could reduce the double standard by making information and subsidies available to low-income persons who might benefit from any reputable non-medical therapies that are locally available.

Such reforms are by no means a panacea for remedying the deficiencies inherent in the two-tiered system. But, if there are any lessons to be learned from the tragic experience of the community mental health movement, one of them may be the realization that there are no quick, inexpensive, or strictly medical solutions for overcoming the inequitable distribution of mental health-care services.

NOTES

1. I will generally employ the term mental "disorders" rather than mental "illness" throughout this chapter because the former concept is non-committal on the controversial issue of whether a medical conception of psychological disturbance is appropriate or not.

2. Srole et al. (1962) also found that persons who had been downwardly mobile were much more likely to be rated as psychiatrically impaired than were those who had moved up in the stratification system.

3. "Stirling County" was a pseudonym adopted by the authors of this study to conceal the identity of the area in Nova Scotia they investigated.

4. For example, see Bradburn and Caplovitz (1965).

5. See, in particular, the study by Harkey, Miles, and Rushing (1976).

6. See Grier and Cobbs (1968) and Greenspan (1983) for critiques of traditional psychiatry from a black and feminist viewpoint, respectively.

7. The classic study documenting this relationship is Brenner (1973).

8. See Rinehart (1975) for a useful discussion of the blue-collar work environment and its psychological consequences.

9. The social sources and political consequences of this pattern are discussed in Della Fave (1980).

10. Scull (1977) has in fact attempted to demonstrate that the impetus for deinstitutionalization was neither the advent of psychotropic drugs nor the belief that it represented a better form of psychiatric treatment. He argues that the real force behind this policy shift was economic; governments perceived it as a way to save large sums of money.

11. American accounts of the rise of the community mental health movement commonly treat it as originating in the U.S. For the record, it should be pointed out that the province of Saskatchewan was among the earliest pioneers of this movement.

12. Kupers (1981) reports cases in his experience as a psychiatrist in public clinics where low-income clients would begrudgingly attend psychotherapy sessions only out of fear that non-attendance might result in termination of their drug prescriptions.

STUDY QUESTIONS

1. How does the relationship between social class and mental disorder correspond with what you have learned in other chapters about the unequal social distribution of physical disease? To what extent do the factors that give rise to high rates of physical illness in the lower class strike you as also responsible for the high rates of mental disorder in this class?

2. Contrast the medical and societal reaction models of mental disorder. What do you see as the main strengths and weaknesses of labelling theory's critique of the medical conception of mental illness?

3. To what extent do you think social class and other types of bias enter into psychiatric diagnosis? Do you think it is possible to devise standards of mental health that are free of such bias?

4. Summarize what Kohn sees as the major differences between middle-class and lower-class value orientations. With a friend or acquaintance whose social class origin is quite different from your own, discuss how each of you was socialized in terms of the distinction between self-direction and conformity. Do the results of this exercise support Kohn's thesis?

5. What social policy implications follow from each of the theoretical interpretations of the relationship between class and mental disorder discussed in this chapter?

6. Unlike the United States, Canada has a universal, government-sponsored health-care system that provides for both hospitalization and private psychiatric treatment. Do you think our health-insurance programmes have substantially weakened the double standard of mental health care? Why or why not?

RECOMMENDED READING

Archibald, W. Peter. *Social Psychology as Political Economy.* Toronto: McGraw-Hill Ryerson, 1978 (esp. pp. 123–185).

Dohrenwend, Bruce P., and Barbara S. Dohrenwend. *Social Status and Psychological Disorder.* New York: John Wiley and Sons, 1969.

Hollingshead, August B., and Frederick C. Redlich. *Social Class and Mental Illness.* New York: John Wiley and Sons, 1958.

Kohn, Melvin L. "Social Class and Schizophrenia: A Critical Review and a Reformulation." In *The Sociology of Mental Illness: Basic Studies,* edited by O. Grusky and M. Pollner, 127–43. New York: Holt, Rinehart and Winston, 1981.

Kupers, Terry A. *Public Therapy: The Practice of Psychotherapy in the Public Mental Health Clinic.* New York: Free Press, 1981.

Scheff, Thomas J. *Being Mentally Ill: A Sociological Theory.* 2nd ed. New York: Aldine, 1984.

Sennett, Richard, and Jonathan Cobb. *The Hidden Injuries of Class.* New York: Alfred A. Knopf, 1972.

REFERENCES

Bradburn, N., and D. Caplovitz. *Reports on Happiness.* Chicago: Aldine, 1965.

Brenner, M.H. *Mental Illness and the Economy.* Cambridge: Harvard University Press, 1973.

Cockerham, W. *Sociology of Mental Disorder.* Englewood Cliffs, N.J.: Prentice-Hall, 1981.

Della Fave, R. "The Meek Shall Not Inherit the Earth: Self-Evaluation and the Legitimacy of Stratification." *American Sociological Review* 45 (1980): 955–71.

Dohrenwend, B.P., and B.S. Dohrenwend. "Social and Cultural Influences on Psychopathology." *Annual Review of Psychology* 25 (1974): 417–52.

Faris, R., and W. Dunham. *Mental Disorders in Urban Areas.* Chicago: University of Chicago Press, 1939.

Gallagher, B., III. *The Sociology of Mental Illness.* Englewood Cliffs, N.J.: Prentice-Hall, 1980.

Greenspan, M. *A New Approach to Women and Therapy.* New York: McGraw-Hill, 1983.

Grier, W., and P. Cobbs. *Black Rage.* New York: Basic Books, 1968.

Grusky, O., and M. Pollner, eds. *The Sociology of Mental Illness: Basic Studies.* New York: Holt, Rinehart and Winston, 1981.

Harkey, J., D. Miles, and W. Rushing. "The Relation between Social Class and Functional Status: A New Look at the Drift Hypothesis." *Journal of Health and Social Behavior* 17 (1976): 194–204.

Hollingshead, A., and F. Redlich. *Social Class and Mental Illness.* New York: John Wiley and Sons, 1958.

Kessler, R. "Stress, Social Status and Psychological Distress." *Journal of Health and Social Behavior* 20 (1979): 259–72.

Kohn, M. *Class and Conformity: A Study in Values.* 2nd ed. Chicago: University of Chicago Press, 1977.

Kupers, T. *Public Therapy: The Practice of Psychotherapy in the Public Mental Health Clinic.* New York: Free Press, 1981.

Langner, T., and S. Michael. *Life Stress and Mental Health: The Midtown Manhattan Study.* London: Free Press of Glencoe, 1963.

Leighton, D.C., J. Harding, D. Macklin, A. Macmillan, and A. Leighton. *The Character of Danger: Psychiatric Symptoms in Selected Communities.* New York: Basic Books, 1963.

Lichtman, R. *Toward Community: A Criticism of Contemporary Capitalism.* Santa Barbara, Calif.: Center for the Study of Democratic Institutions, 1968.

Liem, R., and J. Liem. "Social Class and Mental Illness Reconsidered: The Role of Economic Stress and Social Support." *Journal of Health and Social Behavior* 19 (1978): 139–56.

Myers, J., and L. Bean. *A Decade Later: A Follow-up of Social Class and Mental Illness.* New York: John Wiley and Sons, 1968.

Rinehart, J. *The Tyranny of Work.* Don Mills, Ont.: Longman Canada, 1975.

Scheff, T. *Being Mentally Ill: A Sociological Theory.* 2nd ed. New York: Aldine, 1984.

Scull, A. *Decarceration: Community Treatment and the Deviant.* Englewood Cliffs, N.J.: Prentice-Hall, 1977.

Sennett, R., and J. Cobb. *The Hidden Injuries of Class.* New York: Alfred A. Knopf, 1972.

Srole, L., T. Langner, S. Michael, M. Opler, and T. Rennie. *Mental Health in the Metropolis.* New York: McGraw-Hill, 1962.

Syme, S.L., and L. Berkman. "Social Class, Susceptibility, and Sickness." In *The Sociology of Health and Illness: Critical Perspectives*, edited by P. Conrad and R. Kern, 35–44. New York: St. Martin's Press, 1981.

Szasz, T. *The Myth of Mental Illness.* New York: Harper and Row, 1961.

———. *Ideology and Insanity: Essays on the Psychiatric Dehumanization of Man.* Garden City, N.Y.: Doubleday-Anchor, 1970.

17

THE UTILIZATION OF SOCIAL SCIENCE RESEARCH IN MENTAL HEALTH POLICY:
A Canadian Survey

Robert W. Hetherington
University of Alberta

INTRODUCTION

This chapter has two objectives. The first is to examine the attitude of policy-makers, administrators, and social scientists concerning the place of social science research in the formulation of mental health policy. The second is to examine the use of such information by policy-makers and administrators. Pursuit of these objectives is guided by a consideration of the popular conception that scientists and policy-makers represent two different cultures, and that the resulting differences in beliefs, values, and attitudes hinder effective use of relevant social science knowledge in the resolution of policy issues. Information relevant to the major objectives was gathered from a nation-wide sample of Canadian policy-makers, programme administrators, and social scientists.

THEORY OF TWO CULTURES

There are at least two major schools of thought in the literature on the place of social research in policy. One school, perhaps the most prevalent, maintains that policy can only benefit from input and counsel by social research, which is a force for reason.

This school of thought decries the relatively minor impact which action-oriented research apparently has on decision-making, and leads to schemes to increase the interaction between the scientist and the policy-maker. The second school of thought emphasizes the social scientist as both a critic of and a contributor to pure knowledge. In either role, it is argued, the social scientist must avoid indebtedness to any particular government or sympathy with any social/political cause, because research should not appear to be in the service of either one. Both schools of thought tend to agree, however, on the existence of two cultures. In the former, the response is to devise ways to bridge the gap between them. In the latter, the response is to emphasize the benefits to the discipline of maintaining the unique character of each culture. Scientists who hold the latter view — the separation of science and politics — generally view applied science as an "occupation for second-rate minds." C. P. Snow (1965:32), in commenting on the attitude of "pure" scientists toward "applied" science, said: "We prided ourselves that the science we were doing could not, in any conceivable circumstances, have any practical use. The more firmly one could make that claim, the more superior one felt."

Thus, there is a degree of consensus that two "cultures" do exist — although not everybody would use this term — but there is contention as to whether this state of affairs is natural and desirable. Disagreement is likely to be found among both scientists and policy-makers, and there are policy-makers who would agree with their pure-scientist counterparts: do your scientific work, and if anything useful for policy-making should by chance arise, leave it to us to make use of it.

If two cultures do exist, it is possible to theoretically describe the potential difficulties which might arise in relationships between them. Merton, in an early discussion of this relationship, identified two general problem areas: "scientific" problems concerning the adequacy of social science information for use in meeting practical demands, and interpersonal or interorganizational problems (1949:164).

Merton describes three types of scientific problems: problems of objectivity, of oversimplification, and of tempo. Social science loses much of its credibility if it is perceived to lack objectivity, and this perception is promoted by the fact that social sciences are the most liberal of the academic disciplines (Lipset and Ladd, 1972; Orlans, 1973). Oversimplification refers to the perception that social science must simplify complex policy issues so much that

research is unusable. The problem in reverse is also cited; that social scientists "muddy the waters" by pointing out complexities and uncertainties which do not encourage clear-cut answers (Holzner and Fisher, 1979; Cohen and Lindblom, 1979). Finally, tempo refers to the fact that policy-makers generally want answers more quickly than researchers can provide them. This may lead researchers to provide policy advice before the research is completed, or to shorten the course of research with the potential result that key issues and rigorous procedures are short-circuited. Tempo is much cited in the literature, both by policy-makers as a reason for not using research findings (Rosenblatt, 1968), and by researchers as a reason for not doing good research (Rothman, 1979).

Interpersonal problems are based on conflicting values between policy-makers and researchers. Drawing on the convergence of ideas between Merton and C.P. Snow, it is possible to suggest four conflicting value pairs. First there is the conflict between long-term and short-term solutions, with policy-makers seen as the masters of the short-term solution and scientists as the repositories of long-term foresight. Second is the conflict between the tendency toward scientific rationality and the tendency toward action and intuition; policy-makers are known to act on the basis of their total grasp of a situation and their feelings of what fits politically (Rich, 1977:308), while scientists tend to conclude very little until all the facts are in. Third is the conflict between optimism of scientists, who believe all problems are susceptible to scientific solution, and the realism of policy-makers, who frequently see the scientist's perspective as pathetically naïve. Fourth is the liberal/conservative conflict; part of the liberal perspective of scientists is associated with their willingness to regard as changeable any undesirable part of the system, whereas policy-makers usually must be much more cautious in their orientation to change.

These problems between the two cultures are likely to create tension, lack of communication, misunderstanding, and mistrust. Snow pointed out that where this is the case, policy-makers will tend to use only information from trusted sources, such as friends and associates (Bowman, 1978) and hence are subject to manipulation, since consequent decisions will be based not on scientific alternatives but on the influence of particular scientists (Roberts et al., 1971). Snow emphasized that policy-makers in general cannot discriminate between good and bad research, and in any case, not all scientists can be relied upon to deliver good advice.

Description of some aspects of the gap between the two cultures raises the question of accommodation. If the gap is to be bridged, it may involve movement of policy-makers toward the social science perspective through education of policy-makers in the social sciences. Some researchers have suggested this is occurring already, and that the ability of policy-makers to judge quality of scientific work is improving (Weiss and Bucuvalas, 1980). Movement in the other direction is also possible — that is, accommodation on the part of scientists, for which the rationale is usually phrased: "In order to maximize the utilization of social research in policy, the scientist should become more familiar with the political process." This is based on the belief that social scientists, to a greater extent than other scientists, have an obligation to go beyond the mere production of knowledge to see to its appropriate application in policy (Goodwin, 1966). Whichever way accommodation occurs, there is developing a "third culture," according to Snow, populated by individuals with cross-over experience: that is, social scientists who have policy experience, and policy-makers who have training and experience with social science research.

To the extent that two cultures do exist, it is thought that the appropriate use of social science in policy will be thereby reduced. Researchers have found considerable use, but their research raises the question of definition of "use" (e.g., Roberts et al., 1971; Patton et al., 1977; Rich, 1981; Knorr, 1977). Most of the use demonstrated in the literature is of a diffuse nature involving conceptualization, enlightenment, legiti-

mation, and symbolic applications. Very little is of a specific, instrumental nature. It is thought that measures of use of research information should at the very least reflect two dimensions: first, whether it involves general sources, specific sources, or consultations, and second, whether the information is indeed used to develop policy, or to legitimate it after the fact.

Little empirical literature exists examining the impact of the two cultures on utilization of knowledge. Three studies tend to confirm the importance of cultural gaps in underutilization (Caplan et al., 1975; Dunn, 1980; Badura and Waltz, 1980). These studies also indicate, however, that the gap between the two cultures may be disappearing with the professionalization of the policy-maker community.

Our review of previous work suggests that first, an adequate theoretical framework dealing with relationships between scientists and non-scientists does not exist, and second, empirical work concerning the transfer of knowledge from science research to policy-making is scattered and inconclusive. The most one can say at this point is that important questions have been raised.

RESEARCH QUESTIONS

In this study, through analysis of data from a Canada-wide sample of producers and users of social science information in the mental health field, we are in a position to provide further specification (and tentative answers) to some of the questions raised by the literature:

1. Are there basically two cultures — the scientific and non-scientific — and what characteristics differentiate one from the other?

2. In what ways is social science information predominantly utilized by policy-makers and administrators?

3. What are the predominant motivations for utilization of social science information by decision-makers?

4. How do differences between scientists and decision-makers relate to use or non-use, and to modes of use?

5. What are the major consequences of accommodation between scientists and decision-makers?

METHODOLOGY

In order to provide descriptive and explanatory data on these five issues, a sample of 820 policy-makers, administrators, and social scientists in the field of mental health was drawn from across Canada. All eligible individuals identified from various sources were included. Sources used were:

- federal and provincial government directories,

- the Canadian Hospital Directory,

- university calendars,

- the data bank of the Social Science Council of Canada (social scientists),

- twenty-five informants considered knowledgeable about mental health in their respective regions of the country, and

- responses to questions in the survey which asked for names of people relevant to the study objectives.

Questions were designed to measure concepts relevant to the production and utilization of social science information in the mental health field. Instruments were based on measures used by the Center for Research on Utilization of Scientific Knowledge at the University of Michigan in a previous survey of American policy-makers.

Questionnaires were mailed and interviews conducted in 1978–79.

An overall response rate of 71 percent was obtained, resulting — after 262 were removed from the initial 820 because they were "inapplicable" — in a working sample of 558 cases. The survey was designed to provide an opportunity to study non-response bias, and bias due to data-collection method (i.e., questionnaire versus interviews). Tests for bias revealed no significant bias for non-response or data collection method for socio-demographic or attitudinal variables, but bias was evident for utilization estimates; non-respondents tend to report lower utilization, and those interviewed also tend to report lower utilization. There appears to be a greater impact on the utilization estimates from method of data collection than from non-response. The greatest impact of the bias is likely to occur among administrators.

The sample was classified into three categories: social scientists, administrators, and policy-makers. Respondents were placed into one of the three groups based on their position, their self-report of primary activity, and their experience with research in the mental health area. This resulted in the sample being divided into 125 policy-makers, 214 administrators, and 219 social scientists.

The extent to which the sample is representative of all relevant policy-makers, administrators, and social scientists in the mental health field in Canada is open to speculation. The sampling procedure resulted in certain geographic anomalies, such as underrepresentation in Manitoba, Prince Edward Island, and (at least among policy-makers) in Quebec. Response rates are uneven, ranging from 50 percent in Prince Edward Island to 85 percent in Alberta; they include a rather low 49 percent rate for francophones. Every reasonable effort was made to include all relevant persons, to encourage response from all, and to estimate systematic bias due to non-response and method of data collection. There is some indication that the sample is biased in a manner familiar to most social scientists: those who are "interested" and "in favour of" are more likely to respond than those who are not. Regarding utilization, the study probably indicates more than actually occurs. It is also probable that differences between policy-makers and administrators are underestimated due to the relative makeup of the sample vis-à-vis data-collection techniques.

Table 1. Sample Size and Response Rates

(a) Total Sample

Response Category	Sampling Designation						
	Policy-Makers		Administrators		Social Scientists		Totals
Respondents	144	(67.9%)	211	(64.7%)	203	(83.2%)	558 (71.2%)
Non-respondents	68	(32.1%)	115	(35.3%)	41	(16.8%)	224 (28.8%)
TOTALS	212	(100%)	326	(100%)	243	(100%)	782 (100%)

(b) Response to Questionnaire Survey

Response Category	Type of Respondent (Final Designation for Respondents)						
	Policy-Makers		Administrators		Social Scientists		Totals
Respondents	89	(68.9%)	181	(60.9%)	186	(82.6%)	456 (70.1%)
Non-respondents	40	(31.1%)	116	(39.1%)	39	(17.4%)	195 (29.9%)
TOTALS	129	(100%)	297	(100%)	225	(100%)	651 (100%)

(c) Response to the Interview Survey

Response Category (Interview survey)	Type of Respondent (Final Designation for Respondents) and Response to the Questionnaire Survey					
	Policy-Makers (None interviewed were sent questionnaires)	Administrators		Social Scientists		Totals
		Questionnaire respondents	Questionnaire non-respondents	Questionnaire respondents	Questionnaire non-respondents	
Interview respondents	55 (65.4%)	33 (39.2%)	30 (43.5%)	35 (36.1%)	18 (42.9%)	171 (45.5%)
Interview non-respondents	29 (35.6%)	51 (60.8%)	39 (56.5%)	62 (63.9%)	24 (57.1%)	205 (54.5%)
TOTALS	84 (100%)	84 (100%)	69 (100%)	97 (100%)	42 (100%)	376 (100%)

STUDY OUTCOMES

1. Are there basically two cultures? If so, how are they different?

This issue was presented to respondents directly in the following statement, with which they were invited to agree or disagree: "A major factor affecting utilization of social scientific knowledge is a lack of mutual understanding and interaction between the social scientists' community and the policymakers' community." Responses were on a four-point scale from "strongly agree" to "strongly disagree."

The overall frequency distribution of responses on this variable indicates overwhelming agreement with the statement. If one combines the "strongly agree" and "agree" categories, 92 percent of the total sample is in agreement that two communities do exist, and that this is a major factor affecting utilization of social science information in policy-making. This is the highest agreement found for any of the 29 attitude questions in this study.

It is of interest that Caplan et al. found very much the same type of response when they asked this question of a sample of American policy-makers. The comparison data between Canadian and American policy-makers are shown in Table 2.

The similarities are remarkable. There is nearly universal endorsement of the two cultures theory by both Canadian and American policy-makers in mental health.

Agreement is practically equivalent across the three types of respondents; concurrence is very high. Chi-square tests of significance for the distribution and analysis of variance tests for means do not yield statistically significant differences. There is only a slight tendency for policy-makers to take a more extreme stand than social scientists: 29 percent of policy-makers are in strong agreement, compared with 26 percent of social scientists.

There are no significant relationships between responses to this question and any socio-demographic variables. It is quite interesting, and unexpected, that there is also a lack of relationship between cross-over experience and agreement with the existence of a separation between the scientist and policy-maker communities. One would expect that lack of experience of one member in the other's camp would exaggerate the feeling of separate communities. Contrary to this expectation, the tendency is for the reverse to occur. For example, the percentage of policy-makers without research experience who "strongly agree" with the statement is 25 percent, and the corresponding percentage of those with such experience is 32 percent. For administrators, the shift is even more marked, and in the same direction: 18 percent to 34 percent. Research experience seems to lead decision-makers into virtual agreement with social scientists that there exists a wide gulf in understanding between the two communities.

Table 2. Comparison of Responses by Canadian and American Policy-makers to the Statement "A major factor affecting utilization of social science knowledge is a lack of mutual understanding and interaction between the social scientists' community and the policymakers' community."

	Canadian (N = 120)	American (N = 196)
Strongly agree	29%	27%
Agree.....................	61%	61%
Disagree	8%	12%
Strongly disagree...	2%	0%
$\overline{X}$	1.82	1.95

Further evidence of misunderstanding, lack of trust, and lack of communication between decision-makers and scientists is found in the fact that members of the potential user community have significant doubts or lack of knowledge about the validity and reliability of *infor-*

Table 3. Attitudes of Policy-makers and Administrators toward Scientific Disciplines and Methods of Information Gathering

Scientific Discipline	Percent responding "Very Valid"	
	Policy-makers	Administrators
Physics	40%	40%
Biology	22%	30%
Medicine	17%	21%
Economics	8%	7%
Sociology	7%	6%
Psychology	6%	9%
History	5%	6%
Psychiatry	4%	13%
Anthropology	3%	4%
Political Science	2%	2%

Method of Information Gathering	Percent responding "Very Reliable"	
	Policy-makers	Administrators
Laboratory controlled experiments	19%	25%
Observation in a real-life situation by trained observers	13%	16%
Controlled field experiments	9%	8%
Clinical case histories	5%	10%
Survey research	5%	4%
Public opinion polling	3%	1%
Examination of historical or public documents	3%	3%
Experimental games and simulation	1%	2%
Organizational analysis	1%	3%

mation produced by social science research. These doubts and lack of knowledge are further evidenced by responses to questions about the reliability and validity of specific social science disciplines and information-collection techniques and measures. Some of these data are illustrated in Table 3.

It seems clear that when less than 10 percent of the respondents from the user community rate information supplied by any social science discipline as "very valid," and less than 9 percent rate controlled field experiments as "very reliable," one has identified an area of substantial problems.

The major problem which concerned Snow in characterizing interaction between scientists and policy-makers was not necessarily mistrust or skepticism regarding the validity of scientific information, but rather the inability of policy-makers to distinguish between good research and bad. Answers to the questions on validity and reliability indicate that one third to one half of the respondents from the user community are unable to evaluate social science information.

This skepticism and lack of understanding on the part of policy-makers and administrators is overlaid by other concerns regarding the scientific nature of social science information. The two cultures tend to agree on the existence of significant scientific problems such as lack of objectivity, oversimplification, and lack of fit of information for use by decision-makers. One does not find that the two cultures differ in their perceptions of these problems. The concern regarding objectivity, shared by all, is of particular importance to policy-makers, who apparently believe that the political opinions of researchers affect their research.

With regard to differences in values between social scientists and decision-makers, statistically significant differences were found for two of the four value pairs tested, and in all four, the directions of differences were as predicted. Significant differences were found on the science versus action and the optimism versus realism value pairs; scientists to a greater extent than decision-makers believe in the scientific approach to solution of policy problems, and are more optimistic about the practicality of scientific solutions to those problems. Liberalism/conservatism, tested by subscription to the belief that most problems have individual rather than social causes, was not significant, although 21 percent of the administrators versus 12 percent of the social scientists concurred. Finally, no significant differences were found in orientation toward short-term or long-term solutions, but again 34 percent of the scientists, as compared with 20 percent of the policy-makers, endorsed long-term solutions based on scientific evidence, versus short-term solutions based on a "global feel" for the situation.

In short, our evidence tends to support the idea of two separate cultures. An overwhelming majority of the sample agree to a gulf between science and policy. Decision-makers, while supportive of the need for science in policy, have serious reservations about the validity and reliability of the social science disciplines, information-gathering techniques, and measurement. Scientists and decision-makers agree on the existence of important scientific problems (objectivity, oversimplification, tempo), and tend to subscribe to different values regarding the place of science in policy.

2. In what ways is social science information predominantly utilized by decision-makers?

Three types of utilization were studied: use of general knowledge of social science research, use of specific studies, and use of consultants. Estimates of frequency of use may be a little high in this survey for two reasons. First, the analysis of bias indicates that estimates from questionnaires are likely to be higher than estimates from interviews, and the data are predominantly from questionnaires. Second, the estimate of validity, based on examination of interview information where the respondent was asked to provide examples of types of use, shows that reasonable examples are provided in about 70 percent of the cases. For the remaining 30 percent, claims to utilization may be more wishful thinking than reality.

Given these caveats, utilization data are provided in Table 4.

The evidence regarding the role which social science research information plays in policy decisions strongly suggests that the role is not a vital one. Respondents report much more frequent use of consultants and of *general* knowledge of social research and theory than of specific studies. However, the degree to which these two former uses are really uses of *science* is debatable. General perceptions of facts and relationships which have been established by social science are, one would estimate, erroneous at least as often as they are accurate. Other researchers have also established that this "diffuse" approach to the utilization of social science knowledge is predominant among policy-makers. Some have found reason to be heartened by this finding. For them, social

Table 4. Rates of Reported Utilization of Different Types of Social Science Research Information by Policy-makers and Administrators

USE OF GENERAL KNOWLEDGE OF SOCIAL SCIENCE RESEARCH

Category	Policy-makers	Administrators	Totals
	(N = 105)	(N = 181)	(N = 286)
Very frequently	15.2%	17.7%	16.8%
Frequently	42.9%	42.5%	42.7%
Sometimes	32.4%	29.8%	30.8%
Infrequently	9.5%	7.7%	8.4%
Never	0.0%	2.2%	1.4%
$\overline{X}$	2.36	2.34	2.35
SD	.86	.93	.90

$X^2 = 2.95$, DF = 4, NS: Gamma = −.04; T = .17, NS

USE OF SPECIFIC STUDIES

Category	Policy-makers	Administrators	Totals
	(N = 104)	(N = 179)	(N = 283)
Very frequently	4.8%	2.2%	3.2%
Frequently	26.0%	21.2%	23.0%
Sometimes	32.7%	39.7%	37.1%
Infrequently	26.9%	29.1%	
Never	9.6%	7.8%	8.5%
$\overline{X}$	3.11	3.19	3.16
SD	1.05	.94	.98

$X^2 = 3.23$, DF = 4, NS: Gamma = .06; T = .70, NS

USE OF CONSULTANTS

Category	Policy-makers	Administrators	Totals
	(N = 105)	(N = 179)	(N = 284)
Very frequently	12.4%	6.1%	8.5%
Frequently	34.3%	17.9%	23.9%
Sometimes	26.7%	40.8%	35.6%
Infrequently	20.0%	25.1%	23.2%
Never	6.7%	10.1%	7.8%
$\overline{X}$	2.74	3.15	3.00
SD	1.12	1.03	1.08

$X^2 = 15.81$, DF = 4, P < .01; Gamma = .28; T = 3.12, P < .01

science research provides a framework for the conceptualization of social problems and their alternate solutions; it serves at least as an enlightenment. As a counter-argument to this, the possibility must be considered that such use incorporates an array of disparate half-truths and misperceptions on the part of decision-makers in a hurry for a solution.

The use of consultants to advise decision-makers on the views of social science about particular problems or issues is scarcely more encouraging. Several threads of evidence should be considered here. First, the most frequent users of consultants are policy-makers rather than programme administrators, and it is policy-makers who are shown to have the shortest tenure in office. Second, two of the most frequently mentioned sources of information for these policy-makers are direct contact with friends and associates who are social scientists, and review of in-house working papers. Third, with all potential users, policy-makers share a combination of mistrust of social science information, a suspicion that the personal opinions of social scientists (in particular leftist political beliefs) influence the research, with an inability to judge the quality of social science research on a number of criteria. These threads of evidence should be considered in light of Merton's warning that advice under severe time constraints is not necessarily based on scientific evidence, and of Snow's fear that decision-makers are strongly disposed to put trust in one or another scientific "camp" without being able to judge the scientific merits thereof. Considered together, these items provide a "snapshot" of the decision-maker as characteristically lacking respect for social science, suspicious of the politics involved, and relying heavily on sources of information which can be trusted or controlled — friends and associates (trusted) and in-house working papers (controlled). The potential for misuse of social science information is evident. Least frequently used are specific studies. Used by only three percent "very frequently," this source of information must be regarded as almost negligible, all the more considering that

estimates from this study are likely inflated. It appears that specific studies are not frequently used because there is too great a risk in basing a policy decision on specific studies; it is also likely that specific studies are not available for the issue at hand and that there is generally not enough time to conduct a study to inform the decision. Reliance on specific studies is increased when the policy-maker is academically trained (that is, has a Ph.D.). It is this specific type of input from research to decision-making which is least vulnerable to non-scientific influences, although by no means is it "not vulnerable."

One final note on utilization patterns: the data indicate that use of social science research information is associated with format of the information. Frequent users of this information (defined as those who respond "very frequently" or "frequently" to two of the three types) identify computerized abstracts as a major source of information. Given the relatively poor information systems currently available, it seems that efforts to improve abstracting systems may have a positive impact on utilization rates. However, such abstracts would have to contain within them judgements of study quality in order to aid the decision-maker in overcoming an inability to differentiate good from bad research.

3. What are the predominant motivations for utilization by decision-makers?

The data indicate that instrumental motivations predominate over legitimating motivations in the use of social science information. Instrumental motivations are predicated on use of scientific knowledge to choose among policy alternatives prior to decision-making, whereas legitimating motivations emphasize justification of decisions by bringing scientific knowledge to bear on the issue after the fact. Percentage use of each type in this study by both policy-makers and administrators shows that although instrumental uses are most frequent, legitimating uses are substantial. In fact, both types of use are subscribed to by more than half the respondents, as shown in Table 5.

A differential between policy-makers and administrators is established for frequent use, but in a direction opposite to that which is expected. Policy-makers who are frequent users make greater instrumental use of social science, whereas among administrators who are frequent users, the two types of motivations are equally frequent. One might speculate that, given administrators' need for information for day-to-day decisions, it is more frequently necessary to come to some conclusion regarding an issue, and seek out the scientific literature only afterwards to see if the correct decision was made.

Table 5.

Distribution of sample: (Policy-makers and administrators)		Instrumental Use	Legitimating Use
(1)	Very useful	15.7%	13.9%
(2)		57.7%	47.1%
(3)		21.5%	28.1%
(4)		4.5%	9.1%
(5)	Not useful	0.6%	1.8%

MEAN: 2.17
STANDARD DEVIATION: .76

Although the picture for use of social science information painted in this study is a little gloomy, the information on motivations is encouraging. Combined with support of a majority of policy-makers for the fullest use of social science research by government, the predominance of instrumental motivations implies that this "fullest" use is often turned to rational choices among policy alternatives, rather than providing support for decisions made on some other basis. However, there is reason to believe that the information in this study on motivations for use is subject to bias because of the respondents' awareness of the social acceptability of

claiming instrumental over legitimating motivations. However, the evidence is in line with that produced by previous research. It is an area which could benefit from further research.

4. How do differences between scientists and decision-makers relate to rates and types of utilization?

Despite the evidence that this study provides to indicate that there are significant problems between scientists and potential users of social science information, no relationship is found between recognition of problems and frequency of use of information. In comparing the two cultures, emphasis was placed on perception of scientific problems and on differences in values and beliefs which would be expected to create problems with interpersonal relationships. It was found that scientists and decision-makers perceive scientific problems in very much the same way. However, among users, recognition of scientific problems is unrelated to frequency of use of scientific information. The data seem to suggest that the hypothesized relationship should be stood on its head; that is, frequent use of social science information tends to *result* in greater recognition of problems, rather than greater recognition resulting in more infrequent use.

More information on the recognition of scientific problems was provided in the various ratings of reliability and validity of social science disciplines and data-collection techniques and measures. These ratings demonstrated a significant mistrust by policy-makers and administrators of social science information, but the degree of mistrust on any indicator of reliability and validity did not appear to be related to frequency of use. This is in contrast to previous research, which has concluded that such a relationship does exist and that those policy-makers who rate social science higher on validity and reliability measures make greater use of scientific information. In this sample, approximately one third of the total number of policy-makers and administrators are "frequent users" of social science information, despite perceiving scientific problems. Can it be concluded that the objective quality of social science information makes little difference in frequency of use for policy purposes? It would appear so, since respondents very infrequently indicated that they rejected social science research information because it is faulty. An example of this apparent paradox occurs for data produced by programme evaluations. Three quarters of the decision-makers regard programme evaluation data as "valuable" information, and yet less than 5 percent of them regard it as "very valid and reliable."

There are two possible explanations for this apparent contradiction. One has to do with the predominant use which is made of social science information — in our opinion, use which is not vital to decision-making. Social science information used as general knowledge is not necessarily (or even probably) a critical element in making a decision, but it is contributory, along with many other inputs to the decision-maker. As such, it is not vital that the information be valid. The second type of predominant use — via consultants — places the onus for distinguishing good from bad information on the shoulders of the advisor. Thus, while the decision-maker may be uneasy or ambivalent about the quality of social science information in general, the risk of basing decisions on unreliable information is reduced through consultation with people who are trusted. The third type of use — specific studies — is greatly underplayed by most decision-makers, because here the risk is highest. Again it is noted that the academically qualified policy-maker is significantly more likely to use this latter type of information than are those with less education. If the objective quality of social science information were improved, the use of specific studies would probably increase among those who could tell the difference.

The second explanation has to do with values. Decision-makers, it has been noted, subscribe to the value of science in policy, although not to the extent that scientists do. But the majority are "believers." Strength of this belief turns out to be a relatively good predictor of frequency of use of scientific information. It is possible that this is the crucial element in determining whether or not a decision-maker will make use of social science information, rather than the perceived quality of the information itself. This may be almost a blind faith in the virtues of the scientific approach operating as the driving force behind those decision-makers who continue to frequently use social science information while acknowledging its shortcomings. The faith, however, is in part youthful idealism, since it tends to fade with age.

5. What are the consequences of accommodation between scientists and decision-makers?

The question of accommodation between the two cultures has been addressed both theoretically and empirically in this study. Theoretically, it was proposed that scientists could make a greater contribution to decision-making if they were to become more familiar with the policy-making process; it was also proposed that policy-makers could make more informed and intelligent use of social science information if they were more familiar with science. Empirically, we found that nearly one half of each of the two groups had cross-over experience.

The impact is less direct than theoretically predicted. It was found that scientists with policy experience were more likely than those without it to produce policy recommendations from their research. But it was also found that the relationship between the scientific and policy-making communities is characterized by lack of mutual understanding and communication. Furthermore, the researchers with cross-over experience were not as convinced as those without the experience that knowledge of the policy-making process was essential for social scientists to realize more effective utilization of social science knowledge. It is as if the cross-over experience is a sobering one for social scientists, making them more aware of the problems which con-

Table 6. The Impact of Cross-over Experience on the Utilization of General Knowledge of Social Science Research by Decision-makers

Category	Policy-makers		Administrators		Totals
	No Research Experience	Research Experience	No Research Experience	Research Experience	
	(N = 48)	(N = 57)	(N = 83)	(N = 98)	(N = 286)
Very frequently	6.3%	22.8%	14.5%	20.4%	16.8%
Frequently	37.5%	47.4%	50.6%	35.7%	42.7%
Sometimes	37.5%	28.1%	26.5%	32.7%	30.8%
Infrequently	18.8%	1.8%	6.0%	9.2%	8.4%
Never	0.0%	0.0%	2.4%	2.0%	1.4%
$\overline{X}$	2.69	2.09	2.31	2.37	2.35
SD	.85	.76	.88	.98	.90

$X^2 = 11.94$, DF = 12, NS; Gamma = .06; F = 4.01, P < .01

front the application of scientific knowledge to policy formulation.

The effect of research experience on policy-makers and administrators is to increase rates of utilization (although there is no effect on mode of use), but at the same time it increases the realization of problems in the relationships between social scientists and decision-makers. This increased sensitization of both cultures to the problems which exist between them is a latent function of the cross-over experience. Whereas the manifest function of such experience was theoretically predicted to be a lessening of tensions and mistrust between the two cultures, this prediction did not reckon with the fact that there are objective problems with social science research itself which are actually exacerbated, and not resolved, by greater familiarity of one culture with the other.

Another effect of the cross-over experience on decision-makers is the shift of certain values towards those of the scientific culture. This is the bridging effect which was theoretically predicted, but it is worth noting that virtually all the accommodation occurs on the part of the decision-makers. This value shift on the part of decision-makers is observed for three of the four value pairs tested, and for all four value pairs the maximum separation of the two cultures is observed among those without cross-over experience. Of the two types of experience identified in this study, experience with science and experience with policy, it is the experience with science which has the greatest impact on values and is the most resistant to change.

Finally, it was found that research experience for decision-makers has no discernible effect on judgement of the quality of social science research on a number of criteria. In general, the judgement of those with or without experience is not statistically different, is indicative of mistrust or skepticism, and is characterized by a large number of respondents who are ambivalent. There is no evidence in this study that decision-makers with research experience are more capable of differentiating good and bad research; and, in fact, there is no evidence that they reject faulty information from social science more frequently than decision-makers without this experience.

Table 7. Tentative Answers to the Five Areas of Inquiry

1. Are there basically two cultures — the scientific and the non-scientific — and what are the characteristics which best differentiate one from the other?

   Answer: There appear to be two cultures, separated by differences in values related to the place of science in policy and interpersonal problems related to perceived quality of social science research.

2. What types of utilization of social science information by policy-makers and administrators are predominant?

   Answer: General knowledge of social science research is used "very frequently" by 17% of decision-makers, consultants are used by 8%, specific studies by 3%. These estimates are probably inflated.

3. What are the predominant motivations for utilization of social science information by decision-makers?

   Answer: Instrumental uses, defined as contributing to policy formulation, are endorsed by 73% of decision-makers. Legitimating uses, defined as justifying a policy after it is formulated, are endorsed by 61%.

4. How do differences between scientists and decision-makers relate to use or non-use, and to modes of use?

   Answer: Belief in the value of science in policy is a good predictor of frequency of use by decision-makers. Interpersonal problems related to perceived quality of scientific evidence are unrelated to frequency of use, but lead to greater reliance on trusted resources such as consultants, friends and associates, and in-house research.

5. What are the major consequences of accommodation between scientists and decision-makers?

   Answer: Accommodation appears to reduce differences in values, with decision-makers moving toward greater belief in science in policy. Accommodation raises awareness of interpersonal problems associated with perceived quality of research evidence and "lack of fit."

SUMMARY AND RECOMMENDATIONS

This chapter has outlined some of the findings from a survey of decision-makers and social scientists in Canada. A brief snapshot of the major findings is provided in Table 7.

Policy recommendations to Ottawa, based on these and other findings, included the following:

1. In order to facilitate communication of scientific findings to policy-makers, the federal government should undertake the development of a computerized information system containing abstracts of scientific studies. The system must contain indices of reliability and validity.

2. In order to facilitate communication between decision-makers and scientists, the federal

government should institute a series of conferences on specific topics, involving scientists, decision-makers, and facilitators.

3. In order to meet the perceived lack of availability of reports of federally funded research (we were able to locate 48 of 173 final programme evaluation reports), the federal government should provide a complete collection of final reports through a clearing-house, and should undertake to ensure notification of relevant potential users.

4. In order to counter the perception of poor quality of social science research, a portion of funds distributed to NHRDP and other federal agencies involved with mental health research should be earmarked for basic research, including work on theoretical models, measurement, methods of study design, and execution.

Acknowledgements: This study was supported by Health and Welfare Canada, National Health Research and Development Program (Grant No. 6608–1079–44), with additional support from the Applied Research Unit, Psychiatric Research Division, Saskatchewan Department of Health, and from the Division of Intramural Research, National Center for Health Services Research, Department of Health and Human Services, Rockville, Maryland, USA. The detailed report of the study, from which this paper is derived, has been submitted to the National Health Research and Development Program (NHRDP), Health and Welfare Canada, Ottawa. I wish to thank Gerald E. Calderone Ph.D. of the National Center for his assistance in preparing the final report, and Douglas D. Frey and Jane Dickinson of the Applied Research Unit in Saskatchewan for their assistance in data collection and preparation of preliminary working papers.

STUDY QUESTIONS

1. After reading this chapter, how would you define "cross-over experience" and what are the major implications of such experience for the production and utilization of social science information?

2. One basic hypothesis guiding the study is that greater faith in the reliability and validity of social science research information would be associated with greater utilization of this information. How has this hypothesis been stood on its head, and what *are* the major determinants of utilization?

3. Discuss the meaning and importance of the three types of utilization examined in this study. Why is there "greater risk" associated with use of specific studies?

4. Do you think the perceived problems with social science research information are inherent in the nature of the applied discipline? Are they due to the basically contradictory nature of policy and science, or are they due to misperceptions?

RECOMMENDED READING

Campbell, Donald C., and Julian C. Stanley. *Experimental and Quasi-Experimental Designs for Research.* Chicago: Rand McNally College Publishing Co., 1966.

Caplan, Nathan. "The Two Communities Theory and Knowledge Utilization." *American Behavioral Scientist* 22 (1979): 459–70.

Frank, James E., and Richard A. Smith. "Social Scientists in the Policy Process." *Journal of Applied Behavioral Science* 12 (1976): 104–17.

Horowitz, Irving L. "Social Science Mandarins: Policymaking as a Political Formula." *Policy Sciences* 1 (1970): 339–60.

National Science Foundation. Knowledge into Action: Improving the Nation's Use of the Social Sciences. Report of the Special Commission on the Social Sciences of the National Science Board. Washington, D.C.: U.S. Government Printing Office, 1969.

Pelz, Donald D. "Some Expanded Perspectives on Use of Social Science in Public Policy." In *Major Social Issues: A Multidisciplinary View*, edited by J.M. Yinger and S.J. Cutler, 346–57. New York: Free Press, 1978.

Scott, R.A., and A.R. Shore. *Why Sociology Does Not Apply.* New York: Elsevier, 1979.

Snow, Charles P. *Science and Government: The Godkin Lectures at Harvard University, 1960.* Cambridge, Mass.: Harvard University Press, 1961.

Weiss, Carol H. "Evaluation Research in the Political Context." In *Handbook of Evaluation Research*, Vol. 1, edited by Marcia Guttentag and Elmer L. Struening, 13–26. Beverly Hills: Sage Publications, 1975.

———. "Knowledge Creep and Decision Accretion." *Knowledge: Creation, Diffusion, Utilization* 1 (1980): 381–404.

Weiss, Carol H., and Michael J. Bucuvalas. *Social Science Research and Decision Making.* New York: Columbia University Press, 1980.

REFERENCES

Badura, Bernhard, and Millard Waltz. "Information Behaviour in the German Federal Government: The Case of the Social Sciences." *Knowledge: Creation, Diffusion, Utilization* 1 (1980): 351–79.

Bowman, James S. "Managerial Theory and Practice: The Transfer of Knowledge in Public Administration." *Public Administration Review* 38 (1978): 563–70.

Caplan, Nathan, Andrea Morrison, and Russel J. Stambaugh. *The Use of Social Science Knowledge in Policy Decisions at the National Level: A Report to Respondents.* Ann Arbor, Michigan: Center for Research on Utilization of Scientific Knowledge, Institute for Social Research, University of Michigan, 1975.

Cohen, David K., and Charles E. Lindblom. "Solving Problems of Bureaucracy: Limits of Social Science." *American Behavioral Scientist* 22 (1979): 547–60.

Donnison, David. "Research for Policy." *Minerva* 10 (1972): 519–36.

Dunn, William N. "The Two-Communities Metaphor and Models of Knowledge Use: An Exploratory Case Survey." *Knowledge: Creation, Diffusion, Utilization* 1 (1980): 515–36.

Goodwin, Leonard. "Conceptualizing the Action Process." *Sociology and Social Research* 50 (1966): 377–92.

Holzner, Burkart, and Evelyn Fisher. "Knowledge in Use: Considerations in the Sociology of Knowledge Application." *Knowledge: Cre-*

ation, Diffusion, Utilization 1 (1979): 219–44.

Knorr, Karin D. "Policy Makers' Use of Social Science Knowledge: Symbolic or Instrumental?" Chapter 12 in *Using Social Research in Public Policy Making*, edited by Carol E. Weiss. Lexington, Mass.: D.C. Heath and Co., 1977.

Lipset, Seymour Martin, and Averett Carl Ladd, Jr. "The Politics of American Sociologists." *American Journal of Sociology* 78 (1972): 67–104.

Merton, Robert K. "The Role of Applied Social Science in the Formation of Policy: A Research Memorandum." *Philosophy of Science* 16 (1949): 161–81.

Orlans, H. *Contracting for Knowledge*. San Francisco: Jossey-Bass, 1973.

Patton, Michael O., Patricia Smith Grimes, Kathryn M. Guthrie, Nancy J. Brennan, Barbara Dickey Franch, and Dale A. Blyth. "In Search of Impact: An Analysis of the Utilization of Federal Health Evaluation Research." Chapter 11 in *Using Social Research in Public Policy Making*, edited by Carol H. Weiss. Lexington, Massachusetts: D.C. Heath and Co., 1977.

Rich, Robert F. "Uses of Social Science Information by Federal Bureaucrats: Knowledge for Action Versus Knowledge for Understanding." Chapter 14 in *Using Social Research in Public Policy Making*, edited by Carol H. Weiss. Lexington, Massachusetts: D.C. Heath and Co., 1977.

———. *Social Science Information and Public Policy Making*. San Francisco, California: Jossey-Bass, 1981.

Roberts, A., Judith K. Larsen, and Daryl G. Nichols. *Effective Use of Mental Health Research Information*. Palo Alto, Calif.: American Institutes for Research, 1971.

Rosenblatt, Aaron. "The Practitioners Use and Evaluation of Research." *Social Work* 13 (1968): 53–59.

Rothman, Jack. *Using Research in Organizations: A Guide to Successful Application*. Beverly Hills, California: Sage Publications, 1979.

Snow, Charles P. *The Two Cultures and a Second Look: An Expanded Version of the Two Cultures and the Scientific Revolution*. London: Cambridge University Press, 1965.

Weiss, Carol H., and Michael J. Bucuvalas. "Truth Tests and Utility Tests: Decision-Makers' Frames of Reference for Social Science Research." *American Sociological Review* 45 (1980): 302–13.

18

COMMUNITY PSYCHIATRY: The Institutional Transformation of Psychiatric Practice

Harley D. Dickinson and Glenn Andre
University of Saskatchewan

INTRODUCTION

Since the Second World War there has been a profound transformation of the organization of psychiatric services in Canada and throughout the Western world. The hallmark of this transformation has been a shift from asylum-based to community-based forms of service delivery. This process, usually referred to as the development of community psychiatry, has three related characteristics: a rapid depopulation and reduction in the number of mental hospitals, a swift increase in the number of psychiatric units in general hospitals, and the creation of a network of community-based facilities such as mental health clinics. Table 1 illustrates these trends.

In this chapter we argue that the demise of the asylum and the rise of community psychiatry cannot adequately be understood as simply a cost-cutting response to the "fiscal crisis" of the state, as is claimed by Scull (1979). We also argue that these developments are not simply a manifestation of the medicalization of deviance as is proposed, for example, by Conrad and Schneider (1980). Nor can they be understood as the simple substitution of one form of social control with another, as is suggested by Ralph (1983). Rather, we argue, contemporary psychiatry is characterized by the simultaneous expansion of two distinct but related forms of psychiatric practice. On the one hand, there is a medically dominated, general hospital-based, private-sector psychiatric services system, and on the other, a mental health clinic-based, public-sector psychiatric services system increasingly dominated by non-medically trained professionals such as psychologists and social workers. The basis of this institutional

Table 1. Number and Type of Mental Institutions and Number of Patients, Canada, Selected Years 1937 – 1980–81

Year	Mental Hospitals*		Psychiatric Units in General Hospitals†		Full- & Part-Time Mental Health Clinics & Out-Patient Departments	
	Number of Institutions	Patients on Books (Dec. 31)	Number of Units	Patients on Books	Number	Patients Seen
1937	36	39 420	—	—	—	—
1942	37	44 423	—	—	—	—
1947	38	48 015	—	—	—	—
1952	49	53 689	—	—	—	—
1957	47	50 314	23	598	69	—
1962	61	56 991	52	1 718	151	78 300
1967	60	48 768	70	1 823	218	183 700
1972	66	34 210 (874.3)‡	120	3 129 (28.1)	291	245 583
1977	41	12 591 (583.2)	169	10 742 (34.9)	397	—
1980-81	33	— (586.1)	191	— (31.4)	418	—

* Includes public mental hospitals, public psychiatric hospitals, proprietary hospitals, and after 1952, training schools for the mentally retarded; excludes federal, county, and municipal hospitals.

† Excludes federal psychiatric units.

‡ Figures in brackets indicate average number of patients per day.

— indicates data not available.

Source: Statistics Canada, *Mental Health Statistics, Vol. 1, 1937–1957*, Cat. No. 83-204; Mental Health Statistics, Vol. III, 1962 – 1980–81, Cat. No. 83-205.

bifurcation is the ambiguity about the cause of mental disorders, which appear to be both biological and social/psychological in origin. This unresolved etiological question has resulted in jurisdictional battles between competing professions, and between competing specialities within professions, for control over the diagnosis and treatment of those disorders. The principal objective of this chapter is to examine how various intra- and inter-professional struggles have influenced the institutional development of psychiatry.

This chapter is divided into three sections.

In the first section we critically examine the social control/medicalization of deviance explanations of the development of community psychiatry and the depopulation of the mental institutions. Next, we look at the development of community psychiatry in the province of Saskatchewan. There are two reasons for this. First, Saskatchewan was among the front runners in depopulating and phasing out mental hospitals as well as in developing various community-based alternatives for the care and treatment of those with psychiatric disorders, and thus is of historical interest. Second, because of the structure of the Canadian state, health-care policy remains largely a provincial responsibility. This means that an understanding of health-care policy in Canada requires an understanding of health-care policy at the provincial level. Although the federal government can influence the way in which health-care services will be organized and provided, especially through the structure of funding, the provincial responses to financial incentives and sanctions are often determined by parochial interests and conditions. As a result, the development of community psychiatry in Canada has occurred unevenly and in a somewhat diverse manner in each province. Having said this, however, the general trends apparent in each province are similar and, therefore, an understanding of the development of community psychiatry in Canada can be facilitated through the provincal case study approach adopted here. Based upon the data examined and the literature reviewed, we argue that various attempts to establish the medical nature of psychiatric practice contributed to the depopulation of the mental asylums and, ironically, laid the foundation for the subsequent demedicalization of community psychiatry. The chapter concludes with a brief discussion of likely trends and implications of these developments for the consumers of psychiatric services.

COMMUNITY PSYCHIATRY, SOCIAL CONTROL, AND THE MEDICALIZATION OF DEVIANCE

The most common explanation for the demise of the asylum and the rise of various community-based alternatives is that it was the result of a growth of medical scientific knowledge, and the realization that insanity was really an illness. If insanity was an illness, it then followed that those unfortunate enough to suffer from it should not be further afflicted by being removed from society and locked up in an asylum. Rather, the mentally ill should, like other sick people, be treated by physicians and psychiatrists in the community. Thus, in its most optimistic form, this perception of the development of community psychiatry is accepted as an inevitable triumph of science and humanitarianism and, therefore, an entirely unproblematic development, limited only by a lack of knowledge or resources.

Although this account has an intuitive appeal, some have questioned its adequacy as a complete explanation of these phenomena. Scull (1984), for example, argues that the principal impetus for the depopulation of mental hospitals and the rise of community psychiatry is to be found in some combination of cost-cutting pressure, resulting from a growing fiscal crisis of the state, with the increased social control requirements of advanced capitalist societies. The cost-cutting argument is difficult to sustain, however, in light of empirical evidence which shows that since the advent of community psychiatry, total state expenditures on psychiatric services have not decreased. Scull (1984:143) recognizes this fact and attempts to explain it in terms of state bureaucrats misleading politicians and academic researchers by "statistical juggling and administrative sleight of hand." One is left wondering, however, just who is performing this prestidigitation, and why? Unfortunately, Scull avoids these questions.

There are other limitations to the cost-cutting argument as an explanation of community psychiatry. Perhaps the most significant is that it does not enable one to account for the institutional form of the various community-based alternatives to the traditional mental hospital. Scull's assertion (1984:152) that "it is the pervasiveness and intensity of these [cost-cutting] pressures . . . which account for most of the features of the new system of community 'care and treatment'" can only be accepted as true if one accepts the assumption that decarceration entails the replacement of the mental hospital with nothing whatsoever: the abandonment of problem populations to the "sewers of human misery" (Scull, 1984:153). Although attempts to reduce costs certainly played a part in the depopulation of the mental hospitals, this in and of itself does not afford an explanation of the form taken by the many community-based alternatives, or the particular occupational configuration of the division of labour in community psychiatry.

In this respect, Ralph's (1983) work is more satisfactory. She argues that the rise of community psychiatry marked a radical break with clinical (medical) psychiatry and its replacement by a nationalized form of industrial psychology. She thus implies that community psychiatry corresponds to an almost complete demedicalization of psychiatry. Although this is more adequate than Scull's nihilistic view, as we will see below, it is an argument that is not completely supported by the empirical evidence.

Other social control theorists suggest that control of the mentally ill, and of various other problem populations, is most effectively and economically achieved through a process of "medicalizing" deviance; that is, by transforming badness into sickness. This enables physicians, acting as agents of social control, to individualize social problems and to legitimize control as humanitarian treatment. Freidson (1970:249), for example, suggests that the medicalization of deviance has gone so far as to subsume virtually all other forms of control: "the thrust of the expansion of the application of medical labels has been towards addressing (and controlling) the *serious* forms of deviance, leaving to the other institutions [law and religion] a residue of trivial and narrowly defined technical offences." Szasz (1960) and Illich (1975) add that this social control function is actively adopted by an "imperialistic" medical profession intent upon extending its sphere of influence. Under what conditions does the medicalization of deviance occur?

Conrad (1981) suggests there are five preconditions: (1) some powerful group(s) must define a behaviour as both deviant and a problem; (2) previous or traditional forms of controlling the behaviour must be seen as inadequate or unacceptable; (3) the medical profession must accept the deviant behaviour as being within its jurisdiction; (4) some medically monopolized

form of control/treatment must be available; and (5) ambiguous organic data as to the source of the problem must exist. There are at least two problematic assumptions here. First, it is assumed that possession of a medical degree/licence automatically insures that the work performed is recognized as being medical in nature. Second, it is assumed that the medical profession is homogeneous and unified. An examination of the history of psychiatry reveals that neither assumption is valid.

Since the middle of the nineteenth century, psychiatry has been involved in two interconnected struggles: one with various non-medical therapists who dispute the claim that mental disorders are illnesses (Clark, 1981); and one with other medical specialties like neurology and neurosurgery, which claim that they, and not psychiatrists, should be treating mental illness (Blustein, 1981; Valenstein, 1986). Ironically, the basis of these disputes was and continues to be the ambiguity concerning the cause of mental disorders; mental disorders seem to have both physical and psychological causes. Thus, in opposition to what Conrad (1981) has claimed, ambiguous organic evidence regarding the cause of these disorders can stand as an obstacle to the medicalization of deviance, rather than a necessary precondition to that process. This ambiguity concerning etiology also makes problematic one of Conrad's other preconditions of medicalization; the acceptance of a condition as properly belonging to the practice of medicine by the medical profession itself. Although asylum physicians consistently claimed that mental disorders were illnesses, many within mainstream medicine disputed this claim. Psychiatrists and asylum physicians, therefore, undertook to convince the rest of the medical profession, legislators, and the public at large that insanity was really an illness and that they were really practising medicine.

Although medically trained physicians had gained control of mental asylums and dominated the asylum division of labour by the end of the nineteenth century, we disagree with the claims of Scull (1979) and Conrad and Schneider

(1980) that this marked the complete medicalization of madness, or the integration of psychiatry into the mainstream of medicine. In fact, Grob (1973) and Rothman (1971) demonstrate that at the end of the nineteenth century, psychiatry in the United States was more an administrative profession than a medical specialty. Grob (1973) also points out that in the late nineteenth century, the professional association of medical superintendents of mental asylums in the United States refused to affiliate with the American Medical Association because they saw it as disorganized and largely ineffectual. By the second decade of the present century, this had changed, and psychiatrists were increasingly interested in affiliation and formally establishing the medical nature of their work. In Canada, psychiatry was not recognized by the Royal College of Physicians and Surgeons of Canada as a bona fide specialty until the 1940s (Shephard, 1985:337). The asylum system itself, however, served to distinguish and separate psychiatry from the mainstream of medicine; a distinction that was amplified by the fact that for the most part asylum physicians were state employees rather than self-employed private practitioners.

There were a number of other differences in the nature and organization of psychiatric practice that differentiated psychiatry from the rest of medicine. When institutionalization for therapeutic purposes was deemed necessary by practitioners in other branches of medicine, for example, doctors admitted their patients to hospitals, where they were administered physical treatments in the form of surgery or medications and cared for by trained nurses. In addition, when patients in general hospitals could no longer benefit from continued stay, they were discharged by their physicians, whether or not they were completely cured. The situation was quite different for asylum physicians. To begin with, even though they managed the asylums, asylum physicians generally did not have control over who would be admitted or discharged. Disposition of the insane was largely a legal matter until well into this century. In fact, in most places, commitment and discharge procedures were carried out under legal order. Voluntary admissions or discharges were rare. Throughout the first decades of this century in Saskatchewan, for example, people leaving the provincial asylums were not reported as being discharged; the only reporting categories used were parole, transfer, elopement, and death. So even though asylum physicians maintained that mental disorders were really illnesses, there was little objective evidence for this claim: no physical or biochemical cause could be found for most mental disorders; in most cases, admission and discharge were *legal* rather than *medical* prerogatives; the principal locus of treatment was a remote asylum which was more like a prison than a hospital; and care and treatment were administered by untrained attendants rather than by trained nurses.

These differences compromised the credibility of asylum physicians' claims that their work was really medical in nature and that insanity was really an illness. Thus, asylum physicians undertook to "medicalize psychiatry" and "hospitalize the asylum" (Robertson, 1922). These efforts proceeded along a number of interconnected dimensions: asylums were renamed *mental hospitals*; insanity and madness were renamed *mental illness*; training programmes were established for attendants and they were renamed *psychiatric* or *mental nurses*. In addition, a lobby was undertaken to secure the passage of legislation which would make admission and discharge procedures the same as those in other hospitals, and efforts were made to integrate psychiatric training and research into the mainstream of medicine. Thus, following the First World War, and particularly during the 1930s, much research effort was directed toward discovering effective somatic (organic) therapies for the treatment of mental disorders. It was thought that effective somatic therapies would demonstrate that mental disorders were organic rather than psychological in origin and that this, in turn, would establish the medical nature of psychiatry. The late 1930s thus produced a number of radical somatic therapies, including insulin coma, metrazol shock, electroconvulsive therapy (ECT), and psychosurgery in the form of prefrontal lobotomy and leucotomy. The most significant development in the search for effective somatic therapies, however, was the discovery and use of psychotropic drugs in the early 1950s (Swazey, 1974). This technological development enabled psychiatrists to prescribe chemotherapy for the control of psychiatric symptoms. Because the medical profession had achieved a legislative monopoly over the prescription of drugs in the early part of the twentieth century, and because physicians dominated and controlled the therapeutic work performed in mental hospitals, chemotherapy soon came to supersede all other froms of therapy and treatment, including the other somatic therapies. In fact, the mental hospitals themselves became technologically obsolete in the treatment of psychiatric disorders, and the trend towards depopulation received a further impetus. Even though the discovery of psychotropic drugs enabled psychiatrists to practise medicine like other branches of medicine, it still did not prove that mental disorders had organic causes. Psychiatrists have attempted to gloss over this problem by maintaining that mental disorders are a product of physical, psychological, and social factors. This position, although probably true, results in a problem of legitimacy for the medical profession which has no claim to privileged knowledge or competence in dealing with social-psychological processes. These processes, in fact, are the domain of social scientists and non-medical psychotherapists, who explicitly repudiate medical claims to jurisdiction over these matters. Also, because the definition and disposition of mental disorders is directly related to professional power, pay, and prestige, interprofessional competition and conflict arise over these matters. Thus, the medical domination of the asylum division of labour which physicians had achieved by the end of the nineteenth century was by the middle of the twentieth century being vigorously, and successfully, opposed (Smith, 1954–5).

To briefly summarize, we are suggesting that psychiatry cannot properly be viewed as a unified set of professional practices, and mental disorders cannot be viewed as being completely medicalized. Rather, the nature and cause of mental disorders are ambiguous, and psychiatric practice has developed into two distinct, but related, labour processes: a medically dominated, general hospital- and office-based, private-sector psychiatry, and a public-sector psychiatry, increasingly staffed and managed by social workers, psychologists, and other non-medical therapists working within various community-based facilities such as mental health clinics. The balance of this chapter will be a brief account of this process of institutional bifurcation as it occurred in the province of Saskatchewan.

THE MEDICALIZATION OF PSYCHIATRY AND THE HOSPITALIZATION OF THE ASYLUM

The hospitalization of the asylum refers to various attempts on the part of asylum physicians to replace the prison-like organization of mental institutions with forms and patterns of therapeutic practice prevalent in general hospitals. Robertson (1922:322) suggested that this had been the dominating principle guiding asylum reform in Scotland since at least the turn of the century, although he also noted that its achievement had "not been found in practice to be an easy task." A similar process characterized Canadian psychiatry and it too proved no easy task, although some aspects of the undertaking were simpler than others. Undoubtedly the easiest step in making mental asylums more like hospitals was simply to rename them. Although this transformation was well advanced by the end of the nineteenth century, in Manitoba, for example, it was not until 1910 that mental asylums were renamed mental hospitals with the passage of an amendment to that province's Insane Asylum Act (Edginton, 1986). Saskatchewan's first mental institution, opened in 1914, was from the outset called a mental hospital. It was not until 1922, however, that the notion that a disease process was being treated was legislatively sanctioned with the passage of the Mental Diseases Act. The passage of this Act was warmly welcomed by the medical superintendent of the North Battleford Mental Hospital, who in his report for that year stated that he was "pleased to note that the legislation takes into account that a disease process is being dealt with, rather than a criminal prosecution." Even so, the vast majority of committals were still under legal order.

The next set of major developments in the medicalization of psychiatry in Saskatchewan came in 1930. In that year, a training programme was instituted for mental hospital attendants, and a psychopathic ward for the early treatment of cases of mental illness was opened in Regina General Hospital. The psychopathic ward, although a significant step toward the medicalization of psychiatry, remained a minor subcurrent in the treatment of the mentally ill for the next thirty years. The training programme for attendants also failed to make much of an impact on the treatment of the mentally ill. This was partly because the training programmes themselves were sporadic and inconsistent among institutions and from year to year, and partly because attendants who worked twelve-hour shifts, six days a week, had little time or energy left over for lectures or studying. The establishment of an eight-hour day and a forty-eight-hour week in the mid-1940s eliminated this latter difficulty, and the establishment of a new standardized training programme in 1947 helped solve the former. It was in 1947 that attendants took the name psychiatric nurses. The creation of the new occupation of psychiatric nursing in Saskatchewan was heralded throughout North America as a watershed in the treatment of the mentally ill. This was because psychiatric nurses were employed in the provision of active treatment intended to increase discharge rates. This clearly did away with custodialism, the most prison-like and least medical characteristic of mental hospitals. The new occupation of psychiatric nursing was obviously

successful in its therapeutic activities, as is evidenced by the fact that mental hospital populations began to decrease. It is worth noting that this decrease predates the introduction of psychotropic drugs in the early 1950s. As we saw, it was during the 1930s and 1940s that psychiatry also began to develop many of its more medical treatments, including psychosurgery, insulin shock therapy, metrazol shock therapy, and ECT.

These therapeutic developments, of course, helped integrate psychiatry into the mainstream of medical practice by allowing psychiatrists to treat mental diseases in the same way as other physicians treated physical diseases, namely, through surgery and the prescription of drugs. This process of integration was further advanced by the establishment of a Department of Psychiatry in the Medical College at the University of Saskatchewan in Saskatoon in 1954. At the same time, the provincial Department of Public Health established a psychiatric research unit in the province, which also helped to integrate psychiatry into the mainstream of scientific medicine.

The continued existence of the large, remote mental hospitals as the primary locus of psychiatric treatment, however, perpetuated the isolation of psychiatry from the mainstream of medicine. Thus, in the mid-1950s, plans to construct a third large, 1200-bed mental hospital in Saskatoon were abandoned and replaced with a plan to build a number of small, community-based mental hospitals throughout the province. This came to be known as the Saskatchewan Plan.

THE SASKATCHEWAN PLAN

Provincial psychiatrists thought a number of small, community-based mental hospitals, integrated with general hospitals and institutions for the aged, would not only allow them to improve the quality of treatment, it would also further the goal of medicalizing psychiatric practice. In order to persuade the provincial government to finance this ambitious plan, the province's psychiatrists undertook to secure both professional endorsement. and to generate popular support for the plan. Both strategies were successful. Endorsement of the plan, or of similar plans, appeared in various professional journals and in position papers of the World Health Organization. Popular support was demonstrated through the emergence of a powerful grass-roots movement in the form of the Canadian Mental Health Association (CMHA). The CMHA was a strong advocate of the Saskatchewan Plan, and this support often assumed the form of criticism of the conditions in provincial mental hospitals. Not surprisingly, this resulted in conflict with the provincial government, which, although not opposed to the principle of small, community-based mental hospitals, was unwilling to assume the substantial financial burden such a course of action would entail. It was for this reason also that no amount of professional support and advocacy would persuade the government to go ahead with the plan. This resulted in much conflict between the government and provincial psychiatrists working for the Department of Public Health, who saw the implementation of the Saskatchewan Plan as essential for their professional and career interests.

As stated above, the provincial government was not opposed to the principle of the Saskatchewan Plan and therefore, it joined provincial psychiatrists and other advocates of this plan in lobbying the federal government to include services provided in such institutions as shareable costs under the proposed Hospital and Diagnostic Services Act. When this legislation was enacted in 1957, it specifically excluded psychiatric services provided in mental hospitals, regardless of size. It included as shareable costs, however, psychiatric services provided in general hospitals. This sounded the death knell for the Saskatchewan Plan, and at the same time laid the foundation for the rapid expansion of general hospital psychiatry. One would think that this later development would be enthusiastically welcomed by psychiatrists who had been struggling for decades to integrate their practice with the mainstream of medicine. Ironically, this was not the case. Psychiatrists in the public sector, for example, saw the expansion of general hospital psychiatry as a threat to their career interests, and therefore opposed it. For example, the following statement, made by the Director of Saskatchewan's Psychiatric Services, was reported in the *Saskatoon Star-Phoenix* 21 January 1958: ". . . psychiatric wings in general hospitals have set back by 10 years treatment of mental illness." Such protests, however, were ineffective.

Two further developments in the next few years signalled the successful medicalization of psychiatry. The first was the passage of the Mental Health Act in 1961. This Act, modelled on the 1959 British Mental Health Act, made mental hospital admission and discharge procedures the same as those of general hospitals, and consequently made the disposition of the mentally ill predominantly a medical prerogative. The second development was the establishment of a medical care insurance plan in Saskatchewan which included payment for psychiatric services provided both by psychiatrists and by general practitioners on an outpatient basis. The medicalization of psychiatry throughout the rest of Canada was assured when Dr. D.G. McKerracher, Professor of Psychiatry at the University of Saskatchewan, recommended in his report to the Hall Commission in 1964 that general hospital psychiatry be developed and fostered through the proposed national medicare plan. These recommendations were entrenched in 1966 when medicare was introduced on a national level, and they established the conditions upon which a flourishing private-sector psychiatry developed. Guaranteed payment meant that psychiatrists and general practitioners providing psychiatric services no longer had to worry about receiving payment for services rendered. For many physicians, this made the provision of office-based and outpatient psychiatric services economically feasible for the first time. Thus, since the mid-1960s, there has been rapid growth in the number of psychiatric services provided by physicians on a fee-for-service basis (see Figure 1).

Figure 1: Estimated Rate of Psychiatric Services Provided by Physicians on a Fee-for-Service Basis, Saskatchewan, 1963 to 1985–86

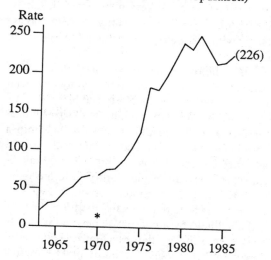

(Services per 1000 Covered Population)

* Change in definition from: "Visit services, consultations, and hospital care rendered in connection with psychiatry or counselling as well as special procedures by a psychiatrist" to "included treatment interviews, group therapy, and counselling."

Source: Medical Care Insurance Commission Annual Reports, 1963 through 1985–86.

At the same time, there was a rapid increase in discharge rates from mental hospitals. This corresponded to a dramatic decrease in the population of mental hospitals, as we saw in Table 1. Saskatchewan, for example, went from one of the highest mental hospital populations per capita to one of the lowest. Smith (1979:114) referring to the reduction in patient numbers at the Weyburn mental hospital between 1962 and 1966, states that it was "probably the most rapid reduction anywhere of a mental hospital population," dropping within that time period from 1478 to 501. By 1971, the mental hospital at Weyburn was closed and replaced by a sixty-three-bed psychiatric centre, and by 1984 the total inpatient population in the province had fallen to 204 persons from a 1944 high of about 4200.

Interestingly, the newly created private-sector psychiatrists opposed the depopulation and phasing out of the mental hospitals because it limited their access to inpatient beds. The provincial government, however, was committed to restricting admissions to inpatient facilities as part of their commitment to cost reduction. The medical profession, far from being unified, was split along a number of dimensions: psychiatrists in private practice opposed the phasing-out of provincial mental hospitals because the reduced availability of inpatient beds threatened their livelihood; government-employed psychiatrists opposed the creation of general hospital psychiatry for the same reason. Ultimately, however, the nature and organization of psychiatric services in this country were not decided on the basis of strictly professional criteria; rather, they were determined by political and economic considerations.

Figure 2: Changes in Psychiatric Service Patterns, Saskatchewan, 1957–1984

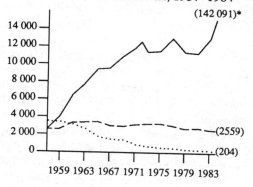

* Total number of community contacts
—— Number of community clients
- - - - Total admissions to all psychiatric facilities
. . . . . Number of patients in mental hospitals

Source: Saskatchewan Health, Annual Reports, 1980–81, 1985.

The rapid depopulation of the mental hospitals and a more rigid admissions policy meant that the number of non-medical occupations employed to provide follow-up services greatly increased and diversified. Personnel in these occupations, particularly social workers, were soon dissatisfied with the subordinate position in which medically trained psychiatrists tried to keep them. This dissatisfaction grew throughout the 1960s, reaching its peak in the early 1970s. At that time, the non-medical occupations were struggling to expand community-based services, and to challenge medical control of public-sector psychiatry. As can be seen in Figure 2, these struggles have been at least partly successful. The number of admissions to inpatient facilities, where medically trained psychiatrists tend to be dominant, has remained relatively constant, while the number of community clients seen in mental health clinics increased rapidly from about 2200 in 1957 to 14 790 in 1984. The 14 790 community psychiatry clients accounted for over 142 000 contacts in that same year. Thus we see the rapid expansion of an increasingly demedicalized, clinic-based, public-sector system of psychiatric services occurring simultaneously with the rapid expansion of a medically dominated, office- and hospital-based, private-sector system. As suggested previously, this renders problematic the claim advanced by Ralph (1983) that deinstitutionalization corresponds to the replacement of one form of social control (medical) by another (non-medical). It makes Scull's contention (1979) that decarceration involves the replacement of the asylum as an institution of social control with nothing at all completely untenable.

This institutional bifurcation was at least partly a result of the struggles of non-medical occupations for autonomy from medical domination of the psychiatric division of labour. In 1972 this challenge was led by social workers at the North Battleford mental hospital, who having recently won the right to see clients by direct referral (thereby achieving independence of medical domination and control), resented attempts by public-sector psychiatrists to revoke this right. Public-sector psychiatrists, who still occupied *all* management positions at that time, tried to re-establish their domination of the psychiatric division of labour by asserting that the

"mental health team" must be headed by a psychiatrist, since only doctors could legally prescribe medications and adequately care for the sick. The social workers countered by claiming that in community psychiatry most people were not ill. Drawing upon the work of Thomas Szasz, the social workers maintained that most community clients really only required assistance with various psychosocial "problems in living."

Psychologists, another non-medical occupation, supported the position taken by the social workers. Tensions at the North Battleford mental hospital continued to mount. The government, fearful that the situation might escalate into a political crisis, intervened on the side of the non-medical occupations by replacing the medical superintendent of the North Battleford mental hospital with a clinical psychologist. This was the first time that an administrative position had been held by a non-physician, and it clearly marked a shift in the psychiatric balance of power. In fact, we suggest that it marked the first substantive step toward the demedicalization of public-sector psychiatry.

The government, realizing that the appointment of a non-medical superintendent of the North Battleford mental hospital would not remove the underlying source of conflict, also established a special committee to look into and make recommendations concerning the distribution of power and responsibility in the psychiatric division of labour. The committee on psychiatric team structure was composed of representatives from the four principal occupations concerned: psychiatrists, social workers, psychiatric nurses, and psychologists. The basic point of contention was control of the psychiatric labour process. Psychiatrists were adamant that mental *illness* required medical treatment and, that therefore, a doctor must be in charge of the psychiatric team. Psychologists and social workers, on the other hand, allowed that while this might be valid for inpatients, it was not generally the case with community clients, who usually only required help with various psychosocial problems of daily functioning. Psychiatric nurses were somewhat ambivalent, although, on the whole, they supported the psychiatrists. It is interesting to note that these two positions encompass and reflect the basic physical-psychological dualism which has characterized psychiatry since its inception and which is derived from the ambiguity concerning the cause of mental disorders. Thus, psychiatrists emphasized the treatment of *mental illness* and the social workers and psychologists emphasized the preservation and development of *mental health*.

Table 2. Total Number of Psychiatrists, Psychologists, and Social Workers in Mental Health Services Branch of Saskatchewan as of March 31, 1970/71–1984/85

Year	Psychiatrists	Psychologists and Social Workers
1970–71	59	89
1971–72	59	92
1972–73	58	75
1973–74	54	84
1974–75	45	83
1975–76	46	85
1976–77	46	85
1977–78	45	88
1978–79	45	88
1979–80	45*	99
1980–81	43*	103
1981–82	42*	110
1982–83	42*	119
1983–84	42*	118
1984–85	42*	123

* Includes 10 Contract Positions

Source: Saskatchewan Health Annual Reports 1970/71 through 1984/85

Although the basic dualism and uncertainty regarding the cause of mental disorders has not been resolved, the struggle for control of the public-sector labour process has been resolved largely in favour of the non-medical occupations. The decrease in the number of psychia-

trists, combined with the increase in the number of non-medical occupations and programmes, is indicative of the demedicalization of public-sector psychiatry (See Table 2). A further and perhaps more significant indication of this trend is the fact that currently at least six of the eight regional directorships, as well as the position of Executive Director, are held by non-psychiatrists. This is a dramatic reversal of the situation which existed in 1970, when all administrative positions were held by psychiatrists. Another indication of this trend toward demedicalization is the fact that with the 1986 passage of a new Mental Health Services Act, the name of the provincial Psychiatric Services Branch was changed to the Mental Health Services Branch. This change of name is a moral victory for the non-medical occupations, because they have long maintained that they are concerned with preserving and promoting *mental health*, as opposed to medically trained psychiatrists, who are concerned with the treatment and cure of *mental illness*. As we saw earlier, name changes, although symbolic, may also be indicative of more fundamental shifts in interprofessional power relations, which may lead to significant changes in the nature and organization of the delivery of psychiatric services.

CONCLUSIONS

Whether the trend towards the demedicalization of psychiatry and the reduction of medical dominance will continue remains to be seen. One of the factors which strongly favours this trend, however, is cost effectiveness. Psychologists, for example, maintain that their fees for assessment and counselling are considerably lower than those charged by physicians. They convincingly claim, furthermore, that they are better trained than physicians for this type of work. They argue that in many cases physicians inappropriately medicate people who are not really ill, but who simply have problems in living. The medical prescription of tranquillizers provides a "quick fix" that does not entail the time and possible embarrassment of the more disclosive social-psychological therapies. The relative ease of the medical approach, combined with the fact that doctors constitute a powerful lobby group that is unrelenting in the defence of its perceived interests, tends to counteract the trend toward demedicalization of psychiatry. Having said this, however, it appears that the trend towards demedicalization is predominant. This trend was greatly encouraged in 1984 with the passage of the Canada Health Act, which makes services provided by various non-physicians eligible for inclusion as insured services within medicare. This greatly enhances the position of non-medical health-care occupations in their struggle for autonomy from medical domination.

The widely accepted notion that individual "lifestyles" are a prime, if not the major, cause of illness may further advance the demedicalization of both public- and private-sector psychiatry. This is because it is now universally held that illness is largely a product of people's bad habits and unhealthy lifestyles. The solution which follows from this assumption is to induce people to modify their behaviour; get them to quit smoking, drink moderately, eat a balanced diet, and exercise regularly. Behaviour modification is the domain of psychology and other occupations with social science backgrounds. Therefore, given the commitment of the federal government to this notion of disease causation, one might expect a further demedicalization of psychiatry, perhaps of health-care delivery in general. Whether this will result in better treatment for the consumers of psychiatric services is an empirical question and remains to be seen. The tendency of both the medical and the non-medical psychiatric professions to seek individualized solutions to social problems, however, leads one to suspect that most therapeutic efforts will be directed towards enabling individuals to cope with problem-producing social conditions and relations, rather than towards changing those conditions. All the psychiatric professions, whether they are medically trained or not, have an interest in perpetuating an individualistic approach to the diagnosis and treatment of mental illness/disorder — their careers depend upon it. Historical evidence leads one to suspect, therefore, that the interests and needs of psychiatric consumers will be subordinated to the needs and interests of providers of psychiatric service, whether they are medically trained or not.

STUDY QUESTIONS

1. Under what conditions can the medicalization of deviance occur? What are the limitations of this concept?

2. Is there some unique aspect of medical work that distinguishes it from other types of health-care work?

3. What is the basic dualism that characterizes notions of mental illness? What impact has this had upon the nature and organization of psychiatric practice?

4. What is the relationship between the depopulation of the asylum and the demedicalization of psychiatry?

5. What are some of the factors which might contribute to a continued demedicalization of psychiatry? What factors might restrict this process?

RECOMMENDED READING

Foucault, M. *Madness and Civilization: A History of Insanity in the Age of Reason.* New York: Vintage Books, 1973.

Scull, A. *Museums of Madness: The Social Organization of Insanity in Nineteenth-Century England.* Middlesex, England: Penguin Books, 1979.

———, ed. *Madhouses, Mad-Doctors, and Madmen: The Social History of Psychiatry in the Victorian Era.* Philadelphia: University of Pennsylvania Press, 1981.

Szasz, T. "The Myth of Mental Illness." *American Psychologist* 15 (1960): 113–18.

———, ed. *The Age of Madness.* New York: Anchor Press, 1960.

Valenstein, E. *Great and Desperate Cures: The Rise and Decline of Psychosurgery and Other Radical Treatments for Mental Illness.* New York: Basic Books, 1986.

REFERENCES

Blustein, B.E. "'A Hollow Square of Psychological Science': American Neurologists and Psychiatrists in Conflict." In *Madhouses, Mad-Doctors, and Madmen: The Social History of Psychiatry in the Victorian Era*, edited by A. Scull. Philadelphia: University of Pennsylvania Press, 1981.

Clark, M.J. "The Rejection of Psychological Approaches to Mental Disorder in Late Nineteenth-Century British Psychiatry." In *Madhouses, Mad-Doctors, and Madmen*, edited by A. Scull. Philadelphia: University of Pennsylvania Press, 1981.

Conrad, P. "On the Medicalization of Deviance and Social Control." In *Critical Psychiatry*, edited by D. Ingleby. Middlesex: Penguin Books, 1981.

Conrad, P., and J. Schneider. *Deviance and Medicalization: From Badness to Sickness.* St. Louis: Mosby Co., 1980.

Edginton, B. "Moral Treatment to Monolith: The Institutional Treatment of the Insane in Manitoba 1871–1919." Unpublished paper, Department of Sociology, University of Winnipeg, 1986.

Freidson, E. *Profession of Medicine: A Study of the Sociology of Applied Knowledge.* New York: Harper and Row, 1970.

Grob, G. *Mental Institutions in America: Social Policy to 1875.* New York: Free Press, 1973.

Illich, I. *Limits to Medicine: Medical Nemesis, The Expropriation of Health.* London: Marion Boyars, 1975.

Ralph, D. *Work and Madness: The Rise of Community Psychiatry.* Montreal: Black Rose Books, 1983.

Robertson, G. "The Hospitalization of the Scottish Asylum System." *Journal of Mental Science* 68, no. 283 (October 1922): 321–33.

Rothman, D. *The Discovery of the Asylum: Social Order in the New Republic.* Boston: Little, Brown and Co., 1971.

Saskatchewan. Department of Public Works, Annual Report, 1921–22.

———. Saskatchewan Health, Annual Reports, 1963–85.

———. Saskatchewan Hospital Services Plan, Annual Reports, 1944–85.

———. Saskatchewan Medical Care Insurance Commission, Annual Reports, 1963–85.

Saskatoon Star-Phoenix, 21 January 1958.

Scull, A. *Museums of Madness: The Social Organization of Insanity in Nineteenth-Century England.* Middlesex: Penguin Books, 1979.

————. *Decarceration, Community Treatment and the Deviant: A Radical View.* 2nd ed. Cambridge: Polity Press, 1984.

Shephard, D.A.E. *The Royal College of Physicians and Surgeons of Canada, 1960–1980: The Pursuit of Unity.* Ottawa: Royal College of Physicians and Surgeons of Canada, 1985.

Smith, C. "From Hospital to Community." *Canadian Journal of Psychiatry* 24 (1979): 113–20.

Smith, H. "Psychiatry: A Social Institution in Process." *Social Forces* 33 (1954–55): 310–16.

Statistics Canada. *Mental Health Statistics, Vols. I and III, 1937, 1942, 1947, 1952, 1957, 1962, 1967, 1972, 1977, 1980–81.* Cat. Nos. 83-204 and 83-205.

————. *Hospital Statistics, 1969–1982–83.* Cat Nos. 82-209 and 82-206.

Swazey, J. *Chlorpromazine in Psychiatry: A Study of Therapeutic Innovation.* Cambridge: MIT Press, 1974.

Szasz, T. "The Myth of Mental Illness." *American Psychologist* 15 (1960): 113–18.

Warren, C. "New Forms of Social Control: The Myth of Deinstitutionalization." *American Behavioral Scientist* 24 (1981): 724–40.

Valenstein, E. *Great and Desperate Cures: The Rise and Decline of Psychosurgery and Other Radical Treatments for Mental Illness.* New York: Basic Books, 1986.

PART VII

HEALTH CARE PROFESSIONS AND THE DIVISION OF LABOUR

INTRODUCTION

The established professions resist and oppose any perceived or actual threat to their monopolistic position either by the state or by other professions and occupations. The first two chapters in this section discuss the medical profession's opposition to midwives and chiropractors, while the dental profession's opposition to a provincial dental plan is discussed in the third chapter.

Midwifery in Canada has re-emerged in two general forms: community midwives who manage home deliveries, and nurse-midwives operating more autonomously within institutions such as hospitals or birth centres. Burtch, in Chapter 19, provides a brief outline of the historical antagonisms between traditional midwives and physicians, and of current applications of legal sanctions to birth attendants. The central theme is that provincial quasi-criminal law — such as the B.C. Medical Practitioners' Act — and the federal Criminal Code have been used to consolidate the powers of the medical profession in managing births. A related point is that the state does not act in merely an instrumental way.

A structuralist interpretation of the role of the state, and especially of its legal apparatus, is applied to current attempts to legalize midwifery practice and place it on a more autonomous footing. Burtch argues that although resistance to the midwifery movement rests upon material and ideological concerns, the public interest is also served by the consequent establishment of controlling general regulation standards of training and professional practice.

The history of the chiropractic profession is a turbulent one spanning the past 80 years. When chiropractic first emerged, orthodox medicine labelled it a "quackery" and "unscientific." However, chiropractic has survived and prospered, particularly in the past two decades. Biggs, in Chapter 20, provides an overview of the chiropractic profession in Canada, documenting the changing social, economic, and legal status of chiropractors. Since the 1960s, chiropractic has gained significant public and official recognition.

The main explanation for the survival of chiropractic has been public support, particularly by the working class. Although chiropractors have lobbied for official recognition for the past 50 years, it was not until the state became involved in the delivery of health care that chiropractors gained wide official recognition, including coverage under universal health insurance. Chiropractors were seen as providing a low-cost service which increased productivity by alleviating back injuries.

However, chiropractic has paid a price for this legitimization: it has been transformed from an alternative health system to a limited neuromuscular specialty. When chiropractic first emerged, it was opposed to orthodox medicine's narrow analysis of disease and to its monopoly over health care. Chiropractic was drawn from everyday practice, which stood in sharp contrast to the more standardized and codified body of scientific-medical knowledge. As chiropractic has become legitimized, it has been forced to adopt a scientific-rational discourse.

Croucher, in Chapter 21, describes the response of a professional association to the introduction of a government-organized children's dental care plan in Saskatchewan. This plan relied on "expanded duty" dental nurses to provide services through clinics based in the school system, working with a minimum of supervision by dentists.

In opposing this plan, the College of Dental Surgeons of Saskatchewan used an ideology containing both "parochial" and "ecumenic" elements. More stress was laid upon the "parochial" issue of the autonomy of the dentist. In this case, this referred to the need for greater supervision of the dental nurse, along with a preference for a service modelled on the existing private fee-for-service model.

By presenting these arguments, the profession overlooked the existing poor dental health of the children of Saskatchewan and the maldistribution in the supply of services.

Objective evaluations of the performance

of the Dental Plan have demonstrated the value-laden basis of the dental profession's ideology. Changes in the epidemiology of dental disease, coupled with a greater supply of dentists, have resulted in the recent "arm's-length" involvement of the profession in the Plan.

19

PROMOTING MIDWIFERY, PROSECUTING MIDWIVES:
The State and the Midwifery Movement in Canada

Brian E. Burtch
Simon Fraser University

INTRODUCTION: THE STATE AND HEALTH CARE

> We are sophisticated enough to see that the law often selects the immoralities with which it chooses to deal on a political basis. The more powerful a group is, the less its immoralities will be legally prohibited. (Wexler, 1976:358)

The status of Canadian midwives has been debated for many decades. In the past 15 years this debate has become more prominent as nurse-midwives have sought greater independence in their work, and community midwives have attended thousands of home births in various Canadian provinces. Barrington (1985:38) estimated that in 1984 just over 100 community midwives were assisting home births in Canada.

This chapter provides an overview of key developments in the contemporary midwifery movement, emphasizing the pivotal role of the state, and especially the provincial governments, since the administration of health care is within their bailiwick, as set out in the British North America Act. The Canadian state has a contradictory position here (Gavigan, 1986). On the one hand, it claims to protect the freedoms of individuals, to ensure equal justice, and to encourage certain forms of competition; on the other hand, the state has limited the freedom of women in reproductive choices, including childbirth (Currie, 1986), and has utilized the criminal sanction for abortion (Gavigan, 1984; Osborne, 1987). Another contradiction emerges with respect to the application of the medical model for pregnancy, a state which is not inherently a disease state.

The orthodox perspective on medicine is largely empirical, disease-oriented, and professional; this leads to minimal emphasis on social theory, non-organic sources of disease, and non-professional action in promoting health (Doyal, 1979). Medical research and practice are to a large extent centred on individual pathology and curative medical treatment. Heroic medicine and high-technology approaches to illness coexist, reinforcing the medical sphere: "The availability of high-technology medicine and the publicising of individual medical breakthroughs (whatever their real value) are important window-dressing in maintaining support for the existing system" (Doyal, 1979:43).

Doyal's analysis also emphasizes the imperatives of production of commodities, the entrenchment of authority relations, and the division of tasks in the health sector along lines of race, class, and gender. A similar analysis of the health-care sector is articulated by the Women's Work Project (1976:19); that is, between 75 and 85 percent of lab technicians, licensed practical nurses, and manual services aides were women, with 80 to 90 percent of the latter occupations comprised of non-white workers (1970 data from New York City hospitals). In their more general analysis of sexual stratification in the Canadian work force, Phillips and Phillips (1983) state that two features of the work force at the turn of the century are still evident: gender differentials in income (women earn approximately 60 percent of men's wages, averaged for full-time work), and the concentration of women's paid employment in specific groupings.[1]

The key to Doyal's analysis, then, is the dialectical relationship between domination and exploitation on the one hand, and changing patterns of health and health services on the other. Her analysis features a distinctly Marxist twist in its interpretation of advances in medicine and improved medical care as either (1) concessions to the working class, thereby mitigating developed class struggle, or (2) a service ultimately on behalf of a dominant class whereby the availability of a healthier, more reliable work force is ensured through health-care programmes and the like.

Spitzer (1983) reviews the emerging theories of law that move beyond simple instrumentalism and economism. Structuralism (exemplified by Althusser) and culturalism (exemplified by E.P. Thompson) are the major competing theories. Both attempt to redefine the nature of relationships among human actors, external structures, and law. A structuralist premise is that although the law is in some sense relatively autonomous, along with other superstructural features of society, the vectors of legal regulation are ultimately traced back to the economic system. The reformulation of this structuralist approach by Poulantzas (1973, 1978) involved a recognition of the role of the law as an apparatus that preserves "real rights" of dominated classes. He added the caveat that these rights are embedded within a dominant ideology.[2]

The relationship between law and the state has thus undergone a contemporary re-evaluation among Marxists and neo-Marxists. As Spitzer (1983:114–117) indicates, the shortcomings of legal economism and of structuralism have generated a more vital paradigm of law in which law arises from an "ideological pool" comprising beliefs and assumptions from all social classes. In turn, the relatively autonomous role of the state — which is not governed by the will of a dominant class but rather exercises power *against* some of its powers — reflects the contradictory nature of legal ideology and the law as practice.

Eisenstein (1981:222) portrays the state as an agency that constrains radical alternatives, including radical feminism. The structure of the state is such that it cannot allow women's equality with men. The "sexual ghetto" of lower-paid occupations is perpetrated by the state as an employer and as an arbiter of social conflicts. Through the agency of law, the state mystifies what women are and what they do; law serves to constrain people's actual options, and yet it can establish "positive rights." Eisenstein recognizes the political power of the state over women while endorsing progressive struggles to secure the recognition of the state. The implications of such struggles are developed in the next section, with specific reference to Canadian midwives.

THE MIDWIFERY MOVEMENT AND THE STATE

The practice of midwifery is a complex phenomenon in Canada and other industrialized societies. While midwifery has been defined generically as the act of attending a person in childbirth, it is better understood as an occupation. In contrast to the traditional (lay) midwife in developing countries, North American midwives include certified nurse-midwives (who tend to practise in hospitals, having completed nursing training followed by a midwifery apprenticeship), and community midwives who attend home births and are generally not members of a professional nurses' association. The techniques of practice and rigours of training vary considerably within these forms of midwifery. Nevertheless, legal regulation of birth attendance influences all forms of midwifery. This regulation is most significant for community midwives whose practice may be a violation of provincial Medical Acts and other quasi-criminal statutes, and community midwives are also more likely to be prosecuted for criminal negligence in the event of death or injury of an infant during labour or delivery.

There are important links between contemporary health-care regulations of midwives in advanced capitalist societies and the historical transformation of birth from a local, private event to a public medical matter. The perception of midwives has historically been negatively stereotypical — as witches, harridans, or meddlesome ignorant women (Donnison, 1977:28–29; Evenson, 1983:313). A closer look at contemporary midwives in a British Columbia study indicates that they are not easily categorized: midwives vary in experience, professional training, and philosophies of birthing and politics, to name only a few aspects.[3]

Common ground for midwives, however, can be determined. First, there seems to be a general agreement that pregnancy is not synonymous with disease. Morbid situations will develop, but birth can generally be managed skillfully and safely with a lower rate of obstetrical intervention, including induction and augmentation of labour, instrumental delivery via forceps or Caesarean section, and the like. Obstetrical intervention is often recast as obstetrical interference.

Second, midwives tend to agree that they could operate more autonomously than is currently provided for under provincial law (which requires the direction of a physician, or a delegation of responsibility from a physician to a non-physician, where applicable). The dependent status of midwives is thus generally seen as contrived, and not associated with legitimate differences in skills between physicians and trained midwives in the management of uncomplicated pregnancies. This dependent relationship is often linked with the economic interest of physicians in attending births and the sense of control that physicians, especially male physicians, can exert over parturient patients and the nursing staff that assist doctors in childbirth care (See Buckley, 1979; Oakley, 1984).

Third, women's right to be informed and to make decisions about maternity care is vital to the midwifery debate. Women should have some say in the location and the manner of birth.

Fourth, the question of iatrogenic (physician-induced) practice is often brought forward. Reliance on such procedures as the lithotomy (prone) delivery position, use of drugs to induce labour and to relieve pain, lack of continuity of care (through the prenatal period, labour, delivery, and after birth), and the overarching ideology that birth is essentially a medical event are all seen as factors contributing to substandard maternity care.

Differences within the movement occur at various points. First, there is an ongoing debate over the importance of nursing training as a prerequisite to midwifery training. Some favour direct entry into a midwifery programme that incorporates some aspects of orthodox nursing curricula, while others maintain that formal criteria are not a necessary condition for midwifery practice. Second, there has been a movement toward establishing guidelines (or standards) for practice. Some midwives' associations discourage their members from managing breech deliveries at home, or insist that women should be transported to hospital if twins are suspected, if amniotic fluid is stained with meconium, or in other atypical circumstances. Others believe that automatic contraindications to midwifery management in domiciliary births are unnecessary and should be left to the midwives' judgement. Another point of disagreement involves the necessity of midwives working with physicians and the delegation of ultimate responsibility for maternal and infant welfare to physicians (e.g., College of Nurses of Ontario, 1983). The counter-position is that midwives should be allowed to work independently of physicians, at least in cases of uncomplicated deliveries (Van Wagner, 1984).

The author's fieldwork on midwifery in British Columbia allows a few impressions on the implementation of midwife attendance. First, community midwives are able to use a variety of resources in conducting their work. There are legal resources available to them through legal advice, sometimes involving litigation, sometimes not. Likewise, there are legal defences available to midwife-defendants. As demonstrated by recent criminal prosecutions of the Halifax midwives and a birth attendant in Victoria (see below), these defences have been suc-cessfully employed against criminal charges. The various court-situated contests over midwifery and birth-related issues have been accompanied by some political support from opposition parties. In Ontario and British Columbia, for example, the provincial New Democratic Parties — through caucus or private members' bills — have supported the legalization of midwifery in their provinces (Cooke, 1984; Stephens, 1984). The National Action Status on the Committee of Women also passed a resolution in 1984 in support of midwifery legalization in Canada (Sweet, 1985). Second, many practising midwives are aided by the material and emotional support of "significant others" — spouses, other midwives, neighbours, family members — which allows them to practise midwifery alongside other responsibilities of income, child care, and the like. Third, opportunities for counter-hegemonic powers are evident. In one instance, recounted to the author by a Lower Mainland midwife, the threat of prosecution for the unlawful practice of midwifery under the Medical Practitioners Act was not followed through, ostensibly because as a politicized midwife she was prepared to muster considerable support in defence of community midwifery (Burtch, 1986).

Fourth, midwives do work in conjunction with sympathetic physicians and other personnel with respect to backup and transfers of women into hospital. Fifth, midwives utilize various forms of medical technology (oxygen for resuscitation, sutures) and a variety of communications devices (the telephone, message recorders, "beepers") to contact fellow midwives, clients, and other concerned parties.

Two other resources that community midwives have developed are media exposure (through letter-writing campaigns to newspapers and contributions to such periodicals as *The Maternal Health News*) and fee increases for birth attendance. The latter resource is especially important in light of the relatively low incomes generated by community midwifery and the economic strain on family earnings. Apparently, the "service" orientation of the mid-1970s has been succeeded by higher fees (approximately $600 for prenatal, labour and delivery, and postnatal care).

These resources must be placed in a larger context of midwifery containment. *Community midwives* remain liable to quasi-criminal prosecution for the unlawful practice of midwifery. They are occasionally faced with the real possibility of criminal prosecution, their personal incomes are far below those of physicians and below those of obstetrical nurses working full-time. *Nurse-midwives* face constraints under the existing law and the policy position of their College and the College of Physicians and Surgeons. Recent initiatives to establish midwifery on a more autonomous footing required the unpaid involvement of nursing professionals on the Low-Risk Clinic in Vancouver. There has also been a reluctance to recognize midwives as midwives, since midwifery is seen as a physicians' monopoly under current legislation.

LEGAL CONSTRAINTS ON MIDWIFERY

The practice of midwifery is, for the most part, both constrained and facilitated by its legal status. A key element in the involvement of the state — through its legal powers — in what was previously a localized, neighbourhood event in North America, has been the assumption that midwifery practice is more hazardous than physicians' attendance. A related assumption is that midwives require supervision by physicians although legislation such as the Midwives' Act in England has established a basis for self-regulation by midwives to a considerable degree. A further assumption of liberal democratic theory is that legal constraints on midwives stem from a public consensus on the appropriateness of restricted birth practices. This includes broad powers of medical practice and self-regulation with respect to medical events. In contrast, there has been a counter-interpretation of medical power as the securing of powerful interests, rather than protection of the general interest in health-related events.

Unlawful Practice of Medicine: Quasi-Criminal Sanctions

The civil status of lay midwives and nurse-midwives in Canada has, with few exceptions, served to limit their practice. In nineteenth-century Ontario, for instance, the right to practise midwifery independently of legislation governing the practice of physic or surgery gradually gave way to the monopolization of childbirth attendance by medical personnel. It is noteworthy that the initial, statutory monopoly status gave way to an explicit recognition of the right of women in Upper Canada to practise midwifery without a licence. Moreover, even as this legislation reintroduced the ban on lay midwifery, enforcement was problematic due to the limited number of doctors and the lack of doctors in what was then a predominantly rural region (Biggs, 1983). Specifically, Section 49 of the Ontario Medical Act held that:

> It shall not be lawful for any person not registered to practise medicine, surgery or midwifery for hire, gain, or hope of reward, and if any person not registered pursuant to this Act, for hire, gain or hope of reward practises or professes to practise medicine, surgery, or midwifery, he shall, upon summary conviction thereof before any Justice of the Peace, for every such offence, pay a penalty not exceeding $100 nor less than $25.

An important qualification at this point in legal regulation was that the alleged illegal practices must in fact trench on medical practice, and that isolated episodes would not sustain a conviction. As J.A. Garrow indicated in *Re Ontario Medical Act* (1906:513),

> The thing practised must, to be illegal, be an invasion of similar things taught and practised by the regular practitioner, otherwise it does not affect the monopoly, and is outside the statute. And it must be practised as the regular practitioner would do it — that is, for gain, and after diagnosis and advice. And it must be more than a mere isolated instance, which is sufficient to prove a "practice."

The obligation to prove more than a single act had been upheld in a number of precedents. In *Regina v. Whelan* (1900) the conviction of a

Toronto midwife under Section 49 of the Ontario Medical Act was reversed on appeal. The Appeal Court found that the Crown had not established that the midwife had practised medicine on more than one occasion, and further that she had not always received financial gain through her actions. The necessity to prove that financial gain was received and that the illegal practice of medicine occurred repeatedly was crucial in the acquittal of the accused in *Regina v. Armstrong* (1911). The judge held:

> Before an accused person can be convicted of falsely pretending to heal the sick, it is necessary that it be shown that the accused was in the habit of so pretending, or at least that there had been continuous treatment, the principle being the same as practising medicine for gain or hope of reward. An isolated case is not sufficient to secure a conviction.

Subsequently, in *Regina v. Cruikshanks* (1914) Justice Simmons confirmed that a single act does not constitute the practice of medicine or a trade.

Nonetheless, as the state has deliberated over birth-related law, the criterion for an offence has been broadened. In Ontario, the common-law rule that "practice" implied repetition of the offending act was altered such that proof of performance of a *single* act in the practice of medicine on one occasion was deemed sufficient to establish the practice of medicine. Another criminal conviction of a midwife in the Northwest Territories was also quashed. In *Rondeau* (1903) the Court held that Section 60 of the Medical Profession Ordinance did not include "midwifery" as a form of practice to be covered along with "medicine" and "surgery." Accordingly, since Section 60 had been composed with reference to the earlier Ontario Medical Act — which prohibited midwifery, medical, and surgical practice by unregistered persons, the Court overturned the conviction.

Legal prohibitions on the practice of medicine thus serve to protect unregistered practitioners to a degree. In a more recent case than the above, an orderly accused of practising midwifery and with practising medicine, both for "hope of reward," was acquitted on both counts. The Court held that the accused orderly had assisted a woman following delivery when no doctor was available to her; that is, he acted under emergency circumstances and did not attempt to charge for his attendance. On the second count, although the accused had on two occasions filled in blank prescription forms, taken patients' temperatures, and given instructions as to treatment, there was no proof of payment or of request for payment by the orderly (*Regina v. Ornavowski*, 1941).

Reference to case law also reveals the opposite effect: persons practising medicine on more than one occasion, and seeking payment for their advice, could be convicted as in *Provincial Medical Board v. Bond* (1890) in Nova Scotia. About two decades later, in a case heard in Saskatchewan, Justice Trant declared that the rights of unregistered practitioners are limited and sharply defined. They must not offer diagnosis, give advice, or prescribe medicines (*Regina v. Raffenberg*, 1909).

The status of Canadian midwives is either unsettled or illegal, with the exception of trained midwives who act as obstetrical nurses, under the supervision of a physician, or nurses who work in remote regions of Canada.

Figure 1 (from Barrington, 1985:140–41) provides an overview of the legal status of midwives.

The practice of midwifery in British Columbia is legally protected as the bailiwick of medical practitioners. Section 72 of the provincial Medical Practitioners' Act stipulates that:

> (1) A person who practises or offers to practise medicine while not registered or while suspended from practice under this Act commits an offence. (2) For the purposes of and without restricting the generality of subsection (1), a person practises medicine who ... (d) prescribes or administers a treatment or performs surgery, *midwifery* or an operation or manipulation, or supplies or applies an apparatus or appliance for the cure, treatment or prevention of a human disease, ailment, deformity, defect or injury... (British Columbia, 1979, emphasis added).

Figure 1. Legal Status of (Non-Physician) Midwives in Canada

Province or Territory	Relevant Legislation	Definition of Practising Medicine	Delegated Powers Re: Midwives	Licensing, Legal Status of Practising Midwives
Newfoundland (& Labrador)	*Midwifery Act* c.235, s.3, s.5(1), s.10			Midwives licensed by Newfoundland Midwifery Board. Legal. Few midwives currently licensed.
Nova Scotia	*Medical Act* s.1(d)(c), s.13, s.37(i), s.40(1)(a)(b), s.40(2).	Includes obstetrics but no mention of midwifery.	College of Physicians not authorized to issue any special licences to midwives.	No mechanism for licensing. Legal/illegal status debatable.
New Brunswick	*Medical Act* 1958. c.74, s.2(1)(c)(d)(e), s.24(1)(a)(b), s.26(k).	A provision states that restrictions on practising medicine do not apply to midwives attending confinements.		No regulation or licensing requirements. No restrictions on midwifery practice. Not illegal.
Prince Edward Island	*Medical Act* M-8, S.27, S.29(2), S.43.	Undefined. Interpreted therefore as common law definition, likely to include obstetrics.	College not authorized to issue special licences.	No mechanism for licensing. Legal/illegal status debatable.
Quebec	*Medical Act* c.46, s.1(c)(d), s.29, s.19(a), s.41(c).	Includes attendance at confinements.	Bureau of Physicians may regulate study and practice of obstetrics by midwives. Has never drafted such regulations.	Likely illegal.
Ontario	*Health Disciplines Act* 1974. c.47, s.1(e), s.45(1)(b), s.50, s.52(1)(a).	Includes obstetrics but the word midwifery removed at last revision.	Council of the College of Physicians can regulate and license midwives. Has not done so.	Legal/illegal status debatable.
Manitoba	*Medical Act* S.M. 1964. c.29.s.1, s.2(2), s.3, s.14(2), s.32, s.46.	Includes the word midwifery.		No provisions for licensing or elective practice of midwifery. Probably illegal.
Saskatchewan	*Medical Professions' Act* M-10, s.2, s.28(1), s.29, s.59, s.70(a)(i), s.75.	Defined by statute to include midwifery.		Likely illegal.
Alberta	*Medical Professions' Act* 1975. c.26, s.1(a)(d)(e), s.18(2), s.23(1)(2)(3), s.26(1), s.64(1)(a), (4), s.66(1).	Includes practice of obstetrics.	Council of the College of Physicians may keep special register for midwives. No midwives are on the Special Register.	Unlicensed midwife may practise where there is no registered practitioner. Otherwise legal/illegal status debatable.
British Columbia	*Medical Practitioners' Act.* c.254, s.71, s.72, s.74, s.84.	Includes midwifery.	Council of the College of Physicians determines qualifications for registrants. Has not registered any midwives.	Likely illegal.
Northwest Territories	*Medical Profession Ordinance* M-10, s.2(b), s.3, s.12, s.13, s.33(1)(b)(i).	Includes obstetrics.	To register, a practitioner must qualify for registration in a province. No midwives so registered.	Legal/illegal status debatable.
Yukon Territory	*Medical Profession Ordinance.* R.O.A58, c.73, s.2(1), 2.8, s.9(1), s.12(1), s.20(1)(b)(j).		To register, a practitioner requires degree from approved medical school.	Legal/illegal status debatable.

Source: Barrington, Eleanor. *Midwifery is Catching*, Toronto: NC Press, 1985. Pp. 140–141.

One episode in which an alternative practitioner (*not* a midwife) was acquitted has been documented in Alberta. In *Regina v. Wong* (1979) the court held that the art of acupuncture was not recognized by the Alberta College of Physicians and Surgeons as a branch of medicine; moreover, acupuncture was not taught in North American medical education. A later conviction of an acupuncturist in B.C. occurred, however, despite the reasoning in *Wong*.

Under Section 83 of the Medical Practitioners' Act the minimum penalty for a first offence for practising medicine or midwifery when unregistered is set at $100 or imprisonment (Section 87); this rises to $300 or imprisonment for a second conviction, and imprisonment only for a third or subsequent conviction.[4] Under Section 73 there are several exceptions to the broad ambit of medical practice set out under Section 72. Specifically, the following practitioners do not practise unlawfully while registered under their respective Acts: chiropractors, dentists, naturopaths, optometrists, pharmacists, podiatrists, psychologists, nurses, and dental technicians. Orthoptic technicians, physiotherapists, and dieticians may also be exempt from Section 72. Emergency procedures are permitted under the Health Emergency Act, domestic administration of family remedies is permitted, and religious practitioners "who practise the religious tenets of their church without pretending a knowledge of medicine or surgery" are exempted under Section 74 of the Act.

Liabilities associated with childbirth become even more complex when one considers the liabilities of parents. In the United States the parents' duty of care has traditionally begun with the birth of a child: there has been no obligation on the part of the mother, for instance, to seek medical assistance prior to the birth of a child. Nevertheless, there appears to be a shift in legal opinion whereby parental failure to obtain medical care in circumstances where such care is clearly warranted ought to be culpable (see Annas, 1978:180). Parental liability is also an issue with respect to responsibility surrounding midwifery attendance in jurisdictions where it is illegal. On one level, Klein (1980:6) indicates that the choice of a birth setting — and, by extension, the choice of birth attendants — is the responsibility of the expectant mother. The Freemont Birth Collective linked their philosophy of parental responsibility and decision-making with a non-hierarchical approach to birth management:

> Working as a team throughout pregnancy and labor, prospective parents and workers all share in the responsibility for the situation. The woman who is pregnant or in labor, and her support people, are the ones who ultimately make the decisions about what to do, how to proceed. Especially because we're not certified in any way, we're concerned that people analyze their level of comfort working with us. We encourage people to educate themselves as much as possible, consult the statistics we have kept, ask us lots of questions, talk to others who have experienced obstetrical care in other settings, and to make conscious decisions to really think about what they want and to make intelligent judgments. (1977:20)

Control over birthing decisions, including who may attend births, can be tied with a general ideological framework of resistance to patriarchy's control over women, and especially its fear of women's power.[5] On another level, legal actions are conventionally brought against the birth attendant, not the expectant mother. This locus of responsibility avoids a direct confrontation with parental rights, at the same time locating the legal conflict as essentially a property dispute pertaining to occupational licensure.

The wide ambit of medicine today corresponds to structuralist imagery of social control: herein the mechanics of touch, palpation, measuring, listening to the pregnant woman or the baby may be construed as the province of licensed physicians or licensed midwives exclusive of parental preferences or the right of women to attend births. A crucial point here is that the consolidation of the "medical gaze" (Foucault, 1973) as a superior method of health care is realized, in part, through legal prohibition and prosecution.

Criminal Prosecution of Birth Attendants

The criminal prosecution of midwives, while less prevalent than quasi-criminal actions launched against midwives, is nonetheless crucial to an understanding of legal encumbrances on midwives: criminal prosecution carries the possibility of severe dispositions, including life imprisonment in Canada in cases involving criminal negligence causing death (Bourque, 1980); moreover, criminal actions appear to be increasing as home birth has become more prominent in recent decades.

A case in point in British Columbia is the prosecution and acquittal of a spiritual healer (and former doctor) on a charge of criminal negligence causing death. In *Regina v. Marsh*, an infant death was attributed to cerebral haemorrhage due to a tear in the tentorium of the skull. This tear was associated with birth trauma, according to the autopsy report (Proceedings at Trial, Oct. 11, 1979:64).

The legal actions which followed this infant death were twofold. First, a charge of criminal negligence causing death was eventually laid against the birth attendant, a former physician who had been dropped from the rolls of the College of Physicians and Surgeons of British Columbia. Second, a quasi-criminal action alleging that her actions contravened the British Columbia Medical Practitioners Act was successfully brought against the defendant (McIntyre, 1983).

Margaret Marsh was acquitted of a charge of criminal negligence causing death. In his Reasons for Judgement, Judge Millward (1980) stated:

Mrs. Marsh first became aware of the unusual and dangerous position of the child when the first foot appeared. By then, the evidence clearly shows it was too late to save the child from the injury that it suffered, or at least on the evidence, it is most unlikely, given the situation, that is, a lack of skilled personnel present, the distance in time and space from the hospital, and the lack of any previous arrangements having been made . . . On that finding, and with reference to the acts or omissions of Mrs. Marsh from the point in time when the foot first emerged, there cannot be a finding of criminal negligence causing death arising out of those acts or omissions, and accordingly, if any criminal liability is to be attached, it must be found in her acts or omissions prior to that point in time. . . . a most important point, in my view, is that there is no evidence whatever of any doubt, in the mind of Mrs. Marsh as to the position of the child at that point.

Accordingly, while Mrs. Marsh may have been incompetent, yet I am faced with the evidence of eminent authorities called both by the Crown and by the Defence, to the effect that even the most expert and experienced practitioners do make mistakes from time to time in detecting the position of fetuses in circumstances similar to those which were obtained here.

I am faced with that clear evidence and a total lack of any positive evidence of a wanton or willful disregard. I am unable to conclude that any act or omission of Mrs. Marsh, prior to the emergence of the foot was indeed negligent, and certainly I am unable to conclude that it was criminally negligent.

Since the 1980 decision in *Marsh*, three midwives faced criminal prosecution in Halifax. The three defendants were charged with criminal negligence causing bodily harm on January 27, 1983 following the transfer of an infant to hospital. This charge was later raised in the summer of 1983, a few weeks after the infant's life support system was disconnected, to criminal negligence causing death.

At a preliminary inquiry to determine whether the defendants would be brought to trial, Judge Gunn decided that the women would not be brought to trial due to lack of evidence. Witnesses at the preliminary inquiry made three key observations: first, that the infant suffered a haemorrhage to the portion of the brain that governed breathing; second, that this injury was not attributable to the midwives' care; and third, that similar injuries have been noted among babies delivered in hospital settings under medical care (Alternative Birth Crisis Coalition, 1984).

The 1986 trial of midwives Gloria LeMay and Mary Sullivan resulted in conviction. This trial represented a break from the tradition of acquittal of midwife-defendants in criminal law in Canada. In finding the defendants guilty of criminal negligence causing death, following recent attempts to assist at a home birth on May 8, 1985, the trial judge concluded that they failed to use reasonable knowledge, skill, and care in managing the birth (Edge, 1986; Mate, 1987). The midwives were each given a suspended sentence, placed on probation for two years, and obliged to perform 200 hours of community service.

Canadian case law reveals few instances in which charges of criminal negligence causing death have been brought against doctors attending births. In *Simard* (1964) the initial conviction of a physician for criminal negligence was quashed on appeal to the Quebec Court of Queen's Bench. The newborn child died of a cerebral haemorrhage a few days following delivery by forceps; however, the appeal judges clearly felt that the facts of the case did not warrant the jury finding of guilt. These facts included the wish of the mother to not be delivered in a hospital but rather at a clinic, her failure to follow Dr. Simard's suggestion of an X-ray for suspected cephalo-pelvic disproportion, and the mother's early departure from the clinic against the doctor's advice. The Court also accepted expert testimony vindicating the use of chloroform and forceps, and rejected contrary opinion on this point.

Civil Suits against Birth Attendants

Malpractice suits against physicians are proportionately fewer on a per capita basis in Canada than in the United States. Coburn (1980:14) reported that while 20 000 malpractice suits were launched in the United States in one year, only 200 to 300 were initiated in Canada. MacIsaac (1976:204), using data from the Canadian Medical Protective Association, reported that between 1966 and 1970 the number of monetary settlements against its members averaged 18 per year; in 1971, only 22 monetary settlements resulted from 131 writs against its mem-

bers. Coburn goes on to suggest that judges in Canada are generally sympathetic to physicians because of a common status. This notion of class affinity is developed further in Miliband (1973), with respect to the British judiciary, and Olsen (1980) makes a similar point. At the same time, there is little evidence of civil suits launched against community midwives by their clients. It is noteworthy, however, that as American nurse-midwives have become established as professionals in institutional (hospital and clinic) settings, they are now increasingly subject to malpractice actions (Sinquefield, 1983).

CONCLUSIONS

There is ample evidence to support the viewpoint that dominant groups invoke their powers to exclude competing groups and that exclusory tactics are intimately connected with powers legitimated by the state (see Giddens, 1982). Approximately 99 percent of births in British Columbia now occur in hospital settings (Tonkin, 1981:11). Hospital-based birth attendance is either directed by physicians or, less commonly, responsibility may be delegated to nursing personnel. Physicians' incomes (on average) remain well above average incomes for North Americans, while as a rule midwives' incomes are markedly lower, especially with respect to community midwifery.

Nevertheless, the available material on midwifery practice in Canada and preliminary data collected by the author reflected initiatives to counter the dominant status of hospital-based obstetrics. Indeed, as has been noted above, attempts to use the courts to prosecute midwives under the Criminal Code have not always been successful. Even quasi-judicial hearings, such as coroners' inquests, do not automatically reinforce the authority of medical control over birth. Two recent coroners' inquiries in Ontario recommended legal recognition of midwives and the establishment of a provincial school of midwifery (Ontario Association of Midwives and the Nurse-Midwives' Association of Ontario, 1983:4).

Legal struggles and the continuing dominance of physician authority in Canadian maternity care touch directly on Balbus's (1978:77) criticism of Western legal ideology for its adherence to formal, abstract equality of citizens despite substantive inequalities before the law. If midwifery is taken as one instance of a "rights struggle," Sumner's (1981) call for further struggles seems apropos, as does Beirne and Sharlet's (1980) observation that struggles for such rights as the right to abortion, prisoners' rights, redress of racial and sexual discrimination, and so forth are to be encouraged.

Theoretically, some have favoured "democratic relativism" (Feyerabend, 1980) as a means of protecting unorthodox forms of medicine and healing and thereby permitting comparisons of the various forms of health care. The point remains that implementation of such a thoroughly pluralistic ideal has not been secured in Western public policy (McRae, 1979). The presence of these specific struggles in maternity care should not overshadow the continuing protection of professional attendance and medical dominance in the Canadian context and elsewhere.

A key point is the yawning gap between the demonstrated ability of midwives to manage uncomplicated deliveries — often with birth outcomes superior to those associated with conventional medical attendance in North America — and the persistence of legal controls that buttress the professional dominance of obstetricians and general practitioners. By vesting policing powers with the Medical Colleges, and through the occasional prosecution of alternative practitioners, the implementation of safe, pluralistic maternity care services remains greatly constrained. As indicated above, however, the rekindling of more autonomous midwifery in community settings and in hospitals is tied with a measure of human agency; so also is the continuing practice of midwifery through limitations on the state and the medical profession.

NOTES

1. See also Eisenstein (1981:209) regarding the low proportion of U.S. women in professional occupations such as law and medicine. The partial segregation of women into occupational groupings — in the health sector and other sectors — is thus linked with market forces. These forces in turn reinforce patriarchal elements in the economy, yet these relations of production in capitalist countries also carry benefits for women, including increased income and consumption levels, greater mobility, and personal independence (Lim, 1983:83).

2. Many contemporary scholars have grappled with the theoretical and practical implications of retaining parliamentary democracy and the rule of law. For a review of some problems associated with idealist and materialist approaches, see Sumner (1981).

3. An elaboration of midwifery practice in B.C. is available in Barrington (1985) and Burtch (1987).

4. It must be kept in mind that the court has the power to dismiss charges against defendants when the information is insufficient. In one instance where a defendant was charged under the British Columbia Medical Act the information alleging the unlawful practice of medicine was quashed. The evidence failed to set forth the act or acts constituting the alleged offences and failed to name the persons with whom the defendant was alleged to have unlawfully practised medicine (Regina v. Kripps, 1977).

5. Gordon and Hunter (1977/78:12) define patriarchy as "a specific organization of the family and society, in which heads of families controlled not only the reproductive labor, but also the production of all family members."

STUDY QUESTIONS

1. Discuss reasons why Canada is the only industrialized nation which has not legally recognized midwifery as an occupation.

2. How have historical restrictions on the licensure of health practitioners affected Canadian midwives? Consider the *number* of midwives now operating autonomously in Canada and the degree to which their work can be criminalized or otherwise regulated.

3. Reconsider stereotypical images of midwifery, especially surrounding competency of midwives and infant safety. Whose interests are served by the charge of "meddlesome midwifery"?

4. Outline possible contradictions between patients' interests and professional interests in maternity care.

5. What does the instance of midwifery lobbying suggest with respect to the place of human agency in political struggles? To what extent is innovation possible? To what extent are alternative measures in health care structured by the state and the professions?

RECOMMENDED READING

Arney, William Ray. *Power and the Profession of Obstetrics*. Chicago: University of Chicago Press, 1982.

Buckley, Suzann. "Ladies of Midwives? Efforts to Reduce Infant and Maternal Mortality." In *A Not Unreasonable Claim: Women and Reform in Canada, 1880s–1920s*, edited by Linda Kealey, 231–52. Toronto: Women's Press, 1979.

DeVries, Raymond. *Regulating Birth: Midwives, Medicine, and the Law*. Philadelphia: Temple University Press, 1985.

Donnison, Jean. *Midwives and Medical Men: A History of InterProfessional Rivalries and Women's Rights*. London: Schocken, 1977.

Doyal, Lesley, with Imogen Pennell. *The Political Economy of Health*. London: Pluto Press, 1979.

Mehl, Louis, Gail Peterson, Michael Whitt, and Warren Howes. "Outcomes of Elective Home Births: A Series of 1,146 Cases." *Journal of Reproductive Medicine* 19, no. 5 (1977): 281–90.

Oakley, Ann. *The Captured Womb: A History of the Medical Care of Pregnant Women*. London: Oxford, 1983.

Spitzer, Steven. "Marxist Perspectives in the Sociology of Law." *Annual Review of Sociology* 9 (1983): 103–24.

REFERENCES

Alternative Birth Crisis Coalition. "News Analysis: Canada Midwives on Trial." *ABCC News* 111, no. 3 (1984): 304.

Anderson v. Chasney and Sisters of St. Joseph, 1949. 2 W.W.R. 337, 57 Man. R. 343, (1949) 4 D.L.R. 71, reversing in part (1948) 4 D.L.R. 458. Affirmed 1950 4 D.L.R. 223 (Can.).

Annas, George. "Homebirth: Autonomy vs. Safety." *Hastings Center Report* 8 (1978): 19–20.

Arney, William Ray. *Power and the Profession of Obstetrics*. Chicago: University of Chicago Press, 1982.

Badinter, Elisabeth. *The Myth of Motherhood: An Historical View of the Maternal Instinct*. London: Souvenir Press, 1981.

Balbus, Isaac. "Commodity Form and Legal Form: An Essay on the 'Relative Autonomy' of Law." *Law and Society Review* 2 (1978): 571–88.

Barrington, Eleanor. *Midwifery is Catching*. Toronto: NC Press, 1985.

Beirne, Piers, and Robert Sharlet. *Pashukonis: Selected Writing on Marxism and Law*. London: Academic Press, 1980.

Biggs, C. Lesley. "The Case of the Missing Midwives: A History of Midwifery in Ontario from 1795–1900." *Ontario History* 75 (1983): 21–35.

Blackburn, Robin, ed. *Ideology in Social Science*. London: Fontana/Collins, 1972.

Bourque, Paul. "Proof of the Cause of Death in a Prosecution for Criminal Negligence Causing Death." *Criminal Law Quarterly* 22, no. 3 (1980): 334–43.

Buckley, Suzann. "Ladies or Midwives? Efforts to Reduce Infant and Maternal Mortality." In *A Not Unreasonable Claim: Women and Reform in Canada, 1880s–1920s*, edited by Linda Kealey, 231–52. Toronto: Women's Press, 1979.

Burtch, Brian E. "Community Midwifery and State Measures." *Contemporary Crises*, no. 10 (1986): 399–420.

Coburn, David. "Patients' Rights: A New Deal in Health Care." *Canadian Forum* 60, no. 699 (1980): 14–18.

College of Nurses of Ontario. "Guidelines for Registered Nurses Providing Care to Individuals and Families Seeking Alternatives to Childbirth in a Hospital Setting." Toronto: CNO (Photocopy), 1983.

Cooke, Dave. "Government Should Recognize Midwifery." *N.D.P. News* 4 December 1984, 30.

Currie, Dawn. "Reproductive Rights: Implications for Feminist Jurisprudence and the State." In *The Administration of Justice*, edited by Dawn Currie and Brian D. MacLean, 35–47. Social Research Unit, Department of Sociology, University of Saskatchewan, 1986.

Donnison, Jean. *Midwives and Medical Men: A History of Inter-Professional Rivalries and Women's Rights*. London: Schocken, 1977.

Doyal, Lesley, with Imogen Pennell. *The Political Economy of Health*. London: Pluto Press, 1979.

Edge, Marc. "Midwives May Face Jail in December." *Vancouver Sun* 10 October 1986.

Eisenstein, Zillah. *The Radical Future of Liberal Feminism*. New York: Longman, 1981.

Evenson, Debra. "Midwives: Survival of an Ancient Profession." *Women's Rights Law Reporter* 7, no. 4 (1983): 313–30.

Feyerabend, Paul. "Democracy, Elitism, and Scientific Method." *Inquiry* 23, no. 1 (1980): 3–18.

Fottler, Myron D., Geoffrey Gibson, and Diane M. Pinchoff. "Physician Resistance to Manpower Innovation." *Social Science Quarterly* 61, no. 1 (1980): 149–57.

Foucault, Michel. *The Birth of the Clinic: An Archaeology of Medical Perceptions*. New York: Vintage Press, 1973.

Freemont Birth Collective. "Lay Midwifery — Still an 'Illegal' Profession." *Women and Health* 2, no. 3 (1977): 19–27.

Gavigan, Shelley. "The Criminal Sanction as It Relates to Human Reproduction." *Journal of Legal History* 5, no. 1 (1984): 20–43.

———. "Women, Law and Patriarchal Relations: Perspectives within the Sociology of Law." In *The Social Dimensions of Law*, edited by Neil Boyd, 101–24. Scarborough: Prentice-Hall, 1986.

Giddens, Anthony. *Profiles and Critiques in Social Theory*. Berkeley: University of California Press, 1982.

Gordon, Linda, and Allen Hunter. "Sex, Family and the New Right: Anti-Feminism as a Political Force." *Radical America* 12, no. 1 (1977/1978): 8–25.

Hamowy, Ronald. *Canadian Medicine: A Study in Restricted Entry*. Vancouver: Fraser Institute, 1984.

Hart, Nicky. "Is Capitalism Bad for Your Health?" *British Journal of Sociology* 33, no. 3 (1982): 435–43.

Klein, Sandra. *A Childbirth Manual*. Victoria, B.C. Photocopy. 1980, 92 pp.

Labonté, Ronald. "Good Health: Individual or Social?" *Canadian Forum* 63, no. 727 (1983): 10–13; 70–91.

Lim, Linda Y.C. "Capitalism, Imperialism and Patriarchy: The Dilemma of Third-World Women Workers in Multinational Factories." In *Women, Men, and the International Division of Labor*, edited by June C. Nash and Maria P. Fernandez-Kelly. Albany: State University of New York Press, 1983.

MacIsaac, Ronald F. "Negligence Actions Against Medical Doctors." *Chitty's Law Journal* 24, no. 6 (1976): 201–6.

Mate, Gabor. "It's Time to Legalize Midwifery." *Globe and Mail* 8 January 1987.

Medical Practitioners' Act, 1979. R.S.B.C.

McIntyre, Greg. "Midwives Ask for Sanction of Law." *The Province*, February 18th, 1983.

McRae, Kenneth. "The Plural Society and the Western Political Tradition." *Canadian Journal of Political Science* 12, no. 4 (1979): 675–89.

Mehl, Louis, et al. "Outcomes of Elective Home Births: A Series of 1,146 Cases." *Journal of Reproductive Medicine* 19, no. 5 (1977): 281–90.

Milbrand, Ralph. *The State in Capitalist Society*. London: Quartet Books, 1973.

Millward, Peter. "Reasons for Judgement." *Regina versus Marsh*. Victoria: County Court of British Columbia, 1980.

Oakley, Ann. *The Captured Womb: A History of the Medical Care of Pregnant Women*. London: Basil Blackwell, 1984.

Olsen, Dennis. *The State Elite*. Toronto: McClelland and Stewart, 1980.

Ontario Association of Midwives and the Nurse-Midwives' Association of Ontario. *Brief on Midwifery Care in Ontario*. Brief submitted to the Health Disciplines Review Committee, Toronto, Ontario (December 1983). Photocopy.

Ontario Medical Act (1906)

Osborne, Judith. "The Crime of Infanticide: Throwing Out the Baby with the Bathwater." *Canadian Journal of Family Law* 6 no. 1 (1987): 47–59.

Phillips, Paul, and Erin Phillips. *Women and Work: Inequality in the Labour Market*. Toronto: James Lorimer and Co., 1983.

Poulantzas, Nicos. *Political Power and Social Classes*. London: NLB, 1973.

———. *State, Power, Socialism*. London: New Left Books, 1978.

Provincial Medical Board v. Bond 1890, 22 *Nova Scotia Reports* 153.

Regina v. Armstrong. *Canadian Criminal Cases*, 18, 72 (Sask.), 1911.

Regina v. Cruikshanks. 6 *W.W.R.* 524, 7 Alta. L.R. 92, 23 C.C.C. 23, 16 D.L.R. 536 (C.A.), 1914.

Regina v. Kripps. 4 *B.C.L.R.* 364 (Provincial Court), 1977.

Regina v. Marsh. (Victoria, B.C.: Unreported), 1980.

Regina v. Ornavowski. *W.W.R.* 103 (Sask.), 1941.

Regina v. Raffenberg. *Western Law Reports*, 12, (1909), 419.

Regina v. Rondeau. *Territories Law Reports*, 5, (1903), 478–83.

Regina v. Whelan. 4 *Canadian Criminal Cases*, 277 (Ontario), 1900.

Regina v. Wong. 6 *W.W.R.* 163 (Prov. Ct.), 1979.

Simard v. the Queen. *Criminal Reports* (Canada), 43, (1964), 70–82.

Sinquefield, Gail. "A Malpractice Dilemma: Defining Standards of Care for Certified Nurse-Midwives." *Journal of Nurse-Midwifery* 28, no. 4 (1983): 1–2.

Spitzer, Steven. "Marxist Perspectives in the

Sociology of Law." *Annual Review of Sociology* 9 (1983): 103–24.

Stephens, Robert. "Ontario Midwives Merit Legal Status, NDPer Says." *Globe and Mail* 16 March 1984.

Sumner, Colin. "The Rule of Law and Civil Rights in Contemporary Marxist Theory." *Kapitalistate* 9 (1981): 63–91.

Sweet, Lois. "Midwives are Battling for their Freedom." *Toronto Star* 8 April 1985, C1.

Tonkin, Roger. *Child Health Profile: Birth Events and Infant Outcome, British Columbia 1981.* Vancouver: Hemlock Printers, 1981.

Van Wagner, Vicki. "The Current Politics of Midwifery in Ontario." Paper presented at the 20th Annual Meeting of the Canadian Sociology and Anthropology Association, University of Guelph, 1984.

Wexler, Steve. "The Intersection of Law and Morals." *Canadian Bar Review* 54 (1976): 351–59.

Women's Work Project of the Union for Radical Political Economists. "USA — Women Health Workers." *Women and Health* 1, no. 3 (1976): 14–23.

20
THE PROFESSIONALIZATION OF CHIROPRACTIC IN CANADA: Its Current Status and Future Prospects

Lesley Biggs
University of Saskatchewan

INTRODUCTION

Chiropractic has been in existence since the turn of the century and represents the largest of the alternative healing systems to orthodox medicine. Chiropractic as well as other occupations such as homeopathy, osteopathy, and naturopathy, have been "labelled" alternative healers because they have been excluded from the official health division of labour. However, chiropractic has not shared the same fate as these other groups: homeopathy and naturopathy have all but disappeared, while osteopathy has been increasingly incorporated into mainstream medical care. In contrast, chiropractic has survived despite persistent and bitter attempts by orthodox medicine to eliminate it, and in recent years, has prospered and flourished.

Despite the significance of chiropractic, sociologists and social scientists in general have ignored chiropractic as a focus of research until very recently. By comparison, orthodox medicine has been scrutinized in microscopic detail not only by social scientists but also by the radio, television, and print media. It is safe to say that information about orthodox medicine permeates our lives, whether it is in the form of a new discovery or as the backdrop for a popular soap opera.

Because chiropractic has been ignored, very little is known about chiropractic therapies and techniques, the organization of its work, chiropractic education, and its political organization. In fact, it is difficult to distinguish between fact and fiction, myth and reality. Often chiropractors and their supporters have embraced chiropractic with evangelistic fervour. Opponents of chiropractic, on the other hand, have been equally zealous in their denunciations of chiropractic theory, philosophy, and practice. The level of hostility between chiropractic and orthodox medicine has led Scotton (1974:32) to compare it to "a holy war between the forces of good and evil."

The purpose of this chapter is to provide an overview of the chiropractic profession in Canada. After a brief introduction to the basic principles and philosophy of chiropractic, we will briefly trace the development of the chiropractic profession in Canada from relatively humble beginnings to its remarkable success in recent years. Finally, we will review the debate between medicine and chiropractic.

SOCIOLOGICAL EXPLANATIONS OF CHIROPRACTIC

Despite the theoretical and numerical importance of the chiropractic profession to medical sociology, there have been few attempts to examine the relationship of chiropractic or alternative healers more generally to orthodox medicine. Before 1970 there were only three sociological articles published on chiropractic (Wardwell, 1952, 1955; McCorkle, 1961). Since the late 1970s there has been a modest and growing interest in chiropractors and other alternative healers. There are two areas of study in the sociology of chiropractic: the first body of literature seeks to develop a profile of chiropractors, their patients, and the organization of their

work (see Hassinger, 1975; Kelner et al., 1980; McCorkle, 1961; Wardwell, 1952, 1955; White and Skipper, 1971; Wild, 1978). The second body of literature, and the more voluminous one by far, is concerned with the professionalization of chiropractic. It attempts to explain the survival of chiropractic despite intense opposition by orthodox medicine.

Both streams of research have been informed implicitly or explicitly by Walter Wardwell's original conceptualization of chiropractic as a marginal profession. Wardwell (1952, 1955) argued that chiropractic occupied a marginal role vis-à-vis allopathic medicine in a number of ways: degree of technical competence, scope of practice, legal status, income, and prestige. According to Wardwell, the marginal status of chiropractic has had important implications for the practice of chiropractic and for its survival as an occupation. In order to cope with their marginal status, chiropractors adopted an "ideology of the oppressed" and attempted to improve their position by lobbying and attacking medical orthodoxy. In addition, though to a lesser extent, sociologists have been influenced by McCorkle's labelling of chiropractic as a "deviant" occupation.

Much of the research on chiropractors has focussed on the motivations, backgrounds, personalities, and career contingencies of chiropractors (Hassinger, 1975; Kelner et al., 1980; McCorkle, 1961; Wardwell, 1952, 1955; White and Skipper, 1971; Wild, 1978). The main question in this body of literature is why someone would choose to enter an occupation which is viewed by many as marginal or deviant. One of the most persistent findings of this literature is that the socio-economic status of chiropractors and their patients has changed.

In the 1950s chiropractors came largely from the working or farming classes. Most researchers have concluded that chiropractic offered the working and lower middle classes a means of upward mobility. However, the most recent and comprehensive study of Canadian chiropractic students by Kelner et al. (1980) indicates that the socio-economic status of chiropractic students is changing. Whereas previous research found that chiropractors were older (many starting a second career), not college-trained, and from working-class families, the present student is young, university-educated, and from a middle-class family. (In comparison, most orthodox physicians have been drawn from the middle and upper classes since the turn of the century.)

In addition to examining the social origins of chiropractors, there has been some interest in their patients. The findings of several studies indicate that chiropractic patients, like the practitioners, were also drawn from the lower-middle income groups (Koos, 1967; McCorkle, 1961; Schmitt, 1978). Recent evidence suggests that in Canada, at least, the socio-economic status of chiropractic patients is also changing. Coulter (1986) has found that chiropractic patients resemble the general population at large and do not disproportionately represent the working class.

The dominant explanation for working-class patronage of chiropractic services is the "sprain and strain" theory; i.e., the working class experiences a disproportionate number of neuromuscular problems. For example, Schmitt (1978) reports that arthritis and rheumatism are more frequently found in the lower-income groups. Schmitt also points out that despite the higher rates of physical injury among lower-income groups, they are less likely to consult with orthopedic specialists. Therefore, in spite of need, specialist utilization is positively associated with income and education (Hewitt and Wood, 1975). Data from Kelner et al. also support the "sprain and strain" theory. The most common problems presented by chiropractic patients were musculo-skeletal, and usually they sought chiropractic care after becoming dissatisfied with the treatments of orthodox physicians.

The psychosocial explanation of working-class patronage of chiropractic services suggests that orthodox medicine has ignored working-class ailments. Wardwell (1980) has pointed out that musculo-skeletal problems were unprob-

lematic for allopathic medicine and has led to the labelling of these patients as neurotics, malingerers, etc. Chiropractic has provided a "legitimate" forum for the expression of these problems.

In addition to the psychosocial explanation and the "sprain and strain" theory, there are several other explanations. The inadequate socialization theory, which is favoured by the medical profession, suggests that chiropractic patients have but a poor knowledge of the "legitimate" health-care system. Schmitt (1978) argues that there is no empirical evidence to support this theory and, in fact, chiropractic patients appear to be discriminating users of the health system. The subcultural theory suggests that patients who utilize chiropractic services follow a belief system congruent with chiropractic theory. Thus, for example, McCorkle (1961) found that the philosophy of chiropractic was consistent with rural Iowan values such as pragmatism, "laying on of hands," and the physicality of work. Koos (1967) in his study of Regionville, a small town in rural America, found that there was an outright hostility towards orthodox medicine from working-class patients.

In conclusion, there is evidence to suggest that a significant change in the socio-economic status of both chiropractors and their patients has taken place within the past two decades. There has also been a remarkable consistency between the socio-economic status of practitioners and clients which has not yet been adequately explained. We can postulate that these relationships are structurally organized. The dominant health-care system is organized in such a way as to give primacy to middle-class health problems while ignoring those of the working class. This structural bias is reflected in the type of problems addressed and the mode of treatment.

Although it is unclear why the middle class has become more accepting of chiropractic services, one possible explanation is that it has begun to reject more orthodox methods of treatment, for example, surgery, for musculo-skeletal problems. In addition, as chiropractic has become legitimated, it has been transformed into a new specialty which is more in line with middle-class expectations of client-practitioner relationships.

The second body of literature has focussed on the professionalization of chiropractic. (For a more extensive review, see Coburn and Biggs, 1986.) In his original work, Wardwell (1952) conceptualized chiropractic as a marginal profession which did not enjoy the same status and rewards as the medical profession. Since Wardwell's pioneering work in the 1950s, there is universal agreement among observers of chiropractic that it has made significant gains in legitimacy, including legal recognition, third-party insurance (both public and private), increased numbers of chiropractors, and increased rates of utilization by a broader spectrum of society.

The chief explanation for the survival of chiropractic is public support for chiropractic and chiropractors' intense lobbying campaigns. (See Wardwell, 1980; Mills and Larsen, 1981; Boase, 1982.) Wardwell (1980) compares chiropractic to a social movement which was able to marshal effective leadership and organization. The financial success of chiropractic, derived from patient and student fees and a variety of other entrepreneurial activities, has enabled the profession to conduct an intense lobbying campaign over many decades.

According to this perspective, the main barrier to the full professionalization of chiropractic lies in its restricted knowledge base (Cobb, 1977; Mills and Larsen, 1981; Wardwell, 1981). The fact that chiropractic is "scientifically unverified" is a major problem. But its critics are aware that the original chiropractic theory has weakened as the basic sciences have come to dominate chiropractic curricula, although at the same time, basic science research has provided some evidence supporting chiropractic theories. However Wardwell (1981) and Willis (1983) regard the scientific status of chiropractic as "ideologically loaded" since chiropractic has been excluded from university and government funding of research. Both Willis and Wardwell

believe that the future of chiropractic will be determined by political and social factors rather than through scientific validation.

Despite the fact that chiropractic has made significant gains in legitimacy, its future remains uncertain. Wardwell (1976, 1980a, 1980b, 1981) distinguishes among four types of health occupations, each denoting a specific relationship to the medical profession. These included: *ancillary workers*, who provide support services and are controlled by the medical profession; *limited medical practitioners*, who have reached a position of accommodation with allopathic medicine (e.g., dentists, pharmacists); *marginal practitioners*, who offer an alternative to the medical profession; and *quasi-practitioners*, who have a fundamentally different epistemological base (e.g., Christian Scientists). In his later writing, Wardwell (1981) adds the category of *parallel profession*, which refers to the "near-equal of medicine" (e.g., osteopathy).

Wardwell discusses the potential pitfalls that each designation engenders for chiropractic. Given the current trend within chiropractic toward the elevation of standards and training and increased public recognition, the most likely avenue for chiropractic is to become a parallel profession. However, as chiropractic theory approaches that of medicine, the differences between the two occupations may, in fact, become indistinguishable. Chiropractic may become incorporated into mainstream medical care as a specialty in neuromuscular problems. Wardwell also points out that the structure of financial reimbursement may shape the practice of chiropractic in the direction of providing a specialized service, i.e., neuro-musculo-skeletal care. In this case, chiropractors will become a type of limited medical practitioners.

Three recent historical analyses of the development of chiropractic in Britain and the United States, Australia, and Canada suggest that chiropractic has been transformed from an alternative healing system to a neuromuscular specialty. Baer, (1984) in his comparison of chiropractic in Britain and the United States suggests that heterodox healing systems can be viewed as a type of revitalization movement. Chiropractic represents a form of social protest against the impersonal nature and technological orientation of regular medicine. According to Baer, chiropractic will be forced to accommodate itself to the dominant group, namely organized medicine. In order to gain legitimacy, chiropractors require the support of strategic elites who are seeking alternatives to capital-intensive medicine. Baier found that in the process of becoming legitimized, chiropractors have redefined their role from comprehensive drugless healers to neuro-musculo-skeletal specialists.

Willis (1983), in his analysis of chiropractic in Victoria, Australia, argues that the medical profession has excluded chiropractic from the division of labour in health services. However, like the chiropractic profession in the United States and Canada, chiropractic in Australia has also moved from a position of exclusion toward legitimation. But Willis argues that this has been at the price of limiting its scope of practice.

The survival of chiropractic in Australia can be partly explained by the establishment of a school which ensured the supply of chiropractors. But Willis maintains that this factor alone does not fully explain the success of chiropractic. Rather, he emphasizes the importance of the wider social and political context of health care.

The main factor in the legitimation of chiropractic was increasing state intervention in health care. The state could not ignore chiropractic because it was able to mobilize public support. At the same time, chiropractic was becoming compatible with the dominant class interests because it was perceived to increase productivity by alleviating back pain and neuromuscular injuries.

Both Baer (1984) and Willis (1983) have found that while allopathic medicine has been forced to accept chiropractic therapy, chiropractic itself has modified many of its earlier claims and beliefs. Chiropractors have rejected its more metaphysical or philosophical aspects in favour of a focus on chiropractic science and technique. Thus, they have redefined their role from

comprehensive drugless practitioners to neuromuscular specialists in the process of becoming legitimized. Moreover, Willis points out that while there may be differences between chiropractic and medical theories, the underlying ideological basis is remarkably similar.

> Medicine with its emphasis on germ theory sees ill health as an individual and biological phenomenon. Chiropractic, emphasizing subluxations, sees it as individual and mechanical. Neither sees it as a social and political phenomenon and rooted in the conditions of [the] existence of capitalist society. (Willis, 1983:198)

In an earlier paper, "Limits to Medical Dominance: The Case of Chiropractic," (Coburn and Biggs, 1986) David Coburn and I attempted to explain the survival and recent success of chiropractic in Canada. One of the main factors which ensured the survival of chiropractic, particularly during the 1920s, was simply public patronage of chiropractic services. We found that the working class in particular strongly supported chiropractic, in part because it offered a therapy which addressed their specific needs, namely musculo-skeletal problems. We also found that segments of the population, again in particular the working class, were vehemently opposed to the medical monopoly over health care; they believed that individuals should have the right to choose their own practitioners.

As indicated above, chiropractic has grown and prospered, particularly since the 1960s. We found that chiropractic has been recognized officially in a number of ways. Like Willis, we concluded that the success of chiropractic was due to state involvement in health care. With the advent of public health insurance, itself a product of working-class pressure, came an increased state presence in health care, and a concomitant move toward the rationalization of health services in order to reduce costs. We argued that state involvement signified a decline in medical dominance, while opening up new possibilities for chiropractors because they provided low-cost services that fit within the new lifestyle paradigm. (See, for example, Canada: M. Lalonde, 1975.) Like Willis, we found a convergence between chiropractic and medical knowledge.

Overall, then, a major portion of the research on chiropractic in other countries and some in Canada indicates that chiropractic is becoming a profession. Earlier analysts have emphasized that the success of chiropractic was due to its lobbying campaigns. More recent analysts do not deny the importance of lobbying, but they stress that in order to understand the development of chiropractic, one must place it within a broader social and political context. In particular, the analysis of chiropractic should include not only its relationship to medicine but also an analysis of the state and the balance of class forces.

In the remainder of this chapter, I will provide some background information regarding chiropractic theory and philosophy. We will then examine the trends in chiropractic legitimacy, which includes an analysis of its legal, economic, and social standing in Canada. Finally we will examine the economic and ideological underpinnings of the debate between chiropractic and medicine.

CHIROPRACTIC THEORY AND PHILOSOPHY

The crucial point at which chiropractic is said to have been discovered was in 1895 in Davenport, Iowa, when Daniel David Palmer, a self-taught magnetic healer, cured Harvey Willard of deafness by giving him an adjustment to the spine. (For a more detailed history see Gibbons, 1977a, 1977b; Dye, 1939; Maynard, 1977.) Palmer subsequently developed the concept of spinal subluxation or a misalignment of the vertebrae, which impinges upon the transmission of nerve energy to the vital organs. Chiropractors locate subluxations by palpating the spine, and remove them through spinal adjustments. Thus, normal nerve transmission is restored.

Chiropractic embraces a holistic view of health, in which mind and body are seen as an integrated unit. Unlike allopathic medicine,

which views disease as an invasion of the body by external agents, Palmer argued that the cause of disease came from within the body. When the body is functioning normally, it is able to combat disease naturally. Palmer referred to the power of the body to heal itself as "Innate Intelligence." The seat of "Innate" is the brain, and the spine and nervous system act as a communication system between the body and Innate. When there is a subluxation in the spine, the flow of Innate is disrupted, hence there is disease (Churchill, 1977). Since the body was able to heal itself, Palmer was opposed to drugs and surgery, because these methods treated symptoms but did not remove causes (subluxations).

Although D.D. Palmer founded the first school of chiropractic, it was his son, B.J. Palmer, known as the Developer, who promoted chiropractic. Like his father, "B.J." possessed a flamboyant, charismatic personality combined with a shrewd eye for business. Under the firm hand of B.J. Palmer, the Palmer School of Chiropractic in Davenport, Iowa, known as the Fountainhead, became one of the largest institutions that trained health practitioners in the United States. Through the collection of student fees and the sale of thousands of pamphlets about chiropractic, B.J. Palmer established a well-financed infra-structure for the promotion of chiropractic.

B.J. Palmer was also responsible for the major schism in the profession between the "straights," who provide "hands-only, spine-only care" and the "mixers" who use a variety of healing modalities, both mechanical and non-mechanical. The schism between straights and mixers occurred in 1924, when B.J. Palmer introduced the neurocalometer, a heat-sensing device for the detection of subluxations. B.J. Palmer demanded that every chiropractor should use the neurocalometer, which could be rented from the school at a cost of $2500 a year.

A second source of contention was B.J.'s concept of subluxation. B.J. believed that nerve compression did not occur below the second cervical vertebra. This led him to develop a technique called "Hole-In-One" which was an

Table 1. Provincial Legislation Governing the Practice of Chiropractic

Province	Statute	Date Passed
Alberta	The Chiropractic Act	1923
Ontario	The Drugless Practitioners Act	1925
British Columbia	The Chiropractic Act	1934
Yukon	The Chiropractic Ordinance	1940
Saskatchewan	The Chiropractic Act	1943
Manitoba	The Chiropractic Act	1945
New Brunswick	The Chiropractic Act	1958
PEI	The Chiropractic Act	1968
Nova Scotia	The Chiropractic Act	1972
Quebec	The Chiropractic Act	1973

Source: Kelner et al. data gathered for chiropractic project. The author would like to thank Professors Kelner, Hall, and Coulter for permitting access to this data.

adjustment at the upper cervical vertebrae. Since subluxations could only occur at this point, B.J. believed that diagnosis was unnecessary. B.J.'s opposition to diagnosis formed the basis of the medical profession's critique, since they regarded this theory as unscientific and verging on medical heresy.

One consequence of these cleavages is that chiropractors in the United States are organized into two national organizations — the American Chiropractic Association (ACA), which represents the mixer tradition, and the International Chiropractic Association (ICA), which represents the straights. In Canada the profession is organized into one association, the Canadian Chiropractic Association (and its provincial counterparts), which represents the mixer tradition.

THE CURRENT STATUS OF CHIROPRACTIC

The medical profession has vehemently opposed chiropractic theory, philosophy, and practice since its beginning. This opposition has led to bitter struggles between chiropractors and allopathic medicine, particularly over licensing, and in some cases chiropractors in the United States and Canada went to jail for practising medicine without a licence. (See Gibbons, 1977; and Biggs, 1985.) However, despite medical opposition, chiropractors have gained significant official sanction in the past 60 years. Chiropractors are now licensed throughout the United States and in all the provinces in Canada with the exception of Newfoundland (where legislation is now being drafted). Chiropractic services are covered under Workers' Compensation Acts in seven provinces. (Quebec, Nova Scotia, and Newfoundland have not included chiropractors under the WCB.)

Since the turn of the century the number of chiropractors (cited in Coburn and Biggs, 1986) has grown from 100 in 1906 (mostly located in North America) to approximately 30 000 worldwide in 1980. There are now 20 000 chiropractors in the United States and approximately 2200 in Canada. Figure 1 indicates that chiropractors are primarily located in Ontario, Quebec, and Western Canada. However, most of the chiropractors are concentrated in just four provinces: Ontario (1033), Quebec (504), British Columbia (270), and Alberta (265). This concentration can be explained by the fact that chiropractors in these provinces were successful in obtaining licensing acts in the early part of this century.

Figure 1: Licensed Chiropractors by Region from 1931–1980

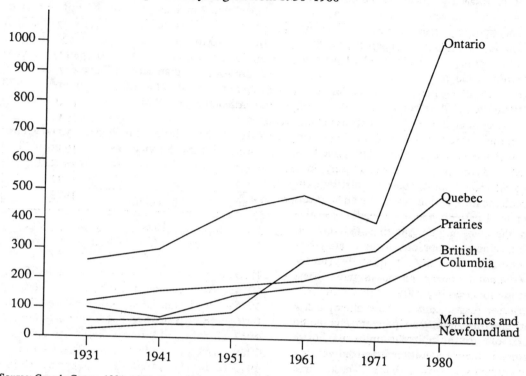

Source: Canada Census 1931–1971; Canada Health Manpower Inventory (1982) for 1973–1980.

The large number of chiropractors in Quebec can be explained by the restricted mobility of francophone chiropractors.

Figure 1 also indicates that there was a significant increase in the number of chiropractors in the postwar period. This jump can be explained by the establishment of the Canadian Memorial Chiropractic College in 1945. Chiropractic education received its initial boost from funding by the Department of Veteran Affairs to demobilized soldiers wishing to acquire a chiropractic education. Under this programme 250 veterans received chiropractic training. After this initial peak, the number of graduates from the CMCC declined to an all-time low of 24 in 1964. The major reason for this decline was that the school became embroiled in a major legal battle with the Toronto Transit Commission. The TTC had expropriated some of the CMCC's property, leaving some of the buildings unfit for

teaching, and as a result the CMCC had a difficult time attracting students. Since the mid-1960s, the CMCC has grown tremendously. Currently there are 600 students enrolled in the programme, with 150 graduates each year.

Not only are there more chiropractors practising in Canada, there are also more people patronizing chiropractors. Data from the Canada Sickness Survey (conducted from 1950–51) indicates that 130 000 persons, or 0.9 percent of the population, visited a chiropractor. In comparison, 43.2 percent of the population visited physicians (either in the office or in a clinic). Although it is difficult to ascertain current utilization rates of chiropractic services, the Canadian Chiropractic Association estimates that utilization ranges from 6 to 10 percent of the population. Recent data from the Saskatchewan Medical Care Commission indicate that in 1973 (when chiropractic services were first covered under the provincial plan) about 5.3 percent of the population received chiropractic care. By 1985–6 this figure had risen to 9.9 percent of the population. In comparison, 80.6 percent and 85.7 percent of the population had visited a physician in 1973 and in 1986, respectively.

Although little is known about chiropractic patients, Coulter (1986) conducted a study of 658 chiropractic patients which provides a socio-demographic profile of chiropractic patients and their use of services. He found that the sample of chiropractic patients closely conforms to the Canadian occupational distribution. His data indicate a strong resemblance between the sample of patients and the Canadian population in the two middle quartiles ($10 000 to $24 999). While chiropractic patients are over-represented in the lowest quartile (under $10 000) and underrepresented in the highest income group (over $30 000).

Coulter also found that chiropractic patients are discriminating patients and go to chiropractors for a limited number of health problems, namely, general back and spine, neck and shoulder, and lower back. These three categories account for approximately 55 percent of all health complaints. The figures for the remaining categories are relatively small but most relate to musculo-skeletal problems.

Chiropractic services were included under state-sponsored health insurance in 1969. Since then, half of the provincial health insurance plans (Alberta, B.C., Manitoba, Ontario, and Saskatchewan) have covered chiropractic treatments. Chiropractors in these provinces are guaranteed payment for the services that they provide. In Saskatchewan, the health insurance plan covers all of the costs of chiropractic care. In the remaining provinces, the health plan covers the cost of services to a maximum amount. For example, in Alberta, the provincial plan covers up to $11.50 for each visit, with a limit of $192.00 per year for single residents and $384.00 for families.

The cost of chiropractic care in Canada was estimated by Statistics Canada to be 128.8 million dollars in 1980. In comparison, the cost of physician services was 227 168.6 million dollars. Table 2 indicates that the cost of chiropractic services has remained relatively constant from 1970 to 1980 and represents 0.5 percent of total health expenditures. In comparison, expenditures on physician services have declined from 16.6 percent of total health expenditures in 1970 to 14.5 percent in 1980.

Table 2. Expenditures on Physician and Chiropractic Services as a Percent of Total Health Expenditures, 1970–1980

Year	Physicians	Chiropractors
1970	16.6	.5
1971	17.6	.6
1972	17.8	.6
1973	17.0	.6
1974	16.2	.6
1975	15.5	.5
1976	14.9	.5
1977	14.9	.6
1978	14.9	.6
1979	14.9	.6
1980	14.5	.6

Source: Canada. Health and Welfare Canada. *National Health Expenditures in Canada, 1970–1982.* Ottawa: Ministry of Supply and Services, 1985.

Tables 3 and 4 compare the costs of chiropractic services in the public (government) sector and in the private sector (primarily private insurance companies). In 1970 chiropractic services represented 0.12 percent of public expenditures and 1.6 percent of private expenditures. By 1980, public expenditures on chiropractic care had increased slightly to 0.5 percent while private expenditures had declined slightly to 1.1 percent. Overall, the private sector has assumed a relatively large proportion of the cost of chiropractic services. In the pre-medicare years many unions had included the cost of chiropractic care as part of collective agreements. Private coverage of chiropractic services has continued in the post-medicare period since all of the provinces,

Table 3. A Comparison of Public and Private Health Expenditures on Physician and Chiropractic Services, Canada, 1970–1980 (millions of dollars)

	1970	1971	1972	1973	1974	1975	1976	1977	1978	1979	1980
PUBLIC EXPENDITURES											
Total health expenditures	4392.0	5217.5	5786.1	6454.6	7676.8	9478.1	10 873.0	11 871.9	12 935.2	14 323.2	16 505.9
Physicians	805.0	1146.8	1265.3	1380.1	1550.0	1820.4	2 027.2	2 217.6	2 433.0	2 723.5	3 127.2
Chiropractors	5.1	7.7	21.1	28.3	31.0	35.9	40.4	45.1	51.3	57.9	66.7
PRIVATE EXPENDITURES											
Total Health Expenditures	1863.9	1904.8	2004.0	2265.7	2570.7	2903.3	3285.7	3660.7	4158.8	4744.0	5672.7
Physicians	235.7	103.6	120.9	103.3	109.6	93.6	76.0	91.4	111.0	119.9	157.4
Chiropractors	29.0	31.7	22.5	21.2	25.8	30.6	37.0	42.7	45.3	57.6	62.1

Source: Canada. Health and Welfare Canada. *National Health Expenditures in Canada, 1970–1982.* Ottawa: Ministry of Supply and Services, 1985.

Table 4. A Comparison of Public and Private Health Expenditures on Physician and Chiropractic Services, Canada, 1970–1980 (%)

	1970	1971	1972	1973	1974	1975	1976	1977	1978	1979	1980
PUBLIC EXPENDITURES											
Total health expenditures	100.0	100.0	100.0	100.0	100.0	100.0	100.0	100.0	100.0	100.0	100.0
Physicians	18.3	22.0	21.9	21.4	20.2	19.2	18.6	18.7	18.8	19.0	18.9
Chiropractors	0.12	0.15	0.36	0.44	0.40	0.38	0.37	0.38	0.39	0.40	0.40
PRIVATE EXPENDITURES											
Total Health Expenditures	100.0	100.0	100.0	100.0	100.0	100.0	100.0	100.0	100.0	100.0	100.0
Physicians	12.6	5.4	6.0	4.6	4.3	3.2	2.3	2.5	2.7	2.5	2.8
Chiropractors	1.6	1.7	1.1	0.9	1.0	1.1	1.1	1.2	1.1	1.2	1.1

Source: Canada. Health and Welfare Canada. *National Health Expenditures in Canada, 1970–1982.* Ottawa: Ministry of Supply and Services, 1985.

with the exception of Saskatchewan, provide only partial coverage for these services.

The average income of Canadian chiropractors in 1977 was $58 000, gross, and net income was about $40 000. (These figures are derived from a survey of Canadian chiropractors conducted by Kelner et al. in 1977.) Twenty-one percent of chiropractors in Canada had gross incomes of over $80 000 in 1977. There is, however, considerable variability in chiropractic incomes across Canada. Chiropractors in the Atlantic provinces had the lowest income (gross) of $32 000 compared to Ontario, which had the highest income of $67 000. Albertan chiropractors follow closely behind those in Ontario, with an average income of $62 000. The remaining provinces conform to the national average.

Overall, the evidence suggests that chiropractic has been very successful in seeking various forms of official recognition. This is in sharp contrast to the turn of the century, when chiropractic was ignored by governments. As a result of its changing fortunes, it is now seen as a legitimate career option for members of the middle class, and patronage of chiropractic services has increased substantially by a broader section of society. In terms of the costs of chiropractic services, chiropractors represent a small fraction of the health-care budget. Nonetheless, chiropractic now offers a financially rewarding career for most of its practitioners.

However, the findings of several studies have indicated that chiropractic has gained legitimacy at a price. Baer (1984), Willis (1983), and Coburn and Biggs (1986) have all argued that chiropractic has dramatically reduced its scope of practice since its early beginnings. Chiropractors no longer claim that they can remove the causes (subluxations) of all diseases; rather they focus primarily on spinal and neuromuscular problems. Indeed, many chiropractors do not claim to be an alternative healing occupation but simply regard themselves as members of the health-care team.

While there is substantial evidence to support the view that chiropractic has reduced its scope of practice, it is not clear why this process should even take place; nor is it clear how this process is mediated. In the final section we will examine the debate between chiropractic and orthodox medicine in order to explicate these processes.

THE DEBATE BETWEEN CHIROPRACTORS AND ALLOPATHIC MEDICINE

There is little doubt that the medical profession in Canada and the United States has vehemently opposed the philosophy, theory, and practice of chiropractic. Allopathic medicine has attempted to deny any official recognition to chiropractic. For example, Dr. John Ferguson, secretary to the Ontario Medical Association in 1917 wrote that osteopathy and chiropractic were "two of the worst impositions on science of modern times" and chiropractic, in particular, was "utter nonsense and humbug." Chiropractic is "completely false," chiropractic theory and education are "absurd," "a complete farce," and "a well-staged fake" (*Canada Lancet*, 1917:54).

However, despite the intense hostility of the medical profession toward chiropractors, there has been little attempt to explain the origins of medical opposition. Implicit in most writings on chiropractic is the assumption that chiropractic was a major economic competitor to the medical profession. That is, orthodox medicine was attempting to maintain its monopoly over health care.

While this may be the underlying reason for medical opposition to chiropractic, some writers have alluded to the fact that it may be based on ideological grounds. Willis (1983) has suggested that chiropractic and other alternative knowledge represents different forms of "knowing." Cobb (1977) argues that chiropractic is based on tacit knowledge while most medical knowledge is based on technical or codified knowledge which is "the hallmark of professionalism."

The distinction between different types of knowledge is further developed by Boehme (1984) in his analysis of midwifery knowledge.

Boehme makes the distinction between two types of knowledge: life-world knowledge, which is knowledge acquired in everyday life; and scientific knowledge, which is characterized by a high degree of formalization and codification. The difference between the two forms of knowledge lies in the context of production and transmission of knowledge. Life-world knowledge is transmitted primarily through tradition and apprenticeship. Scientific knowledge is transmitted through the formal education system, primarily through universities. Thus, using Boehme's categories we can say that chiropractic knowledge represents life-world knowledge while medical knowledge represents scientific knowledge.

Larson (1977) provides a cogent analysis of the relationship between market relations and the production of knowledge. In her view, professionalization is the attempt to translate one order of scarce resources, i.e., specialized knowledge and skills, into social and economic rewards. As a result, a profession maintains a monopoly of expertise in the market and a monopoly of status and privileges in a system of stratification.

According to Larson, the professional project involves two processes: control over the market and collective social mobility. (For the purposes of this chapter we will confine our discussion to the first aspect.) She identifies three preconditions for the establishment of a monopoly of expertise: the production of a homogeneous group of producers, a formal, codified body of knowledge, and finally, market protection through state sanction, i.e., licensing.

The most important factor in determining control of the market is the establishment of formal training over various forms of apprenticeship. The underlying assumption here is that professional services have become commodities which can be bought and sold on the market. Standardized training ensures a uniformity and homogeneity of the product. According to Larson, scientific knowledge appears to offer the best potential for a uniform and standard product because it provides a clear principle of separa-

tion from the "non-standardized empirically trained profession" (Larson, 1977:34). In addition, Larson argues that science is the dominant form of legitimation in capitalist society because it appears to be independent of class interests. Therefore any profession which can claim a monopoly over a "scientific" body of knowledge will be able to assert its superiority over other groupings.

However, Larson believes that the professional project was not possible until the university became the dominant form of "meritocratic legitimation." In Larson's view, the university is the main institution in capitalist society which both mediates and legitimizes social inequality. The university gives the appearance of class neutrality since it is based on universal access and objective methods of evaluation. Thus rewards appear to be matched with merit. At the same time, this appearance legitimizes a monopoly of expertise which justifies higher rewards and thus perpetuates social inequality.

In summary, Larson argues that "credentialling," i.e., the use of examinations or certificates, has become the main strategy by which dominant groups have excluded subordinate groups. In this case, the medical profession has been entrenched in the university system and can claim to possess a body of knowledge which is scientific. These two factors ensure not only the medical profession's dominant position in the division of labour but also its image as objective and independent of specific interests. Therefore, it is in a powerful position to exclude competing health occupations, namely chiropractic, without appearing to be protecting its own monopoly.

In the final section of the chapter we will explore the debate between orthodox medicine and chiropractic over licensing in one province, namely British Columbia. The evidence suggests that orthodox medicine used different strategies in its attack on chiropractic. In its early attempts medicine tried to eliminate chiropractic outright. When these efforts failed, it switched to a more effective means of excluding chiropractic by the strategy of credentialling.

THE DEBATE OVER LICENSING IN B.C. 1910–1934

Much of the early support for chiropractic was based on popular opposition to allopathic medicine's monopoly over health care. For example, in 1920 the B.C. Anti-Vaccination and Medical League sent a strongly worded resolution to the Attorney-General which stated:

> The Provincial Government has no direct authority from the Crown or Mandate from the people to usurp a proprieting [sic] ownership over the bodies of the people and to gratuitously present these rights as a trade asset to an irresponsible Medical Monopoly . . . (Emphasis in the original–Attorney General's Papers, GR 702 M–155–7–2).

There is also some anecdotal evidence which suggests that chiropractors and other drugless healers did, in fact, pose a serious economic threat to allopathic medicine. In a letter to B.C. Premier Tolmie, J.A. Bryant, representative for the drugless therapists, estimated that there were 100 chiropractors practising in B.C. in 1932. According to Bryant, they were each treating 30 patients daily, or 3000 patients in total. While these figures may be somewhat exaggerated, there was a common perception that chiropractors were an important source of competition along with other drugless healers.

Of course, allopathic medicine vigorously denied that chiropractors (and other drugless healers) were a serious economic threat, rather they objected to chiropractic because it was "unscientific." Yet the actions taken by allopathic medicine would strongly suggest that it was protecting its monopoly over health care.

In the early years (1895 to the mid-1920s) the medical profession repeatedly charged and convicted chiropractors of practising medicine without a license. As a result, some chiropractors were fined and, in some cases, jailed. In B.C. between 1914 and 1922, there were 43 chiropractors convicted of practising medicine without a licence, three of whom were jailed.

Allopathic medicine was clearly operating under the assumption that through harassment and intimidation, chiropractors would disappear.

However, in response to medical opposition, chiropractors adopted strategies of solidarism or collective mobilization (Parkin, 1974). This mobilization took two forms. First, the chiropractors organized themselves into associations whose primary purpose was lobbying. In B.C., the chiropractors were divided into two associations: the B.C. Chiropractors' Association, which represented the straights (35 members), and the B.C. Association of United Drugless Therapists (100 members), which represented the mixers.

In addition to chiropractic lobby groups, the B.C. chiropractors were able to mobilize public support. The convictions of 15 chiropractors in 1922 attracted an enormous amount of public attention, which led to the formation of the B.C. Chiropractic Defense League. The League represented a coalition of trade unionists, church groups, and prominent individuals in Victoria and Vancouver. It was very active in lobbying for chiropractic through petitions (one of which had 17 000 names), letters of support to the Premier and his Cabinet, letters to newspapers, and noisy demonstrations on the steps of Parliament. Since the chiropractors were so successful in winning public support, allopathic medicine abandoned tactics which were associated with "class legislation," i.e., monopoly legislation.

Instead the medical profession adopted a new and more effective form of exclusion based on credentialling. Allopathic medicine adopted a two-pronged attack on chiropractic. First, it attempted to discredit chiropractic theory on the basis that it did not conform to current scientific thinking. The central issue between allopathic medicine and chiropractic was over the meaning of diagnosis. Chiropractic diagnosis was based on palpation of the spine, and, therefore, did not require the articulation of a formal body of knowledge. Medical diagnosis was predicated on a more formal and codified body of knowledge which involved the construction of typologies of symptoms into disease categories. As indicated above, standardization is one of the key characteristics of scientific knowledge. Since medical knowledge was able to demonstrate a scientific base, the medical profession was able to construct chiropractic knowledge as "unscientific" and "sheer quackery," refusing to generate "objective" and rational disease categories.

The second tactic used by the medical profession was to ridicule chiropractic educational standards. The length of chiropractic courses ranged from six months to one year. In comparison, allopathic medicine had a lengthy course requirement of four years which by their assertion was of "the highest quality."

Using these two strategies, the medical profession was successful in subordinating chiropractic under the Medical Act in 1922. The passage of this Act reflects the contradictory pressures placed on the state. On the one hand, Legislature was forced to recognize the validity of chiropractic therapy and acquiesce to populist demands. On the other hand, the state had granted allopathic medicine a monopoly on health care, which established the medical profession as the legitimate authority on health matters. As a result, Legislature accepted medicine's criteria of scientific knowledge and acceptable educational standards, rejecting thereby the validity of chiropractic theory, and insisting that chiropractors be "duly qualified" and submit to a common licensing exam.

The chiropractors strongly resisted these attempts at subordination and were eventually successful in forcing the government to establish a Royal Commission on Chiropractic and Drugless Healing in 1931. The mandate of the Commission was to examine the standards of chiropractic collegess, without questioning or investigating the validity of chiropractic theory and therapy. However, Judge Murphy, the sole Commissioner to the Commission, did comment on the debate between medicine and chiropractic. He found that chiropractic and medical theories of disease were diametrically opposed, and concluded that diagnosis "has a very differ-

ent meaning to the chiropractor from what it means to a physician" (*Report*, 1931:7). Murphy argued that diagnosis for the chiropractor means "discovery of subluxation" through palpation. Diagnosis for the physician meant identification of a disease for the purposes of treating it with specific remedies. However, Murphy found that more emphasis had been placed on diagnosis in chiropractic colleges, and the course of study had been lengthened "not because either is regarded as necessary for the practice of chiropractic but because it was expected that legal recognition of chiropractic therapy would thereby be facilitated" (*Report*, 1931:7).

Although Judge Murphy recommended that chiropractors should have a separate act of law which would give them the right of self-government without interference from orthodox medicine, the government refused to introduce the required legislation. After several attempts to introduce private bills, the chiropractors decided to make chiropractic an election issue in 1933. And although it is difficult to ascertain the effect that the chiropractic lobby had on the election results, the Conservative government was defeated and the Liberal government introduced a chiropractic bill soon after the opening of Parliament. The Chiropractic Act passed final reading on March 29, 1934.

As stated above, Larson identified three preconditions for the establishment of a monopoly of expertise: the production of a homogeneous group of producers, a formal, codified body of knowledge, and market protection through state sanctions, i.e., licensing. It is clear that when chiropractic first emerged, it did not meet any of these criteria. Standards for the training of chiropractors were minimal and not uniform. In addition, knowledge of chiropractic was primarily empirically rooted knowledge. Chiropractic diagnosis was based on palpation of the spine and did not require the articulation of a formal body of knowledge.

The "failure" of chiropractic to meet these criteria provided orthodox medicine ample ammunition to eliminate chiropractic. However, it was initially unsuccessful in its bid because chiropractors were able to mobilize public support. The state was forced to recognize the validity of chiropractic therapy but rejected chiropractic theory because it was "unscientific." That is, chiropractic did not conform to the dominant form of cognitive legitimation; namely, a standardized and codified body of knowledge.

The establishment of the Royal Commission on Chiropractic and Drugless Healing can also be seen as a major victory for the chiropractors and the populist movement in general, since under the terms of the Commission, the validity of chiropractic therapy and theory was not open to investigation. However, there is evidence to suggest that chiropractic had already made significant changes in its knowledge base in anticipation of legal recognition. In particular, the length of training in recognized institutions had been extended from one to four years and chiropractors had begun to adopt some medical diagnostic tools.

While the establishment of the Royal Commission can be seen as a victory for chiropractors, the terms of the Commission, namely the establishment of standards, indicate a significant shift in the debate. Whereas previous investigations had focussed on the form of knowledge (i.e., empirical versus scientific knowledge), the establishment of standards denotes an acceptance of a rational-scientific discourse by chiropractors. That is, chiropractic accepted the standardization and codification of its knowledge base in order to become legitimated. As a result, chiropractors were no longer offering an alternative to orthodox medicine, but had accepted the parameters of what was "legitimate" knowledge.

CONCLUSIONS

Despite its early opposition to chiropractic, the medical profession has been forced to live with chiropractors and to a limited extent to accept the techniques of chiropractic, if not its theory. During the 1920s, the main source of chiropractic support was patronage by a working-class clientele. One of the main appeals of chiropractic is that it offered a therapy which addressed the needs of the working class, namely a physical therapy offering relief for musculo-skeletal problems. In addition, the labour movement was opposed to medicine's monopoly over health care.

The main stimulus for the rise of chiropractic during the 1960s was state involvement in health care. Health insurance, itself a product of working-class struggle, meant an increased state presence in health care as the state moved to rationalize health services. As a result, chiropractic moved from a position of "exclusion" to "limitation" (Willis, 1983:200). Chiropractors have reached a position of accommodation with orthodox medicine but provide a limited service.

Through the process of legitimation, chiropractic has been transformed from an alternative healing system to a neuromuscular specialty. Chiropractic in its initial formulation elaborated a cosmology which was in opposition to the dominant cosmology of the medical profession. Chiropractic was opposed to the medical profession's narrow analysis of disease and to its monopoly on health care. Chiropractic knowledge was drawn from everyday practice which stood in sharp contrast to the more standardized and codified body of scientific-medical knowledge. Since medicine was unable to eliminate chiropractors, it developed a more effective strategy of excluding chiropractic through credentialling. Licensing represents the first stage in that process. The establishment of standards forced chiropractors to formulate a set of rules and regulations, which led to the beginning of the codification of chiropractic. In essence, it signified the co-option of chiropractors, since the debate shifted from the form of knowledge to the content.

From the discussion presented in this chapter it is fair to conclude that the chiropractic profession will continue to expand its role in the provision of health services. Chiropractic has not only survived but has grown and prospered over the past few decades. This is reflected both in the increasing numbers of chiropractors and in the number of patients utilizing chiropractic services. Chiropractors are legally recognized in all provinces with the exception of Newfoundland. In addition, chiropractic services are funded through universal health insurance (either in whole or in part) by half of the provinces.

Unlike other health occupations, chiropractic has not been subordinated but remains a "primary contact" practice, i.e., chiropractors do not require a referral from a medical doctor. The main issue facing chiropractors is over the scope of practice. While chiropractors specialize in neuromuscular problems, they also claim to treat visceral problems. This has led chiropractors into a dispute over occupational territory with other health occupations, in particular physiotherapy. While this will be an ongoing struggle, chiropractors have been incorporated into the health-care system as specialists in neuromuscular problems. Thus the debate no longer centres on whether chiropractors will be included in the health division of labour, but rather on how much of the health dollar they will receive.

STUDY QUESTIONS

1. Can you think of any other factors besides the ones cited in this chapter which could account for the rise of chiropractic, particularly during the last two decades?

2. To what extent do you think that the explanation for the rise of chiropractic can be applied to the holistic health movement in general?

3. In what ways do you think chiropractic and other alternative healers may still challenge medical dominance? Will the medical profession be forced to reform in response to these challenges? Why or why not?

4. What other health occupations appear to be grounded in a life-world knowledge base? Are they attempting to professionalize? If so, are they attempting to become scientific? Explain.

5. If scientific knowledge is considered the only legitimate form of knowledge and its production is restricted to the university, what are the implications for the development of alternative (or oppositional knowledge) in the future? Under what circumstances could oppositional knowledge emerge?

6. What do you think will be the future status of chiropractic?

RECOMMENDED READING

Berliner, H.S., and J.W. Salmon. "The Holistic Health Alternative to Scientific Medicine: History and Analysis." *International Journal of Health Services* 10 (1980): 133–46.

Kelner, M., O. Hall, and I. Coulter. *Chiropractors: Do They Help*? Toronto: Fitzhenry and Whiteside, 1980.

New Zealand. *Chiropractic in New Zealand: Report of the Commission of Inquiry, 1979.* Wellington, New Zealand: Government Printer, 1979.

Wallis, R., and P. Morley, eds. *Marginal Medicine.* London: Peter Owen, 1976.

Willis, E. *Medical Dominance: The Division of Labour in Australian Health Care.* Sydney: George Allen & Unwin, 1983.

REFERENCES

Baer, H. "A Comparative View of Heterodox Health Systems: Chiropractic in America and Britain." *Medical Anthropology* 8 (1984): 151–68.

B.C. Royal Commission on Chiropractic and Drugless Healing. Mr Justice Murphy. *Report*. Victoria, B.C.: Charles F. Benfield (King's Printer), 1932.

Biggs, C.L. "Hands Off Chiropractic: Organized Medicine's Attempts to Restrict Chiropractic in Ontario, 1900–1925." *Chiropractic History* 5 (1985): 11–16.

Boase, J. "Regulation and the Paramedical Professions: An Interest Group Study." *Canadian Public Administration* 25 (1982): 332–53.

Boehme, G. "Midwifery as Science: An Essay on the Relationship Between Scientific and Everyday Knowledge." In *Society and Knowledge*, edited by N. Stehr and V. Meja. New Brunswick, N.J., and London: Transaction Books, 1984.

British Columbia Archives. Attorney General's Papers, GR 702 M–155

Canada. Health and Welfare Canada. *National Health Expenditures in Canada, 1970–1982*. Ottawa: Ministry of Supply and Services, 1985.

Canada. M. Lalonde. *A New Perspective on the Health of Canadians*. Ottawa: Information Canada, 1975.

Churchill. "The Evolution of the Primary Theories of Chiropractic." CMCC: Photocopy, 1977.

Cobb, A. "Pluralistic Legitimation of an Alternative Therapy: The Case of Chiropractic." *Medical Anthropology* 1 (1977): 1–23.

Coburn, D., and C.L. Biggs. "Limits to Medical Dominance: The Case of Chiropractic." *Social Science and Medicine* 22 (1986): 1035–46.

Coulter, I. "The Chiropractic Role: Marginal, Supplemental or Alternative Health Care? An Empirical Consideration." In *Health and Canadian Society: Sociological Perspectives*, 2nd ed., edited by D. Coburn et al. Toronto: Fitzhenry and Whiteside, 1986.

Dye, A. *The Evolution of Chiropractic*. Published by author, Philadelphia, 1977.

Ferguson, J. "False Healing Systems, No. 3–Chiropractic." *Canada Lancet* 51 (1917): 54–78.

Gibbons, R. "Chiropractic History: Turbulence and Triumph: The Survival of a Profession." In *Who's Who in Chiropractic International, 1976–1978*, edited by F. Dzaman. Littleton, Colorado: Who's Who in Chiropractic International Publishing, 1977.

———. "Chiropractic in America: The Historical Conflicts of Culturism and Science." *Journal of Popular Culture* 10, no. 4 (1977b): 720–31.

Hassinger, E., et al. "A Marginal Profession in the Rural Areas: The Case of Rural Chiropractors." Unpublished paper, 1975.

Hewitt, D., and P.H.N. Wood. "Heterodox Practitioners and the Availability of Specialist Advice." *Rheumatology and Rehabilitation* 14 (1975): 191–99.

Kelner, M., O. Hall, and I. Coulter. *Chiropractors: Do They Help?* Toronto: Fitzhenry and Whiteside, 1980.

Koos, E. *The Health of Regionville*. New York: Hafner, 1967.

Larson, M. *The Rise of Professionalism: A Sociological Analysis*. California: University of California Press, 1977.

Maynard, A. *Healing Hands*. Jonorum, Mobile, Alabama, 1977.

McCorkle, T. "Chiropractic: A Deviant Theory of Disease and Treatment." *Human Organization* 20 (1961): 20–23.

Mills, D., and D. Larsen. "The Professionalization of Canadian Chiropractic." In *Health and Canadian Society*, 1st ed., edited by D. Coburn et al. Toronto: Fitzhenry and Whiteside, 1981.

Parkin, F. *The Social Analysis of Class Structure*. London: Tavistock, 1974.

Schmitt, M. "The Utilization of Chiropractors." *Sociological Symposium* 22 (1978): 55–74.

Scotton, R. *Medical Care in Australia: An Economic Diagnosis*. Melbourne: Sun Books, 1974.

Wardwell, W. "A Marginal Professional Role: The Chiropractor." *Social Forces* 30 (1952): 339–48.

———. "The Reduction of Role Strain in a Marginal Social Role." *American Journal of Sociology* 61 (1955): 16–25.

———. "The Future of Chiropractic." *New England Journal of Medicine* 302 (1980a): 688–90.

———. "The Future of Chiropractic." *New England Journal of Medicine* 303 (1980b): 401.

———. "Chiropractors, Challengers of Medical Domination." *Research in the Sociology of Health Care* 2 (1981): 207–50.

White, M., and J. Skipper. "The Chiropractic Physician: A Study of Career Contingencies." *Journal of Health and Social Behaviour* 12 (1971): 300–12.

Wild, P.B. "Social Origins and Ideology of Chiropractors: An Empirical Study of Socialization of the Chiropractic Student." *Sociological Symposium* 22 (1978): 33–54.

Willis, E. *Medical Dominance: The Division of Labour in Australian Health Care*. Sydney: George Allen & Unwin, 1983.

21

PROFESSIONS, IDEOLOGY, AND CHANGE:
The Response of Dentists to a Provincial Dental Plan

Ray Croucher
London University

INTRODUCTION

Changes in health-care delivery systems are often assumed to confer benefits on both the consumer and the profession concerned. These may accrue, for example, from the provision of a more universally available service, or one financed through government revenues, and, therefore, with no direct financial penalties upon the patient. The health profession's interests are assumed to complement those of the consumer, and vice versa.

It has become clear, however, that the narrow occupational interests of the health profession do not necessarily coincide with the wider public interest. Apparently contradictory consequences may arise, such as, for example, dentists' opposition to the establishment of a dental programme intended to provide comprehensive dental services to schoolchildren, without financial penalty, through the use of an expanded-duty dental auxiliary. Why would dentists oppose such a plan? What arguments could they use to justify such opposition?

This chapter provides answers to these questions through an examination of the development of a dental plan in the province of Saskatchewan. Although the details of developments discussed are unique to that province, the issues are universal and relevant to any areas where the professionally dominated model of service delivery operates.

The concepts of professionalism and professional ideology, which are useful in explaining the response of dentists to the Saskatchewan Dental Plan, are introduced in the following section. Next is a detailed discussion of the extent and distribution of dental disease, and of the supply of dental services. The dental profession's response to the proposed dental plan is then examined in the light of the previous discussion of professionalism and professional ideology. After a brief evaluation of the Plan's effectiveness, the chapter concludes with a general overview of the changing patterns of dental health and the supply of dentists, and the ways in which these factors are influencing dentists' patterns of practice.

PROFESSIONS AND IDEOLOGY

One way in which professions have set about differentiating themselves from other groups in society is to claim a set of distinguishing attributes. The most commonly accepted attributes are: a prolonged specialized training in a body of abstract knowledge, a commitment to acting in a disinterested and responsible way towards their clients, and the possession of autonomy. Freidson (1970:82) believes that autonomy is the key feature, and defines it as: "a position of legitimate control over work." The profession may exercise autonomy by determining standards of education, by the licensing of professional practice, and by shaping legislation which concerns the profession.

The right of the profession to self-regulation comes through discussion between the professional association and government officials. Hall (1969:75) describes this as being given "community sanction." Through the efforts of the professional association, a monopoly is granted to all members of the profession. The community as a whole believes it will benefit greatly by granting this monopoly.

In addition to self-regulation and professional autonomy, the profession will also seek to define how others should behave in matters concerned with its work. This definition of behaviour may have internal significance to the profession, involving the conditions of work of other people associated in its division of labour. Freidson (1970:48–49), enumerates several conditions of work associated with the medical profession:

1. Much of the technical knowledge which paramedical workers acquire during their training and use in their work tends to have been discovered or enlarged upon or, at the very least, approved of by physicians.

2. The tasks performed by paramedical workers tend to assist rather than to replace the focal tasks of diagnosis and treatment.

3. Paramedical workers tend to be subordinate, in that their work tends to be performed at the request or "order of" physicians, and is often supervised by them.

4. The prestige accorded paramedical occupations by the general public tends to be less than that accorded to physicians.

This definition of behaviour may also be of external significance, that is, outside of the profession, presuming "to tell society what is good and right for the individual and for society" (Hughes 1958:79). Davis (1980:44) notes that "it has generally been the clinician's concept of dental practice that has dominated the deployment of resources and that has also tended to govern our ways of thinking about the problems of oral health in society."

These professional privileges may be legitimated through the use of an ideology — "a set of ideas which explains why professional autonomy is not desired out of self-interest, but is a requirement for offering the best possible service in the public interest" (Daniels, 1973:39).

Presumably, professional ideology will bear out claims to knowledge. Thus, while the division of labour is initially established by associations and legislation, continuous political activity is required to maintain and improve the profession's position in the marketplace and the division of labour surrounding it. The ideology is used to defend the status quo. To limit its basis to purely professional issues would be erroneous. Bottomore (1971:33) emphasizes that "there are many potential sources of ideology: ethnic and linguistic groups, occupational groups, generations, groups resulting from cultural or regional affinities and traditions as well as social classes." Stamm (1978:407) notes that the Canadian climate of entrepreneurial activity has fostered strong independent professions which have chosen to operate in the private sector using a direct-payment fee-for-service arrangement.

Professional socialization is also important, providing not only a body of knowledge but also a set of norms and values. Goode (1957:194) notes that, "though the profession does not produce the next generation biologically, it does so socially through its control over the selection of professional trainees."

The impact of an ideology upon the wider society may be understood in terms of its "parochial" and "ecumenic" content. "Parochial" ideas have particular meaning for the profession, while "ecumenic" ideas are relevant to the concerns of lay persons entirely apart from their dealings with the occupation in question (Dibble, 1963:230). Dibble suggests that the ideologies of higher-ranking occupational groups will often be more widely diffused throughout the society. It follows that the parochial concerns of a professional association may have a greater impact if they are linked to the values held by society at large.

There is a close relationship between these ideas and those of the professional association with which this chapter is concerned, namely, the College of Dental Surgeons of Saskatchewan. Created under the terms of the Saskatchewan Dental Act, it was granted the powers of licensing and disciplining its members. It concerns itself, in addition, with the promotion and protection of the dental health of the public. No conflict of interest is perceived in the simultaneous serving of both public and professional interests.

The above discussion provides a framework for explaining the response of the dental profession to the Saskatchewan Dental Plan. However, it would be useful to first discuss briefly the status of dental health and dental services in Saskatchewan before the introduction of the Plan.

DENTAL HEALTH AND DENTAL SERVICES

While Stamm (1978:408) has noted that "there exists a paucity of data about the prevalence, incidence and distribution of dental disease in Canada," in Saskatchewan, information had been collected which enabled the patterns of dental health and utilization of dental care to be assessed and evaluated. This information revealed that the children of Saskatchewan suffered from poor dental health. A survey of nearly 7000 schoolchildren in 1951 found an average of 3.2 decayed, missing, and filled teeth in one provincial health region, and an average of 2.9 decayed, missing, and filled teeth in another. McPhail et al. (1972:288) reported a survey carried out in 1954 of 3470 schoolchildren aged 7–17 who resided in rural and urban communities in the southern geographical third of the province. It found that only 13 percent of the children examined needed no treatment at all, while 29 percent needed at least four fillings and 8 percent needed at least four teeth extracted. 10 924 six-year-olds were examined prior to treatment at the beginning of the first year of operation of the Saskatchewan Dental Plan. The Annual Report concluded that "the dental health of children enrolled in the Dental Plan is very poor. Enrollees had, on average, 5.01 decayed teeth and only 1.10 filled teeth" (Saskatchewan Dental Plan, 1976:20). Twelve percent of the children examined needed no treatment at all.

For comparison, a survey of children's dental health in England and Wales carried out in 1973 found that six-year-olds had, on average, 3.7 decayed and filled teeth, of which 2.8 teeth were decayed (Todd, 1975:243). Thirty-three percent needed no treatment. These clinical data hid great variations when socio-economic variables were considered. McFarlane (1964:90) had concluded a review of the impact of socio-economic variables upon the utilization of dental health services by noting that "levels of income and education and, in general, position in the social class structure, determine to a great extent the degree of demand for and the utilization pattern of dental services irrespective, relatively speaking, of need." He also found areas of residence to be relevant. This was illustrated by McCormick's study of 11 993 Grade 1–8 schoolchildren, which found that "more than half (57%) of rural Manitoba schoolchildren seek to obtain some dental treatment, but that these children do not necessarily receive all the treatment they require" (1966:285).

It is possible to study these socio-economic variables in Saskatchewan through the data collected as the result of a World Health Organization International Collaborative Study carried out during 1968 and 1969. Data were collected by interview from both urban and rural areas of the province. A total of 3584 interviews with families were conducted (Josie, 1973:29).

The data from this study show a differential utilization of dental services by area of residence. Respondents from the rural area had a markedly lower level of utilization. Only 39 percent had seen a dentist in the previous 12 months, compared to 52 percent of the urban respondents. Sixty-one percent of the rural residents reported not having seen a dentist for one or more years, while only 48 percent of urban residents reported not having seen a dentist one or more years previous. This category includes those who had never seen a dentist. Further analysis showed that 75 percent of the rural respondents who had visited a dentist in the previous month had done so to relieve a symptom rather than for a preventive "checkup," compared to 51

percent of the urban respondents.

Analysis of the factors of age, income of family head, and education of family head emphasize the influence of area of residence upon dental visits.

In the urban area, the youngest age group was two or three times more likely to have seen a dentist in the previous month as its counterpart in the rural area. It might be anticipated that this age group as a whole would make more visits than other age groups, because dental decay is more prevalent among younger people. This is indeed true for the urban area, but not in the rural area, where there was little variation between age groups.

This urban/rural disparity can also be observed when the income and education of the head of the family are considered. In urban areas there was a positive relationship between income, education, and dental visits: those with high incomes (above average) are twice as likely to have visited a dentist in a one-month period as persons from a low-income (below-average) group. Those from households where the head had a university education were about three times as likely to have visited a dentist, as compared to those where the head of the household had only elementary education. This positive relationship between income, education, and dental visits was less pronounced in rural areas.

In summary, the data from the study conducted by the World Health Organization and other studies showed a differential access to services by area of residence, income, and education. It is apparent that the need for dental treatment was not being met. In addition, substantial socio-economic barriers existed to prevent an equitable and accessible utilization of dental services prior to the introduction of the Saskatchewan Health Dental Plan in 1974.

Saskatchewan residents also suffered from an inadequate supply of dental services. The province had never been adequately served by dentists, as measured by the dentist/patient ratio. In Canada as a whole there had been a slight improvement in the ratio from 1957 (one dentist for every 3031 population) to 1973 (one dentist for every 2581 population). Saskatchewan had the second-worst dentist/population ratio of all the Canadian provinces: in 1973 it was one dentist for every 4049 population (Chebib, 1973; Saskatchewan Department of Health: Health Personnel Inventory, 1972–74; College of Dental Surgeons of Saskatchewan, Annual Register, 1975).

There was also a wide variation in the supply of dental services. The two major urban centres, with less than one third of the population, were served by over half the dentists. In 1972, there were 20 rural communities with populations of 1000 or more which did not have a resident dentist (Saskatchewan Debates and Proceedings, 1972–74; Saskatchewan Department of Health: Health Personnel Inventory, 1972–74).

There was apparently little prospect of improving this situation. Prior to the opening of the College of Dentistry in 1968, prospective dentists had to attend dental schools outside of the province, usually in Alberta or Ontario. It was felt that graduated dentists were then reluctant to return to Saskatchewan, having made personal and professional contacts elsewhere. In the years 1972–79, 29 dentists graduated from the newly opened College of Dentistry in Saskatchewan. Twenty-four of them set up practice in the two main population centres (McPhail, 1976:1). It was also apparent that the province suffered from a net out-migration of dentists. While a surplus of 38 new dentists over those retiring was created between 1957–70, there was also a loss of 32 moving out of the province in the same time period. They formed part of the Canadian pattern of westward interprovincial location.

Those dentists working in the province reported a high degree of "busyness." In 1968 the Canadian Dental Association reported that 39 percent of Saskatchewan dentists were too busy to treat all those requesting appointments, and that Saskatchewan dentists were seeing a higher-than-average number of patients — 2991 in that year, compared to the Canadian average of 1926. Seven percent of the province's dentists felt they could have taken on an additional 400 patients each, resulting in perhaps 5600 more patients being served (Canadian Dental Association, 1968).

The nature of dental problems resulted in a minimal division of labour. The dental hygienist was the dental profession's preferred "expanded-duty" auxiliary, being allowed to "work in the mouth" removing hard deposits from the teeth and providing instruction in oral hygiene. The hygienist's predominantly preventive role contributed to improved efficiency and productivity in dental practices. Hygienists worked under the supervision of the dentist, without impinging on the dentist's right to diagnose and plan treatment. However, in 1972, there were only 30 dental hygienists licensed to practise in the province.

THE SASKATCHEWAN DENTAL PLAN: THE GOVERNMENT PROPOSAL

Recognition of Saskatchewan's dental health problems led the government to consider the introduction of a system established in New Zealand in 1921. In that country, dental nurses provided basic dental services to schoolchildren. By 1970, 19 other countries were using a similar auxiliary. A scheme using dental nurses had been in operation in the Yukon since 1962. Following a successful experiment in one Saskatchewan community, proposals for a universal and comprehensive dental service for children aged 3–12 were prepared. This service would be universal in attempting to remove the existing financial and geographic barriers to dental care, and comprehensive in providing as complete a set of services as possible. Use of the school system to provide clinics was proposed to allow easy access to, and treatment of, the child population. It was also anticipated that dental health education could be organized through the school system. The programme would be financed from general provincial revenues with no premiums or individual levies. Recognizing the problems in the supply of dental services, the government proposal advocated the use of an expanded-duty dental auxiliary, the dental nurse, modelled on the New Zealand auxiliary. It was anticipated that 107 such dental nurses would eventually be employed, along with 12 dentists to be designated as Regional Dental Consultants. Rather than providing services, their task would be to monitor the work of the dental nurses. The dental nurse, envisioned as the key person in a clinic, was described by the Proposal (1972:14) as: "the principal officer of a dental clinic and (performing) dental inspections, restorations and extractions within her competence."

THE RESPONSE OF THE DENTAL PROFESSION

An advisory committee was set up by the provincial government, and input invited from the public. Thirty-eight groups or individuals replied, including seven from dental associations. A major feature of the professional response to the government's proposals was to emphasize what have been characterized as "parochial" issues, issues of concern primarily to the profession and the existing organization of dental care. A primary stress was on the necessity for direct "supervision" of the dental nurse. An example of the type of argument used was contained in the submission of the College of Dental Surgeons of Saskatchewan (1973:8) which stated: "a registered dentist must examine the patient and prescribe, preferably in writing, the treatment plan, and delegate appropriate procedures to the nurses. *The flow of communication in this regard must always be from the dentist to the nurse*" (emphasis in original). Supervision had to be direct, as had traditionally occurred. The new Saskatchewan dental nurse posed a threat to the traditional dental division of labour, as the dental nurse would be expected to recognize when a child needed treatment beyond her competence and refer that child to a

dentist.

The professional association acknowledged the need for an auxiliary to assist in the more efficient delivery of dental care, and proposed using the dental hygienist. Hygienists in the province were prepared to accept direct dental supervision, as shown by this quotation from the brief presented by the provincial Dental Hygienists' Association (1973:1): "Dentist not doing examination, diagnosis, and treatment planning . . . is totally inadequate, as we know from our training that you cannot be educated in two years to do real examinations."

Dentist supervision must be of a "direct" nature because, the professional association argued, only the dentist possesses the training and the knowledge to adequately diagnose and treat dental problems.

Associated with the need for direct supervision was an argument for quality. A connection was implied between quality and the already existing organization of dental services i.e., fee-for-service private practice, where the dentist had complete autonomy. The articulation of the issue of "quality" provides an example of the sometimes contradictory nature of the ideas contained in an ideology. While the profession recognized the need for quality dental services, it also deemed itself the only group able to properly assess this, suggesting that the public might be a poor judge: "Any plan that offers services previously not available, is likely to be acceptable to them and viewed with considerable enthusiasm" (Canadian Dental Association, 1973:8). The definition of quality was partial, relating as it did only to the presence of the dentist in supervision but not considering issues like the equitable distribution and supply of dental personnel throughout the province. A quality programme would be more expensive, as it would need to employ more supervisory dentists. It would also delay the introduction of the programme until sufficient labour was available.

"Ecumenic" ideas — those reflecting the values of the wider society — were also articulated, although with much less frequency. One example was the issue of "freedom." The College of Dental Surgeons of Saskatchewan, claiming to protect the public interest, argued that a choice of services be made available, either through schools or using existing dental practices, stating: "The College feels that it should be the right of parents to be able to have a freedom of choice as to who provides services for their children under the plan" (1973:73). The distribution and availability of existing dental services was such that many children had no choice at all. It is interesting to note that the College of Dental Surgeons also proposed the compulsory attendance of parents during treatment.

A second "ecumenic issue" was "personal responsibility" as a key to good dental health: "It is up to the child and his parents to achieve the goal of dental health — it cannot be given" College of Dental Surgeons of Saskatchewan, 1973:29). Two points should be noted. First, many children needed "catch-up" restorative treatment. Second, to place the responsibility solely on the individual is to fail to recognize the impact of many wider social factors, for instance, the use of sugar in food manufacturing, on dental disease. This factor can be tackled most successfully through fiscal measures and innovative nutrition policies (Ringen, 1979).

A third issue used was "universal availability." It was anticipated that the Plan should include all children regardless of economic status, geographic location, race, colour, or creed. However, this "ecumenic" concern conflicted with the more strongly held "parochial" value of "quality": *We feel it is much more important to introduce a programme of the highest possible quality, rather than to institute a universal programme of dubious value* (College of Dental Surgeons of Saskatchewan, 1973:6; emphasis in original).

It should be noted that in presenting these priorities, the dental association was reflecting the feelings of its members. One conclusion of a survey of Saskatchewan dentists conducted in 1972 was that

a preponderance of Saskatchewan dentists contend that examination, diagnosis and treatment planning should be done by a dentist. Certain other duties must be delegated to a dental nurse and performed either under 'in-office' or 'intermittent' supervision of a dentist. (Thomson et al., 1973:53)

DISENTANGLING QUALITY CARE FROM PROFESSIONALISM

Despite the misgivings expressed by organized dentistry in the province, the Saskatchewan Dental Plan started operation in 1974. By the year 1983–84, 161 784 children and adolescents were enrolled in and receiving services from the Plan. After ten years of operation, it was possible to evaluate the validity of the dental profession's ideological claims about the organization of the Dental Plan. In particular, the "parochial" claims that only a high quality of service would be acceptable to the population of the province, and that a quality service could only be provided through a much higher degree of involvement of the dentist, can be evaluated.

An initial evaluation of the quality of service provided by dental nurses was undertaken in 1976. Three academic dentists from outside Saskatchewan assessed the treatment provided for children. An important feature of their study design was the decision to base their sampling on classrooms, and to examine every child in each classroom. This enabled comparisons between the dental work provided by dental nurses and that provided by dentists in private practice. A second important feature was that the examiners worked "blind"; that is, they were unaware of whether the treatment provided for a child had been done by a dental nurse or a dentist. A major finding of this evaluation was that, for whatever type of filling being considered, those placed by dental nurses were significantly superior to those placed by the dentists working in private practice. Of the fillings placed by dentists, 21 percent were rated as "unacceptable" and 1 percent as "superior," while only 4 percent of the dental nurses' fillings were rated as "unacceptable" and 48 percent as "superior."

"Unacceptable" meant that in the opinion of the examiners, the filling should be redone. The evaluators commented in their report upon the issue of supervision. Noting that it had been controversial and that direct supervision of the dental nurse was not provided by a dentist, they concluded: "On the basis of the data presented here, it would be difficult to insist that more direct supervision of dental nurses take place without making the same suggestion in the case of dentists" (Ambrose et al., 1976:15).

A second evaluation was undertaken of the Plan in 1980. The evaluation was based on data routinely collected during the operation of the Plan. For some of the issues involved in the evaluation, it was possible to make comparisons with other provinces.

It was found that enrollment by parents of children in the Plan had averaged 83 percent and that at least three quarters of this group would receive complete care every year. When those children who received only partial care from the Plan were included, along with those who might be receiving treatment from a private dentist, it was suggested that the level of dental-care utilization by Saskatchewan's children might approach 90 percent, higher than anywhere else in North America.

Comparisons with children's dental plans provided in other provinces showed that actual utilization was about 20 percent higher than in Newfoundland, Nova Scotia, and Quebec, and similar to that in Prince Edward Island. It should be noted that the fee-for-service private-practice delivery model is used in the first three provinces, while Prince Edward Island organizes its services for children in a way similar to Saskatchewan.

The costs of providing treatment for each enrolled child were also compared with these other provincial schemes. The evaluator concluded that "costs, despite the provision of more services and wider coverage (utilization) under the Saskatchewan Health Dental Plan, are actually lower than or equal to the costs of the other provincial insurance children's plans" (Lewis, 1981:73).

The most important finding was that a child enrolled in the Plan would be likely to develop less decay and receive less treatment as he or she got older. This has been corroborated by data collected routinely by the Dental Plan, which shows that in 1984–85, a five-year-old child entering the Plan had an average of 2.16 decayed teeth, while an eleven-year-old child had on average only .55 decayed teeth. In addition, the percentage of five-year-old children with no decay and no restorations had increased from 19 percent in 1975–76 to 43 percent in 1984–85 (Young, 1986:828).

The ultimate test of any health programme is its long-term influence on the health status of a population. In this case, the improved long-term oral health status of Saskatchewan's population is being considered. Lewis (1981:vi) concluded that "the performance to date gives early indications of the likely achievement of this long-term goal."

CHANGING PATTERNS OF ORAL HEALTH

The poor dental health of Saskatchewan schoolchildren prior to the introduction of the Plan has been documented, and the drop in dental decay as a result of their being enrolled in and receiving treatment from the Plan has been noted. Just as dramatic as the need for treatment discovered before the introduction of the Plan has been the general decline in decay, identified among both children and adults.

Surveys in Ontario show that in the ten years from 1972–1982 the percentage of "caries-immune" five-year-old children has grown from 42 percent to 57 percent (Ryan et al., 1983:7), while in British Columbia surveys indicate that in 1958–60, 36 percent of five-year-olds had no decay and that in 1980 this had risen to 63 percent (Journal of the Canadian Dental Association, 1982:302).

A survey carried out in Atlantic Canada to assess the dental treatment needs of children aged 6–7 and 13–14 years showed that 21 percent of the younger age group needed no treatment. Data were also collected on socio-economic variables. This showed that children from rural areas, whose parents possessed below-average levels of education and occupational background, were likely to need more treatment than their counterparts from urban areas with parents of above-average levels of education and occupational background (Banting et al., 1985:20). Thus, while there is less overall need for treatment, the socially disadvantaged are still further penalized. This is also the case in global terms. In many developing countries of the world, where sugar consumption is increasing, dental decay is also increasing. Eighty percent of the world's children are found in developing countries. The increase in decay among these children is more dramatic than the declines observed in developed countries (Graves et al., 1985:697).

The reduction in decay in developed countries has been ascribed to the use of fluoride in toothpaste, improved awareness about health in general and oral hygiene in particular, and changes in the nutritional value of foods, as well as the increased availability of dental services (Ryan et al., 1983:7; Graves et al., 1985:698).

The continued socio-economic patterning of dental decay has been indicated. Surveys also show that decay is concentrated in a smaller proportion of children. In Saskatchewan in 1984, 16 percent of the children enrolled in the Dental Plan possessed 75 percent of all the decay (Young, 1986:828), while a national American study (involving 25 000 children) showed that over half of the total decay occurred in only 20 percent of the study participants (Graves et al., 1985:697). In Saskatchewan, services will be increasingly targeted to the needs of this "high-risk" group.

As more people keep more of their teeth for a longer time, increasing attention is being given to improving the gum health of and preventing gum (periodontal) disease in the population. A recent survey of Saskatchewan adolescents concluded that "periodontal disease and factors leading to it . . . are widespread in the population of adolescents in Saskatchewan. Although these

conditions are widespread, on average they were not severe" (Wolfson and Lewis, 1985:489). Many of the early signs of gum disease may be resolved by improved personal oral hygiene; i.e., there is little need for treatment from the dentist or dental nurse. For the population as a whole, the emphasis should be on checking gum disease in its early states by improved oral hygiene. The priority of the profession should be prevention and health maintenance, rather than its traditional role of reconstruction.

At the same time as disease patterns have been changing, the supply of dentists has been increasing. From 1971 to 1981 in Canada the number of dentists grew by 52 percent. This growth came about as a result of more dentists graduating from the expanded educational system. The population of Canada has grown by only 12 percent in the same time period. From 1981 to 2001 the expected increase in dental graduates will be 40 percent, while the population is projected to increase by 19 percent. Although Saskatchewan was underserviced in dental terms in the past, in the future it is expected that the supply of dentists there will grow at a rate above the Canadian average. The dentist/population ratio has dropped from 1:4191 in 1971 to 1:2941 in 1981 to a projected 1:2234 in 2001 (House et al., 1983:89). The number of dentists in the province has grown from 189 in 1961 to 333 in 1981 (McDermott and Oles, 1982:721). Rather than being too busy to take on new patients, dentists are presently facing the challenge of a possible shortage of patients needing the services they have traditionally supplied (Journal of the Canadian Dental Association, 1981:630). The fear is that in the major population centres the supply of dental labour will exceed the demand for dental treatment (McDermott and Oles, 1982:723).

This issue, coupled with a changed provincial administration perhaps more willing to recognize the "parochial" ideological concerns of the profession (Journal of the Canadian Dental Association, 1982:500), may have been responsible for the decision by dentists to become involved in the Dental Plan. From 1981, adolescents aged 14 years and up who were enrolled in the Plan were to receive their dental care in private dental offices. This was presented as a bridging exercise to encourage the transition from the Plan to seeking (and eventually paying for) care from a dentist in private practice upon leaving school. Covered services were provided at no charge to parents.

Three issues emerged from this plan. First the Provincial Department of Health designated schools as either Dental-Plan or general-practice schools. The Dental-Plan schools had care provided by teams of dental nurses (now called "dental therapists") in school clinics, and were situated predominantly in the two major centres of population. General-practice schools were located in rural areas to encourage and support the continuing equitable availability of dental services for the whole population of these areas.

The second issue was the payment mechanism negotiated. This is described as "a modified capitation payment system," which maintains a façade of "at arm's length" involvement by the government. For every adolescent attending a participating dentist, a capitation payment is made to the College of Dental Surgeons of Saskatchewan by the provincial government. In turn, the College has negotiated payment with participating dentists on a fee-for-service basis. By this mechanism, dentists' anxieties about government interference with their professional authority can be smoothed, and their autonomy of practice maintained. The College of Dental Surgeons acts, in effect, as a clearing house, transferring fee accounts from individual dentists to the provincial Department of Health, where they are processed and a payment list generated for return to the College. A cheque is then drawn on the funds previously made available through the capitation payment received from the government. Ninety-five percent of registered general dental practitioners in Saskatchewan take part in the adolescent programme.

Most importantly, there has been no change in the dental profession's perception that it has the prerogative to serve the whole population.

The Dental Plan's involvement with children and adolescents would suggest that dentists might concentrate their efforts towards the adult and geriatric population of Saskatchewan. It may be anticipated that these potential patients have special needs which are not being fully met. If these needs continue to be overlooked, then the government may feel justified in extending denticare to meet them, either through expanded-duty dental nurses or denturists. Additionally, it has been estimated that only 50 percent of the adult population seek regular dental care (McDermott and Oles, 1982:723). Dentists could direct their services to those who are irregular attenders.

CONCLUSION

This paper has described the background of the development of public dental health services in Saskatchewan and the basis of the arguments used to oppose the introduction of these services by the dental profession. It illustrated the use of an ideology based on claims to knowledge in order to protect the basic attributes of professional status: the autonomy to diagnose disease, prescribe treatment, and delegate duties to other members of the dental team. In seeking to justify this status quo, it oversimplified and distorted the reality of dental health for the population of Saskatchewan. Objective evaluations have demonstrated the ability of the Saskatchewan Health Dental Plan to provide a better quality of treatment than that given by dentists. Furthermore, this care has been provided at a lower cost for more members of the child population than in other provinces.

A number of factors have resulted in changes to the operation of the Plan. These have included changing disease patterns, an increasing number of dentists, and growing provincial deficits. Initially these factors resulted in the dentists becoming involved in the Plan in a way designed to preserve the appearance of professional power. In 1987, however, the provincial government of the day effectively eliminated the dental plan as part of a cost-cutting strategy.

That government, itself committed to privatization and deficit reduction, was more receptive to the ideological claims of the dental profession. One consequence of this is that those dental services previously provided free for schoolchildren under the Plan either will not be provided, or will be provided by privately practising dentists on a fee-for-service basis. It might also be expected that the dental health of the population will decline.

An initial argument of this chapter was that the narrow occupational interests of a health profession may not necessarily coincide with the wider public interest. This has been demonstrated in one particular case, where control of the dental division of labour was sought. Other examples exist to further support this argument: the original introduction of the dental nurse in New Zealand (Gruebbel, 1950:425) and the experiment with a dental auxiliary in the United Kingdom (Hallett, 1950:39) provoked similar opposition from the dental profession in those countries.

The introduction of medical-care insurance has shown the medical profession to be concerned about defending its mandate to define the terms of medical practice. During 1962, medical doctors in Saskatchewan went on strike to resist the introduction of medical-care insurance by the provincial government. The intention of the legislation was to provide universal coverage for all of the population, and to furnish a compre-hensive range of medical-service benefits, financed through government revenues. The chief arguments used by doctors related to interference with professional standards and independence. Badgley and Wolfe point out that doctors "wanted a monopoly only if they controlled it, and did not have to negotiate the price of the product they were selling to consumers" (1967:46).

A comparison between the ideology expressed by the Canadian Medical Association in opposing publicly administered and financed medical-care insurance and the ideology of the dental profession in Saskatchewan reveals a similar emphasis on the importance of professional control of change (Croucher, 1976:97; Blishen, 1969:151).

The introduction of the National Health Service in the United Kingdom in 1948 provides a third example of "parochial" professional attitudes. General practitioners went on strike to protest its introduction, and, again, its aim was to make good health care available to the whole population, without a financial barrier (Murray, 1971:1).

These examples suggest that broad comparisons may be made between the ideologies used by different health professions when changes in health-care policy are introduced which are perceived as challenges to their autonomy. On these occasions the needs of the public are displaced by more parochial occupational concerns.

STUDY QUESTIONS

1. Autonomy has been described as a key attribute of professional status. Find examples of its use by other professionals, analyzing why it is being used in each situation.

2. In Saskatchewan, the subordinate members of the dental division of labour, i.e., dental hygienists, readily accepted the claims made by dentists. Need this always be the case? Find examples where this ready acceptance has *not* happened, and try to determine why.

3. It has been suggested that a major source of an ideology was in the process of professional socialization. What other sources of ideology are there, and what role might they play?

4. What data are available on dental health in your province? Have any changes in the organization of dental services evolved as an outcome of this data? Analyze the role played by the dental profession in these changes.

5. What other factors besides the availability of dental services are important for the promotion of good oral health?

RECOMMENDED READING

Davis, P. *The Social Context of Dentistry*. London: Croom Helm, 1980.

Freidson, Eliot. "Professions and Occupational Principle." In *Professions and Their Prospects*, edited by E. Freidson. New York: Sage Publications, 1973.

Gilb, Corinne Lathrop. *Hidden Hierarchies*. New York: Harper and Law, 1966.

Taylor, Malcolm G. "The Role of the Medical Profession in Formulation and Execution of Public Policy." *Canadian Journal of Economics and Political Science* 26 (1960): 108–27.

Thomson, Heather E., J.R. Mann, and C.W.B. McPhail. "Dentists' Attitudes to Prepaid Children's Dental Care Programs and Expanded Duty Dental Auxiliaries in Saskatchewan." *Journal of the Canadian Dental Association* 39 (1973): 47–54.

Wardwell, W.I. "Limited, Marginal and Quasi-Practitioners." In *Handbook of Medical Sociology*, edited by H.E. Freeman, Sol Levine, and Leo G. Reeder. Englewood Cliffs: Prentice-Hall, 1972.

REFERENCES

Ambrose, E.P., A.B. Hord, and W.J. Simpson. *A Quality Evaluation of Specific Dental Services Provided by the Saskatchewan Dental Plan Final Report*. Regina: Saskatchewan Health Dental Plan, 1976.

Badgley, Robin F., and Samuel Wolfe. *Doctors' Strike: Medical Care and Conflict in Saskatchewan*. Toronto: Macmillan, 1967.

Banting, D.W., A.M. Hunt, and J.C. Baskerville. *Summary Report: Atlantic Canada Children's Oral Health Survey*. London, Ontario: Faculty of Dentistry, University of Western Ontario, 1985.

Blishen, B.R. *Doctors and Doctrines: The Ideology of Medical Care in Canada*. Toronto: University of Toronto Press, 1969.

Bottomore, Tom. "Class Structure and Class Consciousness." In *Aspects of History and Class Consciousness*, edited by Istvan Meszaros. London: Routledge and Kegan Paul, 1971.

Canadian Dental Association. *Survey of Dental Practice, 1968*. Toronto: CDA, Bureau of Statistics, 1968.

———. *Brief submitted to the Minister's Advisory Committee on Dental Care for Children, Province of Saskatchewan*. Ottawa: CDA, 1973.

———. "Saskatchewan Facing Manpower 'Crisis.' " *Journal of the Canadian Dental Association* 47 (1981): 630–31.

———. "B.C. Dental Health Survey Reveals Marked Improvement." *Journal of the Canadian Dental Association* 48 (1982): 362.

———. "New Saskatchewan Health Minister Pledges Consultation with Dental Colleges." *Journal of the Canadian Dental Association* 48 (1982): 500.

Chebib, F.S. *Dentists in Canada*. Winnipeg: Publications Office, University of Manitoba, 1973.

College of Dental Surgeons of Saskatchewan. *Brief Submitted to the Minister's Advisory Committee on Dental Care for Children,*

Province of Saskatchewan. Saskatoon, 1973.

————. *Annual Register*. Saskatoon: 1975.

Croucher, R. *Professionalism and Dental Care Legislation in Saskatchewan*. Unpublished Master's Thesis. Saskatoon: University of Saskatchewan, 1976.

Daniels, Arlene Kaplan. "How Free Should Professions Be?" In *Professions and Their Prospects*, edited by Eliot Freidson. New York: Sage Publications, 1973.

Davis, P. *The Social Context of Dentistry*. London: Croom Helm, 1980.

Dibble, Vernon K. "Occupations and Ideologies." *American Journal of Sociology* 68 (1963): 229–41.

Freidson, Elliot. *Profession of Medicine*. New York: Dodd, Mead and Co., 1970.

Goode, William J. "Community Within a Community: The Professions." *American Sociological Review* 22 (1957): 194–200.

Graves, Richard C., and J.W. Stamm. "Decline of Dental Caries: What Occurred and Will it Continue?" *Journal of the Canadian Dental Association* 51 (1985): 693–99.

Gruebbel, A. O. "Dental Public Health Services in New Zealand." *Journal of the American Dental Association* 41 (1950): 275–83; 422–36.

Hall, R.M. *Occupations and the Social Structure*. Englewood Cliffs: Prentice-Hall, 1969.

Hallett, G.E.M. "Public Dental Service in Great Britain With Reference to the New Zealand Scheme." *British Dental Journal* 90 (1950): 38–41.

House, R.K., G.C. Johnson, and F.A. Edwards. "Manpower Supply Study Scenarios for the Future: Dental Manpower to 2001." *Journal of the Canadian Dental Association* 49 (1983): 85–98.

Hughes, E.C. *Men and Their Work*. Glencoe: Free Press, 1958.

Josie, Gordon H., ed. *Report on Basic Canadian Data. World Health Organization International Collaborative Study of Medical Care Utilization*. Saskatoon: Department of Social and Preventive Medicine, University of Saskatchewan, 1973.

Lewis, D.W. *Performance of the Saskatchewan Health Dental Plan, 1974–80*. Regina: Saskatchewan Health Dental Plan, 1981.

McCormick, C.H. "Availability and Utilization of Dental Services by Rural Manitoba Children." *Journal of the Canadian Dental Association* 32 (1966): 275–80.

McDermott, R.E., and R.D. Oles. "Dentist-to-Population Ratios in Saskatchewan: A Realistic Appraisal." *Journal of the Canadian Dental Association* 48 (1982): 721–23.

McFarlane, B.A. *Dental Manpower in Canada*. Royal Commission on Health Services. Ottawa: Queen's Printer, 1964.

McPhail, C.W.B. Personal communication with author, 1976.

McPhail, C.W.B., T.M. Curry, R.E. Hazelton, K.J. Paynter, and R.G. Williamson. "The Geographic Pathology of Dental Disease in Canadian Central Arctic Populations." *Journal of the Canadian Dental Association* 38 (1972): 288–96.

Murray, D.S. *Why a National Health Service?* London: Pemberton Books, 1971.

Ringen, K. "The New Ferment in National Health Policies: The Case of Norway's Nutrition and Food Policy." *Social Science and Medicine* 13C (1979): 33–41.

Ryan, K., and R.M. Grainger. "Reduction in Dental Caries Prevalence and Treatment Needs for Elementary School Children from 1972–1982." *Journal of Ontario Dental Association* 60, no. 5 (1983): 7.

Saskatchewan. *Debates and Proceedings of the Legislature*. Regina: Queen's Printer, 1972–74.

Saskatchewan Dental Hygienists' Association. *Brief Submitted to the Minister's Advisory Committee on Dental Care for Children, Province of Saskatchewan*. Regina, 1973.

Saskatchewan Department of Health. *A Proposal for a Dental Program for the Children of Saskatchewan*. Regina, 1972.

————. *Health Personnel Inventory, 1972–74.* Regina, 1974.

————. Saskatchewan Health Dental Plan. *Report of First Year of Operation.* Regina: Queen's Printer, 1976.

Stamm, J.W. "An Overview of Dental Care Delivery Systems in Canada." *International Dental Journal* 28 (1978): 406–20.

Thomson, H.E., J.R. Mann, and C.W.B. McPhail. "Dentists' Attitudes to Prepaid Children's Dental Care Programs and Expanded Duty Dental Auxiliaries in Saskatchewan." *Journal of the Canadian Dental Association* 39 (1973): 47–54.

Todd, J.E. *Children's Dental Health in England and Wales, 1973.* London: Her Majesty's Stationery Office, 1975.

Wolfson, S.M., and M.H. Lewis. "A Survey of Periodontal Conditions in Saskatchewan Adolescents." *Journal of the Canadian Dental Association* 51 (1985): 486–89.

Young, W. "Targeting Preventive Services in the Saskatchewan Dental Plan." *Journal of the Canadian Dental Association* 52 (1986): 827–30.

PART VIII

NURSES' EDUCATION AND WORK

INTRODUCTION

There has been considerable change in the form and content of nursing education and work. The ramifications of these changes are discussed in this section.

Rejecting theories of modernization and industrialization and stressing the value of a historical materialist and feminist approach, Warburton and Carroll, in Chapter 22, analyze the class and gender implications of hospital nursing by placing it firmly within industrial and domestic social relations that are capitalist and patriarchal. Particular emphasis is placed on nurses' subordination to male physicians and hospital administrators. The class and gender composition of Canadian nursing is illustrated with Canadian Census data, and materials from recent research on Canadian nursing are used to examine the impact of managerial strategies on the nursing labour process, especially those taken in response to the prevailing fiscal crisis of the capitalist state. Nurses' commitment to professionalism and the more recent shift to unionism are studied in the light of their exposure to a process of proletarianization that puts them into situations resembling those of industrial workers. For many of them, this leads to increased class consciousness. Gender issues, however, are becoming more prominent in this field and it may well be that, as in other struggles involving workers in institutions of social reproduction, the pursuit of justice and equality for women will become a major field for political action in the coming decades.

The demand for improvements in the education of nurses has been a continuing focal point in nurses' quest for professional status. Wotherspoon, in Chapter 23, examines the relationship between the development of nursing education in Canada and the nature of control over the nursing profession.

It is argued that concepts of nurses' professionalism are limited by their uncritical acceptance of social structures and occupational practices. Alternatively, it is proposed that nursing be conceptualized according to the social relations which develop around the employment of nurses in health-care work. Viewed in this way, nursing education can be understood as an arena within which competing conceptions of nursing are given shape.

Data reveal that while nurses in this century have made substantial improvements in income levels and working conditions, their subordinate status has been maintained by corporate, state, and medical intervention in health-care policy and nursing education. Despite nurses' efforts to improve their educational qualifications and overall quality of their training programmes, serious inadequacies remain on both accounts. In conclusion, Wotherspoon states that if present trends continue, nurses may become channelled into two separate streams — a highly educated, male-dominated elite, and a feminized pool of less educated nurse practitioners.

Campbell, in Chapter 24, discusses the structure of stress in nurses' work. This chapter is based on research which focusses on the document-based control methods whereby nurses' labour processes can be subordinated to fiscal restraint policies. Hospital nursing in Canada has been reorganized during the last decade by, and in response to, the introduction of documentary systems of managing nurses' work. Management priorities emphasize increased efficiency and productivity — but do so at a cost to both nurses' and patients' well-being. The stress nurses feel arises not only from an increased pace of work, but through losing control over the quality of care they are able to deliver. New nursing management technology such as patient classification, flexible staffing methodologies, and documentary assessment of nursing "quality," even as they improve hospital administration and bring nursing into the era of modern document-based administrative practices, externalize control and bypass nurses' professional judgement.

22

CLASS AND GENDER IN NURSING

Rennie Warburton and William K. Carroll
University of Victoria

INTRODUCTION

In the analysis of health-care systems, nursing is of obvious importance, since nurses provide most of the direct care that hospital patients receive. But the work that nurses do has implications reaching well beyond the issue of health-care delivery. In broad terms, nursing in Canada is a field of work in which one can study the intersection of class and gender relations in advanced capitalist societies. This chapter analyzes the place of nursing within the social relations of capitalist society, drawing out some implications for the consciousness and action of nurses as primarily female workers.

Until recently, sociological approaches to nursing were simply applications of concepts embedded in the theory of "industrial society." According to this approach, in the past two centuries human societies have been undergoing a process of "modernization," characterized by such trends as industrialization, institutional differentiation, increasing affluence and social mobility, and professionalization. This perspective placed great emphasis on the socialization process through which individuals learn the val-

ues and skills appropriate to their roles in a complex social system; it paid little attention to issues of women's oppression and class conflict (Corwin, 1961; Smith, 1981; MacLean, 1974). Nursing was viewed within the distinct social institution of medicine, as a highly specialized occupation whose mainly female practitioners had to be carefully prepared for dedicated, demanding, and responsible tasks requiring high levels of knowledge and expertise and a clear sense of their role in an increasingly complex division of labour. Due to the advancement of medical science and the progress brought about by industrialization, nursing was seen as a quasi-profession aspiring to the status already achieved by physicians, mainly by insisting on higher educational requirements for entry into nursing (Etzioni, 1969). The two professions of nursing and medicine were seen to be mutually interdependent (Diamond, 1984:13). The sexual division of labour, in which female nurses typically worked for male doctors, was attributed to culturally given, normative expectations concerning sex roles, e.g., nurses were mainly women because women were expected to perform mother-surrogate roles, providing tender, loving care (Thorner, 1955; Schulman, 1972; Cockerham, 1982:178).

This sort of uncritical, ahistorical, and optimistic analysis was typical of North American sociology during the period of economic expansion following World War II, when unemployment was minimal, average living standards the highest in the world, and sociologists concerned that their work should remain "value-free," i.e., strictly confined to explaining social behaviour rather than evaluating the quality of contemporary society. In fact, a lot of their sociology, far from being value-free, was actually a justification of the existing structure of society.

In the past two decades several developments have occurred to undermine that approach. The realization on the part of thousands of women that scholarship generally, and sociology in particular, had totally neglected women's oppression has had special significance for research and theory on nurses (Diamond, 1984; Game and Pringle, 1983). The persistence of other kinds of social inequality in North America, especially the disparity between the large incomes of the medical profession and the huge profits of health-sector corporations as compared to the privations of the poor and of ethnic minorities, has led to serious criticism of both the quality of life and the economic structure of capitalism. Studies of the rise of medical dominance and of the "American Health Empire" were part of this development (Freidson, 1970; Ehrenreich and Ehrenreich, 1970; Coburn et al., 1983). One of its main features has been a growing interest in applying Marxist theory, suppressed for decades in North American intellectual discourse with the attack on socialist trade unionism after the First World War and the cold-war McCarthyism which followed the Second (Navarro, 1983). This resurgence of Marxism should not be seen as a fad or the product of extremist radicalism. It is based on the capacity of Marxist analyses to further the explanation of social situations and processes in capitalist societies. Compared to liberal or value-neutral sociology, its strength lies in its concern with historical and dialectical analysis

of the origins of contemporary social structures. Thus, the social relations that presently surround nursing as a position within advanced capitalism are viewed not as the effect of "modernization" but as the provisional outcome of struggles based on opposing interests and unequal power among classes and gender groups.

NURSING AND MODERN CAPITALISM

A basic tenet of Marxism is that to analyze a social practice, we must consider it within the economic, political, and ideological relations of the society in which it appears. In the case of contemporary nursing, this means recognizing that we are dealing with societies where the capitalist mode of production dominates the economy, deeply influences the political system, and appropriates the relations and practices of civil society (Urry, 1981).

The hallmark of capitalism is the selling of the individual's capacity to labour to an employer who uses it to make a profit on the sale of commodities produced by employees, the owners of that labour power. No other economic system throughout human history has operated in this way. In order to establish itself, capitalism had to replace previous modes of production, including feudal agriculture, slavery, and independent commodity production. The latter involves the owner of the means of production using his or her own labour power to produce commodities. Self-employed, "private-duty" nurses who sell their services for a fee are a good example of independent commodity producers. The rise of modern hospitals has reduced their numbers within the nursing labour force from a majority of nurses as recently as 1932 (Weir, 1932) to a minute proportion at present, as Table 1 illustrates. Capitalism's main effect on nursing, therefore, has been to make it a form of wage-labour used in hospitals, that is, to *proletarianize* nurses. Contrary to the beliefs of many nurses and public perceptions of nursing as a profession, nurses are actually skilled members of the working class.

Table 1. Class Composition of Canadian Nurses, 1931–1981

Year	Graduate Nurses				Nurses in Training			
	Wage Earner	Self-Employed	Unpaid	Total	Wage Earner	Self-Employed	Unpaid	Total
1931	47.81	43.06	9.13	100	71.01	0.00	28.99	100
1941	79.52	10.78	9.70	100	45.60	0.00	54.40	100
1951	99.97	0.03	0.00	100	100.00	0.00	0.00	100
1961	96.27	3.71	0.02	100	99.79	0.15	0.06	100
1971	99.12	0.72	0.17	100	99.95	0.00	0.00	100
1981	99.41	0.54	0.04	100	0.00	0.00	0.00	0

Source: for 1931–1971, Census of Canada various years. For 1981, Statistics Canada special tabulation.

At first glance, the establishments in which nurses are employed as hourly wage-earners do not appear to be capitalist, because they do not produce commodities to realize a direct profit, particularly not in Canada, where hospitals are state-funded institutions. But Bellaby and Oribaber (1977:802–3) have demonstrated that hospital treatment is itself a commodity. It has obvious use-value to the patient, but also has exchange-value, inasmuch as it competes with alternatives such as osteopathy, chiropractic, and faith healing, which usually have to be paid for. It also helps to realize capitalist profit by consuming commodities from other branches of the health-care industry: the machines and apparatus of medical technology, pharmaceutical products, etc. Finally, by emphasizing the individual source and nature of medical problems, the impersonal treatment of patients as "cases," and their helpless, subordinate status vis-à-vis physicians and other medical personnel, hospital treatment helps perpetuate the social and psychological conditions on which capitalist corporations depend for their domination of the labour process.

A similar point can be made if we examine hospital treatment from the perspective of nurses. Their work situation in hospitals is structured in terms of capitalist relations of production, which involve the direct subordination of workers to managerial dominance. There is a basic division between rank-and-file and supervising nurses. The latter manage nursing divisions, assisted by Head Nurses, the equivalent of forepersons in industry. Below them are General Duty Registered Nurses, followed by Licensed Practical Nurses, Nursing Aides or Assistants, and student nurses. These objective relations produce support for existing hierarchies of class power and isolate nurses from each other as workers. Campbell's study of hospital nurses in Ontario shows how a two-tiered occupation is being created as those who manage nursing are split off from those who give nursing care (Campbell, 1984:12). The same point was made by Carpenter (1977) in an analysis of nurses' experience in Britain. Head nurses, in particular, are being drawn more and more into management (Campbell, 1984:173). Nurses also supervise and give orders to other hospital workers, e.g., cleaners, orderlies, kitchen staff. We suggest that this ambiguity in their position tends to reinforce their commitment to professionalism and has inhibited the development of a working-class consciousness.

There is still another sense in which hospital nursing must be viewed within the context of an advanced capitalist system. Because they are accountable to governments, modern state-funded hospitals are subject to evaluations of efficiency and cost-accounting like those used in the private corporate sector. In part, this is due to the responsibilities governments feel to ensure that funds are well-spent, but it also places hospitals, and nurses as their primary employees, in competition with other recipients of state funds, including corporations which seek subsidies, grants, research and development funds, highways, cheaper electric power, and other infrastructural services.

In recent years, these competitive pressures have intensified. Economic stagnation and fiscal crisis have prompted governments in the capitalist democracies to shift funding priorities away from the social programmes and demand management of the Keynesian welfare state, to the "supply-side" private investment incentives of neoconservatism (Wolfe, 1983).

In coping with these changing state priorities, hospital management has adopted measures of nurses' work performance, job evaluations, methods of speeding up the delivery of nursing services, definitions of optimum staffing requirements, etc. These "efficiency measures" make excellent sense from the standpoint of hospital administrators, whose objective is to obtain maximum production and consumption for every dollar invested. Campbell's study of measures to produce efficiency among hospital nurses indicates that, though the record-keeping practices yield documented, measurable information, they are wrongly viewed as the neutral application of modern technology in the pursuit of efficiency. They are a means of reinforcing the power of employer over employee, devices of so-called "objective" management which displace nurses' control over their practice (Campbell, 1984). Campbell argues that even though these "accounting" processes may organize higher-status "occupational content" into nurses' work, their most significant effect is an increase in managerial control over nursing knowledge.

In this sense, the incorporation of "efficiency measures" into nurses' labour process may be viewed as an extension of the proletarianization process outlined by Wagner (1980:279), which included creation of "a stable and loyal staff and the development of a hospital

hierarchy based on Tayloristic principles of dividing the work process into the smallest possible components and giving cheaper work to unskilled and semi-skilled workers." The proletarianization of nurses, however, has also entailed a process of *ideological subordination*, similar to that experienced by professionals in profit-making organizations. Employed professionals are increasingly required to faithfully serve "organizational interests, even where basic professional ideals — in this case, of service to clients — are thereby sacrificed" (Derber, 1983:324).

Campbell (1984:182) claims that erosion of the quality of nursing care is one consequence of this subordination. High quality of care can be maintained so long as the staff is adequate to provide good care according to nurses' traditional standards. This includes the chance to take responsibility and enjoy self-respect by applying one's skills and energy to meet a patient's needs. However, Campbell's informants commented that their work had been intensified beyond the level at which they could guarantee good care.

We have obtained evidence which to some extent supports this analysis in a recent survey of 179 Registered Nurses at a large acute-care hospital in Victoria, British Columbia, which was affected by the provincial government's austerity programme of 1982–1984. In response to a question on how often they found the situation of not having enough time to complete all of their nursing tasks stressful, only 10 percent of respondents said "never," 46 percent "occasionally," 31 percent "frequently," and 13 percent "very frequently." Ninety-two percent agreed that the restraint programme had directly affected nurses' working conditions at the hospital. Of these respondents, 77 percent spontaneously mentioned insufficient staffing, 38 percent mentioned bed shortages, and 22 percent mentioned a heavier workload when asked how restraint had affected nurses' working conditions. Similarly, 76 percent of respondents agreed that the government's restraint programme had directly affected patients' safety at the hospital. In describing the effects of restraint on patients' safety, 69 percent of respondents spontaneously cited understaffing, 28 percent cited inadequate monitoring of patients, 26 percent cited patient overcrowding, and 22 percent cited inadequate patient care.

The close connection between nurses' working conditions and the quality of care which they are able to give patients has important implications for their role in class struggles. Insofar as restraint-motivated "efficiency measures" bring an erosion of both working conditions and the quality of care, it is likely that nurses' collective struggles will increasingly centre on these related issues. For instance, the chairperson of the B.C. Nurses' Union Bargaining Committee gave the following description of two of the union's recent contract proposals:

> One of our proposals is for formal recognition of the right of nurses to use the grievance procedure to correct patient care problems. This is something that has been denied us. Another proposal deals with the effects of poor scheduling on us and our patients. Right now, nurses can be required to work eight days, or nights, in a row. We want six to be the maximum, so nurses can give the best possible care without the extra burden of unnecessary fatigue. (Timmivaara, 1986)

Proposals such as these, explicitly linking hospital nurses' interests as workers to the interests of their predominantly working-class clientele, exemplify a broader tendency in the labour movement to establish worker-consumer alliances. As Bernard (1986:382) points out,

> labour is trying to increase its strength by breaking down the separation between producers and consumers. Unions are making issues such as deregulation, centralization, and care of the handicapped into issues of public policy. Workers as the producers and deliverers of services are beginning to recognize that they have expertise and the right to propose their own alternatives.

In their work as deliverers of health care, nurses are in a position to contribute to this widening of the labour movement's agenda.

MALE DOMINANCE, MEDICAL DOMINANCE, MANAGERIAL DOMINANCE, AND NURSES' STRUGGLES

As important as it is to situate nurses in the context of their developing class relations, it is equally crucial to recognize the fact that nursing is a particular form of "gendered labour." Throughout history, healing, caring, and looking after others have been typical of women's activity. As one sociologist put it, "the experience of caring is the medium through which ... women gain admittance into both the private world of the home and the public world of the labour market" (Graham, 1983:30). Together with child care, cleaning, teaching, secretarial and social work, waitressing, and other typical female service jobs, nursing has been a major avenue for women to move out of confined, dependent, domestic roles. The growth of nursing as a feminized occupation in Canada is illustrated in Table 2. Entering nursing, however, has not freed women from patriarchal relationships.

The earliest hospital nurses were either nuns who worked in charitable hospitals, or poor women like Charles Dickens' character Sairey Gamp, who staffed the work-houses where the destitute spent the end of their lives. The nineteenth-century reforms attributed to the influence of Florence Nightingale were efforts on the part of women of the respectable classes to open up working opportunities, mainly for women of bourgeois or petit bourgeois origins who needed alternatives to either marriage or burdensome and inactive spinsterhood (Gamarnikow, 1978:111–12). For this reason, good manners, cleanliness, respectability, and other middle-class virtues and behaviour patterns have been stressed in nursing training.

The granting of opportunities for wage-earning and service occurred within patriarchal settings. Nursing was one of those "natural" spheres of activity for women that was rooted in the institution of the family. According to one proto-feminist speaker in 1885,

Table 2. Gender Composition of Canadian Nurses,* 1901–1981

Year	Percent Female	Nurses† as % of Female Labour Force	Nurses as % of Total Labour Force
1901	100.00	0.12	0.02
1911	97.78	1.54	0.21
1921	98.96	4.36	0.67
1931	100.00	4.79	0.81
1941	99.41	4.63	0.92
1951	98.21	4.36	0.96
1961	96.84	4.79	1.31
1971	95.84	3.53	1.21
1981	95.39	3.79	1.54

* Includes graduate nurses and nurses-in-training
† Includes female nurses only

Source: Census of Canada, various years.

to enlarge the working sphere of woman to the measure of her faculties, to give her a more practical and authorized share in social arrangements which have for their object the amelioration of suffering, is to elevate her in the social scale. (Gamarnikow, 1978)

The Nightingale reformers did not upset the power and control that the medical profession had secured over the health system since the early nineteenth century (Larson, 1977; Coburn et al., 1983). Medical dominance in health care did not simply emerge just as a matter of course or as a simple manifestation of superior knowledge. It involved weeding out the unqualified, obtaining the support of universities and the state, and restricting the activities of competitors like pharmacists — and nurses! (Torrance, 1981:16). Judi Coburn (1981:184) writes of the "housewife-cum-nurse-doctor-apothecary" who, in the 1870s, administered care in remote communities. She points out how women, once independent practitioners, were denied training and thus relegated to a subservient position within the medical profession. Complete subservience to the doctor and silent obedience to his authority were stressed in nursing training. Thus the

development of nursing as a specific location within the division of health-care labour must be viewed as an integral aspect of the rise of medical dominance. As sex-segregated occupations, both medicine and nursing have been historically constructed and ideologically legitimated on the basis of predominant gender relations in capitalist society. Melosh's phrase "The Physician's Hand" captures the essence of nurses' work as subordinate to physicians in the medical hierarchy (Melosh, 1982:6–10). Gamarnikow (1978) claims that nursing is united by a common recognition of the existence and nature of boundaries between itself and medicine, boundaries which reflect unequal professional power and which have been justified by a naturalistic ideology based on an assumed biological basis for the sexual division of labour. She sees medical dominance contained in the limits on access to patients of practitioners of other health occupations, through the monopoly of initial intervention which designates the patient qua patient: "Once the health care process is under way, nursing consists of a variety of tasks, some of which are ordered by the doctor, and others which reflect current ideas about providing a healthy environment" (Gamarnikow, 1978:106). Physicians are not the only patriarchal group with which nurses have had to contend. Hospital administrators and members of governing bodies have also been overwhelmingly male.

The major implication of nurses' status as female employed workers has been their incorporation into hospital settings in subordinate passive roles under the control of male superiors. This situation was facilitated by nurses' adoption of occupational values of dedicated service and commitment to patient care, values rooted in the Christian religious tradition of "sisters of charity" and the devoted activities associated with Florence Nightingale. For several decades in the early part of this century this ideology was instilled into student nurses by an often cruel regime run by autocratic matrons, the appointed representatives of the male-dominated hospital hierarchy. Wagner (1980:200–81) notes how the professional associations fostered loyalty and sympathy for the hospitals and developed an aura of prestige around nursing.

The use of student nurses in hospitals up to the 1930s, paid only in the form of room and board plus training, is one of the most blatant forms of women's exploitation in recent times. For example, student nurses comprised the entire ward staff of the largest training hospital in Canada, working as unpaid, sweated labour. In one case, trained nurses were found to have been paid less than the hospital rat-catcher! A common type of exploitation involved sending student nurses out to do private nursing, the fees being paid to the hospital (Coburn, 1981:189). The Weir Report of 1932 documented frank admissions by nursing school superintendents in Ontario that a cheap labour supply was the prime reason for the existence of training schools.

The low-grade working conditions of hospital nurses in this period were demonstrated by Weir (1932) and by Eaton (1938). According to Weir, inadequate education, low wages, and working hours which were so long that nurses had insufficient time for study and recreation were widely prevalent. Eaton reported twelve-

and sixteen-hour working days as normal. Both of these reports advocated an eight-hour workday for nurses.

Like most other workers, nurses eventually organized to improve their situation. The earliest nurses' groups were formed by the most highly trained, who, in imitation of the medical profession, sought to control the quality of nursing by improving the level of nurses' education and restricting entry to the properly qualified. Judi Coburn compares the struggle for registration to the closed-shop movement among unions. In arguing for protection against lower-paid practical nurses, graduates were not so much seeking professional recognition similar to that enjoyed by lawyers and doctors, but the privileges of the labour aristocracy. In excluding experienced but unqualified practical nurses, the nursing elite in fact helped to perpetuate the exploitation of cheap nursing labour (Coburn, 1981:195). Goldstone (1981:xx) observed in her study of nurses in British Columbia that the graduates who pressed for legalization of nursing registration showed no interest in pressing for improved remuneration or working conditions. They were more concerned with abolishing the oppressive schools of nursing, and in the decades following the passing of nurses' registration acts, a large number of schools in Canada were indeed closed. Nurses' educational aspirations shifted to the pursuit of recognition by universities of nursing as a degree-worthy discipline; the breakthrough came with the establishment of a degree programme at the University of British Columbia in 1919 (Canadian Nurses' Association, 1968).

Concern over working hours led to the struggle for an eight-hour day, pitting nurses against physicians and hospital administrators who were determined to discourage such unionist behaviour (Coburn, 1981:197). The importance of class struggle in understanding modern nursing can be seen further in the organizing which occurred during the Second World War. Nurses across the continent, led by the California State Nursing Association, and faced with competitive rivalry from various trade unions attempting to organize them, responded to their working conditions with collective bargaining measures (Wagner, 1980:288). In Canada, this began with the formation of negotiating committees within nurses' associations. Several labour unions attracted lower-echelon, practical nurses into membership, but Registered Nurses remained opposed to unionization per se. They had, nevertheless, accepted the principle of collective bargaining as a means of resisting managerial dominance.

As bargaining took place and nurses' remuneration increased, a rift developed in the professional associations between those who felt they should confine themselves to clinical issues, improvements in the quality of nursing, professional ethics, etc., and those who identified with the struggle for better working conditions. Many, of course, saw no incompatibility between the two types of activity. The outcome has been the emergence of unions of Registered Nurses in most provinces during the past 15 years. Other levels of nursing, including Licensed Practical Nurses, have joined various hospital workers' unions. An instructive example of nurses' turn toward unionism and collective action arose in British Columbia in 1983 when the nurses' union joined the Solidarity Coalition, an alliance of labour, women's, and community groups, in its protests against the Social Credit government's attacks on social services and trade-union rights. These trends all point to nurses becoming increasingly conscious of their situation as employed workers, albeit with a commitment to professional notions of high-quality service, devotion to duty, and to keeping abreast of improvements in knowledge and nursing skills.

This is not to say, however, that Registered Nurses have acquired a high degree of class consciousness, explicitly aligning themselves with other sections of the working class. As Judi Coburn (1981:200) puts it, nurses have remained "workers who have not seen themselves as workers." She goes on to note how they perpetuate divisions between themselves and other hospital workers by identifying with the status of the medical profession. To Coburn it is not therefore surprising that nurses are still faced with competition from less skilled women whose cheap labour is a boon to hospital administrators.

We have already noted nurses' subordination to male dominance and the class-based authority of doctors and hospital administrators. But their work setting is only one field in which they are subject to the effects of class and patriarchy. The other major arena where these relations are found is the home. Like other women, nurses face varying circumstances on the domestic scene. Some are secondary income earners in fairly wealthy households. Others are single parents or other prime income earners with families. Some live in relatively egalitarian households, others in traditional, patriarchal ones. Whatever the structure of their household, most are heavily involved in domestic labour. We know of no research into nurses' domestic relations, but we expect that they may have an effect on nurses' consciousness of class and gender. In our current research on Registered Nurses in Victoria we expect to throw some light on these issues.

CONCLUSION

In this chapter we have indicated how class and gender relations provide the broad framework in which contemporary struggles of nurses can be understood. By this we do not mean that nurses' efforts to research their delivery of care and to improve the services they offer are not important. Indeed, they are highly significant. But those services are being threatened as the current crisis of the international economy and of capitalist states within it leads to public expenditure cutbacks becoming part of nurses' reality. What, then, of the future?

Unless there is a massive revival of the prosperity that prevailed in the 1950s and 1960s, the quality of nursing and health care generally will be jeopardized, as governments continue to cut back on medical insurance and hospital funding. To the extent that nurses collectively resist the proletarianized working conditions, the pay restraints, and the job insecurity that result from such cutbacks, it is conceivable that increasing numbers of nurses will discover what they have in common not only with other health-care workers but with the rest of the working class. Indeed, as deliverers of human services, nurses are in a position to help broaden the agenda of the labour movement by linking their struggles for improved working conditions to the struggle for improved health care for the population at large. Such linkages have significance precisely because struggles in the sphere of reproduction — whether over health care, education, or the family — have become central to the politics of advanced capitalism (Urry, 1981).

A similar point can be made concerning nurses' role in the struggle for gender justice. As Melosh (1982:219) has noted, nurses' experience of paid work does not merely reinforce women's subordination, it also heightens the contradictions of gender inequality. Unlike housewives, nurses occupy a position of economic independence from which they make indispensable contributions in the social provision of health care. As members of a feminized "semi-profession" subordinate to primarily male physicians and administrators, nurses have considerable scope to challenge and disrupt existing notions of "women's place." This could mean attacking the sexual division of labour on both the industrial and domestic fronts, an enterprise that Maroney (1983:65) deems essential to the long-term solidarity of "a working class that has two sexes."

Sociological projections are always hazardous and usually a source of future embarrassment, as the practical actions of women and men ruthlessly defy our neat causal frameworks. Nevertheless, this analysis does suggest a working hypothesis of modest scope. As skilled female workers engaged in the reproduction of labour power, nurses may play a strategically significant role in the working-class and feminist struggles of the late twentieth century.

STUDY QUESTIONS

1. What ambiguities are found in the class location of nurses?

2. In what ways do nurses face gender subordination?

3. How does class struggle manifest itself among nurses?

4. What are the implications of hospital management "efficiency measures" for the quality of patient care?

5. Examine the shortcomings of mainstream sociology and modernization theory for the study of nursing.

6. Are nurses professionals or skilled workers?

RECOMMENDED READING

Ashley, J. *Hospitals, Paternalism and the Role of the Nurse.* New York: Teachers' College Press, 1979.

Ehrenreich, B., and D. English. *Witches, Midwives and Nurses: A History of Women Healers.* Westbury, N.Y.: Feminist Press, 1973.

Game, A., and R. Pringle. *Gender at Work.* Sydney: George Allen and Unwin, 1983.

Gibbon, J.M., and M.S. Mathewson. *Three Centuries of Canadian Nursing.* Toronto: Macmillan, 1947.

Kramer, M. *Reality Shock: Why Nurses Leave Nursing.* St. Louis: C.V. Mosby & Co., 1974.

REFERENCES

Bellaby, P., and F. Oribaber. "The Growth of Trade Union Consciousness Among General Hospital Nurses." *Sociological Review* 25, no. 4 (1977): 801–22.

Bernard, E. "Labour Tactics Today." In *After Bennett*, edited by W. Magnusson et al., 368–82. Vancouver: New Star Books, 1986.

Campbell, M. "Information Systems and Management of Hospital Nursing: A Study in the Social Organization of Knowledge." Ph.D. Thesis. University of Toronto, 1984.

Canadian Nurses' Association. *The Leaf and the Lamp*. Ottawa: Canadian Nurses' Association, 1968.

Carpenter, M. "The New Managerialism and Professionalism in Nursing." In *Health and the Division of Labour*, edited by M. Stacey et al. London: Croom Helm, 1977.

Coburn, D., et al. "Medical Dominance in Canada in Historical Perspective: The Rise and Fall of Medicine?" *International Journal of Health Services* 13, no. 3 (1983) 407–31.

Coburn, J. "I See and Am Silent: A Short History of Nursing in Ontario." In *Health and Canadian Society*, edited by D. Coburn et al. Toronto: Fitzhenry and Whiteside, 1981.

Cockerham, W.C. *Medical Sociology*. 2nd ed. Englewood Cliffs, New Jersey: Prentice-Hall, 1982.

Corwin, R.G. "The Professional Employee: A Study of Conflict in Nursing Roles." *American Journal of Sociology* 66 (1961): 604–15.

Derber, C. "Ideological Proletarianization and Post-Industrial Labour." *Theory and Society* 12, no. 3 (1983): 309–41.

Diamond, T. "Elements of a Sociology for Nursing: Considerations on Care-Giving and Capitalism." *Mid-American Review of Sociology* 9, no. 1 (1984): 3–21.

Eaton, R. *Report of the Advisory Committee on Labour Conditions in Hospitals*. Victoria: Provincial Secretary and Ministry of Labour, 1938.

Ehrenreich, B., and J. Ehrenreich. *The American Health Empire: Power, Profits and Politics*. New York: Random House, 1970.

Etzioni, A. *The Semi-Professions and their Organization: Teachers, Nurses and Social Workers*. New York: Free Press, 1969.

Freidson, E. *Professional Dominance*. Chicago: Aldine, 1970.

Gamarnikow, E. "Sexual Division of Labour: The Case of Nursing." Chapter 5 in *Feminism and Materialism: Women and Modes of Production*, edited by A. Kuhn and A.M. Wolpe. London: Routledge and Kegan Paul, 1978.

Game, A., and R. Pringle. "Sex and Power in Hospitals: The Division of Labour in the Health Industry." Chapter 5 in *Gender at Work*, edited by A. Game and R. Pringle. Sydney: George Allen and Unwin, 1983.

Goldstone, I.L. "The Origins and Development of Collective Bargaining by Nurses in British Columbia, 1912–76." M.Sc Thesis, University of British Columbia, 1981.

Graham, H. "Caring: A Labour of Love." In *A Labour of Love: Women, Work and Caring*, edited by J. Finch and D. Groves. London: Routledge and Kegan Paul, 1983.

Larson, M.S. *The Rise of Professionalism: A Sociological Analysis*. Berkeley: University of California Press, 1977.

MacLean, U. *Nursing in Contemporary Society*. London: Routledge and Kegan Paul, 1974.

Maroney, H.J. "Feminism at Work." *New Left Review*, No. 141 (Sept.–Oct. 1983).

Melosh, B. *The Physician's Hand: Work, Culture and Conflict in American Nursing*. Philadelphia: Temple University Press, 1982.

Navarro, V. "Radicalism, Marxism and Medicine." *International Journal of Social Services* 13, no. 2 (1983): 179–202.

Schulman, S. "Mother Surrogate — After a Decade." In *Patients, Physicians and Illness*, edited by E. Jaco, 233–34. New York: Free Press, 1972.

Smith, J.P. *Sociology and Nursing*. Edinburgh: Churchill Livingstone, 1981.

Thorner, I. "Nursing: The Functional Significance of an Institutional Pattern." *American Sociological Review* 20 (1955): 531–38.

Timmivaara, S. "Nurses Want Fair Deal." *Victoria Times-Colonist*, 18 May 1986, p. A4.

Torrance, G.M. "Introduction." In *Health and Canadian Society*, edited by D. Coburn et al., 1–28. Toronto: Fitzhenry and Whiteside, 1981.

Urry, J. *The Anatomy of Capitalist Societies*. London: MacMillan, 1981.

Wagner, D. "The Proletarianization of Nursing in the United States, 1932–46." *International Journal of Health Services* 10, no. 2 (1980): 271–90.

Weir, G.R. *Survey of Nursing Education in Canada*. Toronto: University of Toronto Press, 1932.

Wolfe, D. "The Crisis in Advanced Capitalism: An Introduction." *Studies in Political Economy* 11 (1983): 7–26.

23

TRAINING AND CONTAINING NURSES: The Development of Nursing Education in Canada

Terry Wotherspoon
University of Saskatchewan

INTRODUCTION

The first Canadian training school for nurses opened in St. Catharines, Ontario, in 1874. According to "The First Annual Report of The St. Catharines Training School and Nurses' Home, July 1, 1875,"

> the skilled nurse, by minutely watching the temperature, conditions of skin, pulse, respiration, and the various functions of all the organs, and reporting faithfully to the attending physician, must increase the chances of recovery two-fold. (cited in Gibbon and Mathewson, 1947:145)

Clearly, "nursing skill" meant "service" in a dual way, with both the patient and the physician being served. The emergence of the hospital system within the context of burgeoning industrial capitalism set the tone for a nursing force characterized by a unique blend of Christian dedication, Victorian femininity, medical faith, and labour discipline. In this context, nurse training was oriented to produce a cheap, subservient, readily available work force armed with a basic knowledge of hospital and sanitary procedures.

In the 1980s, responsibility for nursing education has been transferred out of the hospitals and into universities and community colleges. A discourse emphasizing faithful service has been supplanted by symposia on credentialling, specialization, nursing research, and medical technology. Nursing, laying claims to professionalism, has proceeded to organize a basis of skill and privilege around a unique body of nursing knowledge.

This chapter is concerned with the development of nursing education in Canada. The transformation which has just been described is interpreted in conjunction with the observation which Celia Davies (1980) makes that nursing education in Britain and the United States emerged as a compromise arising from inadequate resources. In particular, we emphasize the ways in which contradictions in the provision and utility of the education of nurses in Canada have served to limit nurses' position in the Canadian health-care system. Since the nineteenth century, with the emergence of the well-known "Nightingale system," prescient nurses and nursing supervisors have recognized the potential value of training for the establishment of a distinct sphere of nursing activity within the overall health-care system. However, the nature of that training and role has been subject to varying, often conflicting, conceptions by groups within nursing and interests outside of nursing. Ultimately, then, the development of nursing and nurse training must be understood as part of a wider network of social, political, and economic relations.

NURSES AND PROFESSIONALISM

Professionalism is the key concept in most recent analyses of nursing. Nurses are regarded either as constituting a profession, with their traditional low status a relic of the past, or as falling short in their drive to professionalism, in which case the reasons for their failure become the focus of analysis.

A typical expression of the first view is the statement that nursing has been involved in a "progressive development toward professionalism" (Elliott, 1977:69). Three interrelated factors are commonly cited to highlight this apparent evolutionary progress: the specialization and bureaucratization of health care, increasingly sophisticated medical technology, and the growth of nurses' own professional awareness (Innis, 1970; Kelly, 1985). As health care has become a more comprehensive, sophisticated enterprise, new medical knowledge and health-care functions have become unequally distributed among participants in the health-care

system. This has afforded nurses the opportunity to organize and push for increased status and responsibility; nurses have willingly emulated the medical profession with the assumption that full professionalism is an inevitable outcome. In this evolutionary model, the role of education is clear — education is the vehicle for professional status. More education for more nurses, built around a distinct scientific core of nursing knowledge, would allow nurses simultaneously to adapt to a changing world and to occupy a position of enhanced importance in the division of labour in health care (Canadian Nurses' Association, 1986; Rogers, 1978).

As desirable as this image is from a nursing perspective, it fails to analyze adequately the wider context within which nursing operates, and it ignores many of the major constraints which continue to act upon nursing. Arising from the blend of optimism and frustration which has marked nurses' ongoing struggles for status, this viewpoint has interpreted the substantive gains which nurses have made against a backdrop of influential individuals and interest groups which seem to have no enduring connection to other aspects of social structure. The real historical barriers to nursing status seemingly can be dissipated merely through hard work and upgrading of skills on the part of nurses.

The second viewpoint paints a less flattering image of nurses. It takes as its starting point the obstacles which nurses face in their quest for status, and concludes that nurses are at best a semi- or para-profession, most likely doomed to an eternal inferiority to the medical profession (Cockerham, 1986; Wolinsky, 1980). Probably the clearest manifestation of this perspective is the fact that nursing is virtually ignored or given only passing consideration in much of the literature on the sociology of medicine. Against the visible unity and autonomy of the (predominately male) medical profession, the service orientation of the internally divided (predominantly female) nursing ranks seems highly appropriate. This patronizing and accusatory view is expressed clearly by Oswald Hall (1970:12), to whom it seems clear that, to date, nurses have not tried seriously to focus their work efforts in a scientific mould. While medical care has been specializing along new types of diagnosis and treatment at a bizarre speed, nursing has shown no such trend.

We are left with the impression that no matter how strongly nurses have struggled in the past to establish their occupational status, they have not worked hard enough. Ironically, however, this view fits nicely with the first position on nurses' professionalism, differing primarily in the assessment of the likelihood of nurses' success in achieving professionalism.

Unfortunately, the debate over whether or not nursing is a profession tends to divert attention from questions of greater significance. Professionalism is assumed to be a desirable attribute, without any critical appraisal of the conditions within which professionalization occurs or of the strategic importance of professionalism as an ideological position. (See Johnson, 1972 for an extended critique of this approach.) Instead, the circumstances under which the health-care system and the role of nursing within it have developed are attributed to grand, amorphous tendencies like "progress," "technological change," and "interest-group politics" without any sustained analysis of the social relations in which these processes are grounded. Therefore, occupational roles and training are treated as neutral phenomena, given shape by the whims and visions of individuals acting as part of a seemingly natural evolution of social forces.

An alternate explanation of the development of nursing and nurse education focusses on the particular social relations which give shape to and are influenced by nursing. Nurses are recognized as dependent wage earners who pose problems of cost and control to their employers (Cannings and Lazonick, 1975; Warburton and Carroll, this volume). Nursing emerges from and acts upon distinct social structures and practices which are characterized by regular, often contradictory, patterns. Consequently, issues concerning the training and welfare of nurses, although important in their own right, are viewed as meaningful only when interpreted in the context of wider trends associated with health-care organization, policy, and finance.

NURSES AS SALARIED EMPLOYEES

One clear indication of the status of nurses is expressed by the relative incomes of nurses and other health-care workers. As the data in Table 1 indicate, the incomes of nurses have increased steadily both in absolute terms and in comparison with the average income of the Canadian work force as a whole. Of the three tabulated health occupational categories, nurses have made the greatest relative gains. However, nurses' salaries still remain, on average, just below the national average for all occupations and about one quarter of the average for physicians and surgeons.

The most common justification for the latter trend is that medical training is more arduous and is of much longer duration than nurse training. Therefore, in accordance with a functionalist analysis of stratification, the higher salaries of doctors are seen to represent a "payoff" for the years of training and sacrifice undertaken by the individual in order to fill the important medical positions (Davis and Moore, 1945). This correlation between years of training and occupational income is borne out, in broad terms, by general surveys of the labour force which reveal that workers with higher levels of education are likely to be found in higher income categories. (See, for example, the monthly reports issued by Labour Canada under the title of *The Labour Force*.) As such, it serves as a rallying point for nursing advocates who argue that more and better-quality education is necessary for higher status. There are, though, some problems in this analysis. The income-education linkage is more likely to be a product of initial privilege or class power than an indicator of true market value (Bowles and Gintis, 1976). Moreover, the whole question of what constitutes recognized training must be considered. Historically, as we shall see

Table 1. Employment Income for Selected Health Occupations:
Average and Ratio to Average Canadian Occupational Income

| | Health Occupations | | | | | | All Canadian Occupations | |
| | Physicians and surgeons | | Nurses | | Nursing aides, assistants & orderlies | | | |
Year	Average employment income ($)	Ratio to Canadian average	Average employment income ($)	Ratio to Canadian average	Average employment income ($)	Ratio to Canadian average	Average employment income ($)	Ratio to Canadian average
1931	3 095*	3.65*	580	0.68	524	0.62	848	1.00
1941	2 693*	3.10*	596	0.69	486	0.56	868	1.00
1951	2 936*	1.59*	1 107	0.60	1 074	0.58	1 851	1.00
1961	13 836	4.34	2 421	0.76	1 847	0.58	3 191	1.00
1971	25 308	4.69	4 344	0.81	3 572	0.66	5 391	1.00
1981	52 839	3.87	13 036	0.96	9 301	0.68	13 635	1.00

* Figures for 1931 to 1951 do not include income for self-employed physicians and surgeons, and hence are likely to under-represent actual physician and surgeon incomes for those years.

Source: Derived from census data.

below, nurses have been trained on the job, providing cheap hospital labour in a prolonged apprenticeship period which is not rewarded in the same way as is, for example, medical ward experience and internship. At the same time, the fiscal returns and inducements for nurse training are not nearly as significant as a "reward for education" argument would have us believe. In 1975, for example, the mean salary for a public health nurse with both a university certificate in public health nursing and a university degree was $224 *less* than the mean salary for a public health nurse with the same certificate but without the degree (based on data from Statistics Canada, 1976:77). In 1987, staff nurses in Saskatchewan with a baccalaureate degree in nursing received a monthly salary allowance which was only $5.65 greater than that received by staff nurses with a one- or two-year nursing diploma (based on data from the Saskatchewan Union of Nurses, 1986). These examples illustrate that the financial "inducements" in themselves are hardly incentives or rewards for nurses to take the additional two or more years

of formal education that a university degree requires.

A second argument for the relatively low wages which nurses receive is that nurses are much more poorly organized and less assertive than is the medical profession. Certainly doctors have benefitted tremendously from the strength and ability of organizations like the Canadian and American Medical Associations to promote their own interests. In contrast, nursing leaders have chronically lamented the seeming inability of nurses to mobilize into a cohesive, powerful force. Unfortunately, advocates of these arguments tend to regard nurses and doctors as two independent rather than interdependent groups, and to confuse cause and consequence. While the medical and nursing professions each have their unique histories, the picture is incomplete without an analysis of how the medical profession has been able to advance in large part at the expense of nursing, through the subordination and guided development of nursing by doctors, health-care policy-makers and managers, and the structure of health-care systems.

This suggests the need for a relational analysis which can account for contradictions and constraints in nursing development. We can illustrate this type of analysis by returning to Table 1 and taking note of the third category of health occupations, after doctors and nurses. The wage levels of nursing aides, assistants, and orderlies have remained relatively constant, at between 56 and 68 percent of average occupational earnings. This implies that nursing, as an intermediate health occupation, can both exert pressure on and be subject to pressure from at least two levels — doctors and managers from above and auxiliary health-care workers from below. Therefore, by way of example, health-care administrators make decisions influenced by the fact that individual nurses are less costly than physicians but more costly than auxiliary health-care workers. At the same time, nurses have reason to fear that they are potentially more dispensable to the health-care system than are doctors under present circumstances. Nurses, for example, are excluded from legislation which enables physicians and surgeons to prescribe medication or perform surgery. These relations are intensified with the introduction of new medical technology and health-care treatment models which serve to redefine the place and role of various health-care workers. If the diagnosis of a cancer, for example, can be made by a laboratory technician with the aid of a sophisticated instrument, and can be treated with drugs prescribed by a physician, where does the nurse fit in? At another level, a greater integration of the health-care system with other social and educational services could provide opportunities for nurses to enhance their role in health care, or it could have the effect of making nursing a redundant occupation, as social workers, auxiliaries, or other new occupations begin to provide nursing services.

Viewed in this context, nursing education is a significant variable in the development of the health-care system. Education acts as a conduit for nursing knowledge, status, and credentials, but it also serves to stamp into place particular conceptions of nursing. More precisely, while the provision of educational opportunities is generally associated with the advancement of nursing, it is also a factor in the historical subordination of nurses.

WORK AND EDUCATION IN THE CANADIAN CONTEXT

Nursing education, like other forms of vocational training, began outside the formal system of public education in Canada. Mass public schooling emerged through the attempts by nineteenth-century school reformers to ensure the transformation of individuals into morally disciplined political subjects within a sphere of state rule (Curtis, 1983; Corrigan, Curtis, and Lanning, 1987). Vocational training was more strictly concerned with imbuing persons in specific jobs with the competencies and discipline that would make them productive workers. Once established in the throes of industrial development, however, the state public school system was subject to conscription by private capitalist interests concerned with obtaining at public expense a cheap, compliant, and differentiated labour force; schooling thus became penetrated by the logic of vocationalism (Bowles and Gintis, 1976; Schecter, 1977). However, a contradictory dynamic was generated by subordinate social groups which saw in public schooling a vehicle for upward social mobility and participation in hitherto closed political channels (Carnoy and Levin, 1985). A major consequence of the struggles which ensued over the nature and content of state schooling was the emergence in the twentieth century of the education system as the primary channel of individual access to the job market.

The developing linkage between school and work provided a focal point for the energies of competing social interests. The educational credential provided a screening mechanism for employers, a "meal ticket" for individuals, and an instrument to guarantee status for certain prestigious occupational groups such as medical doctors. Little overt challenge was presented to the tacit consensus that formal schooling was a legitimate educational and selective enterprise. Instead, conflict centred around the amounts and content of formal education appropriate to particular occupations or positions in the labour force. As debate concerning how much and what kinds of education a person needed to enter certain jobs began to dominate educational discourse, wider questions about the structures of education and work were no longer issues. The ground rules for work and schooling solidified, with only the details open to contention (Wotherspoon, 1987).

Nurse training, which began in Canada within the hospital system, was absorbed into the state education system only through a protracted series of developments. The interconnection of such factors as the rising cost to hospitals of providing nurse training, corporate and state intervention in the health-care system, and the organized efforts of nurses accompanied a transformation in nursing work away from a strictly supervised feminine servitude to a bureaucratically organized wage-labour force. In the following sections, we outline the development of nurse training in Canada and discuss the nature of the Canadian nursing labour force.

THE DEVELOPMENT OF NURSING EDUCATION IN CANADA

The formal training of nurses in Canada began in the 1870s for the purpose of producing hospital personnel who could adequately carry out doctors' orders (Mussallem, 1965:5–6). In the mid-nineteenth century, nursing was nearly unique as an occupation legitimately open to women. Nursing was established from the outset of the development of medical science as an auxiliary occupation, concerned primarily with "caring" rather than "curing," or hygiene rather than medical treatment (Gamarnikow, 1978; Corea, 1985). The medical division of labour, reproducing the patriarchal structure of the bour-

geois home and workplace, was clear — men were doctors and women were nurses.

Nursing, nonetheless, did present opportunities, however limited, for the career advancement of a select group of women. Early nursing promoters such as Florence Nightingale in Britain, and Isabel A. Hampton in North America, saw that an inexpensive, regimented nursing force could provide the necessary foothold to establish nursing in the health-care process. The advantage of this strategy to solidify nursing status through the promotion of its ethos of service was that nursing could develop as a relatively autonomous enterprise, hierarchically organized around hygienic ideals under the supervision of women (Carpenter, 1977:166–67). However, the development of this autonomy was highly constrained.

Hospital administrators quickly came to appreciate the value of nurses for developing a clientele and providing inexpensive labour. With a nursing force at hand, public hospitals could shift their image and emphasis from providing a repository for the terminally ill to serving as a centre for treatment and recovery. The possibility that patients could be ministered back to health was crucial for an emerging industrial nation which required a continuous supply of able-bodied workers. Hospitals, in becoming important centres of health care, simultaneously began to train and contain nurses. Thus, generally following the pattern of industrialization in Canada, the number of hospital schools of nursing increased from one in 1874 (in St. Catharines) to 20 in 1900, 170 in 1909, and approximately 220 in 1930 (Canadian Nurses' Association, 1968:33; Duncanson, 1970:112).

In this context, nurse training accomplished several contradictory functions. Extending over a two- to three-year period, training programmes ensured that a supply of nurses was continually available for hospital service. The exploitation of the nurse trainee prevailed over educational aims so that lecture and study time was a "privilege" granted only in the interstices of up to 15 hours of daily ward duty (Duncanson, 1970: 112–13; Mussallem, 1965:6). Nurse training programmes dampened the hostilities of doctors who scorned nurses as unskilled and uneducated. At the same time, doctors who were suspicious that they might some day be displaced by trained nurses found that they could advance their own interests by involvement in the nurse training programme as lecturers and moral guardians. Discipline over nurse trainees was further maintained by a highly regimented supervisory structure, constant surveillance facilitated by the establishment of dormitories, the inculcation of virtues of obedience and commitment, and the absence for most trainees of any occupational alternatives.

The advantages in terms of costs and services which nurses offered to the hospital system were also used by nursing leaders in the early part of the twentieth century as levers for gaining certain concessions, including reductions in the workday, specified educational time allocations, formalized instruction, and more standardized curricula (Duncanson, 1970:113; Mussallem, 1965:7). Trained nurses, working to enhance their own status in contrast with untrained nursing personnel, organized local, national, and international associations to provide a body for political lobbying. In 1893, the American Society of Superintendents of Training Schools for Nurses of the United States and Canada was formed by forty nursing-school superintendents in order to push for better-quality and more uniform nursing educational standards. This society laid the groundwork for a dominion-wide nursing organization, the Canadian National Association of Trained Nurses, established in 1908, which in 1924, with 52 affiliated member organizations, became the Canadian Nurses' Association, or the CNA (CNA, 1968:36–38). These organizations focussed the profession's energies on a drive for the establishment of registries of trained nurses, which received some degree of legislative recognition in all nine provinces between 1910 and 1922 (CNA, 1968:38). They also began, especially with the aid of a 1914 Special Committee report on education, a lengthy campaign to have nursing education incorporated into the state

educational system (King, 1970:69).

In the midst of these developments, the fundamental contradiction between state and private demand for low-cost but widespread health-care service on the one hand, and nurses' demands for adequate training and remuneration on the other, intensified. In the early decades of the twentieth century, health-care services were becoming instituted as a regular social provision in conjunction with the rise of a stable national work force. Exacerbating this trend was the success of the medical profession in acquiring greater influence within the health-care system. In this, the medical associations were aided by the large corporate foundations, especially the Carnegie foundation, which sponsored the influential Flexner report of 1910. In the wake of the report, major recommendations to reduce the number of North American medical schools and the supply of medical graduates, and to tighten control over medical education standards were quickly adopted (MacFarlane, 1965:19–21).

The data in Table 2 reveal the impact of these events on the medical and nursing labour forces. The supply of physicians was greatly moderated, especially in the period from 1911 to 1921, when the population per physician ratio actually increased, meaning that there were fewer physicians per capita in 1921 than in 1911. However, medical care was at that time highly labour-intensive so that, with fewer doctors, either patients received less medical attention, doctors worked harder, or other health-care personnel filled the void. The rapid increase in the nursing labour force (which grew by nearly four times between 1911 and 1921, and which has maintained an average annual rate of increase of 52.7 percent between 1911 and 1984, compared to an average annual rate of 7.9 percent for doctors over the same period), suggests the importance of the latter possibility. Lower-cost nurses, trained for dedicated service and disciplined by social and labour market conditions, served, in effect, to subsidize the greater occupational rewards which doctors were in a position to enjoy.

With an expanded and diversified health-

Table 2. Number of Physicians and Nurses, and Population per Physician and Nurse in Canada

| | Physicians | | Nurses | |
| | | Population per physician* | | Population per nurse* |
Year	Number		Number†	
1901	5 442	978	280	19 014
1911	7 411	970	5 600	1 284
1921	8 706	1008	21 385	410
1931	10 020	1034	20 462	506
1941	11 873	968	25 826	441
1951	14 325	976	41 088	325
1961	21 290	857	70 647	258
1971	32 942	659	148 767	146
1981	45 542	538	206 184	119
1984	49 916	506	220 960	113

* Based on census data.

† Registered nurses for 1941 to 1975; census figures for 1931 (graduate nurses) and earlier years (nurses). Excludes Newfoundland prior to 1961; excludes Yukon and Northwest Territories prior to 1941. The 1921 figure includes nurses-in-training.

Source: For 1901 to 1971, Statistics Canada. *Historical Statistics of Canada*, second edition. Ottawa: Minister of Supply and Services, 1983, Series B82–92.

For 1981 and 1984, Health and Welfare Canada. *Canada Health Manpower Inventory*. Ottawa: 1985.

care role, though, nurses were also able to assert more strongly their monetary and educational demands. However, as with doctors, nurses' progress in this regard was highly dependent upon the intervention of external agencies. A university degree programme in nursing, the first in Canada, was established at the University of British Columbia in 1919 and, with the efforts and financial assistance of the Canadian Red Cross Society, public health nursing programmes were developed in six universities by 1920–1921 (King, 1970:70). However, as King (1970: 71–72) indicates, there were serious inadequacies in the early university nursing programmes in terms of both upgrading nursing skill and raising nursing status relative to other university-educated occupational groups: "In the teaching of nursing great emphasis was placed on technical skill, following orders, and adhering to established practice; the intellectual component was subservient to the daily round."

There is evidence, too, of a strong occupational split in nursing between nursing supervisors and instructors who had been trained in and had advanced through the hospital service system and nurses who saw the need to develop the profession through university education and research (King, 1970:73–75). The latter group was given support by George Weir, in the 1932 report *Survey of Nursing Education in Canada*, co-sponsored by the CNA and the Canadian Medical Association. The report's primary recommendation was that nursing schools be removed from hospital control and placed under the auspices of the provincial education systems.

With the onset of the international economic crisis in the 1930s, the fate of this recommendation was suspended between conflicting interests. In the early part of the decade, expenditures on health services declined (Statistics Canada, 1983b), placing increased pressures on the existing health-care system and on its labour force to operate more efficiently. At the same time, these conditions provoked intensified efforts from several quarters for an overall upgrading of the health-care system. Potentially militant trade unions and the unemployed, subject to severe social and economic dislocation, posed a worrisome threat to state and corporate interests. A series of social reform measures, including health-insurance schemes, was introduced by provincial and federal legislatures as part of an attempt to pacify the working class and stabilize economic conditions (Swartz, 1977).

Corporate interests also played a more direct role, primarily through their charitable foundations, which provided financial assistance and funded research for selected health, education, and welfare projects, in order to secure social harmony, develop a stable work force, and promote a favourable investment climate. In the field of health care, the W.K. Kellogg Foundation has a history of prominence, having contributed over 263 1/2 million dollars to various health-care programmes, mostly in the United States, Canada, and Latin America, between 1930 and 1980 (Kellogg, 1979:112). Of that total, 822 thousand dollars were spent between 1944 and 1952 to provide staff, consultative services, and curricular and instructional resources for 12 university nursing schools (ten in the United States and two in Canada), and a grant of over 165 thousand dollars served to establish an experimental undergraduate nursing programme, grounded in basic science training, at the University of Saskatchewan, beginning in 1952 (Kellogg, 1955:143–48).

At the same time, other pressures were mounting to push training of nurses out of the hospitals. Nurses, who in the 1930s often accepted board and lodging from their hospital employers in lieu of full salary payment, began in the 1940s to return to the community and, simultaneously, to demand higher wages (CNA, 1968:34). A similar situation developed for nurses in training who exchanged fees and labour in return for training and services. The Department of National Health and Welfare esti-

mates that by 1960, the average direct annual cost to the hospital per student was one thousand dollars (Mussallem, 1965:40). Because hospitals compensated for this cost by extracting unpaid or underpaid labour from nursing students and by underpaying nursing instructors, a generally unsatisfactory situation prevailed. Moreover, low wages and low levels of government educational assistance made it economically unviable for most nurses and nursing teachers to extend their education beyond the minimal time period required for graduation from basic training, especially when the training programme was prolonged excessively by the priority of work over training in the hospital system. Consequently, it is not surprising that Mussallem (1965), in a study prepared in the early 1960s for the Royal Commission on Health Services in Canada, indicts the nursing education system of the time as haphazard, outdated, educationally unsound, and inadequate for the needs of nurses and the health-care system.

The Royal Commission's report itself recommended a reduction in the time span of the diploma programme from three to two years and a separation of nurse training from hospital demands for nursing service, and stressed that the increasing need for qualified nurses required the co-ordinated development of nursing education programmes integrated into the general system of higher education in Canada and the provinces (Duncanson, 1970:122–23). While the Royal Commission inquiry was being conducted, nurses' organizations, educational institutions, and the Ontario government co-operated in an initiative which led to the establishment in 1964 of a nursing diploma programme at the Ryerson Institute of Technology. By 1968, in the wake of this precedent, 26 nursing diploma programmes were offered in institutions other than hospital schools of nursing across Canada; by 1977, full-time enrollment in community college nursing diploma programmes was 17 789, as compared to 5136 in hospital programmes (CNA, 1981:2; Statistics Canada, 1977). A similar expansion was underway in university degree nursing programmes, with more programmes, greater numbers of students, and the establishment of graduate degree programmes.

NURSING EDUCATION AND THE NURSING LABOUR FORCE IN THE 1980s

The move away from hospital-based nurse training has been associated with a general improvement in the overall status of nurses, but it has not solved several fundamental problems associated with training and maintaining a nursing labour force. There are presently two main educational streams for entry into nursing practice: university degree programmes of three to five years in length, and nursing diploma programmes, offered mainly through the community college system, of one to three years in length. In 1983, there were 118 initial diploma programmes and 21 baccalaureate programmes in nursing in Canada (CNA, 1983:54), compared with 170 hospital schools and 16 university baccalaureate programmes in 1963 (Mussallem, 1965:11). However, despite a recent trend to emphasize the importance of the degree qualification in nursing, in the 1980s about 80 percent of nursing graduates continue to receive their initial training in diploma programmes (see Table 3).

The provision of nursing education through the public education system has ensured that certain levels of funding, facilities, and standards will be maintained for nurse training, sheltered from the vagaries of hospital administration. At the same time, though, new sets of constraints emerge as nursing education is forced to compete for resources with other educational and state priorities. Insofar as the educational credentials of teachers, a major cost factor in post-secondary educational institutions, are linked to promotion and salary scales, nursing education is relatively inexpensive. In 1981, for example, only 5.9 percent of full-time university nursing teachers had completed doctorates, compared with an overall Canadian university teacher average of 61.7 percent (Statistics

Canada, 1983a:58). In addition, such low-cost, highly specific programmes as computer-assisted instruction and self-directed learning modules are becoming prominent features of university nurse education programmes (Crawford, 1978; Hannah, 1978). These programmes, besides reducing the costs of education relative to more open-ended discovery and analysis-based courses, prepare the student for work roles which are highly structured and involve few opportunities for the worker to exercise discretion on the job.

But despite the potentially lower cost of nursing education programmes, there are indications that governments have made only limited commitments to support nurse training programmes, particularly at the university level. If we return to Table 3, we observe that immigration has provided Canada with a major source of trained nurses, especially in the late 1960s and early 1970s during the transfer of nursing education out of hospitals. By importing trained labourers (although not all workers will necessarily become employed in their intended occupations), Canada is able to transfer the cost of educating a substantial pool of workers to the countries of origin and gain in the process a cheap, often docile work force (Bolaria, 1987). Depending upon where the workers are placed in job situations, this will either ensure that lower-paid positions are constantly filled (as opposed to increasing wage levels), or reduce the overall costs of maintaining a trained work force.

The lack of government support for nursing education, especially at the university level, is also revealed in the problems which nurses face in upgrading their basic training. Nurses often discover that they are left out of decisions to introduce, and shut out from training to operate, new medical technology (Wallis, 1978). A recent survey reveals that absence of credit courses for upgrading training at work, lack of time off to attend classes that are offered, and lack of financial assistance are common problems for nurses working in Canadian hospitals and health-care institutions; nurses in at least one institution have even held bake sales and

Table 3. Numbers of Nursing Graduates from Initial Diploma and Basic Baccalaureate Programs in Canada, and Number of Immigrant Graduate Nurses Entering Canada

Year	Number of nurses graduating from Canadian programmes			Number of immigrant graduate nurses*
	Initial diploma programmes	Basic baccalaureate programmes	Total	
1962	6246	148	6 394	1621
1963	6764	171	6 935	1879
1964	7107	154	7 261	1967
1965	7154	206	7 360	2829
1966	7167	220	7 387	3732
1967	7249	273	7 522	4262
1968	7591	300	7 891	3375
1969	7978	381	8 359	3248
1970	8212	413	8 625	2274
1971	9543	515	10 058	989
1972	9596	487	10 083	892
1973	8985	609	9 594	1418
1974	9205	694	9 899	1702
1975	8933	845	9 778	1839
1976	9087	954	10 041	1130
1977	6203	977	7 180	607
1978	5171	1406	6 577	405
1979	5647	1440	7 087	467
1980	6150	1474	7 624	653
1981	6778	1379	8 157	977
1982	6863	1620	8 483	999
1983	6598	1769	8 367	358
1984	6871	1719	8 590	300

* Immigrants who indicated that nursing is their intended occupation.

Source: Health and Welfare Canada, *Canada Health Manpower Inventory* (Annual series, 1969, 1976, 1985); and Helen K. Mussallem, *Nursing Education in Canada.* Ottawa: Queen's Printer, 1965.

auctions in order to raise money for a tuition assistance fund (Allen, 1985:12). Significantly, according to 1983 data, only 25 218 (or 11.6 percent) of the 217 878 registered nurses employed in nursing in Canada have an academic degree (CNA, 1983:29). Moreover, as some of the trends noted above suggest, even the attainment of a university degree does not guarantee that nurses will be prepared to step into decisive, autonomous health-care positions. There does not appear to be a significant change from the days of hospital service for nurse trainees. Nonetheless, there is evidence that the state has channelled funds into specific vocational streams, such as psychiatric nursing and dental nursing, since the 1960s in response to political, economic, and employment relation factors (Dickinson, 1987; Statistics Canada, 1977).

A major consequence of these trends is the possible bifurcation of nursing. In accordance with the degree/diploma distinction, two streams are emerging — one more highly skilled and educated and the other service-oriented and less educated — reminiscent of the separation of trained nurses from untrained nursing personnel in the early part of the twentieth century. This is consistent with the demands of nursing organizations in the 1960s for an increased recognition of the dual educational credential system (CNA, 1968:4), but contains implications for the organization of nursing which may well undermine the very cause nurses are championing.

Hospitals remain the major workplace for Canadian nurses regardless of educational background, employing several times more nurses than do all other categories of nursing employer (see Table 4). However, some variation occurs with respect to educational credentials. Nurses with only basic diploma training are overrepresented in hospitals, nursing homes, and doctors' offices (i.e., while 68 percent of all employed nurses have only basic diploma training, the respective proportions within these workplaces of nurses with basic diplomas are 72, 78, and 80 percent). These are workplaces which tend to be characterized by direct personal or bureaucratic supervision and strict delineation of authority. Conversely, nurses with bachelor's degrees or higher are overrepresented in jobs in community health and in educational institutions, which carry the possibility of greater autonomy and decision-making authority. Similar trends are observable with respect to nursing positions: basic diploma nurses, who predominate numerically, are overrepresented in general-duty nursing positions and underrepresented in directorial, senior supervisory, and teaching positions, while the opposite holds for degree nurses.

A second related aspect of bifurcation is observable in the gender structure of the occupa-tion. Nursing remains an overwhelmingly feminized occupation — in 1983, only 2.3 percent of registered nurses employed in nursing in Canada were male (CNA, 1983:32). Nonetheless, nearly a third (31 percent) of male nurses held directorial, supervisory, or head nurse positions while only 17 percent of female nurses held such positions. Moreover, according to 1981 census data, female nurses earned an average of $850 less in yearly income than their male counterparts (Statistics Canada, 1984).

These conditions are exacerbated by the actions of legislators and administrators empowered with financing and regulating the health-care system, especially in the context of general demands to reduce overall levels of government spending. Health-care services have consumed steadily greater shares of national resources, increasing from $7.8 billion (or 7.4 percent of GNP) in 1972 to $30.1 billion (or 8.4 percent of GNP) in 1982 (Canadian Hospital Directory, 1984:214). Hospital expenditures, in turn, have consumed in the 1970s and 1980s over 40 percent of these total health expenditures, and nursing costs have been a major component of hospital expenditures; in 1980–81, for example, nursing costs constituted 36 percent of the total operating costs of $8.08 billion for Canadian hospitals (Canadian Hospital Directory, 1984:215; 236).

Consequent with the growth of the health-care system have been increasingly sustained legislative and managerial efforts to make the operation of the system more efficient and accountable. Initiatives such as community health centres, prescription drug assistance programmes, and concentration of hospital systems, regardless of their possible medical merits, have the clear effect of increasing the output of hospital workers while shifting some health-care services from hospitals to less expensive and less labour-intensive in-home and community alternatives (Salmon, 1984). At the same time, institutional health care is being reorganized primarily through innovations in the supervision patterns of hospital and nursing-home employees in order to increase centralized managerial

Table 4. Nurses Registered in Canada and Employed in Nursing — Type of Employer, and Position, by Highest Level of Education in Nursing, 1983

Type of employer	Total number	Highest level of education, expressed as percentage of nurses within each type of employment situation or position			
		Registered nurse diploma	Post-basic diploma or certificate	Bachelor's degree	Master's degree or higher
Hospital	130 375	72	19	8	1
Community health	16 325	45	27	27	1
Home for aged, nursing home	11 019	78	17	4	1
Educational institution	4 912	27	15	48	10
Physician's office, family practice unit	4 477	80	15	5	1
Other types of employer	5 998	64	22	12	2
Not stated	3 517	72	28	8	2
Total — percent	100	68	20	11	1
— number	176 623	120 940	34 708	18 816	2 013
Position					
Director, assistant/ associate director	4 386	46	26	22	6
Supervisor/coordinator, assistant supervisor/ coordinator	9 033	56	25	18	2
Clinical specialist	1 367	59	20	13	8
Head nurse	17 174	69	21	8	2
General duty staff	123 889	72	19	8	1
Instructor, professor	4 843	24	15	52	9
Other	8 331	63	20	15	2
Not stated	7 600	69	20	9	1
Total — percent	100	68	20	11	1
— number	176 623	120 940	34 708	18 816	2 013

Source: Derived from Canadian Nurses' Association, *Nursing in Canada 1983*. Ottawa: Statistics Canada and Canadian Nurses' Association, 26, 28.

control and maximize employee productivity (Carpenter, 1977). Nursing, as the largest single category of health-care workers, remains central to the politics and structure of health care in Canada.

The observed tendencies toward bifurcation in nursing suggest that any benefits from a restructured organization of health-care services will be distributed in a highly asymmetrical fashion. Within nursing, males and nurses with degrees, especially post-graduate degrees, are moving into positions likely to serve as bases for further consolidation of authority and resources. While the resources that go into nursing education, as well as nursing initiatives in the direction of credentialling, the development of nursing knowledge, and specialization may serve to upgrade the status of nursing as a whole, they are more likely to be channelled towards the minority of nurses who can use credentials and authority positions to their advantage. If these initiatives do enable nurses on the whole to legitimize their claims to greater proportions of health-care resources, nursing administrators are liable to rely less upon nurses and more upon lower-paid auxiliaries to provide health-care services. The upper stream of credentialled nurses, with the assistance of agencies like the Kellogg Foundation, which has recently funded major projects in nursing research, accreditation, and doctoral studies (CNA, 1983:29–30), may be able to insulate itself from the erosion of the profession as a whole by strengthening its own claims to essential health-care skills and knowledge which it alone possesses.

This trend is represented especially in the recent CNA focus, reinforced through complementary positions advanced by several provincial nursing associations, on "entry into practice" which calls for a minimum requirement of a complete baccalaureate degree as the standard for entry into nursing practice by the year 2000 (CNA, 1982:1; Registered Nurses' Association of British Columbia, 1983). As the CNA itself admits, such a goal seems difficult to attain, given the current slow rate of increase in the proportion of student admissions to degree nursing programmes relative to diploma programmes, and the continuing lack of funds to expand degree nursing programmes (1986:5). Instead, support given to degree programmes and nursing research may be channelled into specialized programmes supporting the small proportion of nursing practitioners who, on the basis of the degree credential, may stake sole

claim to the title of "nurse." At the same time, fiscal and administrative support previously given to nursing diploma programmes is likely to be directed to promoting the expanded production of auxiliary health-care workers. Paradoxically, then, by advancing credentialling and research policies in the interests of the profession as a whole, nurses may be contributing to their own division into a highly skilled and educated nursing elite and a mass of undertrained, low-paid support workers.

CONCLUSIONS

We have observed how the transformation of nursing from a subordinate service occupation into a more specialized and sophisticated profession has been rendered more apparent than real in many key respects through a series of external and internal constraining factors. Education has been a crucial channel for the occupational development of nursing, serving both to advance and to suppress the status of nursing. The pattern of nursing and nursing education in Canada has followed the interplay of nurses' organized efforts to establish their occupation with the development of a Canadian labour force in general and a health-care labour force in particular. The frequent success of corporate, state, and medical interests in guiding the development of nursing has had a significant impact on the present status of nursing as a wage labour force divided by education and gender.

Nurses, though, have come to recognize within the past decade and a half that their status as the largest single health-care occupation is a potential power base (Ferguson, 1985; Lerner, 1985; Mussallem, 1977). By promoting their ability to serve client needs and health-care priorities rather than economic or systemic requisites, while simultaneously avoiding the trap of accepting a professional ideology as a substitute for actual resources, nurses may yet succeed in their quest for status. To this end, nurses are beginning to align themselves with other groups of workers, particularly teachers, who face similar threats and challenges. The consequences of nurses' development of a political strategy are significant, for without a clear analysis of their occupational situation, nurses are likely to suffer, as will the quality of the health services that they are able to provide.

Acknowledgements: The author wishes to acknowledge the contributions of Daniel Jones to the preparation of this paper.

STUDY QUESTIONS

1. Which factors have facilitated the emergence of nursing as a prominent health-care occupation? Which factors have served to constrain the development of nursing in Canada?

2. Discuss the relationship between nursing and the development of the medical profession.

3. What implications have changes in medical technology and in the organization of health-care services had for the development of nursing?

4. Discuss the ways in which the state education system is subject to pressures from various social interests, as illustrated by the example of nursing.

5. How does the development of nursing compare with trends in other related occupations such as teaching and social work?

RECOMMENDED READING

Cannings, Kathleen, and William Lazonick. "The Development of the Nursing Labor Force in the United States: A Basic Analysis." *International Journal of Health Services* 5, no. 2 (1975): 185–216.

Corea, Gena. *The Hidden Malpractice: How American Medicine Mistreats Women*, updated edition. New York: Harper and Row, 1985.

Davies, Celia, ed. *Rewriting Nursing History*. London: Croom Helm, 1980.

Innis, Mary Q., ed. *Nursing Education in a Changing Society*. Toronto: University of Toronto Press, 1970.

LaSor, Betsy, and M. Ruth Elliott, eds. *Issues in Canadian Nursing*. Scarborough, Ont.: Prentice-Hall, 1977.

Stacey, Margaret, Margaret Reid, Christian Heath, and Robert Dingwall, eds. *Health and the Division of Labour*. London: Croom Helm, 1977.

Wotherspoon, Terry, ed. *The Political Economy of Canadian Schooling*. Toronto: Methuen, 1987.

REFERENCES

Allen, Margaret. "Baccalaureate Education Remains an Enigma for Many Nurses." *Canadian Nurse* 81, no. 5 (May 1985): 12.

Bolaria, B. Singh. "The Brain Drain to Canada: The Externalization of the Cost of Education." In *The Political Economy of Canadian Schooling*, edited by Terry Wotherspoon, 301–22. Toronto: Methuen, 1987.

Bowles, Samuel, and Herbert Gintis. *Schooling in Capitalist America*. New York: Basic Books, 1976.

Canadian Hospital Directory. *Canadian Hospital Directory Statistical Compendium*, 1984.

Canadian Nurses' Association. *The Leaf and the Lamp*. Ottawa: Canadian Nurses' Association, 1968.

———. *The Seventh Decade 1969–1980*. Ottawa: Canadian Nurses' Association, 1981.

———. *Entry to the Practice of Nursing: A Background Paper*. Ottawa: Canadian Nurses' Association, 1982.

———. *Nursing in Canada 1983*. Ottawa: Statistics Canada and Canadian Nurses' Association, 1983.

———. "Collaboration Between Nurse Educators in the Use of Nursing Education Resources for the Year 2000." *Entry to Practice Newsletter* 2, no. 5 (October 1986).

Cannings, Kathleen, and William Lazonick. "The Development of the Nursing Labor Force in the United States: A Basic Analysis." *International Journal of Health Services* 5, no. 2 (1975): 185–216.

Carnoy, Martin, and Henry M. Levin. *Schooling and Work in the Democratic State*. Stanford, California: Stanford University Press, 1985.

Carpenter, Michael. "The New Managerialism and Professionalism in Nursing." In *Health and the Division of Labour*, edited by Margaret Stacey, Margaret Reid, Christian Heath, and Robert Dingwall, 165–93. London: Croom Helm, 1977.

Cockerham, William C. *Medical Sociology*. 3rd ed. Englewood Cliffs: Prentice-Hall, 1986.

Corea, Gena. *The Hidden Malpractice: How American Medicine Mistreats Women*, updated edition. New York: Harper and Row, 1985.

Corrigan, Philip, Bruce Curtis, and Robert Lanning. "The Political Space of Schooling." In *The Political Economy of Canadian Schooling*, edited by Terry Wotherspoon, 21–43. Toronto: Methuen, 1987.

Crawford, Myrtle E. "The Curriculum Revision Process — Experienced at the College of Nursing, The University of Saskatchewan." In *Perspectives: Nursing Education, Practice and Research*. Proceedings of the 1978 Annual Meeting of the Western Region — Canadian Association of University Schools of Nursing, The University of Calgary, February 1978, 1–16.

Curtis, Bruce. "Preconditions of the Canadian State: Educational Reform and the Construction of a Public in Upper Canada, 1837–1846." *Studies in Political Economy* 10 (Winter 1983):99–121.

Davies, Celia. "A Constant Casualty: Nurse Education in Britain and the USA to 1939." In *Rewriting Nursing History*, edited by Celia Davis, 102–22. London: Croom Helm, 1980.

Davis, Kingsley, and Wilbert E. Moore. "Some Principles of Stratification." *American Sociological Review* 10 (1945): 242–49.

Dickinson, Harley D. "Vocational Education and the Control of Work: The Case of Psychiatric Nursing in Saskatchewan." In *The Political Economy of Canadian Schooling*, edited by Terry Wotherspoon, 231–51. Toronto: Methuen, 1987.

Duncanson, Blanche. "The Development of Nursing Education at the Diploma Level." In *Nursing Education in a Changing Society*, edited by Mary Q. Innis, 109–29. Toronto: University of Toronto Press, 1970.

Elliott, M. Ruth. "Nursing and Interdisciplinary Practice." In *Issues in Canadian Nursing*, edited by Betsy LaSor and M. Ruth Elliott, 43–72. Scarborough, Ont.: Prentice-Hall, 1977.

Ferguson, Vernice. "Overview of the Concepts of Power, Politics, and Policy in Nursing." In *Power, Politics, and Policy in Nursing*, edited by Rita Reis Wieczorek, 5–15. New York: Springer, 1985.

Gamarnikow, Eva. "Sexual Division of Labour: The Case of Nursing." In *Feminism and Materialism — Women and Modes of Production*, edited by Annette Kuhn and Marie Wolpe, 96–123. London: Routledge and Kegan Paul, 1978.

Gibbon, John Murray, with Mary S. Mathewson. *Three Centuries of Canadian Nursing*. Toronto: Macmillan of Canada, 1947.

Hall, Oswald. "Social Change, Specialization, and Science: Where Does Nursing Stand?" In *Nursing Education in a Changing Society*, edited by Mary Q. Innis, 3–15. Toronto: University of Toronto Press, 1970.

Hannah, Kathryn J. "Overview of Computer-Assisted Learning in Nursing Education at the University of Calgary." In *Perspectives: Nursing Education, Practice and Research*. Proceedings of the 1978 Annual Meeting of the Western Region — Canadian Association of University Schools of Nursing, The University of Calgary, February 1978, 43–56.

Health and Welfare Canada. *Canada Health Manpower Inventory 1985*. Ottawa: Minister of National Health and Welfare, 1985.

Innis, Mary Q., ed. *Nursing Education in a Changing Society*. Toronto: University of Toronto Press, 1970.

Johnson, Terry. *Professions and Power*. London: Macmillan, 1972.

W.K. Kellogg Foundation. *The First Twenty-Five Years: The Story of a Foundation*. Battle Creek, Michigan: W.K. Kellogg Foundation, 1955.

————. *The First Half-Century 1930–1980: Private Approaches to Public Needs*. Battle Creek, Michigan: W.K. Kellogg Foundation, 1979.

Kelly, Lucie Young. *Dimensions of Professional Nursing*. 5th ed. New York: Macmillan, 1985.

King, M. Kathleen. "The Development of University Nursing Education." In *Nursing Education in a Changing Society*, edited by Mary Q. Innis, 67–85. Toronto: University of Toronto Press, 1970.

Lerner, Helen M. "Educating Nurses for Power." In *Power, Politics, and Policy in Nursing*, edited by Rita Reis Wieczorek, 90–95. New York: Springer, 1985.

MacFarlane, J.A. *Medical Education in Canada*, Royal Commission on Health Services Special Study No. 13. Ottawa: Queen's Printer, 1965.

Mussallem, Helen K. *Nursing Education in Canada*, Royal Commission on Health Services Special Study No. 16. Ottawa: Queen's Printer, 1965.

————. "Nurses and Political Action." In *Issues in Canadian Nursing*, edited by Betsy LaSor and M. Ruth Elliott, 154–81. Scarborough, Ont.: Prentice-Hall, 1977.

Registered Nurses' Association of British Columbia. *Entry into the Practice of Nursing in the Year 2000: Position Statement of the Registered Nurses' Association of British Columbia*. Vancouver: RNABC, 1983.

Rogers, Martha E. "Emerging Patterns in Nursing Education." In *Current Perspectives in Nursing Education: The Changing Scene*, Volume 2, edited by Janet A. Williamson, 1–8. Saint Louis: C.V. Mosby, 1978.

Salmon, J. Warren. "Organizing Medical Care for Profit." In *Issues in the Political Economy of Health Care*, edited by John B. McKinlay, 143–86. New York: Tavistock, 1984.

Saskatchewan Union of Nurses. Private correspondence with author, December 1986.

Schecter, Stephen. "Capitalism, Class, and Educational Reform in Canada." In *The Canadian State: Political Economy and Political Power*, edited by Leo Panitch, 373–416. Toronto: University of Toronto Press, 1977.

Statistics Canada. *Compendium of Selected Health Manpower Statistics 1976.* Ottawa: Statistics Canada, 1976.

———. *Survey of Vocational Education and Training 1976–77.* Ottawa: Minister of Supply and Services Canada, 1977.

———. *A Statistical Portrait of Canadian Higher Education From the 1960s to the 1980s: 1983 Edition.* Ottawa: Minister of Supply and Services Canada, 1983a.

———. *Historical Statistics of Canada.* 2nd ed. Ottawa: Minister of Supply and Services Canada, 1983b.

———. *Census of Canada – Population.* Catalogue 92–930. Ottawa: Minister of Supply and Services Canada, 1984.

Swartz, Donald. "The Politics of Reform: Conflict and Accommodation in Canadian Health Policy." In *The Canadian State: Political Economy and Political Power,* edited by

Leo Panitch, 311–43. Toronto: University of Toronto Press, 1977.

Wallis, Mary. "The Technological Society — Its Implications for Nursing." In *Perspectives: Nursing Education, Practice and Research.* Proceedings of the 1978 Annual Meeting of the Western Region — Canadian Association of University Schools of Nursing, The University of Calgary, February 1978, 81–91.

Warburton, Rennie, and William K. Carroll. "Class and Gender in Nursing." This volume.

Weir, George M. *Survey of Nursing Education in Canada.* Toronto: University of Toronto Press, 1932.

Wolinsky, Frederic D. *The Sociology of Health: Principles, Professions, and Issues.* Toronto: Little, Brown and Co., 1980.

Wotherspoon, Terry. "Conflict and Crisis in Canadian Education." In *The Political Economy of Canadian Schooling,* edited by Terry Wotherspoon, 1–15. Toronto: Methuen, 1987.

24

THE STRUCTURE OF STRESS IN NURSES' WORK

Marie L. Campbell
Carleton University

INTRODUCTION

Cost control in the Canadian health-care system has been a major preoccupation of policy-makers since the advent of medicare. Van Loon (1978) noted how cost constraint was translated into administrative action as provinces began to understand the implications for them of changes introduced in 1977 in federal-provincial cost-sharing arrangements. Ontario, for instance, began to cap its grants to hospitals, and by 1981, had taken steps to enforce a policy of no cost overruns in hospital spending. Vayda and others (1979) argue that hospitals have been forced into economizing on service provision. Within hospitals, according to Bennett and Krasny (1977), nursing services began to be an important focus of administrative efficiency measures. New document-based management technologies were being introduced into Canadian nursing to assist these measures. Use of these technologies means that nurses systematically generate information about their work which is then entered into "technological" decision-making processes. Construction of systematic information and its transfer from nurses to management enables

decisions about nursing to be made using "efficiency," as opposed to some other criterion, as the top priority.

This chapter reviews the new technological methods by which hospital managements gain the kind of control needed in order to maximize the usefulness of nursing labour and to thereby improve its efficiency. The analysis casts doubt on the ultimate value of these methods. It is argued that the cost to nurses is so high as to directly undermine their capacity to work effectively. The organization of "efficiency" in nurses' work exacts both a personal and a professional toll. Nurses are expected to accept personal responsibility for delivering safe and sufficient care in conditions which are less and less capable of sustaining it. They experience an increased pace of work and heavier workloads. Even when — or perhaps because — they speed up their work and make personal contributions of their unpaid time in order to cope with these conditions, nurses suffer frustration, anxiety, and self-blame about the care they are able to give. These are the typical features of the now-common work-related stress syndrome which Freudenberger (1975 and 1980) and Vash (1980)

Figure 1. Organization of Cost-Constraint in Hospital Nursing: A Route-Map of Documentary Methods & Results

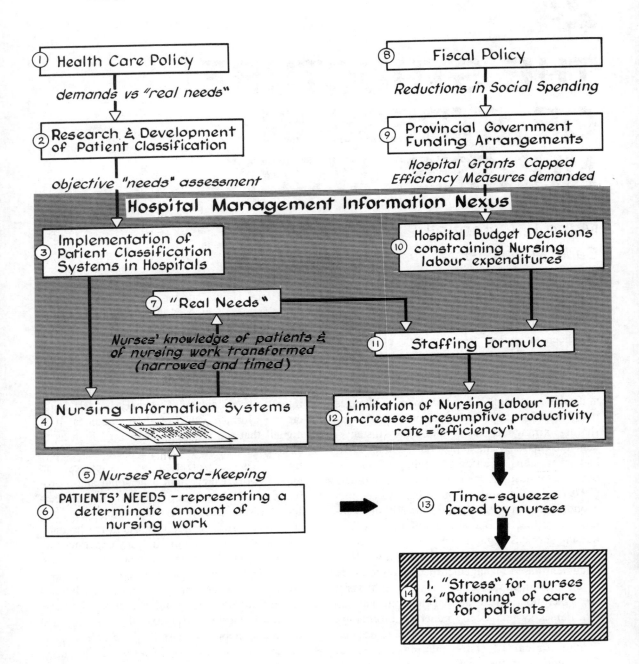

have called "burn-out." The author's own research (Campbell, 1984) shows that such phenomena personally experienced by nurses in their work, while manifesting themselves as "psychological" problems, have an explicitly organized and organizational character. "Efficiency" in the administration of health care is a double-edged sword, cutting nursing labour costs on one side and attacking nurses' physical and mental well-being on the other.

THE STRUCTURE OF MANAGEMENT CONTROL

To understand the structure of stress on nurses, one needs to investigate how efficiency measures have reorganized nurses' work. Figure 1 offers a "route-map" of the structural analysis which links policy and organizational processes to stressful effects.[1] As Smith (1984) has argued, the capacity to organize and control local activities in line with ideas arising elsewhere is a contemporary and distinctive feature of corporate capitalism. The documentary processes described in this chapter help solve a particular problem in hospital management. Until recently, the work of *professional employees* was conducted under professional supervision, relatively free of managerial control. The new methods make it possible for managerial decisions and organizational priorities to be embedded, through objective processes, in nurses' practice. In this way, policy decisions made elsewhere in the health-care system pervade nursing care. Nurses' autonomy from managerial control thus becomes an issue. Nurses' control over their own labour process became problematic only after health-care policy took a direction at odds with nurses' ideas.

Health-care policy deliberations in the 1960s contained rudimentary ideas about the utility of measuring "need" for health services rather than responding to public demand. The notion that Canadians demand more health services than they really need was formalized in policy documents, for example, the *Report of the Task Force on the Cost of Health Services*, pub-

lished in 1970. The recommendations of this report were the launching point for research and development of management systems in which nursing services were to be geared to patients' needs (Vol. 1:43–45). The assumption behind the R and D programmes was that nurses could not be relied on to differentiate "real needs" from patients' excessive demands. Systems of patient classification, such as those developed from work carried out by the Saskatchewan Hospital Systems Study Group (1967, 1968, 1973), were to make determinations of need more objective and rational.

When a patient classification system is implemented in a nursing department, assessment of patients' needs for nursing care takes place *in the management system*, as opposed to individual decision-making by nurses about what to do for individual patients. To nurses who are introduced to a patient classification system, the whole process is represented by a document known as a patient classification form, which they are expected to fill out each day (see Figure 2). Filling out the form puts into motion a process which has a definite effect, at least when it is used as part of a staffing system: nurses are aware that the number of staff made available to do the work on a hospital ward is a reflection of what they have reported in their patient classification forms. Nurses are given to understand that the connection is more direct than is in fact the case; this is what makes their troubles with staffing so distressing. During implementation of patient classification systems, nurses are encouraged to revise the wording on the form, to add new categories, etc., so that it accurately reflects all the important aspects of their care of patients. Later, when they have carefully recorded their knowledge of individual patients, and have received classification ratings which result in too few nurses to do a good job, they are confused. The structure of decision-making remains unclear to them, and the decision itself mysterious. But the system has generated officially sanctioned knowledge founded on what nurses themselves have reported. Nurses are thus implicated in its production in a way

Figure 2. Patient Classification

UNIT: _____ TEAM: _____ TO-DAYS DATE: _____

* For Full Description of Care — Please See Guidelines

Rater: _____

Direct Nursing Care in 24 Hrs.

Time Values:

Factor 1 — 30 min.

Factor 2 — 30-60 min.

Factor 3 — 60-120 min.

Factor E3 — over 120 min.

		PERSONAL CARE				NUTRITION			ACTIVITY			TEACHING & EMOTIONAL SUPPORT				TREATMENT OBSERVATION			TOTAL			PAT. CLASS
		SELF CARE	ASSISTANCE	COMPLETE CARE	OVER 120 MIN. REQUIRED 24 HRS.	MINIMUM ASSISTANCE	PARTIAL ASSISTANCE	NEEDS TO BE FED	MINIMUM SUPPORT	REQUIRES ASSISTANCE	FULLY DEPENDENT	0-30 Min./24 Hrs.	30-60 Min./24 Hrs.	60-120 Min./24 Hrs.	0-30 Min. 24 Hrs.	30-60 Min. 24 Hrs.	60-120 Min. 24 Hrs.	OVER 120 Min. 24 Hrs.	1	2	3	
Rm. No.	Patient's Name	1	2	3	E3	1	2	3	1	2	3	1	2	3	1	2	3	E3				
TOTALS	Team Sub Total	1				2			3			4			5				Team Census			
	Combined Totals	A				B			C			D			E				Unit Census			

that obliges them to deal with its effects on staffing.

To begin to see how nurses' reports are transformed into a seemingly "wrong" organizational decision, one must be aware that the patient classification form is only one piece in a documentary decision-making process. It refers both to previous research and development work and to future decisions on staffing procedures. There is room for a calculated reshaping of nurses' accounts in both those processes. The patient classification form is one of a series of documents in which "what nurses know" is systematically transformed into information with a special character appropriate for semi-automated and objective decision-making. After accumulating, from several documents, specific kinds of information about patients, the form physically travels out of the ward into a central office where compilations are made from it mechanically. (Computer applications can, of course, speed up the processing time, by removing the necessity for paper to be routed around the hospital.)

In patient classification, nurses' knowledge of patients is being used to classify them according to degree of need for nursing care. This record-keeping is carried out in addition to nurses' daily tasks. Nurses categorize what they know about their patients, including the daily plan of work, in the form specially constructed for this purpose. The categories of the patient classification form provide a kind of conceptual template for nurses to mentally scan a particular patient and estimate, according to a standard guide, (see Figure 2) the amount of time a nurse would require to carry out the major features of that patient's therapeutic regime. Nurses need not be familiar with a particular patient to "classify" him or her; they consult and interpret other records in which accounts of care already given, as well as plans for ongoing therapeutic activities, have been provided (Figure 3).

Patient classification has nurses express in concrete terms, tied to actual activities, the amount of time they expect scheduled care of a particular patient to take. Nurses' responses

regarding major features of their patients' needs for nursing intervention indicate "automatically," citing background research, which level of care a patient falls into. Work analysis and time studies (the R and D work) have provided a body of data on the basis of which standard schedules of tasks and standard times per task are defined. Patient classification information supplied by nurses offers the indicators necessary to establish the relation of individual patients to standard interventions, or at least, what is crucial for the management decisions to be taken, to the amount of time which standard interventions take standard nurses to complete in a research setting. These standard times are then substituted for nurses' individual time estimates in calculating staff allocations. This constitutes the first kind of reshaping of nurses' practical knowledge alluded to earlier.

There is yet more manipulation of "what nurses know" before a staffing decision is arrived at. My discussion of the intended uses and unintended effects of document-based decision-making will follow consideration of this second kind of reshaping. The actual staffing decision makes use of more information than nurses' transposed choices about patients' nursing care needs from the classification form. That initial step has produced a generalizable account of "nursing care needs" in an information form ready for processing with budget information to objectively determine staffing levels. It is this capacity of objectivity which makes patient classification useful as a technique for improving "efficiency" of nursing labour. Nurses' pace of work can be adjusted when staffing decisions incorporate patient classification information. A determination is made of the amount of paid labour time which will "match" a given amount of work (estimated in relation to care levels). Reducing slightly the labour time allowed means that nurses have to speed up to handle the designated work.

Matching staff allocations to care levels gives a hospital management more control over a nursing work force. Staffing was formerly a very imprecise procedure. Basic decisions about

Figure 3. A Nurse's Worksheet

INDIVIDUAL CARE PLAN

STANDARD CARE PLANS
IN USE:

DATE	PROBLEMS/NEEDS (NURSING DIAGNOSIS)	EXPECTED OUTCOMES	DEAD-LINES	CHARTING	NURSING ACTIONS

NURSES WORKSHEET   (TO BE COMPLETED IN PENCIL)

DATE	DAILY CLASSIFICATION		DIAGNOSIS:
			DOCTOR:

VITAL SIGNS — DATE

T.P.R.:   APEX:

B/P

INTAKE: OUTPUT:

OTHER:

I.V. THERAPY

PERSONAL CARE: SELF   ASSIST   TOTAL

TREATMENT/THERAPY

ACTIVITY: SELF   ASSIST   TOTAL

NUTRITION: SELF   ASSIST   TOTAL

DIET:

FOOD ALLERGY:

ELIMINATION: SELF   ASSIST   TOTAL

TEACHING NEEDS:

OTHER:

DISCHARGE PLANS/LONG TERM GOAL

how many nurses to assign to a nursing unit depended upon historical experience of the workable ratio between nurses and patients; patient census was the only "hard data" available to modify historical staffing complements. This gave hospital managements very little control over the productivity of their nursing force. Census information (or how many beds were filled each day) revealed nothing about acuity (how ill a patient was); it therefore could not be used to discriminate effectively among differing staff levels needed in units with the same number of patients. Head nurses were previously able to demand additional staff when, in their professional judgement, they needed it. Of course, individual head nurses, like individual staff nurses, would have varying ideas about what amount of care was necessary, how fast nurses could work, and so on; head nurses would also have varying capacities to make their nurses work speedily, and hospital managers had no objective information about which head nurses were more successful in this regard. Particularly, hospitals had no control over nurses' beliefs and commitment to giving "good care." As the policy cited earlier suggested, the costs of health services alarmed Canadian policy-makers into believing that nurses were being too generous, and that their choices should be curbed. Patient classification was the instrument by which this was to be accomplished, although not directly.

To implement changes which would appear desirable from patient classification information, new staffing methodologies have been developed. "Flexible" staffing, for instance, is an innovation which operates on patient classification information. It is a method in which a minimum number of permanent staff are maintained, and "floating" staff are assigned on a daily basis to those units in which classification figures show more staff to be required. This not only provides for efficient use of staff by assigning them where and when they are needed, but it also allows the hospital to make use of cheaper labour, i.e., casual workers not in the permanent work force. Given the local availability of a pool of nurses who are content

with part-time or temporary work, this staffing procedure can be implemented very effectively.

Economical staffing decisions depend on both the way that "real needs" are constructed, and, though to a lesser extent, on how those data are manipulated with budget information. Regarding the first, "real needs" information is a minimized version of what nurses have said about their patients. The "real needs" coming out of the information system are standardized needs, trimmed of individual differences that nurses perceive in patients, and ignoring the fact that individual nurses bring to the workplace their own special characteristics which determine how they will respond to patient needs. Aggregated, "real needs" represent a standardized and minimized estimate of the work contained in a nursing unit (hospital ward) of actual patients. Organizing staffing in relation to "real needs" improves efficiency by making nurses responsible for caring for a determinate number of patients in a determinate amount of paid labour time. In principle, staff allocations can be made precisely, matching exactly the standard time of aggregated "real needs." Thus, every minute of a nurse's paid labour time can presumably be allocated to work that must be done, if the patient is to have his/her minimal needs met. Patient classification in essence gives hospitals the capacity to keep nurses working without any wasted time.

Of course, nursing management is not quite so straightforward as it might appear on paper. For one thing, information about needs is still an estimate, produced daily, in relation to a patient population which is extremely changeable. A patient's medical condition changes all the time, and for reasons of efficiency, hospitals move patients in, through their facilities, and out again rapidly. So the apparent precision which the management system offers is reduced by variations in the work which are not reflected in the objective information. Also, while nurse timing studies have been most successful in assessing those aspects of the work nurses do directly with the patient, it should be kept in mind that nurses' work is by no means limited to the bedside.

They organize and co-ordinate an environment which houses patients and involves many aspects similar to running a hotel; they work in concert with a variety of auxiliary service-providers. In addition, nurses provide a supportive environment for the practice of medicine, and articulate their caring work to physician's orders and practical needs. Nurses take responsibility for managing the patient's entire therapeutic regime, for instance, organizing his or her movements to other hospital departments for special treatments. They are involved with the public, communicating with families and other visitors, some of whom need special attention, instructions, and interpretation. These and many other tasks, apparently peripheral but actually necessary to adequacy of care, are part of nurses' work. In a nursing management system, certain indeterminate features of the work are estimated and are, quite inappropriately, given a quantitative expression in the "real needs" figure.

When standard times were developed, researchers also included in their calculations the varying amounts of time nurses spend "unproductively," that is, not engaged in any observably determinate nursing task. It is assumed that nurses can reduce such "wasted" time if they are organized properly. Hospitals set presumptive productivity expectations when information about patients' needs, standard nursing time, and its costs are compiled and correlated with budget information. A staffing formula brings this information together. The productivity expectation influences the amount of money which can be "saved" on nursing labour. To increase the pressure on nurses to work harder, the staffing formula is shifted to reduce the time allowed for what I have called the indeterminate work. This simply cuts back on the total time estimated for a nurse to complete all needed care. The effect, with a professional work force, is to increase the pace of work. When less time is allocated to labour, nurses take as their own responsibility the additional "cost" of completing the care of patients assigned to them.

Policing how nurses spend their time is not really necessary, as long as they maintain their high level of professional commitment to their patients. When less time is made available for the total care of their patients, not only do nurses speed up, but they work on unpaid time, according to the nurses I interviewed. In addition, they also curtail the range of services and attention they give to patients. This happens through "prioritizing" their work, an approach to nursing which is a professionally sanctioned method of decision-making. That is, nurses, as one of their professional skills, "manage" their work by discriminating between more and less crucial nursing actions. Making decisions about cutting out some of the nursing care their patients actually need puts nurses under even more pressure. It requires a high level of competence to judge which of the list of tasks seen as necessary should be left out, when something has to go. This new responsibility to make rationing decisions, in an ad hoc manner, has nurses at the lowest organizational levels making choices which may have life-and-death implications. Nurses have to make such consequential decisions "on the run," as a matter of daily routine. While nurses have always been on this important front line of decision-making, the pressures on them have increased. Raising nurses' productivity has this contradictory outcome: services are reduced and those reduced services are distributed over more patients.

The efficiency effect has not come about through precise specification and control of the *labour process* of nursing, as is the case in a manufacturing process organized for efficiency. Nursing still has the form of professional work in which the practitioner chooses how to apply knowledge and skills in relation to each patient. It has as well, however, the character of traditional women's work, in which women "take up the slack" to advance a project; the hospital unit is particularly reliant on nurses seeing what needs to be done and doing it, even if it is not in their job description. The nursing programme is laid out in documents, but *how* that work gets done, the specifics of each general task, the order in which they are done, the care and attention to detail, etc., is not defined. "Morning Care," on different occasions even for the same patient, might be a quick face-wash and tidying of the bedclothes, or a complicated bedbath, including time spent helping the patient to dress and move about with tubes, drains, etc., in place. Leaving decisions about what care can be hurried over, skimped on, or deleted completely to overstressed nurses is hardly a rational way to manage health care. In fact, this feature of "efficiency" makes something of a mockery of the previous attention given to measuring and matching "needs" and work accurately.

Yet this is the practical outcome of implementing budget cuts through organizational systems of objective managerial control. The nursing management system described here channels fiscal decisions made elsewhere into nurses' interactions with patients and their families. The system is at once an advance in managerial technology, and a questionable incursion into professional practice. The increasing use of objective management systems in nursing has been part of the corporatization of hospitals and more businesslike management practices. Provincial governments play an active role in encouraging hospitals to implement nursing management-information systems, although the relationship between public hospitals and provincial governments does not allow the government to direct a hospital's actions. Statutory funding arrangements do give the governments certain powers, however. Hospital administrators negotiate annual block grants on the basis of budget forecasts developed from historical data and projected changes. Such negotiations take place in conditions established by political priorities and government fiscal policies. Among other fiscal restraint actions, provincial ministries have required hospitals to demonstrate managerial effectiveness; use of a patient classification system is considered the best way of managing the nursing labour budget. In Ontario, for instance, hospital nursing departments have introduced objective management techniques either to help "rationalize" difficult

staffing decisions made in response to budget cuts or on the recommendation of (invited) Ministry consultation. Taking the Ministry's advice about managerial methods may be a precondition for a favourable hearing in funding talks.[2]

Internal hospital decisions about the amount of the budget allocated to nursing labour are constrained by earlier decisions at the Ministry level, such as the 1981 Ontario decision to stop reimbursing hospital cost overruns. At the hospital level, the nursing labour budget is finally decided in relation to other hospital priorities and pressures, as well as according to the estimates prepared by nursing executives. Nurses' productivity, when treated as indefinitely expandable, certainly presents one solution to funding problems. The staffing decision taken through applying the staffing formula determines what nurses' productivity *must be*. The administrative capability to assess "needs" at the point of service production finally comes down to applying "efficiency." In the "efficiently" organized hospital, there is in fact more work to do than is provided for in purchased hours of labour. This excess must somehow be accommodated through nurses' efforts. The management idea is that not only does less work really need to be done, but that nurses can actually work faster if they are pressured. The management system turns that idea into a staffing quota with a definite productivity expectation.

The new and difficult conditions being organized in hospital nursing have engendered a number of organized responses. For instance, nurses' unions have begun to intervene to help nurses take a collective stand on "safety to practice" issues. Initiated by the Ontario Nurses' Association around a landmark case at Toronto's Mt. Sinai Hospital, several provincial nursing unions have now negotiated "professional responsibility" or "professional accountability" clauses. Such contract provisions provide nurses with routine administrative mechanisms to bring organizational problems affecting their practice to the attention of administrative superiors.[3]

The profession has also acted in response to

the deficiencies recognized in nurses' increasingly pressured decision-making. New systems of programmed decision-making have been developed and implemented through nursing's official regulatory bodies, officially sanctioned nursing school curricula and professional associations. Hospitals have come to see the usefulness of objective assessment of the "quality" of nursing care by these information systems. "Quality assurance," as a management technique, requires yet more record-keeping from nurses, adding to the weight of paperwork for which they are already responsible. To assess its adequacy objectively, that is, documentarily, nurses' work must be conceptualized and recorded in special documents. Not only does this mean an extension of time spent in record-keeping, it also ties nurses even more tightly into the management-controlled, time-constrained version of nursing care. Their "product," at least its documentary reflection, is fully available to management scrutiny. Nurses become individually responsible for results.

Meanwhile, the "quality assurance" system obscures the existence of time pressures on nurses. The staffing system has determined what is enough labour time to supply; the quality assurance system sets objective outcomes for the work. The problem for nurses and their patients occurs with the disparity between the official version of needs and what nurses must actually accomplish in the workplace. Officially and organizationally, the disjuncture between nurses' professional judgement of what needs to be done for adequate care of patients and management's time allotments for the "real needs," can be ignored. "Quality of care" can be and is defined documentarily, within the constraints of any specified and budgeted-for labour time.

With the new professional reliance placed on management information systems, a hospital loses any administrative-level knowledge that a problem exists for nurses and patients. Abstract documentary information, reported through proper channels, replaces procedures for listening to and relying on experienced professionals.

Only nurses at the front line are aware of the disjuncture and what it means. And these nurses are silenced and disempowered by the management information systems and procedures.

Nurses' control over their practice is lost when they no longer have a say in staffing decisions. While nurses continue to be held responsible for the outcome of their work in hospitals, the conditions there are being organized without their control. Working conditions may deteriorate but the demands on nurses remain as high as ever. Nurses' own expectations of themselves as professionals also remain constant. Yet, they also see that learning to fulfill documentary requirements will get them "full marks" on the new documentary monitoring system of "quality of care." Recognition for exercising their judgement, for extending themselves to meet needs they identify in their patients, is systematically erased. Nurses interviewed in the Campbell (1984) study complained that their job satisfaction was declining, both because their work was not valued, and because they felt they were no longer able to care for patients properly. They felt that paperwork had become more important than patient care. Nurses who have other options "flee the profession," as noted in a *Globe and Mail* article (1986). Others carry on through chronic anxiety and self-blame. Talking about how she managed to get through a day's work when she did not have time to care for all her assigned patients, one nurse explained:

> Some patients take a lot more time (than I have to give). When you see that they need it, you have to take time from someone else who doesn't know how much care they are getting. It's not really fair (to the unconscious or confused patient) but that's the way you have to do it. (Campbell, 1984, p. 114)

STRESS

It is in such a context that nurses suffer stress. They absorb, on a continual basis, the risks involved in working with sick people under conditions of fiscal restraint. The pressures on them are exacerbated as they come under increasing (management) scrutiny. Failure to measure up to new demands can be reflected in poor performance evaluations, which have cumulative effects, and might even result in job loss. Walker (1986) gives the following definition of stress:

> The most popular version of the concept is Selye's (1956), which posits a physiological response to internal or external events or "stressors" that cause the body to mobilize for fight-or-flight by releasing adrenalin into the system. Since this is an animal response no longer appropriate to modern life, the body must react in other ways and the person experiences anxiety which must be controlled. This process is generally destructive if extreme, prolonged or frequent. (p. 14)

Burnout is a contemporary term which denotes a person's "response to a prolonged unavoidable and excessive stress in a work situation," according to Walker (1986:15).

The literature which describes and analyzes burnout, Walker has argued, is part of the organization of managerial and therapeutic responses to "the problem." The popularization of this literature makes it possible for readers to recognize a constellation of symptoms, in themselves and others, as burnout. This conceptual framework has administrative usefulness as well, since burnout victims can be fitted into socially acceptable therapeutic categories, and organizationally sanctioned methods of handling workers' problems can then be introduced. The range of responses to burnout runs the gamut from tranquillizers and rest cures for individuals to worker participation in management. In special burnout programmes, workers are taught how to live with the new organizational realities and suffer less pain.

Nurses as a group are exhibiting symptoms of burnout. One of the popular versions of burnout, as applied to nurses, is that professionals, especially those in the "helping professions," demand too much of themselves. The concept of burnout as an explanatory system helps to bypass the structural analysis, with its political implications. The preceding analysis of "efficient" organization of the nursing labour process shows a different side to nurses' stress. Such personally experienced reactions have a definite and consciously planned etiology in the workplace. Pushing this analysis a little farther opens up larger social policy questions behind such organizational change.

We might ask who, in a democratic society, has the right to make the kind of health-care decisions which are being made "technologically" now. Is the Canadian public willing to "save money" in health care by putting its health-care workers and their service product at risk? When the stress symptoms which nurses suffer are restored to their proper administrative context, they direct analysis back to such fundamental questions. Tracing the organizational elements of nurses' problems can be the basis for rethinking the almost universally favourable response to attempts to improve hospital workers' "productivity" and "efficiency" and to bring modern management methods into hospitals. We have seen the latter providing the organizational capacity to erode health services, an outcome of which the Canadian public strongly disapproves. But such an administrative attack on health and social services, instituted through routine, even apparently progressive-appearing, organizational and professional practices, is less visible than cutting programmes, shutting hospitals, or applying user fees. It may, therefore, be harder to resist.

Acknowledgements: The author gratefully acknowledges financial support from two sources: a National Health Student Fellowship for the original research, first reported in a doctoral dissertation; and a Social Sciences and Humanities Research Council Post-doctoral Fellowship during revision of this chapter.

NOTES

1. The account given in this chapter draws on research carried out for my doctoral dissertation (Campbell, 1984). One hospital's nursing information and management systems were studied as an entry point for analyzing how a nursing labour process *could be controlled* through such information-based methods. More than a case study, the research offers a structural analysis of the managerial processes through which funding processes link specific policies to definite outcomes in geographically dispersed organizations. One particular patient classification system, from a possible dozen or so which are in common use across the country, was analyzed and is described here. The claim that I make is that regardless of the particularities of these systems, the *processes* I describe are the same wherever document-based decision-making is done.

2. Unpublished notes for a 1981 update of Buchan's 1979 survey of staffing methodologies in use in Canadian hospitals suggests that this is a more or less standard practice in Ontario. Since then, other provincial governments have made funds available for hospitals to hire private consulting firms to introduce patient classification systems.

3. Clause 10 in the (1984) ONA collective agreement provides the following protection for nurses: "In the event that the Hospital assigns a number of patients or a workload to an individual nurse or group of nurses such that she or they have cause to believe that she or they are asked to perform more work than is consistent with proper patient care, she or they shall ... follow a specified procedure which includes a written complaint, attempting to solve the problem through a hospital committee set up for that purpose, or, failing that, forwarding the complaint to an Independent Review committee empowered to carry out and report on its own investigation." (page 7)

STUDY QUESTIONS

1. This chapter suggests that managing a hospital is not exactly like running a business. Identify some of the differences and some of the similarities. To make hospital management more "business-like," there must be trade-offs; what are they?

2. Physicians' training gives them skills in diagnosing and treating the symptoms which individual patients complain of. New diagnostic technology and improvements in medicine support an approach which focusses on the individual. How would an environmental approach to understanding stress differ from the current medical approach? Why might it be difficult for the medical profession to incorporate such an approach into its practice?

3. Professionals are expected to work independently, to serve their patients or clients, whereas one expects non-professionals to require more supervision and external controls over their work. From what you have read about nurses in this chapter, do you consider them to be professionals? Why? Does the notion of "professionalism" adequately explain the differences in how physicians' and nurses' work is organized?

4. Nurses in Canada are now largely unionized under provincial labour laws. Very few physicians belong to unions. From the chapter, and from what you know about the medical profession, can you suggest why nurses need the protection afforded by collective bargaining more than doctors do?

RECOMMENDED READING

Durber, Charles. *Professionals as Workers: Mental Labor in Advanced Capitalism.* Boston: G.K. Hall, 1982.

Torrance, George. "Hospitals as Health Factories." Chapter 26 in *Health and Canadian Society,* 2nd ed., edited by D. Coburn et al., 479–500. Toronto: Fitzhenry and Whiteside, 1987.

Wahn, Michael. "The Decline of Medical Dominance." Chapter 23 in *Health and Canadian*

Society, 2nd ed., edited by D. Coburn et al., 422–40. Toronto: Fitzhenry and Whiteside, 1987.

Walker, Gillian A. "Burnout: From Metaphor to Ideology." *Canadian Journal of Sociology* 11, no. 1 (1986): 35–55.

White, Rosemary, ed. *Political Issues in Nursing: Past, Present and Future.* Vols. 1 and 2. Chichester: John Wiley and Sons, 1985 and 1986.

REFERENCES

Bennett, James, and Jacques Krasny. "Health-Care in Canada." *Financial Post.* Reprint of series appearing between March 26 and May 7, 1977.

Buchan, Irene. *Nurse Staffing Methodology in Canada.* Ottawa: Canadian Nurses' Association, 1979.

Campbell, Marie L. "Information Systems and Management of Hospital Nursing: A Study in Social Organization of Knowledge." Unpublished Ph.D. Dissertation, Department of Education, University of Toronto, (Department of Sociology in Education, OISE), 1984.

Canada. Committee on the Cost of Health Services. *Task Force Reports on the Cost of Health Services in Canada.* Ottawa: Queen's Printer, 1970.

Freudenberger, H. "Staff Burn-out Syndrome in Alternative Institutions." *Psychotherapy: Theory, Research and Practice* 12 (1975): 17–22.

———. *Burn-out: The High Cost of High Achievement.* New York: Anchor-Doubleday, 1980.

Giovannetti, Phyllis, and Laverne McKague. *Patient Classification System and Staffing by Workload Index: A Working Manual.* Saskatoon: Hospital Systems Study Group, 1973.

Holmlund, B. *Nursing Study Phase 1, University Hospital.* Saskatoon, Hospital Systems Study Group, 1967.

Lipovenko, D. "Hospitals Alarmed as Disgruntled Nurses Flee the Profession." *Globe and Mail, National Edition* 6 December 1986: A4.

Smith, Dorothy E. "Textually Mediated Social Organization." *International Social Science Journal* 36, no. 1 (1984): 59–75.

Sjoberg, K., and P. Bicknell. *Patient Classification Study.* Saskatoon: Hospital Systems Study Group, 1968.

Van Loon, Richard. "From Shared Cost to Block Funding and Beyond: The Politics of Health Insurance in Canada." *Journal of Health Politics, Policy and Law* (1978): 454–77.

Vash, C. *The Burnt-out Administrator.* New York: Springer, 1980.

Vayda, E., R. Evans, and W. Mindell. "Universal Health Insurance in Canada: History, Problems, Trends." *Journal of Community Health* 4, no. 3 (1979): 217–31.

Walker, Gillian. "Burnout: From Metaphor to Ideology." *Canadian Journal of Sociology* 11, no. 1 (1986): 35–55.

PART IX

ENVIRONMENT, WORK, AND ILLNESS

INTRODUCTION

In the realm of medical practice, disease is attributed to "malfunctioning" of the human body, although, increasingly, social-psychological factors are being recognized as influential in disease processes. The treatment model associated with this conception of disease emphasizes that normal, or healthy, functioning can be restored through "technological fixes" and/or individual behaviour modification techniques. This clinical model, although effective with regard to some disease processes, obscures the social nature of disease and undermines the importance of social and work environments to health and sickness. As readings in this section indicate, social and work environments, inequalities of class, production processes, unemployment, lack of job security, social isolation, personal subordination, and exploitation all contribute to ill health.

Chapter 25 by Harding sets out the general, global evidence that supports moving towards an environmental health perspective. It is argued that industrial and other activities that undermine the sustainability of the world's ecosystems will increasingly endanger human health. The fact that much of this activity involves transforming natural substances, and not only the adding of synthetic toxins to the environment, is not accepted as any justification for these dangerous industrial practices.

Next, the environmental degeneration of the Great Lakes and the growing contamination of the Canadian food chain and food supply are discussed to concretely show the interdependence of environmental and human health. In both systems, it is argued, production and consumption for profit encourage such environmental degradation.

Finally, the rising rate of cancer deaths in Canada is explored as an environmental health crisis. The highly individualistic lifestyle approach to cancer prevention and the related biomedical model are rejected in favour of a much more encompassing environmental health approach which would involve the social control and social change of industry. Rising rates of

death from lung cancer and smoking are discussed as a case in point.

The chapter concludes that dominant political ideologies and social sciences have both largely accepted the trade-off of environmental health for economic growth, but that changing broad-based public opinion now provides the opportunity for alliances committed to fundamental alternatives.

Dickinson and Stobbe, in Chapter 26, provide data on the number, rate, and costs of work-related injury, illness, and death in Canada. The authors discuss the individual, technical, and labour process explanations of worker injury and illness. They reject the first two as being incomplete, and hence inadequate as complete explanations arguing that the labour process approach is more satisfactory in explaining workplace injuries and illnesses. This is because the labour process approach highlights the fact that work does not occur in a social, political, or economic vacuum. It is argued that occupational health and safety are not simply an individual, technical, or medical problem, but rather a political issue that has its roots in the nature and organization of the workplace itself.

Bolaria, in Chapter 27, extends the discussion of occupational health and illness to women and racial minority immigrant workers in agriculture, the garment industry, and service jobs. The evidence presented in this chapter shows that farm workers, garment workers, and women domestics, chars, and cleaners are exposed to numerous health hazards. Their living and working conditions are "dangerous to their health." In the case of farm workers, a work environment characterized by unsafe and unsanitary living conditions, exposure to pesticides and herbicides, lack of job security, arduous tasks, and interpersonal subordination, contribute to physical and psychological ill health. The discussion on garment workers indicates that many of the health hazards faced by these workers in factories are also now transplanted to the households, directly exposing the worker's whole family to health risks associated with textile work. It is also evident that women domestics, chars, and cleaners work under conditions which are damaging to their physical and psychological well-being.

Under such conditions, the high accident and illness rates among immigrant workers from the Third World are often attributed to an "accident-proneness" due to their cultural background and their inability to function in an industrial setting. However, it is clear that health problems of farm workers, domestics, chars, and cleaners have essentially nothing to do with their ability to function in an industrial setting. Almost all of these workers are engaged in manual labour.

In conclusion, it is argued that the greater exploitation of immigrant labour is to be understood in the context of objective legal-political vulnerability of this labour force. The health, health care, and safety of these workers is to be analyzed in the context of the organization of labour processes. In the case of an unskilled and easily replaceable labour force, employers are less concerned about the health of the workers. Evidence presented in this chapter suggests that immigrant workers, because of their powerlessness, are subject to harsher working conditions than the indigenous labour force. Gender and race are additional components in class relations in this society — minority workers are exposed to an even more hazardous working environment.

In the last reading in this section, Doran contends that control over the definition of "health" has been increasingly lost by working people. Whereas, in its earlier formulation, health was seen as a political issue in direct opposition to the principles of industrial production, such an articulation no longer exists. Currently, the definition of health is determined by the medico-legal discourse of workers' compensation.

Rather than accepting these definitions of health as natural and self-evident, Doran contends that they are products of certain disciplining techniques which subtly encourage and coerce working people into seeing health in this narrow fashion. As a consequence, workers' infrequent appeals to the remnants of their old experiential language are today rendered irrelevant to any serious discussion of workers' health.

Doran argues that a major locus of this disciplinary power is the structure and content of the workers' compensation form. By carefully designed questions, it continually structures replies so as to conform to Workers' Compensation Board (WCB) definitions of health and illness. Doran also explores the difficulties which result for claimants if appropriate answers are not given. The WCB form serves two purposes: to discipline individual workers and to produce standardized definitions of injuries.

25

ENVIRONMENTAL DEGRADATION AND RISING CANCER RATES: Exploring the Links in Canada

Jim Harding
University of Regina

INTRODUCTION

Environmental health problems involve industrial, military, and other pollutants which detrimentally affect the earth upon which we live, the atmosphere which shields us from cosmic rays, the air we breathe, the water we drink, and the food we eat. When the health of the environment is threatened, it is not only the human species that is endangered; the world's ecosystems, and the detrimental effects of failing to care for them, are shared by all life on this planet.

The notion of environmental health has developed recently in certain parts of the world in response to the acceleration and convergence of environmental crises. Canadian research, politics, and public opinion have lagged behind with regard to the threats to environmental health for a number of reasons, including the seeming vastness of Canada and the associated myth of its infinite natural resources, the relatively small and highly concentrated population, and the dominance of urban living and ideology. All these relate to Canada's political economy, which from its origins has been organized primarily around export of raw materials and staples to the more urbanized and industrialized areas of the United States and Western Europe.

There has been some official recognition, mostly unheeded, of the growing health risks from exposure to environmental contaminants. A decade ago the Science Council of Canada released a report titled *Politics and Poisons*, which focussed on growing knowledge about the risks from asbestos, lead, mercury, oxides of nitrogen, radiation, and vinyl chloride. It noted that these were studied as "separate cause-and-effect models" and, furthermore, that those substances were "not necessarily the six most dangerous or difficult materials which our society handles." It emphasized that: "The impact of collective exposure to the broad spectrum of toxic substances at or below the permissible levels at which each is viewed safe demands serious consideration" (1977:5).

While there have been such pockets of consciousness, the environmental health perspective has mostly been treated as a radical fringe in a society which still tends to act as a junior partner in American-based industrial growth and military dominance. Even the nationalist and anti-war organizations that have emerged to counter growing global disparities, the cold war, and the arms race have failed to grasp the full implications of military-industrial societies (and their hinterlands) for the declining health of the environment. For many years, environmental scientists have warned that some industrial activities (including the use of fluorocarbons in aerosol propellants, supersonic jets, and atomic tests) may reduce the earth's ozone layer which shields us from ultraviolet rays causing skin cancer. The U.S. Environmental Protection Agency has estimated that every percentage point reduction in atmospheric ozone will result in an additional 200 000 cases of skin cancer worldwide.

In the last few years, atmospheric research has confirmed that in a ten-year period there has been a 40 percent decrease in the ozone layer around the South Pole, which has resulted in a "hole" the size of the United States of America. Although natural causes have not been ruled out, the implications for the health of humans and other species are too grave for us not to fundamentally reconsider or stop industrial and consumer use of potential contributors to this damage.

Since human evolution occurred with the aid of the protective layer of atmospheric ozone which built up over eons, it is tantamount to reversing evolution to continue practices which can undermine conditions indispensable to life.

Preparations for nuclear war, of course, are the greatest threat to global environmental health. The use of only a small number of the stockpiled weapons is considered sufficient to create the ecological devastation of a "nuclear winter." It is probably no coincidence that the far-right political groups most committed to the continued dominance of the U.S. military-industrial system are also attacking the evolutionist theories which could provide us with some foresight and ability to prevent such catastrophic events.

Many industrial practices, including those in agriculture, energy and mining, and forestry can, and do, have dramatic negative consequences for ecosystems which evolved over long periods of time. In both the Canadian and U.S. grain belts, for example, a half-century of unecological farming practices has reduced organic matter in the soil, which took thousands of years to develop, by 50 percent (Goldsmith, 1977). Reasons for this include the cultivation of areas not appropriate for agriculture, monoculture, the reliance on annual crops, the export and decline of soil nutrients, dependence upon chemicals, and the growing disregard of conservation practices associated with the increase in farm size and use of farm technology. We have been relatively slow to recognize the environmental damage, as well as the threat to limited food-growing areas in an era of rising world population, from these "modern" agricultural techniques. Famines in Africa are the result of unecological forestry and farming practices, including concentrated land ownership and control (Timberlake, 1985).

There is little awareness of the long-term risks from petroleum-dependent technologies. Manufacturers' additives to petroleum fuel that are based on efficiency, not environmental quality of life (like food additives), are part of this risk. The amount of lead which falls on the Greenland icecap has grown sixteenfold since the turn of the century. Though evidence continues to be amassed that the body burden from lead (especially to children) is increasing, the federal government continues to push back the date for mandatory unleaded gasoline.

The massive world trade and transportation of oil also pose largely ignored threats to the world's oceans. A background paper for the 1972 United Nations Conference on the Human Environment noted that

> of the 2.2 billion tons of oil produced annually in the world, about 10 million tons of related material end up in the oceans from accidental or negligent discharge at sea, from rivers and sewers and — probably the largest source — from the fallout of hydrocarbons emitted on land by motor vehicles. (Main, 1972:9)

Some argue that this cumulative pollution could interfere with the ability of the oceans to sustain life. Moving Canada and other industrial societies to more self-sufficiency in energy — using conservation and renewables — is essential to reverse this trend.

As awareness that uranium mining and nuclear power will threaten environmental health for many thousands of years is also developing (Harding, 1978). The most widely recognized dangers are the production of nuclear weapons, which has been interlocked with the commercial nuclear industry from its beginnings, and the long-lived radioactive wastes that come from both weapons and nuclear power plants. Dangers from the buildup of long-lived (e.g., 250 000 years) radioactive tailings at mine sites, unfortunately, have received less attention. According to Bertell (1985), mounting radioactivity in the biosphere will not only increase cancers, but will weaken the ability of our immune systems to protect us in a declining environment.

This is of particular importance to Canadians, since Canada is presently the world's largest uranium producer. Ten million tonnes of tailings remain as an ecological debt near the ghost town of Uranium City. There are 100 million tonnes of uranium tailings in Northern Ontario; another 25 million tonnes, with much higher levels of radioactivity, are being created at open-pit uranium mines in Northern Saskatchewan.

The debate over nuclear power has polar-

ized those who have an almost religious faith in industrial technology and those who are beginning to rethink social structures and technological designs in more ecological terms. In this polarization, those who see environmentally induced cancers growing with the nuclear and chemical industries have even been called "apocalyptics." Efron (1984:58), discounting the scientific legitimacy of their environmental pronouncements, asserts that the apocalyptics' real "objects of denunciation were man, America, science, technology, industrial production, the profit and market system and economic growth and capitalism." She is particularly concerned about the alleged commitment of the apocalyptics to "the redistribution of American wealth, and the wealth of other great industrial nations, to the Third World countries" (1984:44). She argues, at great length, and apparently with the endorsement of several (unidentified) U.S. scientists, that the dangers of cancer from industrial synthetics have all been based on a logical flaw which forgets that industry "had simply dug up or chopped down the earth's own materials" (1984:121). Criticizing Epstein's list of major industrial carcinogens, for example, she writes:

> Asbestos is a natural mineral; arsenic and chromium are elements and natural metals; and petroleum is a natural fossil fuel. These carcinogens . . . are processed by industry, but they are actually natural substances . . . They are chemicals; everything is chemicals; Epstein is chemicals. (1984:132)

Later she notes that tobacco also is a natural substance. According to her peculiar logic, this means that the smoking industry is less blameworthy for the worldwide epidemic of lung cancer.

Efron's criticisms of many proponents of environmental health is based upon a semantic trick, one used continually by industry itself. Because not as much attention has been given to the natural basis of many industrial and other carcinogens, those created by industry, or those to which industry has greatly increased public exposure, are somehow not valid issues. Her position is all the more indefensible because, even though she discourses extensively about how few chemicals have actually been tested, and how a complete, pure science is not the foundation of concerns about environmental health, she acknowledges that the incidence of cancer and the threat from carcinogens is on the rise (1984:128, 178). Like so many others trying to hide their allegiance to industry behind "pure" science, Efron has simply failed to grasp that this is not an abstract controversy over definitions of "natural," but an issue of increasing environmental health risks.

In the controversy over nuclear energy it would be foolish to deny that uranium is a natural element, or that unmined uranium-bearing ore releases background radiation. It is, however, a most pernicious semantic distortion to call the greatly increased exposure of humans to lung-cancer-causing alpha-emitters from the radon gas in uranium tailings something natural. These tailings have entered the air and waterways through mining and milling practices, and it has been shown that existing technology cannot isolate these or prevent them from moving into biological pathways (Torrie, 1980). It is this transformation of a natural system, and not the fact that there is radioactivity in the earth, that is the crucial environmental health and, I might add, ethical issue. One would have to be slightly mad to say that it does not matter that contemporary industrial practices may be increasing the amount of skin cancer due to their impact on the protective ozone layer, just because ultraviolet rays are naturally created.

THE DECLINING HEALTH OF THE GREAT LAKES

Let us now turn our attention to the decline of one large ecosystem in particular. The degradation of the Great Lakes is probably the greatest assault on the environmental health of any bioregion in Canada's short history. With one fifth of the world's fresh surface water, the Great Lakes are not only a Canadian, but also a global, ecological treasure. Since the time of Canadian and U.S. industrialization, this glorious water

system has been treated as a liquid dump for industrial waste and human excrement. A source of drinking water for nearly 40 million people, and home to many more millions of wildlife, this liquid dump is now rising to haunt us.

Over 1000 chemical and metal pollutants already have been detected in the lake system (Keating, 1986), and the advancing technology of detection has just begun to be applied. These pollutants come mainly from the factories along the lakes and rivers, from agriculture and other run-off, and from the ecologically abnormal concentration of urban population clustered along the lakes.

The extent to which some of these toxins have moved through the Great Lakes is astonishing. In the mid-1970s, for example, taconite, containing cancer-causing asbestos, covered five hundred-square-miles of the Lake Superior lake bed on the American side. There were also traces of the same kind of asbestos on the Canadian side near the intake system for Thunder Bay's drinking water (Harding, 1978). Public concern after asbestos was found in drinking water samples was one of the reasons the city finally built a water filtration system.

Not only many resource industries, but the hub of manufacturing in Canada stretches along the Great Lakes from Hamilton to Oshawa. This so-called "golden horseshoe," Canada's symbol of industrial wealth and power, contains nearly 50 sources of industrial pollution and 30 sources of municipal sewage. For many years, untreated industrial and human wastes were dumped directly into the lake system from both sides of the border.

Referring to Toronto and the lack of ecological consciousness, for example, Keating (1986:D5) notes that

the city's three main rivers are major sewers themselves, polluted with 14 chemicals, including PCBs, at up to 1,400 times the provincial objective for water quality. Along the same heavily settled stretch of Lake Ontario, there are 38 municipal drinking water intake pipes and 25 for industries, including food processing.

In recent years, illness rates in areas adjacent to the 200 or so chemical dumps along the Niagara River were higher than expected. This has resulted in an increase in militant local opposition (Freudenberg, 1984:42–45). The industrial dumps in this area epitomize "the dark side of economic growth" (Capra, 1982). Keating (1986:D5) shows the extent of the problem: "The four biggest, Love Canal, Hyde Park, S-Area and 102nd St., contain 245,000 tonnes of chemical wastes, enough to fill 10,000 tanker trucks stretching bumper to bumper from Toronto to Niagara Falls." The Niagara River provides 80 percent of the water flowing into Lake Ontario, which supplies water for 4.5 million Canadians.

The industries and municipalities polluting the Great Lakes typically claim to have cleaned up their acts and/or deny any responsibility for endangering health. Cancer rates in Canada tend to be higher in the heavily urbanized areas around the lower Great Lakes and St. Lawrence River (especially Montreal Island). It is difficult, however, to establish a causal connection between one pollutant from one polluter and an increase in the rates for particular types of cancer.

Animal studies, however, are useful in this regard, because almost all substances that have been found to cause cancer in humans also do so in other mammals (Epstein, 1978). A Greenpeace study of the relationship between industrial pollutants and mortality and morbidity rates of the endangered beluga whale has found that despite past protective efforts, the beluga population is characterized by a high incidence of diseases such as hepatitis, dermatitis, septicaemia, perforated ulcers, pulmonary abscesses, bronchial pneumonia, and bladder cancer. These diseases are "readily traceable to severe environmental disturbance." According to Greenpeace,

the probable cause of bladder cancer is the carcinogen benzo(a)-pyrene or B(a)P, one of the most dangerous of the polycyclic aromatic hydrocarbon (PAH) chemicals. Besides causing cancer, B(a)P breaks down the immunological system in mammals, producing an AIDS-type syndrome. (Greenpeace, 1986)

The probable source of the carcinogen benzo(a)-pyrene is the Alcan Aluminum plant on the Saguenay River 100 kilometers upstream from the belugas' main habitat. Belugas are not the only victims of this unregulated chemical: it also has been implicated in over 70 cases of bladder cancer among Alcan workers. This chemical assault on the beluga can be seen as an ecological crime in itself and/or as an early warning of similar dangers to humans. Either way it is clearly in the human interest to become more involved in the protection of the health of environments we share with other species.

The consumption of water also threatens the health of the environment. Next to the United States, Canada has the highest per capita consumption of water in the world, over 90 percent of it by industry (including irrigation). This amounts to 4100 litres per capita per day. The U.S. figure is 6300 litres. In Canada's "chemical valley" along the St. Clair River south of Sarnia, nearly 2 billion litres of water are used daily for cooling, mixing, and discharging wastes (Keating, 1986:D5).

In the mid-1970s, 140 cubic metres of water per second were being taken from, but not returned to, the Great Lakes. The amount of water extracted from the Great Lakes, if unchecked, could increase sixfold within 50 years. Authorities are already predicting a lowering of lake levels, with the potential of further destruction of natural habitats and an increased concentration of pollutants by an inhibition of the ability of the lakes to cleanse themselves.

INCREASING CONTAMINATION OF THE FOOD CHAIN

While exposure to water and airborne toxins is cause for growing concern, Epstein (1978:441) claims "food is the most important single source of exposure to a wide variety of synthetic chemicals." Davies' (1986) study of Toronto supermarket food, which found PCB, dioxin, and several other persistent chemicals, confirms this. On the basis of this study, Davies estimates that 86 percent of non-occupational exposure to these chemicals comes from the food we eat.

Food and diet are now considered important causes of cancer, even more important than smoking. It has been estimated that 35 percent of all cancers are related to food and diet (United States Congress, 1981:108). Many factors have been implicated, including fat, meat, and low fibre consumption, elements and chemical reactions in food, deficiencies in essential elements and vitamins, imbalances in diet, certain methods of cooking, environmental pollutants, and industrial additives.

Food additives have been linked to health problems. Pim (1981:27), for example, lists 68 additives used in the Canadian food industry for which "there is some evidence of health effects." They include 18 preservatives, 14 colourants, 10 texture agents, 8 flavourers, 2 acid/base balancers, 1 flour bleacher, and 1 sequestering agent. Also included are 14 common additives, such as monosodium glutamate (MSG), various nitrites, and butylated hydroxytoluene (BHT). These latter alone represent about 20 percent of the food additives permitted in Canada, and do not include any of the hundreds of flavourings currently used (Pim, 1981:37).

Eight of these additives are known or suspected carcinogens, seven others have been found to produce tumours, three have been linked to birth defects (teratogenic), and one has been linked to genetic changes (mutagenic), as well as a range of conditions from allergies to hyperactivity.

The food and chemical industries deny that these additives place humans at risk. Their self-interested viewpoint is that you cannot extrapolate from effects on other animals to humans, or that the amounts are too small to hurt humans. There are too many people, however, who have directly experienced undesirable effects of these additives or seen their children react to them to believe these disclaimers. At present, pressure is mounting to ban the sulphites (widely used in salad bars, canned foods, jams, wines, and beers) because they have been linked to several fatal allergic reactions across Canada. The history of testing and regulation suggests it is more prudent to be suspicious than trusting of these additives, especially when the testing is done by individuals or institutions whose economic interests stand to be affected by the findings (Pim, 1981:43). Since the food laws were tightened up in the mid-1960s, the number of additives presently suspected is about the same as the number of additives that have been removed from use, because since that time a similar number of new additives have found their way into the food supply (Pim, 1981:37). Clearly we are faced with a revolving door of food additives.

Food additives, however, like industrial chemicals, are presumed innocent until proven guilty. Guilt is difficult to establish, often requiring years of exposure and enough victims to be "statistically significant." In some cases, due to legal and regulatory definitions, an additive is not even regulated. Several flavour-enhancers, including MSG (which some consider a psychoactive drug), for example, are not defined as additives, and remain unregulated. One consequence of this is that there is no limit on the quantity of these substances which may be used. Also, since ingredients are simply listed in descending order by weight, a person has no knowledge of the quantity of additives consumed. Some labels are so imprecise, listing only "colours" or "flavours" etc., that it is impossible to know exactly what is being consumed; furthermore, manufacturers and suppliers of bulk foods, baked goods, fast food, and restaurant meals are not required to divulge such information to consumers. This lack of adequate regulation makes a mockery of claims of consumer protection because it is impossible for persons with fatal allergies to some additives to know if those substances are contained in purchased products. Even when ingredients are listed, they may not be reliable or complete; chemicals from packaging materials and residues from agricultural herbicides, insecticides, fertilizers, hormones, and antibiotics, for example, do not have to be listed on labels.

The number of unidentified chemicals consumed is substantial. About 300 chemicals are used in agricultural production. In Saskatchewan alone, farmers spend 250 million dollars annually on a wide range of chemicals. Agricultural chemicals are such big business that Progressive Conservative Premier Grant Devine and others hope to bring the chemical industry to the grain belt as a way of diversifying and stabilizing the economy.[1]

Even in a time of growing environmental consciousness, centralized economic powers and regional disparities lead parochial politicians to go on trying to buy votes by selling the health of the future. People along Lake Ontario, concerned about chemically contaminated drinking water, might even support moving the chemical industry to the Prairies.

The fundamental question regarding food additives is, Why do food products need all those colours, flavours, preservatives, and stabilizers? It is not because this is the best way to produce nutritious food; rather, these substances are used by a food industry wherein production is motivated above all by profit, not by the satisfaction of needs or the protection of health.

CAUSES OF DEATH AND ENVIRONMENTAL HEALTH

Even with the direct evidence of declining environmental health, some people go on believing that this has no bearing on human health. The major causes of death in contemporary Canada highlight the linkages. Ischaemic heart disease, involving restricted arteries, cancer, and cerebrovascular diseases, are among the leading causes of death for all Canadians. Of the five major causes of death, apparently only the categories "all other causes" and "accidents, poisoning and violence" are not linked to environmental health. If the quality of the social environment is related to the larger issues of environmental health, as it must be through

occupational health, however, many of these apparently unrelated causes of death, such as accidents, would also be included as environmentally related.

Statistics Canada recognizes these interconnections in the observation that "the foremost killers are those which are a combination of habits of life, environment, and heredity" (1983:19). There is continuing disagreement, of course, concerning the relative importance of environment versus heredity as causes of death. For mostly economic and ideological reasons, the dominant approach to prevention in recent years has focussed upon the individual's so-called lifestyle. Of the eight risk factors listed by Peron (1985:136), seven — cholesterol, blood pressure, alcohol, smoking, obesity, sedentary living, and not using seatbelts — are lifestyle variables. The fact that "industrial and urban pollution" is treated as only one category also suggests a bias towards a pre-environmental view of health.

This is not to downplay the fatal implications of individually consumed toxins from food, cigarettes, or beverages. However, focussing on "the habits of life" tends to reinforce the treatment orientation of technological medicine, and to emphasize control of the individual rather than control of the institutions of society. The main ideological effect of the lifestyle approach, therefore, has been a general acceptance of the present organization of industry, and its pollution, as a given.

The social control of the individual may be beginning to pay off. There is evidence that lifestyle-related causes of death are starting to contribute less to the overall death rate. A slight decrease in the percentage of all deaths attributable to circulatory ailments, for example, was observed between 1970–72 and 1975–77. This applied to both Canadian men and women born during the same periods (Peron, 1985:156).

Though these small changes (1 percent or less) are not compelling, it is noteworthy that the percentage of all deaths was down for all major causes of death except cancers. Though there were various changes in specific kinds of cancer, and one must be careful of interpreting "cancer" as an aggregate trend since it includes around 200 specific diagnoses, this exception warrants further examination.

ENVIRONMENTAL DEGRADATION AND RISING CANCER RATES

Federal government figures indicate a growth in the role of cancer in the deaths of Canadians throughout the 1970s, both in terms of absolute numbers and as a rate per 100 000 population (see Table 1). The probability of developing some form of cancer is now so high, and apparently continuing to grow, that it should be a major issue of politics and policy. The fact that it is not has much to do with the preponderance of pre-industrial and pre-environmental views of disease.

Table 1. Deaths from Cancer in Canada, 1973–1980

Year	Number	Rate per 100 000
1973	33 069	149.7
1974	33 751	150.4
1975	34 019	149.2
1976	34 832	151.2
1977	36 050	154.8
1978	37 190	158.4
1979	38 584	162.9
1980	39 578	165.3

Source: *Cancer in Canada*, Ottawa: Statistics Canada, 1979 to 1983.

Peron (1985:140) includes calculations of the cumulative incidence of cancer in Canada for the years 1969–72 to all sites of the body for people up to 75 years old. These calculations went from a high of 31.5 percent for males in British Columbia to a low of 20.5 percent for females in Quebec. The highest rate for women, 28.6 percent, was also in British Columbia and the lowest rate for men, 24 percent, was also in Quebec. Remember, these are averages and, therefore, tend to obscure important differences, including rural-urban and regional variations.

Differences in the cumulative incidence of cancer warrant more in-depth analysis. Peron (1985:140) has noted that "the values obtained vary sufficiently to underline the differential vulnerability of provincial populations to various forms of cancer or cancer in general." Thus, one should examine the role of environmental factors, lifestyle factors, and industrial and urban pollutants in the unequal distribution of cancer across Canada.

CANCER, GENDER, AND REGION: THE CASE OF SMOKING

Data indicate there are important gender differences in types and rates of cancer in Canada. In 1981, for example, lung cancer accounted for more deaths among males aged 40–84 than any other cancer. Lung cancers were reported that year as causing one third of all deaths by cancer for men, compared to 12 percent for women. In contrast, in 1981 breast cancer accounted for more deaths among females aged 30–74 than did any other cancer.

This striking comparison shows that men and women have been facing different risks in an era of rising cancer. Not all major cancer trends, however, suggest this. Cancer of the large intestine and rectum accounted for one third of deaths for men 35 and older as well as for women 45 and older. Such things as common diets probably contribute to an equalization of this form of cancer. It is known that the rate of lung cancer among women is getting closer to that of men as they become integrated into the mainstream workforce and adopt such practices as smoking.

There are also important differences in reported deaths from cancer for men and women over their life cycle. This can be shown by contrasting the major sites of fatal cancers for young, middle-aged, and older Canadians. For example, in 1981 for both males and females up to 24 years, leukemia and lymphatic cancers accounted for almost half the fatal cancers. But gender differences became quite pronounced by mid-life. For men 45–49, lung cancer accounted for the most fatal cancers, while for women of these ages this was the case with breast cancer. Gender differences persisted into old age. Lung and breast cancers accounted for the second most cancer deaths for the oldest men and women, those 85 and over; however, prostate and intestinal-rectum cancers accounted for the most cancer deaths in this group, for men and women respectively.

These differences are not necessarily persistent, nor are they well understood. Such factors as kinds of exposure, latency periods for different cancers, effectiveness of treatment, and survival rates, among others, would all have to be carefully considered. Smoking and exposure to airborne carcinogens in the workplace probably explain the higher lung cancer rate in men. This suggests that an understanding of cancer mortality rates requires an understanding of the organization of production and consumption and its role in environmental contamination. The role of smoking, of course, complicates the situation. It seems nonsensical and counterproductive, however, to view smoking simply as an individual, lifestyle problem.

Even federal health researchers acknowledge this. A report titled *Cancer Patterns in Canada 1931–1974*, for example, distinguishes "environmental" from "lifestyle" factors by suggesting that "the exposure of an individual is involuntary to the former but not to the latter" (1977:4). The fact that nicotine is an extremely dependency-producing drug that is widely and persuasively advertised by the cigarette industry, combined with the fact that smoking patterns are characterized by important gender and socio-economic differences, however, suggest that use of the term "voluntary" is quite misleading in the case of smoking.

It is increasingly being recognized that most cancer is environmentally caused. The authors of *Cancer Patterns*, reporting on international variations in cancer mortality rates, for example, stated that "at least 80 percent of all human cancer is environmentally determined and thus theoretically preventable" (1977:3). In spite of this, the debate about lung cancer and smoking is usually depicted in narrower individualistic terms. Worldwide smoking patterns, however, directly relate to the degree to which human activities have become integrated into industrialization. Mass production (e.g., 5000 cigarettes per minute), and mass promotion of tobacco as a commodity for sale and profit may not be a sufficient cause, but they are a necessary cause, of damage from mass heavy smoking. The fact that smoking and lung cancer is increasing as Western production and consumption patterns spread to developing countries, and that smoking and lung cancer are on the increase as women become more integrated into mainstream industrial workstyles, show the stupidity of postulating individualistic reasons for different rates of these fatal cancers.

The view of smoking as fundamentally a lifestyle problem has even been used to try to disprove that environmental cancers are on the rise. For example, it is not that uncommon to attribute rising cancer rates in Canada primarily to lung cancer caused by smoking. On the basis of overall and lung cancer death rates reported in *Cancer in Canada* from 1976–80, however, this is not the case. Lung cancer deaths in that period went from 48.8 to 54.4 per 100 000. The overall cancer death rates for these years rose from 151.5 to 165.3 per 100 000. Subtracting lung cancer deaths from the total cancer deaths accounts for only 5.6 of 13.8 per 100 000, or 40.5 percent of the increase.

This should come as no surprise, since other cancer rates have also been on the rise. Skin cancer (malignant melanoma) for both men and women, for example, doubled between 1951–1970 (*Cancer Patterns, 1931–1974*, 1977: 5). With the interpretation that "excessive exposure to sunlight appears to be a factor" (1977:5), there was a tendency to ignore environmental health, especially the role that a reduced ozone layer may be playing in this trend.

This is not intended to downplay the relationship between smoking and lung cancer but, rather, to suggest this rise constitutes only one part of a larger and more detrimental set of problems of environmental health. There is a sense in which smoking is undeniably an environmental health problem. This is shown by looking at the complete tobacco industry rather than just focussing on individual consumption and risk. This is just what Taylor (1985:252–53) does when he reports that

it has been estimated that around 150 large trees are needed to cure just over one acre of tobacco. (It has been said — although challenged on the grounds that no such calculation is possible — that 300 cigarettes consume one Third World tree.) A quick calculation shows why the horizons are bare; the average size of a tobacco allotment in Rio Grande Do Sul is about four acres. Therefore, in one year, the area's 100,000 tobacco farmers need the wood of 60 million trees — or nearly 1.5 million acres of forest.

The fact that this aspect of the smoking and lung cancer epidemic has not become part of the mass definition of the problem, not even among most anti-smoking environmentalists, goes to show the way in which individualistic biomedical biases permeate the cancer controversy. In fact, smoking, as an activity of production as well as consumption, threatens our health through contributing to environmental degradation in a very direct way.[2]

As stated earlier, significant regional differences in cancer rates continue to be documented. These trends, at the very least, provide descriptive (though not yet explanatory) evidence that cancer must be seen in large part as an environmental health problem.

A volume was prepared on cancer for the *Mortality Atlas of Canada* using cancer mortality by census division for the years 1966–76. One major conclusion was that there was

substantial spatial variation for all cancer sites combined and for several individual cancers including stomach, large intestine (except rectum) and lung. Mortality rates for certain sites such as male lung cancer tended to be high in

major urban areas whereas the high rates for other sites such as stomach tended to occur in rural and semi-rural census divisions. (1980:6)

There are major problems interpreting such spatial differences. The authors estimated that between 1966–71, 10 percent of Canadians 45 years and older moved. Furthermore, there can be the averaging-out of high rates for some groups within census regions. An obvious problem is that the number of smokers within census divisions is not considered, although surveys could be used to help control for this. Lack of standardized data across provinces, the notorious problem of very long latency periods for many cancers, and the fact that mortality data do not indicate actual cancer or survival rates, or account for treatment efficacy, can all further complicate interpretation.

Nevertheless, the extent of some of the spatial differences is suggestive. For all cancer sites the rate for men was "significantly higher in census divisions of several large cities (Winnipeg, Toronto, and Montreal) and several less densely populated census divisions of Quebec" (1980:15). Furthermore, the fact that there was "less spatial variation (for females) than was observed for males" (1980:15) should make us consider the health implications of the division of labour by gender.

Evidence for this exists in Epstein's analysis of the *Cancer Atlas* which lists cancer rates in over 3000 counties in 48 U.S. states. He notes that

males show a striking variation in distribution of cancer mortality rates, with the highest rates of certain cancers in counties with heavy concentrations of petrochemical industries ... The fact that the corresponding cancer rates among women in some cases show less striking variations strongly suggests the cancers in the men are substantially occupational in origin. (1978:50–51)

It is unlikely that the differences in lung cancer rates across Canada can be explained without reference to occupational and industrial exposures. The rates for males were much higher in the densely populated manufacturing areas such as Greater Vancouver, Metropolitan

Toronto, Hamilton-Wentworth, and the Island of Montreal.

Generally, cancer rates for the period 1966–76 were higher in the eastern than western half of Canada. Because of the long latency periods for cancers, the trends probably tell us more about past than present risks to Canadians. Risks from increased use of agricultural chemicals, for example, are likely not yet reflected.

In exploring these gender and regional differences, I am not claiming that the nature of environmentally caused cancer is well understood. I do believe, however, that the evidence and the prerequisites of prevention compel us fundamentally to alter our perspective in order to facilitate such understanding. The importance of this is shown, in particular, when we begin to realize the potential cancers that can come from continued disruptions in global ecological systems such as the ozone layer around the earth. The supreme irony regarding cancer prevention is that we cannot afford the time for pure epidemiological or toxicological research, which requires exposure of large populations, and large numbers of victims, if we are to redirect our social, economic, and political institutions for a more sustainable future.

That is not to say that we cannot or should not learn from these research methodologies. This is possible as long as we continually place the results in the broader context. This is not, however, the way industrial and regulatory bodies usually use the data and tentative conclusions. A few years ago a Task Force report was released on budworm spraying in New Brunswick, one of the most contentious environmental health issues in the Atlantic provinces. Officials supporting expanded spraying across Canada, supposedly as a means to make the exploitation of our diminishing forests more competitive with other lumber-exporting countries, jumped on the conclusion that "a causal link between spraying and any cancer excess has not been established" (Task Force, 1984:138). What was not mentioned was the qualifying statement that "apparent excesses of the incidence [of cancer] for certain anatomical sites

were identified in New Brunswick compared to Nova Scotia. Suggestions of association of the spray programme with some of the anatomical sites cannot be ruled out" (1984:137). Nor did these pro-spraying officials acknowledge the admission by the authors that the study "does not meet current toxicological standards which require two such studies in different species" (1984:137).

OVERCOMING SOCIAL ANTAGONISMS

If we are to change or adequately control activities which jeopardize environmental health, we will have to have a clearer understanding of the roots of these activities. Some people now argue that the roots of environmental decline are more anthropomorphic than industrial and/or capitalist. One of the arguments for this view is that socialist industrial societies, too, have had major environmental health programmes. Certainly, the U.S.S.R. has proven able to bring devastation to major ecosystems, as the accident at its electrical and military nuclear power plant at Chernobyl in 1986 attests.

The critical study of environmental health certainly requires a vigilantly independent stance. The anthropomorphic ideology which is associated with the dominance of nature (including humankind), however, is probably part of the industrial epoch. Capitalist and socialist forms of production and consumption both have originated and developed with this epoch. Due to the fundamental commitment of capitalism to exploitation, expansion, centralization, and profit, however, the prospects for an environment-compatible post-industrial socialism seem greater.

That is not to say that the seeds of such politics or economics are within today's ruling communist, socialist, or social democratic parties or governments. For the most part these have been as fully committed to the assault on environmental health as have the ruling capitalist parties. Both have been assisted by the conventional assumption of growth-oriented economics that

> public expenditure on health is "social" expenditure, involving "wealth-consumption." Thus the need to safeguard health, e.g., by safety or pollution-control measures is seen as a cost. Measures to create a healthier physical and social environment which would enable people to live healthier lives are not recognized as productive investment in society's most important resource and capital asset, namely its people. (Robertson, 1985:10)

The dominant social sciences have been no more sensitive to the realities of environmental health. For the most part, all social sciences accept, as an unstated assumption and value, domination of nature as a necessary condition for economic growth. Furthermore, most social scientists have an urban and northern hemispheric perspective on the world, and tend to be more removed from the devastation brought to environmental health at the front end of extraction, or at the point of production. It has been indigenous people, trade unions at the shop level, and peace groups who have brought to light the military-industrial links behind environmental devastation.

By the mid-1980s, opinion polls suggested that most Canadians were beginning to break from the aspect of the dominant ideology of industrial capitalism that traded off environmental health for economic growth. Over 80 percent in a 1984 poll indicated they "do not believe that environmental laws should be relaxed to achieve economic growth [and feel] that protecting the environment is more important than keeping prices down." Over 90 percent believed "that every major economic project should be proven environmentally sound before it can go ahead" (Environment Canada, 1986:20). This shows a trend towards support for prevention instead of clean-up.

Ecosystems do not operate in terms of the antagonisms between economic classes, genders, town and country, or the northern and southern hemispheres. It was just a matter of time, therefore, before our ecological interdependence was recognized. How much this recognition of interdependence will contribute to the resolution of the antagonisms which underlie the environmental health crisis and cancer epidemic facing humankind will depend upon our ability to organize effective alliances for this purpose.

NOTES

1. This is the same logic which informed previous attempts by NDP Premier Blakeney to develop and expand uranium mining and refining. Blakeney's plan, which failed due to an unexpected public opposition, was to diversify the provincial economy by building a uranium refinery in the south of the province.

2. The steady depletion of the world's forests, particularly the rain forests of Central and South America, constitutes one of the greatest ecological crimes of all times. This is not only destroying the regional habitats of indigenous people and many of the world's endangered species; but also, if unchecked, will permanently disrupt the globe's photosynthesis cycles of oxygen creation and carbon absorption. Since these forests are the "winter homes" of many of Canada's summer song birds, these too are now at risk.

STUDY QUESTIONS

1. In what major ways do the environmental health perspectives differ from the more biomedical views of sickness and health?

2. What evidence exists for linking rising cancer rates or other illnesses to environmental degradation?

3. What are the major consequences of viewing smoking and lung cancer as a problem of environmental health rather than simply of lifestyle?

4. What social and economic ideologies do you think presently inhibit the achievement of global environmental health?

5. What do you think are the major implications of the environmental health perspective for social science in Canada?

6. What do you think are the main problems with Canada's existing system for protecting environmental health?

RECOMMENDED READING

Bertell, R. *No Immediate Danger: Prognosis for a Radioactive Earth*. London: Women's Press, 1985.

Canada. *State of the Environment Report for Canada*. Supply and Services, 1986.

Capra, Fritjof. *The Turning Point: Science, Society and the Rising Culture*. New York: Simon and Schuster, 1982.

Epstein, S. *The Politics of Cancer*. San Francisco: Sierra Club Books, 1978.

Freudenberg, N. *Not in Our Backyards: Community Action for Health and the Environment*. New York: Monthly Review Press, 1984.

Goldsmith, E. "The Future of an Affluent Society — The Case of Canada." *Ecologist* 7, no. 5 (June 1977): 160–94.

Howard, R. *Poisons in Public: Case Studies of Environmental Pollution in Canada*. Toronto: James Lorimer and Co., 1980.

Keating, M. *To the Last Drop: Canada and the World's Water Crisis*. Toronto: Macmillan of Canada, 1986.

Pim, L. *Additive Alert: A Guide to Food Additives for the Canadian Consumer*. Toronto: Doubleday Canada, 1981.

Taylor, P. *The Smoke Ring — Tobacco, Money and Multi-National Politics*. London: Sphere Books, 1985.

Troyer, W. *No Safe Place*. Toronto: Clarke, Irwin and Co., 1977.

REFERENCES

Bertell, R. *No Immediate Danger: Prognosis for a Radioactive Earth*. London: Women's Press, 1985.

Canada. Environment Canada. *Canada's Environment: An Overview*. Supply and Services, 1986.

———. *State of the Environment Report for Canada*. Supply and Services, 1986.

———. Health and Welfare Canada. *Major Causes of Cancer Deaths in Canada*, 1981.

———. Health and Welfare and Statistics Canada. *Mortality Atlas of Canada*, Vol. 1: Cancer, 1980.

———. National Health and Welfare. *Cancer*

Patterns in Canada, 1931–1974. Bureau of Epidemiology, March 1977.

———. Statistics Canada. *Cancer in Canada, 1979 to 1983*.

———. Statistics Canada. *In Sickness and in Health: Health Statistics at a Glance*. May 1983.

Capra, Fritjof. *The Turning Point: Science, Society and the Rising Culture*. New York: Simon and Schuster, 1982.

Crawford, R. *Sickness as Sin*. New York: Health PAC Bulletin No. 80 (January–February 1978): 10–16.

Davies, K. *Human Exposure Routes to Persistent Toxic Chemicals in the Great Lakes Basin: A Case Study*. Toronto: Department of Public Health, 1986.

Doyal, L., et al. *Cancer in Britain*. London: Pluto, 1983.

Efron, E. *The Apocalyptics: Cancer and the Big Lie*. New York: Simon and Schuster, 1984.

Epstein, S. *The Politics of Cancer*. San Francisco: Sierra Club Books, 1978.

Franson, R.T., et al. *Canadian Law and the Control of Exposure to Hazards*. Science Council of Canada, Background Study No. 39, (October 1977).

Freudenberg, N. *Not in Our Backyards: Community Action for Health and the Environment*. New York: Monthly Review Press, 1984.

Goldsmith, E. "The Future of an Affluent Society — The Case of Canada." *Ecologist* 7, no. 5 (June 1977): 160–94.

Greenpeace. *A History of the Beluga Whales in the St. Lawrence*. Vancouver: Pamphlet, 1986.

Harding, Jim. *The Ecology of Health*. A paper presented to Consumer Health Organization of Manitoba, Winnipeg, March 17, 1984.

———. "Mercury Poisoning." In *Sociology: A Critical Perspective*, edited by Ryerson. Toronto: Holt, Rinehart and Winston, 1983.

———. "The Worldwide Public Health Hazards of the Nuclear Industry." *Alternatives* (Winter 1978).

———. "Asbestos in the Great Lakes." *New Ecologist* No. 2 (March–April 1978)

Higginson, J. "Present Trends in Cancer Epidemiology." In *Canadian Cancer Conference*, 40–75. Toronto: Pergamon of Canada, 1969.

Howard, R. *Poisons in Public: Case Studies of Environmental Pollution in Canada*. Toronto: James Lorimer and Co., 1980.

Keating, M. "Soiling the Sweetwater Seas." *Globe and Mail* 18 October 1986: D5.

———. *To the Last Drop: Canada and the World's Water Crisis*. Toronto: Macmillan of Canada, 1986.

Main, J. *Pollutants: Poisons Around the World*. New York: United Nations, 1972.

New Brunswick Task Force on the Environment and Cancer. *Final Report*. Ministry of Health, Government of Province of New Brunswick, March 16, 1984.

Peron, Y., and C. Strohmenger. *Demographic and Health Indicators: Presentation and Interpretation*. Ottawa: Statistics Canada, November 1985.

Pim, L. *Additive Alert: A Guide to Food Additives for the Canadian Consumer*. Toronto: Doubleday Canada, 1981.

Policies and Poisons: The Containment of Long-Term Hazards to Human Health in the Environment and in the Workplace. Science Council of Canada, Report No. 28, October 1977.

Robertson, J. *Health, Wealth and the New Economics: An Agenda for a Healthier World*. New York: Intermediate Technology Group of North America, 1985.

Starrs, C. *Environmental Ethics and Beyond: The Human Side of the Non-Environment Relationships*. Ottawa: Public Policy Concern, January 1982.

Taylor, P. *The Smoke Ring — Tobacco, Money and Multi-National Politics*. London: Sphere Books, 1985.

Timberlake, L. *Africa in Crisis: The Causes, The Cures of Environmental Bankruptcy*. London, England: Earthscan, 1985.

Torrie, R.D. *Uranium Mine Tailings — What the Record Shows: A Review of Evidence Presented to the British Columbia Royal Commission on Uranium Mining.* Presented to Select Committee on Ontario Hydro Affairs, Toronto, Queen's Park, August 6, 1980.

Troyer, W. *No Safe Place.* Toronto: Clarke, Irwin and Co., 1977.

United States Congress, *Assessment of Technologies For Determining Cancer Risks From the Environment.* Washington, D.C.: Office of Technology Assessment, 1981.

26

OCCUPATIONAL HEALTH AND SAFETY IN CANADA

Harley D. Dickinson and Mark Stobbe

University of Saskatchewan

INTRODUCTION

Work is one of the leading causes of injury, disease, and death in Canada. Every 30 seconds in this country, a worker is injured on the job. Each year, nearly 1000 people are killed on the job, and several thousand more die as a result of diseases caused by their work. Work trails only heart disease and cancer as a cause of death in Canada (and contributes to many cases of these diseases). Canadian workers are twice as likely to die from their work as from automobile accidents (Reasons et al., 1981:4).

Table 1 shows the number of occupational injuries in Canada from 1975 to 1985. During this period 5 646 777 workers received injuries that forced them to take time off work. Another 6 153 085 received injuries requiring medical attention. In 1982, the last year for which figures are available, over 15 million work days (or 1.5 days per worker) were lost due to injuries received on the job. These figures, as large as they are, may actually underestimate the number of work injuries, since they include only those for which workers' compensation payments were made. Because about 20 percent of Cana-

dian workers are not covered by Workers' Compensation Boards (WCB), injuries and illnesses suffered by these people do not appear in the statistics. Also, in some cases, employers will transfer injured workers to "light duty" positions without a reduction in pay if they agree not to report their injuries. This helps employers minimize their WCB assessment rates, and at the same time provides workers with greater incomes because of the difference between wage rates and WCB compensation rates. This practice contributes to the underreporting of worker injury rate.

Table 2 shows the reported proportion of workers injured on the job in Canada. The injury rate tends to increase between 1975 and 1980. Between 1981 and 1983 it drops, after which time it again increases. Part of the drop in the early 1980s can be attributed to the 1982 recession which reduced employment in high-risk occupations such as mining, logging, and manufacturing, rather than to any overall improvement in workplace safety conditions. Another related factor which may have contributed to this decline was the growth in the number of persons employed in lower-risk service

Table 1. Work Injuries* in Canada

Year	Disabling Injuries	Non-Disabling Injuries	Total Injuries	Work-Days Lost ('000s)
1975†	441 008	547 147	988 155	11 000§
1976‡	473 726	572 062	1 045 788	11 800§
1977	456 803	586 267	1 043 070	11 400§
1978	485 245	592 297	1 077 542	12 100
1979	537 102	630 118	1 167 220	13 100
1980	567 921	648 272	1 216 193	14 500
1981	585 410	622 208	1 207 618	15 800
1982¶	518 405	495 799	1 014 204	15 380
1983¶	490 503	461 585	952 088	N/A
1984¶	521 746	501 718	1 023 464	N/A
1985¶	568 408	495 582	1 063 990	N/A

* Includes some claims for occupational disease.
† Data for the Northwest Territories and Yukon not available.
‡ Data for the Northwest Territories not available.
§ Estimate.
¶ In 1982, Alberta WCB shifted payment of medical costs to the Alberta Health Care Insurance Division. This resulted in an underreporting of an estimated 80 000 non-disabling injuries per year.

Sources: *Employment Injuries and Occupational Illnesses, 1972–1981* (Ottawa: Labour Canada, 1984) and Worker Compensation Board *Annual Reports* for ten provinces and two territories for 1982–1985.

Table 2. Estimated Rate* of Occupational Injuries in Canada

Year	Employment in Canada ('000s)	Disabling Injuries per 100 Workers	Non-Disabling Injuries per 100 Workers	Total Injuries per 100 Workers
1975	9 284	4.75	5.90	10.65
1976	9 477	5.00	6.04	11.04
1977	9 651	4.73	6.07	10.80
1978	9 987	4.86	5.93	10.79
1979	10 395	5.17	6.06	11.23
1980	10 708	5.30	6.05	11.35
1981	11 006	5.32	5.65	10.97
1982	10 644	4.87	4.66	9.53
1983	10 734	4.57	4.30	8.87
1984	10 907	4.76	4.57	9.33
1985	11 339	5.01	4.38	9.39

* Rates are understated since Statistics Canada estimates of employment are used. Not all persons employed in Canada are covered by Workers Compensation. The understating of rates is estimated to be approximately twenty percent.

Sources: From *Labour Force Annual Averages*, 1975–1983. Statistics Canada Cat. No. 71-529 and *The Labour Force*. Statistics Canada Cat. No. 71-001 (Dec. 1984 and Dec. 1985).

industries. The partial recovery in industries of Canada's primary and secondary sector after 1983 is accompanied by an increase in injury rates. The injury rates as shown in this table are underreported because of the reasons discussed above, and because of the way the rate itself is calculated. The population base used is the total number of persons employed. Since only about 80 percent of the working population are covered by compensation boards, this results in an underrepresentation of up to 20 percent. Even with this underrepresentation one in ten workers in Canada is injured in any year and one in 20 is disabled as a result of an injury received at work.

Table 3 shows the number of work-related fatalities in Canada. Both the number of fatalities and the fatality rate have tended to decline over the past decade. Suschnigg (1985) suggests that this decline in part may be attributable to the changing composition of the Canadian work force and the reduction in the length of the work week, rather than to a general improvement in safety conditions. The proportion of workers employed in the relatively safe service industries has been increasing. This results in a reduction in the aggregate fatality rate. In addition, as the work week has shortened, risk expressed as a proportion of the total number of people employed declines because the same amount of risk is spread over a greater number of workers. This leads Suschnigg to conclude that the risk of death during any given hour on the job in most industries is just as high now as it was 50 years ago.

The data discussed up to this point have dealt almost exclusively with injury and death due to accidents. The extent of occupationally related disease in Canada is substantial but largely unknown. There are a number of reasons for this.

First, there are long latency periods between exposure to disease-causing agents and the appearance of symptoms. In the case of most occupationally caused cancers, ten to 20 years elapse between first exposure to a carcinogen and diagnosis of the disease. This can make it very difficult to assign causality to a specific case of cancer.

Table 3. Occupational Fatalities in Canada

Year	Total Fatalities*	Fatality Rate per 100 000 Workers†
1975	1172	12.62
1976	1058	11.16
1977	943	9.77
1978	999	10.00
1979	1059	10.19
1980	1041	9.72
1981	960	8.72
1982	1025	9.63
1983	819	7.63
1984	798	7.27
1985	818	7.23

* Includes compensated deaths for occupational disease and deaths of workers on pension for earlier disabling injury where death was the result of the injury. Understates total occupationally caused deaths by excluding most deaths due to occupational disease.

† Understates fatality rate since not all workers are covered by WCB. Estimate of understatement is approximately 20 percent.

Sources: *Employment Injuries and Occupational Illnesses, 1972–1981* (Ottawa: Labour Canada, 1984); Workers' Compensation Board *Annual Reports*, all provinces and two territories 1982–85; *The Labour Force.* Statistics Canada Cat. No. 71-001.

Second, there is almost no pre-testing of new chemicals to determine their long-term safety for exposed workers. When this is combined with a long latency period, a substance might be considered "safe" for decades, when in fact it is causing many cases of disease. Widespread use of PVCs, for example, began during World War II, but it was not until 1974 that their extremely carcinogenic nature was confirmed (Mendelkoff, 1979:52–56; Epstein, 1978). Sentes (1985) has argued that in addition to this problem, there is reason to doubt the reliability and validity of exposure-level settings as they are currently established.

Third, most workers, and many employers, do not know to which chemicals they are being exposed, since, in order to protect "trade secrets," the ingredients of many industrial chemicals are not disclosed (Sass and Butler, 1979; Doern, 1977; Franson et al., 1977).

Fourth, the sheer quantity of chemicals used in industry makes monitoring almost impossible. There are over 12 000 toxic chemicals presently used in Canadian industry and the rate of introduction of new substances exceeds the existing capacity to assess their safety. These difficulties are compounded when one considers the possible synergistic effects. That is, two chemicals may be harmless in themselves, but exposure to both of them may be extremely dangerous. Since such safety testing as does occur is limited to single substances, any combined effects remain unknown (Ison, 1978).

Fifth, physicians are not in general trained to identify occupational causes of illness. Most medical schools in Canada devote little time to occupational diseases and their causes. This lack of training for physicians raises the possibility that many occupationally caused diseases are not diagnosed as such. This problem may also be compounded by the fact that company physicians are under pressure not to diagnose illness as being occupationally caused (Walters, 1985).

Sixth, physicians and compensation-board officials tend to assume that the absence of positive data requires a "negative assumption" (Ison, 1978) in assigning disease causation to a patient's occupation. Unless a person can prove that he or she was exposed to a known toxic or carcinogenic substance for a long period of time at a high exposure level, physicians usually reject the suggestion that the illness was occupationally caused. This is compounded by the tendency on the part of physicians to assign greater importance to "lifestyle" factors, such as smoking, drinking, drug use, and diet, in the causation of disease than to occupational or environmental factors. When a worker who smokes suffers from a respiratory disease, for example, it is generally assumed that it is the smoking, and not any factors at work, that is to blame (Sterling, 1978).

Despite these difficulties in determining which diseases are occupationally caused, there is much evidence to suggest that the workplace is the site of several epidemics. Epidemiological studies indicate that exposure to asbestos that has already occurred in the United States, for example, will result in 19 000 cases of mesothelioma (a previously rare form of cancer of the lining between the lung and the chest cavity), 55 000 cases of lung cancer, and 65 000 cases of asbestosis between 1980 and 2009 (Walker et al., 1983). A study by Canadian researchers Howe and Lindsay (1983) reveals various risks for a wide range of Canadian workers. Bartenders, for example, are 6.35 times more likely to die of buccal or larynx cancer than is the average Canadian, farmers are 2.61 times more likely to die of stomach cancer, butchers are 4.41 times more likely to die of cancer of the rectum, and service-station attendants are 5.29 times more likely to die of bladder cancer.

Although cancer is a leading cause of death, estimates vary as to what proportion of cancer is occupationally related. A joint study conducted in the United States by the National Cancer Institute (NCI), the National Institute of Environmental Health, and the National Institute of Occupational Safety and Health suggests that up to 40 percent of cancer deaths are occupationally related (NCI, 1978). Other researchers estimate that only about 5 percent of cancer deaths are related to occupation (Howe and Lindsay, 1983). If these divergent estimates are applied to Canada, then somewhere between 2200 and 16 000 Canadians annually die from cancers caused by substances they are exposed to at work.

Cancer is not the only fatal occupationally caused disease. Workers also die from silicosis caused by exposure to silica dust, from neurological damage caused by exposure to lead, from heart attacks caused by exposure to glycerine, excessive stress, and/or exertion, and from byssinosis caused by exposure to cotton flax or hemp dust. Many, if not most, of the deaths from these and other causes are never reported as occupationally caused, and so victims or their families are never compensated.

Besides the fatal diseases, a host of other minor ailments can be caused by work. Stress, for example, which is often job-related, has been implicated in a number of conditions ranging from ulcers to heart disease. Early symptoms of chronic stress can include indecision, reduced appetite, weight loss, irregular bowel movements, headache, backache, skin rashes, insomnia, nervousness, tremors, poor memory, and irritability (Stellman and Daum, 1973). Causes of job stress can include physical surroundings such as noise and vibration, rate of work for repetitive tasks, work scheduling and shift work, fatigue, and emotional and psychological pressures from such things as unclear demands from supervisors or concern for job security (Lowe and Northcott, 1986). The personal costs of work-related injury and illness are associated with staggering social costs.

The direct financial cost of work-related injury, illness, and death is great. Table 4 shows the payments made by Workers' Compensation Boards to injured workers or their survivors. The total payment reached $2 544 535 000 in 1985. This amounted to 1.14 percent of Canada's total wage bill. The costs of occupational injuries have been increasing steadily since 1975, both in terms of dollars and as a proportion of the total wage bill.

As large as these amounts are, they represent only a small proportion of the financial cost of occupational injury and illness. Workers suffer from uncompensated wage loss and loss of earning potential. Employers suffer losses from decreased production, equipment damage, and retraining costs. Governments pay for increased utilization of medical and hospital services, and for increased use of welfare services by those who have been injured or made ill on the job, but who receive little or no WCB compensation. Governments also lose the tax revenues that healthy workers generate. Labour Canada (1984:4) estimates the indirect costs of occupational injury and illness to be four times the

direct costs. This would raise the total cost in Canada in 1985 to over $12.5 billion.

A report prepared for the Economic Council of Canada (Manga et al., 1981) estimated the indirect costs could exceed the direct ones two-to tenfold. If the higher estimate is accurate, work-induced injury and disease would have cost the Canadian economy about $28 billion in 1985 — close to the amount of the federal deficit in that year.

Although it is clear that the personal and the societal cost of work-produced injury and illness is great, it is not clear why work should be so dangerous and unhealthy. The balance of this paper will be an examination of three different explanations of occupational injury, illness, and death. We will begin by looking at the individualistic explanations and the solutions that follow from this approach. Next we look at technical explanations and proposed solutions. Although both these explanations have an intuitive appeal, we suggest they are inadequate as complete explanations for occupational injury and illness, because they fail to examine the broader context within which work is organized and occupational injuries and illnesses occur. We conclude the chapter with a brief outline of the labour-process approach, which views worker injury and illness as at least partly a consequence of the nature and organization of work itself.

EXPLANATIONS FOR OCCUPATIONAL INJURY, ILLNESS, AND DEATH

Individual Explanations

The extent of occupational illness, injury, and death outlined in the preceding section raises two basic questions: What is the cause of occupational injury and illness? and How can it be reduced?

The most common answer to the first question is that workers themselves are to blame. That is, workplace injuries or illnesses are often attributed to the carelessness, laziness, and/or

Table 4. Compensation Benefit Payments in Canada

Year	Medical* Aid ('000s)	Compensation for Lost Earnings ('000s)	Pension ('000s)	Total Benefits ('000s)	Total Payroll (Millions)	Benefit Payments per $100 Payroll†
1975‡	137 275	337 241	182 719	657 235	86 727	0.76
1976§	163 039	411 766	200 276	775 081	100 059	0.77
1977	174 225	454 380	230 276	858 881	110 379	0.78
1978	199 598	496 787	301 110	997 495	120 030	0.83
1979	212 383	575 858	316 308	1 104 549	135 274	0.82
1980	251 479	709 110	392 448	1 353 037	153 671	0.88
1981	318 245	837 597	471 414	1 627 256	176 568	0.92
1982	359 416	1 017 635	588 703	1 965 754	188 221	1.04
1983	354 876	983 461	807 254	2 145 591	188 221	1.04
1984	373 746	1 096 484	827 254	2 145 591	197 632	1.09
1985	424 372	1 163 056	957 107	2 544 535	224 095	1.14

* Includes medical aid and rehabilitation expenses.

† Rate is understated since Statistics Canada statistics on payroll are used. Not all payroll earned by workers is covered by Workers Compensation. Estimate of underreporting is 20 to 30 percent.

‡ Data for the Northwest Territories and Yukon not available.

§ Data for the Northwest Territories not available.

Sources: *Employment Injuries and Occupational Illnesses 1972–1981* (Ottawa: Labour Canada, 1984); Workers Compensation Board *Annual Reports*. All Provinces and Territories. 1982–1985; *Estimates of Labour Income*, Statistics Canada Cat. No. 72-005 (Quarterly).

stupidity of workers. The most popular version of this approach is the "accident-prone" worker thesis. The concept of accident-proneness emerged from research done during the First World War. Researchers at the Industrial Fatigue Research Board studying accident distribution among munitions factory workers observed that of a total of 301 accidents, 169, or 56 percent, were suffered by only 68 workers, or just under 11 percent of the work force. In the same period, 448 workers had no accidents. By assuming workplace tasks and conditions to be homogeneous and static for all workers, it was concluded that different accident frequency groupings "indicate that varying individual susceptibility to 'accident' is an extremely important factor in determining the [accident] distribution" (Greenwood and Woods, 1919; Greenwood and Yule, 1920; Newbold, 1926). Subsequent researchers

have attempted to identify the physiological or psychological attributes of individuals that dispose some workers to accidents more than others. They have had little success. Rather than being able to predict which workers are most likely to have accidents, identification is done after the fact. Thus, if a worker has had an accident, he or she is then labelled accident-prone and in effect blamed for causing it.

The prevention strategy that emerges from this notion of causation is to protect the worker from him or herself. The worker must be educated, begged, cajoled, or intimidated into working safely, and the workplace must be rendered "foolproof." In addition, accident-prone workers must be screened and eliminated from the workplace before they hurt themselves or others.

Individualized explanations also exist for occupational illnesses as well as for injuries. The most common is the notion that lifestyles outside of work are the primary causes of degenerative or chronic diseases. For example, smoking, rather than breathing asbestos fibres or radon gas, is seen as the cause of lung cancer in exposed workers. Alcohol consumption, rather than exposure to toxic chemicals at work, is seen as the cause of liver ailments. This view is institutionalized. The British Columbia WCB, for example, has ruled:

> Where a person claims compensation in respect of bronchitis and emphysema the Board considers the history of heavy or significant cigarette smoking a strong influence that this is due to the smoking and not to the nature of his employment. (quoted in Sterling, 1978:438)

The implication here is that occupationally caused disease does not exist, or at best is of little significance. It follows then that the way to eliminate disease among workers is to convince them to give up their vices and unhealthy personal habits.

Another variant of the individualized victim-blaming approach is to focus not on a worker's accident-proneness or bad habits, but on physiological characteristics. It has been suggested, for example, that miners of below-average physical stature are to blame for the high lung cancer rates among Ontario uranium miners. According to Holmes (1982:9) this is because shorter miners "exposed their lungs to larger doses of airborne carcinogens," having to "breathe more rapidly than their taller colleagues to perform the same amount of work." This increased exposure, he argued, resulted in higher cancer rates. Among other things, Holmes recommended that "pre-employment examinations could be used to restrict shorter workers from jobs where lung cancer risk from carcinogens is high."

Though the particular test which Holmes has proposed has not been widely accepted in the scientific community, the logic underpinning it has. Much research attention has been devoted to means of identifying so-called hypersusceptible workers. Hypersusceptible workers, it is argued, are characterized by physiological or genetic traits which render them more susceptible than other people to the harmful effects of certain substances. Again, the fault for illness is seen to reside within the individual worker. According to the logic of this theory, the correct way to eliminate occupational disease is through advance screening of workers, using an array of genetic tests. Although much research has gone into the development of these tests, as yet they have not been widely accepted by industry. This is due partly to their ineffectiveness in actually predicting which workers will develop diseases, partly to worker and union opposition, and partly to a fear on the part of employers of the legal implications of certifying workers as not easily susceptible to a substance, and subsequently having them develop related diseases. Some corporations, however, have used the tests to establish hypersusceptibility to a substance after toxic injury has occurred, and have then used the information to argue against payment of compensation claims (Green, 1983; Severno, 1980).

Individualized explanations for occupational injury or disease have predominated, and most preventive strategies have been based upon them. They possess a certain common-sense appeal. At the lowest level of analysis, almost any accident can be traced to a single action, which if done or not done, would have precluded it. Usually only some workers in a given workplace develop a disease, so that there is a temptation to examine the personal differences between those that are and those that are not afflicted. Little attention is paid to the disease-producing conditions. Despite all the attempts to prevent occupational injury and illness based upon the individual notion of disease causation, however, occupational injury and illness continue to be serious problems. This suggests a number of possibilities: that efforts have been correct but insufficient, that workers are too stupid for prevention efforts to be of any use, or that the underlying view of causation is inadequate. If this last point is true, one must question why then it persists. One possible explanation is that it serves some function for those that propagate it: blaming workers for their injuries, diseases, and deaths results both in the obscuring of the real causes, and the refusal to recognize the injustice inherent in occupational injury, illness, and death based on the claim that they are the product of the workers' own actions or lack of action.

Technical Explanations

Another explanation for occupational injury, illness, and death changes the focus from the individual worker to the physical reality of the workplace. From this perspective, injuries are blamed on such things as the design of machines, physical conditions such as light, heat, or noise, fatigue produced by the length of the working day or shift scheduling, and so on. Occupational diseases are held to be the product of exposure to harmful substances or conditions. From this perspective, the correct preventive strategy is to design the workplace on sounder ergonomic principles and to control exposure to harmful substances.

The preventive efforts based upon this approach have been more successful than those based upon the previously discussed individualistic approaches. Better lighting, for example, has proven more effective in reducing accidents than simply urging workers to watch where they are walking, and reduced exposure to known poisons has proven more effective than trying to determine which workers will get sick or die first. Indeed, some diseases have been completely eliminated. At the turn of the century, for example, matchmakers suffered a degenerative disease known as "phossy-jaw" in which the jawbone of the worker disintegrated because of exposure to the phosphorus used in making matchheads. The disease was eliminated by changing the material used in the manufacture of matches.

Proponents of this view of causation and related means of prevention tend to argue that technical capability and level of knowledge of a hazard are the primary determinants of safety. Hazards that are known will be dealt with, if possible. As technology improves and scientific knowledge develops, there will be a corresponding improvement in the health and safety of workers. The principal actors in this scenario are physicians, toxicologists, engineers, and safety experts.

The proponents of a strictly technical conception of health and safety, however, overlook the political and economic dimensions of the occupational health and safety issue. It is not only technical capability which determines the level of risk. Many studies have shown a direct correlation between the pace of work, for example, and the number of injuries. The pace of work is set by management, which is under constant pressure to increase it regardless of the implications for worker health or safety. Nor is the level of scientific knowledge the principal criterion used to determine which substances are used or how. In the first century A.D. in Greece for example, observers noted that slaves who wove asbestos into cloth developed a disease which left them short of breath and often eventually killed them. In the late nineteenth century, European researchers were warning of the dangers of asbestos and the first definitely reported case of asbestosis occurred in 1906. In 1918, the Prudential Life Insurance Company of New York became so firmly convinced of the hazards of the substance that it stopped issuing insurance policies to asbestos workers. In subsequent years, dozens of scientific and medical studies conclusively established the link between asbestos and lung diseases such as asbestosis, lung cancer, and mesothelioma. Despite this mass of evidence, the first legal exposure standard in North America was not established until 1970 (Tartaryn, 1979:15–60). Examples such as these are numerous and indicate that technical explanations on their own do not suffice for a complete understanding or explanation of occupational injury and illness. For this reason attention will now be turned to a third approach to this topic.

Labour Process Explanations

Although it is obvious that particular types of substances used in the workplace have an impact upon workers' health and safety, the technical approach discussed above fails to ask some of the most interesting sociological questions, such as, Who decides what type of technology is introduced into a particular labour process? When? How? What are the implications of this control for worker health and safety? Answers to these questions require an examination of the nature of interpersonal relations in the workplace.

The most important of these is the one between employer and employee. There are, however, others. These include: (1) intramanagement relations; that is, relations among various strata of management; (2) interoccupation relations, or the relations among the various occupations constitutive of a given labour process; and (3) intra-occupation relations, which consist of the relations among various factions of the same occupational group. It is our contention that a complete explanation of different types and rates of occupational illness and injury requires an analysis of these various relations with a particular focus on the distribution of power in the workplace. That is, in order to understand the patterns of work-related injury and illness it is necessary to know who has the power to determine the terms, content, conditions, and substances used in any given work setting. Although the several kinds of relations mentioned above are important in this regard, it must be kept in mind that the relationship between employers and employees (the employment relation) is the one central to the capitalist labour process and the one which influences all other relations.

The employment relation develops when one category, or class, of people sells its labour power (i.e., its actual physical and mental capacity to work) to another category, or class, or people in order to secure an income. Within the context of the employment relation, the employer attempts to control the labour power of employees in order to reduce the costs of production and/or to increase worker productivity. This is generally achieved through two related means: the extension of the occupational division of labour, and the development and application of "labour-saving" technology.

The Division of Labour, Technology, and Worker Health and Safety

It has long been recognized that worker productivity can be increased by extending the occupational division of labour. Adam Smith, in his famous 1776 work *The Wealth of Nations*, argued that the increased productivity which resulted from the extension of the occupational division of labour in any industry was the result of three factors: (1) the increased dexterity which workers develop when they perform only one, or at most a few, tasks; (2) the time saved by not having workers change types of work; and (3) the invention and application of "labour-saving" technology which is facilitated by specialization, and which allows one worker to do the work of many. Charles Babbage, in the nineteenth century, agreed the above were important for explaining increases in productivity, although he added that breaking down a job into a series of simplified tasks also contributes to cost reduction by allowing employers to substitute less skilled and less expensive labour power for more skilled and more expensive labour power (Braverman, 1974:79). While the simplification and repetition of tasks, achieved through the extension of the division of labour, contributes to greater worker productivity and reduced costs, it also results in work becoming more boring and monotonous for the worker. This may in turn result in workers becoming inattentive and careless and thereby, more susceptible to accidents. It is important to note that this idea is different from the notion of the "dumb worker" examined earlier. We are suggesting here that the nature and organization of work may itself contribute to the creation of "stupid" and "accident-prone" workers — that these characteristics are not necessarily brought to the workplace, but rather produced by it. This is not a novel concept. Adam Smith argued that the development of the capitalist division of labour would, unless the state intervened, contribute to the general stupefaction of the majority of workers:

> In the progress of the division of labour ... the great body of the people, come to be confined to a few very simple operations, frequently to one or two. But the understandings of the greater part of men [sic] are formed by their ordinary employments. The man whose life is spent in performing a few simple operations, of which the effects too are, perhaps, always the same, or very nearly the same, has no occasion to exert his understanding, or to exercise his invention in finding out expedients for difficulties which never occur. He naturally loses, therefore, the habit of such exertion and generally becomes as stupid and ignorant as it is possible for a human creature to become ... (Smith, [1776] 1937:734)

Thus, within the context of the capitalist employment relation, productivity increases and costs are reduced by breaking a work process down into its component parts and then dealing out a small number of these simplified tasks to individual workers. In this process, workers become less skilled and more easily replaced. Both these characteristics are amplified by the development and application of "labour-saving" technology. This is because control over the nature and pace of work is built into the machinery itself and, thereby, discretion in these matters is removed from the workers and transferred to management. This entrenches the division between mental and manual labour. Management uses this division to secure a monopoly of knowledge which, in turn, is used to further subdivide and simplify the work process. Braverman (1974) refers to this process as "deskilling."

The deskilling of labour tends to destroy the distinctions of skill and craft which various occupations have used to protect their position within the workplace and the labour market. The simplification of tasks, all things being equal, reduces all labour to a common level, and makes the substitution of one worker by another a relatively simple task for employers. In such a situation, employers, interested primarily in increasing productivity and reducing the costs of production, will have limited incentive to respond to workers' health and safety concerns.

Conversely, deskilled workers who are easily replaceable will have little power to ensure that their concerns are addressed. One would thus expect that in those industries or firms where workers have little power and limited control of the labour process, there will more likely be higher accident and illness rates. A recent study of two European Chrysler plants supports this view, leading to the conclusion that "the best protection of the safety and health of workers comes from a strong and effective organization on the shop floor" (Grunberg, 1983:621). The ability of workers to organize for their own protection, however, is a political, and not simply an individual or technical issue. Thus, a complete solution to the problem of occupational health and safety must also be sought at the political level.

CONCLUSION

In this chapter we have suggested that occupational health and safety is not simply an individual, technical, or medical problem. Rather it is a social and political issue rooted in the nature and organization of the workplace itself. Any explanation, or preventive strategy, that fails to take this into consideration will be incomplete, and hence, inadequate. Recognition of this has led some to argue that the major obstacles to the creation of safer and healthier workplaces are inadequate laws and/or inadequate law enforcement. In a recently released report, the Law Reform Commission of Canada criticized the government on both counts. The report also suggests that the Canada Labour Code "places a lower value on the life, health, and bodily integrity of an individual in the workplace than on that of an individual outside it." It goes on to state that "given the inherently unequal distribution of power and authority as between employers and employees, the reverse should be the case" (*Globe and Mail*, 22 January 1987:2).

Although the criminalization of occupational health and safety violations might contribute to a reduction in the number of accidents and illnesses produced by any particular employer, it still fails to address the broader question of the distribution of power and resources within the workplace and, more broadly, in society. Until these issues are addressed, work for many Canadians will continue to be unsafe.

STUDY QUESTIONS

1. What are the main limitations of individualistic theories of the causes of occupational injury and illnesses?

2. What factors do the technical theories of causation ignore?

3. Do labour process theories adequately deal with the limitations of the individualistic and technical explanations of occupational injuries and illnesses?

4. What would be the main components of an adequate prevention strategy for occupational illness and injury?

5. Explain the argument that occupational injury and illness are a political as well as a medical and technical problem.

RECOMMENDED READING

Braverman, H. *Labor and Monopoly Capital: The Degradation of Work in the Twentieth Century.* New York: Monthly Review Press, 1974.

Manga, P., R. Broyles, and G.T. Reschenthaler. *Occupational Health and Safety: Issues and Alternatives.* Technical Report No. 6. Ottawa: Economic Council of Canada, 1981.

Reasons, C., L. Ross, and C. Paterson. *Assault on the Worker: Occupational Health and Safety in Canada.* Toronto: Butterworths, 1981.

Sass, R. "Occupational Health and Safety: Contradictions and the Conventional Wisdom." In *Politics Versus Ecology in Canada,* edited by W. Priess. Toronto: University of Toronto Press, 1978.

Tartaryn, L. *Dying for a Living: The Politics of Industrial Death.* Ottawa: Deneau and Greenberg, 1979.

REFERENCES

Braverman, H. *Labour and Monopoly Capital: The Degradation of Work in the Twentieth Century.* New York: Monthly Review Press, 1974.

Doern, G.B. "The Political Economy of Regulating Occupational Health." *Canadian Public Administration* 20, no. 1 (1977): 1–35.

Epstein, S. *The Politics of Cancer.* San Francisco: Sierra Club Books, 1978.

Franson, R., A. Lucas, L. Giroux, and R. Kenniff. *Canadian Law and the Control of Exposure to Hazards.* Background Study No. 39. Ottawa: Science Council of Canada, 1977.

Globe and Mail. "Soft policing of workplace safety criticized by panel on law reform." 22 January 1987, 1–2.

Green, J. "Detecting the Hypersusceptible Worker: Genetics and Politics in Industrial Medicine." *International Journal of Health Services* 13, no. 2 (1983): 247–64.

Greenwood, M., and H. M. Woods. *The Incidence of Industrial Accidents upon Individu-*

als with Special Reference to Multiple Accidents. Report No. 4. London: Industrial Fatigue Research Board, 1919.

Greenwood, M., and G.A. Yule. "An Inquiry into the Nature of Frequency Distributions Representative of Multiple Happenings with Particular Reference to the Occurrences of Multiple Attacks of Disease or Repeated Accidents." *Journal of the Royal Statistical Society* 83 (1920): 255–71.

Grunberg, L. "The Effects of the Social Relations of Production on Productivity and Workers' Safety: An Ignored Set of Relationships." *International Journal of Health Services* 13, no. 4 (1983): 621–33.

Holmes, C. "Lung Cancer Rates and the Heights of Miners." *Journal of Occupational Medicine* 24, no. 1 (1982): 1–10.

Howe, G., and J. Lindsay. "A Follow-up Study of a Ten-Percent Sample of the Canadian Labour Force: Cancer Mortality in Males, 1965–73." *Journal of the National Cancer Institute* 70 (1983): 37–44.

Ison, T. *The Dimensions of Industrial Disease.* Kingston: Industrial Relations Centre of Queen's University, 1978.

Labour Canada. *Employment Injuries and Occupational Illness, 1972–1981.* Ottawa: Labour Canada, 1984.

Lowe, G., and H. Northcott. *Under Pressure: A Study of Job Stress.* Toronto: Garamond Press, 1986.

Manga, P., R. Broyles, and G. Reschenthaler. *Occupational Health and Safety: Issues and Alternatives.* Technical Report No. 6. Ottawa: Economic Council of Canada, 1981.

Mendelkoff, J. *Regulating Safety.* Cambridge: MIT Press, 1979.

National Cancer Institute. "National Cancer Institute/NIEHS Draft Summary Report on the Incidence of Cancer from Occupational Factors." *Occupational Safety and Health Reports* 8 (1978): 1090–91.

Newbold, E.M.A. *A Contribution to the Study of the Human Factor in the Causation of Acci-*

dents. Report No. 34. London: Industrial Health Research Board, 1926.

Reasons, C., L. Ross, and C. Paterson. *Assault on the Worker: Occupational Health and Safety in Canada.* Toronto: Butterworths, 1981.

Sass, R., and R. Butler. *Industrial Chemical Labelling.* Regina: Saskatchewan Department of Labour, 1979.

Sentes, R. "The Politics of Health Standards Setting." In *The Politics of Work in the West: Historical and Contemporary Perspectives,* edited by H.D. Dickinson and B. Russell. Saskatoon: Social Research Unit, 1985.

Severno, R. "The Genetic Barrier: Job Benefit or Job Bias." *New York Times* 3–6 February 1980, 1.

Smith, A. *The Wealth of Nations.* 1776. Reprint. New York: Random House, 1937.

Statistics Canada. *Estimates of Labour Income.* Cat. No. 72-005.

———. *Labour Force Annual Averages, 1975–1983.* Cat. No. 71-529.

———. *The Labour Force, 1984–1985.* Cat. No. 71-001.

Stellman, J., and S. Daum. *Work is Dangerous to Your Health.* New York: Vintage Books, 1973.

Sterling, T. "Does Smoking Kill Workers or Working Kill Smokers (or) The Mutual Relationship Between Smoking, Occupation and Respiratory Disease." *International Journal of Health Services* 8, no. 3 (1978): 437–52.

Suschnigg, P. *Industrial Politics in Canada, 1926–1981: A Function of Economic Change, Unemployment, and Labour Strength.* Unpublished Ph.D Dissertation, Department of Sociology, York University, 1985.

Tartaryn, L. *Dying for a Living: The Politics of Industrial Death.* Ottawa: Deneau and Greenberg, 1979.

Walker, A., J. Laughlin, E. Friedlander, K. Rothman, and N. Dreyer. "Projections of Asbestos-Related Disease, 1980–2009." *Journal of Occupational Medicine* 25, no. 5 (1983): 409–25.

Walters, V. "The Politics of Occupational Health

and Safety: Interviews With Workers' Health and Safety Representatives and Company Doctors." *Canadian Review of Sociology and Anthropology* 22, no. 1 (1985): 57–79.

Workers' Compensation Board, *Annual Reports*. All Provinces and Territories, 1975–1982.

27

THE HEALTH EFFECTS OF POWERLESSNESS: Women and Racial Minority Immigrant Workers

B. Singh Bolaria
University of Saskatchewan

INTRODUCTION

Foreign workers now constitute a significant part of the labour force in many developed countries. These workers have become a permanent part of the economic structure of many countries, and their labour cannot be relinquished. The volume, composition, and immigrant status of these workers vary, however, depending upon the labour force needs and other structural requirements of the economies of the labour-importing countries. The influx of workers, as well as their immigrant status, is controlled by immigration laws and regulations. Internationally, the direction of flow is from the periphery to the core countries. Canada is one of the major users of "foreign" labour.

These workers, precisely because of their legal-political status as "foreigners," have become an important and perhaps sole source of labour in certain sectors of the Canadian economy. Some workers are imported for specific tasks in specific sectors where because of low pay, arduous work, and an unsafe and unhealthy environment, indigenous workers are unwilling to work. One of the areas in which foreign workers have become a permanent structural necessity is the agricultural sector, where employers "have difficulty in attracting and retaining workers." The effect of immigration regulations and contractual obligations is to make foreign workers reliable, dependable, and docile farm labour. In addition, they are not protected by any labour legislation. Foreign workers, with very little legal or political status, are, from the employer's point of view, ideal labour. On the other hand, for these workers, this distinctive legal-political status has significant effects on health and other areas. These are discussed in this chapter.

FOREIGN LABOUR: POWERLESSNESS

Foreign workers can be broadly classified into landed immigrant settler labour, migrant contract labour and transient workers, and illegal or undocumented workers.

It is the immigration laws and regulations which set criteria for admission and determine the legal status of foreign labour; that is, whether the workers are migrant or immigrant, which in turn determines their political status.

Landed immigrants are those workers who have "lawful permission to come into Canada to establish permanent residence." A permanent resident is "a person who has been granted landing, has not become a Canadian citizen or has not lost his permanent resident status" (Canada, Employment and Immigration, 1984:100). Landed immigrants are entitled to seek employment and enjoy many legal rights. However, they are not citizens. They are entitled to apply for citizenship after a three-year residency in this country. It is precisely this probationary period which is of significance in the context of this chapter.

The new Immigration Act has given the state the right to impose many restrictions on permanent residents, such as the power to dictate almost any type of "terms and conditions" for six months for new arrivals (Act S.14), power to photograph and fingerprint permanent residents (Act S. 115 [1][n]), and to refuse re-entry unless he or she has obtained a "returning resident permit" (Act S.25). Some of these provisions were contained in the Chinese Immigration Act in the 1920s and 1930s. However, the current regulations apply to all permanent residents (Law Union of Ontario, 1981:47).

A permanent resident can also be deported on somewhat vague grounds — simply if a police or immigration officer has "reasonable grounds to believe" that he or she will commit an indictable offence (Act S. 27 [1][a] and 19 [1][d]). Failure to willingly support oneself or one's dependents also constitutes grounds for deportation (Act S.27 [1][f]).

Many of these clauses have been seriously questioned by the Canadian Civil Liberties Association, which has told the government that it is "concerned about rendering permanent residents . . . deportable on the basis of 'reasonable grounds to believe' [they] are likely to engage in criminal activity." The Association is of the opinion that "this country owes such persons something more precise than an exercise in prophecy. The removal of such people from this country on the basis of anticipated anti-social conduct should require at the very least, certain proved anti-social acts" (Canadian Civil Liberties Association, 1977:13).

The implications of these clauses in the legislation are quite serious for the legal-political rights of landed immigrants. Immigrants are reluctant to engage in union activity and/or complain about working conditions lest they be considered subversive. Participation in "undesirable" activities may also jeopardize approval of the citizenship application. Thus, the existence of these clauses is likely to be intimidating for new arrivals, particularly unskilled, uneducated, racial minority, and women workers.

In addition to needing immigrant workers, Canada also relies upon migrant workers under the Non-Immigrant Employment Authorization Program. An employment authorization is "a document issued by an immigration officer whereby the person to whom it is issued is authorized to engage or continue employment in Canada" (Canada, Employment and Immigration, 1984:100).

At a broader level, non-immigrant employment authorization regulations were introduced in 1973 to allow admission of non-immigrants for employment. Since the implementation of this programme, thousands of workers have come to Canada to work.

The data on immigrant and non-immigrant workers for 1978–84 are reported in Table 1. It is quite evident that more foreign workers are now being brought to this country as migrants rather than as immigrants. For the years 1978–1984, migrant workers have far exceeded immigrant workers.

Table 1. Immigrant and Non-Immigrant Workers, Canada, 1978–1984

Year	Immigrant Workers	Non-Immigrant Workers (Employment Authorizations)
1978	35 080	63 320
1979	47 939	94 420
1980	63 403	108 871
1981	56 978	126 583
1982	55 482	125 901
1983	37 119	130 717
1984	38 500	143 979

Source: Canada, Immigration Statistics, Employment and Immigration 1984 (*Annual Report*).

Temporary work authorizations are given only if the immigration office is satisfied that no Canadian citizen or permanent resident is available for the job in question. This means that, in most cases, jobs will be either menial and low-paying, such as domestic or farm work, or highly skilled and specialized. Also, the work authorization is specific to the job and for a determinate time period (Law Union of Ontario, 1981: 113–14). It is crucial to note that these non-immigrant workers have been allowed to enter Canada even when there is high unemployment.

Canada continues to import migrant contract workers to supplement the labour force in agricultural and service sectors (Bolaria, 1984a; Bolaria and Li, 1985).

Migrant workers are in a vulnerable position. As the Law Union of Ontario states (1981:115):

> The bargaining power of temporary workers is practically non-existent, since their presence in Canada is dependent on their continued employment by their employer. Such people often experience deplorable working conditions, long working hours and low wages.

The working conditions of these workers are often compared to those of the "guest workers" in many European countries who fill the most menial and low-paying jobs. As long as such workers continue to put up with the situation, and Canadian employers continue to have virtually unlimited access to this "captive and powerless labour force," working conditions and wage levels are not likely to improve. (Economic Council of Canada, 1978:126).

In addition to temporary status in this country, migrant workers have other constraints imposed by restrictive contractual obligations which tie them to a particular job. The vulnerability and, consequently, the compliance of migrant labour is achieved through the control of political boundaries, immigration laws, and contractual obligations.

In addition to landed immigrants and migrant workers, illegal or undocumented workers now constitute a significant part of the labour force in many countries. Officially, these workers do not exist. Illegal status and the threat of deportation assure their compliance, docility, and cheap labour. These workers are in a weaker position than any others.

Thus, a very large segment of the labour force in Canada at any given time is in quite a vulnerable position. Immigration laws and contractual obligations place all foreign workers in a distinctly disadvantaged position in political and economic relations; racial discrimination places additional specific pressures on non-white workers, which indigenous Canadian workers are not subjected to (Miles, 1982). Though minorities and women are now employed in diverse occupations, in certain areas of the labour market there is still a disproportionately high representation of minority workers and women. For instance, racial minority workers comprise a substantial portion of the agricultural labour force in British Columbia and Southern Ontario. Almost all of these workers are newly arrived immigrants or migrant contract workers. The numbers of women workers are disproportionately high in the service sector, domestic work, and garment work (which includes both factory and in-home textile work). In these sectors, workers are not adequately protected by labour legislation.

This inadequacy of legal protection ensures the powerlessness of workers in the workplace. Due to the lack of political rights (the right to vote, for example), these workers cannot influence the institutions which subordinate them.

The exploitation of immigrants is repeatedly documented (Berger and Mohr, 1975; Castells, 1975; Bolaria, 1984a, 1984b; Carney, 1976). Contrary to popular assumption, this is not due to some *natural* docility of workers determined by their personality or cultural background: rather, it is dictated by the vulnerable circumstances — legal and political — of immigrants.

Most of these workers would not work or continue to work in undesirable, low-paying jobs if they were at liberty to sell their labour in the open market. However, many of the alternative job opportunities are closed to them, and their subordinate status is unreasonably prolonged through immigration regulations and contractual obligations. For example, one of the contractual obligations in the case of seasonal agricultural workers requires that these workers "not work for any person without the prior approval of the employer, the Government's agent and the Canada Employment and Immigration Commission." Conditions of employment for domestic workers similarly restrict job mobility (Arnopoulos, 1979; Law Union of Ontario, 1981; Task Force on Domestic Workers, 1981).

An unofficial period of grace (in obtaining such approvals) may be allowed for change of job. This is a discretionary practice and "its availability and length are nowhere specifically set forth or guaranteed, adding to the employee's uncertain position" (Task Force on Immigration Practices and Procedures, 1981:26).

Immigration authorities are quite aware of the necessity to minimize employment opportunities for non-immigrant workers to ensure that they continue to work as domestics. Arnopoulos (1979:25) notes: "Senior immigration officials say privately that this policy of employment authorization was introduced because women will work as live-in domestics only if they have no choice." This statement is borne out by the fact that landed immigrants admitted for employment in household service occupations invariably leave these jobs soon after their entry into Canada (Task Force on Immigration Practices and Procedures, 1981).

When people need jobs, they have to take what is available to them. A domestic worker is dependent upon her employer for wages, a dwelling place, and most importantly, for her continued stay in this country. Many women are afraid that they might be deported if they complain about their working conditions (Task Force on Domestic Workers, 1981). Even among those who enjoy some protection under the law, few can afford to spend time to press for their rights. For many workers, coming to Canada is a chance to escape the poverty and unemployment of home and to earn a regular wage, however menial and low-paying the available jobs might be. Their economic needs thus make them susceptible to exploitation. A labour force composed mostly of women and racial minority workers can be hired cheaply (Brown, 1983:106).

The powerlessness of these workers also results from the absence of union organization in the workplace. Many work in isolation from other workers; this is particularly true, of course, of domestic workers and in-home textile workers (Task Force on Domestic Workers, 1981; Johnson and Johnson, 1982).

In summary, immigration laws, contractual obligations, lack of protection by labour legislation, lack of alternative job opportunities, poverty and unemployment in the country of emigration, and the absence of union organization place many foreign workers in a vulnerable position and render them powerless vis-à-vis the employer.

THE HEALTH EFFECTS OF POWERLESSNESS

The Canadian labour market is characterized by occupational, gender, and racial stratification and segmentation (Royal Commission, 1984).

Often, foreign workers either "end up" in, or are specifically brought in to fill, positions in sectors where there is a shortage of Canadian labour or where Canadian workers are unwilling to work. For example, migrant workers are specifically imported for seasonal work in agriculture. Another area where there is a disproportionately high concentration of women and racial minorities is domestic and textile work.

In some sectors, all workers, whether foreign or Canadian, are in a disadvantaged and powerless position vis-à-vis their employers because of lack of union organization, lack of minimum wage coverage, lack of health and safety legislation and Workers' Compensation Board regulations, and so forth. Foreign workers (recently arrived immigrants and migrant workers on work authorizations, for example), because of their tenuous legal-political status are even more disadvantaged and powerless than are indigenous workers. Therefore, immigrant labour assumes special significance for the employers. As Sassen-Koob (1980:27) states: "Immigrant workers can then be seen as one basic factor in the reproduction of low-wage, powerless labour supply, and not simply as a quantitative addition to cheap workers."

The interest of the employer lies in procuring labour that is not only cheap, but also, that can be consumed under specific conditions. These conditions have to do with the organization of work and the control of the production process, which is primarily a product of the outcome of the historical struggle between labour and capital. Labour has had some victories, but the production process under capitalism is still characterized by the primacy of management control. The institutionalization of this control varies with the nature of the production process. In the case of low-cost labour, management's control rests primarily on the powerlessness of the workers (Sassen-Koob, 1980).

In the following section, the health effects of this powerlessness are discussed, with a primary focus on farm labour, domestic workers, and garment workers both in factories and in the household.

Farm Labour: A Bitter Harvest

Workers are exposed to unsafe and unhealthy working conditions not only in industrial-sector production but also in the agricultural sector. Farming in North America is the third most dangerous industry (Reasons et al., 1981), and possibly the least protected in terms of acceptable labour standards. The agricultural sector in the United States and Canada makes extensive use of the low-cost labour provided by racial or ethnic minorities (Burawoy, 1976; Waitzkin, 1983; Sharma, 1982; Sharma, 1983; B.C. Human Rights Commission, 1983).

From their employers' perspective, immigrant and racial minorities have been ideal farm workers. At the beginning of this century, when farmers in British Columbia faced a shortage of labour and a consequent increase in labour costs, they petitioned the government for more immigrant labour. As a consequence, 10 000 Japanese and 5000 East Indians were allowed to enter Canada to supplement the agricultural labour force (Sharma, 1982; B.C. Human Rights Commission, 1983). Presently, most farm labour in British Columbia is composed of various vulnerable minorities — East Indians, Chinese, Native Indians, francophones, and migrant youth (Sharma, 1982; Sharma, 1983; B.C. Human Rights Commission, 1983). There has been a circulation from one labour pool to another of a similarly vulnerable labour force, consisting primarily of racial minorities or recently arrived immigrants. The survival of the small-scale production units and the profit margins of the larger units depend upon the availability of this labour pool.

The agricultural labour force is supplemented by migrant labour under the Non-Immigrant Work Authorization Program (initiated in 1973) and the Seasonal Agricultural Workers' Program (initiated in 1966). These workers provide a valuable labour force for many producers and "meet identifiable shortfalls in the available supply of Canadian workers for the harvesting of fresh fruit and vegetable crops and the processing of these same commodities"

(Canada Employment and Immigration Commission, 1981:2). Ontario continues to be the primary destination for temporary farm workers (Immigration Statistics, 1980–84).

Table 2. Non-Immigrant Work Authorizations in Agriculture and Landed Immigrants Destined for Agriculture, 1973–84

Year	Non-Immigrant Work Authorizations in Agriculture*	Landed Immigrants Destined for Agriculture†
1973	9 208	3 079
1974	10 408	2 637
1975	9 841	1 511
1976	8 937	1 162
1977	8 149	1 215
1978	8 260	937
1979	8 738	1 597
1980	8 773	2 462
1981	16 479	2 931
1982	9 229	2 187
1983	8 290	1 419
1984	8 067	1 170

Source: * Figures for 1973–79 computed from data made available through Employment and Immigration Canada, Saskatchewan Regional Office; 1980–84, Immigration Statistics, Employment and Immigration Canada. Figures for 1980 and 1981 were based on the sum total of work authorizations in agriculture issued to "long-term" and "short-term" visitors. The former refers to visitors remaining in Canada for more than one year, the latter to those for one year or less. For 1982 and 1984, no such distinction was made in the published reports.
† Immigration Statistics 1973–84, Employment and Immigration Canada.

Table 2 shows the number of non-immigrant work authorizations issued in agriculture between 1973–1984. With the exception of 1981, when 16 479 migrants were in Canada on work authorizations, the number of temporary immigrants in agriculture ranged between 8000 and 10 000, while the number of landed immigrants destined for agriculture ranged between 1000 and 3000. A large proportion of these tem-

porary workers are Caribbean blacks or Mexicans.

Long before the introduction of non-immigrant work authorizations, foreign workers had been admitted to meet the seasonal labour demand in agriculture. The Seasonal Agricultural Workers' Program helps to create a versatile labour pool for farmers harvesting highly perishable fruit and vegetable crops. In light of the experience with the Caribbean countries, a similar bilateral programme was established with Mexico in 1974. In 1976 the Caribbean programme was extended to include the Eastern Caribbean Islands. As Table 3 indicates, since 1973 both the number of worker-participants and the number of job vacancies filled have ranged from 3000 to just under 7000.

In terms of the total agricultural labour force, foreign workers represent under 5 percent of the paid agricultural labour force at any one time; these workers, nevertheless, provide valuable service for a large number of agricultural producers (Canada Employment and Immigration Commission, 1981).

The deplorable working conditions of both the domestic transient farm labour and migrant imported workers are well documented (Sanderson, 1974; Labonte, 1980, 1982; Sandborn, 1983; Canada Department of Manpower and Immigration, 1973; Report of the Special Committee on Visible Minorities in Canadian Society, 1984; Sharma, 1982; Kelly, 1983; B.C. Human Rights Commission, 1983). Workers and their families are often exposed to harmful substances on the farms. There is inadequate or no enforcement of the Health Act regulations concerning physical danger, occupational diseases, pesticides, and a high risk of injury. Farm workers are also not adequately protected in terms of minimum wage legislation, working hours, and overtime wages (Report of the Special Committee on Visible Minorities in Canada, 1984).

Both the living and working conditions of farm workers contribute to their ill health. A 1973 federal task force report on the seasonal migrant farm workers in Ontario uncovered instances of "child labour, sick, pregnant, and

Table 3. Program Arrivals (Vacancies) Filled by Caribbean and Mexican Seasonal Agricultural
Workers (by Country and Year)

Year	Caribbean Arrivals	Mexican Arrivals	Total Worker Arrivals (Vacancies Filled)
1966	277	—	277
1967	1 077	—	1 077
1968	1 258	—	1 258
1969	1 545	—	1 545
1970	1 379	—	1 379
1971	1 488	—	1 488
1972	1 638	—	1 638
1973	3 426	—	3 426
1974	5 731	195	5 926
1975	6 237	382	6 619
1976	5 597	580	6 177
1977	5 063	510	5 573
1978	5 080	550	5 630
1979	5 304	584	5 888
1980	5 325	676	6 001
1981	5 230	670	6 900
1982	4 819	691	5 510
1983	3 952	612	4 564

Source: Canadian Employment and Immigration, Labour Market Planning and Adjustment, July 1980; Canadian Employment and Immigration Commission, 1983, 1984.

otherwise unfit adults working in the fields; and of entire families working with only the head of the family being paid" (Sanderson, 1974:405). The task force was "shocked, alarmed, and sickened" by the working conditions, wage levels, malnutrition, non-existent health facilities, and the "undescribable squalor" of living conditions which migrant farm workers had to endure (Canada, Department of Manpower and Immigration, 1973:17; Sanderson, 1974). There were many cases discovered of violations of the Immigration Act, Child Labour Act, human rights, and minimum sanitation standards. Employers, of course, benefitted from family labour and were "delighted" to have foreign workers with large families (Canada, Manpower and Immigration, 1973).

The working and living conditions of farm workers in British Columbia are similar to the conditions which minority workers face in Ontario. Farm workers in British Columbia, exploited by the labour contracting system, face long hours of work, low wages, with no overtime pay or benefits, unhealthy working conditions, lack of toilet or drinking water facilities on many farms, crowded and dangerous housing, and exposure to chemicals and pesticides in the field (Sharma, 1982; Canadian Farmworkers' Union, 1980; Labonte, 1980, 1982–83; Kelly, 1983).

Due to the lack of day-care facilities, incidents of childrens' deaths due to drowning in buckets of drinking water in the shacks, or in unfenced ponds, have been reported (Sharma, 1982; Sharma, 1983). The coroner's jury which, in August 1980, investigated the death of a child who had rolled off a bunk and drowned in the water bucket, recommended that immediate steps be taken to establish standards for farm labour housing. The irony is, however, that standards, established in 1946, do exist, which are not being enforced (B.C. Human Rights Commission, 1983).

Farm workers are not covered under the Workers' Compensation Board (WCB) regulations. The B.C. government in May 1982 had decided to protect farm workers through implementation of such measures as WCB inspection of farms, safety standards, and pesticide control. However, the government reversed its plan in March, 1983. This decision, ironically, came during a coroner's jury inquest into the pesticide poisoning death of a farm worker. The jury ruled that the death was "preventable homicide" (*Vancouver Sun*, 18 March 1983; Pynn, 1983; Koch, 1983). The extension of the WCB regulation to farm workers was opposed by the B.C. Federation of Agriculture on the grounds that it would be costly, unrealistic, and impractical (*Victoria Times-Colonist*, 12 March 1983). Failure to establish legal protection for farm workers in this case to a large extent affects racial minority workers.

The agricultural labour force is composed primarily of racial minority workers, "marginal" domestic workers, newly arrived immigrants, and migrant contract workers, all of which are low-paid, seasonally employed, and transitory. In the case of families, subsistence wages can be earned only through the labour of the whole family. Not only parents, but children and very old members of the family also work in the field and are exposed to all the health hazards. Because families need work to survive, and complaints or resistance to intimidation or abuse means loss of jobs, these workers are less likely to report cases of violation of the Labour Relations Act.

Union organization has been difficult in the case of farm workers due to racial, cultural, and linguistic barriers and divisions and the abundant availability of foreign labour brought in with the support of the state. The formation of the Canadian Farmworkers' Union (CFU) in 1980 was the first serious attempt to organize farm workers. The union membership is estimated as over 10 percent of the labour force (Pynn, 1983). Through the CFU, farm workers are fighting for their rights in the workplace and lobbying for inclusion of farm workers under the Payment of Wages Act, child labour laws, workers' compensation, and so forth (Glavin, 1980).

Entire families work and in effect live in the fields, in crowded, unhealthy, and unsanitary accommodations — without clean drinking water or proper wash-up facilities. In some cases workers have to pay high rents for "housing accommodations" provided by the farmers. These are usually small, overcrowded, and insalubrious firetraps without in-unit bathrooms or running water (Sharma, 1982:13). A survey of 270 farm workers in 1982 revealed that a large proportion of the accommodations (about 80 percent) had no proper wash-up facilities, and 44 percent had no access at all to shower facilities (Matsqui, Abbotsford Community Services, 1982). This study also revealed that farm workers are exposed to dangerous pesticides:

- Eight out of ten farm workers regularly suffer from direct contact with pesticides and a majority (55 percent) have been directly sprayed.

- Eight out of ten farm workers have had to work immediately after a spraying.

- Over a quarter have had their living quarters sprayed with pesticides.

- Seven out of ten farm workers have become physically ill after a direct spraying, yet only 3 percent received medical help provided by their employers.

- Almost one fifth frequently breathe pesticide fumes while working.

Many of the workers spend long hours in the fields and therefore have prolonged periods of exposure to pesticides. As many of the pesticides are carcinogenic, farm workers suffer from many ill effects of exposure to spraying. The Matsqui study revealed that 90 percent of the workers had experienced one or more symptoms of pesticide spraying. For instance,

- 44 percent suffered skin rashes

- 47 percent suffered itching

- 50 percent reported headaches

- 35 percent experienced dizziness

- 17 percent suffered from gastro-intestinal problems

- almost 60 percent of the children working in the fields experienced the same sorts of symptoms

- almost half reported various central nervous system disorders

- one out of five had missed work owing to work-related health problems

The majority of the workers did not speak English and many of them did not receive information or instructions on health hazards of pesticides. A vast majority (over 80 percent) ate their lunches in the sprayed field areas. One writer has commented that "the living and working conditions of Canadian farm labourers (especially in B.C.'s Fraser Valley) bear a closer resemblance to those of Third World peasants than to those of the average Canadian worker" (Labonte, 1982–83:6). Also, pesticide safety regulations are either not enforced, or non-existent altogether. There is continued use of pesticides that have never been adequately tested for safety, and cases of severe pesticide poisoning and death are not uncommon.

One of these involved a twenty-year old man who, after two hospital admissions within a month for poisonings, was re-admitted in a life-threatening comatose state that persisted for six days. It was caused by the ingestion of the extremely lethal organophosphate, methamidophos (tradename Monitor), and the highly toxic fungicide, donoseb (tradename Top-Killer). The medical health officer investigating the case, according to a story in the October 9 *VAN-*

COUVER SUN, "is leaning towards the theory that behavioural changes caused by gradual exposure to toxic pesticides may be the only explanation for the mystery of why Deol (the farmworker) consumed the chemical." Deol died four weeks later, never regaining consciousness, a day after the B.C. Medical Association joined the Canadian Farmworkers' Union and other Organizations in calling for better regulatory safeguards. (Labonte, 1982–83:6–7)

Studies of farm workers in the United States have also pointed to their grim health status. Their life expectancy is 20 percent less than that of the average American, and infant mortality among their children is 60 percent above the national average (U.S. Congress, 1972). Other evidence from the United States indicates that "farmworkers have an injury rate due to toxic chemicals almost three times as high as injuries of all types for workers in other industries" and "farmworkers lost twice as many hours due to pesticide-related illnesses than hours lost by manufacturing workers due to all causes" (B.C. Human Rights Commission, 1983:22).

In the face of all the ill effects of pesticides, the "agrichem" business flourishes, and continued use of many pesticides is allowed despite the fact that they have not been properly tested and, in some cases, are known to be carcinogenic (Goff and Reasons, 1986; B.C. Human Rights Commission, 1983).

As noted above, agricultural workers fare very badly as regards general living conditions, being housed in labour compounds — typically unsanitary, unsafe, and overcrowded accomodations; this, combined with long hours of arduous work tend to produce ill health. Working conditions are equally stressful: the misery of the material, social, and environmental deprivations, racial subordination, long-distance migrations and uprooting from stable traditional cultures and disruption of community ties, all contribute toward psychological distress and mental disorders (Doyal and Pennell, 1979; Eyer, 1984; Waldron et al., 1982). Kuo and Tsai (1986:133) state that

an excessive amount of social stress among immigrants — resulting from social isolation, cultural conflicts, poor social integration and assimilation, role changes and identity crisis, low socio-economic status, racial discrimination — has led to a high prevalence of ill health and psychological impairment among them.

It should be noted that the health hazards in the fields vary according to the type of farming. In addition to exposure to various chemicals, farmers and farm workers undergo excessive exposure to commercial solvents, sunlight, and heat. Those who work with animals are at risk from bacterial and viral infections (George, 1976). Prairie farmers and farm workers suffer from serious lung diseases, particularly those who handle wet or mouldy grains and hay. The most common are: farmer's lung, due to inhalation of mouldy grain dust, grain dust asthma, and silo filler's lung. Respiratory problems are likely to be higher among farmers and farm workers who handle wet and mouldy grains or hay. Their incidence is higher still among those who work with inadequate equipment for drying and storing grains and hay. On small and less profitable farms, which are likely to have inadequate equipment, the labour of the entire family is essential to survival. Under these circumstances, the incidence of respiratory and other symptoms associated with handling of mouldy and wet grains and hay is likely to be higher among the family members (George, 1976).

Chronic back injury is one of the commonest occupational diseases among farm workers who work with short hoes. As Waitzkin (1983:15) states: "the short hoe's human toll is crippling back disease for thousands of farmworkers; the main injuries are slipped discs and degenerative arthritis of the spine." Waitzkin (1983:15) further states that "these problems occur in younger workers who do stoop labour, and their physical effects are irreversible. Since migrant workers most often lack educational opportunities and frequently know little English, farmworkers' back usually means permanent economic disability" — although this is a preventable disease. However, migrant workers are an easily replaceable work force. A reserve army of migrants is available to take the place of

workers who are crippled by back injuries or who resist conditions of their work. As Waitzkin (1983:15) states, "powerlessness resulted from lack of organization; individual farmworkers had no alternative to the crippling effects of the short hoe, because resistance meant loss of work."

In summary, workers are exposed to health hazards not just in the industrial workplace, but also in agriculture. Both the living and working conditions of farm labour are "dangerous to their health." Unsafe and unsanitary living conditions and exposure to dangerous pesticides and other detrimental agents contribute to excessive physical health problems, injuries, and premature death. These circumstances also damage workers' psychological health. Insecure and depressing working conditions, social isolation, and racial subordination all contribute toward psychological distress and mental disorders. The health hazards vary according to the type of farming. For instance, those who work with animals are at risk from bacterial and viral infections. Other farm workers suffer from serious lung diseases and chronic back injuries. Farm workers are inadequately protected by labour legislation and health and safety regulations.

Women Workers: Home Sewing and Domestic Servants

Because of increased employment of women, there is considerable interest in the effects of employment on women's health. They face many chemical, biological, and physical health hazards in the workplace. Even apparently safe female-dominated occupations, such as service, clerical, sales, teaching, and health, are associated with significant hazards (George, 1976; Waldron, 1983). For instance, women health workers face many health hazards, such as an increased risk of viral hepatitis, back strain, and exposure to anaesthetic gases which can cause spontaneous abortions (Waldron, 1983). Women workers are exposed to chemicals in dry-cleaning and laundry establishments, and hairdressers and beauticians have increased risk of respiratory disease due to extended exposure to hairsprays (Blair et al., 1978). Dental hygienists, technicians, and assistants are exposed to anaesthetics, radiation, and mercury (George, 1976). Sales clerks, constantly on their feet, suffer from varicose veins and run an increased risk of contagious diseases because of constant contact with the public. Teachers are susceptible to mumps, measles, influenzas, and performance stress. Pregnant women face special problems at the workplace, as many substances are dangerous to the baby (Waldron, 1983; Messing, 1983; George, 1976). In manufacturing industries, female workers are exposed to occupational carcinogens. In the garment industry, where a very high proportion of workers are women, exposure to cotton fibres and dust puts workers at a high risk of developing brown lung, or byssinosis (Harris et al., 1972; Merchant et al., 1973). Eye irritation and strain are common health problems in a number of industries, including textiles and electronics (Hricko and Brunt, 1976). Due to the dual responsibility of job and care of the family and the home, many employed women experience stress (Johnson and Johnson, 1977).

The above brief account covers only some of the health hazards faced by employed women; there are many additional physical, chemical, and biological health hazards which women workers face in these and other work settings (Stellman and Dawn, 1973; Stellman, 1977; Hricko and Brunt, 1976; Newhouse, 1967; Newhouse et al., 1972; Miller, 1975).

Attention has been focussed primarily on the paid work force; however, women also face numerous health hazards in their own homes. Many of these hazards are the same as at the outside workplace: accidents, stress, and exposure to chemicals, laundry detergents, and solvents. The risk of accidents may be as high for homemakers as for women in the labour force (Krute and Burdette, 1978). Like the latter, homemakers experience stress, though for different reasons: social isolation and the monotonous and unrewarding nature of housework are primary contributors (Ferree, 1976; Oakley, 1974). Homemakers are more likely than employed women to report such health problems

as asthma, allergies, heart disease, and restricted activity and bed rest due to illness and psychiatric impairment (Waldron, 1983). One study indicates higher suicide rates for homemakers than for employed women (Cumming et al., 1975).

Besides homemaking, women also engage in paid labour in their own households. Because of economic necessity to supplement family income and lack of day-care facilities, and to combine their family responsibilities with work, many women are now engaged in such "contract work" and "employed labour." Home work appeals to women housebound by child care and other responsibilities; it is attractive to the employers as a means of lowering their labour and other overhead costs, particularly in enterprises which are threatened by unions and international competition. Home work is being promoted "with the ideology of liberation through self-employment. Touted as a way of escaping the ills of modern 9–to–5 work, it is promoted as a way for women to 'have it all' — children, family and job" (Berch, 1985:41). Households have become little cottage industries and all the health hazards faced by workers at the workplace are now transplanted into the households. The garment industry illustrates this point.

In an attempt to lower the labour costs and improve competitive advantages, there has been a restructuring and reorganization of garment production in several countries (Lipsig-Mumme, 1987; Morokvasic et al., 1986; Johnson and Johnson, 1982), specifically in those where the garment industry is faced with shortages of low-cost labour and higher labour costs. To preserve the rate of profit against labour shortages and higher labour costs, two basic strategies are used: increasing the intensity of labour exploitation (i.e., increasing workers' productivity), and/or resorting to low-cost labour (Portes, 1979). The search for low-cost labour takes two primary forms: (1) establishing firms where such labour is available, and (2) importing such labour to replace or supplement the local labour force. Not all enterprises can take advantage of these strategies. The first option is available only to the monopolistic firms. It is evident that the corporations which have ability to move elsewhere are doing so (NACL, 1979), and the ability of transnational corporations to relocate in cheap labour areas (or their threats to do so) is being used to impose wage cuts, harsher working conditions, and undervaluation of labour power on employees (Dixon et al., 1982). On the other hand, there are the small, competitive firms, which lack capital and resources, and are therefore mostly dependent upon availability of low-cost labour in the local market. This labour force consists largely of immigrant and migrant women.

To reduce labour costs, one common strategy used by employers is restructuring of garment production, in effect achieving deindustrialization and deunionization by shifting work to individual households. There has been a renaissance of home sewing. In the home, as in the factories, it is usually women who do this work, because they are the ones who have sewing skills. The textile and garment industries are characterized by gender-typed low-wage jobs and are major employers of minority and immigrant women (Reasons et al., 1981; Johnson and Johnson, 1982; Lipsig-Mumme, 1987; Morokvasic et al., 1986; George, 1976).

Workers in the textile industry face numerous health hazards. Numerous chemicals used in this industry for dyeing, shrinking, and waterproofing fabrics have known health hazards (George, 1976); many are teratogenic and carcinogenic. Textile workers are affected by excessive noise in the workplace, sore backs caused by long hours of sitting at sewing machines, injuries from broken needles, skin, nose, and eye irritations, headaches and dizziness, and even psychological changes because of certain chemicals and liquids used in the industry (George, 1976).

Workers are also exposed to large quantities of lint, dust, and fabric scraps (Reasons et al., 1981; Johnson and Johnson, 1982; George, 1976). Inhalation of cotton fibres and cotton dust presents the risk of developing brown lung, or byssinosis. The common symptoms of this respiratory problem are shortness of breath, cough, and chest tightness (George, 1976). Textile workers may also face risk of asbestosis, now commonly recognized among workers exposed to asbestos, which may be used in the production of curtains and rugs. Scarring of lungs, reduction in size and elasticity of lungs, lowered lung capacity, cough, and breathlessness are common signs of asbestosis (George, 1976). Asbestos may also cause certain cancers — lung cancer, mesothelioma, and gastrointestinal cancers (Stellman and Daum, 1973; Newhouse et al., 1972).

The above overview should give some indications of the working conditions and health hazards faced by workers in the garment industry. A British Columbia Ministry of Labour study of the garment industry observed that "the very fact that the industry cannot recruit personnel from the mainstream of the labour force raises some questions regarding working conditions in the industry." Other studies on the working conditions of the immigrant women employed in the garment industry point to poor working conditions, job hazards, low wages, and high stress for the workers (Arnopoulos, 1979; White, 1979).

Unsatisfactory as the work environment and working conditions are for the factory workers, the working conditions for workers in their households are even worse — loose piecework rates, low overall wages, irregularity of work, irregular and unpredictable working hours, and uncertain income (Johnson and Johnson, 1982). As Morokvasic et al., (1986:406) state, "sewing is often considered only as an extension of women's 'natural' and unpaid domestic tasks, so that women can be expected to do the work for nothing or for extremely low wages." Immigrant women, because of cultural, linguistic, and legal barriers, may not be able to sell their labour in the open labour market. They also have fewer options because of domestic responsibilities (family and child care). For some there may be other structural barriers: gender discrimination combined with racism increases their vulnerability (Morokvasic et al., 1986).

Home workers are exposed to health risks similar to those faced by factory workers. However, in this case, the whole family suffers the hazards of fabric dust, lint, and accompanying allergic symptoms. Home workers, like their counterparts in the factories, suffer from back problems from sitting and sewing for long hours without breaks (Johnson and Johnson, 1982). Economic necessity and the lack of paid sick leave forces many to work even when they are not well. As Johnson and Johnson (1982:81) state: "If she wants to earn money, she must keep working. This means that many home workers continue to do their sewing even when they are ill." Pressure to meet the deadlines and fulfill the quotas creates severe stress for the home workers. These women must also balance the competing demands of two roles of homemaker and home worker. As home sewing is messy work, it adds to existing cleaning and housework pressures and thus constitutes an additional source of stress (Johnson and Johnson, 1982).

Home workers constitute an individually isolated (working alone in their own homes) and vulnerable labour force. These workers are characterized as "invisible segments of production," "captive and underpaid labour force," "invisible labour force," and "clandestine employment" (Lipsig-Mumme, 1987; Morokvasic et al., 1986). These conditions contribute to home workers' powerlessness. Their vulnerability is primarily due to their status as immigrants, and to inadequate legal protection in the workplace. As Johnson and Johnson (1982:121) state:

> It is not by chance that the homeworker labour force is comprised mainly of isolated, immigrant women with young children. This is a vulnerable population that would be unlikely to stand up for its own rights, even with the protection of additional employment standards legislation.

Home workers are usually considered as "sub-contractors" and not workers. This situation permits the evasion of health and safety regulations, if indeed any regulations exist at all. It also allows the employers to evade labour regulations, if any.

In summary, while attention has been focussed primarily on the paid work force, women also face numerous health hazards in their own homes. To supplement household income while meeting other domestic responsibilities, numerous homemakers engage in employed labour in their homes, into which many of the health hazards faced by workers at the workplace are now transplanted. In this case, not only the worker, but the worker's whole family is exposed to health risks.

Women Domestics, Chars, and Cleaners

Women continue to be concentrated in the traditional gender-typed occupations. In fact, the percentage of women in clerical, sales, service, health, and teaching slightly increased during the seventies from 71 percent in 1971 to 74 percent in 1981 (Statistics Canada, 1984). A large number of women work part-time. In fact, between 1971 and 1981, there was a 59 percent increase in the number of women who worked part-time — from 1 million to 1.6 million (Statistics Canada, 1984).

Table 4. Immigrant and Non-Immigrant Service Workers, 1980–1984

Year	Immigrant Workers	Non-Immigrant Workers (Employment Authorizations)
1980	4 648	17 610
1981	4 250	26 780
1982	4 195	21 596
1983	3 816	22 217
1984	5 235	27 042

Source: Canada, Immigration Statistics, Employment and Immigration, 1980–84. Non-Immigrant Employment Authorizations for 1980–81 include "short-term" and "long-term."

Many women also work in low-paid, low-

Table 5. Service-Sector Jobs by Gender for Workers under the Non-Immigrant Employment Authorization 1980–84

	% Women Workers	% Women Workers in Service Jobs	% Service Jobs Occupied by Women	Total Service Workers	Total Women Workers Employment Authorization	Total Employment Authorization
1980	27.3	45.7	80.1	17 610	30 873	113 272
1981	24.5	40.8	78.7	26 780	51 587	210 550
1982	27.8	47.4	76.8	21 596	34 982	125 897
1983	26.8	46.2	73.1	22 217	35 106	130 711
1984	27.1	45.9	66.2	27 042	38 959	143 979

Figures for 1980 and 1981 are on the sum total of employment authorizations issued to "long-term" and "short-term" visitors. The former refers to visitors remaining in Canada for more than one year, the latter to those for one year or less. For 1982–84, no such distinction was made in the published report.

Source: Immigration Statistics, 1980–84, Employment and Immigration Canada.

status, arduous service-sector jobs. For instance, janitors, chars, and cleaners, ranked tenth among the top ten occupations for women in 1981. Many foreign workers on non-immigrant work authorizations are being admitted to Canada to supplement the service sector's labour force. As Table 4 indicates, the number of non-immigrant workers admitted for service-related jobs far exceeds the number of landed immigrants destined for the service sector. Furthermore, women constitute a significant proportion of this work force. As Table 5 indicates, while during the years 1980 to 1984, the number of women workers on work authorizations was between 24.5 percent and 27.8 percent of admissions, the proportion who ended up in service jobs ranged from 40.8 percent to 47.4 percent. However, of particular significance is the proportion of service jobs occupied by women — from 66.2 percent to 80.1 percent.

It is apparent that many jobs in the service sector are filled by temporary foreign women workers. The presence of these workers is particularly crucial in some occupations. For example, due to undesirable working conditions, low wages, and low value placed upon domestic work, Canadian workers and landed immigrants are unwilling to accept and keep jobs as live-in domestics (Buckley and Nielsen, 1976; Hook, 1978; Ballantyne, 1980; Arnopoulos, 1979; Law Union of Ontario, 1981). There is a chronic shortage of Canadians for these jobs. Landed immigrants admitted for employment in household service occupations invariably leave these jobs soon after their entry into Canada (Task Force on Immigration Practices and Procedures, 1981). Consequently, it is foreign workers on non-immigrant work authorizations who constitute the chief segment of this labour force. For instance, in 1980, 11 555 "domestic" employment authorizations were issued: 6160 for "domestic occupations," such as maid domestic, housekeeper, personal attendant; the remaining were child-care occupations, such as babysitter, child nurse, parent's helper (Task Force on Immigration Practices and Procedures, 1981:48). Visible minorities are heavily represented in paid domestic work (Royal Commission on Equality in Employment, 1984).

Domestic workers confined to individual households are an "invisible" work force. Live-in domestic workers face almost all conceivable employment problems — low wages, long working hours, stress and loneliness, work while being ill, and sexual abuse (B.C. Human Rights Commission, 1983; Law Union of Ontario, 1981; Hendleman, 1964; Boldon, 1971). In most instances, live-in domestics were paid less than the minimum wage (Hook, 1978; B.C. Human Rights Commission, 1983). Even if they are paid minimum wage, one third of their income is deducted for room and board (*Star-Phoenix*, 2 April 1987).

These conditions for domestics prevail partially due to the deficiency of labour legislation and the gap between regulations and enforcement, and partially due to the general attitude toward domestic work. As a representative of an organization set up to advance the rights of domestic and other workers in Ontario states: "It all stems from the general feeling that it's OK to pay people less because what happens in the house is not really work" (*Star-Phoenix*, 2 April 1987). A brief submitted to the B.C. Human Rights Commission (1983:26) by the Committee for the Advancement of the Rights of Domestic Workers (CARDWO), reflects similar attitudes experienced by workers.

> People look upon us as nothing. They ask us why we leave our country to come and clean someone else's house. They don't look on it as the same job as working in a hospital, hotel or nurses' home, cleaning and making beds. The only difference with it is that those of us who are domestics live in the home where we work. We have long working hours. Some don't get any holidays. That's because we are not covered by the Labour Act. It's up to the good will of our employer to pay us.

Many workers must continue working even when they are ill or pregnant because of inadequate legal provision for sick leave or maternity leave. As one domestic worker in her brief to the British Columbia Human Rights Commission (1983:28) states:

> For two weeks I was sick with flu and fever, but I still had to work. I'm a hard worker and my employers know when I'm not feeling well, but they never gave me even a day off. They never said, "Stay in bed, you're not well".
>
> I have to get up, prepare the supper, clear up — going up the stairs, you could see I was weak. I had lost weight.

> If I were in my own country, I wouldn't go to work. But because I am here, if I don't work, they could say, the Immigration could say, "Leave tomorrow!"

Besides becoming domestic workers, women end up as chars, janitorial helpers, chambermaids, nurses' aides, and in restaurants as dishwashers and cook's helpers (Sharma, 1982). All these jobs are low-status, low-paid, and unhealthy. Chars may not have the stigma of a live-in domestic, but they face similar disadvantages and exclusion from labour legislation. Long hours of work can lead to many health problems, and the insecurity of the job is worrisome. Again, to quote from a CARDWO brief (B.C. Human Rights Commission, 1983:30):

> The work is exhausting and boring (but then again, so are most jobs). I come home from work with sore feet, an aching back and a deadened mind. I'm lucky in that I don't work full time. But a lot of women have a family to support or debts to pay off, and they have to work long hours. Then end up with bad backs and varicose veins and not a moment for themselves. No time and a half for overtime, either.
>
> The lack of security is another big problem ... Sometimes I worry, what if I get sick? What about when I'm old? And for women with children, these worries are even heavier.

Women must endure in silence personal humiliation at the hands of the employers. As a woman in the CARDWO brief states (B.C. Human Rights Commission, 1983:31):

> We are considered dumb, incompetent, and untrustworthy ... and every day in smaller ways, I'm treated as if I'm not a real person, with a mind, feelings and dreams of my own. That kind of attitude really makes me angry, but I have to keep my mouth shut unless I want to risk losing my job.

It is evident that the working conditions of women domestics, chars, and cleaners are damaging to physical and psychological health. Long working hours, stress and loneliness, low social status, and the ever-present threat of unemployment all contribute toward physical illness and psychological distress. Domestics and chars suffer from sore feet, aching backs, and varicose veins. Job insecurity creates anxiety and worries about the future. Interpersonal subordination and humiliation — being considered stupid, incompetent, and untrustworthy — may produce additional "psychosocial injuries."

SUMMARY AND CONCLUSIONS

The discussion presented in this chapter shows that farm workers, garment workers, women domestics, chars, and cleaners are exposed to numerous health hazards. Their living and working conditions are "dangerous to their health." In the case of farm workers, unsafe and unsanitary living conditions, exposure to pesticides and herbicides, lack of job security, arduous tasks, and interpersonal subordination each contribute to their physical and psychological ill health. Our discussion of garment workers indicates that many of the health hazards faced by them in factories are also now transplanted to the households. This directly exposes the whole family to health risks associated with textile work. It is also clear that the conditions in which women domestics, chars, and cleaners work are damaging to their physical and psychological well-being.

Under such conditions, the high accident and illness rates among immigrant workers from the Third World are often attributed to "accident-proneness" due to their cultural background and their inability to function in an industrial setting. However, evidence suggests that "immigrants and indigenous workers tend to fall into separate categories with immigrant workers consistently filling the most dangerous jobs" (Lee and Wrench, 1980:563). Their job-related accidents have "less to do with immigrants themselves than the tasks they perform and the environment in which they find themselves. The reason is technical, rather than psychological or cultural" (Lee and Wrench, 1980:563). For instance, the health problems of farm workers, garment workers, domestics chars, and cleaners have essentially nothing to do with their ability to function in an industrial

setting. Almost all of these workers are engaged in manual labour.

In many sectors, all workers, foreign or Canadian, are in a disadvantaged and powerless position vis-à-vis their employers because of the absence of union organization, inadequate labour legislation, insufficient health and safety regulations, and so forth. Foreign workers, however, because of their particular legal-political status, are even more disadvantaged than the indigenous labour force.

These workers are a low-cost labour force whose vulnerability stems from various economic, social, legal, and political considerations, and not from some natural docility of their gender or racial and cultural background. Among farm workers, garment workers, domestics, chars, and cleaners, a failure of legal protection seriously affects women, racial minorities, and immigrant workers.

This lack of protection might seem surprising at first glance, even if only because good health and physical fitness are important to maintain high worker productivity and a stable labour force. As Marx wrote: "When capitalist production lengthens the hours of work, it shortens the lives of the workers." However, employers' concern about workers' health depends upon the reproduction costs, availability, and replaceability of the work force. Workers who become ill are sent home, and quickly replaced by healthy workers at little or no cost to the employers or the state. When labour is plentiful and can be easily replaced, employers will be less concerned about the health of employees (Schatzkin, 1978). Access to foreign workers assures an almost infinite supply of labour. The workers on non-immigrant work authorizations may be characterized as a "bonded forced-rotational" system of labour procurement (Bohning, 1974; North, 1980). Health screening tests assure the supply of physically fit immigrant labour.

In conclusion, the greater exploitation of immigrant labour must be understood in the objective context of workers' legal-political vulnerability. The health, health care, and safety of workers must be analyzed in the context of the organization of labour process. Evidence from selected cases, namely agricultural workers and textile workers, suggests that immigrant workers, because of their powerlessness, are subjected to harsher working conditions than is the indigenous labour force. Gender and race compound workers' disadvantages — minority workers and women are exposed to an even more hazardous working environment.

STUDY QUESTIONS

1. Discuss specific occupational health problems faced by women because of their concentration in gender-typed jobs in the labour market.

2. Discuss the health hazards faced by women and their families because of the revival of home sewing.

3. Explain the low health status of women and racial minority immigrant workers in agricultural and service-sector jobs.

4. Discuss the specific health hazards faced by farm workers.

5. How does "employed wage labour" in the household contribute to women's physical illness and psychological distress?

RECOMMENDED READING

Brown, Carol A. "Women Workers in the Health Service Industry." In *Women and Health: The Politics of Sex in Medicine*, edited by Elizabeth Fee, 105–16. Farmingdale, New York: Baywood Publishing Co., 1983.

Fee, Elizabeth, ed. *Women and Health: The Politics of Sex in Medicine*. Farmingdale, New York: Baywood Publishing Co., 1983.

Lee, Gloria, and John Wrench. "Accident Prone Immigrants: An Assumption Challenged." *Sociology* 14, no. 4 (1980): 551–56.

Majka, L.C., and T.J. Majka. *Farm Workers, Agribusiness and the State*. Philadelphia: Temple University Press, 1982.

McDonnell, Kathleen, ed. *Adverse Effects: Women and the Pharmaceutical Industry*. Toronto: Women's Press, 1986.

Waldron, Ingrid. "Employment and Women's Health: An Analysis of Causal Relationships." In *Women and Health: The Politics of Sex in Medicine*, edited by Elizabeth Fee, 119–38. Farmingdale, New York: Baywood Publishing Co., 1983.

REFERENCES

Arnopoulos, S.M. *Problems of Immigrant Women in the Canadian Labour Force*. Ottawa: Canadian Advisory Council on the Status of Women, 1979.

Ballantyne, Susan. *Domestic Workers: Proposals for Change*. Toronto: University of Toronto, Faculty of Law, 1980.

Berch, Bettina. "The Resurrection of Out-Work." *Monthly Review* 37, no. 6 (November 1985): 37–46.

Berger, John, and Jean Mohr. *A Seventh Man: Migrant Workers in Europe*. New York: Viking Press, 1975.

Blair, A., P. Decoufle, and D. Grauman. "Mortality Among Laundry and Dry Cleaning Workers." *American Journal of Epidemiology* 108 (1978):238.

Bohning, W.R. "Immigration Policies of Western European Countries." *International Migration Review* 8, no. 2 (1974): 155–63.

Bolaria, B. Singh. "Migrants, Immigrants, and the Canadian Labour Force." In *Contradictions in Canadian Society*, edited by John A. Fry, 130–39. Toronto: John Wiley and Sons, 1984a.

———. "On the Study of Race Relations." In *Contradictions in Canadian Society*, edited by John A. Fry, 219–47. Toronto: John Wiley and Sons, 1984b.

Bolaria, B. Singh, and Peter Li. *Racial Oppression in Canada*. Toronto: Garamond Press, 1985.

Boldon, Bertram. "Black Immigrants in a Foreign Land." In *Let the Niggers Burn!* edited by Dennis Forsythe, 22–40. Montreal: Black Rose Books, 1971.

British Columbia Human Rights Commission. "What This Country Did to Us, It Did to Itself." *A Report of the B.C. Human Rights Commission on Farmworkers and Domestic Workers*. February 1983.

British Columbia Ministry of Labour. "Manpower Analysis of the Garment Industry." Victoria, B.C., 1974.

Brown, Carol A. "Women Workers in the Health Service Industry." In *Women and Health: The Politics of Sex in Medicine*, edited by Elizabeth Fee, 105–16. Farmingdale, New York: Baywood Publishing Co., 1983.

Buckley, Helen, and Soren T. Nielsen. *Immigration and the Canadian Labour Market*. Research Project Group, Strategic Planning and Research, Manpower and Immigration, 1976.

Burawoy, Michael. "The Functions and Reproduction of Migrant Labour: Comparative Material from Southern Africa and the United States." *American Journal of Sociology* 81 (March 1976): 1050–87.

CARDWO (Committee for the Advancement of Rights of Domestic Workers). *Submission to B.C. Human Rights Commission, June 17, 1982.*

Canada. Department of Manpower and Immigration. *The Seasonal Farm Labour Situation in Southwestern Ontario — A Report*. Photocopy, 1973.

Canada. Employment and Immigration. *Annual Report 1982–83*. Ottawa, 1983.

———. *Immigration Statistics*. Ottawa, 1984.

Canada. Employment and Immigration Commission. *Commonwealth Caribbean and Mexican Seasonal Agricultural Workers' Program: Review of 1979 Payroll Records*. Labour Market Planning and Adjustment Branch. Hull, Quebec. Photocopy, 1981.

———. 1980 Review of Agricultural Manpower Programs. Labour Market Planning and Adjustment (June). Photocopy, 1981.

Canada. Department of Manpower and Immigration, *The Immigration Program: 2*. (Green Paper), 1974.

Canada. House of Commons. *Equality Now! Report of the Special Committee on Visible Minorities in Canadian Society*. Ottawa, 1984.

Canada. Royal Commission. *Equality in Employment*. Ottawa: Minister of Supply and Services, 1984.

Canada. Task Force of Immigration Practices and Procedures. *Domestic Workers on Employment Authorizations — A Report*. Ottawa: Supply and Services, 1981.

Canadian Civil Liberties Association. *Brief to the House of Commons Standing Committee on Labour, Manpower and Immigration, June 2, regarding Immigration Bill C–24*. 1977.

Canadian Farmworkers' Union. *Support British Columbia Farmworkers*. 1980.

Carney, John. "Capital Accumulation and Uneven Development in Europe: Notes on Migrant Labour." *Antipode* 8, no. 1 (1976): 30–36.

Castells, Manuel. "Immigrant Workers and Class Struggles in Advanced Capitalism: The Western European Experience." *Politics and Society* 5 (1975): 33–66.

Cumming, E., C. Lazer, and L. Chisholm. "Suicide as an Index of Role Strain Among Employed and Non-Employed Married Women in British Columbia." *Canadian Review of Sociology and Anthropology* 12 (1975):462–70.

Dixon, Marlene, S. Jonas, and Ed McCaughan. "Reindustrialization and the Transnational Labour Force in the United States Today." In *The New Nomads*, edited by Marlene Dixon and S. Jonas, 105–15. San Francisco: Synthesis Publications, 1982.

Doyal, Lesley, and Imogen Pennell. *The Political Economy of Health*. London: Pluto Press, 1979.

Economic Council of Canada. *For a Better Future*. Ottawa, 1978.

Eyer, Joseph. "Capitalism, Health and Illness." In *Issues in the Political Economy of Health Care*, edited by John B. McKinlay. New York: Tavistock Publications, 1984.

"Farm Safety Rules Scrapped." *Victoria Times-Colonist*, 12 March 1983: A8.

"A Fatal Mistake." *Vancouver Sun*, 18 March 1983: A4.

Ferree, M.M. "Working Class Jobs: Housework and Paid Work as Sources of Satisfaction." *Social Problems* 23 (1976): 431–41.

George, Anne. *Occupational Health Hazards to Women*. Ottawa: Advisory Council on the Status of Women. October, 1976.

Glasbeek, H. "The Work Place As A Killing Ground." *This Magazine* 16, no. 2 (May 1982): 24–27.

Glavin, Terry. "Breaking the Back of Back-Breaking Labour." *Canadian Dimension* (August 1980).

Goff, Colin H., and Charles E. Reasons. "Organizational Crimes Against Employees, Consumers, and the Public." In *The Political Economy of Crime*, edited by Brian D. MacLean. Scarborough, Ontario: Prentice-Hall, 1986.

"Group Threatens to Sue Ontario For Domestic

Rights." *Star Phoenix*, 2 April 1987: 9B.

Halliday, Fred. "Migration and the Labour Force in the Oil Producing States of the Middle East." *Development and Change* 8 (1977): 263–91.

Harris, T.R., J.A. Merchante, K.H. Kilburn, et al. "Byssinosis and Respiratory Disease of Cotton Mill Workers." *Journal of Occupational Medicine* 14 (1972): 199–206.

Hendleman, Dan. "West Indian Association in Montreal." Unpublished M.A. thesis, Department of Sociology and Anthropology, McGill University, 1964.

Hook, Nancy C. *Domestic Service Occupation Study*. Department of Family Studies, University of Manitoba. 1978.

Hricko, A., and M. Brunt. *Working for your Life: A Woman's Guide to Job Health Hazards*. Berkeley: Labour Occupational Health Program, 1976.

Hull, Diana. "Migration, Adaptation, and Illness: A Review." *Social Science and Medicine* 13A (1979): 25–36.

INTERCEDE (Internation Coalition to End Domestic Exploitation). The Status of Domestic Workers on Temporary Employment Authorization. A Brief Submitted to the Task Force on Immigration Practices and Procedures. 1981.

Johnson, C.L., and F.A. Johnson. "Attitudes Toward Parenting in Dual-Career Families." *American Journal of Psychiatry*, 134 (1977): 391–95.

Johnson, Laura C., and Robert E. Johnson. *The Seam Allowance*. Toronto: Women's Education Press, 1982.

Kelly, Russell. "Bitter Harvest." *New West Review*, November, 1983.

Koch, Tom. "Farm Poison Death Government's Fault, Jury Says." *Vancouver Province*, 17 March 1983, B1.

Kreckel, Reinhard. "Unequal Opportunity Structure and Labour Market Segmentation." *Sociology* 14, no. 4 (1980): 525–50.

Krute, A., and M.E. Burdette. "1972 Survey of

Disabled and Non-disabled Adults: Chronic Disease, Injury and Work Disability." *Social Science Bulletin*, April 1978: 3–16.

Kuo, W.H., and Y. Tsai. "Social Networking, Hardiness and Immigrants' Mental Health." *Journal of Health and Social Behavior* 27 (June 1986): 133–49.

Labonte, Ron. "Of Cockroaches and Berry Blight." *This Magazine* 15, no. 6 (December 1982–January 1983): 4–9.

———. "The Plight of the Farmworkers." *Vancouver Sun*, 25 August 1980.

———. "Racism and Labour: The Struggle of British Columbia's Farmworkers." *Canadian Forum*, June–July, 1982.

Law Union of Ontario. *The Immigrant's Handbook*. Montreal: Black Rose Books, 1981.

Lee, Gloria, and John Wrench. "Accident Prone Immigrants: An Assumption Challenged." *Sociology* 14, no. 4 (1980):551–56.

Lipsig-Mumme, Carla. "Organizing Women in the Clothing Trades: Homework and the 1983 Garment Strike in Canada." *Studies in Political Economy* 22 (1987): 41–71.

Majka, L.C., and T.J. Majka. *Farm Workers, Agribusiness and the State*. Philadelphia: Temple University Press, 1982.

Matsqui, Abbotsford Community Services. "Agricultural Pesticide and Health Survey Results." A Project of the Matsqui, Abbotsford Community Services. October, 1982.

Merchant, J.A., et al. "Dose Response Studies in Cotton Textile Workers." *Journal of Occupational Medicine* 15 (1973): 222–30.

Messing, Karen. "Do Men and Women Have Different Jobs Because of Their Biological Differences?" In *Women and Health: The Politics of Sex in Medicine*, edited by Elizabeth Fee, 139–48. Farmingdale, New York: Baywood Publishing Co., 1983.

Miles, Robert. *Racism and Migrant Labour*. London: Routledge and Kegan Paul, 1982.

Miller, A. "The Wages of Neglect: Death and Disease in the American Work Place." *American Journal of Public Health* 65, no. 11 (1975): 1217–20.

Morokvasic, Mirjana, Annie Phizacklea, and Hedwig Rudolph. "Small Firms and Minority Groups: Contradictory Trends in the French, German, and British Clothing Industry." *International Sociology* 1, no. 4 (December 1986): 397–420.

NACL (North American Congress on Latin America). "Undocumented Immigrant Workers in New York City." *Latin America and Empire Report* 12, no. 6 (Special Issue, 1979).

Navarro, Vicente. *Crisis, Health and Medicine*. New York: Tavistock Publications, 1986.

Newhouse, Muriel. "The Medical Risks of Exposure to Asbestos." *The Practitioner*, No. 199 (1967).

Newhouse, Muriel, et al. "A Study of Mortality of Female Asbestos Workers." *British Journal of Industrial Medicine* 29 (1972): 134–41.

North, D.S. "Non-immigrant Workers: Visiting Labor Force Participants." *Monthly Labor Review* 103, no. 10 (1980): 26–30.

Oakley, A. *The Sociology of Housework*. New York: Random House, 1974.

Portes, Alejandro. "Labour Functions of Illegal Aliens." *Society* 14 (September–October 1979): 31–37.

Pynn, Larry. "Exempting Farmers From Safety Rules Attacked." *Vancouver Sun*, 11 March 1983.

———. "Coroner Urges Pesticide Laws." *Vancouver Sun*, 16 March 1983: A1.

Reasons, Charles E., Lois Ross, and Craig Peterson. *Assault on the Workers*. Toronto: Butterworths, 1981.

Sandborn, Calvin. "Equality for Farmworkers — A Question of Social Conscience." A Submission to the Legislative Caucus of the Provincial New Democratic Party. 1983.

Sanderson, G. "The Sweatshop Legacy: Still With Us in 1974." *Labour Gazette* 74 (1974): 400–17.

Sassen-Koob, Saskia. "Immigrant and Minority Workers in the Organization of the Labour Process." *Journal of Ethnic Studies* 8, no. 1

(1980): 1–34.

———. "Towards a Conceptualization of Immigrant Labour." *Social Problems* 29, no. 1 (1981): 65–85.

Schatzkin, Arthur. "Health and Labour Power: A Theoretical Investigation." *International Journal of Health Services* 8, no. 2 (1978): 213–34.

Sharma, Hari. "Race and Class in British Columbia — The Case of B.C.'s Farmworkers." *South Asian Bulletin* 3 (1983): 53–69.

Sharma, Shalendra. "East Indians and the Canadian Ethnic Mosaic: An Overview." *South Asian Bulletin* 1 (1982): 6–18.

Statistics Canada. "Canadian Women in the Workplace." *Canada Update*, from the 1981 Census, Vol. 2, no. 3 (January 1984).

Stellman, J.M. *Women's Work, Women's Health*. New York: Pantheon Books, 1977.

Stellman, J.M., and S.M. Daum. *Work Is Dangerous to Your Health*. New York: Pantheon Books, 1973.

U.S. Congress. *Hearings on Migratory Labor*. Washington, D.C.: U.S. Government Printing Office, 1972.

Waitzkin, Howard. *The Second Sickness*. New York: Free Press, 1983.

Waldron, Ingrid. "Employment and Women's Health: An Analysis of Causal Relationships." In *Women and Health: The Politics of Sex in Medicine*, edited by Elizabeth Fee, 119–38. Farmingdale, New York: Baywood Publishing Co., 1983.

Waldron, Ingrid, M. Nawotarski, M. Freimer, J. Henry, N. Post, and C. Wittin. "Cross-Cultural Variation in Blood Pressure: A Quantitative Analysis of the Relationships of Blood Pressure to Cultural Characteristics, Salt Consumption and Body Weight." *Social Sciences and Medicine* 16 (1982): 419–30.

White, Julie. *Women and Unions*. Ottawa: Ministry of Supply and Services, 1979.

28

CANADIAN WORKERS' COMPENSATION: Political, Medical, and Health Issues

Chris Doran
University of Saskatchewan

INTRODUCTION

Although it is generally acknowledged that the establishment and operation of Workers' Compensation Boards (WCBs) constitutes a significant political victory for working people, the profound limitations of this system of health care have yet to be fully analyzed. In this chapter, I will examine the ways in which the contemporary administration of workers' compensation legislation encourages workers' "health" to be conceived in a way that is very narrow, compared with the much more radical understanding of it current in the days before the advent of state-administered WCBs. Specifically I suggest that medico-legal discourse today establishes the parameters within which workers must understand their health. WCB legislation, by encouraging an individualized and "accident"-oriented notion of "ill health," pre-

vents workers from formulating their health in the more holistic terms which they had used in the early nineteenth century. At that time, industrial capitalism itself was seen as the cause of their ill health — not because it produced accidents in the workplace, but because it led, much more seriously, to the general debilitation of their health. Health, as formulated then, was an aspect of people's lives to be preserved, not compensated. Today, however, because WCBs encourage workers to see their health in a much narrower fashion, such legislation, I contend, contributes to the perpetuation of industrial capitalism. My claim is that, despite the obvious advantages which come from the rise of workers' compensation legislation, an equally important loss has been suffered: workers have the battle to preserve their health at the expense of industrial production.

In order to substantiate this claim, I will

develop two lines of argument. First, I will suggest how the early concern with "health" was transformed into the narrower concern with "accidents" and "diseases," which then led to the passage of the first workers' compensation legislation. Second, I will demonstrate how through a proliferation of medico-legal discourse, WCBs today continually discipline workers into seeing their health in these limited ways. As a consequence, working people's understanding and control over their own bodies is continually being rendered invalid and incompetent.

THE INITIAL STRUGGLES FOR WORKERS' HEALTH

Although exploitation of working people is by no means unique to the early nineteenth century, there were particular hardships for workers dictated by the escalating industrial production of this period. The English theorist Ricardo's conceptualization of political economy in terms of an insistence upon longer production hours in factories was enthusiastically embraced by the emerging class of factory owners. Consequently, workers were with increasing frequency forced into working sixteen or more hours per day. Under such conditions, it was quite obvious that the deterioration of their health resulted directly from the nature of their work. They responded by formulating their health as a political issue, to be addressed by reducing the length of the working day. The following petition from young factory operatives to the second British Royal Commission into Factory Labour of 1833 nicely illustrates this experiential understanding of their health problems:

> We want more time for rest, a little play, and to learn to read and write. Young as we are, we find that we could do our work better if we were to work less time, and were not so weighed down by the long continuance of our toil. (Fraser's Magazine, 1833:714)

With regard to this Royal Commission, Fraser's Magazine (1833:715) also noted that no "dictum of their report [can] convert the present system

of factory labour, unaltered, into one consistent with health and long life." Yet this is exactly what the state attempted to achieve. By introducing a system of factory inspection, as well as the "relay" system, (which allowed the hours worked by children to be reduced, while allowing the total hours worked by any factory to remain largely unchanged), the state tried to protect, albeit unequally, the interests of both employers and employees. As a consequence, the 1833 Factory Legislation occupies an ambiguous role in the history of workers' health protection. Although it is often viewed as constituting a great victory for the working class, at the time, it was seen as a great disappointment by most workers engaged in this struggle. A major explanation of this disappointment, I contend, is that with the passage of the 1833 Factory Legislation, health became a phenomenon to be *regulated* rather than protected (Doran, 1986). That is, working people's health starts being transformed into a calculable cost to employers.

The consequences of this transformation are profound. Today, workers' health-care demands are generally understood as in no way challenging the basic tenets of industrial capitalism. Employer control over the workplace has never been seriously threatened by them. Indeed, when political demands concerning health and safety are made by workers' organizations, they are typically formulated within the broad parameters of workers' compensation legislation; that is, demands are made for the inclusion of more diseases, for higher rates of compensation, and so on. However, characterizations of the workplace such as those made by nineteenth-century workers in their radical demands for health preservation cannot today be taken seriously. The following quotation from Navarro (1980:532) makes this point:

> The docs keep telling me there's nothing wrong with the place where I work. I guess they're supposed to know it all because they've had a lot of education and everything. I'm no expert like they are, but I sure as hell know there's something wrong in that mill and the other guys are saying the same thing. One thing I know for sure is that place is killing us.

As illustrated here, formulations of health problems which are not couched in today's dominant medico-legal discourse are all too readily ignored, whereas in the early nineteenth century, a statement such as the above, regardless of the language, would have been treated quite seriously in evidence given to royal commissions.

One major reason for the pervasiveness of medico-legal definitions of health and illness today is, quite simply, that within the workers' compensation system, this type of understanding has produced generally accepted health benefits for workers. The dominance of this expert body of knowledge, however, means that workers' own conceptions of their health problems are discounted.

The years from 1833 to 1897 mark the period in which working people's radical claims concerning their health give way to an acceptance of their health as a phenomenon to be defined by various bodies of expertise. By the 1890s, the majority of working people conceptualized their health primarily in terms of "accidents," as defined by state bodies, such as the factory inspectorate and royal commissions (Doran, 1986: chaps. 3 and 6). "Accidents" now become the "natural" way of understanding workers' health problems. It is this focus upon "accidents," rather than on the general state of health, that guides workers' compensation policy. As a consequence, and within a relatively short period, workers' experiential understanding of "health" is lost, replaced by a state-inspired preoccupation with "accidents."

The balance of this chapter is concerned with examining how this conception of health only in terms of accidents and diseases is continually managed and promoted by present-day WCBs. It comprises two main sections. In the first section, I describe how the WCB form produces mediated versions of workers' bodies through the processes of classification and normalization. I argue that these processes encourage working people to understand their health and illness in individualized medico-legal terms, which will pose little threat to the continuation of industrial capitalism. The second main section is a specific examination of how these processes take place with reference to the problem of injured backs, and is followed by some general concluding comments.

COLLECTING "STRUCTURED INFORMATION"

Workers' Compensation Board officials make decisions that continually transform working people's experiential understanding of their own bodies into the language of medical science. It is my contention that the forms used by the workers' compensation board are a powerful means by which this transformation is *continually* enacted at both the individual and the organizational level. At the individual level, the form quite simply both seduces and disciplines workers into accepting that version of health and illness constituted by medical expertise. The seduction lies mainly in monetary compensation, while disciplinary action usually takes the form of requests for clarification of injuries, demands for further medical examination, and delays in payment. These disciplinary mechanisms are put into motion whenever injured workers report their injuries in ways deemed unacceptable by WCB officials. Workers' understanding of the causes and nature of their injuries are never accepted outright. In all cases, they are subjected to expert medical inquiry and interpretation. As a consequence, WCB officials deal with a mediated version of the worker, one which is silent and passive, rather than with the actual person. Even at the level of appeals against the board, decisions are again primarily based on the mediated body. Evidence submitted at this stage, like information in the claimant's original file, has to be produced systematically, and must give an "objective" description of the body in question.

The form not only portrays a body, it also combines with other information-gathering forms to produce new "medical" ways of understanding the body. For example, as Table 1 dem-

Table 1. The Rise of the "Back Injury"; A Comparison of Workers' Compensation Schemes of Classification 1947 and 1985

Nature of Injuries in Respect to Accidents Reported During the Year 1947		Number of Claims Reported by Part of Body in 1985	
Amputation without infection	129	Back	14 199
Amputation with infection	3	Fingers	7 399
Bruises	4 687	Toes, feet or ankles	6 325
Burns and scalds	764	Chest, hips or shoulders	5 724
Cuts, lacerations without infection	7 094	Multiple injuries	4 728
Cuts, lacerations with infection	1 202	Hands or wrists	4 418
Eye injuries	3 098	Arms	3 544
Strains and sprains	4 820	Knees	3 475
Fractures without infection	2 171	Head or neck	3 373
Fractures with infection	4	Eyes	3 266
Fractures with infection causing amputation	1	Non-personal damage	3 071
Hernia	298	Legs	2 227
Industrial diseases	84	Body systems	794
Silicosis	13	Unclassified	83
Heat exhaustion	13		
Frostbite	69	Total	62 626
Drowning	4		
Overcome by fumes	48		
Nature unknown	21		
Burns with infection	63		
Dislocation	139		
Lead poisoning	1		
Trench mouth	1		
Unclassified	1 137		
Total	25 864		

Source: Alberta Workmen's Compensation Board Annual Report 1947:24.

Source: Alberta Worker's Compensation Board Annual Report 1985:10.

N.B. The purpose of displaying these two charts is not to compare types of injuries across a 40 year period, but rather to illustrate the different ways in which injuries came to be conceptualized in this time period.

onstrates, over a period of time, "backs" have become a new category for understanding workers' illnesses. Even more importantly, as we will see later, "backs" have become a new area in which medical science must devalue workers' knowledge of their own bodies. Medical science today increasingly puts definitions on workers' bodies so as to make them conform to the logic of its own language.

Figure 1. An Employer's Report

WCB

WORKERS' COMPENSATION BOARD
BOX 2415, EDMONTON, ALBERTA
T5J 2S5

EMPLOYER'S REPORT OF ACCIDENT OR INDUSTRIAL DISEASE

ANSWER ALL PERTINENT QUESTIONS SIGN ON REVERSE AND MAIL TO THE BOARD WITHIN 24 HOURS

THIS SPACE FOR WCB USE ONLY

EMPLOYER'S ACCOUNT NO.
OCCURRENCE CLASS
CLAIM NUMBER
EMPLOYER'S AREA CODE
AMOUNT OF PERSONAL COVERAGE

WORKER'S LAST NAME

DATE AND HOUR OF ACCIDENT   19   AT   A.M. ☐ P.M. ☐

FIRST NAME(S)

EMPLOYER'S FULL NAME (PROPRIETORS, PARTNERS OR CORPORATIONS)

FULL ADDRESS

TRADE NAME

POSTAL CODE

MAILING ADDRESS

POSTAL CODE

SOCIAL INSURANCE NO.   MARITAL STATUS   DATE OF BIRTH DAY. MON./YR.   SEX F ☐ M ☐

WAS WORKER INJURED ON THE EMPLOYER'S PREMISES?   YES ☐   NO ☐

TYPE OF INDUSTRY   PHONE NO.

STATE ADDRESS WHERE ACCIDENT HAPPENED IF NOT THE SAME AS EMPLOYER MAILING ADDRESS

STREET, PLANT, MILL OR SITE NAME

DATE AND HOUR ACCIDENT FIRST REPORTED DAY/MON   19   AT   A.M. ☐ P.M. ☐

DID ACCIDENT OCCUR IN ALBERTA?   YES ☐   NO ☐   IF NO, PROVINCE?

WHAT TIME DID WORKER COMMENCE WORK?   A.M. ☐   P.M. ☐

WORKER'S OCCUPATION

NAME OR ADDRESS OF ATTENDING DOCTOR OR HOSPITAL

HEALTH CARE INSURANCE NO.   PROVINCE

1.   DESCRIPTION OF ACCIDENT - ATTACH SHEET IF NECESSARY

A.   WHAT HAPPENED TO CAUSE INJURY?

B.   WHAT WAS THE WORKER DOING?

C.   WHAT MACHINE, TOOL, EQUIPMENT OR MATERIAL WAS THE WORKER USING?

D.   STATE ANY INVOLVEMENT OF GAS, CHEMICAL OR EXTREME TEMPERATURE.

2.   NATURE OF INJURY - IF INDUSTRIAL DISEASE, GIVE DETAILS

A.   WHAT PART OF THE BODY WAS INJURED? (HAND, EYE, BACK ETC., STATE LEFT OR RIGHT)

B.   WHAT TYPE OF INJURY WAS SUSTAINED? (BURN, FRACTURE, BRUISE ETC.)

3.   QUESTIONS ANSWERED "NO" REQUIRE FULL EXPLANATION - ATTACH SHEET IF NECESSARY

A.   WERE THE WORKER'S ACTIONS AT THE TIME OF INJURY FOR THE PURPOSE OF YOUR BUSINESS?   YES ☐   NO ☐

B.   WERE THEY PART OF THE REGULAR WORK?   YES ☐   NO ☐

C.   ARE YOU SATISFIED THE INJURY OCCURRED AS STATED?   YES ☐   NO ☐

D.   WAS FIRST AID RENDERED? IF YES, STATE WHEN AND BY WHOM.   YES ☐   NO ☐

4.   A.   DO YOU HAVE AN ACCOUNT ESTABLISHED WITH THIS BOARD? IF YES, QUOTE FILE NUMBER.   YES ☐   NO ☐

B.   DOES THIS WORKER HAVE PERSONAL COVERAGE WITH THE BOARD? IF SO, PLEASE QUOTE HIS ACCOUNT NUMBER.   YES ☐   NO ☐

C.   IS THE INJURED PERSON A PARTNER IN THE BUSINESS?   YES ☐   NO ☐

D.   IS THE INJURED PERSON A DIRECTOR OF THE CORPORATION? IF YES, SPECIFY.   YES ☐   NO ☐

E.   DOES HE EMPLOY HIS OWN WORKERS? IF YES, EXPLAIN.   YES ☐   NO ☐

5.   IS WORKER OFF WORK, OR WAS HE OFF WORK LONGER THAN DAY OF ACCIDENT. IF YES, COMPLETE REVERSE.   YES ☐   NO ☐

C 040   05 86   COMPLETE REVERSE AS INDICATED AND SIGN IN SPACE PROVIDED

Producing a Worker's Body as a Document

Although workers' bodies may be the object of a WCB's attention, what constitutes the body is generated from the information in workers' files. Typically, this will include at least three forms: (1) the worker's report of the injury, (2) the employer's report, and (3) the doctor's report (see Figures 1 and 2). If the injury is anything besides the most ordinary, it will also include other documentation in the form of memos, reports, etc. This documentary evidence stands as the body, and constitutes the primary focal point of this mediation.

Although the file produces a body which is represented documentarily and linguistically, this transformation of the body into the text is not simply a representation of the facts, as the workers' compensation system would like us to believe. Instead the form is normatively organized to portray workers' health problems in a particular fashion. By the way it uses language, it disciplines workers into seeing themselves only in certain ways. This process has two aspects: classification and normalization. Through the use of a particular classification system, as exemplified by the actual words used, the WCB form demonstrates what type of health problem is meaningful, and therefore eligible for compensation. This leaves no medium through which injured workers can call attention to health problems which fall outside the narrow parameters of "accident" or "disease"; the actual design of the questions subtly coerces workers into transforming their complaints into "normal" "accidents" and "diseases" for the purposes of compensation. Classification and normalization are the processes by which the mediation of workers' knowledge takes place, and it is to these processes that attention is now turned.

The Classification Process

I have already suggested that at the beginning of the nineteenth century, a concern with accidents and diseases was not a natural part of working people's understanding of their health. Instead,

they formulated a much more radical concept; that the factory system was responsible for the general deterioration of their health. Nevertheless, the compensation system deals more in "accident" and "disease" than "health". Both categories have proven problematic for WCBs and their claimants, yet legislative efforts, rather than reformulating the classification system, have been directed towards more accurately defining "accidents" and "diseases." In other words, the mediation of working people's knowledge is increased by the further transformation of their language into categories necessitating expert definition.

Accidents and Diseases

Legally, most WCBs today compensate for more than just commonplace accidents. The Alberta WCB, for example, compensates for injuries occasioned by intended malevolence against the worker, chance events, disablement, and occupational diseases. Yet in terms of how the worker's form is worded, there is absolutely no suggestion of this fact. The form by its design makes meaningful only one interpretation of "accident," the one typically concerned with *trauma*. Consequently, other features of the accident definition, such as disablement, are rendered marginal. For example, the only box available for the claimant to describe his injury asks "How did the accident happen and what injury did you receive?" In a 1982 case, the claimant was forced to respond, "It was not an accident, it was a health problem due to the carbon black and dust allergies in both my hands and legs."[1] Here the claimant is forced to disregard the form's classification scheme so as to report his ailment.

This notion of "accident" as portrayed in WCB forms is a powerful tool and acts not only to discourage workers from filing claims for anything other than typical traumatic occurrences, but also to encourage adjudicators to see the problem in this narrow way. Consequently, "normal" injuries for the board usually mean traumatic accidents. The following exchange from the Tysoe Commission (1966:184) illustrates this. With regard to a particular claim the

Figure 2. A Worker's Report

WORKERS' COMPENSATION BOARD
BOX 2415, EDMONTON, ALBERTA
T5J 2S5

WORKER'S REPORT OF ACCIDENT

MAILING ADDRESS

COMPLETE AND RETURN FORM AT ONCE

PLEASE PRINT YOUR FULL NAME, ADDRESS, SOCIAL INSURANCE NUMBER, EMPLOYER'S NAME AND ADDRESS IN AREA BELOW IF NOT SHOWN CORRECTLY AT RIGHT

LAST NAME

FIRST NAME(S)

MAILING ADDRESS

HEALTH CARE INSURANCE NUMBER   PROVINCE

POSTAL CODE

SOCIAL INSURANCE NUMBER   PHONE   MARITAL STATUS   DATE OF BIRTH   OCCUPATION

EMPLOYER'S NAME   EMPLOYER'S MAILING ADDRESS   EMPLOYER'S PHONE NO.

1 A.   DATE AND HOUR OF ACCIDENT   THE   DAY OF   , 19   AT   O'CLOCK   M.

   B.   WHEN DID YOU REPORT THE ACCIDENT TO YOUR EMPLOYER?
                                                          NAME   TITLE

   C.   WHO DID YOU REPORT TO?

   D.   IF NOT REPORTED IMMEDIATELY, GIVE REASON.

   E.   IN WHAT CITY, TOWN OR PLACE DID THE ACCIDENT HAPPEN?

   F.   DID IT HAPPEN ON THE EMPLOYER'S PREMISES?
        STATE EXACTLY WHERE.

2   WAS THE WORK YOU WERE DOING FOR THE   YES ☐   NO ☐   WAS IT PART OF YOUR REGULAR WORK?   YES ☐   NO ☐
    PURPOSE OF YOUR EMPLOYER'S BUSINESS?

3   HOW DID THE ACCIDENT HAPPEN AND WHAT INJURY DID YOU RECEIVE? DESCRIBE FULLY.   MARK PART INJURED
    (STATE RIGHT OR LEFT, IF APPLICABLE).

                                                                                    Right   Left

IMPORTANT PLEASE LIST ANY WITNESSES.

NAME   ADDRESS

C 060 05.86   COMPLETE BOTH SIDES - THIS FORM MUST BE SIGNED ON REVERSE

Commissioner states that he was "a little puzzled how an accident has anything to do in a heart case." The respondent from the WCB attempts to explain:

> [Respondent]–I think the difficulty in these cases arises by reason of the application that is made, the claim that he makes — and it is the form of application, of course, which we supply — it is our form 39, Mr. Commissioner, and it says, "That I am the widow of (x) who died on a certain day, as a result of accident which occurred on such and such a day" and in this particular application she probably included the day of accident and that's what Mr. Tufts was trying to say, well, was there any accident on that day?
>
> [Commissioner]–Because that really isn't the question at all, is it, in heart cases?
>
> [Respondent]–Well, it could be.
>
> [Commissioner]–Well, I suppose it could be, but –
>
> [Respondent]–You mean whether the injury is a result of his employment?
>
> [Commissioner]–Yes.
>
> [Respondent]–Yes, that's right. I think it is fairly obvious, Mr. Commissioner, that this shouldn't be written this way, but I suppose we let ourselves be misled by the form of application.

With regard to industrial disease, there are a number of points to make. Although certain diseases have been compensated since the inception of the Workers' Compensation Act, it is only recently that the term has appeared on the initial application form. In the 1930s in Alberta, neither employers' nor employees' reports made reference to industrial disease; contemporary forms include industrial disease, but on the employer's form only! Consequently, workers suffering from industrial disease and wanting to make a claim have to ignore the form's classification schemes.

For example, in order to make a claim for asbestosis, one recent claimant was forced to answer in reply to the question "How did the accident happen and what injury did you receive?" (See Figure 2) as follows: "I started insulating in the 1950s and when I was applying insulation material (including asbestos), I was exposed to heavy concentrations of fine particle dust." The nature of his injury is displayed before him as apparently marginal, because he finds it difficult even to file his complaint. Instead of responding to the classification "accident" which appears on the form, he is forced to reply quite differently: by immediately recalling his occupational history.

In these examples, the power of classification has been demonstrated. The system of compensation is set up so that claimants and adjudicators are encouraged to see and understand compensation in only a certain way. The prime consideration of working people in 1833 — their health — is now virtually eliminated from the design of the form. Their concern with the debilitating effect of industrial life itself is now rendered marginal, yet what they considered relatively unimportant, the question of traumatic accidents, is now the number-one priority.

In addition, distinctions which have been introduced by amendments to the legislation are not always conveyed by the structuring of the form. The form still displays a prominent concern with traumatic accidents, even though the legal definition of "accident" has been widely extended. It might be contended here that although the form does not state all the possible diagnoses which render a worker eligible for compensation, this does not prevent him from making an application. My point, however, is that the design of the form subtly disciplines working people into a certain perception of what constitutes a meaningful, compensable, "normal" injury. From that, they also understand that any injury which does not fall into this "normal" category requires more work. With regard to the claim for asbestosis examined previously, the claimant, with the assistance of his union, produced a nine-page work history in order to substantiate his claim for compensation. Workers know they must work harder to get compensation for those injuries not seen as "normal."

Granted, the manner of presentation of industrial injury is limited on any conceivable form, yet because the form always puts forward a preferred version of injury, injuries which do not fit this categorization system become less meaningful; they cannot easily be understood within the form's framework. Again, it might be argued that this presentation reflects the typical ratio of accident cases to industrial disease cases and, thus, can be justified as reflecting what exists in the population. Yet, as I have suggested, working people's present understanding of health, primarily in terms of "accidents," was not common at the beginning of the nineteenth century. They have been seduced and disciplined into accepting this idea over a considerable period of time. My further claim is that the design of the form significantly reinforces this thinking.

The Normalization Process

Immense care and skill go into the manufacture of forms, since questions on forms are designed to elicit rather specific answers. In addition, the spacing and sequencing of questions allow us to guess the form's preferred answers. Let me take, as a common example, the "Employer's Report of Accident or Industrial Disease" form (see Figure 1). Notwithstanding its name, in terms of the questions which it contains there is an obvious imbalance: the "Description of Accident" section is broken down into four subsidiary questions, while industrial disease gets mentioned only once, in the following context: "Nature of injury — if industrial disease, give details." Thus the form, by its design, prefers accidents over diseases, and because the form is conventionally treated as information-seeking rather than intrusionary in intent, this structuring rarely leads to overt complaints.

However, this notion of the explicitly designed form is not lost on claimants. The form encourages claimants to believe that there are standard answers which will ensure compensation; ones which produce "normal" injuries. Their problem then becomes to determine which type of answers will get rewarded. For example, workers typically know that answers ought in some way to demonstrate the work-related

nature of the complaint. Let me illustrate this by displaying the problems which arise when such constraints are ignored.

Because there is a standard question on the workers' claim form which asks "How did the accident happen?", an answer like "Came home after work, bent over to up something then pain on lower part of back" may not immediately indicate the appropriate connection. The question not only presupposes a certain type of injury, but it does not allow space for the citing of extenuating criteria which might make the case compensable. With regard to the case above, we get the following extenuating circumstances, given in a subsequent letter of clarification to the board:

> My doctor examined me and he too felt the cause of my injury was not the mere fact of my bending over to pick up an ice scraper. He felt the actual source of the injury was the work I had been doing in the previous eight hours of work.

The point here is not that the claimant does not know enough to express the complaint clearly, but that the form itself demands only certain answers and not others. At the level of this form the WCB tries to subtly deter any type of nonconformity. In the example above, the answer did not conform to bureaucratic standards of relevance and resulted in the request for clarification. In other words, the claimant was punished, in a subtle yet irritating manner. A classic petty bureaucratic penalty was imposed: delay of payment until a clarification had been given.

With regard to the asbestosis case introduced earlier, attempts to answer the questions it asks appear nonsensical because they expose the underlying assumptions which went into the compilation of the form. They display how industrial disease simply cannot be reported on the standard form. For example, the following questions and answers (see Figure 2, questions D and F) on the worker's claim form display the irrelevance of this form to cases of industrial disease:

Q. When did you report the accident to your employer?

A. Never because I didn't know until recently that I had a serious lung injury (asbestosis)

Q. If not reported immediately, give reason.

A. Didn't know I had asbestosis until I went to doctors recently when I was sick and found I had chest problems.

Industrial diseases are not considered important enough to be included on the standard form, either in the title of the worker's form, or in the actual design of the questions used.

Although it seems strange that such a fundamental feature of workers' compensation is so difficult to report, this is not accidental; on the contrary, these forms are very carefully worded, but the wording and the structure are geared to what a WCB might see as the more relevant features of an injury. The form itself does not encourage anomalies. It sets the task of the claimant to transform his injury into one which is bureaucratically acceptable and normal.

Because the form demands only certain ways of describing injuries, these descriptions, although treated as factual, have a peculiar constitutive quality: they become "normal" injuries. Consequently, other, non-traumatic injuries such as stress and back pain are constituted as being marginal. This is not so much a consequence of the nature of such injuries but rather a product of their exclusion by the workings of the form.

THE FORM AND MEDICAL SCIENCE

The WCB form is not only the principal mechanism for disciplining and classifying individual workers. It is also instrumental in producing whole new categories of people who must be brought under the monitoring eye of medical expertise. Thus medical science takes problems defined in lay discourse, and subjects them to redescription and reclassification in its own terms. In this course of redescribing, it also forces us to accept this new way of seeing,

because this is an accurate "scientific" description. Workers' back problems are an excellent example of this process.

Mediating Backs

Holt (1983:69–73), in a recent review of "work-related back problems," lists a number of investigations into the problems of back injuries which have emerged in recent years. In his summary, he shows that " 'compensation cases for low back pain' have routinely been featured as 'measures of back problem.' " Compensation forms thus are not only used for extracting information from individual claimants, they can also be used to produce the scientific problem of "back injury" itself. They form the input into medical studies on back problems, and are instrumental in the production of new scientific classifications of "back injuries."

Such scientific facts and classifications are then applied to the everyday context of workers' health. But because medical science has taken over a previously meaningful language common to workers, it acts as a power over them. Workers' knowledge of their own bodies is continually being rendered invalid, and the discourse on their own pain irrelevant. They now must subject themselves to the discipline of medical science, which "objectively" knows their condition. Let us examine this process.

Medical science defines back injuries as a problem, and one which it is capable of solving. It also assures us that its intervention into the arena of back pain is primarily in the worker's best interests. Having once established back pain as a problem, medical science then proceeds to try to control it. The attempt is made first to investigate and observe phenomena so as to diagnose the problem scientifically, and then to explain it. As Holt (1983:11) points out, however, "There is no standard definition of back problem in the literature." In order for medical science to be able to "help" working people, it must first "define" the back problem. Currently, no accepted definition exists, and consequently, back problems have not yet been mediated.

Although back injuries have been compensated by the board since its inception, it is only recently that they have become the subject of intense scientific investigation. The Alberta Workers' Compensation Board, for example, routinely labelled back injuries as "sprained back" for the purposes of description. For example, in the 1930s, cases such as "slipped and strained back," "sprained back," "sprained back after slip," were routinely reported in compensation claims (Compensation claims Nos. 1920, 2263, 2326, Compensation Files, Glenbow Museum, Calgary). But it was not until after the 1940s that they became problematic, as seen in Table 1. They first became a publicly known topic when they were articulated as a "problem." For example, in the 1952 British Columbia Royal Commission into Workmen's Compensation, back problems appear, but not under their own classification. Instead we find them under the heading of "Medical Division: Basis of Conflicts, Intervertebral Disk Issue."

By 1966, backs have become formulated under the separate classification of "Back Injuries" and that section in the Tysoe Commission Report (1966:222) states: "Labour, industry, and the Board are in agreement that cases of back injuries are numerous and contentious and present particularly difficult problems." With the extension of the legislation around this time, to include "disablement" under the rubric of accident, bad backs started to cause a different type of problem. As Tysoe (1966:225) remarked,

There are two areas of potential controversy. One is the true nature and extent of the disability and the other the causal relationship or work connection. Although both are vexations, the latter is the more troublesome and the greatest cause of disputes between workmen and the board.

He goes on to describe the nature of this latter problem.

The stress of the doctors seems to be on the difficulty of determining whether it was the work or something else that was the cause ... I find it impossible to convince myself that it is just (i.e., fair) to differentiate between two workmen who have performed the same type of work for the same length of time and who end

up with like back disabilities simply because one of them can point to a tripping or slipping while the other cannot. (Tysoe, 1966:227)

Backs are constituted as a problem because the law has recently extended the meaning of "accident" to include non-traumatic occurrences. Yet medical expertise lags behind. In a certain sense, the problematization of backs exists now as a creation of the discourse of compensation itself. With the aim of helping the worker by easing the general criteria for eligibility, the compensation board simultaneously creates another problem, that of work-relatedness: whether the injury was caused by work or not. This becomes a problem not so much for WCBs, but for medicine. Medicine is now encouraged to engage in the task of making decisions concerning the contribution to back problems of work.

On further investigation, this problem can be seen as a dispute over two different types of descriptive account, that of the worker and that of the expert, as seen in the following:

Time after time a worker on the job, especially in an industry like the forest industry or a sawmill where the day-to-day work entails some fairly substantial pulling or lifting, an employee will go along week after week or year after year with no problem. In the normal course of their employment suddenly their back gives out. Unless this man truthfully or untruthfully says that he slipped or that he was pushing or pulling something and something fell on him, he does not get compensation. (Tysoe, 1966:174)

* * *

Now we do not lightly dismiss a workman's complaints in regard to his back or any other part; but we are very reluctant to assess or to pay a pension based only on complaints, without some objective evidence to back them up. (Tysoe, 1966:222)

Here the difference between these two discourses is made clear: WCBs require more than the workers' knowledge of their back injury, demanding "objective evidence" and this, of course, can only be provided by medical science. The stage is set for medicine to enter and produce an "objective" injured back. In the case above, the issue becomes one of converting the worker's definition of a back injury into a medical one.

A report in the *Globe and Mail* in June 1985 indicated just how medicine was about to attempt this conversion:

> A University of Alberta researcher has designed a machine to scientifically measure what a sore back means in terms of disability ... Dr. Shrawn Kumar of the University of Alberta's department of physical therapy proposes to collect data on healthy backs that can be compared to information on diseased or injured backs, thereby delineating degrees of impairment and creating a way to quantify rehabilitation.

Although medical research is done in the sincere hope that it can produce not only knowledge of back pain, but a cure as well, a concomitant and *unavoidable* consequence of this research is that the back must be subjected to standard definitions. In this attempt to come up with objective criteria of pain, working people's knowledge of their own back pain is transformed into the language of medical science. Via this transformation of their experiential language, working people are continually being rendered powerless with regard to these aspects of their health.

CONCLUSION

In this chapter I have tried to show that control over the definition of "health" has been increasingly lost by working people since the early nineteenth century. Whereas their earlier construction of health was in political terms in direct opposition to the principles of industrial capitalism, such an articulation no longer exists. Today, health is seen in exactly those terms put forward by the medico-legal discourse of the workers' compensation system.

Rather than accepting these definitions of health as natural and self-evident, I have contended that they are products of certain disciplining techniques which subtly encourage and coerce working people into seeing health in this narrow fashion. As a consequence, workers' infrequent appeals to the remnants of their old experiential language are rendered irrelevant to any serious discussion of workers' health problems today.

A major locus of this disciplinary power is the structure and content of the workers' compensation form. I have shown how it continually structures replies so as to conform to WCB definitions of health and illness. I also explored the difficulties which result for claimants if appropriate answers are not given. The WCB form is not only used to discipline individual workers, however; it is also used by medicine to help produce standardized definitions of injuries for the working population as a whole. In both cases, what we see happening is the general process of mediating workers' bodies, such that increasingly today, their own knowledge of their health is invalidated.

NOTE

1. This response to a WCB form's question, and the others which follow in this paper, are all taken from actual recent claims applications dealt with by the Alberta Workers' Compensation Board.

STUDY QUESTIONS

1. Examine other "blank forms" and suggest the assumptions which are tacitly incorporated into their design.

2. Discuss what is meant by the comment above that "appeals to the remnants of their old experiential language become rendered irrelevant ... today."

3. Discuss how political problems of the nineteenth century have been transformed into administrative ones in this century, with regard to the topic of workers' health.

4. Speculate on other ways in which working people have been seduced into seeing their experiential language as in many ways deficient.

5. Explain what is meant by the term "structured information". In what ways does it have power over injured workers?

6. What is the notion of mediation? Explain with reference to workers' compensation.

RECOMMENDED READING

Finer, S.E. *The Life and Times of Sir Edwin Chadwick.* London: Methuen and Co., 1952.

Fielden, J. *The Curse of the Factory System.* Frank Cass and Co. Ltd., 1969.

Leyton, E. "The Bureaucratisation of Anguish: The Workmen's Compensation Board in an Industrial Disaster." In *Bureaucracy and World View*, edited by Handelman and Leyton, 70–134. St. John's, Newfoundland: Institute of Social and Economic Research, Memorial University of Newfoundland, 1978.

United Kingdom Parliament. *Report from the Select Committee on the Bill to Regulate the Labour of Children in the Mills and Factories of the United Kingdom. (Volume XV)*, 1831–2.

REFERENCES

Alberta Workmen's Compensation Board. *Annual Report.* Edmonton, 1947.

Alberta Workers' Compensation Board. *Annual Report.* Edmonton, 1981.

Alberta Workers' Compensation Board. *Annual Report.* Edmonton, 1985.

Canada. *Parliamentary Debates.* (Volume 19), 1833.

Aarsteinsen, B. "How much disability lies in a bad back?" *Globe and Mail* 5 June 1985.

Bartrip, P., and Burman, S. *The Wounded Soldiers of Industry.* Oxford: Clarendon Press, 1983.

British Columbia Royal Commission Inquiry into Workmen's Compensation. 1952.

"The Commission for Perpetuating Factory Infanticide." *Fraser's Magazine* (June 1833): 707–15.

Doran, C. *Calculated Risks: An Alternative History of Workers' Compensation.* Unpublished Ph.D diss., University of Calgary, 1986.

Holt, P. *Work-Related Back Problems: A Review of Recent Research Evidence.* Alberta Workers' Health Safety and Compensation, 1983.

Navarro, V. "Work, Ideology and Science: The Case of Medicine." *International Journal for Health Services* 10, no. 4 (1980): 523–50.

Tysoe, C.W. *Commission of Inquiry, Workmen's Compensation Act: Report of the Commissioner.* British Columbia: Queen's Printer, 1966.

PART X

CURRENT ISSUES

INTRODUCTION

There is an increasing recognition that social conditions and social contradictions foster and contribute to many illnesses in society. Because of the close linkages between medicine and society, any meaningful discussions of health and illness, health-care delivery systems, and policy alternatives cannot be divorced from the consideration of the political, economic, social, and ideological structures in the society. The chapters in this section illustrate this by a number of diverse cases. For instance, one of the primary contradictions in this society is between profits and health. Illness is exploited for a variety of purposes by a number of groups, including profit-making corporations. Chapter 29, *Profits and Illness: Exporting Health Hazards to the Third World*, by Bolaria, and Chapter 30, *Profits First: The Pharmaceutical Industry in Canada*, by Lexchin, explore the linkages between the corporate drive for profits and production of illness-generating conditions.

Sustained corporate profits generally require expansion, low production costs, cheap labour, diversification, and creation of new markets. During the past few years, awareness of the devastating effects of health hazards in the work environment, and occupational and environmental carcinogens has increased in advanced capitalist countries. Legislation regarding environmental standards and occupational health and safety regulations in some industries potentially limits corporate profits. Rather than complying with environmental and occupational safety and health standards, some corporations are relocating their enterprises (in particular industries involving health and safety hazards) to Third World countries where regulations concerning environmental and occupational health and safety are either inadequate or non-existent. Consequences for the workers in those countries are ill health, shorter life span, and "accidental" death. Potential health hazards also extend far beyond the workplace, because of dumping of hazardous waste and other pollutants in the environment. Evidence presented in Bolaria's

chapter also shows that the chemical and pharmaceutical industries, in their drive for profits and new markets, are engaged in dumping of dangerous and banned drugs and chemicals in the Third World. Promotion of bottle-feeding has contributed to malnutrition, ill health, and high infant mortality rates in many countries.

The primary thesis of Lexchin's chapter is that the driving force behind the pharmaceutical industry is profits; ethical considerations are secondary. Lexchin notes that because of foreign domination, opportunities for manufacturing, exporting, and research in the Canadian pharmaceutical industry are severely constrained. However, the pharmaceutical industry is one of the most profitable in Canada. Pharmaceutical companies have been able to achieve this position by limiting price competition and replacing it with product competition. Lexchin argues that product competition also forms a key element in the orientation of many of the research activities of this industry. Development of new drugs is guided by the potential for profit rather than health. Pharmaceutical companies exercise a major influence over prescription practices of physicians and "stocking practices" of pharmacists, which affect their sales and profits.

Weston and Jeffery in Chapter 31 discuss the influence of institutions and social forces external to medicine in the perception and definition of and reaction to AIDS. The authors posit that the social issues are overriding the medical issues of disease, with the result that AIDS is being seen less as an illness or medical condition than a sensationalized social phenomenon. Weston and Jeffery in this chapter discuss AIDS in the context of Western society's views of sexuality and of sickness, and the role which religious institutions, the state, and medicine play in the control of deviant behaviour. Several factors have shaped public perceptions and reactions to AIDS, including marginality of the groups considered at risk, the rise of the political right, and the fact that currently science has no cure for AIDS.

Roy in Chapter 32 presents a discussion of medical and clinical ethical issues in the overall context of societal values, ethics, and morality. Questions abound in this area. When should efforts to prolong or to save a patient's life be stopped? What are the criteria for such decisions? Can they be uniform in a morally and culturally pluralistic society? How is the responsibility for such decisions to be shared? If it is morally justified in specific circumstances to let a patient die, why is it not morally justifiable to hasten the same patient's death? Roy discusses these questions, addressing diverse medical problems such as active euthanasia, and withholding treatment from the very old, terminally ill or comatose patients, and severely malformed newborns.

Individual lifestyles and consumption patterns are now widely invoked as explanations of the present increase in many chronic and degenerative diseases. As these explanations and the attendant solutions are being given wide publicity through the mass media and professional journals and are increasingly gaining acceptance, they are bound to have far-reaching consequences in the provision of health services and health-related policy issues. Bolaria in Chapter 33 argues that the promotion of this "new perspective" — individual etiology and individual solutions — is consistent with the basic societal tenets of "bourgeois individualism and freedom of choice" and that its promotion in the face of health-care crises is more than coincidental. Bolaria goes on to argue that it obscures the extent to which health and illness depend upon socially determined ways of life, obfuscates the social causes of disease, shifts responsibility for health and illness back onto the individual, individualizing what is essentially a social problem, and promotes a course of action oriented toward changing individual behaviour and lifestyles rather than addressing deficiencies in existing social, economic, and political institutions and the health sector.

Change of individual behaviour and promotion of self-care prevention through health education are important parts of the strategy to reduce health-care costs. The burden of health-care crises may be borne by individuals to the extent that they accept the proposition that illnesses that are actually the result of environmentally induced conditions can be solved individually by self-care and "wise living."

29

PROFITS AND ILLNESS: Exporting Health Hazards to the Third World

B. Singh Bolaria
University of Saskatchewan

INTRODUCTION

Capitalism is becoming increasingly global in character. Multinational corporations know no particular native country. Monopoly capital, primarily in the form of multinationals, in its search for profits and capital accumulation does not stop at national boundaries, and capital investments are no longer confined to domestic sources, raw materials, or labour. Sustained corporate profits generally require expansion, low production costs, cheap labour, diversification, access to cheap resources, and new markets. Third World countries are increasingly being invaded by profit-motivated enterprises because the business climate in many of these countries is most favourable for profits and capital accumulation. While multinationals reap enormous profits, the industrial production process and the marketing practices of some corporations have had significant effects on the health of the populace in those countries. This chapter explores the linkages between the corporate drive for profits and the social production of illness, drawing on the literature dealing with pharmaceutical and chemical industries, the food industry and its promotion of infant formula, and industrial enterprises involved in the production of dangerous products and dumping of hazardous wastes and other pollutants in the environment.

EXPORT OF INDUSTRIAL HEALTH HAZARDS

As hazardous industries come under increasing scrutiny in the advanced industrial nations, some corporations are locating their production plants in Third World countries. Legislative action regarding environmental standards, and occupational health and safety regulations in hazardous industries potentially threaten corporate profits. Rather than complying with costly safety and health standards at the workplace and environmental pollution-control regulations, dangerous industries move to locations where such standards are either inadequate or non-existent and where cheap, unorganized, and uninformed labour is plentiful. The magnitude of the flight of "runaway hazardous industries" and the export of jobs is of such proportions that a bill was introduced in the United States Congress "to establish a Commission on Unemployment Caused by the Dispersion of Hazardous Industry" (H.R. 9505, 94th Congress, 1st Session).

The governments of underdeveloped countries, on the other hand, are willing to provide tax shelters, relaxed environmental, health, and safety standards, and other "incentives" to attract these industries and jobs (Castleman, 1979, 1981, 1983; Butler et al., 1978; Elling, 1977; Hassan et al., 1981). They try to outbid each other to provide "pollution havens," to industrial polluters (Barnett and Muller, 1974). For example, one advertisement by the Government of Mexico read:

> Relax. We've already prepared the ground for you. If you are thinking of fleeing from the capital because the new laws for the prevention and control of the environmental pollution affect your plant, you can count on us. (cited in Elling, 1977:218)

The factors above have encouraged some multinationals to relocate their hazardous enterprises to Third World countries, and thus to avoid costly compliance with environmental pollution-control regulations and health safety standards. When a hazardous product is banned in one country and not in others, this creates what Castleman (1983:5) calls "the double standard in industrial hazards"; that is, double standards in health protection, whereby workers and communities in Third World countries are exposed to dangers which would not be tolerated in the advanced countries. The consequences for workers and their families are ill health and eventually death. Health hazards extend far beyond the workplace. The dumping of hazardous waste and other pollutants in the environment adversely affects community and public health.

Increasingly, a variety of industries are locating their hazardous industrial plants in the Third World (Castleman, 1979, 1981; Elling, 1977; Myers, 1981; Laporte, 1978; Berman, 1986). For the purposes of this paper, however, a few examples will suffice to demonstrate the double standard in production of hazardous materials and in health protection.

The asbestos industry is one which has received considerable attention in this regard. The dangers of asbestos, known as far back as Ancient Greece, had been public in America since 1900. By 1919, insurance companies in the United States and Canada were already refusing to sell life insurance policies to asbestos workers (Berman, 1986). Exposure to asbestos is known to cause lung cancer, cancer of the gastrointestinal tract, and mesotheliomas (Selikoff et al., 1964, 1979). Asbestos products, such as insulation and automotive friction products, are linked to increased risk of cancer. The widespread public recognition of the dangers of asbestos in the advanced countries has had a number of positive effects, such as the establishment of occupational health and safety standards, health warnings on asbestos products, and so forth.

Historically, most of the world's asbestos manufacturing has been done in the advanced industrial nations. But now that these nations are applying increasingly costly health and safety production standards, a significant proportion of manufacturing has shifted to countries without adequate health and safety standards. For instance, while up to 1970 the United States did most of its own asbestos manufacturing, since then its import of asbestos textiles has increased significantly, particularly from Mexico, Taiwan, and Brazil (Elling, 1981; Castleman, 1979).

While workers in the Third World suffer from ill health, the manufactured asbestos is profitably being exported to the markets of the advanced countries. As Castleman (1983:6) notes: "In such cases, the export of the uncontrolled or poorly controlled hazardous process nets enough savings (in fixed costs, operating costs and liabilities) to more than offset increased shipping costs."

One of the countries from which manufactured asbestos is imported to the United States is Mexico. An American-based company (Amatex) operates two asbestos textile plants in Mexico. The asbestos fibre used in these mills comes from Canada. A reporter who in March 1977 visited one of the plants (the Agua Prieta plant just across the border from Douglas, Arizona) along with an industrial health specialist gave the following account of the working conditions (Yoakum, 1977, cited in Castleman, 1979:576):

> Asbestos waste clings to the fence that encloses the brick plant and is strewn across the dirt road behind the plant where children walk to school. Inside, machinery that weaves yarn into industrial fabric is caked with asbestos waste and the floor is covered with debris. Workers in part of the factory do not wear respirators that could reduce their exposure to asbestos dust.

In September, 1977, a Texas television team visited the other Amatex plant in Ciudad Juarez and reported the following (Castleman, 1979:576):

> A worker, whose identity was concealed, said that he had not been warned that he could develop a fatal disease from breathing asbestos. He went on to describe the plant as having no dust controls in the dustiest parts, and said no provisions were taken by management to provide workers with functioning respiratory protection or a change of clothes for work. Dust levels in the plant were not monitored; in the U.S. plants, Amatex has been required since 1972 to monitor fiber levels in the workplace air at least twice a year and to make the data available to workers.

In addition to Mexico, Taiwan, South Korea, and Brazil also supply asbestos textile to the United States. Health and safety regulations to protect workers from asbestos in these countries are either not enforced, or are inadequate, or do not exist at all. For example, in Mexico there are no specific regulations to protect workers from asbestos or to control asbestos pollution of air and water. Castleman (1979:578) further notes that "there are no specific health regulations for asbestos in South Korea. Taiwan's ceiling limit of 2 milligrams per cubic meter of air

amounts to classifying asbestos as little more than a nuisance dust."

Data from asbestos plants in other Third World countries provide additional evidence of the double standard in health and safety protection. Sluis-Cremer (1970) reported a high incidence of asbestosis among South African asbestos miners. Castleman (1981), in an article entitled "Double Standards: Asbestos in India," reports on two asbestos plants — the Shree Digvijay Cement Company in Ahmedabad and Hindustan Ferodo in Bombay. Both these plants are associated with Western multinationals.

Johns-Manville, the American asbestos corporation, helped to build the Ahmedabad plant and supplied "technical know-how, designs, drawings, specifications, and planning data and with all other technical information and engineering assistance including the erection and supervision of the project" (Castleman, 1981:522). The Indian company is tied to Johns-Manville by myriad business connections. Workers were exposed to health hazards in and around the factory that would never be permitted in the West. Untreated wastes littered the areas surrounding the company.

> The road to Shree Digvijay Plant was lined on both sides by asbestos cement waste. A high wall surrounded the factory. Outside, untreated waste water emptied into a trench piled with solid asbestos waste on either side. Solid waste from the plant littered the neighbourhood where houses stand — indeed some of the houses were made from hunks of asbestos-cement pipes and scraps of corrugated asbestos-cement sheets. Children played on the wastes around their homes. (Castleman, 1981:523)

It must be noted that in the United States, of course, asbestos companies must meet stringent regulations by the U.S. Environmental Agency (EPA) in the discharge of wastes (Castleman, 1981).

Workers and the public are exposed to hazards in other respects. While is is well known that cutting and working with asbestos cement exposes people to hazardous dust, yet no such warning labels were placed on asbestos products of this plant. Castleman (1981:523) further notes:

> It is ironic that thousands of American workers have brought suit against Johns-Manville for not putting warning labels on the asbestos products it sold in the U.S. until 1964. Yet Shree Digvijay's asbestos-cement products, made from fibers that Johns-Manville sold to the company, carried no labels in 1980.

When a senior vice-president for health of Johns-Manville was shown pictures of the Indian plant he said "That is criminal," yet the 1979 annual report of the company glibly states: "Asbestos fibre enjoyed one of its best years due primarily to strength in overseas markets where most of the fibre is used in asbestos-cement construction materials" (Castleman, 1981:523).

The Bombay plant makes asbestos textiles and asbestos brake and clutch linings. Turner and Newell, a British asbestos company, owns 74 percent of Hindustan Ferodo. Based upon information provided by a well-informed local source, Castleman (1981:523) writes:

> Inside the plant, only workers in the fluffing and carding areas are issued with respirators. Here the asbestos dust is like the dust "behind a bus on a dirt road in the dry season." Workers are not told about the hazards of asbestos and often do not wear the respirators. They receive an "inconvenience allowance" for working in this section.
>
> The same source says that simple "housekeeping" measures are not employed in the plant: floors are "dry-swept," creating dust; the same lockers hold overalls and the worker's own clothes, which are thus contaminated; workers receive regular medical examinations but are not told the results. Day labourers who carry away dust that the ventilation system traps have no protection; they are covered with dust.

These two Indian asbestos plants, according to Castleman, illustrate a fundamental point; that is, that "life-saving medical and engineering technology that should be exported along with dangerous technology is often left behind. It is time for responsible members of the business world to step forward and make a commitment not to profit by such abuses" (Castleman, 1981:523).

In addition to occupational safety and health and numerous environmental regulations, the asbestos industry in advanced countries faces higher-priced, more organized, and more informed labour. Major corporations are also facing lawsuits and mounting compensation costs for past failures to protect the lives of their workers. For instance, faced with liability lawsuits by victims or their relatives, the Johns-Manville Corporation in August 1982 "filed for bankruptcy in order to avoid paying for what they called a potential multi-billion-dollar liability exposure, leaving thousands of asbestos victims out in the cold" (Berman, 1986:254). Many victims of asbestosis have died before receiving any compensation (Lueck, 1983). Faced with greater legal and production costs in the advanced countries, the international asbestos industry is expanding into the Third World, where there are increasing opportunities, particularly in asbestos-cement construction materials. Canadian asbestos-mining firms and firms from other countries are installing plants for the production of asbestos construction material (Castleman, 1983). Labour in Third World countries is weak, open to accepting low wages, and perhaps less likely to complain about working conditions or to file liability lawsuits. For example, the enormous wage differential in the textile industry is one of the reasons for the United States Capital company to locate production in Asian and other countries (Chossudovsky, 1981). Third World workers are additionally exploited by long working hours and compulsory overtime work without overtime pay. There is also a more frequent use of labour of women and children, who are generally paid low wages. The increased intensity of labour, which means an overworked labour force, has further increased the incidence of accidents and fatalities at the workplace (Navarro, 1986:105–140).

Though the asbestos industry provides one of the clearest examples of export of hazards from industrialized to the poor countries, it is by no means the only one to practise it. Numerous other industries which are required by health and safety standards and environmental regulation to implement costly methods to reduce workers' and the community's exposure to hazardous materials are also locating their production plants in the poor countries. A significant proportion of benzidine dye industries, mercury mining industries, lead- and arsenic copper-producing smelters, mineral, vinyl chloride, pesticide, textile, and microelectronic industries are either locating their production plants in the poor countries or are exporting banned products to these countries (Castleman, 1979, 1983; Castleman and Vera Vera, 1980; Laporte, 1978; Geiser, 1986; Elling, 1981).

The Seveso catastrophe in northern Italy in 1976 received worldwide attention (Laporte, 1978). The plant, owned by the Swiss-based Givaudan Corporation (a subsidiary of Hoffman-LaRoche), manufactured trichlorophenol. On July 10, 1976, this plant emitted into the atmosphere one of the most toxic substances extant, TCDD, or dioxin, which was "accidentally produced during trichlorophenol synthesis." Laporte (1978:619) gives the following description:

> On July 10, 1976, a cloud of products in the form of an aerosol emanated from a plant of the firm Icmesa north of Milan. These products, which originated from an uncontrolled chemical exothermal reaction, were deposited on a vast zone in the municipalities of Desio, Seveso, Meda, and Cesona. On July 12, rabbits, chickens, and dogs began to die, and on the 15th 4 children were admitted to hospital, as they presented serious forms of dermatitis observed in a great number of individuals, although mainly among children. On July 16, the mayor of Seveso asked the population not to eat vegetables from the gardens of this region, where industrial and residential areas are mixed. On the same day workers of Icmesa decided not to return there. Only on Sunday, July 18, that is to say 9 days after the release, the plant was officially closed, after declaration by those responsible that the toxic cloud contained 2,3,7,8-tetrachlorodibenzo-p-dioxin (TCDD or dioxin).

There have been such accidents in a number of countries since 1949. However, this was the first accident where people in the neighbourhood of the plant were exposed to TCDD and surrounding soil was contaminated. In previous cases the contamination was confined to the plant. The Seveso plant did not have a heat-control mechanism or holding tank backup, standard safety features without which excessive buildup of heat in the reactor will cause an explosion. The workers were not made aware of potential dioxin hazards. Castleman (1979:596) further notes that "it is highly doubtful that this Swiss-owned plant would have been allowed to operate in Switzerland."

An even more scandalous disaster took place in Bhopal, India, in 1984, where over 2800 people were killed, and over 200 000 injured when poisonous methyl isocyanate gas was emitted from the Union Carbide plant there.

Some hazardous products are being exported with the assistance of governmental agencies. Because of lack of hard (i.e., foreign) currency, some poor countries cannot afford to pay for the products. In some instances, the United States, through "foreign aid" programmes, has helped the multinationals to export banned products. For instance, the U.S. Agency for International Development (AID), as part of the U.S. assistance programme, exported the pesticide leptophos, known to have caused serious nerve damage among workers in Texas. It is important to note that it was not registered for use in the United States "because the manufacturers withdrew the application for registration after reports of delayed neurotoxicity became widely publicized. However, it was exported to many Third World countries" (Shaikh and Reich, 1981:740). In Egypt, during the early 1970s, leptophos was considered to have caused the death of one farm worker, poisoning of several other field workers, and numerous deaths among water buffalo. The export of this product was halted in 1976 when it was known that the health of the American workers who produced the pesticide was seriously damaged (Shaikh and Reich, 1981). Heptachlor, chlordane, and DDT are other pesticides (banned or in the process of being banned in the United States) that AID shipped to Third World countries (Milius, 1976; cited in Castleman, 1979). Since 1957, the shipment of pesticides under the AID programme has amounted to over $500 million (Curry, 1977; cited in Castleman, 1979). U.S. law allowed this export of pesticides which are banned in the States to other countries (Weir, Schapiro, and Jacobs, 1979; Norris, 1982; Eckholm and Scherr, 1978).

In 1975, the United States Agency for International Development was sued by four public interest groups for funding the export of DDT and other pesticides which had been banned in the United States. As Shaikh and Reich (1981:740) state: "That lawsuit challenged the double standards of a government's restricting the use of specific chemicals abroad, especially in the Third World." This suit did lead to some tighter restrictions on pesticide use.

Another product which received considerable attention was the export of "Tris" — flame-retardant material used to treat children's pyjamas. The United States Consumer Product Safety Commission banned the sale of Tris-treated garments in April 1977 in the United States, but in October 1977 "the Commission ruled that it had no authority to restrict the export of Tris pyjamas if they were properly labelled and marked for export" (Shaikh and Reich, 1981:740). It took the Commission another seven months, and the export to developed and underdeveloped countries of 2.4 million Tris-treated garments, to impose a ban on export.

There are other ways in which multinationals expose people in the Third World to hazardous and dangerous chemicals. Because of the awareness and concern in the advanced countries about dangers of toxic chemical wastes, the Third World countries are also increasingly becoming dumping grounds for hazardous wastes (Castleman, 1983). If people are not directly exposed to hazardous industries and dangerous production processes at work, they become victims of toxic chemical dumps.

While some corporations withhold information under the guise of protecting trade secrets, health authorities in poor countries are also sadly lacking in knowledge of dangerous chemicals. As Castleman (1983:13) observed, in one case "a government occupational health specialist had never heard of benzidine. Another found nothing wrong in a survey of an asbestos plant, and postulated that the 'Asian body is immune' to the dangers of the dust." If health "specialists" cite the immunity of Asian body, the directors of corporations refer to cultural stereotypes. The director of Hoffman-LaRoche, after the Seveso catastrophe, commented to a Swiss audience: "Everybody knows that the Italian people, and especially women, are always complaining; it is known that the Italians are extraordinarily emotional. . ." (Laporte, 1978:630).

Hazardous products and industries are being exported to the poor countries with adverse affects on the health of the populace in those countries. Yet, as Elling points out, the impact of these hazards is likely to be even more serious for workers of the underdeveloped countries. Elling (1981:219) states:

> The poorer nutritional levels of workers associated with higher rates of debilitating disease, the absence of union organisation, the lack of official awareness of, concern for, and action in relation to pollution and occupational health hazards, the newness of workers to the industrial environment, the lack of industrial health services and personnel, and still other conditions relating to the underdeveloped countries themselves are all factors leading to the hypothesis that occupational health hazards resulting from industrialisation will be at least as great and probably greater in the underdeveloped countries than has been the case in developed countries.

In summary, the evidence shows the industrial double standard by which the workers and communities in Third World countries are exposed to hazards not tolerated in the advanced countries. This double standard is manifested in a number of ways, including the export of hazardous industries, hazardous products, and toxic and dangerous wastes. The health, safety, and environment of people in the importing countries are being constantly threatened by the profit-motivated multinationals.

MULTINATIONAL PHARMACEUTICALS AND THE HEALTH OF THIRD WORLD PEOPLE

A small number of multinationals dominate the worldwide pharmaceutical industry. These multinationals are mainly based in the advanced capitalist countries — the United States, Great Britain, Germany, and Switzerland (Bodenheimer, 1984). The pharmaceutical industry is one of the most profitable in North America (Ehrenreich and Ehrenreich, 1971). Almost one quarter of the gross revenues of the pharmaceutical industry are spent on product advertising and other activities such as funding for medical literature and educational conferences. Thousands of "detail" men and women promote the products in the offices of doctors and pharmacists (Goddard, 1973; Bell and Osterman, 1983; Vance and Millington, 1986; Silverman and Lee, 1974). The capital accumulation drive leads to a perpetual quest of new profitable markets. With the saturation of the industrialized world with drugs, the Third World is a rapidly developing market for the pharmaceutical industry (Bader, 1979; Yudkin, 1980). According to one source, over 85 percent of drug patents in the Third World are held by foreign companies (Agarwal, 1978). A large proportion of the health budgets of many underdeveloped countries (from 20–30 percent up to 50 percent) is consumed by pharmaceutical expenditures, as compared to 10 percent for most of the advanced countries (Yudkin, 1980; Agarwal, 1978). Pharmaceutical expenditures are substantially higher in the primary care sectors. In the case of Ghana, Barnett et al., (1980:479) write:

> Pharmaceutical expenditure in Ghana accounts for about one-third of the total recurrent costs of the Ministry of Health, but in isolation this figure is a misleading indicator of economic importance. In the primary care sector up to

75–80 percent of the running cost of a health center may be accounted for by pharmaceuticals, and because the Ghanaian currency is heavily overvalued, even these proportions understate the true value of resources used on important drugs.

Multinationals reap huge profits from their production and sales in the Third World. When the drug multinationals set up local production plants in the Third World, they also benefit from the exploitation of cheap labour in those countries (Bodenheimer, 1984; Murray, 1974; McCraine and Murray, 1978). Additionally, multinationals charge their subsidiaries excessively high prices for drugs, thereby increasing the return on their investments. For instance, in India, foreign drug companies have usually shown the highest profits of any foreign manufacturer (Agarwal, 1978). These profits are generally transferred to the home base of the corporations (Agarwal, 1978). While the pharmaceutical industry reaps huge profits, the use of modern drugs benefits only a small urban elite. Multinationals are also engaged in promoting and dumping drugs in the Third World which either are not yet approved for sale or are banned in the developed countries. Third World countries are fighting what the Director-General of the World Health Organization (WHO) has called "drug colonialism" (Agarwal, 1978).

The inappropriate, unregulated promotion and marketing of pharmaceuticals have received a great deal of attention. Silver (1972:223) observed:

> We sell drugs, supplies and equipment abroad ... Outdated vaccines or drugs that can't be sold in the United States are still sold abroad. Items that are forbidden for sale in the United States because they are considered dangerous, poisonous, or useless are also sold abroad. The Food and Drug Administration's writ does not run in the other countries and some foreign countries where these items are sold have no equivalent control. The entrepreneur's conscience is not touched because his motto is still "caveat emptor": business must maximize profits.

As noted before, the Third World is a rapidly expanding market for the multinational pharmaceutical companies. This market is created by the activities of the drug manufacturers themselves. As Yudkin (1980:455) states, "this market has been to a large extent developed by the intense promotional activities of the drug companies themselves. In addition to normal marketing methods, these companies indulge in techniques which would be neither acceptable nor legal in developed countries." Misinformation, exaggerated claims, suppression of information on adverse reactions, and incorrect indications are all used to sell drugs in the poor countries. Based upon his work in the United States and Latin America, Silverman (1977:159) concluded:

In nearly all of the products investigated in this study, the differences in the promotional or labeling material were striking. In the United States, the listed indications for each product were usually few in number, while the contraindications, warnings, and potential adverse reactions were given in extensive detail. In Latin America, the listed indications were far more numerous, while the hazards were minimized, glossed over, or totally ignored. In some cases, only trivial side effects were described, but potentially lethal hazards were not mentioned.

Silverman (1977:157) adds:

The differences were not simply between the United States on the one hand and all the Latin American countries on the other. There were substantial differences within Latin America, with the same global company telling one story to Mexico, another in Central America, a third in Ecuador and Columbia, and yet another in Brazil.

Another work by Silverman, with Lee and Lydecker (1982), titled *Prescriptions for Death: The Drugging of the Third World*, indicates that the products which are banned or never approved in the industrialized countries are being widely promoted in the poor nations with exaggerated claims of their effectiveness, and minimal warning of the dangers of serious or lethal side effects or potential risks of the products. These practices are also documented by Yudkin (1978, 1980).

Despite much publicity about the activities of multinationals in the Third World, the marketing of inappropriate and dangerous and potentially toxic drugs continues. Many of the underdeveloped countries do not have legislative provisions to control advertising. For instance, in Tanzania, there is no legislation to "either require the listing of side-effects and contraindications of drugs or control the claims which are made on their behalf" (Yudkin, 1980:460). Drug companies in Tanzania are engaged in hazardous promotion of Aminopyrine and Dipyronen compounds. These compounds are painkillers with temperature-lowering properties, but they can also severely depress the production of white blood cells (Yudkin, 1980). In the United States these drugs are recommended for use only by patients with terminal malignant disease. However, in the 1978 edition of an American medical reference book funded by the drug industry, 34 such compounds are listed, and the stated indications included toothache and dysmenorrhea (Yudkin, 1980).

While "hormone pregnancy tests," because of the association between these drugs and fetal malformation, have been restricted elsewhere, some of these drugs were still being promoted in Tanzania in 1977 (Yudkin, 1980).

One of the most recent examples of irresponsible drug promotion in the Third World is the marketing of Cibalgin (an analgesic made in Switzerland) in Mozambique. The drug is sold over the counter and is frequently taken for headaches (Hammond, 1980). The drug may indirectly be fatal, as it reduces the victim's resistance to other infections. Cibalgin contains amidopyrine, which as far back as the 1920s was known to cause agranulocytosis, a fall in white blood cells that leaves the patient susceptible to potentially fatal secondary infections (Hammond, 1980). It may be noted that amidopyrine was placed under prescription control in the United States as early as 1938; its use was banned in Australia in 1964, and it was recently withdrawn from the market in Sweden and Britain. It is also banned in West Germany, Japan, and Switzerland (Hammond, 1980). Despite its ban in many advanced countries and its well-known risks, in Mozambique, amidopyrine was still being promoted actively by Ciba (one of Switzerland's three largest pharmaceutical firms) as late as 1979 (Hammond, 1980).

Lower promotional standards also allow the inappropriate use of drugs. For instance, the drug chloramphenicol has since the 1950s been restricted for use in a narrow range of life-threatening infections, owing to its serious side effects, such as aplastic anaemia (Shaikh and Reich, 1981). While in the United States this drug is promoted for only limited indications, most notably for typhoid fever, Silverman found that in Mexico, Ecuador, and Colombia, chloramphenicol was being promoted for such diverse ailments as tonsillitis, bronchitis, urinary-tract infections, eye infections, and yaws. Silverman (1977:159) also states:

> In the United States, physicians are warned that use of chloramphenicol may result in serious or fatal aplastic anemia and other blood dyscrasia. Physicians in Mexico are given a similar warning in the promotional material for Parke-Davis' Chloromycetin, but no warnings are listed for the same product in Central America.

Some powerful tranquillizers (Mellaril) are being promoted for a host of minor neurotic disorders not mentioned in promotional materials in the United States. These additional indications include minor behavioural disorders such as inability to adapt in school, insomnia, and nail-biting. Mellaril's adverse reactions were disclosed in the United States and a few in Mexico, but none in Central America, Colombia, or Ecuador (Silverman, 1977).

Recommended dosage of drugs is another area of abuse. For instance, the recommended dosage of Migrail (for migraine) was twice as high in Asia and Africa as in the U.S. or U.K. (Medawar, 1979). Pharmacists substitute one drug for another because they do not have the prescribed drug in stock (Silverman, 1976), and in some instances provide patients with only one day's supply of antibiotics.

In a 1977 list of essential drugs published by the World Health Organization (WHO) only

16 antibiotics were included. A study by Gustafsson and Wide (1981) revealed that in only two of eight countries were fewer than 200 varieties of antibiotic sold. About one third of these were drug combinations of questionable value. Frequently doctors were not given adequate information about the adverse drug effects. As drug compounds could be obtained without prescription, it further increased the high potential risk for misuse of antibiotics in these countries. Gustafsson and Wide (1981:32) conclude: "Thus, our review of the antibiotics marketed in Central America and Mexico shows that many irrational and possibly dangerous combinations are still available."

Yet another area of abuse is the dumping of drugs whose shelf life has expired, or of products which fail to meet the quality standards of the advanced countries (Medawar, 1979).

Yudkin (1978) found double standards in listing information by the manufacturers in the British and African versions of the Monthly Index of Medical Specialities (MIMS). Chloramphenicol was again being promoted for respiratory-tract and other minor ailments in the African version of MIMS. Some other examples of double standards are listed by Yudkin (1978:811):

> Aminopyrine and dipyrone are antipyretic analgesics which may produce agranulocytosis with a mortality as high as 0.57%. In the United States they are licensed for use only in patients with terminal malignant disease in whom safer antipyretics have been unsuccessful. In African M.I.M.S. (November, 1977), 31 preparations containing these drugs were recommended as analgesics for minor conditions. Package inserts claim they have a "wide margin of safety" (Avafortan, Asta Werke) or that "their safety has been proven and confirmed in over 500 publications throughout the world" ("Buscopan Compositum" containing dipyrone, Boehringer Ingelheim).
>
> Anabolic steroids may produce stunting of growth, irreversible virilisation in girls, and liver tumors. They are used in Britain to treat osteoporosis, renal failure, terminal malignant disease, and aplastic anaemia. In African M.I.M.S., they are promoted as treatment for malnutrition, weight loss, and kwashiorkor ("Decadurabolin", Organon), as appetite stimu-

lants ("Winstrol", Winthrop), for exhaustion states ("Primobolan Depot", Schering; "Dianabol", Ciba Geigy), and for "excessive fatiguality" in schoolchildren ("Dianavit", Ciba Geigy).

Melrose (1982) and Muller (1982) also provide evidence indicating double standards and inappropriate use of medications. For example, Muller revealed the use of diuretics to treat kwashiorkor (childhood malnutrition) and Melrose found the promotion of anabolic steroids as appetite stimulants in the poor countries.

While the U.S. label for Dipyrone products (painkillers) reads "should be restricted to use in serious or life-threatening situations," in Brazil the material reads "an indispensable supplement in the initial and continuing treatment of very varied minor ailments" (Ledogar, 1975:32–33). Ledogar names some other toxic drugs which were being sold without proper warning in other countries, after they had been banned in advanced countries. For instance, Dithiazanine Iodide was banned in the United States and France by the mid-sixties. According to Ledogar (1975:30–31) "In the areas outside the jurisdiction of the FDA, Pfizer's marketing tactics have not been interfered with in the same way. Under brand names like Netocyd and Dilbrin, the drug was being promoted in many countries of Latin America as late as 1974 as a broad-spectrum antiparasitic agent."

Pharmaceutical company representatives put enormous pressure on doctors and health administrators to sell their products. Physicians in the underdeveloped countries are pressured to prescribe unnecessary, expensive, and even dangerous and harmful drugs. Promotional expenditures of drug companies in underdeveloped countries far exceed those in developed countries. For instance, in Tanzania, there was one drug company representative for every four doctors as compared to one representative for every 20 doctors in Britain (Yudkin, 1980). Other promotional methods used to sell drugs include: gifts and drug company parties for doctors, free samples to doctors and hospital pharmacies, and gifts to the Ministry of Health and its institutions (Yudkin, 1980).

Drug company representatives encourage physicians "to use proprietary names, and are regaled with terrifying tales of the non-equivalence of generic brands" (Yudkin, 1980). Dowie (1979) reports various strategies used by companies to increase the market of drugs, such as name change, listing products "for export only," dumping the whole factory (relocation of production), and formula change.

The pharmaceuticals not only engage in unethical promotion practices, that is, exaggeration of the benefits and minimization of the dangers of drugs, but also engage in what Victora (1982) characterizes as "statistical malpractice in drug promotion." His study revealed that the drug companies in Brazil use faulty research designs, analysis, and presentation of evidence to impress upon physicians the quality of their products. Thus, doctors are influenced to prescribe drugs which may be potentially hazardous to patients' recovery and health. Inappropriate and irrational use of drugs is promoted by advertisement (Vance and Millington, 1986).

Intensive promotion activities have created extensive markets for Western drugs in the poor countries, where people in fact cannot afford to pay for expensive and mostly inappropriate and non-essential items. In Zaïre, even when the multinational drug companies did import essential drugs, these cost far more than available generic alternatives. In some cases the average difference in price between the multinational and generic products was 300 percent. In the case of iron pills, the difference was staggering: $32 versus $2.60 for 1000 iron pills (Glucksberg and Singer, 1982).

In Zaïre, three fourths of the drugs imported by multinational pharmaceutical companies consisted of expensive and non-essential items. Also, "two drug firms imported and promoted the sale of ominopyrone-dipyrone analgesic-antipyretics, drugs now rarely used in Western industrialized countries because of potentially fatal complications" (Glucksberg and Singer, 1982:381). Ninety-five percent of the drug import budget of Zaïre was spent on non-essential drugs. The importation of agranulocytosis-causing drugs exposed Zaïre's population to serious hazards.

A study of 25 health clinics and 37 local pharmacies revealed that these facilities lacked essential drugs (e.g., antiparasitic agents, as most children have serious parasitic infestations) but had abundant supplies of hazardous and expensive drugs. Over three fourths of drug supplies consisted of brand names rather than generic drugs. Glucksberg and Singer (1982:386) conclude: "Zaïrians will continue to pay exorbitant costs for nonessential and often dangerous drugs, and be denied access to safe and inexpensive agents capable of controlling endemic diseases. Thus, they will continue to pay more for the possibility of dying."

The governments of developed countries often help the multinationals to export banned products to the Third World countries. For example, after deaths of 17 women in the United States, when the intrauterine contraceptive Dalkon Shield was banned in the United States, it was sold to the U.S. Agency For International Development (AID) to be sold in developing countries (Dowie, 1979). Similarly, Depo-Provera, a highly questionable contraceptive, was sold to AID for marketing in the Third World (Ehrenreich, Dowie, and Minkin, 1979).

Even when the activities of the multinationals in the promotion of inappropriate and dangerous drugs are known, these companies continue to exploit the poor countries and expropriate the health of the populations. As Ledogar (1975:39) states: "Just as manufacturers are often quick to recommend a drug for a new indication, they can be very slow to modify or remove outdated indications from their foreign labelling and promotion." It must be noted in passing that the physicians in the advanced countries as well are not immune to the practices of the pharmaceutical industry. For instance, Bell and Osterman (1983), in a study of Compendium of Pharmaceuticals and Specialties (CPS), a reference publication widely used by physicians in Canada for drug prescribing, found that this publication exaggerated the benefits and underestimated the adverse effects of many drugs.

High on the list of profit-making products are vitamins and mineral supplements, which are being promoted in advanced as well as developing countries. People with normal diets do not need any supplement; "much of the additional vitamin intake is simply excreted through the kidneys, and accordingly America is said to have probably the most nutritious sewage in the world" (Silverman et al., 1982:74). Many of the supplements do little or no harm, except to the pocketbooks of the individuals consuming them. In the Third World the situation is different, however. As Silverman et al. (1982:75) state: "The problem for the poor people of the Third World — which means most of the people — is not a shortage of vitamins, it is a shortage of food." Multinationals are also engaged in the promotion of toxic and numerous other irrelevant and inappropriate concoctions (Silverman et al., 1982).

The health of the Third World may be endangered in other respects by pharmaceutical companies shifting their initial clinical testing of new drugs to the poor countries. Poor people both in the advanced and developing countries have served as "guinea pigs" for new products. Initial trials of birth control pills were conducted on women in Puerto Rico in 1953, and the major U.S. clinical trials involved Mexican and black women (Heller, 1977). Another example of this exploitation is a well-known study — known as the Tuskeegee trials — in which the "course of natural history" of syphilis was observed by allowing poor black men to go through the whole course of this disease without treatment (Braithwaite, 1984). It is very likely that as the risks of "human experimentation" become widely known and the availability of "defenceless" human subjects becomes increasingly difficult that initial trials will be carried out on poor and uninformed individuals in the Third World.

In summary, the Third World is a rapidly expanding market for the pharmaceutical industry. This market to a large extent is developed by the intense promotional activities of multinationals through the mass media, professional journals, physicians, and health-care institutions. Misinformation, exaggerated claims of benefits of drugs, suppression of information on adverse and lethal side effects, incorrect indications, and other unethical practices are used to increase consumption of drugs in the poor countries. Many of these practices are not permitted in the advanced countries. While multinationals reap large profits, the health of the Third World is being endangered by irrelevant, toxic, and inappropriate medications.

COMMERCIOGENIC MALNUTRITION: INFANT FORMULA

In recent years a body of literature has been growing on the operations of the multinational agribusiness, the availability of food, and nutritional levels in the Third World. Considerable attention has been focussed on the association between increased bottle-feeding and high infant mortality rates in the Third World.

Evidence indicates that since the Second World War there has been a decline in breast-feeding in many Third World countries (Elling, 1981; Bader, 1981; Jelliffe and Jelliffe, 1977; Jelliffe, 1971, 1979; Manderson, 1982). This decline is attributed to a number of factors, including the multinational agricultural and food industry's aggressive marketing of infant formula and the concomitant "occidentogenic" (derived from Western culture) influences (Elling, 1981; Bader, 1981; Latham, 1979; Garson, 1977; Jelliffe and Jelliffe, 1977). Studies dealing with this subject point out "the way in which 'modern' sexual images of uplifted breasts as well as lies about convenience, safety, and economy have been used in worldwide campaigns with complicity of hospital-based medical personnel who give free formula sample on discharge" (Elling, 1981:3).

The social and cultural attitudes regarding the body and sexual attractiveness have contributed to the decline in breast-feeding. As Bader (1981:237) writes,

> the breast has been gradually transmogrified from its nutritional role into a cosmetic and sexual symbol, and some women fear unjustifiably that breast-feeding will ruin the shape of their breasts. Nursing in public, a common sight a decade ago in most parts of the developing world, is rapidly disappearing as the modesty accompanying changes in attitude grows.

Other advertising portrays bottle-feeding as a convenience to free working mothers from the constraints of feeding. Breast-feeding is considered a "backward" custom and bottle-feeding is associated with modernity. Claims are also made that bottle-feeding is safer and healthier for babies and that breast-feeding is incompatible with mothers' shapeliness (Latham, 1979). In addition to these social and cultural factors, the export of dry milk under the "Food for Peace" and other international food programmes has also contributed to the decline in breast-feeding (Wade, 1974). These feeding programmes were ostensibly designed to alleviate malnutrition in the poor countries. But Doyal and Pennell (1979:128) state:

> Even when the poor are able to obtain imported food it may sometimes do them more harm than good. A particularly striking instance of this is the export of baby milk to the third world. This has been freely distributed as aid in underdeveloped countries, but has done more to aid the assiduous efforts of multinational companies to promote bottle feeding, than to alleviate malnutrition.

In their search for new markets and sustained corporate profitability, multinationals are the most powerful promoters of infant formula in the Third World. Rather than alleviating malnutrition, the promotion of infant formula has led to what Jelliffe calls "commerciogenic malnutrition" (Jelliffe, 1972). The decline in breast-feeding, attributed primarily to advertisement by the multinationals, and its health effects are described in some detail by Jelliffe and Jelliffe (1977:249–250):

> All major infant food firms, especially the large international concerns, have continually carried

out advertising and promotional campaigns in competition with each other in less-developed countries since World War II. Without any doubt whatsoever, they have been one of the major factors responsible for the present decline in breast-feeding in areas where bottle-feeding is neither economically nor hygienically feasible. They have therefore also been responsible in considerable measure for the present rise in such regions in the prevalence of marasmus and diarrheal disease in infants, resulting in high mortality, costly and prolonged treatment, and considerable risk of permanent brain damage.

In addition to advertisement of infant formula in the mass media, the multinationals promote bottle-feeding through so-called milk nurses and milk banks (Jelliffe and Jelliffe, 1977; Bader, 1981). Milk nurses often get access to maternity wards, even when it is against the rules, visit mothers in their homes, and offer advice and free samples to new mothers. Some studies point to the questionable practices used by milk nurses to promote their products (Ledogar, 1975; Grenier, 1975). They are expected to provide information about child care, but a Jamaican study revealed that "most mothers felt that the nurses had offered very little information unrelated to the Company's products" (Ledogar, 1975:138).

Milk banks are sales outlets in the clinics and hospitals. They are supposed to sell infant milk at reduced prices to poor parents. However, they end up as another device for expanding the practice of artificial feeding and marketing for the food companies (Ledogar, 1975).

Milk companies also carry on marketing activities through the provision of free teaching materials, posters, pamphlets, and free samples to "assist in the running of the clinic." Posters donated by the infant food industry "decorate" the walls of clinics and hospitals (Jelliffe and Jelliffe, 1977). Such free literature is notorious for misrepresentation (Grenier, 1975). The companies make misleading claims in advertising and promote infant formula as an ideal substitute for mother's milk.

The milk companies influence health institutions and health professionals by their "sponsorship" of professional activities. As Jelliffe

and Jelliffe (1977:250) state, "milk companies, as with the pharmaceutical industry, have become adept at what is to them low-cost molding of professional opinion by 'manipulation by assistance' and by 'endorsement by association'."

The promotional techniques used by the manufacturers of infant formula "are much like those of drug companies that conceal hazards, exaggerate claims, and dump dangerous drugs on other countries" (Silverman et al., 1982:117). These promotional techniques were condemned by every member of the United Nations but the United States (Silverman et al., 1982).

Aggressive marketing, Western cultural influences working through advertising techniques, marketing of infant formula through nurses and milk banks, sponsorship of professional associations, and assistance to clinics and hospitals all encourage the decline of breast-feeding and increased infant malnutrition, illness, and death. Bottle-feeding of babies in the poor countries is dangerous for a number of reasons. Maternal poverty in itself is a cause of malnutrition in those countries. Millions of children suffer from kwashiorkor and eventually die from malnutrition (Bader, 1981). In the first instance, poor people can ill afford to buy the infant formula milk. Because of this budgetary pressure there is a tendency to constitute the formula with too much water, in order to make it last longer. This, of course, reduces its nutritional value. As a consequence, the baby becomes undernourished and more susceptible to infections. Second, there is the problem of obtaining clean water with which to mix the formula. Additionally, the unsanitary living, cooking, and washing facilities and lack of refrigeration further increase the baby's chances of infections and diarrhea. Consequently, the baby is unable to absorb even diluted milk, meaning that he/she becomes even more undernourished and more susceptible to infections and eventual death.

The mother's milk, on the other hand, not only has more nutrition but provides natural immunological protection, which is crucial because of unsanitary living and environmental conditions of poor families. Bader (1981:239) emphasizes this point:

> The protection functions of human milk are, of course, of even greater importance in the developing countries, where in many cases the community is impoverished and where there are low educational levels, highly contaminated environments, and insufficient culinary equipment for the sanitary preparation and storage of food.

Numerous studies indicate infant morbidity and mortality to be higher among bottle-fed than breast-fed babies. In the Third World, millions of cases of malnutrition and infectious disease are attributed to artificial feeding (Manderson, 1982; Bader, 1981; Lappe and Collins, 1977; INFACT, no date). It is estimated that one million babies in poor nations die each year because of bottle-feeding (INFACT; Silverman et al., 1982).

In summary, in the quest for new markets and sustained corporate profitability, promotional techniques used in the Third World by the manufacturers of infant formula are much like those of the pharmaceuticals. The promotion of infant formula has led to "commerciogenic malnutrition," which has contributed to increased infant morbidity and mortality in the poor nations.

SUMMARY AND CONCLUSIONS

This chapter has explored the linkages between the corporate drive for profits and the social production of illness, drawing primarily upon the literature dealing with multinationals involved in the production of hazardous products, pharmaceutical and chemical industries, and the food industry and its promotion of infant formula. It is evident that the health, safety, and environment of people in the Third World are being constantly threatened by the profit-motivated multinationals.

The evidence presented in this chapter shows the double standards in industrial hazards and in health and safety practised by multina-

tionals in Third World countries. Workers and communities in the poor nations are being exposed to dangers which are not tolerated or are illegal in the advanced countries. These double standards are manifested in a number of ways, including export of hazardous industries, export of hazardous products, and dumping of toxic wastes. The Third World is also a rapidly expanding market for the pharmaceutical industry. Unethical and often illegal promotional activities, most of them not permitted in advanced countries, are used to increase consumption of irrelevant and inappropriate medications. The promotional techniques used by the manufacturers of infant formula are much like those of the pharmaceuticals. The decline of breast-feeding and the promotion of artificial feeding has led to "commerciogenic malnutrition," which has contributed to the increased infant morbidity and mortality in the Third World.

Living in the poor countries is in itself a liability. Material poverty, unsanitary conditions, and low nutritional levels all lower resistance to disease, contributing toward ill health and high morbidity and mortality rates. In this context, the impact of additional imported hazards is likely to be even more serious. However, the full impact of exposure to some industrial hazards may not be statistically evident. Workers may succumb to other, "natural" causes of deaths before they die of diseases with long latency periods, such as asbestosis and cancers. Every now and then the public may learn of dangerous industries when accidents occur, as in Seveso, Italy and in Bhopal, India where the death and destruction are immediately evident.

Though this chapter has primarily focussed on Third World countries, it has important implications for occupational and environmental health and safety in advanced countries. The ability of multinationals to relocate their production from the advanced to the poor countries may discourage the workers (for fear of losing their jobs) from pushing for more stringent health and safety standards at the workplace. Similarly, the communities which depend upon a single industry (company towns) may be reluctant to push for strict pollution emission and waste-disposal standards for fear of loss of industry. It is quite evident from the material presented in this chapter that rather than implementing costly health and safety standards, the multinationals will export their hazardous industries to those countries where regulations are either inadequate or non-existent. Workers, therefore, may be faced with the dilemma of employment versus health and safety.

Workers in Third World countries find themselves in an even more difficult situation, because of higher unemployment, lack of unions, and inadequate health and safety and environmental standards. So long as the multinationals can move their enterprises to areas of low production cost (and evidence presented above showed that they are being "invited" by the poor countries), they are less likely to implement those health and safety standards which would interfere with profits. Therefore, occupational health and safety and public health in the advanced countries cannot be divorced from occupational health and safety and public health in the poor countries. Because of this, health becomes a global rather than a national issue.

Even pesticides which are banned in advanced countries and are exported to the Third World indirectly affect the public health in the advanced countries. These pesticides are sprayed on crops and are "returned" to advanced countries through imported food and other products. This is dubbed the "boomerang effect."

Health is a global issue in other respects. The recent nuclear accident in Chernobyl, U.S.S.R., clearly demonstrates that such accidents have impact far beyond the borders of a particular nation. Nuclear explosion knows no particular national boundaries and nuclear fallout does not recognize national borders.

STUDY QUESTIONS

1. Outline the factors conducive to the export of hazardous industries from the developed to Third World countries.

2. Discuss the linkages between the corporate drive for profits and the social production of illness in the Third World.

3. Because of the "global reach" of the multinationals, occupational and environmental health and illness are a global rather than a national issue. Discuss this statement.

4. Discuss the adverse health effects (infant morbidity and mortality) of aggressive marketing of infant formula with particular reference to Third World countries.

5. Discuss the double standards used by multinational pharmaceutical and chemical companies, and their health effects in the Third World.

RECOMMENDED READING

Castleman, Barry I. "The Exporting of Hazardous Factories to Developing Nations." *International Journal of Health Services* 9, no. 4 (1979): 569–606.

Castleman, Barry I., and Manuel J. Vera Vera. "Impending Proliferation of Asbestos." *International Journal of Health Services* 10, no. 3 (1980): 389–403.

Chossudovsky, Michael. "Human Rights, Health, and Capital Accumulation In the Third World." In *Imperialism, Health and Medicine*, edited by Vicente Navarro, 37–52. Farmingdale, New York: Baywood Publishing Co., 1981.

Elling, Ray H. "Industrialization and Occupational Health in Underdeveloped Countries." *International Journal of Health Services* 7, no. 2 (1977): 209–35.

Silverman, M. *The Drugging of the Americas.* Berkeley, California: University of California Press, 1976.

Silverman, M., et al. *Prescription for Death: The Drugging of the Third World.* Berkeley, California: University of California Press, 1982.

Warnock, John W. *The Politics of Hunger: The Global Food System.* Toronto: Methuen, 1987.

REFERENCES

Agarwal, Anil. *Drugs and the Third World.* London: Earthscan Press, 1978.

Aidoo, Thomas Akwasi. "Rural Health Under Colonialism and Neo-Colonialism: A Survey of Ghanaian Experience." *International Journal of Health Services* 12, no. 4 (1982): 637–57.

Bader, Michael B. "Breast-Feeding: The Role of Multinational Corporations in Latin America." In *Imperialism, Health and Medicine,* edited by Vicente Navarro, 235–52. Farmingdale, New York: Baywood Publishing Co., 1981.

———. "Hustling Drugs To The Third World: Let the Buyer Beware." *The Progressive* (December, 1979): 42–46.

Barnett, Andrew, Andrew Lacey Greese, and Eddie C.K. Ayivor. "The Economics of Pharmaceutical Policy in Ghana." *International Journal of Health Services* 10, no. 3 (1980): 479–99.

Barnett, R.J., and R.E. Muller. *Global Reach: The Power of the Multinational Corporation.* New York: Simon and Schuster, 1974.

Bell, R. Warren, and John W. Osterman. "The Compendium of Pharmaceuticals and Specialties: A Critical Analysis." *International Journal of Health Services* 13, no. 1 (1983): 107–18.

Berman, Daniel M. "Asbestos and Health in the Third World: The Case of Brazil." *International Journal of Health Services* 16, no. 2 (1986): 253–63.

———. *Death on the Job.* New York: Monthly Review Press, 1978.

Bodenheimer, Thomas S. "The Transnational Pharmaceutical Industry and the Health of the World's People." In *Issues in the Political Economy of Health Care,* edited by John B. McKinlay, 187–216. New York: Tavistock Publications, 1984.

Bodenheimer, Thomas, Steven Cummings, and Elizabeth Harding. "Capitalizing on Illness: The Health Insurance Industry." In *Health and Medical Care in the U.S.: A Critical Analysis,* edited by Vicente Navarro, 61–68. Farmingdale, New York: Baywood Publishing Co., 1977.

Braithwaite, John. *Corporate Crime in the Pharmaceutical Industry.* London: Routledge and Kegan Paul, 1984.

Brandt, Allan M. "Polio, Politics, Publicity, and Duplicity: Ethical Aspects in the Development of Salk Vaccine." *International Journal of Health Services* 8, no. 2 (1978): 257–70.

Bryant, J. *Health and the Developing World.* Ithaca, New York: Cornell University Press, 1969.

Butler, J., D. Giovannetti, M. Hainer, and H. Shapiro. "Dying For Work: Occupational Health and Asbestos." *NACLA Report on the Americas* 12 (1978): 1039.

———. "International Hazards: You Can Run But You Can't Hide." *NACLA Report on the Americas* 12 (March–April 1978): 20–30.

Canada: Lean Now, But Future Bright. *Asbestos* 62 (1981): 12–13.

Castleman, Barry I. "The Double Standards in Industrial Hazards." *International Journal of Health Services* 13, no. 2 (1983): 5–14.

————. *Asbestos: Medico-Legal Aspects.* New York: Harcourt Brace Jovanovich, 1985.

————. *Asbestos: Medical and Legal Aspects.* New York: Law and Business, 1984.

————. "Double Standards: Asbestos In India." *New Scientist* (February 26, 1981): 522–23.

————. "The Export of Hazardous Factories to Developing Nations." *International Journal of Health Services* 9, no. 4 (1979): 569–606.

————. "The Export of Hazardous Substance." *International Journal of Health Services* 9, no. 4 (1979).

Castleman, B.I., R. Madan, and R. Mayes. "Export of Industrial Hazards to India." *Economic and Political Weekly*, Bombay, 13 June 1981, 1058–59.

Castleman, B.I., and M.J. Vera Vera. "Impending Proliferation of Asbestos." *International Journal of Health Services* 10, no. 3 (1980): 389–403; also in *Health and Work Under Capitalism: An International Perspective*, edited by Vicente Navarro and D.M. Berman, 123–37. Farmingdale, New York: Baywood Publishing Co., 1983.

Chossudovsky, Michael. "Human Rights, Health and Capital Accumulation in the Third World." In *Imperialism, Health and Medicine*, edited by Vicente Navarro, 37–52. Farmingdale, New York: Baywood Publishing Co., 1981.

Cleaver, H.M. "The Contradictions of the Green Revolution." *Monthly Review* 24, no. 2 (1972): 80–111.

Curry, B. "U.S. is Changing Emphasis in Aid To Developing Nations for Pesticides." *Washington Post*, 14 May 1977, (cited in Castleman, 1979).

Dixon, Marlene, and Thomas Bodenheimer, ed. *Health Care in Crisis.* San Francisco: Synthesis Publications, 1980.

Dowie, Mark. "The Corporate Crime of the Century." *Mother Jones*, November 1979, 23–49.

Doyal, Lesley, and Imogen Pennell. *The Political Economy of Health.* London: Pluto Press, 1979.

"Drug Use In The Third World." *Lancet* (December 6 1980): 1231–32.

Eckholm, E., and S.J. Scherr. "Double Standards and The Pesticide Trade." *New Scientist* 16 (February 1978).

Ehrenreich, B., and J. Ehrenreich. *The American Health Empire: Power, Profits and Politics.* New York: Random House, 1971.

Ehrenreich, Barbara, Mark Dowie, and Stephen Minkin. "The Charge: Gynocide." *Mother Jones* 4 (1979): 25–37.

Elling, Ray H. "The Capitalist World-System and International Health." *International Journal of Health Services* 11, no. 1 (1981): 21–51.

————. "Industrialization and Occupational Health in Underdeveloped Countries." *International Journal of Health Services* 7, no. 2 (1977): 209–35.

Garson, B. "The Bottle Baby Scandal: Milking The Third World For All It's Worth." *Mother Jones* 2, no. 10 (1977).

Geiser, Kenneth. "Health Hazards in the Microelectronics Industry." *International Journal of Health Services* 16, no. 1 (1986): 105–20.

Glucksberg, Harold, and Jack Singer. "The Multinational Drug Companies in Zaïre: Their Adverse Effect on Cost and Availability of Essential Drugs." *International Journal of Health* 12, no. 3 (1982): 381–87.

Goddard, J.L. "The Medical Business." *Scientific American* 229, no. 9 (1973): 161–66.

Grenier, T. *The Promotion of Bottle Feeding by Multinational Corporations: How Advertising and the Health Professionals have Contributed.* International Nutrition Monograph Series. No. 2. Ithaca, New York: Cornell University, 1975.

Gustafsson, Lars L., and Katarina Wide. "Marketing of Obsolete Antibiotics in Central America." *Lancet* (January 3 1981): 31–33.

Hammond, Karl. "Third World Still Hooked On Western Drugs." *New Scientist* 13 (March 1980): 811.

Hassan, A., et al. "Mercury Poisoning In Nicaragua: A Case Study of the Export of Environmental and Occupational Health Hazards by a Multinational Corporation." *International Journal of Health Services* 11, no. 2 (1981): 221–26.

Heller, T. *Poor Health, Rich Profits: Multinational Drug Companies and the Third World.* London: Spokesman Books, 1977.

Hosenball, Mark. "Karl Marx and the Pajama Game." *Mother Jones* 4 (1979): 47.

Hudecki, Stanley. "Infant Formula Distribution in Third World Needs Greater Consideration." *West Hamilton Journal*, 22 April 1981: 7.

Hughes, R., and R. Brewin. *The Tranquilizing of America.* New York: Harcourt Brace Jovanovich, 1978.

Infant Formula Action Coalition. (INFACT), (no date): 1–8.

Jelliffe, Derrick B. "Commerciogenic Malnutrition." *Food Technology* 25 (1971): 55–56.

———. "Commerciogenic Malnutrition." *Nutrition Review* 30, no. 9 (1972): 199–205.

———. "Commerciogenic Malnutrition? Time for Dialogue." *Food Technology* 25, no. 153 (1979): 55–56.

Jelliffe, D.B., and E.F.P. Jelliffe. "Human Milk, Nutrition, and the World Resource Crisis." *Science* 188, (1975): 557–61.

———. "The Infant Food Industry and International Child Health." *International Journal of Health Services* 7, no. 2 (1977): 249–54.

Klass, A. *There's Gold in Them Thar Pills.* Middlesex, England: Penguin, 1975.

Lall, Sanjaya. "The International Pharmaceutical Industry and Less Developed Countries, With Special Reference To India." *Oxford Bulletin of Economics and Statistics* 36, no. 3 (1975): 143–72.

———. *Major Issues in Transfer of Technology to Developing Countries: A Case Study of the Pharmaceutical Industry.* Geneva: U.N. Conference On Trade and Development, 1975.

———. "Medicines and Multinationals: Problems in the Transfer of Pharmaceutical Technology to the Third World." *Monthly Review* 28, no. 10 (1977): 19–30.

Lall, Sanjaya, and Senaka Bibile. "The Political Economy of Controlling Transnationals: The Pharmaceutical Industry in Sri Lanka, 1972–76." In *Imperialism, Health and Medicine*, edited by Vicente Navarro, 253–82. Farmingdale, New York: Baywood Publishing Co., 1981.

Lang, R.W. *The Politics of Drugs: A Comparative Study of the British and Canadian Pharmaceutical Industries, 1930–70.* London: Saxon House, 1974.

Laporte, Joan-Ramon. "Multinationals and Health Reflections on the Seveso Catastrophe." *International Journal of Health Services* 8, no. 4 (1978): 619–32.

Lappe, Frances, and Joseph Collins. *Food First.* Boston: Houghton Mifflin, 1977.

Latham, M.C. "International Perspective On Weaning Foods: The Economic and Other Implications of Bottle Feeding and the Use of Manufactured Weaning Foods." In *Breastfeeding and Food Policy in a Hungry World*, edited by D. Raphael, 119–27. New York: Academic Press, 1979.

Ledogar, Robert J. *Hungry For Profits: The U.S. Food and Drug Multinationals.* New York: IDOC/North America, 1975.

Leng, Chee Heng. "Health Status and the Development of Health Services in a Colonial State: The Case of British Malaya." *International Journal of Health Services* 12, no. 3 (1982): 397–417.

Lueck, T.J. "Manville Thriving in Bankruptcy, Shielded from Asbestos Law Suits." *New York Times* 25 October 1983.

Manderson, Lenore. "Bottle Feeding and Ideology in Colonial Malaya: The Production of Change." *International Journal of Health Services* 12, no. 4 (1982): 597–616.

McCraine, Ned, and Martin J. Murray. "The Pharmaceutical Industry: A Further Study in Corporate Power." *International Journal of Health Services* 8, no. 4 (1978): 573–88.

Medawar, C. *Insult or Injury? An Enquiry into the Marketing and Advertising of British Food and Drug Products in the Third World.* London: Social Audit Ltd., 1979.

Melrose, Dianna. *Bitter Pills: Medicine and the Third World Poor.* Oxford: Oxfam, 1982.

Milius, P. Various articles, *Washington Post* 1,2,3,4,8,9,14,26 December 1976. (cited in Castleman, 1979).

Mintz, Morton. "The Dump That Killed Twenty Thousand." *Mother Jones* 4, (1979a): 43–44.

———. "If There are No Side Effects, This Must be Honduras." *Mother Jones* 4, (1979b): 32–33.

Muller, Mike. *The Health of Nations.* London: Faber and Faber, 1982.

———. "Selling Health or Buying Favour." *New Scientist* 3 (February 1977): 266–68.

Murray, Martin J. "The Pharmaceutical Industry: A Study in Corporate Power." *International Journal of Health Services* 4, no. 4 (1974): 625–40.

Murray, Robin. "The Internationalization of Capital and the Nations State." *New Left Review* 67 (1971).

Myers, Johnny. "The Social Context of Occupational Disease: Asbestos and South Africa." *International Journal of Health Services* 11, no. 2 (1981).

Navarro, Vicente. *Crisis, Health, and Medicine.* New York: Tavistock Publications, 1986.

Nicolson, W. J., G. Perkel, and I. J. Selikoff. "Occupational Exposure to Asbestos: Population At Risk and Projected Mortality — 1980–2030." *American Journal of Industrial Medicine* (1982): 259–311.

Norris, R. *Pills, Pesticides and Profits: The International Trade in Toxic Substances.* New York: North River Press, 1982.

"Old Deceptions, New Strategies: Nestlé Tries to Beat Back Boycott." *Dollars and Sense* 67 (May-June 1981): 12–14.

Selikoff, I.J., and D.H.K. Lee. *Asbestos and Disease.* New York: Academic Press, 1978.

Selikoff, I.J., E.C. Hammond, and H. Seidman. "Mortality Experience of Insulation Workers in the United States and Canada." *Annals of the New York Academic of Science* 330, (1979): 91–116.

Selikoff, I.J., J. Churg, and E.C. Hammond. "Asbestos Exposure and Neoplasia." *Journal of the American Medical Association* (1964): 22–26.

Shaikh, Rashid, and Michael R. Reich. "Haphazard Policy on Hazardous Exports." *Lancet* (October 3, 1981): 740–42.

Silver, G.A. "Lessons From Abroad: Comparison in Health Policies." In *The Politics of Health*, edited by D.Carter and P.R. Lee. New York: Medcom Press, 1972.

Silverman, Milton. *The Drugging of the Americas.* Berkeley: University of California Press, 1976.

———. "The Epidemiology of Drug Promotion." *International Journal of Health Services* 7, no. 2 (1977): 157–66.

Silverman, Milton, Philip R. Lee, and Mia Lydecker. "Drug Promotion: The Third World Revisited." *International Journal of Health Services* 16 no. 4 (1986): 659–67.

———. *Prescriptions For Death: The Drugging of the Third World.* Berkeley: University of California Press, 1982.

Silverman, Milton, and P.R. Lee. *Pills, Profits and Politics.* Berkeley: University of California Press, 1974.

Sluis-Cremer, G.K. "Asbestos in South African Asbestos Miners." *Environment Research* 3 (November 1970): 310–19.

Tataryn, L. *Dying For a Living.* Toronto: Deneau and Greenberg, 1979.

Vance, Michael A., and William R. Millington. "Principles of Irrational Drug Therapy." *International Journal of Health Services* 16, no. 3 (1986): 355–61.

Victora, Cesar G. "Statistical Malpractice In Drug Promotion: A Case Study From Brazil." *Social Science and Medicine* 16 (1982): 707–9.

Wade, N. "Bottle Feeding: Adverse Effects of Western Technology." *Science* 184 (1974): 45–48.

Wall Street Journal. 8 April 1980: 1.

Waitzkin, Howard. *The Second Sickness.* New York: Free Press, 1983.

Warnock, John W. *The Politics of Hunger: The Global Food System.* Toronto: Methuen, 1987.

Weir, David, Mark Schapiro, and Terry Jacobs. "The Boomerang Crime: It Comes Home in Your Coffee, Your Bananas . . ." Mother Jones 4 (1979):40–48.

Yoakum, G. "Workers Inhale Deadly Asbestos." *Arizona Daily Star*, 27 March 1977.

———. "Asbestos Pressure Dwindles." *Arizona Daily Star*, 30 May 1977.

Yudkin, John S. "The Economics of Pharmaceutical Supply in Tanzania." *International Journal of Health Services* 10, no. 3 (1980): 455–77.

———. "Wider World: Provision of Medicines In a Developing Country." *Lancet*, (April 15, 1978): 810–12.

30

PROFITS FIRST:
The Pharamceutical
Industry in Canada

Joel Lexchin, M.D.
Toronto

INTRODUCTION

The pharmaceutical industry is no different from any other enterprise in a capitalist economy; its primary motivation is profit. Although the *Principles and Code of Marketing Practice* of the Pharmaceutical Manufacturers' Association of Canada[1] states that "the calling of a pharmaceutical manufacturer is one dedicated to a most important public service, and such public service shall be the first and ruling consideration in all dealings" (1972:3), the practical ethics of the industry can be summed up by a quote from W.M. Garton, president of PMAC: "The pharmaceutical industry has never claimed to be motivated by altruism, but rather by profit for survival" (1980).

The incompatibility between public service and private interests becomes evident when the stated ethics of the industry clash with the realities of turning a profit. In 1975, medical reports began appearing which warned that sudden withdrawing of a drug called propranolol, marketed by Ayerst Laboratories as Inderal and used for treating high blood pressure and angina (heart pain), could lead to heart attacks in some cases. Warnings to that effect were appearing in advertisements in American medical journals, but not in Canadian ones.[2] When asked about this discrepancy by a reporter for the *Globe and Mail*, a representative of Ayerst said: "This is of no concern to the consuming public . . . We're getting into more complex drugs. We can't inform the public on them all" (Bell, 1975:F5). At that time Inderal was the twelfth most frequently prescribed drug in Canada.

Another, more recent, example of how drug companies put profit above health involved Eli Lilly's anti-arthritis drug benoxaprofen. In 1980, this drug was marketed in Britain under the trade name Opren.[3] Lilly organized an aggressive promotional programme for Opren and very quickly the drug was enjoying large sales. However, shortly after the drug appeared on the shelves of chemists' shops, Lilly's British subsidiary informed British health officials of the first of eight deaths resulting from suspected adverse reaction to Opren that occurred between May 1, 1981, and January 1982. In February 1982, nine months after the first known British death, benoxaprofen was evaluated by the Canadian Health Protection Branch as safe for use in Canada.[4] Presumably, Lilly was hoping that benoxaprofen would sell as well in Canada as it did in Britain. In its submission to the HPB, Lilly did not mention the eight deaths in Britain connected to benoxaprofen. Other omissions from Lilly's initial documentation included suspected adverse drug reaction reports compiled in 1981 by U.S. doctors participating in Lilly-sponsored tests with benoxaprofen, and the results of a Lilly-sponsored study, presented in Paris in June 1981, showing that dosages of benoxaprofen had to be modified for elderly patients. Lilly officials did not provide the HPB with any of this critical information about their product until just before reports of the deaths in Britain were going to appear in the *British Medical Journal*.

FOREIGN DOMINATION

According to the Report of the Commission of Inquiry on the Pharmaceutical Industry (*Eastman Report*) there were 131 pharmaceutical companies operating in Canada at the end of 1982 (1985:40). Although 60 percent of all these enterprises were Canadian-owned, domestically controlled firms accounted for less than 16 percent of the value of factory shipments valued by the *Eastman Report* at over $1.4 billion in 1982 (1985:42). This foreign domination of the Canadian industry is further illustrated by examining the makeup of the top 45 companies operating in this country. Only four of these companies were Canadian-owned and the largest of these, Novopharm, ranked just twenty-second in terms of sales.[5]

The Canadian pharmaceutical industry is one of the most foreign-dominated in the world. According to a chart in the *Eastman Report* (1985:248) domestic firms were expected to supply a greater percent of the market in 1985 in countries like Argentina, Iran, the Philippines, and Spain than they were in Canada. Out of the 25 countries listed, Canada ranked twenty-first in terms of domestic control of the market. This

high degree of foreign control, as we will see in the next section, allows the multinationals to manipulate their profit levels in Canada. It also has serious consequences for pharmaceutical manufacturing in this country. Information from the Bureau of Policy Co-ordination, a section of the Department of Consumer and Corporate Affairs, shows that between 1967 and 1981 Canada's contribution to the world output of pharmaceuticals fell from 2.6 to 1.6 percent (1982:5). Pharmaceutical manufacturing in Canada has always been minimal. Even in the late 1960s, 85 percent of manufacturing was confined to the conversion of imported material into final-dosage form. The reason why manufacturing has declined even further is that the multinationals are finding that they can generate greater profits by consolidating production in other countries. An analysis of import and export figures confirms that the multinationals are centralizing their production. Between 1968 and 1977, the country which had the largest relative gain in exports to Canada was Puerto Rico. The rise in imports from Puerto Rico was the result of U.S. companies moving their manufacturing operations there to take advantage of tax concessions. Gordon and Fowler have found that "for Canada, importing fine chemicals had been the rule, but what took place during the seventies was the massive transfer abroad of the secondary stages of drug manufacture, including the production of the end product" (1981:50).

The ability of Canadian branch plants to export drugs is also circumscribed by foreign control. With the patents on most drugs foreign-owned,[6] subsidiary companies of the parent patentees control the market within their own jurisdictions. Export has to be limited to those areas of the world where patents are not taken out, areas, in other words, that are commercially insignificant. Having a successful Canadian operation takes second place to achieving an optimal overall international performance. This situation leads to the finding by the Department of Industry, Trade, and Commerce that Canadian subsidiaries are usually "not encouraged or permitted by the head office to assume responsibility for exports of their products" (1980:5).

A study by Burstall, Dunning, and Lake for the Organisation for Economic Co-operation and Development has concluded that in countries where the industry is dominated by foreign multinational companies, the prospects of developing a viable indigenous pharmaceutical sector, actively engaged in international operations, are very limited (1981:100).

Research and development in Canada are also severely constrained because of foreign domination. The Department of Industry, Trade, and Commerce found that pharmaceutical research carried out in Canada is only about 40 percent of that which could be expected based on Canada's share of the world market for drugs (1980:18). A survey of 55 of the largest pharmaceutical companies in Canada discussed in the *Eastman Report* found that only five of these firms did any substantial amount of research (1985:422). The reason for the lack of research in Canada is simple: multinationals concentrate their research facilities almost exclusively in their home countries. Taylor quotes Donald Davies, chairman of Ayerst McKenna and Harrison: "Virtually all companies do most of their research in their home country . . . German companies do the bulk of their research in Germany, and French companies do their work in France. That's just the way it is" (1983:B1). The OECD study by Burstall et al. (1981:213) and the *Eastman Report* (1985:423) both confirmed the truth of Davies' statement.

PROFITS IN THE PHARMACEUTICAL INDUSTRY

The Canadian subsidiaries of multinational drug companies, and the industry in general, have been extremely profitable. A 1983 report by the investment firm of Walwyn Stodgell Cochrane Murray Ltd. of Toronto called the pharmaceutical industry "a particularly attractive area for long-term investment. The field is characterized by high profitability and consistent growth. Favorable demographics assure that this growth will continue well into the foreseeable future" (1983:142). An examination of Table 1 will show the accuracy of this statement.

Over the thirteen-year period 1970–1982, pharmaceutical firms were over 90 percent more profitable than manufacturing companies in general. The *Eastman Report* concluded that profit levels in Canada were generally higher than in most other well-developed countries in the world (1985:277).

As robust as these profits seem, it is quite likely that they are an underestimate of the industry's true profit picture. The 1964 Report of the Royal Commission on Health Services said that "the earnings of the Canadian drug industry are not a satisfactory test of the overall pricing policies of the industry because they are understated" (1964:679). This statement recognizes that multinational firms tend to charge the most advantageous "cost" of raw materials supplied by their plants in other countries, so as to have lower profits in high-tax countries than in low-tax countries. Gordon and Fowler provide evidence to back up this contention (1981:46, 72, 73). They concluded that the terms under which resale products (finished products that are imported into Canada for sale), raw materials, and business services were transferred from foreign parents to Canadian subsidiaries were designed to transfer profits out of the Canadian subsidiaries. In 1976, the cost to Canadian subsidiaries for resale products was 73.4 percent of sales. This figure, which is more than twice the production cost in the United States on these products, provides the parent companies with substantial profits.[7]

In 1980, the Department of National Revenue launched an industry-wide audit of the international transactions of the pharmaceutical industry. The results of this audit were cited in a study by the Department of Consumer and Corporate Affairs. A sampling of 14 major drugs in Canada, covering the period 1977 to 1979,

Table 1. Rate of Return on Capital Employed, Before Taxes, 1970–1982

Year	Pharmaceutical Manufacturing (%)	All Manufacturing (%)	Rank of pharmaceutical industry out of 87 manufacturing industries
1970	20.9	8.2	3
1971	23.8	9.5	2
1972	23.8	10.8	3
1973	22.3	15.2	11
1974	25.0	17.3	8
1975	22.6	13.4	10
1976	19.4	11.7	13
1977	18.7	10.8	13
1978	20.4	12.8	12
1979	24.9	16.2	10
1980	27.1	14.7	4
1981	27.8	11.9	1
1982 (prelim)	26.1	3.3	2
Average	23.3	12.0	7

Source: Statistics Canada. *Corporate Financial Statistics — Detailed Income and Retained Earnings Statistics for 182 Industries.* Ottawa: various years.

revealed that prices charged by one subsidiary to another subsidiary of the same company were more than triple the prices paid for the same drugs when the transaction was between two independent companies (1983:16). Findings of this sort led a representative of the department to comment in the *Globe and Mail* that "profits were not being reported in Canada but somewhere else" (Westell, 1980:B1). Leslie Dan, president of Novopharm, believed that because of the government audit, $20 to $25 million in additional tax reassessments were filed and promptly paid by several companies in order to avoid court action (1982:64–5).

Looking at the figures in Table 1 and considering all the evidence just presented suggesting that these figures are an understatement of the industry's true profits, it would seem difficult to deny that there are huge sums to be derived from manufacturing pharmaceuticals. But the Pharmaceutical Manufacturers' Association of Canada repeatedly claims that the high profits

are an accounting illusion created by the standard accounting practice of treating research and development expenditures as expenses against current income rather than capitalizing these outlays as an investment item (1975:18). However, as Gary Gereffi, professor of sociology at Duke University, makes clear, the accounting explanation of high profitability is inadequate for several reasons (1983:192). First, the accounting bias is not just confined to the pharmaceutical industry but is present in all "discovery-intensive" industries such as oil and gas and in industries with high levels of research and development expenditures. Under certain circumstances the accounting rate of return could actually underestimate rather than overestimate the "real" or economic rate of return. Second, as we have just seen, under any method of calculating profitability, the declared profits of the industry in Canada are likely to be artificially depressed. Finally, by allowing pharmaceutical companies to treat research and development costs as a current accounting expense, the government is, in effect, granting them an indirect fiscal subsidy to encourage their risk-taking efforts. This accounting method thus serves to raise the drug firm's profitability in fact as well as on paper. Temin showed that even after "correcting" profits by treating research and development expenditures as an investment, the drug industry was still one of the most profitable of any around (1979:445).

The other major argument that the pharmaceutical companies use to counter charges of excessive profits is to maintain that these profits are necessary because theirs is an inherently high-risk industry. A fairly typical example of this type of defence comes from an early president of the PMAC, Dr. W.W. Wigle: "And it's risky. Almost 200,000 substances are investigated each year, but only one in every 7,000 compounds yields a usable drug — after seven years' research and an investment of $700,000"[8] (1969:441–2).

Dr. Dale Console, a former medical director of the multinational company Squibb, testified before a United States Senate Subcommittee about the true risks involved in researching and marketing drugs: "They [the drug firms] stress that there are many failures for each successful drug. This is true since it is the very essence of research. The problem arises out of the fact that they market so many of their failures" (1960:10372–3).

In a study by Orr, 71 Canadian manufacturing industries were ranked on the basis of risk. The drug industry ranked sixty-seventh, showing itself to be almost the lowest-risk industry in Canada (1974:39–49). The Special House of Commons Committee on the price of drugs concluded:

> [A] review of the evidence before this Committee seems to indicate that, in comparison to manufacturing in general, the effects of losses on the pharmaceutical firms as a group does not indicate the presence of greater risk. In fact . . . the pharmaceutical industry in Canada has been increasingly less risky as compared with manufacturing in general. (1967a:71)

COMPETITION IN THE PHARMACEUTICAL INDUSTRY

One of the major reasons that the pharmaceutical industry has been able to sustain such high profit levels is the absence of price competition for most products. Figures in the *Eastman Report* show that, on average, when there is more than one firm selling a drug that the ensuing competition results in a halving of the cost of the drug.[9] Looking at Table 2, which examines the effects of competition in Ontario and Manitoba, we see that the greater the number of companies making a drug, the greater the price differential between the lowest- and the highest-priced versions of that drug.

However, for most drugs on the Canadian market, there is no competition. Of 1474 drug preparations[10] listed in the 1985 *Ontario Drug Benefit Formulary*, only 376 were available from more than one manufacturer.

In the place of price competition, the industry has given us product competition. In product competition, drugs are promoted not on the basis of costing less than other, equivalent products, but on the grounds that they are superior to them in their action, whether or not that is in fact the case. Companies identify successful drugs sold by their competitors, then expend large quantities of money in an attempt to invent comparable alternative drugs, circumventing existing patented formulas and securing their own product for which they too can obtain a patent.

Product competition is a formidable entry barrier into therapeutic classes,[11] especially for small companies. In order to develop a new patentable product, a company must be able to expend substantial capital, initially on research, and later, on marketing; smaller companies, lacking the necessary funding for this, are therefore denied entry into the market. The formidability of the entry barrier into the pharmaceutical manufacturing industry was illustrated in Orr's 1974 study of 71 Canadian manufacturing industries. The entry barrier was measured against the

Table 2. Effect of Competition on Drug Prices

ONTARIO 1985								
No. of suppliers of drug	2	3	4	5	6	7	8	10
Price of least expensive brand as a percent of most expensive brand	81.3	71.6	60.4	55.2	42.3	26.1	36.3	27.5

Source: Calculated from: *Ontario Drug Benefit Formulary*, January 1985.

MANITOBA 1985					
No. of suppliers of drug	2	3	4	5	6
Price of least expensive brand as a percent of most expensive brand	73.5	49.2	48.0	29.4	17.4

Source: Calculated from: *Manitoba Drug Standards and Therapeutics Formulary*, January 1985.

following five characteristics: empirically observed ability to meet capital requirements, intensity of advertising, intensity of research and development, risk, and level of concentration within the industry. Of the 71 industries, the pharmaceutical industry had the twelfth-highest entry barrier (1974).

The net result has been a high level of concentration within therapeutic classes. Among the large firms, a pattern of specialization has emerged that tends to break companies into smaller, rather exclusive groups. Each group shares a therapeutic class such as antibiotics or steroids. The PMAC tries to draw attention away from this type of concentration by talking about overall industry concentration statistics.

The top four drug manufacturers, all foreign-controlled, accounted for less than 25 percent of total pharmaceutical industry shipments in 1982. A PMAC-sponsored study by J.J. Friedman & Associates weighed this figure against the comparable figure of 50 percent for all Canadian manufacturing industries and proclaimed that "drug manufacturing is relatively unconcentrated" (1981:60–61). However, these statistics ignore the relatively high degree of concentration in therapeutic classes. The *Eastman Report* listed sales in 14 therapeutic classes in 1984. In 11 of these 14, four companies accounted for over 50 percent of sales[12] (1985:131).

RESEARCH IN THE PHARMACEUTICAL INDUSTRY

The multinational pharmaceutical companies are also able to maintain high profit levels by directing their research efforts towards certain targets. In an article in the *New England Journal of Medicine*, Van Woert stated that a representative of the United States Pharmaceutical Manufacturers' Association confirmed that, in general, drug companies do not undertake research on relatively uncommon diseases, because drugs to treat them would generate insufficient profits (1978:904). The same idea was echoed in 1980 by Joseph Williams, president of Warner Lambert, who was quoted by Gray as saying that "Our [that is, Warner Lambert's] focus is to develop major drugs for major markets" (1981:791).

Pharmaceutical companies rarely do research on drugs which do not have the potential to generate large sales and ultimately large profits. One of the major factors that go into determining the profit potential of a drug is whether or not it is patentable. If a drug can be patented, then the company has a monopoly on its sales until the patent expires — 20 years in major markets like the United Kingdom, the United States, and West Germany.[13] One example of how patentability affected the development of useful drugs is in the pharmaceutical development of lithium, a medication that may be very beneficial in the treatment of manic-depressive disorders. Reports of lithium's effectiveness began appearing as long ago as 1949. However, lithium, a naturally occurring element, cannot be patented. Gershon and Shopsin reported that only when it was found that lithium could be compounded into a patentable slow-release form did the drug companies start researching and manufacturing it (1973).

In testimony before the Special House of Commons Committee, the province of Alberta severely criticized the effect of patents on applied research:

> Hence patents have not only induced a distortion between basic and applied research, but in making the latter budgets relatively too large have induced wasteful duplication of effort and the misdirection of effort toward rivalry-oriented molecular manipulation. (1967b:2444)

In an industry where product, not price, competition is the chief form of rivalry, it is essential to keep churning out new products. Pierre Garai, an advertising executive and a staunch supporter of the pharmaceutical industry and the free enterprise system in general, recognized this reality.

> No manufacturer of drugs can afford to restrict his production to genuinely significant pharmaceutical innovations. There simply aren't enough of these around in any given fiscal year or, for that matter, any dozen fiscal years. It should therefore surprise no one that we find slight modifications of existing products marketed by the bushel, a veritable blizzard of parity products slugging it out as each company strives to extend its share of the market, endless polypharmaceutical combinations of dubious merit, and a steady outpouring of new chemical entities whose advantages, to say the least, remain to be established. (1964:194)

Garai was writing over 20 years ago but the situation is scarcely any different today. According to figures in the *Eastman Report*, at the end of 1982 there were 922 new molecular entities being investigated in the United States for their potential medicinal use. Of these only 23, or 2.5 percent, were deemed to have significant therapeutic value and 802, or 87 percent, were assessed as offering little or no therapeutic value (1985:242).

In more concrete and specific terms we can look at the plethora of anti-inflammatory (anti-arthritis) and benzodiazepine (minor tranquillizer) drugs currently available in Canada. There are 11 arthritis medications on the market and 14 benzodiazepines. For a minority of patients this kind of choice is beneficial because for them only one particular anti-inflammatory or only one particular minor tranquillizer will work; but in the vast majority of cases, there is no clinical difference among any of the anti-inflammatories or benzodiazepines. The reason that the Canadian market is flooded with these products, with new ones continually being introduced, is simply that they are drugs with huge markets. In 1982, there were six anti-inflammatories among the 25 top-selling drugs in the country; this class of drugs generated just under $100 million in sales. As the population ages, the market for these products will continue to grow. In that same year there were almost 10 million prescriptions[14] written for benzodiazepines, and according to Dr. Una Busto of the Ontario Addiction Research Foundation, the use of these drugs is also growing (1986:184).

In terms of research it is clear that the pharmaceutical industry puts its money where it is likely to generate more money, and not necessarily where the health need is.

THE PHARMACEUTICAL INDUSTRY AND THE MEDICAL PROFESSION

Doctors, through their associations and their journals, are all prime objects of attention for the drug companies. Doctors are the ones who prescribe medicaments, and it is their prescriptions that translate into sales and profits for the pharmaceutical houses. It is not surprising, then, that the companies actively seek to influence medical students early in their careers. Martin Shapiro went to medical school at McGill in the early 1970s and wrote about his experiences in *Getting Doctored* (1978). At the end of the first year, Eli Lilly offered students a stethoscope, reflex hammer, tuning fork, and doctor's bag, all free of charge. Pekkanen quotes Dr. Harold Upjohn, the vice-president of Upjohn, on why companies are so willing to bestow gifts upon medical students: "You know why they give them. No question about it. They want doctors to be interested in prescribing their brands" (1976:15). Drug companies also use "giveaways" to influence interns and residents training in hospitals. Between 1970 and 1974, Hoffman LaRoche gave away to Canadian hospitals 174 million units of its tranquillizer Valium, worth an estimated $5 million at market price. One reason for Roche's uncommon act of apparent generosity was to head off competition from Horner's Vivol.[15] But Roche was also particularly anxious to get its products into hospital pharmacies with a view to influence the prescribing habits of the physicians in their private practice.

The systematic bestowal of gifts does not cease once young doctors embark on their practices. There are always rulers, paperweights, notepads, paintings, photographs, books, and a variety of trinkets available to doctors, free for the asking. Drug companies pay handsomely for the right to set up booths at medical conferences. Their fees provide a considerable chunk of the financing for these meetings, thus keeping down the cost to the individual doctor.

Dr. Philip Berer described the bazaar-like atmosphere at one conference of family physicians he attended in October 1983 (1983:6). The doctors attending were issued lottery cards. If they spent their time at the conference "usefully," as judged by company salespeople, they received a red dot for good performance. Twenty-five red dots on a lottery card made it eligible for a draw; the winners received $100 from the participating companies. At the same conference, a sleeping-pill manufacturer challenged doctors to press a button in the shortest time possible after the salesperson said "Go." The leaders' scores and names were posted prominently and at the convention's end a winner was declared.

In 1983, the drug companies spent almost $209 million promoting their products, with the vast proportion of those expenses being directed at doctors.[16] On a per doctor basis, the companies spend about $5000 annually. The reason for all the advertising is, of course, the same as in any industry — to sell the product and increase profits. In an analysis of the Canadian pharmaceutical market, Pazderka and Rao concluded that the most significant determinant of a drug's share of a therapeutic market was the amount spent on promoting that drug (1981). Nordic Biochemicals, soon after the company was founded in 1951, found out this fact of economic life the hard way. It tried to limit advertising to simple announcements in a few of the main medical journals. While the company maintained this policy, it teetered on the brink of disaster. However, as the head of Nordic told the Restrictive Trade Practices Commission that once the company accepted the "facts of life" with respect to promotion it began to prosper (1963:226).

The money spent on promotion has a pronounced effect on physicians. Fassold and Gowdey surveyed doctors in southwestern Ontario. Sixty-five percent rated drug company salespeople (known in the trade as "detailers") as good or excellent for reliability. A significant minority, 37 percent, also rated detailers as good or excellent with respect to their knowledge of drugs. Twenty-four percent indicated that it was detailers who influenced them to use a drug for the first time and for 4 percent it was direct mail advertising or journal advertisements (1968). In another survey of Ontario primary care physicians by Dunn et al., over 15 percent considered drug company literature an important source of continuing medical education (1982).

This dependence on promotion was reflected in doctors' prescribing of three different drugs — an antibiotic, an appetite suppressant, and a tranquillizer. Fassold and Gowdey found that 48 percent of general practitioners prescribed the appetite suppressant on the basis of the manufacturer's promotion versus 5 percent who based their prescriptions either on a colleague's or consultant's recommendation or on post-graduate education. The comparable figures for the antibiotic were 23 and 19 percent. Only for the tranquillizer did the professional sources outweigh manufacturer's promotion as the reason for trying the drug (1968).

There is a grave problem in doctors' reliance on commercial sources, that is, industry sources, for information about drugs. In an article on pharmaceutical promotion, Lexchin found that in all of the studies done on the rela-

tionship between advertising and prescribing the conclusion was the same. The more doctors rely on commercial sources for their information, the less rational they are as prescribers: they are more likely to prescribe the wrong drug in the wrong formulation for the wrong reason in an incorrect dosage for an inappropriate length of time (1987). Lexchin links heavy promotion of antibiotics, ulcer medications, and antihypertensives with widespread irrational use of these drugs. The *Globe and Mail* reported that in an appearance before the House of Commons Health Committee, the head of the Health Protection Branch charged that the hard-sell tactics used by drug companies to "flog" their products were a major reason for the medical complications and deaths related to drug overuse and adverse reactions (1974:8).

THE PHARMACEUTICAL INDUSTRY AND THE PHARMACISTS

Pharmacists are also important to the profits of the drug industry. In cases where more than one company makes a drug, when pharmacists are presented with a prescription they are free to dispense any company's brand of that drug, regardless of which particular trade name the doctor has written on the prescription.[17] The only time the pharmacists cannot substitute is if the doctor has written "no substitution" on the prescription. However, just because pharmacists have the power to substitute does not always mean that they will do so.[18] Pharmacists generally make their decision on which brand to dispense depending on which products they have in stock and which products yield the greatest profit margin. If pharmacists do not choose a certain company's brand then obviously sales for that company are going to suffer. Therefore, it is in the interest of companies to encourage pharmacists to stock their products and to ensure that the pharmacist reaps a good profit from their sale.

There have been reports in British Columbia and Alberta that as inducements to purchase their products, pharmaceutical companies have been offering pharmacists gifts such as free trips to Paris, silver ingots, and television sets. This practice is not confined to the multinational companies; it is also found among Canadian-owned firms. In a *Vancouver Sun* story by Kieran and Fitterman, Jack Kay, a vice-president of Apotex, the second largest Canadian-owned company, admitted that Apotex had offered such inducements to pharmacists, but went on to say that the practice was going on across Canada. Gordon Postlewaite, director of professional relations for the Pharmaceutical Manufacturers' Association of Canada, also quoted in the same article, sidestepped the issue by claiming that "as an association we cannot require that our members do anything with respect to prices" (1986:A–1, A–2).

To encourage pharmacists to dispense their brand of a drug, companies engage in what is called "discount pricing" or "discount competition." Under a provincial drug plan, drug X will be listed in the provincial formulary[19] as selling for, say, $10.00 per 100 pills. That figure is the amount that the pharmacist is supposed to have paid the drug company for 100 pills, and that is the amount the pharmacist will be reimbursed by the government if the pharmacist dispenses the 100 pills to someone covered by the province's drug programme. The pharmacist's profit theoretically derives from the dispensing fee.[20]

Under discount pricing, however, the drug company will sell its product for, say, $2.00 per 100 instead of the listed $10.00. The government still pays the pharmacist $10.00 and the pharmacist pockets the extra $8.00 as pure profit.[21] The drug companies are willing to discount their drugs because the bigger the pharmacists' profit margin, the more likely they are to dispense that particular company's brand of drug X, thereby increasing the company's market share. Indeed, it is in the direct interest of the drug companies to inflate the prices for their products listed in the provincial formularies, because the larger the profit margin for the pharmacist, the greater the incentive to use the company's brand. As in

the case of inducements, discount pricing is not restricted to the multinationals but is also practised by the generic companies. A 1983 news story by Peter Calamai estimated that discount pricing was costing provincial drug plans across Canada $40 to $60 million annually (1983:1, 2).

While the interactions between the pharmaceutical industry and pharmacists do not have any negative effects on people's health, they obviously have profound negative effects on the cost of drugs.

PUBLIC POLICY AND THE PHARMACEUTICAL INDUSTRY

Both federal and provincial governments have been involved with the pharmaceutical industry through efforts to control the costs of drugs. In 1962, Alberta was the first province to allow a pharmacist to substitute a generic or brand-name equivalent for the drug named in the prescription. The PMAC replied by having an article published in the *Canadian Medical Association Journal* disparaging the quality of generic drugs. The Swiss multinational Ciba unsuccessfully challenged the legislation in the courts.

In 1970, the Ontario government announced its first programme aimed at lowering drug costs, PARCOST (Prescriptions At Reasonable Cost). The basic goal of the programme was to get doctors and pharmacists to choose the least expensive brand of a drug. PARCOST was not a particularly aggressive scheme, since there was nothing compulsory about it. Nevertheless, the drug industry felt threatened, and R.G. Robb, the marketing director of Lilly, predicted that the end result of the programme would be "minimum acceptable quality, reliability and service" (1970:27). Some drug companies were reportedly supplying doctors with rubber stamps and labels saying "no substitution."

In the early years of the first Manitoba New Democratic Party government, the Advisory Committee on Central Drug Purchasing and Distribution published its findings in the *Klass Report* (1972). Some reasonably progressive recommendations were included on methods for controlling the prices of drugs. Highlighted in the *Report* was a recommendation to set up a committee to prepare a Manitoba formulary of equivalent brand-name drugs along with the respective prices of these medications. A Crown corporation was to have been established for the purpose of province-wide central purchasing, and distribution to pharmacies, of the most widely used drugs on this list. In the end, the government did not go ahead with bulk purchasing, but did pass a law allowing pharmacists to substitute. Furthermore, the substitute could not be sold at a price higher than that of the lowest-priced equivalent drug. After this legislation passed, Dr. W.W. Wigle, the president of the PMAC, made a thinly veiled threat to the Manitoba government. The text of Dr. Wigle's remarks was published in a letter from one D. Harper that appeared in *Drug Merchandising*:

> It will remain to be seen how much value would be put on the Manitoba market by research-oriented companies. It is each company's decision whether the size of their Manitoba market will merit the cost of properly servicing that market. If they can't meet the prices they could be forced out of business. In the long run, the patients of the future will suffer. (1972:74)

During the 1970s, other provinces initiated programmes to control drug costs to the consumer. Saskatchewan introduced North America's first universal drug coverage programme. Saskatchewan also picked up on the recommendation in the *Klass Report* and implemented a scheme of province-wide purchasing for high-volume drugs. Manitoba brought in a plan to refund up to 80 percent of the cost of prescription drugs after the first $50 and British Columbia enacted legislation similar to Manitoba's, but with a $100 deductible.

In 1969, the federal government amended the Patent Act to allow for compulsory licensing to import drugs still under patent.[22] This action came after three major federal reports, from the Restrictive Trade Practices Commission (1963),

the Royal Commission on Health Services (1964), and the Special Committee on Drug Costs and Prices (1967), had all concluded that Canadian drug prices were among the highest in the world. The first of these reports had simply recommended abolishing patent protection for prescription drugs altogether, but the latter two advocated compulsory licensing.

The PMAC mounted a campaign against compulsory licensing, estimated by Lang to have cost $200 000 to $250 000 annually (1974:59). While the Special Commons Committee was meeting, the PMAC had a representative at all the meetings of the Committee to provide information to the Conservative members of the Committee. After the Committee reported, Dr. Wigle threatened that if this recommendation was acted upon, the large companies operating in Canada would close down their plants (1967:1361). During the parliamentary debate on the bill allowing compulsory licensing, the PMAC and its supporters were once again active, placing all their resources at the disposal of the Conservatives. PMAC representatives stationed themselves in the Commons gallery and would periodically rush down to pay phones, contact the PMAC office, and then forward information or questions to the Tories on the floor of the Commons.

In the end, all of the lobbying efforts on the part of the multinationals were to no avail and Bill C–102, allowing compulsory licensing to import, passed on March 28, 1969. However, the multinationals were determined to make sure that the legislation would not work and American Home Products Ltd. immediately challenged the bill in court. At first, the company attempted to prevent the application of the law by seeking an order of prohibition against the Commissioner of Patents. This action delayed the implementation of the legislation for a year. When the case reached the Ontario Court of Appeals in March 1970, it was dismissed within fifteen minutes. By 1971, of the 60 licences issued, there had been 43 appeals before the courts.

The other major federal project to reduce costs has been the drug quality assurance programme, known as QUAD.[23] Started in 1971, this was a fourfold programme involving: drug analysis, inspection of manufacturers' plants, efficacy tests and assessment of manufacturers' claims, and an information system to advise pharmacists, doctors, and the public of test results. Generic and brand-name drugs were to be compared for quality and effectiveness and the results published in a periodical sent free to all physicians. The initial response of PMAC companies to the QUAD programme was to boycott it and refuse to submit to voluntary intensive examination.

W.M. Garton, the 1978 president of the PMAC, voiced the general reaction of the multinationals to government plans for price reduction, as opposed to insurance plans that would cover drug costs without affecting their price or limiting their availability:

> Such well-intentioned policies presented disincentives to the further extension of an industry oriented towards innovation, investigation and development in Canada . . . It is an unfortunate observation that many were, and continue to be based as much on emotional or political factors as on a careful consideration of objective evidence and we have consequently witnessed the "stretching of the skin of science to fit the drum of political necessity." (1978:7)

SUMMARY AND CONCLUSION

The thesis of this chapter has been that the driving force behind the pharmaceutical industry is the profit motive; ethical considerations are secondary.

The Canadian pharmaceutical industry is heavily foreign-dominated and as a result, opportunities for manufacturing, exporting, and research are severely constrained. Over the years the pharmaceutical industry has been much more profitable than Canadian manufacturing industries in general. None of the rationales that the industry uses to justify this level of profit has any basis in fact. The companies have been able to achieve this position primarily by limiting price competition and replac-

ing it with product competition.

Product competition is also a key element in the orientation of much of the research carried out by the industry. Instead of trying to develop drugs that have the greatest health potential, the companies generally direct their research efforts towards developing drugs with the greatest profit potential. The central goal of this research strategy is for firms to identify highly profitable drugs produced by competitors and then to develop their own version of these products. The end result is a proliferation of virtually identical drugs, none of which is superior to the others in any significant way.

The medical profession, at all levels, is constantly courted by the pharmaceutical companies. Doctors receive endless little gifts, the costs of their conferences are underwritten, and drug companies spend hundreds of millions of dollars on pharmaceutical promotion directed at them. The ultimate goal of all this attention is of course to persuade physicians to prescribe in a manner that will increase the sales and profits of the drug companies. Unfortunately those doctors who are so influenced are the ones who prescribe the least appropriately or correctly; and the health of their patients suffers accordingly.

Pharmaceutical companies, both multinational and Canadian-owned, have complex economic relations with the pharmacists. They offer inducements to pharmacists to stock certain brands of drugs, and undercut officially listed prices in order to allow pharmacists to increase their profit margins. While these measures do not affect health, they do increase the cost of drugs to the consumer.

Provincial and federal governments have attempted to control drug prices by fostering price competition among companies, and have introduced programmes to ease the burden of drug costs to various segments of the population. Where the drug companies have viewed government action as a threat to their profits, the response has usually been to predict a decline in the quality of drugs and the ultimate demise of the Canadian pharmaceutical industry.

NOTES

1. The Pharmaceutical Manufacturers' Association of Canada currently has about 65 member companies, including all the large multinationals operating in Canada. Only 4 or 5 of its members are Canadian-owned companies. The Canadian Drug Manufacturers' Association represents 17 Canadian-owned companies, the largest of which is Novopharm.

2. Since then such warnings have also been included in advertisements in Canadian medical journals.

3. In Canada and the United States, the drug was called Oraflex.

4. The Health Protection Branch is the division of the Department of National Health and Welfare charged with monitoring the safety and efficacy of prescription drugs. Before the HPB allows a drug to enter the Canadian market, the manufacturer has to present it with evidence that the product is both safe and effective for human use.

5. The *Eastman Report* gives Novopharm's 1982 sales at $22 296 000. The leading company that year was American Home Products, with sales of $94 704 000 (1985:174–82).

6. In the mid-1960s, the Royal Commission on Health Services found that of 395 patents on 14 "important pharmaceutical products" only 9, or less than 3 percent, were held by genuine Canadian firms (1964:656).

7. In 1976, resale products accounted for almost 20 percent of sales in Canada.

8. Currently, industry spokespeople quote a figure of $50 to $100 million as the cost of developing and marketing a new drug.

9. One of the studies done for the *Eastman Report* examined the actual savings that competition produced in a sample of 32 multiple-source drugs. The 1983 sales of these drugs amounted to $216.0 million. Without competition the cost would have been $426.6 million (1985:315).

10. This figure includes different dosage forms of the same drug and different formulations of the same drug; for instance a drug may be marketed as pills, capsules, solutions, creams, or ointments.

11. A "therapeutic class" consists of drugs used in the treatment of a particular problem or disease, such as arthritis or ulcers. All drugs can be placed into one or more therapeutic classes, depending on how many uses the drug has.

12. The *Eastman Report* also evaluated submarket concentration in alternative ways and the figures produced from these assessments showed a lower level of concentration than the ones obtained by an analysis of therapeutic classes (1985:135–42). While all of these methods have their limitations, they all showed that submarket concentration was higher than overall industry concentration.

13. The situation in Canada is somewhat different, owing to the existence of compulsory licensing. Under this system, introduced in 1969, a company wishing to import a drug that is still under patent protection in Canada can apply to the Commissioner of Patents in Ottawa for a licence to import the drug. The licence is almost always granted whether or not the patent holding company agrees, hence the term compulsory licensing. In return for losing its monopoly the patentee receives a royalty of 4 percent of sales from the company granted the licence. (The companies

taking out compulsory licences are often collectively referred to as "generic firms" and their products, whether or not they have their own trade names, are called "generic drugs.") Therefore, in Canada, the monopoly period may be very much shorter than the 17 years of patent protection that drugs are granted. What happens in Canada does not affect the research decisions of the multinational drug companies, as Canada represents only about 1.5 percent of the world pharmaceutical market. The major incentive to do research and development lies in the profits to be derived from selling pharmaceuticals in the major world markets — Western Europe, the United States, and Japan — which represent 33, 25, and 17 percent of world sales respectively. For more information about research and patents as they apply to Canada, see Lexchin (1984:95–102, 162–81).

14. Dollar sales of anti-inflammatories and the number of prescriptions for benzodiazepines were both calculated from figures in the *Eastman Report* (1985:174–83).

15. Valium is Roche's trade name for the benzodiazepine diazepam. In 1970, Horner was granted a compulsory licence allowing it to import and market its own version of diazepam called Vivol. Roche executives expected Vivol to sell for 25 percent less than Valium, and so to head off competition used a marketing technique known as "filling the pipes." Just prior to the entry of Horner's product, Roche "flooded the market" with Valium at a low price so that Horner would be unable to establish Vivol in the market for a period of time.

16. $209 million represented 16.7 percent of sales, compared with less than 4 percent being spent on research.

17. The trade name of a drug is the name that a company has given to its particular version of that drug. Drugs also have a true scientific name, called the "chemical name," and a generic name, which is an abbreviated scientific name and can be used in prescribing, naming, and identifying the drug. For example: Miltown is Horner's trade name for a tranquillizer. The generic name is "meprobamate" and the chemical name is "2-methyl-2-propyl-1, 3-propanedioldicarbamate." Besides prescribing by the trade name, doctors may also prescribe by the generic name. If they do, then pharmacists are again free to pick any company's product.

18. In Saskatchewan, for certain multiple-source high-volume drugs, pharmacists must dispense a particular brand unless the physician has written "no substitution" on the prescription.

19. A provincial formulary is a listing of all the drugs covered under the provincial drug plan. All provinces publish a formulary except Alberta, British Columbia, and Prince Edward Island. Ontario's formulary is widely used in British Columbia. For more information about the provincial drug plans see the *Eastman Report* (1985:395–406).

20. The dispensing or professional fee is the amount that pharmacists charge for their professional services.

21. Discount pricing does not take place in British Columbia and Saskatchewan, where pharmacists are reimbursed for their actual acquisition costs. At the end of 1986, Ontario had also moved to such a system.

22. Compulsory licensing to manufacture had been around ever since 1923. Under this provision of the Patent Act, companies in Canada wishing to manufacture a drug still under patent here could get a licence to do so. There are very few licences of this type issued, primarily because of the cost of setting up a plant to manufacture a drug just for the small Canadian market.

23. The program's name was later changed and the "A" came to stand for assessment rather than assurance.

STUDY QUESTIONS

1. How would you account for the foreign domination of the Canadian pharmaceutical industry?

2. Besides increasing competition, what other methods could be used to control drug costs?

3. If the profit motive for researching new drugs were removed, how do you think that would affect the development of drugs?

4. Speculate on how the involvement of the medical profession with the pharmaceutical industry may have affected physicians' ability to be objective about the benefits of pharmaceuticals.

RECOMMENDED READING

Commission of Inquiry on the Pharmaceutical Industry. *Report*. Ottawa: Minister of Supply and Services Canada, 1985.

Gordon, M., and D. Fowler. *The Drug Industry: A Case Study in Foreign Control*. Toronto: James Lorimer & Co., 1981.

Klass, A. *There's Gold in Them Thar Pills*. Middlesex, England: Penguin, 1975.

Lang, R.W. *The Politics of Drugs*. Westmead, England: Saxon House, 1974.

Lexchin, J. *The Real Pushers: A Critical Analysis of the Canadian Drug Industry*. Vancouver: New Star Books, 1984.

————. "Pharmaceutical Promotion in Canada: Convince Them or Confuse Them." *International Journal of Health Services* 17, no. 1 (1987): 77–87.

REFERENCES

Advisory Committee on Central Drug Purchasing and Distribution, *Report*. Province of Manitoba, 1972.

Bell, P. "Ayerst man disagrees with FDA warning." *Globe and Mail* 12 June 1975.

Berger, P.B. "The masters of the giveaway." *Globe and Mail* 3 December 1983.

Bureau of Policy Coordination. *A Policy Analysis of the Compulsory Licensing of Pharmaceutical Patents in Canada*. Ottawa: Department of Consumer and Corporate Affairs, September 1982.

Burstall, M.L., J.H. Dunning, and A. Lake. *Multinational Enterprises, Governments and Technology: Pharmaceutical Industry*. Paris: Organisation for Economic Co-operation and Development, 1981.

Busto, U., P. Isaac, and M. Adrian. "Changing Patterns of Benzodiazepine Use in Canada: 1978 to 1984." *American Society for Clinical Pharmacology and Therapeutics* 39 (1986): 184 (abstract).

Calamai, P. "Hidden drug profits total $50 million a year." *Sault Star* 21 October 1983.

Canada. House of Commons. Special Committee of the House of Commons on Drug Costs and Prices. *Second (Final) Report.* Ottawa: Queen's Printer, 1967a.

––––––. *Minutes of Proceedings and Evidence, No. 33.* Ottawa: Queen's Printer, 1967b.

Commission of Inquiry on the Pharmaceutical Industry. *Report.* Ottawa: Minister of Supply and Services Canada, 1985.

Consumer and Corporate Affairs Canada. *Compulsory Licensing of Pharmaceuticals: A Review of Section 41 of the Patent Act.* Ottawa: 1983.

Dan, L.L. "The Drug Industry in Canada: A Position Analysis." *Business Quarterly* 47 (Autumn 1982): 62–71.

Department of Industry, Trade, and Commerce. *The Health Care Products Industry in Canada.* Ottawa: 1980.

Dunn, E., J.I. Williams, A.M. Bryans, et al. "Continuing Medical Education in Ontario: A Primary Care Perspective." *Canadian Family Physician* 28 (1982): 1327–33.

Fassold, R.W., and C.W. Gowdey. "A Survey of Physicians' Reactions to Drug Promotion." *Canadian Medical Association Journal* 98 (1968): 701–5.

Friedman, J.J., & Associates. *Pharmaceutical Prices in Canada: Guiding Principles for Government Policy.* Ottawa: Pharmaceutical Manufacturers' Association of Canada, 1981.

Garai, P.R. "Advertising and Promotion of Drugs." In *Drugs in Our Society*, edited by P. Talalay. Baltimore: Johns Hopkins Press, 1964.

Garton, W.M. "The Pharmaceutical Sector in Canada — Its Environment and Performance." *Drug Merchandising* 111 (January 1978): 6–7.

––––––. Personal communication with the author. 26 May 1980.

Gereffi, G. *The Pharmaceutical Industry and Dependency in the Third World.* Princeton: Princeton University Press, 1983.

Gershon, S., and B. Shopsin. *Lithium: Its Role in Psychiatric Research and Treatment.* New York: Plenum Press, 1974.

Gordon, M., and D. Fowler. *The Drug Industry: A Case Study in Foreign Control.* Toronto: James Lorimer & Co., 1981.

Gray, C. "The Pharmaceutical Industry: Promoting Research in the 80's." *Canadian Medical Association Journal* 124 (1981): 787–92.

"Hard-sell tactics linked to drug-related deaths." *Globe and Mail* 10 April 1974.

Harper, D. "No Threat Made by Dr. Wigle." *Drug Merchandising* 53 (September 1972).

Kieran, B., and L. Fitterman. "Probe set in gifts to druggists." *Vancouver Sun* 18 March 1986.

Lang, R.W. *The Politics of Drugs.* Westmead, England: Saxon House, 1974.

Lexchin, J. *The Real Pushers: A Critical Analysis of the Canadian Drug Industry.* Vancouver: New Star Books, 1984.

––––––. "Pharmaceutical Promotion in Canada: Convince Them or Confuse Them." *International Journal of Health Services* 17, no. 1 (1987): 77–87.

Orr, D. "An Index of Entry Barriers and Its Application to the Market Structure Performance Relationship." *Journal of Industrial Economics* 23 (1974): 39–49.

Pazderka, B., and R.C. Rao. *Market Share Competition in the Canadian Prescription Drug Industry: A Comparison of Several Theoretical Markets.* Kingston, Ontario: Working Paper 81–8, School of Business, Queen's University, September 1981

Pekkanen, J. "The Impact of Promotion on Physicians' Prescribing Patterns." *Journal of Drug Issues* 6 (1976): 13–20.

Pharmaceutical Manufacturers' Association of Canada. *Principles and Code of Marketing Practice.* Ottawa: 1972.

––––––. *The Performance of the Canadian Pharmaceutical Manufacturing Industry.* Ottawa: 1975.

Restrictive Trade Practices Commission. *Report Concerning the Manufacture, Distribution and Sale of Drugs.* Ottawa: Queen's Printer,

1963.

Robb, G.W. "Product and Service Less Than Best." *Drug Merchandising* 51 (October 1970): 27–8.

Royal Commission on Health Services. *Report.* Ottawa: Queen's Printer, 1964.

Shapiro, M. *Getting Doctored.* Kitchener: Between the Lines, 1978.

Taylor, P. "Generics a bitter pill for big drug firms." *Globe and Mail* 16 July 1983.

Temin, P. "Technology, Regulation, and Market Structure in the Modern Pharmaceutical Industry." *Bell Journal of Economics* 10 (1979): 429–46.

U.S. Senate. Committee on the Judiciary, Subcommittee on Antitrust and Monopoly. *Hearings on Administered Prices in the Drug Industry.* Washington, D.C.: U.S. Government Printing Office, 1960.

Van Woert, M.H. "Profitable and Nonprofitable Drugs." *New England Journal of Medicine* 298 (1978): 903–5.

Walwyn Stodgell Cochran Murray Ltd. "For a Pill, Like to Try One from the U.K.?" *Investor's Digest* May 10, 1983.

Westell, D. "Pharmaceutical industry picked for audit by national revenue." *Globe and Mail* 5 May 1980.

Wigle, W.W. "A Pharmaceutical Industry in Canada?" *Canadian Medical Association Journal* 97 (1967): 1361.

———. "Drug Costs." *Canadian Medical Association Journal* 100 (1969): 441–2.

31

AIDS: The Politicizing of a Public Health Issue

Marianne Weston and Bonnie Jeffery
University of Regina

INTRODUCTION

Because of the incompleteness of medical science's current understanding of the disease and because there are ethical and political implications yet to become apparent and to be addressed, the present chapter cannot possibly deal comprehensively with the issue of AIDS. By the time it appears in print, cures for the disease may be closer, preventive measures better understood, and altogether different issues associated with the disease may have come to the forefront. Nonetheless, Conrad and Schneider's (1980) concept of the "medicalization of deviance" provides a useful theoretical framework in which to analyze some of the reasons for the present definitions and meanings associated with AIDS. A cursory examination of popular journalism dealing with AIDS would lead us to conclude that the disease is often associated with "badness" rather than "sickness" labels. The professional literature dealing with AIDS is also replete with sometimes subtle, sometimes not so subtle, designations of "badness." This chapter will examine some of the non-medical factors which have contributed to AIDS being defined in a negative sense.

AIDS IS AN ILLNESS

There is a great deal of fear, uncertainty, and mythology surrounding AIDS. It is important that any discussion of AIDS firmly establish it as a disease prior to an examination of the processes which have influenced its meaning.

AIDS is a widely used acronym standing for an infectious disease called acquired immune deficiency syndrome. The disease was named in 1982, although Mass (1985:56) indicates that the first case of AIDS came to the attention of the United States Public Health Service's Centers for Disease Control (CDC) in late 1979. By 1981, as an increasing number of cases from both coasts were reported, it was clear to U.S.

public health authorities that something more than individual cases of an unknown disease was occurring. According to Parent (1985:22), the first case of AIDS in Canada was reported in February of 1982.

AIDS is caused by a retrovirus known as lymphadenopathy-associated virus (LAV) or human T-cell lymphotropic virus type III (HTLV-III). LAV was discovered by the French scientist Luc Montagnier in 1983; one year later, the American scientist, Robert Gallo, discovered HTLV-III. Since then, the appropriate naming of the virus has been widely debated. In September 1986, the *Canada Disease Weekly Report* (CDWR) (Sept.13, 1986:169) adopted the International Committee on Taxonomy of Viruses' terminology of "human immunodeficiency virus" (HIV). *Nature* magazine (1986:325) has recently reported that another, similar, virus may also be responsible for causing the disease.

Most of those who have been identified as carrying the virus do not have AIDS. Mass suggests that depending on who is estimating, between one and three in ten persons who carry the virus will develop full-blown AIDS (1985:63). Recent Canadian media reports, on the other hand, suggest this proportion may be 50 percent.

AIDS itself is a breakdown in the body's immune system. Those who develop what clinicians refer to as "frank" or "full-blown" AIDS become vulnerable to a number of serious and frequently fatal so-called opportunistic diseases and malignancies. The most frequent of these diseases are Kaposi's sarcoma (KS) and a protozoan infection of the lungs called Pneumocystis carinii pneumonia (PCP). KS, PCP, and many of the other opportunistic infections to which AIDS predisposes the body are relatively infrequent in persons who have healthy immune systems. Because there are many different causes of immune deficiency, there continues to be some uncertainty about the exact definition of AIDS, but most agree that only those patients who show symptoms of the major complications associated with severe and otherwise unex-

plained immune deficiency — such as KS or PCP — qualify for the diagnosis of AIDS.

According to the *Canada Diseases Weekly Report*:

> Persons with a diagnosis of AIDS are those with the more severe manifestations of infection with HIV. These cases meet strict criteria of definition and are those reported to provincial and national surveillance programs. HIV infection in these cases is accompanied by one or more opportunistic infections and/or rare cancers such as Kaposi's sarcoma. (September 13, 1986:159)[1]

What is excluded from this official definition are the numbers of those with AIDS-related complex (ARC). These people have less specific or milder manifestations of HIV.

Those who are infected with HIV but are asymptomatic are also excluded from the official reporting procedures. It is recognized that these people are able to transmit the virus and therefore the estimates of these numbers are important in developing projected incidence of AIDS.

At present it is believed that from 9 to 30 percent of persons with ARC will develop full-blown AIDS over a period ranging from months to several years. Many ARC patients have recovered, however, and one wonders if the level of fear associated with AIDS would be quite so high if the conditions known as ARC had been included in the original definition of AIDS.

INCIDENCE AND TRENDS OF AIDS

In order to discuss the statistics related to current incidence and projected trends of AIDS, we must first examine how the disease is defined for the purpose of official reporting. Canada has adopted the CDC case definition that was first published in September 1982, which includes persons with more severe cases of HIV infection but excludes those with ARC.

The United States Department of Health and Human Services, in the *Morbidity and Mortality Weekly Report* (MMWR) noted that its recently revised definition of AIDS includes a recommendation "that CDC develop more inclusive definitions and classifications of HTLV-III/LAV infection for diagnosis, treatment and prevention, as well as for epidemiologic studies and special survey" (June 28, 1985:374). Although the U.S. definition was revised in June 1985, the case definition for national reporting continues to focus on or include only those with severe manifestations of infection.

According to Mass, at present the mean survival time of an AIDS patient is 18 months and 85 percent of those diagnosed in 1981 in the United States have since died from the disease (1985:63).

In Canada, AIDS was included for the first time in January 1986, on the list of notifiable diseases compiled by Statistics Canada. As of July 14, 1986 the National AIDS Centre surveillance programme in Canada had received reports of 638 cases of AIDS. By November 17, 1986 the *Canada Diseases Weekly Report* listed the number of AIDS cases at 786 (November 29, 1986). The sex distribution of cases indicates that men are 15 times more likely than women to have contracted the disease; the majority of cases (90 percent) are people between the ages of 20 and 49. The risk factors for exposure to HIV are as follows:

Homosexual/bisexual activity	81.8%
Use of intravenous drugs	0.4%
Blood transfusions	3.6%
Heterosexual contact with person at risk of infection	1.8%
Unknown	2.5%

(CDWR, November 29, 1986)

Global reporting of AIDS through the World Health Organization (WHO) began in August 1985. Seventy-seven countries are reporting, with the U.S. data accounting for about three quarters of all cases. As of November 1986, 34 448 cases of AIDS had been reported to the WHO Global Control Programme (CDWR, January 10, 1987).

It is important to note that there is no known cure for AIDS, nor is there a vaccine which will prevent transmittal of the virus. Med-ical science has not yet discovered why some persons who carry the virus develop AIDS and others do not. As discussed later, this fact undoubtedly influences the more tenuous hold which the medical profession has on the definition of the illness. Because its knowledge and technology have not yet developed a cure for those with the disease, in the case of AIDS, the medical profession has been denied the power and control it has with regard to other diseases.

HISTORICAL CONTEXT OF SEXUALITY AND SICKNESS

In order to further our understanding of the various meanings which have been associated with AIDS, we must examine historical definitions of both sexuality and illness. Although AIDS is known to be transmitted in non-sexual ways, it is its sexual transmission that has most greatly influenced its meaning in Canada and the United States. The connection between AIDS and sexuality is firmly and inextricably reinforced through public reporting of aspects of the illness.

Conrad and Schneider (1980:27) have defined three major paradigms which have influenced deviance and therefore sickness and sexual behaviour designations throughout history. These models trace the definitions of unacceptable behaviour from deviance as sin, to deviance as crime, to deviance as sickness. These historical changes are very closely related to the influence of the Church, the state, and medicine as a profession.

Not only have the definitions of deviant sexual behaviour and sickness changed over time, but the agents of social control which have been brought to bear on these deviant states and practices have also changed. It is critical, then, to discuss the relationship between the dominant view of sexuality and the views of the disease called AIDS. Furthermore, we must examine how these views, represented by various interest groups, have impacted on each other within this decade to change our labels for both sickness and sexuality.

Historically, every culture has had its own definitions of approved versus deviant sexual behaviour. What is considered deviant sexual behaviour has varied among cultures at similar points in history as well as within cultures over time. Anthropological and historical studies would seem to indicate that there are few sexual practices which have been historically and universally taboo.

Just as our definitions of what is acceptable or unacceptable sexual behaviour have changed, so too have the labels assigned to such behaviour. Prior to the nineteenth century, approved sexual practices were defined and controlled by the Church. Words such as "good" and "evil" or "virtue" and "vice" were used to distinguish that behaviour which was considered to be good or acceptable. Underlying these words was the fundamental notion of deviant sexual behaviour being defined as sin. When the definitions of acceptable or approved sexual behaviour came to be legitimized through the state, the enforcement of such behaviours was achieved through the criminal justice system. Consequently, certain sexual behaviours or practices which previously had been defined as "sinful" were now defined as "criminal."

The development of the post-industrial society resulted in an increasing reliance on and faith in scientific discovery and knowledge. Science had been added to the list of agents of social control and biologists began to define "degenerative" or "maladaptive" sex as opposed to species-enhancing or adaptive sex. Psychologists also began to label certain sexual practices as "abnormal" or "pathological" and more recently, as neurotic, immature, or aberrant. The medical profession became the watchdog of scientific standards, and at the beginning of the twentieth century began to attain increasing control over definitions of acceptable sexual behaviour. Gagnon (1977:26) notes that the transition from religion to the state and then to the medical profession as primary agent of social control has coincided with the move from collective or societal to personal justifications for various sexual behaviours.

Until recent times, we have had collective justifications for sexual conduct even though the source (i.e., Church, state, medical profession) of the collective justification has changed. Since the 1950s, a far more individualistic perspective on sexuality has developed. The collective definition for appropriate sexual behaviour has less appeal today because it has come to conflict with the sexual activity of the majority. Sexual practices are now defined in terms of individual preference, and popular views of sex see it as joy, play, intimacy, and recreation. This shift in the way we define or justify our sex practices has also changed the way we perceive the purpose of sex. The current trend toward individual rather than collective decisions about the purpose of sex has meant that the agents of social control have not been able to cast their net as widely. As sex has come to have more individual purposes, various sexual practices have come to be defined as "conventional" and "unconventional," or "satisfying" and "unsatisfying." These terms are much less loaded than words like "immoral," "criminal," or "pathological." When freed from the constraints of collective definitions, violations of the sexual norms are either not considered very important or, at the very least, are seen as an individual and private decision. Katchadourian and Lunde (1975:9) also support this idea and note that society now distinguishes between public and private sexual behaviour. Those behaviours or practices conducted in private between consenting adults are considered beyond the scope of societal regulation. The ability of a collective view of sexuality to be imposed on individual behaviour and choices has been diminished, except in times of crisis. While it may be too early to judge, there are signs that AIDS has become the crisis which may precipitate a move back to a collective rather than an individual definition of acceptable sexual behaviour. The widespread fear of AIDS may allow the Church, state, and/or the medical profession to re-impose control over the definition of acceptable sexual behaviour.

Historically, disease or illness has been conceptualized as a symptom of sin and as a punishment for moral corruption. Sontag (1978:47), for example, notes:

> With the advent of Christianity which imposed more moralized notions of disease, as of everything else, a closer fit between disease and "victim" gradually evolved. The idea of disease as punishment yielded the idea that a disease could be a particularly appropriate and just punishment.

Various cultures and historical periods have defined specific diseases and illnesses differently, and our culture's views and labels have changed over time.

Several writers have discussed the increasing medicalization of society and the implications of this trend. Some, such as Illich (1976:13–14), see the increasing involvement of the medical profession in all aspects of life as a negative trend.

> During the last generation the medical monopoly over health care has expanded without checks and has encroached on our liberty with regard to our own bodies. Society has transferred to physicians the exclusive right to determine what constitutes sickness, who is or might become sick, and what shall be done to such people. Deviance is now "legitimate" only when it merits and ultimately justifies medical interpretation and intervention.

Conrad and Schneider (1980:246–47), when discussing the "medicalization of deviance," point out some of the positive aspects that can be the result of the growing medical involvement in the definition and control of human conditions and social problems. They argue that the medicalizing of social problems such as alcoholism and juvenile delinquency removes both the burden of responsibility and the stigma attached to the condition from the individual. The condition or social problem is depoliticized and thus exempt from punitive consequences.

Talcott Parsons (1951) has pointed out that the labelling of someone as ill serves to conditionally legitimate the condition, thus exempting the individual from normal responsibilities to whatever extent may be necessary in order to get well. Society does not hold individuals responsible for their illnesses, although they are expected to want to get well and to co-operate with a physician to that end. Medicine both defines the sick role and acts as the agent of social control in limiting certain behaviours of the individual. An overriding theme in the medicalization of behaviours or conditions is one of humanitarian concern. While it is difficult to object to the notion of caring for others, the humanitarian concerns can promote the view of individuals being "victims." Moreover, the assumption that a medical definition is always neutral and objective ignores the reality of the power that society has granted to the medical profession.

Some authors have questioned the idea that those who are ill are not punished or are exempt from moral judgements. Zola (1972:490), for example, writes:

> Most analysts have tried to make a distinction between illness and crime on the issue of personal responsibility. The criminal is thought to be responsible and therefore accountable (or punishable) for his act, while the sick person is not. While the distinction does exist it seems to be more a quantitative one rather than a qualitative one, with moral judgements but a pinprick below the surface.

Conrad and Schneider also argue that social judgements are very much connected to moral judgements because "they are related directly and intimately to the moral order of society" (1980:35).

While there is a great deal of evidence that the medical profession has been successful in increasing its domain and in destigmatizing those conditions it defines as illnesses, this does not hold true when we examine the reactions to AIDS. In the public mind, sexually transmitted diseases, and AIDS in particular, continue to have associations of immorality. Thus the majority of those with AIDS bear a double burden. They face the future with the grim knowledge that medical science has not yet discovered a cure for their illness. They also face the reactions of others, both those in their social circle and the general public, who have come to identify the disease with homosexuality. Until the development of what have been considered "innocent" AIDS cases, i.e., those not resulting from homosexual contact, many viewed AIDS as punishment for homosexual behaviour. The medical profession's control over the meanings of illness and deviance becomes tentative, especially when sexuality comes face to face with germs.

Homosexuality in the Western world prior to the twentieth century was initially viewed as sinful. With the gradual relinquishment of the Church's power to the state, it became defined as a criminal activity. Later, through what Illich (1976:47) calls the increasing "medicalization of life," behaviours and events such as childbirth and menopause which had previously been defined as normal became defined as sickness. Homosexuality also came to be defined as an illness, to be subjected to cure rather than punishment. The medicalizing of homosexuality and the accompanying belief that it was an illness to be cured provided the basis for the decriminalization of homosexual relations. During the 1970s, the homosexual community increased its organizing and lobbying efforts to both decriminalize and demedicalize homosexuality. This led to both its removal from the Criminal Code of Canada and from the American Psychiatric Association's DSM classification in the same decade.[2]

With the advent of AIDS, however, it can be argued that many of these more progressive attitudes are being undermined. In the Western world, AIDS has been very clearly defined as a "homosexual" disease. In fact, it has been referred to as the "homosexual plague." This understanding of the disease grew out of the fact that the first cases of AIDS recognized in the United States were among homosexual men. In fact, although it was never officially termed thus, AIDS was known in the beginning as GRID (gay-related immune deficiency). The emphasis of the American scientists on the epidemiology rather than virology is undoubtedly a significant factor in the disease's association with a lifestyle rather than a micro-organism. Clearly, gay men are not the only victims of the disease, but in both statistical and political terms they are the most significant. As Altman (1986:39) points out: "Among gay men AIDS has become an omnipresent nightmare ... AIDS haunts us both asleep and awake, and it changes not just our behaviour but our very conceptions of who we are and our belief in ourselves."

Homophobia has surfaced more publicly as the fear about AIDS increases. What we are witnessing is the blaming of homosexuality for a disease. Rather than viewing the illness as primarily a medical condition, the public views and reactions have spilled over into the area of sexuality, and allowed the opportunity for a variety of interest groups to launch anti-gay campaigns.

THE MARGINALITY OF THE RISK GROUPS

To a great extent, the way society has dealt with AIDS, the allocation of research dollars to it, and the treatment AIDS patients receive, all depend on the fact that those whom the disease strikes have been in large part marginal members of society. They are members of unpopular, even mistrusted groups. They lack both resources and power. In more recent times, the popular media have begun to talk of the "innocent" victims of the disease (hemophiliacs, babies, those who receive blood transfusions, and heterosexual partners of AIDS carriers). This promotes the false impression that there are groups who are "guilty." These are the marginal communities of homosexuals, drug users, prostitutes, and less clearly, Haitians.

The marginality of homosexuals, the most prominent risk group, is best exemplified by the fact that many of them are to some degree in violation of the law or at least are not afforded equal protection under the law. In the United States, homosexuality is still illegal in many states. In Canada, homosexuals are not protected under human rights legislation and thus can be fired from jobs or be denied employment or housing on the grounds of their sexual orientation. If this happens, they have no recourse to the courts.

Drug users may be the most marginal of all of the groups at risk. They are perhaps the poorest, are clearly engaged in illegal activity, are unorganized, and have no power as an identifiable group. Society has little understanding of the factors and culture which underlie drug use, and attempts to reach users and change the practice of needle sharing may prove to be difficult. Drug users have received the least attention as a risk group. Their numbers are likely underestimated since those who both engage in homosexual practices and are intravenous drug users are classified in the homosexual or bisexual category only.

The immigrant populations mentioned in Canada's health pamphlets and who once formed a risk group in both Canada and the United States are also clearly marginal. The Haitian community in both countries tends to be poor, lacks access to the media, and does not speak English well; furthermore, some of its members are living in the country illegally. Despite their marginal status in North America, Haitians do have status as a nationality. Thus, in part because of increasing pressure from Haitian government officials, both the United States and Canada removed Haitians from their risk group classification in 1985. A second factor which no doubt influenced this action was medical science's inability to find a scientific basis for the classification. Since they could not determine why Haitians were at risk, the medical profession's authority to control and define the disease was clearly capable of being undermined.

It has been claimed that Haitians were the only group classified on the basis of who they were rather than what they practised. While this is to some extent valid, most of the medical literature and certainly the popular media constantly refer to risk groups as homosexual men, bisexual men, drug users, and hemophiliacs. These are clearly words which identify *groups*, not practices. The Centers for Disease Control in the United States continue to use terms associated with groups, although in Canada the Laboratory Centre for Disease Control talks of homosexual/bisexual practices.

If the medical profession had been focussed on minimizing the further stigmatization of already marginal groups, practices and situations which facilitate transmission would have been emphasized, rather than particular group identities.

Haitians, unlike the other groups at risk, protested their classification and despite the fact of being a low-status marginal group in the United States and Canada, their status as a nationality lent a certain power to their claim. Altman (1986:74) points out, however, that their removal from the "at risk" list has done nothing to alleviate the discrimination against them, and it is difficult for Haitians to either obtain or retain jobs or housing. Then again, their high-risk status often remains subtly alluded to, as in Canada's AIDS pamphlet (1986), which states: "AIDS has also occurred among recent immigrants from some areas in the Caribbean and Central Africa where AIDS is widespread."

With the appearance of AIDS in the heterosexual community, a new group, prostitutes, began to be scapegoated for its spread. Western society has had a history of scapegoating prostitutes for both social problems like family breakdown and diseases such as venereal disease. As Adams (1986:27) points out: "In 1918 and 1920, 18,000 American prostitutes were rounded up and committed to prison hospitals to protect the health of American troops (who presumably were incapable of protecting themselves)."

The lengths to which American and Canadian society will go to quarantine (incarcerate) prostitutes remains to be documented but already one prostitute who carries the virus has been arrested in Canada. Further evidence of scapegoating is that public health and other authorities as well as the media seem almost singularly concerned with prostitutes' transmittal of the disease rather than worrying about how to protect them from the risk of receipt of the virus

from bisexual men. As Adams (1986:27) states, prostitutes "are more often seen as receptacles of and transmitters of the virus" rather than being recognized as persons at risk of contracting the disease.

Marginality is clearly linked to lack of resources and power, although this varies among different groups. As Altman (1986:39) states: "One of the reasons that the perception of AIDS has been so closely linked to gay men is that no other affected group has comparable political will and resources to deal with the issue."

Drug users have no resources to deal with the issue and if they did, the illegality of their activities and their very addiction would make them unlikely to organize. The Haitian community also lacks resources, and in any case, in the past tended to use whatever resources and status they had to deny that they were at risk. Prostitutes, by the nature of their profession, also find it difficult to organize and to be perceived as a credible voice. However, in the last few years some steps have been made in this direction in order to argue for the removal of prostitution from the Criminal Code of Canada. Ironically, their failure to effect Criminal Code changes may make it even more difficult for them to congregate in order to discuss issues affecting them, and thus their risk of contracting the AIDS virus may be increased.

In relative terms, the gay community is the least marginal. It has large numbers in some locales, it has the skills and resources, and it has organization upon which to build. As Altman (1986:39) suggests, however, the need and competence with which the gay community has organized itself against the disease only serves to reinforce the perception of AIDS as connected with homosexuality. Other factors, such as the early detection of AIDS in only homosexual men, the U.S. concentration on the epidemiology of the disease, the tendency of the media and the New Right to promote the association of the disease with homosexuals by referring to it as "the gay plague," the homophobia in general of Western society, the large proportion of cases among homosexual or bisexual men,

and the historical context within which the disease occurred all served to further label the disease as primarily a "gay" issue. Not until less marginal members of the general population, which included children, hemophiliacs, recipients of blood transfusions, and the partners of bisexual men began to contract the disease did it become recognized as a public health issue.

THE NEW RIGHT

AIDS has come to the public's attention at the same time as the New Right is gaining increasing political power. Control of sexuality has always been a dominant theme of the right, which believes that medical technology (birth control and cures for syphilis and gonorrhea) has served to free our sexuality from the moral agents of social control. They blame sexual liberation for massive social problems such as family breakdown, teen pregnancies, and disease; and thus advocate for a return to traditional values (i.e., sex for procreation and only within marriage) and punitive social controls to enforce these values.

While at times the New Right's agenda has seemed badly out of step, it cannot be dismissed. From time to time, it has had the power to appeal to the latent guilt that even the most liberal carry, which is predicated on the historical meanings we have attached to both sexuality and disease.

The New Right, because homosexuality violates its value system, promotes homophobia, playing on the general population's suspicions of those who are different. The spokespersons of the movement, already associating homosexuality with numerous signs of social decay, were quick to seize upon the appearance of AIDS as further proof of their position. They have resurrected the language and meanings associated with religion as the agent of social control, and directed it at homosexuals. In so doing they have added to the public's tendency to associate the disease with gayness rather than with health practices.

Examples of the New Right's determination to combine religious and medical meanings to provoke hatred of homosexuals abound. Both Altman (1986) and Patton (1985) cite numerous American examples. For example, Altman quotes a Nevada minister as saying: "I think we should do what the Bible says and cut their [homosexuals'] throats" (1986:68). As an example of the strength of morality even among some professionals themselves, Altman quotes from an article by Dr. James Fletcher in the *Southern Medical Journal*:

> A logical conclusion is that AIDS is a self-inflicted disorder for the majority of those who suffer from it. For again, without placing reproach upon certain Haitians or hemophiliacs, we see homosexual men reaping not only expected consequences of sexual promiscuity, suffering even as promiscuous heterosexuals the usual venereal diseases but other consequences as well.
>
> Perhaps, then, homosexuality is not "alternative" behaviour at all, but as the ancient wisdom of the Bible states, most certainly pathologic. Indeed from an empirical medical perspective alone, current scientific observation seems to require the conclusion that homosexuality is a pathologic condition. (1986:66)

In Canada, the *Regina Leader Post* allows Reverend John Bergen regular paid advertising which promotes hatred of homosexuality and links this lifestyle to AIDS. The New Right has even taken its campaign door-to-door and for the first time in many years specifically anti-homosexual literature is being distributed to households in a major Saskatchewan city. R.E.A.L. Women of Canada is distributing a pamphlet targeting homosexuals as promoters of AIDS which states:

> The new findings on AIDS have destroyed the idea that the "gay rights" movement doesn't injur [sic] anyone, and that what they do is their "own business." Homosexuals are a medical threat to their own sex, to those who require blood transfusions, to the promiscuous and their unknowing spouses.

The effect of the New Right's rhetoric has been to burden the disease with even more symbolic baggage to ensure it is firmly anchored as a homosexual issue rather than as a health issue.

Their appeals have also served to fuel both fears and hatred at a time when political will, the ability to be non-judgemental in the development of public education programmes, and rationality are needed.

The public's reaction to the need for education on this health issue, as distinct from their reaction to the need for education to combat the issue of teen pregnancy, has been ironic in light of the right-wing conservative agenda. While on the one hand, there are numerous examples of the power of the right to blame the victims of the disease and to label it as punishment for immorality and promiscuousness, on the other hand, the disease and the nature of its prevention is wresting away the control which the right previously exercised to deny young people access to birth control and explicit information on sexuality.

While the fight is just beginning, it would appear that explicit discussion of sexual practices and information on condoms will be mandated in school programmes by many provinces. Those concerned about teen pregnancy have fought for many years to have schools provide information on birth control methods, but success has been minimal. Now it would appear that AIDS will provide the impetus for dissemination of this information, and education will go beyond the classroom to widespread media campaigns as well.

Making reliable information on how to prevent AIDS available to the general public is, at face value, a positive step. Although by denying our young people access to information, we have exposed them to unwanted pregnancies, those who have the power in most provinces are not willing to similarly deny specific information about sex, drug use, and alternative lifestyles to those engaged in sex outside of marriage, when the consequences may entail death.

Just how positive this move is will likely be measured by the extent to which "safe sex" education can be integrated into a broader programme of education on sexuality. Standing alone, this education runs the risk of entrenching fear and hatred of homosexuality and of promoting anti-sex attitudes. To the extent that sex becomes increasingly associated with death, it may in the end support the New Right's ethics after all.

SUMMARY AND CONCLUSIONS

Previous sections of this chapter have discussed some of the reasons for the medical profession's inability to bring the definition of AIDS firmly under its control. What, then, are the implications? Medicalizing a social problem such as alcoholism works to hold the moralists and the state at bay. Defining alcoholism as an illness removes blame from individuals and means that treatment and rehabilitation rather than jail or damnation are the preferred ways of controlling alcoholic behaviour. There is, however, no effective treatment or cure for AIDS. The blaming of specific marginal groups for the spread of AIDS supports the view that the "medicalization of deviance" has not occurred with this disease.

With the dawn of 1988, AIDS is receiving increased public attention. This will make it somewhat easier to follow the power struggle for control over the meaning of AIDS, although the media themselves play a major role by controlling information. It is clear that moral leaders, the state, and the medical profession are all vying for position with regard to control of the disease and its meanings. At present, morality seems to have the upper hand, probably because frightened societies tend to seek scapegoats onto which to project their anxieties. Susan Sontag (1978:87) notes the results in *Illness as Metaphor*:

> Trying to comprehend "radical" or "absolute" evil, we search for adequate metaphors. But the modern disease metaphors are all cheap shots. The people who have the real disease are also hardly helped by hearing their disease's name constantly being dropped as the epitome of evil.

Scapegoats are almost always marginal groups of one kind or another. In this case it is the gay male community which has been blamed for propagating the epidemic, despite the fact that in many African countries males and females are equally affected. Prostitutes will

likely be the next victims of this scapegoating.

Fear of the disease will continue in the face of the expanding number of cases and the lack of a cure. Both of these will work against the dominance of the medical profession's perspectives and its ability to give the humanitarian protection of the sick role.

Of course, we all need to be concerned about AIDS, but we can react to disease on the basis of scientific and medical facts, or we can react with fears which create community and social tensions and which ultimately compound the effects of the disease itself. Because the meaning and, therefore, our reactions to AIDS are not firmly established, moral leaders, the state, and the medical profession will all continue to interact to define the general public's view of the disease.

Not only will the dominant agents of social control vie amongst themselves for power, but also within themselves. The law (state) usually operates in one of two ways. The first is to protect the sick from discrimination, thereby entrenching the sick role. If the state decides to protect those with AIDS rather than holding them responsible for the disease, we will likely see anti-discrimination laws enacted[3] or court interpretations of human rights codes and the Canadian Charter of Rights to include protection to those with AIDS.

If on the other hand, the state chooses to ignore individual rights in favour of protecting the public's health, we will see a number of punitive measures such as antibody testing as a marriage requirement, exclusion of antibody-positive children and teachers from schools, jailing of prostitutes with antibodies, and, as authors such as Hancock and Carim (1986) have suggested, quarantine. These authors quote Ben Schatz, the lawyer who heads the National Gay Rights Advocates in the United States, and who posits the extreme case:

> I wouldn't rule out the possibility of concentration camps for gays in America. One would like to think that such things would not be possible because this is the 20th century but, on the other hand, the most gross violations of human rights have occurred in the 20th century. The fact is

that once fear gets hold of people, it's very hard to shake it. (1986:185)

The physician as official designator of the sick role can also take on one of two functions. The first is a gatekeeping function which usually works to exempt the sick from school or jobs without penalty. Because AIDS victims are the subject of such widespread discrimination due to fear and misunderstandings, this role is presently being exercised to allow inclusion rather than exclusion. For example, Saskatchewan's "Guidelines for Schools and Day Care Services" states:

> Infection with AIDS should not prevent a person from being employed or working in a school except as determined by the personal physician and MHO (Medical Health Officer) in consultation with the individual. In cases where employment is a health risk to the school population as determined by the personal physician and MHO, the MHO will advise the Director of Education. (p. 4)

While the physician's function is often to protect the sick, he or she can also become an agent of society rather than of sick individuals. This is the more likely role in times of fear. If AIDS becomes defined as a public health problem requiring radical intervention, the physician will undoubtedly become the agent of the state, determining who should be segregated from the rest of society and the nature of the segregation environment.

Present overtones of sexual morality and judgement mask the fact that AIDS is an illness, and work against the ability of major institutions to offer the protection of the sick role. These overtones also work against useful prevention strategies and tend to promote control strategies. The only way of preventing disease, at time of writing, requires alteration of sexual practices and of needle-sharing practices. Educating the general public will require explicit information and discussion of condom use, oral, anal, and vaginal intercourse, drug use, and other topics generally considered taboo.[4]

Those who are well deserve education; those who are sick deserve protection. AIDS offers us the chance to measure the degree to which we are an "enlightened" humanitarian society. One cannot truly capture the personal experience and suffering of those who are ill with AIDS, nor of those who have lost family members or friends. The disease will ultimately heighten the vulnerability of those at risk and those suffering from the disease, or else it will cause more firmly entrenched civil rights protections for them. Those with power will decide.

NOTES

1. The retrovirus that is believed to be the cause of AIDS has been known by a variety of names. It is referred to in the literature as LAV (lymphadenopathy-associated virus) and HTLV-III (human T-cell lymphotropic virus type III) and LAV/HTLV-III (a combined abbreviation). The *Canada Diseases Weekly Report*, in its September 13, 1986 publication, reports that the Executive Committee of the International Committee on Taxonomy of Viruses endorsed the term "human immunodeficiency virus" or HIV and recommended that it be used to replace the other designations. The name HIV is now used by the *Canada Diseases Weekly Report* and in all World Health Organization's publications and documents.

2. The Diagnostic and Statistical Manual of Mental Disorders (DSM) is the official classification of psychiatric disorders of the American Psychiatric Association. In DSM-I (1952), homosexuality was defined as a form of sexual deviation under the category of "Sociopathic Personality Disturbance." DSM-II (1968), still defines homosexuality as a sexual deviation but it was changed to fall within the general category of "Personality Disorders and Certain Other Non-Psychotic Mental Disorders." The DSM-III (1980) was

changed as a result of a referendum of APA in 1974, and homosexuality became defined as "Homosexual-Conflict Disorder" (Conrad and Schneider, 1980:193, 208–9).

3. According to Leonard (1985:30), Los Angeles and West Hollywood, California have enacted local ordinances expressly prohibiting discrimination in employing persons with AIDS unless the employer can show that absence of AIDS is a bona fide occupational qualification.

4. For example, in January of 1988 the Canadian Broadcasting Corporation (CBC) still prohibits any advertisements for contraception. They have, however, indicated they would be willing to examine the possibility of airing advertisements on disease barriers. Either way, the object will be a condom, but no one will be allowed to indicate that it can be used to prevent pregnancies, only that it can reduce the risk of contracting AIDS.

STUDY QUESTIONS

1. To what extent does the media's discussion of AIDS contribute to the stigmatizing of those who have the disease?

2. Are there other health issues which the medical profession has been less than successful in bringing under its control? What are some of the reasons for its lack of success?

3. Are there any examples you know of AIDS, or AIDS antibody tests being used to discriminate against risk groups or sick individuals?

4. Do you think that insurance companies have the right to deny coverage to those with seropositive blood or those who are homosexual? What factors are likely to motivate their decision?

5. What are some of the potential implications of applying the Charter of Rights to those who are afflicted with AIDS?

RECOMMENDED READING

Altman, Dennis. *Aids in the Mind of America.* New York: Anchor Press/Doubleday, 1986.

AMA Management Briefing. *AIDS: The Workplace Issues.* New York: AMA Membership Publications Division, 1985.

Conrad, P., and J.W. Schneider. *Deviance and Medicalization: From Badness to Sickness.* St. Louis: C.V. Mosby Co., 1980.

Patton, Cindy. *Sex and Germs.* Boston: South End Press, 1985.

Sontag, Susan. *Illness as Metaphor.* Markham, Ontario: Penguin Books, 1978.

REFERENCES

Adams, Mary Louise. "Politics, Women and AIDS." *Horizons* 4, no. 9 (September 1986): 21–23.

Altman, Dennis. *AIDS in the Mind of America.* Garden City, New York: Anchor Press/Doubleday, 1986.

Canada. Health and Welfare Canada. *AIDS in Canada: What You Should Know* Cat. no. H46-121, 1986.

———. *Canada Diseases Weekly Report,* Vol.

12, no. 37 (September 13, 1986); Vol. 12, no. 48 (November 29, 1986); Vol. 13, no. 1 (January 10, 1987).

Conrad, P., and J.W. Schneider. *Deviance and Medicalization: From Badness to Sickness*. St. Louis: C.V. Mosby Co., 1980.

Gagnon, J.H. *Human Sexualities*. Glenview, Illinois: Scott, Foresman and Co., 1977.

Hancock, G., and E. Carim. *AIDS: The Deadly Epidemic*. London: Victor Gollancz Ltd., 1986.

Illich, I. *Limits to Medicine: Medical Nemesis, The Expropriation of Health*. Toronto: McClelland and Stewart, 1976.

Katchadourian, H.A., and D.T. Lunde. *Fundamentals of Human Sexuality*. Holt, Rinehart and Winston, 1975.

Leonard, A.S. "The Legal Issues." *AIDS: The Workplace Issues*. New York: AMA Membership Publications Division, 1985: 28–46.

Moss, Lawrence. "Medical Answers About AIDS." *AIDS: The Workplace Issues*. New York: AMA Membership Publications Division, 1985: 55–76.

"New Human Retroviruses: One Causes AIDS..." *Nature* 320, no. 3 (April 1986): 325.

Parent, Grey. *The AIDS Phenomenon: A Medical Mystery*. Toronto: Toronto Sun Publishing Corporation, 1985.

Parsons, T. *The Social System*. New York: Free Press, 1951.

Patton, Cindy. *Sex and Germs*. Boston: South End Press, 1985.

R.E.A.L. Women of Canada. *Laws Protecting Homosexuals on "Sexual Orientation" Legislation*. Toronto: Pamphlet, no date.

Saskatchewan Advisory Committee on AIDS. *Information on AIDS: Guidelines for Schools and Day Care Services*. Pamphlet, no date.

Sontag, Susan. *Illness as Metaphor*. Markham, Ontario: Penguin Books, 1978.

United States. Department of Health and Human Services. Centers for Disease Control. *Morbidity and Mortality Weekly Report*, Vol. 34, no. 25 (June 28, 1985).

Zola, I.K. "Medicine as an Institution of Social Control." *The Sociological Review* (November 1972): 487–504.

32

DECISIONS AND DYING: Questions of Clinical Ethics

David J. Roy
Center for Bioethics of the Clinical Research Institute of Montreal

INTRODUCTION

The concept of "dying with dignity" has during the last ten years dominated medical practice, medical ethics, and medical law. It is often far from clear what this slogan should mean in hospitals that have become theatres for the deployment of a complex life-prolonging technology requiring the services of many specialized persons. The sick, and possibly dying, person represents a cluster of clinical challenges woven into the pattern of a unique personal history. That history of desires, plans, achievements, loves, and hopes, not just health and biological survival, are thrown into question when devastating illness strikes and death threatens. That unique person, certainly weak and possibly frightened and confused, should be not only the object of the clinical decisions that have to be made, but also the norm of the fundamental human choices that define the meaning of clinical activity at the extremes of life. However, who is to make these choices and how are they to be made in a highly pluralistic society and highly specialized hospitals?

The reappearance of groups promoting active euthanasia and "rational suicide" reveals levels of desperation that mark profound societal discord about eminently important matters. The questions abound and recur. When should efforts to prolong or to save a patient's life be stopped? What are the criteria for such decisions? Can they be uniform in a morally and culturally pluralistic society? How is the responsibility for such decisions to be shared? If it is morally justified in specific circumstances to let a patient die, why is it not morally justifiable to hasten the same patient's death?

These and related questions challenge the ethos, morality, and ethics of individuals and communities within a pluralistic society. We do not all share the same governing perceptions, assumptions, and beliefs about the origin, destiny, meaning, liberties, and moral imperatives of human life. These are elements of an *ethos* that sets the foundation of moral living and determines a hierarchy of values. We often do differ quite sharply about what is of greater or lesser importance in life, about which values may be sacrificed and which are to be maintained, perhaps at any cost. If a *morality* is based upon governing values, then we differ morally, at times profoundly so, in our society.

An ethos and a morality need a system of *ethics*. An ethics works out the judgements that have to be made when moral design confronts constraints on the real possibilities available to individuals and societies. Ethics applies the norms shaped by fundamental perceptions and governing values to resolve value conflicts in a real world marked by limitations. These may affect the range of real possibilities open to people, as well as their personal and moral development.

CLINICAL ETHICS

Value conflicts at the bedside frequently arise from uncertainty about how best to care for the gravely ill and dying, when available treatments affect patients' clinical needs and total life interests in quite different ways. The key question of clinical ethics is, How can we help this particular person live or die in a way that preserves his or her dignity, and ours as well?

Using the patient as a battlefield for contending moral persuasions and traditions totally undermines the method of clinical ethics. This method centres on the patient as the primary norm for the resolution of uncertainties and differences of view about treatment options. The patient's biography — his or her clinical course, relationships, beliefs, life plans, and overall life interests — constitute this primary norm. The skillful use of this norm requires the most accurate description of the patient possible. The results of laboratory tests and diagnostic imaging portray only a part of the whole patient.

The maxim of clinical ethics is: each case contains its own resolution. Understand the patient as comprehensively as possible, and the balance of elements required to resolve the ethical dilemma or conflict will emerge.

It is difficult to obtain a comprehensive understanding of a patient, particularly in large tertiary-care hospitals, without engaging in wide-ranging communication. This means attending to, and inviting the mutually corrective interplay of, all informed and pertinent points of view: those of the patient, if lucid and competent, and those of the physicians, nurses, family members, and other participants in the clinical drama.

The challenge of clinical ethics is to construct this dialogue and sustain it until the play of one view against another leads to a comprehensive grasp of the essentials, and to an acceptable consensus on what should be done or avoided. The most striking feature of these dialogues of clinical ethics is that people of widely disparate backgrounds and philosophies can come to agree on what is best for this particular patient, when the patient is incapable of expressing his or her own mind.

The ethical uncertainties, issues, and dilemmas of modern medicine are inextricably bound up with the unique circumstances of particular cases. Though general propositions and principles define moral perimeters, they do not of themselves decide concrete cases. The specific norms required for such cases are not prefabricated and available for deductive application; they have to be constructed slowly and inductively from discriminating judgements about individual patients and the unique problems of specific clinical trials. Without such norms, general principles remain mute about what they command, prohibit, or permit.

This, then, is the situation of ethics in clinical practice and research. General principles need the resolving power of specific norms to focus on the detail of individual cases. The norms are designed inductively from ethical judgements constructed to fit these cases as equitably as possible. The construction of practical judgements, rather than arguments, is essentially interdisciplinary work. Case reasoning, which constitutes a return to a method of moral thinking favoured by leading minds in ancient Greece and medieval times, has helped medicine to extricate ethics from the deadlock of interminable discourse about matters upon which people are likely never to agree. This understanding of clinical decision-making incorporates Toulmin's observation (1981:32) that we can often agree on practical judgements about what should or should not be done without being able to agree on the rationales for such judgements.

THE INSTITUTIONALIZATION OF DYING

People today usually die in places equipped with a massive and complex technology capable of supporting and prolonging life, frequently only life in the biological sense, when cures and returns to health and vitality are no longer possible. Terminally ill and dying patients may be technologically bound to biological existence beyond the moments when they could have died conscious and in mastery of their ultimate moments of life. Philippe Ariès (1974:88–89) has described the situation that has arisen because of our new life-prolonging technologies and our uncertainty about when this technology is out of place.

> Death has been dissected, cut to bits by a series of little steps, which finally makes it impossible to know which step was the real death, the one in which consciousness was lost, or the one in which breathing stopped. All these little silent deaths have replaced and erased the great dramatic act of death, and no one any longer has the strength or patience to wait over a period of weeks for a moment which has lost part of its meaning.

Dying today means dying with medicine's complex technology and with its technologists. One rarely dies on one's own. Dying has almost become a team activity, an interdisciplinary performance. People do not simply die, nor do they die simply. Their dying calls for decisions. However, the dying person is often not the central action, nor the decision-maker, but an object of custody about whom others make decisions.

The kinds of decisions that have to be made for and with dying persons are not purely technical. They become an intrinsic component of the event of dying. Depending on the content and mode of these decisions, some people will have the chance to die well, masters of their dying, not alone and not lonely. Others may die before their time, without a chance to fully experience their dying. Others may die too late, reduced to biological systems that have to be tended. Some may die uninformed and unenlightened, caught trying to play Scene One when the curtain is about to be rung down. Still others may die, who could have lived.

Decisions with such consequences are eminently moral. They cannot be made without calling upon and expressing our deepest values and beliefs about what is truly worthwhile in life. People may differ profoundly on such matters. Consequently, even once we move beyond negligence, insensitivity, incompetent pain control, mindless medical intervention, reflex applications of medical technology, and medical paternalism, "dying with dignity" remains as a plea for compassionate understanding, as a category of controversy, and as a symbol of a quest for a moral and societal consensus. The consensus, not to be identified with uniformity, is growing and includes space for those who differ from established views.

DYING WITH DIGNITY: A MODEL

Blaise Pascal has said that a human being, even when subjected to the laws of nature that dictate descent into death, remains superior to the entire universe. This is so because a human being can know that he dies, while the universe knows nothing about what it does. Though the dignity of a human being does not consist in thought alone, how can one's dying be an expression of human and personal dignity if it has no chance to be the final expression of the meaning one has given to life and to love?

A *model of dying* with dignity would include *at least* the following elements. Dying with dignity would mean:

- dying without a frantic technical fuss and bother to squeeze out a few more moments or hours of biological life, when the important thing is to live out one's last moments as fully, consciously , and courageously as possible;

- dying without that twisting, racking pain that totally ties up a person's consciousness and leaves one free for nothing and for no one else;

- dying in surroundings that are worthy of a human being who is about to live what should be one's "finest hour." The environment of a dying patient should clearly say: the technical drama of medicine has receded to the background to give way to the central human drama, the drama, as the poet would say, of a unique human being "wrestling with his God";

- dying in the presence of people who know how to drop the professional mask and relate to others simply and richly as human beings;

- dying with one's eyes open. No games, no pretense. We find and give to one another the courage to admit what is happening. A human being who can do this is already ahead of dying and superior to death;

- dying with one's mind open. The really hard questions that rattle the bedrock of our dreams and hopes face us unanswered at the time of dying. To die, firmly holding on these questions, to refuse to latch in to some little myth designed to render these questions harmless and to rob them of their power to echo through the soul, is what dying with an open mind demands;

- dying with one's heart open. This I saw in a young woman dying of cancer. She gave us something of herself that reached beyond her death and that death could not take away. She made us want to live courageously and to live for others.

Dying is meant to be an act of life, an act of integration, and an act of communication. Professional skills are there to serve the achievement of these acts. At this moment, professional authority gives way to the new authority that appears in a person who rises to the demands of dying with unique and personal dignity.

Of course, reality is always too varied and complex to fit neatly into any one model of what dying with dignity means. What does respect for dignity demand or permit when patients are young and in deep, irreversible coma, or are old and in deep, irreversible dementia? Is there dignity in the act of denial, in a person's steadfast refusal to admit, at least publicly, that death is imminent? Can anger and rebellion be as dignified as serene acceptance?

We would do well to go slowly in fixing the modes of dignity in dying. The one attitude we must criticize is thanatological totalitarianism, the idea that there is only one right way to die.

WHEN IS A PERSON DEAD?

Many people still find it difficult to grasp the relationships among the various proposed concepts of brain death. There is also a residual reluctance to accept fully that brain death is "real" death. This holds true despite the growing consensus over the past twenty-five years among informed members of the medical, nursing, and legal professions that death can be diagnosed reliably on the basis of precise neurological criteria. These criteria are required when continuing circulation and respiration, maintained by prolonged intensive life support, are no longer definitive signs of life.

However, a brain-dead body, *with intensive care life-support*, can breathe, circulate blood, digest food, filter metabolic waste products, maintain body temperature, grow new tissue, and support fetal life. Many people today do find it conceptually perplexing and ethically perturbing to declare and treat as dead a patient whose body can still do all these things and show all these signs of life. For example, Mark Siegler (1982:1101–2) has claimed: "The death of the brain seems not to serve as a boundary; it is a tragic, ultimately fatal loss, but not death itself. Bodily death occurs later, when integrated functioning ceases."

A number of principles are generally recognized and respected today throughout the world when brain death concepts and criteria are used to ascertain that a patient with artificially maintained respiratory function and continuing cardiovascular function is, in fact, dead.

Roy et al. (1986:161–68) have developed the argument showing how irreversible apneic coma, a state marked by deep unconsciousness, unresponsivity, and the inability to breathe spontaneously, shapes the central concept of brain death. Death should not be declared on the basis of neurological criteria unless the cause of this coma is known or the coma is known not to result from events or agents that produce reversible coma. There is general agreement that the fulfillment of these conditions cannot be judged on the basis of only one criterion or test. A set of criteria and a battery of tests are required. It is generally admitted now that patients fulfilling all these conditions will never regain consciousness or the capacity to breathe, and invariably suffer stoppage of the heart and electroencephalographic activity in a matter of days, despite continuing artificial maintenance of respiratory function.

The major current of thought underlying this clinical notion of death is represented notably in the document of the Conference of Medical Royal Colleges and their Faculties in the United Kingdom (1976:1069–70). Christopher Pallis (1983:284–87), in articulating this trend of thought, emphasizes that *permanent functional death of the brain stem means death of the brain as a whole, that death of the brain as a whole is death of the human being, and that brain stem death can be diagnosed reliably on the basis of clinical criteria.*

If one adopts this view of death, stopping the respirator after proper diagnosis of brain stem death is not the same thing as allowing someone to die. Rather, it is a medically and ethically justified refusal to continue uselessly treating someone who is already dead. If consent has been given for the donation of organs, it is justifiable according to this view of death to reconnect the brain-stem-dead patient to the respirator to preserve organs until they can be removed for transplantation.

Those holding the view that death means death of the whole organism will resist disconnecting a respirator until the heart of a patient with brain stem death comes to a final stop. It is also unlikely that they would countenance removal of organs for transplantation while the heart is still beating, despite proven total irreversible loss of brain stem function. The idea underlying this opposition, as Wainwright Evans et al. explain (1980:1022) is that brain stem death defines "a very grave prognosis ... but must not be confused with a diagnosis of death."

MAY WE ALLOW OR HELP THE OLD TO DIE?

When an old person is in an irreversible state of advanced senility of the Alzheimer's type, we witness development in reverse. These persons cannot think, reason, decide, choose, speak, communicate, or maintain interpersonal relationships. The question may be phrased sharply: If biological existence in these older persons short-circuits the achievement of their higher human purposes, need we make major medical efforts to maintain this biological existence? Need we give antibiotics to cure pneumonia to a patient now fallen into a state of irreversible advanced senility?

Morally justifiable acts in one kind of relationship may be immoral in another. The doctor-patient relationship obviously justifies high-risk invasions of the bodily integrity of human beings, acts that would be criminal outside this relationship. What acts does the medical mandate justify when a patient is deteriorating beyond medicine's ability to cure? Are there any moral limits to the measures a doctor may take to alleviate pain, suffering, and a lingering process of dying? A patient, conscious and lucid, may request rapid and painless death from a doctor. In certain extreme cases of cancer, with respect to certain unsalvageable infants, and when faced with certain irreversibly senile patients in a state of painful and prolonged dying, doctors themselves may ask whether waiting for death to occur defines the limit of their moral and professional duty.

Several years ago, Dr. J. Freeman (1972:904–5) asked: "In those rare instances where the decision has been made to avoid 'heroic' measures and to allow 'nature to take its course', should society not allow physicians to alleviate the pain and suffering and help nature to take its course — quickly?" Freeman's question was in reference to the care of neonates. But the times when this question arises are not rare in the care of the old who are chronically ill and degenerating cerebrally as well.

How is such a question to be answered? By measuring the proportion of benefits to damages? In this event, whose benefits and damages enter into the ratio? Only those of the patients? Do we need a broader view, and should we seek to answer the question by considering the long-term consequences of an act of "mercy" that amounts to killing those patients who fail to die rapidly enough for their own good, or perhaps, for the good of others? Should a society give such power to doctors or to any profession? If we were to justify some acts of humanitarian infanticide or geronticide, are we also capable of establishing generally acceptable and non-arbitrary limits to the putative medical mandate to shorten "useless dying curves" by direct termination of life? Do we try this as an experiment and closely monitor the results? Do we, on the basis of a fear that "things might get out of hand," arbitrarily decree that no one, doctors included, is ever morally justified in terminating a patient's life?

Some, perhaps many, would hold that such a decree is not arbitrary at all. It would simply be an expression of the most basic of all principles, namely, that no human being has dominion over the life of another. However, as the Australian film "Breaker Morant" demonstrated, in war, situations arise that fall outside all existing rules. Surely similar situations arise in medicine? Should we then recognize these situations as exceptions to the argument that no human has dominion over the life of another, act accord-

ingly, and avoid public discussion of acts that cannot be generalized and hence cannot be regulated by any rule or law?

THE SEVERELY MALFORMED NEWBORN

Contemporary neonatal intensive care units are the scene of an increasingly intense debate. The issue, in its crudest and most unqualified form, is: to treat or not to treat seriously defective newborn babies. At an earlier period, many or even most of these babies would simply have died, indeed, quite quickly. Because at the time little could be done for these babies, there was little that had to be decided.

Things have changed. Medicine has advanced. Many of these babies now need not die as a direct and quick result of their defects at birth. Their lives can now be "saved" — or at least prolonged for a very significant period.

In some cases, the prolongation resulting from medical treatment amounts to little more than an extension of the dying process. The anencephalic and hydranencephalic child, or the child with major neurological and multi-system defects are examples.

In other cases, vigorous and prolonged medical treatment will save the infant's life. The child, and later, the teenager and young adult will, however, be more or less handicapped. Depending on the circumstances, the handicap will be physical and/or mental in character. Babies born with spina bifida and myelomeningocele are examples.

In a third set of cases, babies are born with a physical defect which can be treated successfully, and is lethal if left untreated. These babies, however, are also marked by other sorts of defect that are not lethal but are also at the moment, untreatable. Such, frequently, are the Down's syndrome babies.

It is with respect to babies such as these that the question of selective non-treatment, with death as a consequence, arises in contemporary neonatology. Some hold tenaciously to a "sacredness of life" principle and argue that no selection whatsoever should be made. Every effort to prolong every infant life should be made. Others hold with equal tenacity to a "quality of life" principle and use measures of natural endowment at birth to prognosticate or guess future levels of I.Q., productivity, etc., of the given infant.

The best possible medical decisions for these babies surely call for attention to a host of concrete physiological and neurological factors. The ultimate basis for a decision in these matters, nevertheless, is moral in character. The medical community is divided in opinion and conflicting treatment policies are proposed and followed precisely because of a deep divergence of view on the worth or value of these babies.

Those who hold absolutely to a given "sacredness of life" principle tend to forget that this sacredness covers a curve or spiral of development, described by Lonergan (1958:664) as follows: "Man develops biologically to develop psychically, and he develops psychically to develop intellectually and rationally." Ignorance of this principle can generate a misplaced passion for the sacred. One may then proceed to overlook the purposes and limits of medicine, and to treat malformed infants aggressively, when prolongation of dying and suffering is the only likely outcome.

Another extreme is reached when fixation on the estimated future quality of life motivates non-treatment decisions that mean death for babies who, despite disabilities, would have had chances of attaining levels of genuine human development. We should never allow infants to die because it is in someone else's interests for the child to do so. Some lives, of course, simply cannot be lived. When damage at birth is great and irreversible, withholding life-prolonging treatment is quite justifiable. Life-prolonging measures are not meant to be used simply to prolong dying and suffering.

ACTIVE EUTHANASIA

Some detect a radical inconsistency when a justifiable decision to allow a patient to die is combined with passive waiting for this death to occur. Robert Reid (1977:18) has urged: "If a designated aim of medicine is that a child should die, why should it not be more humane to make it die?" Over ten years ago, a conference on critical issues in newborn intensive care, as Jonsen (1975:758) reports, asked the question: Is it ever right to intervene directly to kill a dying infant?

When we withhold treatment from defective babies and patients because we cannot cure them and because treatment would, at bottom, signify our initiative in prolonging a dying process, we are admitting the limits of what we are able to do medically for these patients. We at the same time admit the ethical limits of what we should do to them. When we kill such patients, however, we assume a mandate to eliminate suffering by eliminating the sufferer. This mandate assumes a total power of dominion over the sufferer because it assumes a total responsibility for the sufferer's life. The least that can be said for such a mandate is that it carries the burden of its proof. The next thing to be said is that such a mandate *requires justification*. The existence of such a mandate has to be demonstrated.

However, no demonstration that medicine has such a total mandate has ever been given. In fact, the cardinal beliefs and positions of Western civilized thought on the uniqueness and autonomy of every individual human being have consistently rejected the totalitarian premises of such a mandate. If there are technical limits on what we can effectively do, medically, *for* a defective newborn, there are also definite ethical limits on what we can do, ethically, *to* such a child in his or her name and on the basis of our interpretation of what is in his or her best interests.

Humanitarian euthanasia is based on a view of unlimited medical responsibility for patients' lives. However, the premise of ethical medical practice should be that doctors intervene as little as possible in any human life. Every such intervention has to be justified, even if this justification is often smoothly implied in the initial contacts that establish a given doctor-patient relationship, or is explicitly given in negotiations of informed consent. Decisions for non-treatment, with death the result, may, in a range of circumstances, signify precisely respect for the principle of limited intervention and for limitations on medicine's power to do good for patients. The additional step of humanitarian euthanasia implies an absolute imperative to intervene in a human life, the very point denied by the non-treatment decision.

Killing patients to relieve them of pain or suffering is ethically unjustified, has been rejected generally in civilized societies, and is hardly necessary. Intelligent administration of modern analgesics permits an adequate control of pain.

Suffering, of course, is more than the experience of pain. Memories, lost opportunities, guilts, dated moments of hurt or betrayal, the fragility of one's most unforgettable loves and joys, and unfulfilled dreams are all as unique as the days, times, places, and persons to which they are bound. Suffering is the message between unwritten lines of a singular personal biography. Humanitarian euthanasia is no substitute for compassion, that unique ability to join hands with another human being at the crossroads of our greatest vulnerability.

PROLONGING LIFE: ETHICAL CONSIDERATIONS

We have all been very eloquent in recent years about patient autonomy. We marshall increasing legal support for our public moral claims that it is a patient's right to refuse life-prolonging treatment, if and when that treatment conflicts with personal beliefs about how his or her life is to be lived. We generally support the value of self-determination in the face of potential or threatening dictatorial uses of medical technology.

However, *we do not always find it easy to live in the same categories as those in which we think.* Publicly, we think about patients in terms of autonomy and rights to self-determination. Frequently, we live and act in the categories of paternalistic protection and moralistic commitment to a "you must live at all cost" ethic.

Difficult clinical, ethical, and legal issues arise when we face decisions about withholding or discontinuing aggressive life support to allow persons living with undamaged brains or nervous systems to die. The issues are somewhat different, though no less difficult, when others have to make such decisions for patients whose consciousness is too perturbed to permit them to express their own minds. A resolution of these issues may generate conflict between the principles of philosophical and medical ethics, the current state of the law and jurisprudence, the maxims of clinical experience, and the variant moral persuasions and perceptions of people in societies as pluralistic as our own.

The Patient's Will as Norm

If confusion or pathological depression, as contrasted with rational depression, can be excluded, many would hold to the principle, formulated by Cassem (1976:155), that "the will of the patient, not the health of the patient, should be the supreme law." The Law Reform Commission of Canada (1983:32), in the same vein, has proposed an amendment to the Criminal Code to prohibit any relevant paragraph of the code from being interpreted as requiring a physician "to continue to administer or to undertake medical treatment against the expressed wishes of the person for whom such treatment is intended."

The Vatican Declaration on Euthanasia (1980:9–10) gives additional support to the value of self-determination and reflects the view that refusal of life-prolonging treatment is not equivalent to suicide. The relevant proposal states that

> one cannot impose on anyone the obligation to have recourse to a technique which is already in use but which carries a risk or is burdensome. Such a refusal is not the equivalent of suicide; on the contrary, it should be considered as an acceptance of the human condition, or a wish to avoid the application of a medical procedure disproportionate to the results that can be expected, or a desire not to impose excessive expense on the family or the community.

Proportionality Ethics

The proportionality rule, as concisely stated by Cassem (1976:155–56), affirms that life-prolonging treatments are contraindicated "when they cause more suffering than benefit." The Law Reform Commission of Canada (1983:32) has suggested that physicians are not bound by the Criminal Code to administer treatments that are therapeutically useless or are not in the patient's best interests.

Adamant holding to a "sacredness of life" principle may lead one to overlook the purposes and limits of medicine, as will as the limits of a patient's physical and moral resources. Medicine has reached its limits when all it can offer is an extension of function that is experienced by the patient to be a prolongation of dying rather than an enhancement of living.

The Vatican Declaration on Euthanasia (1980:9–10) proposes that it is ethically justifiable to discontinue the use of advanced life-prolonging techniques, "where the results fall short of expectations." Direct appeal is made to the proportionality rule when this document directs attention to the fact that patient, family, and staff may judge that "the techniques applied impose on the patient strain or suffering out of proportion with the benefits which he or she may gain from such techniques."

Withholding and Discontinuing Treatment: An Equivalence

Some find it easier to withhold life-prolonging treatment than to discontinue such treatment once started. However, the conditions that would ethically justify a decision not to start life-prolonging treatment for a patient exercise the same ethical force when they obtain only after treatment has been started. In Cassem's succinct words (1976:156) "stopping treatment is ethically no different from never starting it."

CONCLUSION

The preceding considerations rest on the assumption that biological life is not an absolute value, and that death is not an absolute evil. A moment comes, at different times for different patients, when technologically aided efforts to extend life may interfere with higher personal values, and should give way to other forms of care. These concepts call for a community of concern, care, and co-operation that unites the patient, family, and physicians in a search for the decision that best honours and protects patients, their dignity, and their unique hopes.

STUDY QUESTIONS

1. Is a patient's refusal of life-prolonging treatment, for example, hemodialysis for irreversible, terminal kidney disease, equivalent to suicide?

2. If withholding or discontinuing life-prolonging treatment is justifiable in certain situations, why is active termination of the patient's life in the same situations generally considered to be unjustifiable?

3. Should potentially lethal infections, for example, pneumonia, be treated in old per-

sons who are in a state of deep, irreversible senility?

4. When children are born with serious congenital malformations, should doctors respect parental refusal of life-saving treatment for these children? Always? Only in certain situations?

5. Under what conditions is it justifiable to a doctor to instruct health-care personnel not to resuscitate a patient in the event of cardio-respiratory arrest?

RECOMMENDED READING

Ariès, Philippe. *Western Attitudes Toward Death: From the Middle Ages to the Present.* Baltimore: Johns Hopkins University Press, 1974.

Cassem, N. "When Illness is Judged Irreversible: Imperative and Elective Treatments." *Man and Medicine* 2 (1976): 154–66.

Jonsen, A.R., et al. *Clinical Ethics.* New York: Macmillan, 1982.

Law Reform Commission of Canada. *Euthanasia, Aiding Suicide, and Cessation of Treatment.* Ottawa: Minister of Supply and Services Canada, 1983.

Roy, D., S. Verret, and C. Roberge. "Death, Dying, and the Brain." *Critical Care Clinics* 2, no. 1 (1986): 161–72.

Trowell, H. *The Unfinished Debate on Euthanasia.* London: SCM Press, 1973.

Wanzer, S.H., et al. "The Physician's Responsibility Toward Hopelessly Ill Patients." *New England Journal of Medicine* 310 (1984): 955–59.

REFERENCES

Ariès, Philippe. *Western Attitudes Toward Death: From the Middle Ages to the Present.* Baltimore: Johns Hopkins University Press, 1974.

Cassem, N. "When Illness is Judged Irreversible: Imperative and Elective Treatments." *Man and Medicine* 2 (1976): 154–66.

Conference of Royal Colleges and Faculties of the United Kingdom: Diagnosis of Brain Death. *Lancet* 2 (1976): 1069–70.

Freeman, J. "Is There a Right to Die — Quickly?" *Journal of Pediatrics* 80 (1972): 904–5.

Jonsen, A.R., et al. "Critical Issues in Newborn Intensive Care: A Conference Report and Policy Proposal." *Pediatrics* 55 (1975): 756–68.

Law Reform Commission of Canada. *Euthanasia, Aiding Suicide, and Cessation of Treatment.* Ottawa: Minister of Supply and Services Canada, 1983.

Lonergan, Bernard. *Insight: A Study of Human Understanding.* New York: Longman, 1958.

Pallis, C. "The Arguments about the EEG." *British Medical Journal* 286 (1983): 284–87.

Reid, Robert. "Spina Bifida: The Fate of the Untreated: Euthanasia?" *Hastings Center Report* 7 (1977): 18.

Roy, D., S. Verret, and C. Roberge. "Death, Dying, and the Brain." *Critical Care Clinics* 2, no. 1 (1986): 161–72.

Siegler, M., and D. Wikler. "Brain Death and Live Birth." *JAMA* 248 (1982): 1101–02.

Toulmin, S. "The Tyranny of Principles." *Hastings Center Report* 11 (1981): 31–39.

Vatican Congregation for the Doctrine of the Faith. *Declaration on Euthanasia.* Rome, 1980.

Wainwright Evans, D., and L.C. Lum. "Brain Death." *Lancet* 2 (1980): 1022.

33

THE POLITICS AND IDEOLOGY OF SELF-CARE AND LIFESTYLES

B. Singh Bolaria
University of Saskatchewan

INTRODUCTION

The 1974 working paper by Minister of Health Marc Lalonde, *A New Perspective on the Health of Canadians*, brought attention to the health risks associated with individual lifestyles and consumption patterns. It was contended that since the major risk factors in mortality are controlled by the personal discretion of the individual, there would be a considerable decrease in mortality if people would simply focus their attention on changing those aspects of their lifestyles and consumption patterns which are injurious to their health. As Lalonde (1974:26) argued,

> individual blame must be accepted by many of the deleterious effect on health of their respective lifestyles. Sedentary living, smoking, overeating, driving while impaired by alcohol, drug abuse and failure to wear seat-belts are among the many contributors to physical or mental illness for which the individual must accept some responsibility and for which he should seek correction.

Self-care and lifestyles also received prominent attention in a recent policy paper, *Achieving Health for All: A Framework for Health Promotion* (Epp, 1986). This paper refers to three major challenges that are not adequately addressed by current health policies and practices: (1) to reduce inequalities in health and health care, (2) to increase the prevention effort, and (3) to enhance people's capacity to cope with chronic conditions, disabilities, and mental health problems (Epp, 1986:398–99). Health promotion is offered as the way to meet these challenges, and is defined as "the process of enabling people to increase control over, and to improve, their health" (Epp, 1986:400). One of the mechanisms considered intrinsic to health promotion is self-care, which "refers to the decisions taken and the practices adopted by an individual specifically for the preservation of his or her health ... simply put, encouraging self-care means encouraging healthy choices" (Epp, 1986:401). Balanced diet and regular exercise are examples of self-care. The second mechanism considered intrinsic to health promotion is mutual aid — people working together, helping and supporting each other, or forming self-help groups. The third health mechanism is the creation of healthy environments, which in fact received very little attention in the policy paper, where it was acknowledged that "environmental change becomes by far the most complex and the most difficult of the three mechanisms or kinds of actions required for the promotion of health" (Epp, 1986:403). The policy paper tends to stress individual lifestyles, self-care, self-help groups, and other factors more in the individual's sphere of control than environmental factors which require societal intervention.

This perspective, which has become extremely popular not only in Canada but also in other countries (Doyal and Pennell, 1979; Navarro, 1986; Waitzkin, 1983), tends to downgrade the importance of the physical and social environment to the individual's health. The underlying assumption is that the basic cause of much ill health is the individual.

Even with respect to deaths due to motor vehicle accidents and other accidents and suicides, the Lalonde paper states: "Since all these causes are mainly due to human factors, including carelessness, impaired driving, despair, and self-imposed risks, it is evident that changes in these factors are needed if the rates of death are to be lowered (Lalonde, 1974:14). Consider further the "self-imposed" risks regarding circulatory diseases discussed in this paper: "While the causes of circulatory diseases are various, there is little doubt that obesity, smoking, stress, lack of exercise and high-fat diets, in combination, make a dominant contribution" (Lalonde, 1974:15).

This emphasis on lifestyles over social environment is symptomatic of what William Ryan has called "blaming the victim" syndrome. More importantly, as Berliner (1977:119) maintains, "focusing on lifestyles serves only to reify the lifestyles as an entity apart from the social conditions from which it arises." Berliner (1977:119) further argues: "Discussing changes in lifestyle without first discussing the changes in the social conditions which give rise to them, without recognizing that the lifestyle is derivative, is misleading and, in effect, is victim blaming."

Individual lifestyles and consumption patterns are now widely invoked as explanations of the current increase in many chronic and degenerative diseases. As these explanations and the attendant solutions are being given extensive publicity through the mass media and professional journals, thus becoming popularized and gaining greater acceptance, they are bound to have far-reaching consequences in health decisions and the provision of health care. As such, they merit serious analysis and consideration. The promotion of this strategy — individual etiology and individual solutions — in the face of the national health-care "crisis" is far from coincidental. Suffice it to state here that it obscures the extent to which health and illness depend upon socially determined ways of life, obfuscates the social causes of disease, shifts responsibility for health and illness back onto the individual, individualizing what is essentially a social problem, and promotes a course of action oriented toward changing individual behaviour and lifestyles rather than the existing social, economic, and political institutions and the health sector.

As the following discussion reveals, this is not a "new perspective"; rather, it is consistent with the basic tenets of bourgeois individualism and freedom of choice which have been with us for some time. Our discussion further reveals that this ideology, which pervades clinical medicine, is consistent with prevailing ideologies in the social sciences and with their application to the analysis and explanation of various social issues, as well as the attendant policy formulations.

INDIVIDUAL ETIOLOGY IN MEDICINE

This section evaluates the implications of the clinical paradigm, widely accepted in medical practice, that defines health and illness in individual terms, independent of the social context in which they occur. Turshen (1977:46) states: "This paradigm takes individual physiology as the norm for pathology (as contrasted with broader social conditions) and locates sickness in the individual's body." Contemporary medicine operates on a mechanistic and individualistic model in which individuals are "atomized" and decontextualized for treatment. Under such a paradigm,

> a living organism could be regarded as a machine which ought to be taken apart and reassembled if its structure and function were fully understood. In medicine, the same concept led further to the belief that an understanding of disease processes and of the body's response to them would make it possible to intervene therapeutically, mainly by physical (surgery), chemical, or electrical methods. (McKeon, 1965:38)

This approach basically ignores the fact that much ill health is rooted in the structure of society itself. Many diseases are considered to have a "specific etiology"; that is, the specific causes are sought in the body's cellular and biochemical systems. This individual-centred concept of disease has led to an essentially curative orientation, whereby people can be made healthy by means of "technological fixes" (Renaud, 1975). Technical solutions are offered to many problems which stem from social conditions (Fee, 1977).

Furthermore, the major response to many of the psychological disorders has been pharmacological — antidepressants, anti-anxiety agents, stimulants, and tranquillizers (Waldron, 1977; Katz, 1972; Stroufe and Stewart, 1973; Fee, 1977). These are generally prescribed to women, who consume large quantities of these drugs (Fee, 1977; Harding et al., 1977).

Many diseases are viewed as malfunctions, mere technical defects in the body's machinery, and many treatments are oriented toward restoring the "normal" functioning of the human body. Rather than removing the external causes of illness, medical technology is used to destroy the capacity of the body to register reaction to these causes.

Ironically, many treatments for a variety of stress-related illnesses act not by removing the causes of illness but by destroying the capacity of the organ to respond to the cause, often by removing the organ or by severing its connection with the brain. Thus "ultimate cures" for ulcer are vagotomy or removal of the duodenum; a response to hypertension may be blockage of the sympathetic nervous system; a response to severe mental disturbance may be psychosurgery. (Eyer and Sterling, 1977:34)

There has been increasing criticism of the clinical paradigm, especially as applied to psychiatric treatment (Illich, 1976; Dubos, 1968; Powels, 1973; Szasz, 1961; Laing, 1970; Doyal and Pennell, 1979; Waitzkin, 1983; Navarro, 1986). Nonetheless, this orientation has a pervasive and continuing influence in medical practice (Turshen, 1977).

Much of the research into non-psychological, or physical, illnesses reflects this orientation as well. There has been heavy emphasis on individual treatment and etiology of disease rather than on social and environmental factors, such as occupational and environmental exposure to pollutants, chemicals, and other harmful agents.

In some areas of medicine this individual etiology is taking extreme forms. For instance, in the area of occupational health, genetic screening is being done in some petrochemical industries in order to detect those workers whose genetic makeup may make them more susceptible to various toxins. The assumption made in genetic screening programmes is that certain workers get ill because of their genetic background and structure rather than because of exposure to toxins at the work place. This shifts the responsibility for disease back onto the individual, promoting a victim-blaming epidemiology. As one union leader said, "I think that in the 1980's we are going to see a lot of victim blaming. The emphasis will be not on so much what you work with, it will have to do with who your mother and father were" (cited in Navarro, 1984:113).

Similarly, in the case of some cancer research, the major emphasis, both in research and educational campaigns, is placed on individual responsibility and behaviour, such as smoking and personal habits (Greenberg and Randal, 1977). Little attention is given to environmental factors, such as pollutants and carcinogens, which are more and more being recognized as the agents most responsible for cancer: it is estimated that environmental factors are involved in the etiology of about 80 percent of all cancers (Waitzkin, 1983). Yet in many educational campaigns the emphasis is on the individual preserving his or her own health. Information on environmental and occupational carcinogens is rarely included in these campaigns. As Greenberg and Randal (1977) indicate, the American Cancer Society "has shown scant interest in the carcinogenic effects of air and water pollution, drugs and food additives. Its look-the-other-way attitude closely resembles that of the drug and chemical industries, with which many of its directors — all unpaid volunteers — are directly or indirectly associated." This attitude has changed little since 1977.

It is clear from the above discussion that a mechanistic-individualistic conception of disease, which engenders a disease-centred, high-technology, medical orientation is pervasive in medical practice and research, absolving economic and political systems from the responsibility for disease, and denying its social foundations.

INDIVIDUAL LIFESTYLES AND ENVIRONMENT

Despite the prevalence of this approach which conceals the social context of disease, there is considerable evidence which suggests that many diseases are environmentally generated, by the workplace in particular.

Workers constantly face hazardous working conditions, conditions which can hardly be attributed to their lifestyles. Workplace-related illnesses and accidents account for millions of days of lost work in Canada and far exceed the number of days lost due to strikes and lockouts (Rinehart, 1987; Jangula, 1986). For instance, in 1981 there were 1.2 million work injuries among the slightly more than 9 million workers in Can-

ada, a rate of nearly 13 injuries per 100 workers. Forty-eight percent of these injuries involved loss of work. The total number of work days lost was 15.8 million (Jangula, 1986). Thousands of workers work in unhealthy environments, where they are exposed to poor ventilation, inadequate safety, excessive dirt, radioactive dusts, and other pollutants. Some of these pollutants are directly linked to various debilitating and fatal diseases such as asbestosis, silicosis, and black lung. In addition to these pulmonary diseases, many types of cancer are associated with environmental conditions (Cairns, 1975; Hammond, 1974; Goff and Reasons, 1986).

Occupational diseases are, for the most part, environmentally determined. The priority of profits over occupational safety and workers' satisfaction is clearly responsible for disease-causing work environments (Miller, 1975; Waitzkin, 1983).

The nature and organization of work, job factors, and job attributes appear to have important relationships to the individual's general well-being (Coburn, 1975). Bosquet (1977:102) writes:

So deep is the frustration engendered by work that the incidence of heart attacks among manual workers is higher than that in any other stratum of society. People "die from work" not because of it is noxious or dangerous ... but because it is intrinsically "killing."

Other investigators have shown a correlation between general economic conditions, such as the unemployment rate, and cardiovascular and other mortality (Eyer, 1975, 1977; Brenner, 1971). Research evidence shows substantial health differences between the employed and the unemployed. The unemployed, for instance, report higher levels of psychological distress, more symptoms of depression, higher anxiety levels, and generally more health problems than the employed (D'Arcy and Siddique, 1985; Grayson, 1985). This observation is particularly significant in view of the current employment situation in Canada. The high unemployment rates in Canada are accompanied by increases in long-term unemployment — that is, for six months or longer (Parliament, 1987). The number of Canadians experiencing long-term unemployment more than tripled between 1980 and 1983. In 1985, 28 percent of unemployed Canadians were in the long-term unemployment category (Parliament, 1987). There was a dramatic drop in employment levels for men aged 55–64 between 1975 and 1985 (Lindsay, 1987). Because of the ever-present threat of unemployment, many workers may be reluctant to complain about conditions at the workplace. Under these circumstances, workers are faced with a choice between working in an unsafe and unhealthy workplace and not working at all.

Many factors in the work environment serve to produce conditions which are widely known as "stress-related diseases." Many of these stress-related diseases, such as heart disease, can be seen as originating from the needs of the production process itself.

The competitive nature of the production process, the continuous demand for an increase in efficiency, the need for a flexible and free labour force, unemployment, and job security, all contribute to general stress in the population.

This is evident in the disruption of the social environment. Eyer and Sterling (1977) argue that economic and cultural forces in capitalist society, which mould competitive, striving individuals and disrupt communal ties, create stress. Increasingly, stress is being recognized as a variable in the creation of ill health. Stressful effects of disruption of co-operative relationships and traditional cultures are manifested in high blood pressure and increases in blood cholesterol and fat levels (Sterling and Eyer, 1981; Waldron et al., 1982). Elevated blood fats and cholesterol levels increase the risk of cardiovascular diseases, which dominate modern excess mortality.

While competitiveness often leads to success in the capitalist work environment, at the same time much research has shown that it is a prime determinant of heart disease. Individual behaviour patterns have been identified as one of the strongest risk factors in heart disease. In the literature, studies have shown that the chance of

a person with "Type A" behaviour (aggressive, competitive) having a heart attack is two to five times higher than that of a person with "Type B" behaviour (co-operative, easy-going, relaxed, passive). The Type A behaviour pattern has become common and is associated with an increase in mortality from coronary heart disease (Rosenman et al., 1970, 1975). Independent of the effect of other risk factors, Type A alone increases the risk of coronary heart disease (Jenkins and Zyzsanski, 1980). This is because Type A "gathers" the other risk factors. As Ayer (1984:31) states:

> Part of this increased risk is because type-A "gathers" the other risk factors: smokers tend to be type-A, and type-A's smoke heavily; blood pressure and cholesterol are both elevated in type-As. This association provides evidence for the linkages suggested ... between work demands, behaviour, drug consumption; and physiological changes.

This indicates a contradiction between the needs of the economic system and what is healthy for the individual. It is in the interest of the individual, then, to practise Type B behaviour, but the interest of the system demands that individuals maintain Type A behaviour (Eyer, 1975). This suggests that the health effects of individual behaviour must be examined in the context of the social conditions from which the behaviour arises.

Competitiveness and orientation towards achievement become ideals; this is achieved through socialization in schools, religion, education, and cultural values (Bowles and Gintis, 1977). As noted earlier, social disruptions are the price of maintaining a free and flexible labour force. To correct for such disruptions would hinder the capitalist pursuit of profits and productivity. Similarly, as Eyer and Sterling (1977:37) state, "mass relaxation by the majority of men who share coronary-prone behaviour patterns would undermine productivity, the profits of capitalist firms, and thence the growth process itself."

Those in this society who do not exhibit competitive achievement orientation may be considered as "maladjusted," and the individuals blame their failure on their own lack of initiative. Therefore, the primary adaptation is competitive achievement orientation. There are those who cannot adapt or for whom the cost of adaptation is too high. The cost takes many forms other than coronary heart disease. The massive social and personal stresses engendered by the capitalist system may lead to drug and substance abuse. For instance, alcohol consumption is higher among groups with higher rates of unemployment, family breakup, and migration (Eyer, 1977; Egger, 1980). Other work-induced problems are ulcers, mental illness, and even suicide (Eyer and Sterling, 1977).

In addition to these factors, there is considerable evidence to show the effect of poverty on morbidity and mortality (Statistics Canada and Health and Welfare Canada, 1981; Wilkins and Adams, 1983; Wigle and Mao, 1980). Other evidence indicates the association of poverty with malnutrition, retarded growth, psychomotor retardation, emotional disturbance, and visual difficulties. These problems are even more acute among the Native people, where poverty is combined with added exposure to environmental disruption (Special Senate Committee on Poverty, 1971; Shah and Farkas, 1985).

Native people are subject to more pollutants than the general population because they frequently live in environmentally unsafe areas. Mercury poisoning of rivers and lakes at some Indian reserves in Ontario has received a great deal of publicity (Castrilli, 1982; Smith and Smith, 1975). The Native people of the White Dog and Grassy Narrows reserves were found to have 40 to 150 times more mercury in their blood than the average Canadian (McDonald, 1975; Moore, 1975). This problem is not confined to Northwestern Ontario. The *Medical Post* reported that there were 15 badly contaminated areas in Canada (Cassels, 1975). The release of toxic chemical wastes is creating a physical environment harmful to public health.

Yet the reaction of the Ontario Minister of Health was to blame the people for a lack of concern for their own health. The Minister said

he was "tired of people complaining about health hazards facing Indians in Northwestern Ontario while the complainers go on killing themselves with ... diseases of choice by exercising too little and smoking too much (Moore, 1975:16). Apparently, according to him the "real" problem is the Native people.

> One of the biggest frustrations the Government has faced in trying to cope with the problem is the attitudes of the Indians. 'We've just got to get through to them that they shouldn't eat certain fish', he said. (Moore, 1975:16)

It may be noted here that most mercury pollution is caused by industrial enterprise. The Minister, however, is concerned about the Native attitudes and behaviour of the public rather than the attitude of the Reed Paper Company and that of his own government. Again, it is the "blaming the victim" syndrome.

The differential use of medical services by the poor is often attributed to their lack of knowledge, lack of readiness to use services, lack of positive values toward health, cultural impediments, and "fear" of immunization programmes and dental clinics. Though it is phrased somewhat differently, again the attempt is to shift the responsibility for not benefitting from services back onto the poor people — to blame the victim.

This approach to analyzing "social problems" is not confined to the health sector alone. It has been used in the sociological study of racism, education, inequality, welfare, and poverty. For instance, sociologists, for the most part, focussed on the poor, analyzing their attributes and their way of life (culture) and lifestyles. Rather than looking into the socio-political and economic conditions which create inequality, poverty is explained in terms of personal attributes and deficiencies of the poor and their inappropriate ways of life. This view is best represented in Oscar Lewis' "culture of poverty" thesis (Lewis, 1966). Numerous variations of this perspective appear in other areas in the form of functionalist theory, the I.Q. argument, achievement syndrome, and personal pathologies, to mention just a few (Davis and Moore,

1945; Rosen, 1956; Davis, 1975).

The review of selected studies presented above has demonstrated the medical emphasis on individual lifestyle over environment. There is evidence, however, which suggests that a change in lifestyle and elimination of so-called self-imposed risks might reduce mortality rates by only a small proportion. A Special Task Force to the Secretary of Health, Education and Welfare report indicates:

> In an impressive 15 year study of aging, the strongest predictor of longevity was work satisfaction. The second best predictor was overall "happiness." ... Other factors are undoubtedly important — diet, exercise, medical care and genetic inheritance. But research findings suggest that these factors may account for only about 25% of the risk factors in heart disease the major cause of death...

In summary, this focus on individual lifestyle and self-imposed risks tends to downgrade the importance of social and environmental factors in the production of illness. As noted above, massive social disruptions, unemployment, conditions in the workplace, requirements of the production process, and stress account for a great deal of illness. In the face of this evidence, this singular emphasis on individual etiology and individual solutions has important ideological and policy implications, which are discussed below.

IDEOLOGICAL AND POLICY IMPLICATIONS

It must be pointed out that the individual-centred approach — individual etiology and individual solutions — is being promoted in many Western countries. For example, a DHSS (1976:62–63) report in Britain states:

> The prime responsibility for his own health falls on the individual. The role of the health professions and of government is limited to ensuring that the public have access to such knowledge as is available about the importance of personal habit and at the very least, no obstacles are placed in the way of those who decide to act on that knowledge.

Another exponent of individual epidemiology is a well-known health economist, Fuchs, who states (1974:151) that "the greatest potential for improving health lies in what we do and don't do for and to ourselves. The choice is ours." This message that health depends upon what we choose to do and not to do is being promoted in other papers and publications (see Cohen, 1987; Association of American Medical Colleges, 1984; White, 1987; Carlson, 1975; Vickery and Fries, 1976).

In times of economic constraints, when the situation becomes even more critical and the health-care crisis deepens, government programmes promoting this type of individual emphasis gain dominance over others. An attempt is made "to shift the responsibility for disease back onto the worker, in this case through victim-blaming epidemiology and of individual solutions for the workers" (Berliner, 1977:119). As Doyal and Pennell (1979:296) put it: "Thus it is said that individuals are to blame for their own health problems and it is up to them to adopt a healthier life-style. The Victorian notion of 'undeserving poor' is being replaced by the equally inappropriate notion of 'the undeserving sick'." This has strong implications for health-care policy. And as Ryan states: "It is a brilliant ideology for justifying a perverse form of social action designed to change, not society, as one might expect, but rather society's victim (Ryan, 1971:7).

The health promotion strategies and educational campaigns are primarily oriented toward changing individuals and their life-styles. Relatively little attention is given to the transformation of the physical and social environment and the health-care system. For instance, Epp's policy paper says relatively little about creating a healthy environment (McDowell, 1986), and Epp considers "health promotion as an approach that complements and strengthens the existing systems of health care" (Epp, 1986:396). The need for legislative action to curb the harmful effects of the environment and to have a critical look at the health-care system is increasingly being recognized.

Change of individual behaviour and promotion of "self-care prevention" through health education are an important part of the strategy to reduce health-care costs. The DHSS (1976:22) Priorities Report states: "Preventive medicine and health education are particularly important when resources are tightly limited, as they can often lead to savings in resources in other areas." Similarly, Epp, in his health policy promotion paper, (1986:406–7) states that

> there is the question of allocating resources during times of scarcity. The availability of financing is obviously a critical question for each of us. Canada has performed fairly well in controlling the growth of health care costs; however, cost control is a matter of continuing concern. The pressure created by an aging population and the growth of incidence of disabilities in our society will take a heavy toll on our financial resources. We believe, however, that the health promotion approach has the potential over the long term to slow the growth in health care costs.

This response to crises in health care strengthens "the ideological construct of bourgeois individualism by which one is responsible for one's wealth or lack of it, for one's work or lack of it, and for one's health or lack of it" (Navarro, 1978:206), and thus it masks the social nature of disease. By focussing on workers' lifestyles and habits it diverts attention from unhealthy and unsafe work environments; by concentrating on safe driving and seat belts it ignores the automobile industry and unsafe cars, and by concentrating on individual diet it diverts attention from food monopolies and potentially harmful food additives (Berliner, 1977). As Navarro (1976:207) states,

> an ideology that saw the "fault" of disease as lying with the individual and that emphasized the individual therapeutic response clearly absolved the economic and political environment from the responsibility for disease and channeled potential response and rebellion against that environment to an individual, and thus less threatening level. The ideology of medicine was the individualization of a collective causality that by its very nature would have required a collective answer.

However, a focus on social, economic, and political institutions will bring into question the legitimacy of the whole system and its health sector. By promoting individual responsibility, this strategy serves as a legitimizing function and distracts attention from the illness-generating economic and social environment.

The policies are primarily geared toward changing lifestyles; this is achieved through educational campaigns. Popularization of this strategy, in the long run, would be instrumental in preparing the populace to accept further reductions in health services — "to tighten their medical care belts" (Berliner, 1977:116). It is likely to have adverse effects. Healthy lifestyles, "wise living," and self-care are fine, but cannot substitute for professional health services when they are required (Waitzkin, 1983). With regard to Epp's health promotion policy paper, McDowell (1986:448) states:

> Self-care and the assistance of neighbours are laudable, but are made here to sound like a cheap alternative to professional health care . . . Epp is trying to reduce the demand for health services, rather than the need for them.

Therefore, the burden of health crises may be borne by individuals to the extent that they are willing to accept the proposition that what are actually to a great extent socially, economically, and politically caused conditions can be solved individually either by medical intervention or by self-care and changes in lifestyle. This approach promotes a policy of "health education in prevention and clinical medicine in cure," rather than drawing attention to the organization of health-care delivery systems, or the nature, function, and composition of the health sector in this society and the overall economic and political forces which determine the state of healthiness.

CONCLUSIONS

In this chapter we have presented an analysis of one of the strategies — focus on lifestyles and self-imposed risks — being largely popularized by the state and media at the present time in the area of health care. The promotion of this strategy in the context of the current health debate is more than coincidental. Our discussion indicates that this approach is consistent with the basic tenets of "bourgeois individualism and freedom of choice," and its singular emphasis on the individual obscures the extent to which health and illness are perceived as arising from socially determined ways of life. Thus, responsibility for health and illness depends on behaviour modification by individuals rather than on changing the existing social, economic, and political institutions and the health sector.

At a broader political level, this strategy serves to legitimate existing class relations and the dominant political and economic structures. The popularization of this ideology, in the long run, would be instrumental in preparing the population to alter its expectations regarding health care and, perhaps, accept reductions in health services (Crawford, 1977). On the other hand, challenging existing social, economic, and political institutions is likely to bring into question the legitimacy of the whole system and the health sector.

The burden of health crises may therefore be borne by individuals to the extent that they accept the proposition that illnesses that are actually the result of environmentally induced conditions can be solved individually by self-care or "wise living."

A final point must be made. In this chapter we are not presenting a social deterministic behaviour model. It would be absurd to argue that individuals have no control over their lives and that individual lifestyle has no significance whatsoever for individual health. What is important, however, is the recognition that individual lifestyle choices are not made in a vacuum. Instead, individual choices are limited by structural conditions — social, political, and economic forces. Many individuals live and work in unhealthy environments. Changes in personal lifestyle can do nothing to correct the unhealthy surroundings. For the unemployed, their joblessness and associated health problems can hardly be blamed on their lifestyles. As has been noted earlier in this chapter, unemployment is causally related to a number of physical and mental illnesses and to numerous social problems. It is also crucial to note that lifestyle modification campaigns have been more effective in modifying the health-related behaviour (smoking cessation, for instance) of better-educated and higher-income groups; these are also likely to have stable employment patterns, health workplace environments, better nutrition, and perhaps more leisure and relaxation time. There are grounds to believe that changing "at risk" behaviour of certain individuals may improve their state of health. However, this cannot be used as a substitute for improving the social and economic conditions that are responsible for so many of their health problems. Therefore we have criticized the political and ideological undercurrents inherent in the approach which continues to "atomize both causation and solution to illness" and the policy implications of changing individual behaviour and not the social and economic environment.

STUDY QUESTIONS

1. "By seeking the causes of social illness in the behaviour of individuals, social scientists end up blaming the victim." Discuss this statement and present and support your position.

2. The burden of health crises may therefore be borne by individuals to the extent that they accept the proposition that illnesses that are actually the result of environmentally induced conditions can be solved individually by self-care or "wise living." Discuss this statement.

3. Discuss the ideological and policy implications of the promotion of the causal role of lifestyles and self-imposed risks in relation to

health and disease.

4. How would the popularization of individual lifestyles and self-imposed risks in relation to

health and illness, in the long run, be instrumental in preparing the population to alter their expectations regarding health care and, perhaps, accept reductions in health services?

RECOMMENDED READING

Berliner, Howard S. "Emerging Ideologies in Medicine." *Review of Radical Political Economics* 9, no. 1 (Spring 1977): 116–24.

Crawford, Robert. "You are Dangerous to Your Health: The Ideology and Politics of Victim Blaming." *International Journal of Health Services* 7, no.4 (1977): 663–80.

Epp, Jake. "Achieving Health For All: A Framework for Health Promotion." *Canadian Journal of Public Health* 77, no. 6 (November-December 1986): 393–407

Eyer, J. "Capitalism, Health and Illness." In *Issues in the Political Economy of Health Care*, edited by John B. McKinlay. New York: Tavistock Publications, 1984.

Eyer, J., and Peter Sterling. "Stress-Related Mortality and Social Organization." *Review of Radical Political Economics* 9, no. 1 (Spring 1977): 1–44.

Lalonde, Marc. *A New Perspective on the Health of Canadians*. Ottawa: Information Canada, 1974.

Waitzkin, H. "Recent Studies in Medical Sociology: The New Reductionism." *Contemporary Sociology* 5 (1976): 401–5.

REFERENCES

Association of American Medical Colleges. "Physicians for the Twenty-First Century. Report of the Project Panel on the General Professional Education of the Physician and College Preparation for Medicine." *Journal of Medical Education* 59, no. 11 (1984): 1–208.

Berliner, Howard S. "Emerging Ideologies in Medicine." *Review of Radical Political Economics* 9, no. 1 (Spring 1977): 116–24.

———. "A Large Perspective on the Flexner Report." *International Journal of Health Services* 5 (1975): 573–92.

Blackburn, R., ed. *Ideology in Social Science*. New York: Random House, 1973.

Bosquet, M. *Capitalism in Crisis and Everyday Life*. Sussex: Harvest Press, 1977.

Bowles, Samuel, and Herbert Gintis. *Schooling in Capitalist America*. Basic Books, 1977.

Brenner, M. Harvey. "Economic Changes and Heart Disease Mortality." *American Journal of Public Health* 61 (1977): 606–11.

———. "Health Costs and Benefits of Economic Policy." *International Journal of Health Services* 7 (1977):581–623.

Cairns, J. "The Cancer Problem." *Scientific American* 233, no. 18 (1975):64–72.

Canada. Senate. Special Senate Committee on Poverty. *Poverty in Canada*. Ottawa, 1971.

Carlson, Rick. "The End of Medicine." New York: Wiley/Interscience, 1975.

Cassels, Derek. "Minamata" *Medical Post* 30 September 1975.

Castrilli, J. "Control of Toxic Chemicals in Canada: An Analysis of Law and Policy." *Osgoode Hall Law Journal* 2 (June 1982): 322–401.

Coburn, David. "Job-Worker Incongruence: Consequences for Health." *Journal of Health and Social Behaviour* 16 (1975): 198–212.

———. "Work and General Psychological and Physical Well-Being." *International Journal of Health Services* 8, no. 3 (1978): 415–35.

Cohen, Lynn. "Responsibility for Health Shift From Doctors and Hospitals, Conference Told." *Canadian Medical Association Journal* 136, no. 3 (February 1, 1987): 282–85.

Crawford, Robert. "You are Dangerous to Your Health: The Ideology and Politics of Victim Blaming." *International Journal of Health Services* 7, no. 4 (1977): 663–80.

D'Arcy, C., and C.M. Siddique. "Unemployment and Health: An Analysis of Canadian Health Survey Data." *International Journal of Health Services* 15, no. 4 (1985): 604–35.

Davis, Kingsley, and Wilbert E. Moore. "Some Principles of Stratification." *American Sociological Review* 10 (April 1945): 242–49.

Davis, Nanette J. *Deviance.* Dubuque, Iowa: Wm. C. Brown Co., 1975.

Department of Health and Social Security (DHSS). *Prevention and Health: Everybody's Business.* London: HMSO, 1976.

———. *Priorities for Health and Personal Social Services in England.* London: HMSO, 1976.

———. *The Way Forward.* London: HMSO, 1977.

Doyal, Lesley, and Imogen Pennell. *The Political Economy of Health.* London: Pluto Press, 1979.

Drietzel, Hans Peter, ed. *The Social Organizations of Health.* New York: MacMillan Co., 1971.

Dubos, R. *Man, Medicine and Environment.* Harmondsworth: Penguin Books, 1968.

Egger, G. "Psychosocial Aspects of Increasing Drug Abuse: A Postulated Economic Cause." *Social Science and Medicine* 14A (1980): 163–170.

Ehrenreich, Barbara, et al. "Health Care and Social Control." *Social Policy* (May-June 1974).

Epp, Jake. "Achieving Health For All: A Framework for Health Promotion." *Canadian Journal of Public Health* 77, no. 6 (November-December 1986): 393–407.

Eyer, Joseph. "A Diet-Stress Hypothesis of Coronary Heart Disease Causation." *International Journal of Health Services* 9 (1979): 161–68.

———. "Capitalism, Health and Illness." In *Issues in the Political Economy of Health Care*, edited by John B. McKinlay. New York: Tavistock Publications, 1984.

———. "Hypertension as a Disease of Modern Society." *International Journal of Health Services* 5 (1975): 539–58.

———. "Prosperity as a Cause of Death." *International Journal of Health Services* 7, no. 1 (1977): 125–50.

———. "Social Causes of Coronary Heart Disease." *Psychotherapy and Psychomatics* 34 (1980): 75–87.

Eyer, Joseph, and Peter Sterling. "Stress-Related Mortality and Social Organization." *Review of Radical Political Economics* 9, no. 1 (Spring 1977): 1–44.

Fee, Elizabeth. "Women and Health Care: A Comparison of Theories." In *Health and Medical Care in the U.S.: A Critical Analysis*, edited by Vicente Navarro, 115–32. New York: Baywood Publishing Co., 1977.

Fuchs, Victor. "Health Care and the United States Economic System." *Milbank Memorial Fund Quarterly* 50, no. 2, part 1 (1972): 211–37.

———. *Who Shall Live?* New York: Basic Books, 1974.

Greenberg, D.S., and J.E. Randal. "Waging the Wrong War on Cancer." *Washington Post*, 1 May 1977.

Goff, Colin H., and Charles E. Reasons. "Organizational Crimes Against Employees, Consumers, and the Public." In *The Political Economy of Crime*, edited by Brian D. MacLean. Scarborough, Ontario: Prentice-Hall, 1986.

Grayson, Paul. "The Closure of a Factory and Its Impact Upon Health." *International Journal of Health Services* 15, no. 1 (1985): 69–93.

Hammond, E.C. "Epidemiologic Basis for Cancer Prevention." *Cancer* 33, no. 6 (1974).

Harding, J., N. Wolf, and G. Chan. "A Socio-Demographic Profile of People Being Prescribed Mood-Modifying Drugs in Saskatchewan." Regina: Alcoholism Commission of Saskatchewan, November 1977.

Illich, Ivan. *Limits to Medicine: Medical Nemesis, The Expropriation of Health.* New York: Pantheon, 1976.

Jangula, Gordon. "Occupational Health and Safety: A Human Rights Perspective." In *The Struggle For Justice: A Multi-Disciplinary Approach*, edited by Dawn Currie and Brian MacLean, 240–55. Saskatoon Social Research Unit, 1986.

Jenkins, C.D., and S.J. Zyzsanski. "Behavioral Risk Factors and Coronary Heart Disease." *Psychotherapy and Psychosomatics* 34 (1980): 149.

Katz, R.L. "Drug Therapy: Sedatives and Tranquilizers." *New England Journal of Medicine* 286, (1972).

Kotelchuk, David, ed. *Prognosis Negative: Crisis in the Health Care System.* New York: Vintage, 1976.

Laing, R.D. *The Politics of Experience and The Bird of Paradise.* Harmondsworth: Penguin Books, 1970.

Lalonde, Marc. *A New Perspective on the Health of Canadians.* Ottawa: Information Canada, 1974.

Lewis, Oscar. *La Vida.* New York: Random House, 1966.

Lindsay, Colin. "The Decline in Employment Among Men Aged 55–64, 1975–85." *Canadian Social Trends* (Spring 1987): 12–15.

Mahler, H. (Director-General of WHO). "Address At the Opening Ceremony of the International Conference on Health Promotion in Industrialized Countries, Ottawa, 17–21 November 1986." *Canadian Journal of Public Health* 77, no. 6 (November-December 1986): 387–89.

McClelland, D. *The Achieving Society.* New York: Free Press, 1961.

McDonald, Marie. "The Massacre at Grassy Narrows." *Maclean's*, 20 October 1975.

McDowell, Ian. "National Strategies for Health Promotion." Letters to *Canadian Journal of Public Health* 77, no. 6 (November-December 1986): 448.

McKeon, T. *Medicine in Modern Society.* London: Allen and Unwin, 1965.

McKinlay, John B., ed. *Issues in the Political Economy of Health.* New York: Tavistock Publications.

Miller, A. "The Wages of Neglect: Death and Disease in the American Work Place." *American Journal of Public Health* 65, no. 11 (1975): 1217–20.

"Miller Fed Up." *Globe and Mail* 16 October 1975.

Miller, Lawrence G. "Negative Therapeutics." *Social Science and Medicine* 9 (1975): 673–77.

Moore, Steve. *Mercury Poisoning, Native People and Reed Paper Company.* Toronto Alliance Against Racism and Political Repression, Pamphlet No. 1, no date.

Navarro, Vicente. "The Crisis of the Western System of Medicine in Contemporary Capitalism." *International Journal of Health and Services* 8, no. 2 (1978).

———. *Crisis, Health, and Medicine.* New York: Tavistock Publications, 1986.

———. *Health and Medical Care in the U.S.: A Critical Analysis.* New York: Baywood Publishing Co., 1977.

Parliament, Jo-Anne. "Increase in Long-Term Unemployment." *Canadian Social Trends* (Spring 1987): 16–19.

Powels, J. "On the Limitations of Modern Medicine." *Science, Medicine and Man* 1, no. 1 (1973): 1–30.

Renaud, Marc. "On the Structural Constraints to State Intervention in Health." *International Journal of Health Services* 5, no. 4 (1975): 559–71.

Rinehart, James W. *The Tyranny of Work.* Toronto: Harcourt Brace Jovanovich, 1987.

Rosen, Bernard C. "The Achievement Syndrome: A Psychocultural Dimension of Social Stratification." *American Sociological Review*

21 (1956): 203–11.

———. "Race, Ethnicity, and the Achievement Syndrome." *American Sociological Review* 24 (1959): 47–60.

Rosen, R., M. Friedman, R. Strauss, C. Jenkins, S. Zyzsanski, and M. Wurm. "Coronary Heart Disease in the Western Collaborative Group Study: A Follow Up Experience of Four and One Half Years." *Journal of Chronic Diseases* 23 (1970): 173.

Rosenman, R., R. Brand, C. Jenkins, M. Friedman, R. Strauss, and M. Wurm. "Coronary Heart Disease in the Western Collaborative Group Study: The Final Follow Up Experience of Eight and One Half Years." *Journal of the American Medical Association* 233 (1975): 872.

Ryan, William. *Blaming the Victim*. New York: Vintage Books, 1971.

Shah, C.P., and C.S. Farkas. "The Health of Indians In Canadian Cities: A Challenge to Health-Care System." *Canadian Medical Association Journal* 133 (1985): 859–63.

Smith, E.W., and A. Smith. *Minamata*. New York: Holt, Rinehart and Winston, 1975.

Statistics Canada and Health and Welfare Canada. *The Health of Canadians: Report of the Canadian Health Survey*. Catalogue 82-538E. Ottawa, 1981.

Sterling, P., and J. Eyer. "Biological Basis of Stress-Related Mortality." *Social Science and Medicine* 15E (1981): 3–42.

Stroufe, L.A., and M.A. Stewart. "Treating Children with Stimulant Drugs." *New England Journal of Medicine* 289 (1973): 409.

Szasz, T. *The Myth of Mental Illness*. New York: Harper and Row, 1961.

Turshen, Meredith. "The Political Ecology of Disease." *The Review of Radical Political Economies* 9, no. 1 (Spring 1977): 45–60.

United States. Special Task Force to the Secretary of Health, Education and Welfare. *Work in America*. Cambridge, Mass.: M.I.T. Press, 1973.

Vickery, D.M., and J.F. Fries. *Take Care of Yourself: A Consumer's Guide to Medical Care*. Reading, Mass.: Addison-Wesley, 1976.

Waitzkin, Howard. *The Second Sickness*. New York: Free Press, 1983.

Waldron, I. "Increased Prescribing of Valium, Librium, and Other Drugs — An Example of the Influence of Economic and Social Factors on the Practice of Medicine." *International Journal of Health Services* 7, no. 1 (1977): 37–62.

Waldron, I., M. Nawotarski, M. Freimer, J. Henry, N. Post, and C. Wittin. "Cross-Cultural Variation in Blood Pressure: A Quantitative Analysis of the Relationships of Blood Pressure to Cultural Characteristics, Salt Consumption and Body Weight." *Social Science and Medicine* 16 (1982): 419–30.

White, Franklin. "The Environment of Medicine in the 21st Century: Implications for Prevention and Community Approaches." *Canadian Medical Association Journal* 136, no. 6 (1987): 571–75.

———. "A Voluntary Perspective on Health Promotion — The Role of Non-Government Organizations, Particularly in the Voluntary Sector." *Canadian Journal of Public Health* 77 (November-December 1986): 431–36.

Wigle, D.T., and Y. Mao. *Mortality by Income Level in Urban Canada*. Ottawa: Health and Welfare Canada, 1980.

Wilkins, R., and O. Adams. *Healthfulness of Life*. Montreal: Institute on Public Policy, 1983.

PART XI

CONCLUSIONS

34

MEDICINE, HEALTH, AND ILLNESS: Current Issues and Future Prospects

Harley D. Dickinson and B. Singh Bolaria
University of Saskatchewan

The creation of a universal, comprehensive system of prepaid hospital and medical care insurance in Canada was widely heralded as a great accomplishment, which indeed it was. Proponents of medicare saw this as a way not only to eliminate inequalities in access to health-care services, but also to eliminate inequalities in health status. It was thought that removing financial barriers to necessary hospital and doctor services would encourage the poor, and other marginalized groups in society, to seek medical treatment, and that this in turn would result in an overall improvement in peoples' health. Critics of medicare argued that the removal of financial barriers would result in a massive increase in demand for health-care services that would in turn bring financial ruin to the country. Advocates of medicare countered with the argument that although there would certainly be an initial increase in utilization rates and costs as the poor "caught up," this would be followed by a real reduction in both, thanks to a general improvement in the health status of the population.

Presumably a healthier population would require fewer health-care services. As we have seen throughout this book, neither the most optimistic proponents of medicare, nor the most pessimistic of opponents, were entirely correct. Although medicare has contributed to the reduction of financial barriers to health-care services and to a general improvement in health status, inequalities of access and health status continue to characterize Canadian society. As a result medicare cannot be counted an unqualified success. On the other hand, neither is it an unmitigated disaster. Although utilization rates and costs continue to rise, there is no indication that they are out of control, or that they are the result of frivolous or unnecessary utilization on the part of users. Because of the somewhat ambiguous nature of available data concerning the effectiveness and efficiency of medicare, one is left with the conclusion that perhaps we do not yet fully understand (or possibly cannot control) all the factors and forces influential in determining health status, or the nature and organization of health-care delivery. This brings us to the role of sociology.

With regard to medicine, there are two types of sociology: sociology for medicine and the sociology of medicine. Generally the sociology for medicine has been enlisted to serve the needs of the medical profession. Its task has been to describe how various social and cultural factors influence people's perceptions of health and illness, patterns of help-seeking, and illness behaviour, with a view to improving the clinical effectiveness of doctors and other health-care professionals. On the other hand, the sociology of medicine has traditionally been concerned much less with solving the practical problems of various clinical specialties than with two areas: the social dimensions of health and illness, and the ways in which the nature and organization of the health-care services system influence the effectiveness and efficiency of health-care delivery. As Strauss (1957:203) noted, "these two types of medical sociology tend to be incompatible with each other." This is largely because an adequate sociology of medicine often entails exposing inconsistencies between professional theory and practice and rhetoric and reality. It will also often entail the demonstration of how various vested interests and patterns of practice militate against the achievement of an effective and efficient health-care delivery system or a healthy environment. The various chapters in this book are contributions to the development of the sociology of medicine.

The fact that health and illness are influenced by social and economic factors is nothing new. It has long been known that there are four possible etiological relationships between social conditions and disease: "social conditions (a) may create or favor a predisposition for a disease; (b) may themselves cause disease directly; (c) may transmit the causes of disease; and (d) may influence the course of a disease" (Rosen, 1963:44).

If this is true, then one would expect people living in different societies, or people occupying different positions within the same society, to be characterized by different rates of illness, different types of illness, and different life expectan-

cies. Indeed, this is exactly what one does find. As we have seen, within contemporary Canadian society, morbidity and mortality rates vary according to age, gender, race, region of residence, occupation, income, and class. These differences are even more striking when one examines differences between societies or within the same society at different points in time.

Eyer (1984), for example, provides a brief historical overview of average life expectancy. He reports that the average life expectancy for late Ice-Age hunters and gatherers was about 38 years. The rise of agricultural society was probably associated with a drop in average life expectancy to 30 or 35 years, although the total population that could be supported was much larger than in pre-agricultural societies. By the end of the European Middle Ages, the world's population had grown to approximately 500 million. The average life expectancy for rural dwellers at that time was still about 35 years, although it was lower for those living in cities. Since the sixteenth century, world population has increased to just about 5 billion people, with most of that growth occurring since the nineteenth century. Part of this increase is explained by "the extension of the average life expectancy at birth to over seventy years in advanced countries and to forty, fifty, or sixty even in the poorest areas of the periphery, in Africa and South Asia" (Eyer, 1984:25). In Canada, for example, the average life expectancy at birth for females has increased from 62.1 years in 1931 to 79 years in 1981. For males in Canada during that same time period, the average life expectancy at birth increased from 60 to 71.9 years.

It is generally agreed that the improved life expectancy characteristic of modern industrial societies is primarily the result of improvements in nutrition, sanitation, food handling and storage, and immunization. Thus, changes in social and economic organization and technology and the development of public health practices have had a tremendous impact on life expectancy and morbidity patterns.

Given that the origin and causes of disease

and health are influenced, if not determined, by social factors, then it follows that preventing illnesses or influencing the course of diseases requires that attention be paid to the social and economic environment of the patient. Failure to do so results in the partial, symptom-relieving approach to care and cure which characterizes modern medicine. There are many, including some doctors, who have deplored the limitations of the medical model which sees disease and illness as specific entities caused by specific agents and which advocates a curative, rather than a preventive approach to treatment. These critics have suggested that overcoming this limitation requires educating doctors about the social dimensions of disease. Even where this educational approach has been tried, however, it has failed to achieve any significant transformation in the nature and organization of medical practice.

This is not surprising inasmuch as the basic conceptual foundation of modern medicine, if not antithetical to the consideration of social factors, at least makes it easy to ignore them. Rosen (1963:42), for example, points out that with the development of medical bacteriology, one of the foundations of modern medicine, "it was not difficult to overlook the patient and his environment, and to emphasize the cause-and-effect relationship between germs and disease." This same development led Emil Behring to declare in 1893 that "the study of infectious diseases could now be pursued unswervingly without being sidetracked by social considerations and reflections on social policy" (Rosen, 1963:42). Undoubtedly the avoidance of "social considerations and reflections on social policy" has contributed to the current crises in both health and health-care delivery.

As we have seen, the major improvements in life expectancy which have occurred throughout the nineteenth and twentieth centuries are not primarily attributable to the development of institutional medicine. In fact, studies have shown that certain aspects of medical practice may be hazardous to people's health. When doctors in Los Angeles County, for example, withdrew their services for a five-week period in 1976, the death rate fell by 15 percent. It rose well above its usual level when doctors resumed practice, eventually returning to normal levels. Roemer and Schwartz (1979:217) conclude that the decline in the death rate "could not readily be attributed to causes other than the withholding of elective surgery." Although they are careful to indicate that their findings do not support the claim advanced by Illich (1976) that medical care as a *whole* does more harm than good, they make it clear that medically unnecessary elective surgery does. The notion advanced by Illich that the abolition of organized medicine would in itself result in improvements in health status seems ludicrous and cannot be seriously entertained. Having said this, however, it should also be pointed out that the organization of medical education and practice is undoubtedly in need of reform.

Much of the available evidence indicates that at least some aspects of medical practice are intended to increase doctors' incomes more than to promote the health status of the population. It also appears that doctors' discretionary power to mobilize health-care resources contributes to the rising cost of health-care services. Thus, the failure to develop a more rational health policy and a more effective and efficient health-care system is not the result of a lack of information or analysis. Rather, the health-care system remains inefficient and ineffective because of the lack of political will "to resolve the competing and conflicting interests among powerful actors" that have a stake in maintaining a certain status quo (Mechanic, 1981:1). Thus, health policy and the nature and organization of health-care delivery are the product of competing and conflicting interests that do not necessarily have the promotion of health or the treatment of disease as their primary objectives. The interests of these various groups and classes are not simply free-floating. Rather, they are the product of social and economic structures which give them shape and substance. The various strategies and tactics used by interested parties are similarly shaped and influenced by the position that different classes and groups occupy within the socio-economic system. Thus, not all the interested parties are on an equal footing. As a result of unequal distribution of economic and political resources, certain groups and classes are more likely to be successful in defining the nature of the problems to be solved and the nature of the solutions to be pursued. Perhaps more importantly, they are also more likely to achieve their objectives and to have their interests realized. Those who ally themselves with that segment of the capitalist class which has a direct interest in the nature and organization of health-care delivery, for example, are more likely to achieve their objectives than those groups and classes that oppose the power of capital. This is not meant to imply that the form and content of health-care delivery are simply the product of capitalist interests. On the other hand, any account which ignores the dominance of capital and the drive for profits is incomplete and, hence, unsatisfactory.

Drug companies, private insurance companies, and medical and hospital supply firms, for example, can all be argued to have profitability as their primary interest. And although profits may not necessarily be incompatible with good health, nor do they necessarily go hand in hand with it. For example, drug companies, in an attempt to capture a market and maximize profits, may make inadequately tested drugs available for use. Perhaps the best known example of this occurred with the drug Thalidomide. In the 1960s Thalidomide was marketed as an anti-nausea drug for pregnant women. Tragically, one of the side effects of its use was severe physical deformity for the children of hundreds of those mothers. Although the drug industry claims that the Thalidomide tragedy was an unfortunate aberration that could never happen again, the argument is unconvincing, because the structural pressures to maximize profits remain unchanged. The industry also is being deregulated, which means that the safeguards intended to protect the public from the marketing of dangerous products are being relaxed in order to make the industry even more

profitable than it is already. Under these conditions it seems likely that some unsafe and inadequately tested drugs will be marketed to consumers.

Other actors in the health-care field include doctors' organizations and those of other health-care workers and professionals. We have already seen that in a fee-for-service payment system, where income is dependent upon the number of services provided, there is a tendency on the part of health-care professionals to provide as many services as possible, whether or not they are necessary from a health standpoint. In some cases, of course, this has little or no impact on the patient's well-being: furthermore, it is an extremely inefficient use of health-care resources. In other cases, such as elective surgery, it can be fatal. The only way to put a stop to these abuses and inefficient practices is to make doctors and other health-care workers accountable to some independent agency. Doctors historically have opposed any reforms of the health-care system which threatened their professional power and autonomy. Politicians have generally been unwilling or unable to successfully challenge this professional dominance, although recently there is some indication that it is weakening, at least in certain respects.

Medical schools and research facilities, hospital associations, proprietary nursing homes, various voluntary associations such as the Canadian Cancer Society, the Red Cross, the Lung Association, etc., the state, various political parties and, of course, the public are some of the other actors, or combatants, in the health-care arena. All of them have various interests and objectives that determine the form of health-care policy as well as the content of health-care delivery. It appears that in many cases the achievement of those objectives and the satisfaction of those interests may stand as obstacles to the prevention of illness or the treatment of disease. The consumers of health-care services are the only group with an exclusive interest in the establishment of an effective and efficient health-care system. But the primary consumers of health-care services are members of the working and middle classes — those who are the least able financially to mobilize the resources necessary to realize that goal.

Government is the only institution in society that has the legislative power to develop a rational, integrated health policy and to transform the structure of health-care delivery. Currently, however, governments at both the federal and provincial levels seem to have abrogated their responsibility for policy formulation in this area. To the extent that a health policy can be said to exist, it encompasses nothing more than a commitment to privatization and cost containment. Rather than solving the problems of the health sector, it seems likely that this strategy will further fragment and disintegrate the Canadian health-care system. This will not only increase the power and influence of various sectional interests; at the same time, it will shift more health-care costs onto the individual. This in turn will result in the emergence of a two-tiered system, wherein those who can afford to pay will get whatever health-care services are available, and those that cannot will go without. Politicians are aware that medicare is consistently rated as the most popular government programme by the public: this, combined with pressures to reduce government spending and various other pressures, often results in politicians publicly supporting medicare, while at the same time allowing the system to be eroded.

As we have seen, with regard to certain types of services, this could have real health benefits; however, the denial of access to health-care services simply because of inability to pay is intolerable to those committed to the principles of social equality and justice. Furthermore, making services inaccessible does nothing to improve the efficiency or effectiveness of the health-care delivery system, despite the claims of the proponents of privatization. Privatization may reduce *government* expenditures on health care, but this means increased personal expenditures for those who can afford it, and unavailability of services for those who cannot.

Devotees of cost containment usually do not deny this. They claim, however, that the cur-

rent economic situation, and especially the size of government deficits, leaves no choice. The claim that the health-care system is in a financial crisis, which is widely accepted as a self-evident truth, needs to be critically examined. The fact that more than 30 billion dollars per year are spent on health care is, of itself, no indicator of a crisis. There is no way, in fact, that one can determine if too much or too little is being spent on health care simply by looking at the absolute amounts expended. Those decisions are moral and political in nature. Thus, to say that too much is being spent on health care means that one thinks those funds should be spent on something else. Although some people will support an idea for purely ideological reasons, that is, because they think it is the right thing to do, usually the main proponents of an idea have real political or economic interests at stake. With regard to the notions that too much is being spent on health care and that privatization will solve the fiscal crisis, it is readily apparent that there are many political and economic advantages for the main advocates of these policies, which include private insurance companies, drug companies, other health-sector businesses, pro-business political parties, governments, and many doctors. Similarly it is apparent that there are few benefits for most consumers of health-care services. Whether defenders of medicare and the principles upon which it rests can successfully organize and mobilize to protect and extend the availability of affordable and appropriate health care for all remains to be seen. Success in this regard will depend in part on the availability of information and knowledge, which brings us to the issue of the role of sociology in general, and medical sociology in particular.

As we have seen in the various chapters in this book, sociology can make a contribution to our understanding of illness, health, and health care in a number of ways and in a number of areas. Although there can be many different objectives underpinning any particular piece of research, the ultimate goals are to improve the health status of the population and to improve the efficiency and effectiveness of the health-care system. The achievement of these goals often involves challenging vested interests and established patterns of living and working. We have already seen how much social scientific knowledge has been drawn upon to try to persuade people to modify unhealthy lifestyles. Unfortunately, social scientific knowledge and expertise have also been even more effectively used by private industry to persuade people to consume a vast array of unhealthy and dangerous products ranging from alcohol and tobacco to air-polluting automobiles and high-fat fast food. These economically motivated "manufacturers of illness" are largely responsible for many of the bad habits which are the object of recent lifestyle campaigns (McKinlay, 1981). One of the tasks of sociology is to broaden the conception of the social etiology and ecology of health and illness to include analyses of the economic structure of society and the ways in which it is implicated in the creation of health and illness. This will include analyses of occupational safety and health issues, especially examinations of the impact of work organization and technology on the health of workers. Related to this is a need to examine both the direct and indirect health effects of the manufacture and marketing of various products. In these times of capital restructuring, there also needs to be more study of the relationship between unemployment and illness. The relationships among economy, environment, and health status also promise to be a critical area of investigation. It appears that unless some hard decisions are taken, certain industrial and military practices may be leading us towards an environmental tragedy of unprecedented proportions that will, in turn, have major repercussions for morbidity and mortality patterns.

Another area of research for medical sociology is the nature and organization of medical and health-care work. It is becoming increasingly clear that health-care professionals, although motivated by concern for the well-being of patients and clients, are also influenced by purely professional concerns that are themselves influenced by their patterns of practice and remuneration. As we have seen already, in some circumstances, consumer interests are subordinated to the non-medical concerns of various health-care professionals. Sociological studies of how patterns of work organization influence patterns of service provision will provide useful insights into how health-care services can be organized to be more efficient and effective from the point of view of consumers. As previously mentioned, there are limits to reform. Just as socio-economic structures are implicated in morbidity and mortality patterns and are influential in giving form and content to the health-care system, so too these same structural factors limit the extent and effectiveness of reform. It is now apparent, for example, that inequalities of health status cannot be eliminated simply by removing inequalities of access to health-care services. So long as class, gender, generational, racial, and other forms of inequality persist in society, there will be inequality of health status. It is in this sense that health and illness are political, economic, and social phenomena as well as medical problems. By theorizing and analyzing the nature of the links between health, illness, health-care delivery, and the structure of society, medical sociologists can make an important contribution to both medicine and sociology.

REFERENCES

Eyer, J. "Capitalism, Health and Illness." In *Issues in the Political Economy of Health Care*, edited by J.B. McKinlay, 23–59. London: Tavistock, 1984.

Illich, I. *The Limits to Medicine: Medical Nemesis, The Expropriation of Health.* Toronto: McClelland and Stewart, 1976.

McKinlay, J.B. "A Case for Refocusing Upstream: The Political Economy of Illness." In *The Sociology of Health and Illness: Critical Perspectives*, edited by P. Conrad and R. Kerns, 613–33. New York: St. Martin's Press, 1981.

Mechanic, D. "Some Dilemmas in Health Care Policy." *Milbank Memorial Fund Quarterly/Health and Society* 59, no. 1 (1981): 1–16.

Roemer, M.I., and J.L. Schwartz. "Doctor Slowdown: Effects on the Population of Los Angeles County." *Social Science and Medicine* 13C, no. 4 (December 1979): 213–18.

Rosen, G. "The Evolution of Social Medicine." In *Handbook of Medical Sociology*, edited by H.E. Freeman, S. Levine, and L.G. Reeder, 17–61. Englewood Cliffs, N.J.: Prentice-Hall, 1963.

Strauss, R. "That Nature and Status of Medical Sociology." *American Sociological Review* (April 1957): 200–204.

NOTES ON CONTRIBUTORS

Seema Ahluwalia is a Sessional Lecturer, Department of Sociology, University of Saskatchewan. Her publications and current research interests are in the area of victimization of women and domestic violence, among others.

Glen Andre is a graduate student, Department of Sociology, University of Saskatchewan. His current research interests include Canadian health-care policy with a special focus on psychiatry.

Lesley Biggs is Assistant Professor in the Department of Sociology, University of Saskatchewan. She has written several articles on chiropractic and midwifery and is presently researching the rise and fall of medical dominance in Canada.

Brian E. Burtch is on the Faculty of the School of Criminology, Simon Fraser University. He has co-authored, with Richard Ericson, *The Silent System: An Inquiry into Prisoners who Suicide*, (Centre of Criminology, 1979), as well as a number of articles on prison clinical services, the state and criminal justice, and the practice and politics of midwifery.

Marie L. Campbell teaches in the Social Administration and Policy Program, School of Social Work, Carleton University. Currently she holds a post-doctoral research fellowship from the Social Sciences and Humanities Research Council. Her academic interests and publications are in the areas of workload management in social services and the management of nursing work.

William Carroll is Associate Professor in the Department of Sociology at the University of Victoria. His research interests include the political economy of Canada and class and gender relations.

Ray Croucher teaches and is a Research Fellow at the Dental School, University College, London, England. He is currently studying the issue of compliance and self-care in adult dental patients.

Dawn Currie is Assistant Professor in the Department of Sociology at the University of Saskatchewan. Her academic interests and publications are in the areas of feminist theory, reproductive decision making, and women and the legal process. She also co-edited, with B.D. MacLean, *The Administration of Justice*, (Social Research Unit, 1986).

Chris Doran is Assistant Professor of Sociology at Memorial University. His current interests include the history of workers' compensation, occupational health and safety, and socio-legal studies.

B. Gail Frankel is Assistant Professor of Sociology, University of Western Ontario. Her research and publications are in the areas of determinants of the utilization of health care and psycho-social factors affecting the course and outcome of disease processes.

James S. Frideres is Professor of Sociology at the University of Calgary. He has published widely in the area of of ethnic relations, and with A. Anderson has co-authored *Ethnicity in Canada*, (Butterworths, 1981). He has also written *Native People in Canada*, (Prentice-Hall, 1983).

Karen R. Grant is on the Faculty of the Department of Sociology, University of Manitoba. Some of her academic interests and publications are in the areas of health policy, gender differences in lifestyles and health status, and medical technology and the transformation of the doctor-patient relationship.

Jim Harding is Associate Professor, School of Human Justice, University of Regina. His research interests and publications are in the areas of uranium mining and environmental health, drug- and alcohol-related problems, and social policy.

David A. Hay is Associate Professor, Department of Sociology, University of Saskatchewan. He has published in the areas of research methods and drug- and alcohol-influenced behaviour, and is currently involved in a study of farm women and work.

Robert W. Hetherington is Professor of Sociology, Department of Sociology, University of Alberta. His contribution to this book represents an aspect of his long-term interest in technological transfer, begun at UCLA with the development of the Databank of Program Evaluations in Mental Health, and continued at the National Center for Health Services Research in Washington, D.C. with the development of an information system on organizational research in hospitals.

Bonnie Jeffery is on the Faculty of Social Work, University of Regina, where she has held a number of administrative positions, including Director of the Social Administration Research Unit. Her research and writing focus on the analysis of social policy and social welfare.

Joel Lexchin has been a practising physician in Nova Scotia, Ontario, and New Zealand. He is a member of the Medical Reform Group of Ontario. He has written numerous articles on all aspects of the pharmaceutical industry, including a book titled *The Real Pushers: A Critical Analysis of the Canadian Drug Industry*, (New Star Books, 1984).

Brian D. MacLean is Assistant Professor, Department of Sociology, University of Saskatchewan. His recent publications include *The Islington Crime Survey*, (Gower, 1986), which he co-authored with T. Jones and J. Young; *The Political Economy of Crime*, (Prentice-Hall, 1986), and *The Administration of Justice*, (SRU, 1986), which he co-edited with D. Currie.

Herbert C. Northcott is Associate Professor and Associate Chair (Graduate) in the Department of Sociology, University of Alberta. His publications, teaching, and research focus on the sociology of health and health care and on the sociology and demography of aging. His recent publications include (with G. Lowe) *Under Pressure: A Study of Job Stress*, (Garamond Press, 1986).

Scarlet Pollock is Assistant Professor, Department of Sociology and Social Anthropology, Dalhousie University. Her research and publications are in the areas of gender relations and sexuality. She co-edited (as Friedman), with E. Sarah, *The Problem of Men*, (Women's Press, 1982).

David J. Roy is a physician and founder and Director of the Center for Bioethics of the Clinical Research Institute of Montreal. His research activities are in the area of ethical issues in clinical medicine and biomedical science, and he is editor-in-chief of the Canadian-based *International Journal of Palliative Care*. In 1985–86 he was one of Canada's three representatives to the summit nations' meetings on bioethics.

H. Michael Stevenson is a member of the Department of Political Science, and Associate Director of the Institute for Social Research, York University. He is co-investigator of the 1986 National Survey of Canadian Physicians and of a study of medical group practice in Ontario.

Mark Stobbe is a former hardrock miner who has studied at the University of Saskatchewan and McMaster University. He has an interest in occupational health and safety and has written a number of academic and journalistic articles on the subject.

James Stolzman is a member of the Department of Sociology and Social Anthropology, Dalhousie University. His areas of academic interest are the sociology of mental disorders, social stratification, and social theory. He is currently engaged in research on Therafields, a psychotherapeutic movement in Ontario.

Vera Ingrid Tarman is doing graduate work at the University of Toronto as well as lecturing part-time at McMaster University. Her research interests include aging in society and institutional care for the elderly.

Joann M. Trypuc is Director of the Ontario Hospital Association. Her research interests include women's issues and health care, the effects of plant shutdown on workers and their families, and gender differences in health.

K. Victor Ujimoto is Professor and Research Associate, Gerontology Research Center, University of Guelph. He has published numerous articles on Japanese Canadians, multiculturalism, and aging ethnic minorities. He also co-edited, with G. Hirabayashi, *Visible Minorities and Multiculturalism: Asians in Canada*, and at present is researching comparative aspects of aging Asian Canadians.

Rennie Warburton is Associate Professor, Department of Sociology, University of Victoria. His research interests include the structure of Canadian society and feminist analysis. His publications include articles on holiness, religion, nationalism in Canada and Switzerland, and white-collar workers in British Columbia.

Marianne Weston is a researcher for Saskatchewan Women's Resources, a non-governmental organization serving women's groups in the province. She was previously employed by both Saskatchewan Health as a researcher and the Faculty of Social Work, University of Regina as a research associate. She is the author of a major lifestyle study of Saskatchewan adolescents.

A. Paul Williams is in the Department of Health Administration, University of Toronto, and is a Visiting Research Fellow at the Institute for Social Research, York University. He is co-investigator of the 1986 National Survey of Canadian Physicians and of a study of medical group practice in Ontario.

Terry Wotherspoon is Assistant Professor of Sociology at the University of Saskatchewan. His current research emphasizes education and the labour process of teaching and other professions. He also has a number of publications including, as editor, *The Political Economy of Canadian Schooling*, (Methuen, 1987).